Roman Pottery in Britain

Paul A. Tyers

B T Batsford Ltd, London

© Paul A. Tyers 1996

First published 1996

All rights reserved. No part of this publication may be reproduced, in any form or by any means, without permission from the Publisher

Designed and typeset by Vaughan Collinson Design
and printed in Great Britain by Butler and Tanner Ltd.,
Frome, Somerset

Published by B.T. Batsford Ltd
4 Fitzhardinge Street, London W1H 0AH

A CIP catalogue record for this book is available from the British Library

ISBN 0 7134 7412 2

CONTENTS

List of illustrations   iv
List of tables   viii
Acknowledgements   ix
Introduction   x

PART ONE

1   A brief history of Roman pottery studies   1
1.1   The beginnings of the study   1
1.2   From Dragendorff to Camulodunum   8
1.3   From Camulodunum to CBA10   19
1.4   The modern era of Romano-British pottery studies   22

2   Sources for the study of Roman pottery   24
2.1   Site assemblages   24
2.2   Kiln assemblages   26
2.3   Typology   29
2.4   The analysis of clay   30
2.5   Experimental archaeology and ethnography   33

3   The role of pottery in Roman archaeology   36
3.1   Pottery as chronology   36
3.2   Pottery and economics   38
3.3   Pottery and function   42
3.4   Pottery and potters   45

4   A short history of Roman pottery in Britain   48
4.1   Roman pottery in pre-Roman Britain   48
4.2   The Late Iron Age pottery of Britain   52
4.3   The Claudio–Neronian period   56
4.4   Flavian–Trajanic   61
4.5   From Hadrian to Severus   66
4.6   The third and fourth centuries   70
4.7   The end of Roman pottery in Britain   77
4.8   Byzantium and the western seaways   80

PART TWO

Atlas and guide to Roman pottery in Britain   83
Introduction to the Atlas   83
Amphoras   85
Terra sigillata   105
Mortaria   116
Imported wares   135
Romano-British fine wares   166
Romano-British coarse wares   180

Appendices

1   Resources for the study of Romano-British pottery   202
2   The processing of Roman pottery from excavations   204
3   The Atlas distribution maps   206
4   Principal Roman emperors from Augustus to Honorius   207

Glossary   208
Bibliography   210
Index   226

LIST OF ILLUSTRATIONS

1	E. T. Artis directing excavations	3
2	Charles Roach Smith	4
3	An expedition to the Upchurch Marshes	5
4	Forms of samian ware with their possible Latin names	6
5	Decorated terra sigillata types illustrated by Haverfield	10
6	Bushe-Fox's Wroxeter mortarium type-series	12
7	Thomas May at Richborough	14
8	Analysis of Thomas May's tables	14
9	Mark Reginald Hull	18
10	John Gillam	21
11	Transformation of the pottery assemblage	24
12	Factors affecting the composition of a ceramic assemblage	25
13	Residuality in assemblages from Chester-le-Street	26
14	The principal components of a pottery kiln	27
15	The distribution of Romano-British pottery kilns	29
16	Ruralization of the pottery industry	30
17	Thin-section analysis	31
18	Heavy mineral analysis	32
19	Discriminant analysis of Köln and Nene Valley sherds	32
20	Experimental kiln firing	33
21	Samian plate and cup ratios in Boudiccan destruction horizons	36
22	Analysis of ceramic assemblages using pie-slice	37
23	Seriation of Gillam's types	39
24	Samian supply to London	41
25	Fluctuation in the Roman pottery industry	42
26	Functional analysis of pottery from Segontium and Chelmsford	44
27	Graffiti usage on Romano-British sites	46
28	Distribution of Massiolite amphoras	48
29	Distribution of Breton pottery and Dressel 1A amphoras in Britain	49
30	Sources of pottery imports to Britain *c.* 100BC–AD43	52
31	Principal pottery types at Prae Wood, and pedestal urns	54
32	Sources of pottery imports to Britain *c.* AD43–AD100	58
33	The coarse pottery assemblage made by immigrant potters at Usk	60
34	Movements of Verulamium-region potters	61
35	The development of coarse wares in southern Britain	62
36	The development of coarse wares in the Midlands	63
37	The 'legionary ware' industries in western Europe	64
38	Movements of potters in Britain *c.* AD120–AD200	66
39	Sources of pottery imports to Britain *c.* AD100–AD180	68
40	Mortarium supply to Inveresk	70
41	Sources of pottery imports to Britain *c.* AD180–AD250	70
42	Sources of pottery imports to Britain *c.* AD250–AD400	72
43	Sources of pottery in the Guernsey shipwreck	73
44	Mortarium supply to Vindolanda	74
45	Industries producing everted-rim jars and flanged bowls	75
46	The origins of Housesteads ware	76
47	Distribution of imported pottery in western Britain	82
48	Provinces and regions of the Roman Empire	83
49	Sites in Britain with records of Roman pottery	84
50	Letter codes for 100km National Grid squares	84
51	Amphoras: dating of principal classes	86
52	Dressel 20 amphoras and allied types	88
53	Dressel 20 amphoras and allied types: overall distribution	88
54	Dressel 1 amphoras	89
55	Dressel 1 amphoras: British distribution	89
56	Dressel 1 amphoras: overall distribution	90
57	Dressel 2–4 amphoras: overall distribution	90
58	Dressel 2–4 amphoras	91
59	Mid-Roman Campanian amphoras	91
60	Mid-Roman Campanian amphoras: British distribution	92
61	Pascual 1 amphoras: British distribution	92
62	Pascual 1 amphoras	92
63	Pascual 1 amphoras: overall distribution	93

List of Illustrations

64	Rhodian (Camulodunum 184) amphoras	93
65	Rhodian (Camulodunum 184) amphoras: British distribution	94
66	Gauloise flat-based amphoras	95
67	Gauloise flat-based amphoras: British distribution	96
68	Gauloise flat-based amphoras: overall distribution	96
69	Gauloise 12 amphora	96
70	Gauloise 12 amphoras: British distribution	96
71	Haltern 70 amphora	97
72	Haltern 70 amphoras: British distribution	97
73	London 555 amphora	98
74	London 555 amphoras: British distribution	98
75	Dressel 7–11 'salazon' amphoras	99
76	Dressel 7–11 'salazon' amphoras: overall distribution	99
77	Richborough 527 amphora	100
78	Richborough 527 amphoras: British distribution	100
79	Richborough 527 amphoras: overall distribution	100
80	Camulodunum 189 ('carrot') amphoras	101
81	Camulodunum 189 ('carrot') amphoras: British distribution	101
82	Kapitän II ('Hollow foot') amphoras	102
83	Kapitän II ('Hollow foot') amphoras: British distribution	102
84	British B4 amphoras ('micaceous jars')	102
85	British B4 amphoras ('micaceous jars'): British distribution	103
86	British B4 amphoras ('micaceous jars'): overall distribution	103
87	North African cylindrical amphoras: British distribution	104
88	North African cylindrical amphoras	104
89	North African cylindrical amphoras: overall distribution	105
90	Terra sigillata kiln sites	106
91	Terra sigillata or Samian wares: dating of principal forms	107
92	Terra sigillata or Samian wares	108
93	Terra sigillata or Samian wares	109
94	Terra sigillata or Samian wares	110
95	Italian-type ('Arretine') sigillata: British distribution	111
96	Italian-type ('Arretine') sigillata: overall distribution	111
97	South Gaulish (La Graufesenque) terra sigillata: overall distribution	112
98	South Gaulish (Montans) terra sigillata: overall distribution	112
99	Central Gaulish terra sigillata: overall distribution	113
100	East Gaulish terra sigillata: overall distribution	114
101	Colchester terra sigillata	115
102	Colchester terra sigillata: overall distribution	116
103	Romano-British mortaria: major potteries and kilns	116
104	Mortaria: dating of principal industries	117
105	Aoste mortaria	117
106	Aoste mortaria: British distribution	118
107	Aoste mortaria: overall distribution	118
108	Corbridge mortaria	118
109	Corbridge mortaria: distribution of principal potters	119
110	Colchester mortaria	119
111	Colchester mortaria: distribution of principal potters	120
112	Eifel region mortaria	120
113	Eifel region mortaria: British distribution	121
114	Italian mortaria	121
115	Italian mortaria: British distribution	121
116	Italian mortaria: overall distribution	122
117	Lincolnshire mortaria	122
118	Lincolnshire mortaria: overall distribution	123
119	Mancetter-Hartshill mortaria	124
120	Mancetter-Hartshill mortaria: distribution of stamps of principal potters	124
121	Dates of principal Mancetter-Hartshill mortarium potters	124
122	New Forest mortaria	125
123	New Forest mortaria: overall distribution	125
124	North Gaulish (Pas-de-Calais) mortaria	126
125	North Gaulish (Pas-de-Calais) mortaria: distribution of stamps of principal potters	126
126	Nene Valley mortaria	127
127	Nene Valley mortaria: overall distribution	127
128	Oxfordshire white-ware mortaria	128
129	Oxfordshire white-ware mortaria: overall distribution	129
130	Rossington Bridge mortaria	129
131	Rossington Bridge mortaria: overall distribution	130
132	Rhône valley mortaria	130
133	Rhône valley mortaria: British distribution	130
134	Soller mortaria	131
135	Soller mortaria: British distribution	131
136	Soller mortaria: overall distribution	132

List of Illustrations

137 Verulamium-region mortaria	133
138 Dates of principal Verulamium-region mortarium potters	134
139 Verulamium-region mortaria: distribution of stamps of principal potters	134
140 Wilderspool mortaria	134
141 Wilderspool mortaria: distribution of stamps of principal potters	135
142 Imported wares: dating of principal classes	135
143 Argonne ware	136
144 Argonne ware: British distribution	136
145 Argonne ware: overall distribution	136
146 Central Gaulish black-slipped ware	137
147 Central Gaulish black-slipped ware: overall distribution	138
148 Trier black-slipped ware ('Moselkeramik'): overall distribution	138
149 Trier black-slipped ware ('Moselkeramik')	139
150 Central Gaulish colour-coated wares: British distribution	140
151 Central Gaulish colour-coated ware	140
152 Central Gaulish glazed ware	141
153 Central Gaulish glazed ware: British distribution	141
154 Central Gaulish glazed ware: overall distribution	141
155 Central Gaulish coarse micaceous ware	142
156 Central Gaulish coarse micaceous ware: overall distribution	142
157 Central Gaulish fine micaceous wares	143
158 Central Gaulish fine micaceous wares: British distribution	143
159 Central Gaulish fine micaceous wares: overall distribution	144
160 Céramique à l'éponge	144
161 Céramique à l'éponge: British distribution	145
162 Céramique à l'éponge: overall distribution	145
163 E ware: British and Irish distribution	145
164 E ware	146
165 E ware: overall distribution	146
166 Lower Rhineland (Cologne) colour-coated ware	147
167 Lower Rhineland (Cologne) colour-coated ware: British distribution	148
168 Lower Rhineland (Cologne) colour-coated ware: overall distribution	148
169 Lyon ware	149
170 Lyon ware: British distribution	149
171 Lyon ware: overall distribution	149
172 German marbled wares	150
173 German marbled wares: British distribution	151
174 Late Roman Mayen ware	151
175 Late Roman Mayen ware: overall distribution	152
176 Late Roman Mayen ware: British distribution	152
177 North African red slip ware	153
178 North African red slip ware: British distribution	153
179 North African red slip ware: overall distribution	153
180 North Gaulish grey wares	154
181 North Gaulish grey wares: British distribution	155
182 North Gaulish grey wares: overall distribution	155
183 Phocaean red slip ware	156
184 Phocaean red slip ware: British distribution	156
185 Pompeian-Red ware – fabric 1	157
186 Pompeian-Red ware – fabric 1: British distribution	157
187 Pompeian-Red ware – fabric 1: overall distribution	158
188 Pompeian-Red ware – fabric 2	158
189 Pompeian-Red ware – fabric 2: British distribution	158
190 Pompeian-Red ware – fabric 3	159
191 Pompeian-Red ware – fabric 3: British distribution	159
192 Pompeian-Red ware – fabric 3: overall distribution	159
193 South Gaulish colour-coated ware	160
194 South Gaulish colour-coated ware: British distribution	160
195 Spanish colour-coated ware	160
196 Spanish colour-coated ware: British distribution	161
197 Spanish colour-coated ware: overall distribution	161
198 Gallo-Belgic wares	162
199 Gallo-Belgic wares	163
200 Gallo-Belgic wares: overall distribution	163
201 Terra rubra: British distribution	165
202 Terra nigra: British distribution	165
203 Eggshell terra nigra	166
204 Eggshell terra nigra: British distribution	166
205 Romano-British fine wares: dating of principal classes	166
206 Colchester colour-coated wares	167
207 Colchester colour-coated wares: overall distribution	168

List of Illustrations

208 Hadham red-slipped wares	169
209 Hadham red-slipped wares: overall distribution	169
210 London-Essex stamped wares	170
211 London-Essex stamped wares: overall distribution	170
212 The 'London ware' style: overall distribution	170
213 The 'London ware' style	171
214 New Forest slipped wares	172
215 New Forest slipped wares: overall distribution	173
216 Nene Valley colour-coated wares	174
217 Nene Valley colour-coated wares	175
218 Nene Valley colour-coated wares: overall distribution	175
219 Oxfordshire red/brown-slipped wares	176
220 Oxfordshire red/brown-slipped wares	177
221 Oxfordshire red/brown-slipped wares: overall distribution	178
222 South-east English glazed ware	179
223 South-east English glazed ware: overall distribution	179
224 Romano-British coarse wares: dating of principal classes	180
225 Alice Holt/Farnham grey wares	181
226 Alice Holt/Farnham grey wares: overall distribution	182
227 South-east Dorset black-burnished 1	183
228 South-east Dorset black-burnished 1	184
229 South-east Dorset black-burnished 1: overall distribution	185
230 Rossington Bridge BB1	186
231 Rossington Bridge BB1: overall distribution	186
232 Black-burnished 2	187
233 Black-burnished 2: overall distribution	188
234 Crambeck wares: overall distribution	188
235 Crambeck wares	189
236 Dales ware and Dales-type ware	190
237 Dales ware and Dales-type ware: overall distribution	190
238 Derbyshire ware	191
239 Derbyshire ware: overall distribution	191
240 Late Roman grog-tempered wares: overall distribution	191
241 Late Roman grog-tempered wares	192
242 South Midlands shell-tempered wares	193
243 South Midlands shell-tempered wares: overall distribution	193
244 North Kent shell-tempered storage jars	194
245 North Kent shell-tempered storage jars: overall distribution	194
246 Portchester fabric D: overall distribution	194
247 Portchester fabric D	195
248 Savernake-type grey wares: overall distribution	195
249 Savernake-type grey wares	196
250 South Devon burnished ware	196
251 South Devon burnished ware: overall distribution	197
252 Severn Valley wares	198
253 Severn Valley wares	199
254 Severn Valley wares: overall distribution	199
255 Verulamium-region white ware	200
256 Verulamium-region white ware: overall distribution	201
257 Structure of a pottery recording system	205

LIST OF TABLES

1	Principal publications on Romano-British pottery by Charles Roach Smith	4
2	Principal reports on Romano-British kilns and kiln sites	5
3	Quantification of Roman pottery from sites in Cranborne Chase	8
4	Principal publications on terra sigillata	9
5	Major publications on Romano-British pottery by Thomas May	15
6	Principal publications of Romano-British kiln and kiln assemblages	16
7	Volumes on Romano-British pottery published by BAR	23
8	The growth in the number of Roman kiln sites identified in Britain	27
9	Romano-British wares identified	27
10	Modes of pottery production	34
11	The distribution of graffiti by type of vessel	45
12	Amphoras from Hengistbury Head	50
13	The archaeological contexts of Dressel 1 amphoras in Britain	50
14	Principal pottery imports into pre-Roman Britain	52
15	Late Iron Age coarse-ware assemblage at Puddlehill	55
16	Pre-Flavian fine-ware imports to Britain	57
17	Amphoras and contents from 1970 excavations at Sheepen	57
18	Imported mortaria in pre-Flavian Britain	58
19	Immigrant potters operating in pre-Flavian Britain	59
20	Techniques in 'legionary ware' industries in Britain	65
21	Colour-coated industries following Lower Rhineland traditions	68
22	Romano-British samian and other moulded wares	68
23	Bar Hill ware assemblage	69
24	Types of pottery imported to Britain *c.* AD250–400	72
25	Types of pottery in the Guernsey shipwreck	73
26	Major late Romano-British industries	77
27	Comparison of sherd types of Roman material from Roman and Saxon contexts	79
28	Types of imported pottery in western Britain	81
29	Roman measures of capacity	87
30	Typology of Gaulish amphoras	94
31	Principal terra sigillata type-series	105
32	Colchester sigillata potters	114
33	Principal Corbridge mortarium potters	119
34	Principal Colchester mortarium potters	120
35	Principal Lincolnshire mortarium potters	122
36	Principal Mancetter-Hartshill mortarium potters	123
37	Principal North Gaulish mortarium potters	127
38	Principal Nene Valley mortarium potters	127
39	Principal Rossington Bridge mortarium potters	130
40	Principal Verulamium-region mortarium potters	132
41	Principal Wilderspool mortarium potters	135
42	Principal Central Gaulish black-slipped forms	138
43	Principal Trier black-slipped ware forms	139
44	Classification of Central Gaulish glazed-ware forms	140
45	Classification of *la céramique à l'éponge* forms	144
46	Classification of E ware forms	145
47	Classification of Lower Rhineland colour-coated ware forms	148
48	Classification of Lyon ware forms	150
49	Classification of Late Roman Mayen ware forms	152
50	Pompeian-Red ware fabrics	156
51	Gallo-Belgic wares: concordance and dating of principal forms	164
52	Classification of Colchester colour-coated forms	168
53	Classification of New Forest slipped ware forms	173
54	Classification of Nene Valley colour-coated ware forms	173
55	Classification of Oxfordshire red/brown-slipped ware forms	178
56	Classification of South-east English glazed ware forms	178

List of Tables

57 Classification of South-east Dorset BB1 forms   185
58 Classification of Crambeck ware forms   188
59 Classification of Late Roman grog-tempered forms   191
60 Classification of South Midlands shell-tempered ware forms   192
61 Classification of Portchester D ware forms   195
62 Classification of Severn Valley ware classes   197
63 Classification of Verulamium-region forms   201

ACKNOWLEDGEMENTS

A work of synthesis such as this inevitably relies on the work of many other students of the subject, both contemporaries and predecessors. For permission to reproduce original illustrations I would like to thank Anne Anderson (166), Paul Arthur (222), Colchester and Essex Museum (9), Michael Fulford (122,214), Kevin Greene (152), Neil Holbrook, Paul Bidwell, Christopher Henderson and Exeter City Museums (227–8, 250), the London Archaeologist (64, 68), the London and Middlesex Archaeological Society (82, 232, 255), Prof. W. H. Manning, the University of Wales Press and Board of Celtic Studies (33, 75, 169, 193, 195), the Museum of London (134, 146, 149, 213), the Peterborough City Museum and Nene Valley Archaeological Research Committee (126, 216–17), the Society of Antiquaries of London (3, 7, 12, 73, 101, 198–9, 206), the Surrey Archaeological Society (82, 232, 255), and Christopher Young (128, 219–20). The illustrations by Mr J. P. Gillam (105, 108, 110, 117, 119, 236, 238) are reproduced by permission of the Society of Antiquaries of Newcastle upon Tyne and Mr Andrew Gillam. Most of the data incorporated on the maps in the Atlas has been collected from published sources, but I would like to thank Jane Timby and Marc Pomel for access to data included in their unpublished theses (210, 202, 240). The text does not take account of any publications after January 1994.

I would like to thank the many individuals and organisations who contributed to the production of this book, often unknowingly: the staff of the libraries of the Institute of Archaeology (University College London), the Joint Library of the Hellenic and Roman Societies (London) and the Society of Antiquaries of London for their unfailing assistance; Maggie Darling and Barbara Davies (of the City of Lincoln Archaeological Unit), Joanna Bird, Michael Fulford and Peter Kemmis Betty, for their comments on early drafts of the Atlas pages or text, much to their improvement; Barbara West, for her sterling work mounting the illustrations; Christopher Harvey for his assistance during the final processing of the PostScript files; John Dore, for tracking down the photograph of John Gillam (10); Mr A. Tyers and Mr J. Bailey for the loan of items of office equipment; David Brown of Oxbow Books (Oxford); Michael Rhodes, for drawing my attention to the Burkitt engraving (3); Clive Orton, Alan Vince and Harvey Sheldon, for many small points of advice and comments; and, finally, Juliet Bailey, for tea and sympathy.

INTRODUCTION

If you visit an archaeological excavation on a Roman site in Britain, you may be guided around the trenches and the sequence of activity will be explained to you. Buildings come and go, pits are dug and filled, roads are shifted and floors laid out, as the ground-level slowly rises. Some of the people you see may be digging furiously with pick and shovel, demolishing walls or clearing topsoil; others will be delicately clearing surfaces, or drawing plans. Beside the excavators in the trenches you may see trays and bags where they are collecting all the objects as they work their way through each successive layer.

Some of the muddy lumps in the trays are recognizable even from a distance as bones, or bits of brick and tile. To one side of the excavation area you see someone washing the lumps and laying them out to dry in trays. There seems to be rather a lot. You move across and finger a few pieces. Many of the smaller ones, and some bigger ones, are sherds of pottery. Red, white, black, and all shapes and sizes; some very fine and glossy, others dark and coarse; some plain, some with raised decoration on the surfaces. You follow the line of drying trays across the ground. It leads towards one of the site huts. Someone is sitting outside with pen and ink, marking numbers and letters on all the sherds, not looking very happy.

Go inside the hut and there is more pottery – pottery in boxes, bags and trays, on shelves, on the floor, under the table. Some sherds sit in splendid isolation in plastic bags that are too big for them. The labels inside the bag are covered in numbers, letters and symbols. On the tables there are sherds laid out like a three-dimensional jigsaw puzzle. Some sherds are sitting at odd angles in trays of sand, and the pots are beginning to take shape from the fragments. The walls of the hut are decorated with faded photocopies of drawings of pottery, annotated with numbers and letters. Record sheets and cards are being filled in. Bags of sherds are being weighed, measured, counted, catalogued. There may be someone transferring streams of the letter and number codes on to a computer.

You pause a moment and listen. There are strange mutterings. 'It's a Drag 18, 70 to 100.' 'Is it Peacock's fabric one?'

The occupants of the hut might be brought out, like performing seals, to show their tricks. How did we date the large pit? The pottery suggests it is later than AD 70 but before 120. And where did the pottery come from? Well, the majority is local – produced within 10km of here – but we have these imports from Gaul and Italy, and these are from Baetica. Baetica? That was a Roman province in southern Spain, near Seville. What was the pot used for? As a container for olive-oil. So Spanish olive-oil was being used here during the Roman period? Well, it certainly looks like that.

WHY BOTHER WITH POT?

A well-fired ceramic is one of the most indestructible of materials. In most soil conditions pottery will survive with little obvious physical deterioration for thousands of years. On archaeological sites of the Roman period, pottery is the commonest of finds. But why do we bother doing anything with it? What uses, actual or potential, can be made of ceramic data in Roman archaeology?

The most common use of pottery is probably as a means of *dating* sites. Pottery (and many other artefacts) will change their shape or character with the passing of time. Just as the pottery in common use in the nineteenth century differs from that of today, so the pottery of the first century differs from the second. The changes are partly due to changing technology or sources, partly to developing tastes and fashions.

Pottery is not inherently datable, but relies on the building up of a web of connections between types and contexts that are dated from other evidence. In the Roman period that usually means dating by historical reference, inscriptions or coinage. Thus the burnt levels in Colchester, London and St Albans that are identified as the destruction wrought by Boudicca in AD 60/61 – a historically attested event – provide a horizon against which we can test whether a particular variety of pot is already in circulation. Some types are already present in these levels, but others may appear later in the sequence, so were not introduced until after that date. Of course, this only works if the original identification is correct, and the excavated fire horizon is not some accidental conflagration a decade or so later.

A similar process applies to, for instance, the pottery assemblages from the strings of forts founded and occupied during campaigns such as that along the Rhine frontier under the Emperor Augustus, or the Agricolan occupation of Scotland, for which we have written evidence. The pottery from these sites shows which types were in circulation at those periods – with the same proviso that the identification and dating of the sites is correct. Sometimes the historical sequence is less certain, or open to different interpretations, such as the sequence of occupation on the Antonine Wall in Scotland where the historical references are ambiguous. Pottery assemblages may be assigned to one 'historical' period, and then another, with consequent shifts in the dating of a type.

There will also be significant assemblages of pottery that have no historical context, but may be dated by other means, perhaps coins. Generally, a coin gives the lowest possible date for an assemblage. A coin of AD 139 in a pit shows that it cannot have been filled before that date, but does not tell us how long after that date this was done. Of course, as with the 'historically dated' groups, there is always the possibility of redeposited material. Perhaps earlier levels were disturbed or truncated during digging in ancient times, and pottery that had already been buried for twenty or thirty years was mixed with later pottery and coins, and dumped in a pit. Once a satisfactory framework has been established then this is precisely the sort of thing that pottery can help to untangle, but in earlier stages of a study it will tend to make the dating of some types rather fuzzy.

However, once established, the date of a type can be transferred from one site to another. If a samian pot is found in Boudiccan destruction levels at London, it may suggest a similar date (plus or minus some margin) for an identical pot at a site without any historical horizon. This in turn may suggest dates for the other pottery types in a feature, which in turn may date other features, other types and so on. Keeping track of this nightmarish web of connections is by reference to established typological series, fabric types, named potters and dies (where appropriate) or stylistic trends.

Individual pottery forms develop and change through time. To take just one example, the ring-necked flagons from the potteries operating in the St Albans area during the first and second centuries AD start off (in the period AD 70–100) with a flaring trumpet-shaped mouth with evenly spaced, equally sized rings. From about AD 120 the topmost ring swells to become larger, more rounded and more prominent than the others. A couple of decades later a new variety appears, where the rings form a short expanding mouth. This sequence of developments is dated by reference to the stratified sequence in London and St Albans, dated by a combination of coins and externally dated pottery types such as samian wares. But the dated sequence of flagons can now be used on sites elsewhere in the region, perhaps where samian and coins are rarer.

With a certain amount of experience, most ceramicists will begin to recognize not only a Flavian flagon type, but also the character of a Flavian assemblage. Some wares may be largely confined to assemblages of a certain date – or the balance of two or more wares (with some declining towards extinction, with others rising towards their peak) may suggest the place of a group in the sequence, and hence its date. These feelings can be expressed formally as the percentage in the group, using some measure of the quantity of pottery, but for some day-to-day purposes a rather looser impressionistic assessment may be all that is possible.

It is implicit in this that the sources of pottery change with time, just as much as the shape of the individual pieces. This brings us to the topic of *economics and trade*, the second major use that is currently made of pottery data. At some periods the majority of pottery in use on a site will be from sources that are relatively close, while at others it may be from far away.

The distribution patterns of pottery give us information about the differing marketing roles of, for instance, small towns versus regional capitals, or the relative benefits of river versus land transport. The proportions of the assemblage on each site from known sources will vary. If we have data from many sites we can see how the amount of pottery found drops off with distance from the source – this is known as the decay rate. Fluctuating proportions of the assemblage will be imported into Britain from sources in Gaul, Spain, Italy and elsewhere around the Mediterranean.

Patterns of the long-distance movements of goods around the Empire have been used to investigate the importance of the Roman State authorities in the opening and maintenance of official supply routes, particularly from Gaul and the Mediterranean through to the armies stationed along the northern frontiers, including Britain. Many of the pots that moved long distances functioned as transport-containers for oil, wine and other specialized commodities, such as fish-sauces. The origins of these changed with time, and we can see in the pots the physical evidence of the agricultural investment and development in successive regions, that is also described by ancient historians. The State probably had an important role, for in securing supplies for its troops and administrators and the corn supply for Rome, it encouraged production and exports from, for instance, the North African provinces. This led to the wide distribution of African amphoras and other wares around the Mediterranean, and their appearance as far away as Britain. Pottery in these cases may be an indestructible marker for the movement of perishable goods and materials, such as foodstuffs, that have now dis-

Introduction

appeared from the archaeological record.

Transport-containers were not the only *function* of pottery. Most would have been used for the storage, preparation or service of food. Comparisons between the range of pottery types in use on sites of the same period, or different areas of a single site, may show that different functions were being carried out. There are indications that urban and rural assemblages differ significantly, as do the assemblages from different parts of the country. This type of functional analysis is still in its infancy – indeed the relevant data is only now starting to become available in any quantity – but it is likely to be a fruitful area of research.

Of course, not all differences are purely functional, they have a *social context* as well. Higher-status sites may have access to a wider range of pottery types and perhaps some of higher quality. But does our classification have any bearing on questions of value and desirability? If we look at the distribution of ownership marks we find them most commonly on finer wares such as samian, perhaps suggesting that they were indeed more highly valued. What is not so clear with questions of either status or function is whether we should be concerned with differences between features on a site, or only dealing with differences between sites, or even at a multi-site level.

Another use made of ceramic data is its use in the study of *site formation*. Periods of truncation or levelling on a site may result in the Roman sherds being recycled through a number of deposits, until they come to a final rest in a much later level. Successive episodes of disturbance may affect the sherds, perhaps making them smaller, rounding the corners or abrading the surfaces. In some cases, analysis of the Roman sherds in medieval or post-medieval deposits can give valuable clues about the activity on the site, and the Roman material is here being used as a marker for these processes.

Most of the topics introduced above will be discussed in more detail in chapters 2 and 3 of this book. The history of Romano-British pottery studies is discussed in chapter 1. Chapter 4 gives an overview of the development of the pottery industry on historical lines.

The major pottery types which are encountered in the narrative are described in the Atlas (pp. 83-201). Each entry has a description, distribution map and illustrations, with comment on dating and sources, and a bibliography for further reference. While far from exhaustive, the Atlas entries cover the major types of Roman pottery encountered in Britain (both imports and locally produced) and some rarer items that are important for the historical narrative.

PART ONE

1 A brief history of Roman pottery studies

The study of Roman pottery has a long history in Britain. Its role has developed as the aims of archaeology and Romano-British studies themselves have changed, and new techniques and tools have become available. For most of the twentieth century pottery held a key place in the dating of Roman sites and the study of trading patterns, both within the province and within the rest of the Empire. Love it or hate it – and there are plenty more than willing to take up cudgels on both sides of the argument – pottery cannot be ignored by the student of Roman Britain.

This chapter gives a historical overview of Romano-British pottery studies. The diverse approaches taken up to the end of the nineteenth century are summarized in section 1.1. The foundations of the subject can be considered to have been laid by 1900, and developments from then until the 1970s are described in sections 1.2 and 1.3. There were significant increases in the quantity of pottery that was being recovered from the large-scale urban excavations during the 1960s. This, a range of new techniques and the new questions that were being asked of the pottery, combined to form the modern approach to the subject. These themes are introduced in section 1.4, and considered individually in more detail in chapters 2 and 3.

1.1   THE BEGINNINGS OF THE STUDY

Roman pottery would doubtless have been a fairly common find in the towns and fields of Britain in the centuries following the Roman occupation, turning up in ditch digging and building work whenever Roman sites were disturbed. The views of those who found any sherds are unrecorded, and there are very few clues. But we do know that samian sherds, for instance, are excavated occasionally on sites of the Viking and early medieval period, and they may be shaped and pierced. Perhaps they were collected for their bright red colour, and used as amulets or talismans. At least a part of the thin scatter of Roman pottery recorded from Ireland is likely to have been carried there long after the Roman period for some such purpose (Warner 1976).

In 1586, the antiquary William Camden compiled his great survey of the history and topography of the British Isles, *Britannia*, the model for many succeeding antiquarian studies. Among his catalogues of Roman monuments, coins and readings from inscriptions we find mention of 'urnes'. Urn burial, that is, the burial in pots of cremated remains, was the subject of *Hydriotaphia* (1658), by Sir Thomas Browne, a noted religious and scientific writer. Some of the vessels he described are Roman in date, but his concerns lay not with the pot but the religious implication of the customs and ceremonies they had formed a part of. Some years later an account of his discovery of pots and a kiln at Brampton, Norfolk, was published (Browne 1712). These are likely to have been Roman, for the site lies in the middle of one of the county's largest kiln fields (Swan 1984, fiche 495).

Roman pottery and structures must have turned up frequently during new building work in the country's cities. Only rarely have records of such events survived down to the present day. The diary of one John Conyers, an apothecary based in Fleet Street, which is now preserved in the British Museum (*Sloane* MSS 958, f.105 ff.), records his observations in and around the City of London following the Great Fire of 1666. Conyers' manuscripts for 1673 and 1677 record the discovery, during the digging of the foundations of St Paul's Cathedral, of large quantities of pottery of many different types, and a number of kiln structures, including four arranged in a cross with a common stoke-hole (Marsh 1981, 195-7, with refs; Swan 1984, fiche 485). The drawings of the pots and the descriptions he gives allow us to recognize samian, colour-coated, mica-dusted and various types of local coarse wares. Readings of some of the stamps on the samian vessels are given. For Conyers these stamps recorded not the maker of the pots but the users – thus the stamp OF.PRIMANI showed that the vessel was intended for the First Legion. Conyers' observations, despite their deficiencies, remain an important record of pottery manufacturing in this area of London, and it was not for three centuries that the rest of the picture could be filled in.

Pudding pans and samian vessels
The early volumes of the Society of Antiquaries' journal *Archaeologia* (founded in 1774) contain a number of papers on the subject of Roman pottery discovered in Britain. Volume V

A brief history of Roman pottery studies

(for 1779) includes a paper by Thomas Pownall entitled 'Memoire on the Roman earthen ware fished up within the mouth of the River Thames'. It had been observed that fishermen living along the north coast of Kent had among their household effects, a number of complete Roman vessels. Investigation by Pownall and his brother revealed that the source of these vessels lay off the coast at a sand-bar known as Pudding Pan Sand. Many sherds and fewer complete vessels had been recovered from this site, and they seemed to be particularly easy to 'catch' after storms. The general opinion in the district was that the pottery came from a wreck on the sands.

Pownall's instinct was to turn to the Classical sources for an explanation of this phenomenon. Firstly, he suggested that Pudding Pan Sand should be equated with one of the islands in the Thames estuary listed in Ptolemy's *Geography*, and he pointed to the occasional bricks that had been recovered from the same area as evidence of a sunken building. The pots themselves, with their fine red surfaces, he called 'Ionian or Samian', citing a Dutch scholar, Samuel Pitiscus, as his source (A. K. B. Evans 1981, 522–3, 531 fn.12). Pownall concluded that the material derived from a 'manufactory' making holy vessels and suggested that the stamps on the vessels – and he had only seen examples stamped ATTILIANI – were to certify their origin. Attilianus, in this scenario, was the director of a guild of potters, such as that set up by King Numa, the second of Rome's seven legendary monarchs (Plutarch, *Numa*, 17; Pliny, *Natural History*, xxxv, 46).

There were two rejoinders to this paper in the next volume of the journal (volume VI, for 1782). Edward Jacob pointed out that more than one stamp was present among the material from Pan Sand, and repeated the local view that there was a wreck on the site (1782). George Keate disputed that the material represented a manufactory and a college of potters and suggested that the vessels were not solely for religious purposes. He concluded that 'they might have baked puddings and pies, stewed meats, or served for tarts or custards. And the unenlightened fishermen have very sensibly and very uniformly applied them to these purposes, till the ardour of the antiquary rescued them from their hands' – a splendid example of the role of ethnographic observation in the service of Roman pottery studies (Keate 1782). Before we leave Pudding Pan Sand, we should note that the name of the sand-bar is almost certainly derived from the frequent discoveries of these Roman 'pudding pans' in the vicinity – the only place in Britain named after a Roman pottery type.

Undeterred by his experiences at Pudding Pan, Pownall returned to the subject of Roman pottery in 1787 in his description of a red-ware bowl with moulded decoration found at Sandy, Bedfordshire. The vessel was almost complete, and an illustration, 'made by a young lady', accompanies the paper. Pownall went on to describe the material thus:

I must now inform the Society that pottery of this very fabrique, with exactly similar mouldings and ornaments, is at this day found in Provence and Languedoc, particularly at Aix and Nismes; at Vienne in Dauphine; and in many parts of France; and also in many parts of Switzerland ... This fabrique was usually called the Samian, mentioned by Pliny, XXXV, 46 ... originally made at Samos, but afterwards ... at Rome.

So, to Pownall's satisfaction at least, the link was made between the British material, the extensive continental distribution and the references in the Classical texts.

Alongside such Classically based interpretations of excavated pottery, there were others who produced simple catalogues of material. An early example of such a report is that by Combe and Jackson on the material recovered during rescue archaeology in advance of sewer construction in Lombard Street and Birchin Lane (London). Their paper includes many of the elements that were to become commonplace in Roman pottery reports – several pages of illustrations, a catalogue of the material, with descriptions of the fabrics, and lists and drawings of stamps on both 'coral-coloured ware' (that is, samian – not everyone was convinced by Pownall's view on this ware) and mortaria (Combe and Jackson 1787, 126 and 130; Orton, Tyers and Vince 1993, 6–7, fig. 1.1). In the precise illustrations of the mortaria several can still be recognized as the stamps of potters we now know to be from the Verulamium region industry, such as SOLLUS and SECUNDUS.

So even at this early date we can distinguish two strands in the approach to Roman ceramics. Firstly, there is the attempt to relate the material to the broader picture of Roman Britain gleaned from other sources, in this case the Classical literature, and if possible to use the vessels to illustrate some aspect of that picture. Secondly, there is the publication of assemblages more or less for their own sake and as a record of what had been found during archaeological investigations. The later history of the subject can be seen, in part at least, as the interplay between the competing requirements of these two poles of endeavour.

Edmund Tyrell Artis

The next major advances in the study of Roman pottery in Britain took place in the Nene valley in the 1820s. Edmund Tyrell Artis (1787–1847) was house steward in the Northamptonshire home of Earl Fitzwilliam, and later counted the Duke of Bedford among his patrons. His early interest was not in archaeology but in geology. He amassed a large collection of Coal Measure fossil plants, which was sold to the British Museum in 1825, and published a volume of plates on his discoveries in the same year. He was elected as a Fellow of the Geological Society in 1824, sponsored by the

A brief history of Roman pottery studies

distinguished geologist William Buckland, Canon of Christ Church, Oxford and later Dean of Westminster. Among his other talents, Artis was also an accomplished artist and illustrator, and the Northamptonshire rural poet John Clare was part of his circle (Tomlinson 1974; Crowther 1984).

Artis commenced excavations in the vicinity of Castor, near Peterborough, in 1821 and uncovered extensive remains of Roman occupation including kilns and other traces of pottery manufacturing (1). He published a collected volume of fine plates illustrating his discoveries in 1828, entitled *The Durobrivae of Antoninus Identified and Illustrated*. He interpreted the site as the Durobrivas listed in *Iter V* of the *Antonine Itinerary*, a Roman document listing routes and posting stations across the Empire. The plates were never accompanied by a text in Artis's own hand – apparently because of the high costs of publication and distribution of the plates, borne by Artis out of his own funds. Almost twenty years later, Charles Roach Smith published an account of a paper given by Artis to a meeting of the newly founded British Archaeological Association in Canterbury in 1845, which described the results of Artis's excavations, and his interpretations of the pottery manufacturing carried out there (Smith 1845).

After his excavations in the 1820s, Artis spent more of his time on business activities, including the purchase and management of a restaurant in Doncaster which catered for the racing fraternity. He recommenced large-scale excavations on the Duke of Bedford's estate at Sibson (Northants) from 1844 (Artis 1847), a campaign during which he was deserted by his labourers due to inclement winter conditions. Artis illustrated a wide range of vessels from his Castor excavations, but in particular a series of beakers and flasks which were generally dark in colour, with white fabrics, and often decorated with scrolls or other simple motifs in white slip, or more complex barbotine figures representing hunting scenes, with stags and hounds. In consequence of Artis's work such vessels became known as Castor ware (or, more rarely, Durobrivan ware). It was soon recognized that this type of ware was abundant on many sites in Britain, but was also found in some quantity in France (Smith 1845, 8-9) and in consequence Castor ware became more of a stylistic term than the description of the product of a particular industry.

In addition to describing the pottery from Castor, Artis was also concerned with the structure of the kilns and their operation. He performed experiments to attempt to duplicate the colour and texture of the Roman pottery, and made calculations about the number of workmen – he suggested 2000 – employed in the potteries. These concerns seem to reflect the very practical outlook of a man who had dealt with such problems throughout his life.

Artis and Roach Smith apparently intended to collaborate in the publication of a supplementary volume of text and illustrations to accompany *The Durobrivae*. They placed a call for subscribers to *An Account of Discoveries of Roman*

1 *E. T. Artis directing excavations of a Roman pottery kiln at Castor*

A brief history of Roman pottery studies

Remains, at and near Castor, in the County of Northampton in volume 2 of the *Journal of the British Archaeological Association* (for 1846), repeating the offer in volume 3, at a price 'not to exceed one guinea'. This venture seems to have been terminated by Artis's death in the December of 1847. He is buried in the churchyard at Castor, in the heart of the Nene valley.

Charles Roach Smith

Charles Roach Smith (1806–90) was perhaps the leading antiquary of his generation, and a prolific writer, publisher and correspondent (**2**). He was born in the Isle of Wight, and as a young man was apprenticed to a pharmacist in Chichester. He arrived in London to carry on his trade in 1827, and remained there until retirement in 1855, when he moved to Strood in north Kent. His period in London – very much the London of his near contemporary, Dickens – coincided with much reconstruction and rebuilding in the capital, including the building of the sewerage system, the arrival of the railways and the demolition of the picturesque but inadequate medieval Old London Bridge. Roach Smith was often on hand to observe operations and acquire antiquities from the workmen for his collection.

From the 1840s, Roach Smith published a series of papers on Roman pottery (**table 1**), in both Britain and France (which he visited often), and amassed a large collection of Roman objects from London, including large numbers of samian vessels. His 1848 paper 'On the red-glazed pottery of the Romans' – that is samian or terra sigillata in modern parlance – is the first of any consequence to tackle the problems

2 Charles Roach Smith

of a single class of Roman pottery written in English. He described in some detail the form, fabric, stamps and decoration of the ware. The majority of the British material, he suggested, was manufactured in Gaul, citing as evidence the fact that most of the potters' names found in British collections could be paralleled in collections from Trier, Tours and elsewhere in France, and the presence of kilns, stamps and moulds at Lezoux and other sites. A few specimens from Britain were considered to be better matched by the vases from Arezzo, in Tuscany, that had then only recently been published by Fabroni (1841). The most common sigillata forms are illustrated by a series of fourteen vessels, drawn in a plain but informative style, and almost to scale. Roach Smith was well aware of the works of earlier writers on this subject, such as Pownall, and their reliance on Pliny and other ancient texts as support for the identification of Samos as the source of this ware. Now, however, we can see a willingness, almost a delight, in testing the words of the Classical authors with the facts of archaeology – with drawings, catalogues, and distributions of real pottery from real places. The spirit of the age shows through.

He sold this collection to the British Museum in 1855 for £2,000, where it remains at the core of the pottery collections of the Romano-British department. His approach to pottery studies, and he should probably be considered as its

Date	Title
1845	*On Roman potters' Kilns and pottery discovered, by Mr E. T. Artis, in the county of Northampton*
1847	*On Roman pottery discovered on the banks of the Medway, near Upchurch, Kent*
1848	*Potters' marks discovered in London*
1848	*Roman sepulchral remains found at Strood, in Kent*
1848	*On the red-glazed pottery of the Romans, found in this country and on the Continent*
1855	*Romano-British pottery*
1864	*Remains of Roman potteries on the banks of the Medway, and the Nen; and in London*
1877	*Roman pottery at Gravesend*
1880	*Roman potters' kilns discovered near Colchester*
1882	*Site of Roman potteries on the banks of the Medway*

Table 1 *Principal publications on Romano-British pottery by Charles Roach Smith*

first significant exponent in this country, was described in one of his papers on the subject (Smith 1845):

> It is of the first importance to be able to classify and appropriate these various kinds of pottery; because, apart from the interest they afford as illustrations of an early art, they often serve to direct research, encourage the investigation of ancient remains, and contribute towards forming correct opinions upon objects less known which may be discovered in connection with them. A simple urn, or even a fragment of an urn, insignificant as in itself it may be, and even useless when dissociated from the circumstances under which it was discovered, gains an importance when placed in juxtaposition with authenticated facts, and may supply a link in a chain of evidence.

Roach Smith wrote several papers on the subject of the Roman potteries on the banks of the Medway, in the vicinity of Upchurch, and thus introduced the subject of Upchurch ware to the archaeological literature. Roman pottery was abundant among the creeks and dykes of the north Kent marshes – sometimes as single isolated vessels, sometimes as layers 'a foot thick' and extending over great distances. The wares from Upchurch were generally black or dark grey in colour and the forms included beakers and jars which often had incised, rouletted and barbotine decoration. This material could be recovered at low water by probing the bed of the creeks with sticks and poles. We have evocative accounts of an expedition by yacht from Chatham to the marshes by Roach Smith and his party in May 1846, when the afternoon was spent very agreeably, dabbling about in the mud and the water (Smith 1883, 214–16; T. Wright 1852) (3).

Date	Author	Site
1675	Conyers	London
1828	Artis	Nene Valley (Northants)
1851	Jewitt	Headington (Oxon.)
1852	Wright	Upchurch (Kent)
1853	Akerman	New Forest (Hants)
1868	Roach Smith	Upchurch (Kent)
1873	Bartlett	New Forest (Hants)
1878	Joslin	Colchester (Essex)

Table 2 *Principal reports on Romano-British kilns and kiln sites up to 1880*

Roach Smith's 1864 paper on Upchurch concludes with brief descriptions of the Romano-British pottery kilns then known to him, and there are additions listed in a later paper on the kilns discovered at Colchester in 1877 (1880). Together these form the first attempt to construct a gazetteer of Romano-British pottery kilns. It is notable that many of the major pottery industries, particularly of the later Roman period, are in this list – New Forest, Oxfordshire, Alice Holt, the Nene Valley, Colchester – and were thus already recorded, if far from understood, by the 1880s (**Table 2**).

The illustrations in Roach Smith's many papers were always

3 *An expedition to the Upchurch Marshes, August 1851: engraved by A. H. Burkitt*

A brief history of Roman pottery studies

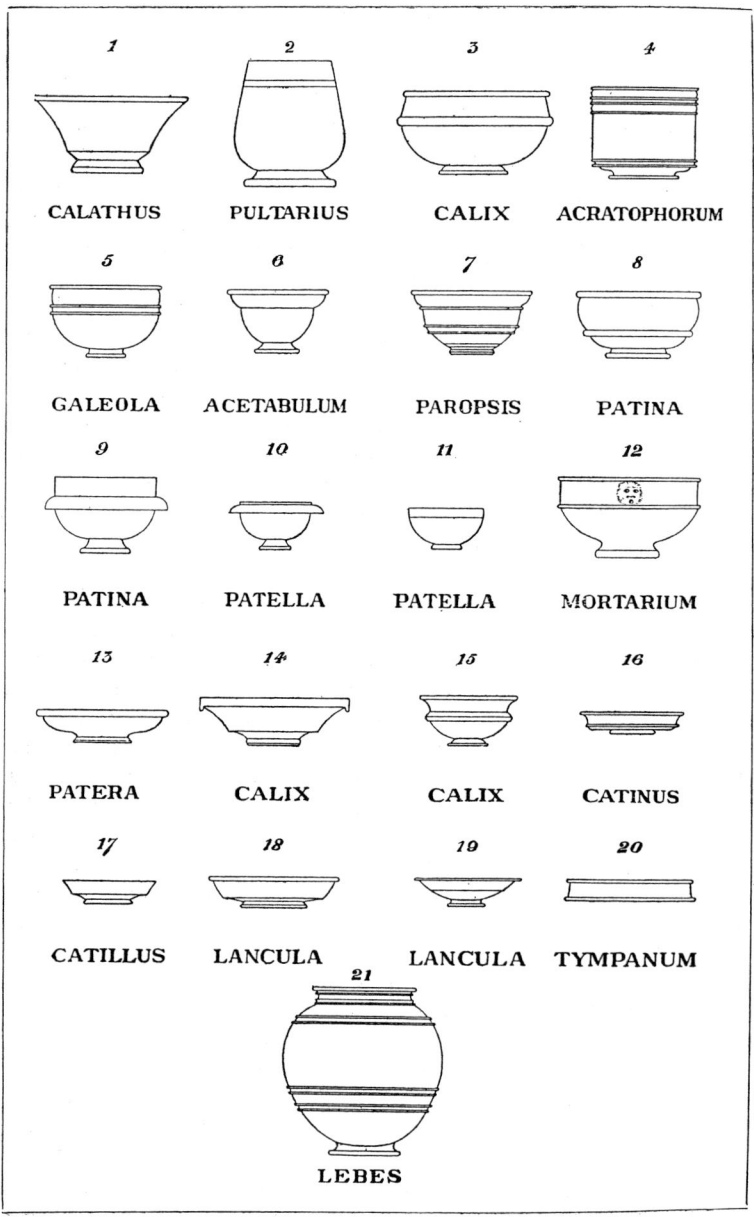

4 *Forms of samian ware with their possible Latin names (from Cuming 1891)*

of a high standard and were to be continually recycled (along with many of his ideas) through other publications for many decades (e.g. T. Wright 1872, 224–50). His work on red-glazed pottery is certainly the highpoint of the mid-nineteenth-century study of Roman ceramics in Britain.

Roach Smith was not, of course, alone in his work on Roman pottery at this period. One of his contemporaries was Llewellyn Jewitt. Jewitt was an interesting character, who at the beginning of his career had been an illustrator for Thomas Bateman, one of the nineteenth century's great barrow diggers.

Jewitt's later interests were more in pottery as an art and craft than in its archaeological value, and in 1878 he published *The Ceramic Art of Great Britain from the Prehistoric Times Down to the Present Day*, a massive compendium of obscure ceramic knowledge. Jewitt's principal archaeological contribution was a report on a group of kiln material from Headington in Oxfordshire (1851). He took particular care over his analysis of the mortaria in the group, illustrating sections of sixteen vessels from Headington and a selection (drawn to the same scale and style) from other sites – Iffley (Oxfordshire), London (including samian examples, from Roach Smith's collection), Caerleon, Castor and Keston. He comments:

> Comparison of specimens from various localities may assist us in appropriating the varieties to the potteries where they were manufactured, and it is in hope of calling forth notices and observations on the subject of sections that the present examples have been given. If a collection of the rims themselves, from all parts of the country, could be made, and arranged together, we should then be enabled to localize them at a glance; but such a desideratum is not likely to be acquired.

Jewitt foresees here not only the possibility of a type-series for a single class of pottery (in this case, for mortaria), but also fabric collections of the type that became *de rigueur* during the 1970s – and also a hint of the difficulties that would be encountered in maintaining them. It is perhaps to be regretted that his later interests took him off down the route to *The Ceramic Art* rather than to some further development of his ideas on the treatment of archaeological ceramics.

Parts of the descriptive language still in use were already in place by the middle of the nineteenth century. The term 'roughcast ware' as a description of a common decorative technique where fine clay or sand particles are applied to the vessel surface, seems to derive from an 1871 paper by H. Syer Cuming on material from Wilderspool. He cites the similarity between the technique and the 'rough-casting' applied to the surface of rustic edifices. The sherds in question are illustrated particularly clearly by an early form of photographic reproduction. For forms, terms derived from Latin sources, such as *amphora* and *olla*, were used widely from the 1850s, often prompted by the descriptions published in the Classical dictionaries of the period. This process culminates in Cuming's own analysis of samian ware (1891). He describes and illustrates twenty-one forms (4) in the ware and attempts to assign a Latin name to each. References to Classical authors from Alciphron to Varro are drawn in to illustrate the possible uses to which each might have been put on the Roman table.

General Pitt Rivers

The later nineteenth century was a time when intellectual endeavour was advancing on many fronts. The new sciences of archaeology, ethnography and anthropology drew inspiration from Darwinism, the theories of the social evolutionists, geology and other pure sciences. From this rich soup of ideas a man like Pitt Rivers drew freely and easily. Lieutenant-General Augustus Henry Lane Fox Pitt Rivers (1827–1900) had been born into one of the outer branches of a large landed family, but due to a series of unexpected deaths, came to inherit (in 1880) large estates in Cranborne Chase, Dorset, as well as the Pitt Rivers surname. Prior to this his earlier career had been as an officer in the army, and he had accumulated large collections of ethnographic objects, particularly weapons.

In his writings, Pitt Rivers displays a considerable concern with cultural evolution, and his principal tools were classification and 'typology' – a word he claimed, with some justification, to have invented (1891, 116). Pitt Rivers wrote extensively about the evolution of weaponry, tools and other implements and organized his collections of artefacts on evolutionary lines, and the underlying subtext of much of his writings was the concern to demonstrate that cultural evolution (rather than revolution) was the natural order of things. His foremost contributions to archaeology are to be found in the four privately published, blue-bound and gold-tooled volumes of *Excavations in Cranborne Chase*. In the preface to volume 3 (published in 1892) he expounds his views on the value and function of ceramics for the archaeologist. It is worth quoting at length from this, for it expresses in the General's usual clear and down-to-earth tones the potential of pottery studies:

> Vessels of pottery in prehistoric and Roman times, were subject to breakage, as are now our less fragile and more durable ones; the pieces were not carried away by the dustman, as is now the case, but were scattered and trampled into the soil. In the course of time, the fragments have broken up into smaller bits, of a more or less uniform size, so that by counting the pieces of different qualities, a good idea may be formed of the different kinds of fictile ware in use at the time. Then, as now, the better class of earthenware was used by the better class of people, so that by calculating the percentage of each kind, some notion may be formed of the comparative wealth of the inhabitant of any site that may be explored. I have found this practically, to be of use in my explorations. In places occupied by the Roman Conquerors of the Island, Samian pottery and other pottery of a hard quality, is found in a much larger proportion than the commoner kinds, used in Romano-British Villages of the poorer sort, some of which was made in local kilns, and some probably, even cooked in an ordinary turf fire, as was still the practice in the Hebrides, until a comparatively recent date. The grains of stone, quartz, sand, flint, shell, and other substances, mixed up, in considerable quantities, in pottery of the commoner kind, to prevent its cracking in the fire, may be traced to their original beds, and will probably afford, when properly studied, a clue to the district in which the vessels were fabricated, and when the kilns were discovered, the distribution of their products will be a means of tracing the trade routes, that were frequented at the time. These lines of distribution may almost be hunted over fields, so widely was the pottery diffused and so permanently

A brief history of Roman pottery studies

are the little bits preserved in the soil.

A good knowledge of the local kilns will therefore add greatly to our knowledge of earthworks; but investigations into the sites of ancient potteries can hardly be said, as yet, to have become so serious a study as the subject demands. As a rule, when kilns have been discovered and described, no attempt has been made to classify the different kinds of pottery found in them. I admit that the identification and classification of fragments of pottery is difficult, but not so much so, as to discourage the attempt.

Viewed in this light, the study of the ceramatist becomes a serious one, well worthy of taking its place by the side of that of the numismatist, to which it is to some extent allied; for if the date of the various qualities of pottery, in any district, can be determined by means of coins found in local kilns, then, as the pottery is so much more widely diffused, the knowledge acquired in this way is made available over a large area.

In these few paragraphs are introduced many of the themes of the succeeding century of Romano-British pottery studies – the concerns with quantification, fabric classification, distributional studies, the identification and study of kiln sites, the incorporation of ethnographic data, and the analysis of functional and social variation between assemblages.

The practical application of many of these ideas can be seen in the same volume, where the Roman ceramics from three sites in Cranborne Chase are described and compared (**table 3**). The pottery is classified by a combination of fabric (e.g. samian wares, New Forest hard wares) and form (rims with twisted rope-pattern, bead rims) and quantified by sherd count. The discussion of the data points out the varying percentage of samian, New Forest and bead-rim jars, and interprets some of these as differences caused by the status of the sites, others as due to the effects of distribution from production sites. The pottery is illustrated in a series of plates, with scale drawings and rim sections. However, as with many other aspects of Pitt Rivers's work and ideas, his views on pottery analysis did not have the impact that might have been expected on the succeeding generation (Bowden 1991, 162–5). To take just the pottery illustrations, many published during the last two decades of the century failed to reach the standards of Pitt Rivers, even to the extent of failing to draw to scale, and in style they seem to have more in common with those earlier in the century.

The next advance in Roman pottery studies, when it came, was not from within British Victorian science, but from the pen of a German scholar.

1.2 FROM DRAGENDORFF TO CAMULODUNUM

Terra sigillata

In volume 96 of the German archaeological journal *Bonner Jahrbücher*, for 1895, is a paper entitled simply 'Terra sigillata'. It is probably one of the most influential archaeological papers ever written, particularly if we were to employ such a currently fashionable criterion as citation counting. The author, Hans Dragendorff (1870–1941), had studied at Bonn where he was a pupil of Siegfried Loeschcke, another major figure in Roman pottery studies. He excavated widely in Greece and the Near East and was later Secretary General of the influential German Archaeological Institute. His work on

| | Woodcuts 27721 | | Rotherley 18932 | | Woodyates 28489 | |
Total number of fragments found	No.	Per cent	No.	Per cent	No.	Per cent
Red samian pottery	585	2.11	437	2.3	248	0.9
Imitation samian	0	0	0	0	166	0.6
Total samian	585	2.11	437	2.3	414	1.5
New Forest hard ware	218	0.78	17	0.09	1141	4.0
New Forest cream-coloured ware	27	0.1	1	0.005	1075	3.8
Rims with twisted-rope pattern	186	0.67	51	0.27	55	0.19
Handles	90	0.32	66	0.35	92	0.32
Basin-shaped rims with high-ridge – exclusive of other forms of basin-shaped rims	586	2.11	26	0.14	504	1.8
Eyelets or loops for suspension	81	0.29	151	0.79	8	0.03
Bead rim	599	2.16	283	1.50	10	0.03

Table 3 *Quantification of Roman pottery from sites in Cranborne Chase (after Pitt Rivers)*

terra sigillata has rightly been described as the foundation of the scientific study of Roman pottery, and this is perhaps all the more remarkable when we consider that he was only aged twenty-five when it was published. Dragendorff preferred the term terra sigillata (literally 'moulded earth') to the samian of British archaeological writings and this has since been almost universal in the continental literature.

At the heart of Dragendorff's paper (1895) is an account of terra sigillata production in Italy (Arretine ware) and Gaul, and related pottery types such as Campanian ware, Megarian bowls and 'Belgic' wares (including terra nigra and terra rubra). The discussion of the Arretine and Gaulish sigillata is accompanied by illustrations of the fifty-five principal types. These figures were a new departure. Most were drawn in a consistent style which showed the section of the vessel on the left-hand side of a centre line, and the external view on the right. There are catalogues of the potters' stamps recorded on the different forms and suggestions about their respective dates. The latter were largely based on the appearance of the forms or potters on German sites which were dated by reference to the historical record – the dates of campaigns or building activity on the German frontier – or by their association with coins. The principal decorative schemes are also analysed, classified and dated where possible. These vessel illustrations form the basis of the Dragendorff samian type-series – now usually abbreviated to Drag or simply Dr.

Three years after Dragendorff's paper, Francis Haverfield, the leading archaeologist of Roman Britain, appended a short paper, 'Notes on samian ware', to his report on the excavations at Birdoswald on Hadrian's Wall (1898). He drew attention to the recent work of the German school:

> In Germany various archaeologists, notably Hettner, Koenen, and Dragendorff, have attempted to classify chronologically the various sorts of Samian by examination of shape, ornament and general technique. The attempt has aroused little attention or imitation in England, and in the following notes I wish to make what, however scanty and inconclusive, will at least be a beginning of the enquiry in Britain.

Haverfield proceeded to describe finds of samian from sites on Hadrian's Wall in relation to Dragendorff's discussion of the chronology of the types. He illustrated his paper with a small selection of figures taken directly from Dragendorff's plates, but paired with illustrations of the same types from Roach Smith's 'Red-glazed' paper of 1848 (**5**).

Haverfield discussed the distribution of the samian bowls of forms Drag 37, 30 and 29 (although he does not refer to them by Dragendorff's numbers). The wide diffusion of the Drag 37 type, which was common on Hadrian's Wall sites, is contrasted with that of the Drag 29 and 30 forms, which were absent on and near the Wall, but fairly common in the south, at London or Colchester for instance. Throughout the paper Haverfield refers to the German dating evidence described by Dragendorff, and is at pains to demonstrate that it could also be applied to British finds. The note concludes with a drawing of a single samian plate from Birdoswald, illustrated in the style of Dragendorff – perhaps the first application of this technique to British material.

Date	Author	Title
1895	Dragendorff	*Terra sigillata*
1904	Déchelette	*Les vases céramiques ornés de la Gaule romaine*
1907	Knorr	*Die verzierten Terra Sigillata Gefasse von Rottweil*
1908	Walters	*Catalogue of the Roman Pottery in the Department of Antiquities in the British Museum*
1909	Loeschcke	*Keramische Funde in Haltern*
1913	Ritterling	*Das frührömische Lager bei Hofheim im Taunus*
1914	Atkinson	*A hoard of samian ware from Pompeii*
1919	Knorr	*Töpfer und Fabriken verzierter Terra-Sigillata des ersten Jahrhunderts*
1920	Oswald & Davies Pryce	*Introduction to the study of terra sigillata*

Table 4 *Principal publications on terra sigillata, 1895–1920*

The progress of sigillata studies on the Continent continued through the publications of Déchelette and others – works which are still fundamental to the subject (**table 4**). Some of these reports concerned a particular type or class of ware, while others were essentially site reports which provided a type-series or particularly well-dated assemblages. The result was a growing appreciation of the value of samian as a source of dating evidence. Samian reports in Britain came swiftly to conform to a standard pattern, with separate treatments of the stamped, decorated and plain wares. The catalogue of the British Museum collection by H. B. Walters, which included the vast collection of London samian acquired from Roach Smith in 1856, was one of the most influential (Walters 1908). Walters' introduction included a general description of the principal wares and their sources, supported by detailed bibliographic references. He also republished two plates from Dragendorff's type-series (1–55) and, following the lead of Déchelette (who had added types 56–77 to Dragendorff's series) and Knorr (who added form 78), Walters added three new forms (Walters 79–81).

A brief history of Roman pottery studies

5 *Decorated terra sigillata types illustrated by Haverfield in 1898*

The increasing confidence with which samian was being dated did not go entirely unchallenged. In a paper given in 1910 Haverfield attempted to catch, or at least slow down, the hare he had raised in 1898 (1911). He pointed out the undoubted difficulties that accompanied any attempt to assign vessels to sources, or date them, simply on the strength of a consultation of the fast-expanding literature. Moreover, the dangers were compounded when only the interpretations were published and not illustrations of the material in question. Haverfield's plea was as much for the publication of the primary data as for caution in its interpretation.

The publication of *An Introduction to the Study of Terra Sigillata* by Felix Oswald and T. Davies Pryce in 1920 shows how far the study of sigillata had advanced in the quarter-century since Dragendorff's paper. Oswald and Pryce (or O&P) was a systematic, comprehensive survey, treated 'from a chronological standpoint', covering vessel forms and decoration and the development of the industry. On pp. 39–46 they listed the now considerable number of dated sites and assemblages in Britain, Gaul and Germany that formed the basis of much of the dating of both forms and decorative styles. In the 1930s Oswald published indices to both figure types and potters' stamps on sigillata (F. Oswald 1931; 1936). The comprehensive bibliography and extensive illustrations made O&P the fundamental study of the terra sigillata for many years to come (the book was reprinted in 1966) and it remains the only comprehensive work in English on the subject.

Coarse wares
These developments in the dating, analysis and presentation of samian ware naturally had some effect on the coarse wares that accompanied them. Writing in 1902 on the finds from the Roman fort at Gellygaer, John Ward included three plates of scaled drawings, explicitly described as 'after a German manner' (1903, 75). He felt it necessary to explain this decision: 'each figure representing at once an elevation of the exterior and the interior and a section of one side. These drawings may not have the pleasing effect of the usual perspective views, but they have obvious advantages.' The illustrations encompassed both coarse wares and samian, and the dating of the latter was discussed in relation to both the German evidence and Haverfield's comments on the Birdoswald material. The Gellygaer material had been collected under rather difficult circumstances, and Ward suspected that the amphoras and samian were over-represented in the assemblage due to their 'largeness' and 'brightness' respectively. He sought to compensate for these biases by confining his quantification to the coarse-ware types, and presented a table showing the proportions of the principal forms present (ibid., 83).

Ward's general book on the Roman archaeology *The Roman Era in Britain* (1911) includes a chapter on Roman pottery. He describes 'red-glaze' samian wares with reference to Dragendorff's types. The coarse wares are not illustrated 'in the German manner' but with full profiles. The vessels are grouped into broad categories (jars, bowls, jugs etc.) but it is notable how little chronology can be included in the descriptions at this stage. Instead he concentrates on relating these categories to vessels recorded in the Classical literature such as *ollae, amphorae, ampullae* and *pelves*.

Another theme running through discussion of pottery at this period is the possibility of separating out the Roman and Celtic elements in the decoration of the vessels. This was not only a comment on artistic taste, but went back to questions about quite how 'Roman' the culture of Roman Britain had become, and how deep the process of Romanization went. Haverfield (1915, 48–51) concluded that Roman designs had 'stifled' Celtic art, although more recent writers have preferred instead to emphasize the flowing Celtic lines of the decoration on many of the same pots that Haverfield had considered as purely Roman.

The report on the excavations at Newstead in southern Scotland, by James Curle, was published in 1911. The work at this fort had identified two phases of occupation and consequently it was possible to distinguish Flavian pottery from Antonine with reasonable confidence. Curle's approach to the pottery was based around a type-series (of 49 types) which covered both samian and coarse wares, illustrated by 'sectional drawings' on plates, but supplemented by groups of sherds drawn in perspective, with sections, inset in the text and 'family portraits' of the more complete vessels in photographs. In overall appearance and arrangement the effect is remarkably similar to that of contemporary German publications such as the Haltern report of 1909 (Loeschcke 1909) or Emil Ritterling's studies of the pottery from Hofheim (1913) and Wiesbaden (1909). With the exception of the Castor wares and a few vessels identified as possible imports, no attempt was made to source the majority of the non-sigillata wares, and the discussion concentrated instead on identifying parallels for the forms in both Britain and Germany. The solid Newstead volume remains one of the key British publications of this period, and two of Curle's samian forms (15 and 21) have become the references for types that are not covered in the standard Dragendorff–Déchelette–Walters series.

J. P. Bushe-Fox
A major influence on Romano-British pottery studies in the period from 1910 was Jocelyn Plunket Bushe-Fox (1880–1954). He had worked with Flinders Petrie on the excavations at Meydum, in Egypt (Drower 1985, 312), where he would undoubtedly have been exposed to Petrie's approach to ceramic analysis. Petrie had been studying the pottery from his Egyptian sites in detail since the 1880s. His particular contribution had been the recognition that assemblages of pottery could be ordered on the basis of the co-occurrence of types (Petrie 1899; Orton, Tyers and Vince 1993, 11, 189). Types that frequently occurred together should have similar date-ranges,

A brief history of Roman pottery studies

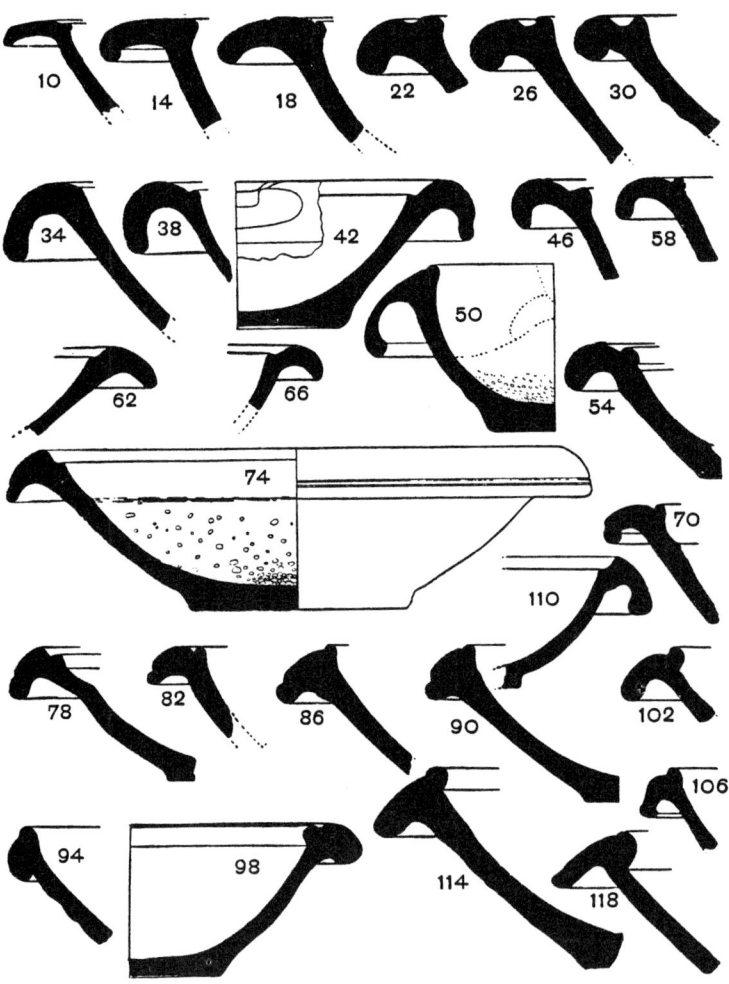

6 *Bushe-Fox's Wroxeter mortarium type-series, 1913*

and conversely assemblages that had a high proportion of types in common should be of similar date. Petrie employed this approach to ordering (known as seriation) to closed grave groups.

Bushe-Fox's first report on Romano-British pottery was his study of the material from the fort at Corbridge in 1911 (Bushe-Fox in Forster and Knowles 1912). He was particularly concerned to date the coarse wares from the site, recognizing that this would be important on other sites where samian and coins were scarce, but also noted that the dates in the north of the country may not hold good for the south. The pots were drawn in the now-conventional profile and section pattern, and this passed without comment or explanation. His next work was the Roman town at Wroxeter, where a campaign of excavation was financed through the Society of Antiquaries between 1912 and 1914. The results were published with remarkable promptness in volumes 1, 2 and 4 of the newly founded series of Research Reports from that Society (Bushe-Fox 1913a; 1914; 1916).

The introduction to the first pottery report notes specifically the similarity between the early material from Wroxeter and the Corbridge assemblage (Bushe-Fox 1913a, 68–9), with a higher proportion of dissimilar types in the later levels. The pottery is not published in stratified groups, but rather as a series of selected items from dated layers. The major contribution of the first Wroxeter report was a typology of mortaria (ibid., 76–80). Bushe-Fox laid out his reasoning thus:

> It has been evident to excavators of Roman sites that the mortarium underwent considerable alterations at different periods. At Corbridge, Newstead, Poltross Burn and elsewhere, efforts have been made to assign the different types to their respective periods, but the result is still far from complete. One of the chief difficulties has been

the lack of any publication in which a sufficient number of specimens has been brought together showing clearly the different types and their variations.

This is all strangely reminiscent of Jewitt's words some sixty years previously in his discussion of the mortaria from the Headington kilns (above p. 7). The Wroxeter types were numbered in such a way as to allow for future insertions (e.g. 10, 14, 18, 22, ... 242), although as with many such schemes, nobody seems to have taken up the offer (**6**).

Bushe-Fox commented that the illustrations were not intended as a dated type-series, but a means of collecting the data from which one could be constructed in the future. Evidently he envisaged the application of an ordering technique to the numbered types following the Petrie model. His principal concern was clearly with chronology and the source of the vessels was of lesser concern. The descriptions of the mortaria did not include any assessment of fabric, but one form stamped by G. ATISIUS SABINUS (type 50) is picked out as a possible import – and we now know this to be a product of Aoste in France – and three (types 70, 74, 78) are paralleled with similar forms from the province of Rhaetia (southern Germany): the first reference to the so-called Rhaetian or raetian style in Britain (Hartley in Robertson 1975, 241–4).

The second Wroxeter report (Bushe-Fox 1914) continues with the study of the coarse wares, concentrating again on the chronological implications and extensively cross-referenced to British and German parallels. In the report on the plain samian wares, three new forms are described and illustrated which, it was claimed, filled gaps in the standard Dragendorff–Déchelette–Walters series (ibid., 43). However, these forms (which might have been labelled *Bushe-Fox* 82, 83 and 84) did not become incorporated into the standard typology and, unlike Walters' 1908 extensions, have completely disappeared from the sigillata literature. Nevertheless this episode, and the 1913 mortarium typology, gives us insight into Bushe-Fox's methodology and approach: the identification of types or forms to allow comparison between sites, backed up by stratified sequences.

Bushe-Fox also wrote a paper which pursued Haverfield's comments on the sigillata from Birdoswald and considered once more the dating of the earliest Roman occupation of Scotland. Again drawing heavily on German publications he concluded that on sites where Drag form 29 was found in any quantity 'the date is probably not later than the early years of Domitian' (Bushe-Fox 1913b, 296). On this basis he identified sites in Scotland that were probably occupied during the campaigns of Agricola.

It was at this time that developments in Romano-British pottery studies attracted the attention of the young R. E. M. (later Sir Mortimer) Wheeler. Recently graduated from University College London, he applied for and won the newly established Franks studentship in archaeology in 1913. His topic was the Roman pottery of the Rhineland and he spent the summer of that year drawing pottery in German museums. Service on the Western Front intervened in his plans, but in 1919, when the then Major Wheeler was stationed near Cologne after the Armistice, he again had time to turn his attention to the problems of Roman ceramics (J. Hawkes 1982, 49–50, 74). His thesis, submitted later that year, was unfortunately never published.

Thomas May

Bushe-Fox became Inspector of Ancient Monuments in 1920 and continued to excavate and publish in the Society of Antiquaries Research Reports series. His volumes on Hengistbury Head (Dorset), Swarling and Richborough (Kent) include extensive pottery reports and his collaborator and illustrator on many of these projects was Thomas May (**7**). May was prominent in the Romano-British pottery scene from the turn of the century until 1930. His earliest work, such as the reports on excavations at Wilderspool (1897) or *Warrington's Roman Remains* (1904), is rather uninspiring, from a ceramicist's viewpoint. Even the pottery from the kilns he excavated is not illustrated, a lack that has continued to vex students of the material down to the present day. But his catalogue of the collection of York Museum is perhaps the first of a major provincial museum and can be seen now as the beginnings of a regional survey.

The influence of the flow of the major German publications of Roman pottery on the study of coarse wares can be seen particularly clearly in the York catalogue. In Part 1 (published in 1909) May laid out the scheme for the succeeding catalogue (which was to be published in successive volumes of the Transactions of the Yorkshire Philosophical Society). He declares his intention to use the same headings as Walters' 1908 British Museum catalogue, 'for the sake of uniformity with generally accepted systems of naming and dating'. The Romano-British wares would be classified under the headings of Castor, Painted New Forest and Upchurch ware. Parts 1 and 2 of the catalogue proceeded, using Walters' headings for the terra sigillata. However, the Romano-British wares (published in volumes dated 1910 and 1911) were clearly reorganized in response to the publications from Germany that had appeared in the year or so since the scheme for the catalogue was laid out in Part 1.

The introduction to the first of the reports on the coarse wares (1910) gives some flavour of the impact of these new studies on Thomas May, and his approach to the material before him.

> Widening knowledge of Roman ceramics has shown that the use of the terms Samian, Castor, Upchurch and Salopian, as class names for the wares to which they are usually applied, should be abandoned. They

A brief history of Roman pottery studies

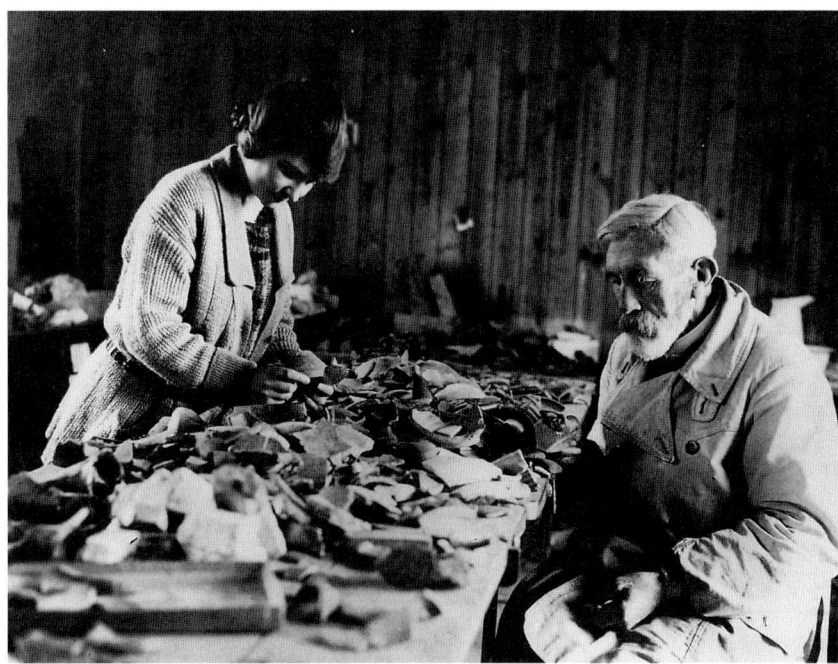

7 *Thomas May at Richborough, c. 1925*

have already been discarded as misleading or inadequate by the latest investigators in this country, and they are unknown to, or regarded as obsolete by Continental archaeologists, whose labours have rendered a more systematic classification possible.

The classification of Roman provincial pottery according to individual character – form, ornamentation, material and technique – which is the prevailing one among Continental archaeologists, is likewise requisite in dealing with the York collection, in order to be useful or complete. This is owing to the fact that the productions of local potteries of the Roman period in our museums are often indistinguishable, and that some of the most important centres of production in Britain are still unknown or unexplored.

May thus proposed to dispense with the classification based on catagories such as Castor and Upchurch wares, and replace these with a classification based on manufacturing techniques. A necessary prerequisite to this was some understanding of the processes employed. Both the third and last parts of the York catalogue contain résumés of the principal methods of 'glazing and colour coating' on which the York classification was based. Although some of this may now seem a little dated (such as the assertion that red sigillata was fired twice – once in biscuit form and again when slipped), these paragraphs represent one of the first attempts to apply some of the ideas developed by the German archaeologists of the period to Romano-British ceramics. As May himself points out, an approach to the classification of pottery based on technology

was immediately appealing to the writer of a museum catalogue, because all the material to be included would fall somewhere within the structure, whereas the few wares that had been defined at this period left many vessels without any obvious label to attach to them.

As a solution to the problems of dating pottery, May concentrated on the shape of the vessels, and was clearly aware that changes in vessel form were, in part at least, a reflection of date. His point of departure was the observation that vessels of the same general type (such as beakers and flagons) which were late Roman often exhibited a rather elongated character

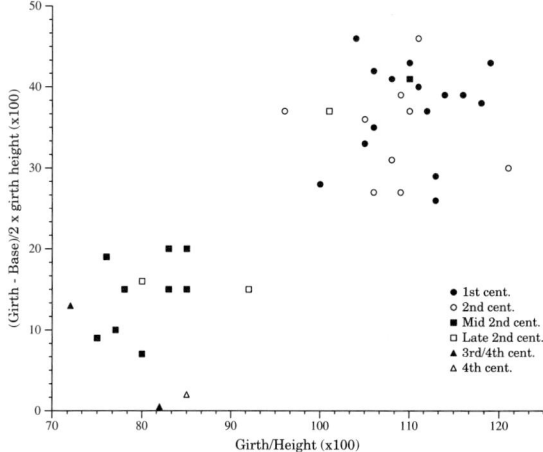

8 *Analysis of Thomas May's tables of standard proportions for jars*

14

when compared with their early Roman counterparts. Although the terms in which this is described seem to betray an aversion to the later Roman product (the 'neatness, regularity and fitness of form' of the early Roman pottery is contrasted with the 'top heavy, clumsy, later vessels'), May compiled and presented a number of *Tables of Standard Proportions* for the principal vessel classes and suggested that they could be used as a reference standard for determining approximate dates (8).

The data are presented in simple tabular form, but nevertheless this ranks as an early application of simple numerical analysis to the problems of Romano-British pottery typology.

Date	Subject
1897–1907	Warrington and Wilderspool (Ches.)
1909–12	York Museum catalogue
1911	Elslack (Yorks.)
1916	Silchester collection (Reading Museum) catalogue
1917	Tullie House Museum (Carlisle) catalogue
1921	Hambleden villa (Bucks.)
1922	Sandford (Oxon.) kiln group
1922	Templeborough (Yorks.)
1930	Colchester and Essex Museum catalogue
1931	Ospringe (Kent)
1931	Tiddington (War.)

Table 5 *Major publications on Romano-British pottery by Thomas May*

May's later work (**table 5**) included substantial catalogues of the Silchester collection in Reading Museum (1916) and the collections of the Colchester and Essex Museum (1930). The publication of the latter was sadly delayed for many years and was certainly starting to look a little dated when it finally appeared. These later works extended the tables of standard proportions but his ideas in this respect seemed to have little impact on other students of Romano-British ceramics, who continued to describe the development of forms in written rather than numerical form. Indeed it is sometimes suggested that May himself had little grasp of the notions of typological development (G. Webster 1977, 318). May's final work was at Tiddington near Stratford-on-Avon in 1930, having moved to a house adjacent to the excavation for the purpose, and where he died in 1931.

Despite May's major contributions in bringing the collections of Reading and Colchester Museums to publication and his knowledge of material from many parts of the country (a coverage that few writers on the subject before or since could match), his abandonment of the search for wares within the material in favour of classifications based on technology can be seen, in retrospect, to have been a mistake and ultimately such an approach led nowhere.

Collingwood's survey of 1930

1930 saw the publication of R. G. Collingwood's *The Archaeology of Roman Britain*, the first general survey of the state of Romano-British archaeology since Ward's *The Roman Era in Britain* in 1911. Alongside a consideration of the historical and structural evidence from the province, Collingwood included two chapters on pottery. The first was concerned with terra sigillata and was written in collaboration with T. Davies Pryce. This brief survey included illustrations of the thirty most common types and variants and a short list of the potters most likely to be encountered in Britain with comments on their dates, cut down from the larger catalogues in Oswald and Pryce.

The remainder of the pottery was covered in a chapter by Collingwood. He starts with a description of his methodology:

> Before proceeding to the discussion of the individual types, it is well to explain what is meant by a type. These pots – often very rough pieces of work made by people with little training and under conditions little favourable to uniformity either of pattern or of quality – show only feeble and intermittent tendencies towards standardization. Each potter did much what he pleased, and each pot was a new thing. The archaeologist who begins to collect and classify the forms of coarse pots soon finds that he is dealing with an infinite variety of fluctuating shapes each passing over into others by gradations that are at first hardly perceptible. It is impossible to draw up a complete list of these shapes; it is impossible even to do for coarse pottery what Dragendorff did for Samian, and draw up a list complete enough for practical purposes. All one can do is to select, out of the welter of forms, a number of more or less recognizable fixed points, and use these as trigonometrical stations for a more detailed survey whose complication must be very great.

He presents a series of 94 types, intended as an aid for both the beginner and the trained archaeologist faced with the task of publishing a group of pottery. The type vessels were only drawn from sites and contexts which fulfilled three criteria: (1) the vessels were from sites in Britain, (2) they were from securely dated contexts or from sites with a a known and short period of occupation and (3) they were properly published, so that the reader could verify the writer's statements. The list of key sites used in the type-series reads as a roll-call of the principal published excavations of the preceding twenty years – Newstead, Hardknot, Brecon (Segontium), Caerleon, Gellygaer, Corbridge, York, Huntcliff, Poltross Burn,

Birdoswald, Throp, Wroxeter and Richborough. The legacy of Bushe-Fox and May, and the investigators of the archaeology of the Welsh and northern frontiers, can be seen in this list. The importance of dating frontier sites and the material from them, sometimes aided by dated monumental inscriptions, references in the Classical literature and so on, had led to a rather more systematic approach to the ceramics from such sites (Wallace 1990).

Collingwood notes that verbal descriptions are no substitute for the handling of pottery. He accepts the validity of Castor and New Forest wares as divisions, but others, such as Salopian and Upchurch wares, are regarded as inadequate. Two new terms were proposed: Rustic ware – which was dated to the Flavian period because of its rarity in the north and Scotland – and Huntcliff ware, named after a signal station on the Yorkshire coast where it was first recognized. The coarse vesicular fabric of Huntcliff ware (described as 'native') had a limited distribution in northern England, and Collingwood commented on the evident survival of such techniques into the later Roman period.

Kiln sites and fabrics
Alongside the publication of dated assemblages, there was increasing attention to the evidence of pottery production. In 1930 W. F. Grimes published the results of the excavations that had taken place some years earlier at Holt (Denbighshire/Clwyd). As a part of his report (1930) he produced 'a topographical list of Romano-British pottery sites' and, for the first time, an analysis of the kiln structures. His typology remained in general use until the 1950s, but the catalogue (of 101 sites) remained the only published annotated gazetteer until 1984.

Until the 1930s the number of published Romano-British pottery kilns and assemblages was very limited. Thomas May had published the material from Sandford (part of the Oxfordshire industry) in 1921, but perhaps the most interesting product of this period was Heywood Sumner's accounts of his excavations in the New Forest. George Heywood Mauroir Sumner (1853–1940) was a professional artist and illustrator, an associate of William Morris and participant in the Arts and Crafts movement; on his archaeological side he was a follower of Pitt Rivers. His characteristic illustrations are a feature of all his studies of Wessex archaeology (Coatts and Lewis 1986).

The results of his almost single-handed excavations in the New Forest potteries were given in a series of booklets published between 1917 and 1927, and gave substance to the products of an industry whose presence had been known since the 1850s. Although his interpretation of much that he observed, but perhaps particularly the kiln structures (Swan 1973), requires some amendment, his drawings of the Sloden potters carrying their wares to market through a misty woodland scene on pack-ponies is a delightful bonus.

During the 1930s the number of kilns and kiln groups excavated and published rose steadily (**table 6**). Of particular importance were the first reports on the large late Roman industries of east Yorkshire at Crambeck, Knapton and Throlam. The second Crambeck report (Corder 1937) included a gazetteer and distribution map of known specimens of Crambeck ware, and an assessment of the dating for the industry, drawing on evidence from the Wall forts, and the pottery from signal-stations on the Yorkshire coast which had been published by M. R. Hull in 1932. In 1939, J. P. Gillam published a paper on Derbyshire ware. Expanding on a suggestion made by Collingwood some years earlier (1930, 235, type 74), Gillam described a hard grey pimply fabric (which had hitherto often been erroneously identified as medieval) produced in the Derbyshire region during the third and fourth centuries AD. The distribution of the ware (which was listed and mapped) extended as far as the Wall forts. These two papers together heralded many of the themes which were to come to the fore in the post-war period; the concerns with the identification of wares, rather than simply typology, the use of the northern sequences to date industries further south and the compilation of distribution maps are all seen here.

Date	Site	Author
1928	Crambeck (Yorks.)	Corder 1928
1930	Throlam (Yorks.)	Corder 1930
1932	Caistor-next-Norwich (Norfolk.)	D. Atkinson 1932
1932	Knapton (Yorks.)	Corder and Kirk 1932
1935	Corfe Mullen (Dorset.)	Calkin 1935
1936	Dorchester (Oxon.)	Harden 1936
1936	St Albans (Herts.)	Wheeler and Wheeler 1936
1937	Crambeck (Yorks.)	Corder 1937
1937	Little London (Notts.)	A. Oswald 1937
1941	Cowley (Oxon.)	R. J. C. Atkinson 1941
1941	St Albans Pit 6 (Herts.)	Corder 1941
1944	South Carlton (Lincs.)	G. Webster 1944

Table 6 *Principal publications of Romano-British kiln and kiln assemblages, 1928–45*

Swarling and Belgic pottery
One of Bushe-Fox's excavation campaigns of the 1920s was at the site of a Late Iron Age cemetery at Swarling, in Kent (1925). The pottery included wheel-thrown pedestal urns and other forms decorated with cordons and grooves. The assemblage was combined with that from nearby Aylesford, which had been published by Sir Arthur Evans in 1890, into the Aylesford–Swarling style. The distribution of the style was listed (pp. 27–9): 'The bulk of this pottery has been found in

Kent, Essex, and Hertfordshire, and it is evident that the people to whom it belonged did not penetrate westward ... into the midlands, or further north than Northamptonshire.' The dating of the vessels was achieved largely through the associated metalwork (particularly the brooches) and the chronology of the continental prototypes for some of the pottery types, such as the pedestal urns. The interpretation of the style was essentially historical, and drew support from Julius Caesar's narrative on his two forays in Britain and the background data on the island he supplied in *De Bello Gallico*.

Bushe-Fox suggested that the origin and diffusion of the Aylesford–Swarling style could be linked with the history of Cassivellanus (Caesar's principal opponent during his British campaigns of 55 and 54 BC) and his successors (Bushe-Fox 1925, 39). This was contrasted with the styles current south of the Thames, such as at Silchester among the tribe of the Atrebates. The relationship between pottery style and population groups is implicit throughout, but it was also recognized that the Aylesford–Swarling style was a significant influence on coarse wares of the early Roman period throughout south-east England.

Further refinement of the chronology of later Iron Age pottery styles, and data on the chronology and character of pre-conquest imports from the Roman world, came in 1936 with the publication of the Verulamium report by R. E. M. and T. V. Wheeler. In addition to extensive excavations within the confines of Roman Verulamium (St Albans), the Wheelers had investigated the massive earthworks at Prae Wood and Wheathampstead. Substantial assemblages of pottery were recovered from both sites, and illustrated and described in some detail in the report (Wheeler and Wheeler 1936). The assemblages fell into two groups; firstly those which were composed solely of wares of the Aylesford–Swarling style and their coarser counterparts (described collectively as Belgic) and secondly those where these types were joined by vessels of 'Italic or Italianate wares' – that is sigillata and other plates, cups and beakers of continental manufacture. It was suggested (with reference to German sites such as Haltern) that the Italic element appears from *c.* 15 to 10 BC and thus marks a dividing line between Belgic pottery before and after that date. The following astute warning is issued:

> In dating a Belgic group, the archaeologist is thus thrown back upon a criterion – the presence or absence of Italic or Italianate wares – which is easy on the positive side but demands utmost caution on the negative side. A group which contains an Italic form or fragment tells to some extent its own story; but a group which does not contain such a fragment must obviously be extensive and thoroughly representative of a site before it can be used as evidence of a pre-Augustan date.

Sigillata and other imported fine wares of the Augustan and Tiberian periods are by no means abundant in south-eastern England, and even less so outside the region. The 15–10 BC 'marker' can only be employed as a means of dividing assemblages chronologically with care. In many cases the absence of such wares is as likely to be due to the status, function or geographical location of a site, as it is to its date. This was not always fully appreciated by later writers.

The Roman pottery from the Wheelers' excavations at Verulamium was not considered in the same detail as the pre-Roman, and indeed this has often been a point of criticism levelled at their report (Frere 1972, 3; G. Webster 1977, 317). Against this we must weigh the value of the publication of the domestic pre-conquest assemblages from Prae Wood and Wheathampstead, which remain a major contribution to the archaeology of the pre-Roman period.

Camulodunum

In many respects the pottery report of the 1930s with the longest-lasting impact has been that on the material from the Colchester (Roman *Camulodunum*) excavations of 1930–9 – although the final reports on much of the material did not see the light of day until 1947 and 1963. The excavations – in advance of road construction – were beyond the north-western edge of the Roman colonia, but within the confines of the earlier dyke system, in an area known as Sheepen. There were known to be Roman pottery kilns in the vicinity and large groups of pre-conquest material had also been recovered from the site. The excavations were directed by C. F. C. Hawkes (then assistant keeper at the British Museum) and M. R. Hull, curator of the Colchester and Essex Museum.

Mark Reginald (Rex) Hull's (1897–1976) early archaeological work, as an undergraduate at Durham University, had been on Hadrian's Wall. In 1925 he contributed a short report on the pottery from the excavations at Rudchester (Hull in Brewis 1925) and wrote a very important survey of the pottery from the late Roman signal stations on the Yorkshire coast (not published until 1932). In the latter he compared the assemblages from five small sites – Scarborough, Huntcliff, Goldsborough, Filey and Long Whins – classified the material in a series of thirty-six types and presented a table showing the counts of these on the five sites (Hull 1932, 250). This remained the only quantified pottery report from east Yorkshire for over five decades.

In 1927 Hull moved south to Colchester, where he remained for the rest of his career (9). He soon started publishing papers on the Roman Colchester. The annual Colchester Museum Reports include drawings and descriptions of pottery brought into the museum for identification, and material recovered during site watching and field walking in the district. During the years of the Sheepen excavation there were interim reports by Hull on the material from the season's work, complete with lists of stamps on terra sigillata and Gallo-Belgic wares, and illustrations of the major pottery types, which often reappeared many years later as type vessels in the final report. By

A brief history of Roman pottery studies

9 *Mark Reginald Hull at Colchester Museum*

any standards these are exceptional pieces of scholarship.

The major contribution of the Sheepen excavations to pottery studies were twofold; firstly, the recovery of large assemblages of material of the Augustan–Claudian period, and secondly, the excavation of a series of pottery kilns, dating from the first through to the fourth century (but largely later second and third century). The first full report on the excavations did not appear until 1947, when the *Camulodunum* volume was published (C. F. C. Hawkes and Hull 1947). Although it is evidently largely a product of the pre-war years, the preface is dated 30 June 1945. The substantial ceramic report (over 120 pages) takes the form of separate type-series for sigillata (s1–s25) and the other wares (1–275, with some numbers vacant). The distribution of these types through the six phases of activity defined on the site is illustrated by a *Chronological table of incidence of forms*.

The text includes a particularly thorough assessment of the Gallo-Belgic wares (terra rubra and terra nigra) with a detailed survey of the published literature (pp. 202–5). Many of the imported types are cross-referenced to published continental examples and, additionally, there are specific references to vessels examined in museums in France, Germany and the Low Countries, the product of study tours in the mid-1930s. Some of the material referred to seems not to have survived the 1939–45 war. The Camulodunum material (or Cam as it is generally referred to) remains to this day one of the key assemblages of the Augustan–Claudian period in Britain – and indeed far beyond these shores. The pottery was divided and stored by type and a search through the Sheepen material, until recently housed in the museum in Colchester's Norman castle, has formed part of the studies of most students of early Roman pottery in Britain.

The Sheepen excavations also revealed a series of kilns, overlying the earlier Roman occupation. The earliest kilns dated to the period of Boudicca, but the majority belonged to the period from the mid-second to early third century AD. Of particular interest was the identification in 1933 of a kiln for the firing of terra sigillata, associated with the distinctive kiln-fittings of tubes, moulds for the decorated wares and quantities of wasters and seconds. An account of the kilns, complete with illustrations of the decorated wares, the figure types and stamps of the plain-ware potters, appeared in the next Colchester Museum Report, and also in a paper in the journal *Germania* (Hull 1934). There were also workshops producing a whole range of colour-coated wares, mortaria and other types. The final report on these discoveries did not appear until 1963 (Hull 1963) and this remains one of the most thorough assessments of a pottery production site in Britain.

The chronology of the Sheepen site, and particularly the dating of the beginning of the occupation, depended to a great extent on an assessment of the sigillata. The Sheepen forms could not be paralleled at the German camp of Oberaden (thought to have been occupied *c.* 12–8 BC) but there were plentiful matches with Haltern, then considered to have been abandoned in AD 16 (C. F. C. Hawkes and Hull 1947, 28–9). A date of *c.* AD 10 was suggested as most likely for the start of activity at the site. Many years later the dating of the German camps was amended, and a controversy also grew up around Dressel 1 amphoras in the Sheepen assemblage (*Cam* form 181), whose latest production should antedate AD 10 by two decades (Sealey 1985, 101–8).

Jewry Wall, Leicester

The excavations at the Jewry Wall site, Leicester, were, like Camulodunum, work of the pre-war years that was not published until later (Kenyon 1948). The large pottery report was divided into two parts – a typology and a series of dated deposits. The report relies heavily on the use of parallel searching in the study of the coarse wares. The fifty-six sites listed in the introduction include most of the major pottery reports published in the previous half-century. They are distributed throughout the country, with a certain bias towards the north and west.

Parallels for the shape of a vessel were sought in other published reports and the references were listed. The cumulative impression gathered from the parallels for the date of the form was noted. The danger of such an approach was, firstly, the drawing together of unrelated items into a single group. There was no certainty that the same shapes were made by potters in widely spaced parts of the country at the same period, and, in general, regional traditions tended to be subsumed beneath a single global view. Secondly, there was the danger of a certain circularity of argument. It was relatively easy for the confusion caused by a poorly dated piece to trickle down through the system to influence the dating of an assemblage that was far away in both time and space.

The process of parallel searching in some cases resulted in reasonably clear dating for some types, supported by evidence from around the country; in other cases it was less satisfactory. It can be seen that the lack of any study of fabrics was reducing the value of the exercise. In effect the Jewry Wall report stands as a summary of the state of Romano-British ceramic studies by the mid-1940s prior to the major advances in the recognition of fabrics, wares, and regional traditions of the following decades.

Summary

The decades between the publication of Dragendorff's 'Terra sigillata' and the eve of the Second World War saw a series of major advances in the study of Roman pottery in Britain. We have the first attempts at synthesis by Ward in 1911 and Collingwood in 1930, built on the foundations of increasing quantities of published material from sites of all periods. Both authors, however, regret their inability to produce a super-Dragendorff series covering Romano-British wares.

Sigillata had come to take a prime role as chronological evidence on many sites. Typology, and the cross-referencing of forms between sites (sometimes very widely spaced geographically), were seen as the major tools for study and dating. Although many of the major industries, particularly those of the later Roman period (such as Oxfordshire, New Forest, Alice Holt and the Yorkshire industries), were represented by significant publications, there was relatively little concern with distribution. Doubts were apparent about the value of many of the wares that had been described in the nineteenth century – e.g. Upchurch, Castor and New Forest – and most preferred to talk of 'Castor-type' wares, without any implied attribution to a source. At the end of the period we have Gillam's work on Derbyshire ware – the precursor of many fabric-based studies in the post-war decades.

1.3 FROM CAMULODUNUM TO CBA10

The result of the increasing quality and quantity of the evidence from kiln sites in the 1940s was a growing appreciation of the regional character of Romano-British pottery, and of the coarser wares in particular. The focus shifted more to regionally based studies, and the kiln structures themselves, and the approach taken in the Jewry Wall report (for example) of searching for parallels across the entire country was becoming increasingly inadequate.

Gillam's types

The prospects for a large-scale regional survey were more advanced in the north of England and Scotland than elsewhere. Building on the foundations laid by Curle's Newstead report, and Bushe-Fox's work at Corbridge, a series of pottery reports through the inter-war years had begun to expose the ceramic sequence. Pottery (but samian in particular) was in regular use as a means of correlating the occupation of the sites on the frontier zone (E. Birley 1977, 1-3). Collingwood, for instance, had relied on the evidence from northern sites in his 1930 typology.

The appointment of John Gillam (1917–86) to the University of Durham in 1947 opened up a new phase in pottery studies in the north, resulting in a series of reports on assemblages from Corbridge and elsewhere in the region (**10**). His earliest synthetic studies were considerations of the problems of dating pottery in the second and fourth centuries (1949; 1951a) but the publication of *Types of Roman Coarse Pottery Vessels in Northern Britain* in *Archaeologia Aeliana* for 1957 marks a significant advance in Romano-British coarse pottery studies. The core of the paper was the illustration of 350 types (samian and amphoras were excluded from consideration) which were cross-referenced to 134 dated groups. Gillam's *Types* was reissued as a separate booklet in 1968 and again in 1970, on each occasion with amended dating of some types or groups. The long-term survival and value of the study had been ensured by the publication of the lists of dated groups for each type. This allowed Gillam (and others) to reassess the date of a type in the light of developments in the understanding of the stratigraphy of a particular site. In this it is far in advance on the superficially rather similar, but earlier, work of Gose (1950) on pottery types in the Rhineland, which does not include any site cross-referencing.

The use of Gillam's *Types* in southern Britain requires a certain amount of care and discrimination. At some periods, particularly during the second century, a significant proportion of the pottery in use on the northern frontier was produced around the Thames estuary or in the south-west, and in such cases the application of Gillam's dates might be appropriate. Even then the earlier or later production of a type which was only exported to the north for a limited period had to be considered.

The relationship between the northern frontier and its sources of supply had been particularly well illustrated in another paper by Gillam, which had been given before the Roman Frontier Congress in Austria in 1955 (1956). He produced maps showing the British distribution of seven classes of mortaria, Castor ware hunt cups, Crambeck ware, black-burnished wares, Dales ware and Derbyshire ware, as well as a distribution map of the mortarium kilns that were *supplying*

A brief history of Roman pottery studies

Corbridge. This was the largest collection of such maps that had yet been published, and showed the advances that could be made in the study of trade within the province, against the firm background of regional studies.

Philip Corder and kiln assemblages

Another influential publication of this period was *The Structure of Romano-British pottery kilns* by Philip Corder (1957). The bulk of the paper naturally concerns the structure of the kilns themselves, and presents a large number of kiln plans arranged in a simple typology. However, the introduction draws out some more general themes in pottery studies, and in particular that of chronology. Describing the process of dating pottery, Corder comments:

> It has been usual in such an event to fall back on typology, and to cite parallels for the forms of vessels from another part of the province. While it is undeniable that there were fashions in the shapes of vessels, as there are to-day, and that therefore a typological series might be built up by scrupulous reliance upon site-evidence, it should be recognized that only approximate dating can be achieved by typology, which has sometimes proved very misleading. Where, however, it is possible to assign pots to the source of their manufacture, and to date the kilns where they are made, either by associated coins, or by the occurrence of their products in dated stratified deposits, much greater precision can be hoped for. The debris found in or near kilns normally consists of ´wasters´ rendered unsaleable during manufacture. Since the life of any kiln is very short, the chance of survival of sherds on a pottery site is much less than that on an occupation site. The discovery of pottery kilns and a detailed study of their products is thus of prime importance, not merely for the light it may throw on one of the major industries of the province, but as the only means whereby many sites are to be dated at all.
>
> There is no more urgent task facing students of Roman Britain than the discovery of pottery kilns and the classification and publication of their products, and their distribution.

Corder foresees the implementation of typologies for single wares defined at production sites, rather than typologies which span across numerous fabrics, and defined at consumption sites. This is clearly quite different from the approach of, for instance, the Jewry Wall report. It is also suggested that when such corpora are available the presentation of pottery evidence would be reduced to a 'neat tabulation' of a numismatic report. Such hopes have yet to be fulfilled, indeed the trend seems to be rather in the opposite direction.

The effects of the increasing quantities of data from kiln sites could be seen, for example, in the approach to mortaria, and particularly mortarium stamps. Since the eighteenth century, pottery reports had included illustrations and comments on mortarium stamps. From the 1870s reference could be made to the mortarium stamps published in the CIL volumes from Britain, Gaul, Germany and Italy, and parallels were sometimes drawn between the readings on mortaria and other wares such as sigillata or amphoras. Particular attention had always been given to those mortaria from Britain with the counterstamp LUGUD, which suggested that they were produced at a site named *Lugudunum*. This had long been taken to be a reference to Lyon, in France (e.g. Walters 1908, 551), although the absence of any examples of these stamps from Lyon, or indeed anywhere else on the Continent, had not gone unnoticed. In 1944, when Felix Oswald described the mortaria from his excavations at *Margidunum* (East Bridgeford, Notts.), he pointed to the lack of evidence from Lyon, but (inexplicably) went on to suggest that the stamps were a reference to Leyden in Holland (*Lugdunum Batavorum*) although the evidence for either stamps or production waste was no better there (F. Oswald 1944). A stamp of Albinus, one of the LUGUD potters, had been found in association with a kiln at Radlett, in Hertfordshire, as early as 1898 (Page 1898, 161), but this was thought to indicate that this 'imported' vessel was being used as a model by the potters working there (Birley in Kenyon 1948, 214), rather than the perhaps more obvious conclusion that it was made in the kiln. The stranglehold that an apparently incontrovertible written reference held over the interpretation of the material remained strong.

Excavations at Brockley Hill (Middlesex) in 1947 revealed a large quantity of kiln waste, including flagons, jars and bowls, and a large number of mortaria. The publication on the material, by K. M. Richardson (1948), included a specialist report by E. Birley on the mortarium stamps. Birley asserted that mortaria in the group were imported continental products. However, Richardson's descriptions of the firing faults on the mortaria, such as the heavy burning (also seen on other wasters in the same context) and the detached spouts, seem to betray some doubts in her mind about this attribution, and a preference to take the assemblage at face value as a single coherent group of local products. By the early 1950s the increasing data from Brockley Hill, including the publication of a die-stamp of the potter Matugenus (Suggett 1955) left no doubt that it was a major centre of mortarium manufacture, and that the LUGUD potters used the same fabric and operated from within the same region.

The scientific analysis of pottery

The increasing concerns during the 1950s and 1960s with assigning vessels to their source, and building up distribution, patterns naturally led to an interest in the more sophisticated techniques of scientific analysis (for background, Orton, Tyers and Vince 1993, 140–51). The major stimulus to fabric

20

studies came from the geological sciences. The use of the petrological microscope to study pottery in thin-section was applied widely to material in the southern United States from the 1940s, most notably by Anna Shepard (1956). Hodges had published the results of thin-section analysis of British pottery in 1962, but it was not until later, with the work of Peacock, that the technique was applied extensively to Roman material (Peacock 1967a; Peacock in Cunliffe 1971). Peacock followed up his work on Romano-British coarse wares with a major paper on the fabrics and sources of amphoras in pre-Roman Britain (Peacock 1971). Other more general techniques from material science were also applied to the problems of Roman pottery, such as a major study of mortaria using spectrographic analysis (Richards 1959; K. F. Hartley and Richards 1965).

The need to bring some order to the terminology used in the increasing number of reports led to the publication of the *Student's Guide to Romano-British coarse pottery* by the Council for British Archaeology in 1964, edited by G. Webster (1964). This provided a glossary of the principal names given to vessel shapes, thumbnail sketches of the major fabrics and wares, and a bibliography organized by region and country, annotated with comments on the dating of some of the major published assemblages. The second edition of Collingwood's *Archaeology of Roman Britain* (Collingwood and Richmond 1969) included a chapter on coarse pottery with illustrations of some of the principal forms drawn from Gillam's *Types*, and selections from the products of the principal industries. The chapter on samian ware was by B. R. Hartley. The principal sources, forms and decorative techniques are described, with notes on dating. This concise and practical summary of the ware enjoyed particularly wide circulation as a reprint of the chapter was published by the Hertfordshire Archaeological Society. A much-thumbed copy of this slim orange volume was to be found in many pot sheds during the 1970s. Both this and the *Student's Guide* distilled information on Roman pottery into a more easily accessible form, for a wider audience. The pace of excavation was beginning to accelerate and resources, as always, had failed to keep up. The role of volunteers and amateurs was becoming increasingly important and the processing and illustration of the large pottery assemblages now becoming commonplace, was one of their ever-present tasks.

CBA10

The general state of the art at the beginning of the 1970s is particularly well documented by the papers given at a weekend conference sponsored by the Council for British Archaeology and held at New College, Oxford in March 1972. The proceedings were published with admirable promptness the following year (A. Detsicas, (ed) 1973) as *Current Research in Romano-British coarse pottery*, generally referred to as CBA10. Among others, the volume contains valuable papers by J. P. Gillam on the sources of supply of pottery to northern sites (a follow-up to his 1956 and 1957 work), K. F. Hartley on mortaria, and a major study by R. A. H. Farrar of the sources of black-burnished wares. K. T. Greene's paper on the pottery from the Neronian legionary fortress at Usk

10 *John Gillam at Corbridge, 1980 (photograph by P. Moffat)*

explored the continental origins of the coarse-ware types made there by potters attached to the legion. This paper opened up the way for a new assessment of the relationship between Romano-British and continental coarse wares, and was a major stimulus to others searching for outside influences on their material. In all, CBA10 shows how far Roman pottery studies had progressed, and in particular how the concern for the identification of fabrics and wares, and hence the collection of data on production and distribution, had come to take centre stage.

1.4 THE MODERN ERA OF ROMANO-BRITISH POTTERY STUDIES

The developments in Romano-British pottery studies since the 1970s will be considered in more detail in the following chapters, which describe the principal resources available (sections 2.1–2.5) and the major uses that have been made of Roman pottery data in the service of Romano-British archaeology (sections 3.1–3.4). The period from the late 1960s is marked by the mushrooming of large-scale urban and rescue archaeology and the consequent increases in the quantity and quality of ceramic material that had to be handled by the new regionally based archaeological units. Alongside laboratory scientific techniques, such as thin-sectioning, there was the increasing use of simpler tools, such as a low-powered binocular microscope to identify and describe pottery fabrics.

In retrospect the difference, as much as anything else, was the acceptance that fabrics were not confined to the major named wares (such as Castor or New Forest) but were a tool for the analysis and classification of all the material from a site. Many units set up their own processing systems, often based on the models described by Peacock (1977a) or Orton (1979). There were three principal elements to these schemes. Firstly, the fabric type-series, usually referred to by number or letter codes, was physically represented as sample sherds in some form of ordered storage system with a record card or sheet for each holding the description and other characteristics of the individual fabrics. Secondly, the pottery from stratified contexts was catalogued and a record made of the presence and quantity of each ware, again usually on a proforma sheet (see appendix 2). Finally, illustrations of vessels in drawing books or sheets were cross-referenced to the fabrics and the stratified contexts. Although it had been generally appreciated since the 1970s that the quantification of pottery was 'a good thing', there had been rather less agreement on the optimum system (or systems) to apply. A persistent problem, peculiar to Romano-British pottery, has been the removal of some specialist classes of pottery such as samian or mortaria prior to any quantification, and consequently their non-appearance in the final statistics.

These three legs – fabric, quantification and form – supported much of the work on pottery in Britain during the 1970s and '80s – it became the dominant paradigm. The results of this approach can be seen in a series of major reports such as those on Chelmsford (Going 1987), Exeter (Holbrook and Bidwell 1991), Gloucester (Hurst 1985) and Milton Keynes (Marney 1989). The same fabric type-series (such as those from Gloucester and Chelmsford) are often applied to the material from a number of sites in an area. These regional fabric databases were built up using the same classification system, and can be used to investigate ceramic supply to sites of different character (Griffiths 1989) or the distribution of local kilns as well as the distribution of the nationally recognized wares.

In parallel with the analysis of fabrics from sites has been a continuing concern with kilns and kiln sites. Some of the major industries of the later Roman period, whose presence had been apparent for a century or more, were finally dealt with in the 1970s and '80s. Among this unfinished business was the New Forest industry, tackled in a monograph by Fulford (1975a) and the Oxford industry by Young (1977a). The pottery of the Upchurch Marshes – the haunt of Roach Smith – was finally given some substance by Monaghan (1987a). Castor ware (now normally referred to as Nene Valley colour-coated ware) received attention from a number of authors (e.g. Howe *et al.* 1980).

The kiln structures themselves were studied by V. G. Swan in a report published by the Royal Commission on Historical Monuments in 1984 (Swan 1984), but whose roots lay in one of the meetings in the run-up to the Oxford conference of 1972. The scope of *The Pottery Kilns of Roman Britain* was wider than its title suggested, for the volume also included a wide-ranging discussion of the development of the Romano-British pottery industry, identifying the relationship between the industries and the outside (continental) influences. The heart of this study was a gazetteer of over 1300 certain or probable pottery kilns or kiln groups, including references to much otherwise unpublished information. This remarkable body of data, unfortunately only made available in microfiche, is unparalleled as a study of the physical remains of an industry of the Roman period, from any province of the Empire. The potential of kilns and kiln evidence will be described in section 2.2.

Progress through the 1970s may be traced through a series of collected works and monographs in the burgeoning British Archaeological Reports (BAR) series (**table 7**).

To mention just a few among these volumes, there were papers by Hartley on first-century mortaria (K. F. Hartley 1977), Greene on the origins and affinities of the Holt assemblage and the legionary ware style (1977), Arthur on the hitherto neglected topic of Romano-British glazed wares (1978) and Marsh on the patterns of samian supply to London and the rest of the province (1981). In general there was a move away from concerns with chronology *per se* towards tackling topics such as distribution and trade or the functional and social context of pottery production and use (e.g. Fulford

1977a; Gillam and Greene 1981). The mechanisms behind the observed patterns at the level of both the individual industry (Hodder 1974), or of inter-provincial trade (Fulford 1977b), were examined. The distribution of pottery types in the same geographical region, but on sites of different types (e.g. towns, forts, rural settlements) has been investigated by several writers searching for socio-economic correlates (Loughlin 1977; J. Evans 1988). The interplay between pottery distribution patterns and the location of kiln sites is investigated by Millett in relation to the civitas boundaries (1990). In 1992 Going highlighted the apparently cyclic fluctuations in Roman pottery production and supply and the effects of this on, for instance, site dating. These topics shall be examined further in sections 3.1 and 3.2. At the heart of these studies was the growing number of published pottery distributions and, increasingly, a body of quantified data. As ever, pottery remained – in Orton's splendid phrase – the 'playground of ideas' (Orton, Tyers and Vince 1993, 33).

Date	Author/Editors	Title
1975	Fulford	New Forest Roman pottery
1977	Young	The Roman Pottery industry of the Oxford region
1977	Dore & Greene	Roman pottery studies in Britain and beyond
1978	Arthur & Marsh	Early fine wares in Roman Britain
1981	Anderson & Anderson	Roman pottery research in Britain and north-west Europe

Table 7 *Volumes on Romano-British pottery published by BAR, 1975–81*

The search for guidelines

The increasing quantities of pottery excavated and studied naturally led to some consideration of standards of recording and processing. The Department of the Environment (who funded much post-excavation work) and the Study Group for Romano-British Pottery collaborated on the production of *Guidelines for the Processing and Publication of Roman Pottery from Excavations* (Young 1980).

The recommendation in the *Guidelines* can, in retrospect, be seen as a rather blunt tool – they laid down the minimum standards for the maximum report. No guidance was given on sampling from a large assemblage, and it was assumed that all material would be reported to the same standard (p. 8).

In consequence it was perhaps inevitable that the recommendations in the *Guidelines* were only partially implemented, and many units (either by design or force of circumstances) instituted a two-level system of pottery recording. The full recommendations were applied in some form to only a subset of the material recovered; the remainder (perhaps the majority) being recorded at a lower level of detail. With the aid of computers these simpler records formed an important resource in their own right, and could often assist in the formulation of questions that might be answered by recourse to a more detailed analysis, when funds, time and so forth permitted. The 1980 *Guidelines* introduce the topic of computer storage of data on pottery with comments on the cost of computer time and programming time (Young 1980, 6). There was a flurry of activity with home-grown packages, mostly written in spaghetti-like BASIC, in the early 1980s but by the end of the decade many users had access to some form of off-the-shelf word-processing, database and statistics packages. The ability to retrieve quickly and accurately from large databases has to some extent encouraged the collection and recording of data which would only be of value in such a computerized environment (e.g. Tyers and Vince 1983 on the systems used on London pottery). However, the integration of information on ceramics with other classes of finds data, which should have been simplified, only rarely occurs. Even cross-referencing between pottery and site phasing seems to be more complex than it should be. More sophisticated analytical and presentational tools (such as geographical information systems) are rarely applied, although much pottery data is ideally suited to analysis by such systems.

The Fulford/Huddleston report, 1991

Growing pressures on the funding of post-excavation work, and some disillusionment with the quality of some of the results of work on pottery in the 1980s, led, at the end of the decade, to a review of the current state of Romano-British pottery studies for English Heritage, which was the successor to the Department of the Environment in archaeological funding (Fulford and Huddleston 1991). This drew on data from two sources: (1) an analysis of 74 site reports published between 1972 and 1989, and (2) interviews and questionnaires from nineteen units and other organizations responsible for pottery work. The extent of the different approaches to quantification, sampling, fabric and form classification in the published reports is documented in a series of tables, and the state of knowledge about pottery production and supply across the country is described. The report identified a number of general priorities for future work on Romano-British pottery and made recommendations about recording and reporting procedures which (at the time of writing) are still being followed up.

However, the general political context of the report did not pass without comment (Greene 1992a) and the fate of pottery reporting, and indeed any other form of serious finds analysis, in the Brave New World of competitive contract archaeology has yet to be seen.

2 Sources for the study of Roman pottery

In this chapter we shall look at the potential tools available to the student of Roman pottery, describing the advantages, disadvantages and potential of each in turn. The assemblages from excavated sites are the raw material of most archaeological investigations, and pottery is no exception (section 2.1). Kiln sites or production sites require special treatment for they bring with them their own set of problems and potential (2.2). The form and fabric (or clay) of a pot both have a major contribution to make to our study (2.3–2.4), and finally we shall look at the value of experimental archaeology and the study of pottery production in the modern world and the recent past in the domain of ethnography (2.5).

2.1 SITE ASSEMBLAGES

The site assemblage is the bread-and-butter of most work on pottery. In the earlier history of pottery studies the site assemblage was exploited principally for its chronological value. More rarely were the other factors that contributed to the character of the assemblage, or to the differences between assemblages, considered, although the potential impact of the status of the inhabitants or the functions carried out on a site were understood by writers such as Pitt Rivers.

Transforming the assemblage

The history of both the single vessel and the ceramic assemblage between its point of use, and the work-table of the twentieth-century archaeologist is long and complex. We can view the voyage as one of a series of states, linked by processes that move pottery (and any other artefact) from one another (11). Thus a vessel in use (*life assemblage*) becomes broken (*death assemblage*) – and some non-random sample of these become incorporated in archaeological deposits (*the archaeological assemblage*), perhaps on more than one occasion. The material recovered from archaeological excavation is in turn only a proportion of that which was buried, the *archaeological sample*.

The processes that move objects from one state to another, in the jargon these are usually known as *transforms* (Schiffer 1976), can affect the pottery for either a short period of time or over many centuries. Thus the transforms responsible for cre-

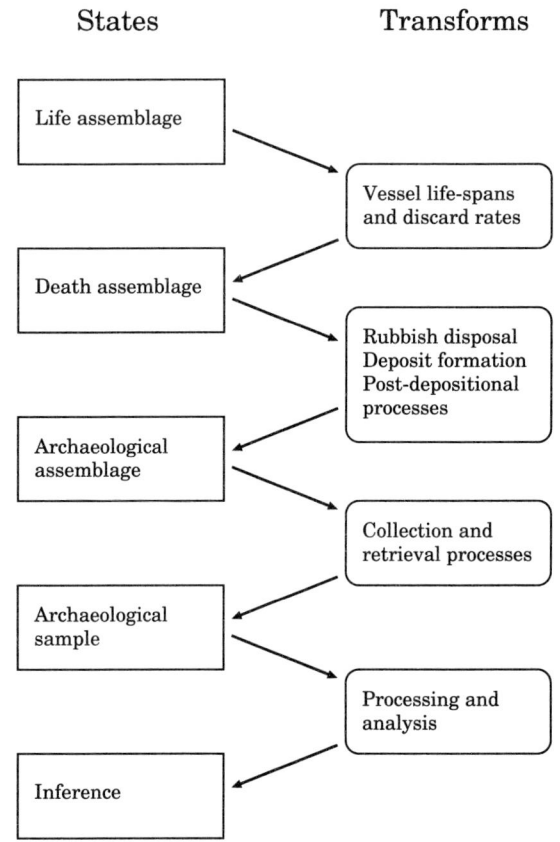

11 *Transformation of the pottery assemblage*

ating the death assemblage, that is the mechanisms that lie behind the breakage and discard of pottery, have an instantaneous effect (a vessel is complete one moment and broken the next), but the different rates at which these processes occur within the pottery assemblages alter the balance of the death assemblage, compared to the life assemblage. Thus vessels with long lifespans, such as large storage jars that do not get moved about very much, will be less represented in the death assemblage than the same number of vessels that are regularly handled and perhaps structurally more prone to breakage, such as drinking cups or cooking pots. The topic of lifespans of pottery is one of regular interest to ethnographers and several useful studies have been published (e.g. Bedaux and van der Waals 1987). We might expect lifespans to vary from one site to another, even for the same types. Sites with ready access to pottery supplies, either because of their location (in close proximity to production sites) or their economic status (higher-status sites may perhaps have a faster throughput of pottery) may tend to be rather less careful with their pottery than sites without these advantages.

A long-term process affecting the composition of the assemblage might be the effects of exposure and weathering on the pottery lying at or near the surface of the ground, such as that collected in field surveys. Here the sherds may have been exposed to many centuries of weathering, frost action, and ploughing and other agricultural activities. Some pottery types can cope much better with these conditions than others – some indeed completely disintegrate (Swain 1988).

It will be clear from the foregoing that what may have started out as a clear difference in the life assemblage, is likely to become somewhat blurred and distorted when passed through the various transforms. The proportions of pottery broken and discarded on the site will not be the same as those of the pottery in use; pottery from different layers and features becomes mixed; the assemblage retrieved by the archaeologist will be, in turn, biased, in that certain types of sherds, such as sherds of particular colours and sizes, may be collected preferentially. So we have the problem of selecting the appropriate tools for comparing between assemblages, and highlighting patterns that require interpretation. The value of any interpretation we place on the assemblage before us is only as good as our ability to compare it with others. The principal tools will be statistical analysis, and the precondition is a method of quantifying assemblages in a way that allows meaningful comparisons to be made. A single assemblage of pottery is impossible to interpret. We cannot say if type X or Y is over or under-represented unless we have comparative data available. We must know something about what to expect in the 'average' assemblage before we can pick out the unusual, and proceed to attempt an interpretation.

The history of pottery quantification in archaeology has been reviewed by Orton (1993). The topic became one of lively debate from the 1960s when the increasing quantities of pottery being recovered from the deep urban excavations brought home the necessity of simultaneously managing both the

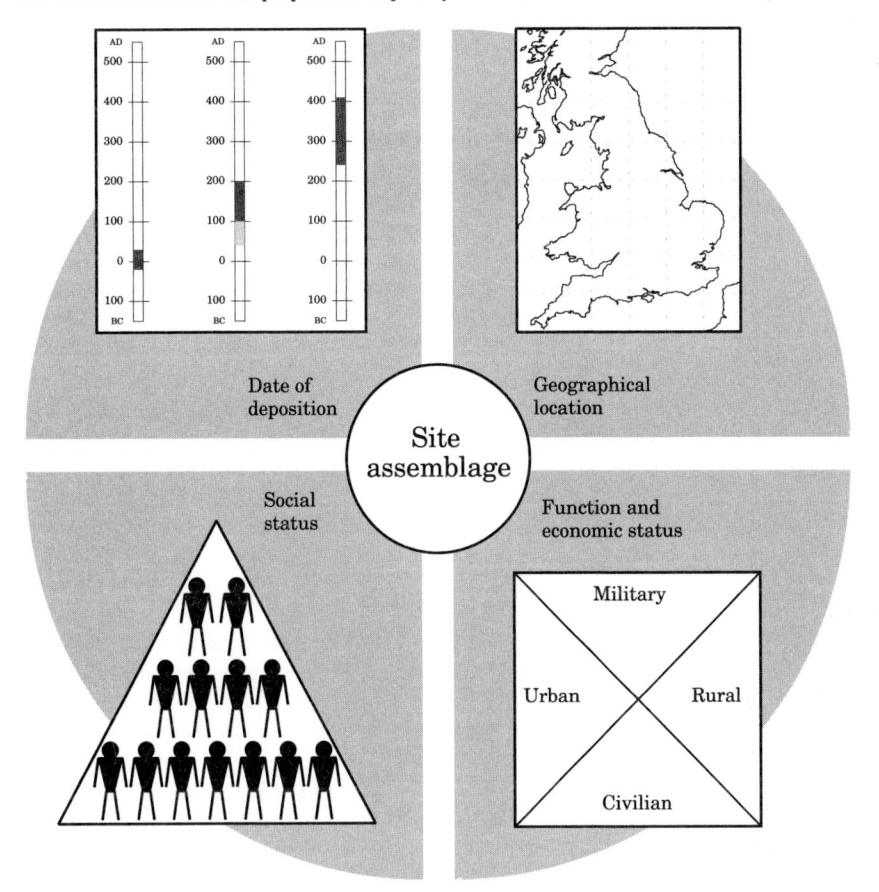

12 Factors affecting the composition of a ceramic assemblage

material and data, and making some sense out of it. The role of quantification will be discussed again in the section 3.1, on chronology.

The principal factors affecting the composition of the life assemblage on a site are discussed in later sections. These are:

1. The geographical location of the assemblage: the location of the site in relation to centres of production, supply routes and marketing centres (see 3.2).
2. The date of deposition: in addition to changes in the position of forms or decoration, there is the changing pattern of supply through time (3.1).
3. Function: the range of activities on a site will affect the range of pottery types in use (3.3).
4. Social factors: sites of differing social or economic status in the same region will have access to a different range of supplies. Similarly the status of types or forms may change from one level to another, so flagons in the first century BC may be a high-status type, but are commonplace by the end of the first century AD (3.3).

So, to some extent the task is one of placing an assemblage (be it the site, feature or context) in its position in the multi-dimensional space whose axes are time, function, status and location, viewed through the filter of site-formation processes, retrieval conditions and analytical procedures (**12**).

Site formation and pottery

Most of the discussion above has been concerned with looking at patterns in the archaeological record with the purpose of working back through the transforms to investigate the processes that were operating in the past to create the original ceramic assemblages. Running in parallel with this there is the possibility of looking at the transforms that were operating on the site to investigate site-formation processes. In this case, some of the physical characteristics of the sherds will tell you something of the archaeological deposits in which they are found. The criteria usually chosen are those that are likely to have been affected by the history of the sherd after it was discarded but before it came to its final resting-place, such as the size, rounding, degree of water rolling and abrasion. One general assumption behind such studies has been that pottery which passes through several periods of disturbance will tend to become smaller with time (Bradley and Fulford 1980) although this is evidently not a universal rule, but something that needs to be examined on a site-by-site basis. In some cases it may be a change in the average sherd size (perhaps expressed as the average weight of a sherd) of residual material from one phase to another that suggests that the material being incorporated into a deposit comes from a different source. Such 'new' residual material may be from the disturbance of earlier deposits on the site.

These and other problems and possibilities are aired in a paper on residuality by Evans and Millett (1992). They conclude that two factors probably influence the level of residual material; firstly the rate of contemporary supply (which can perhaps be measured by recording the numbers of sherds per unit-volume of archaeological deposit, and secondly the type of context, and particularly whether it is depositional or the product of the cutting or truncating of early deposits, which in turn reflects the contemporary activity on the site. Both of these are worthwhile areas of interest, although the extra resources necessary to record the additional data are not inconsequential. The interest in these phenomena extends beyond the immediate confines of the Roman levels on the site. Evans and Millett describe several cases where study of the Roman pottery residual in medieval and later deposits aids with the interpretation of these levels.

In a post-medieval sequence from Chester-le-Street (**13**) the average sherd weight of Roman pottery falls initially (phases 5–12) but rises steeply in phase 13, when there was stone-robbing from the underlying Roman buildings and truncation of Roman levels. At this point the average size of the Roman sherds in these levels rises, because of the mixture of new material, and is greater than that of the contemporary, post-medieval, material from the same contexts.

There are regular pleas in the literature for more investigation of such problems, and the work has indeed much potential. However, it is probably true to say that this is the type of project that is regularly discussed (often at the instigation of site directors and archaeological field staff) but only rarely executed, and even more rarely brought to any sort of satisfactory conclusion with useful results.

2.2 KILN ASSEMBLAGES

Since Corder's 1957 paper on kiln structures, the study and publication of kiln assemblages has been a major aspect of

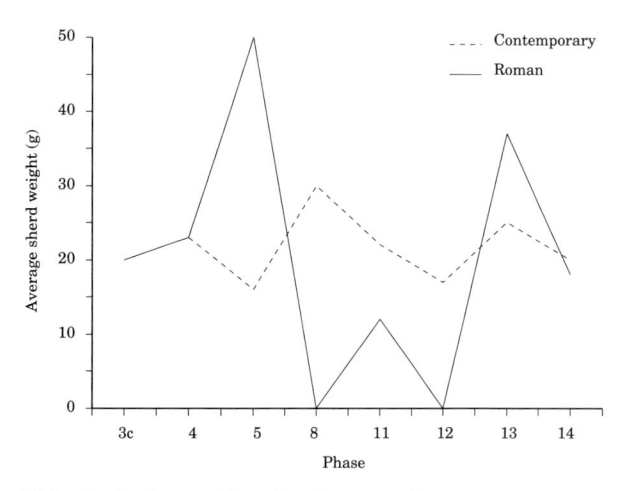

13 *Residuality in assemblages from Chester-le-Street*

Sources for the study of Roman pottery

Table 8 *The growth in the number of Roman kiln sites identified in Britain*

Date	Number	Source
1864/1880	13	Roach Smith
1930	101	Grimes
1956	122	OS Map of Roman Britain, 3rd edition
1978	146	OS Map of Roman Britain, 4th edition
1984	365	Swan/RCHME gazetteer

Romano-British pottery study. It was seen that by dating kilns and their production, either directly or via external stratified assemblages, the pitfalls of dating by 'parallel searching' could be avoided. The rise in the number of recorded kilns is illustrated in **table 8**. Alongside this has been a dramatic increase in the number of named wares, which have at least regional significance, in addition to the vast number whose only label is some code or number (**table 9**). The potential of kilns and kiln assemblages will be examined under four headings: (1) the dating of production, (2) kiln structures and equipment, (3) the distribution of kiln sites and (4) the study of production assemblages.

Table 9 *Romano-British wares identified*

Date	Number	Source
1930	4	Collingwood
1976	15	Webster, *Student's Guide*, 3rd edition
1980	32	Young, *Guidelines*
1986-92	162	JRPS bibliography

Dating kiln assemblages

When we turn to the problems of dating, several features of the archaeology of kiln sites conspire to reduce their chronological value. This is true whether we are attempting to give a date-range to the activity on a site, or to define a series of phases of production. Firstly, the proportion of externally datable material, such as samian, on kiln sites is often pitifully small, and particularly so on sites in rural locations. Coins also seem relatively uncommon, so conventional approaches to archaeological chronology may not be available.

Secondly, the nature of the stratigraphy on many kiln sites tends to reduce the chronological value of much of the material recovered. The relatively small number of closed kiln assemblages which contain the debris from the last firing, should be contrasted with the bulk of the pottery on kiln sites which comes from waster heaps or dumps. Waster heaps may accumulate over a period of time, perhaps intermittently, and may also be moved about to make way for later activity, such as new kilns. Wasters are often incorporated within the kiln structures themselves. There are ethnographic records of wasters being used to cover kilns during firing, as sealing and insulation and this also seems probable on Roman kiln sites. There is thus the possibility of much shovelling about of waster heaps, incorporating and mixing the material from several phases of production activity.

Often there will be smaller closed assemblages from elsewhere on the site, such as groups from pits or wells, that may be used as a 'control' to divide up the bulk of the material from the larger dumps. On sites that are only partially investigated – and the majority of excavation still concentrates on the kiln and its immediate environs – it is possible that pottery from earlier phases of production located in unexcavated areas may be present, but unrecognized as such.

Kiln structure

Although the Roman period is the first when kiln-fired pottery

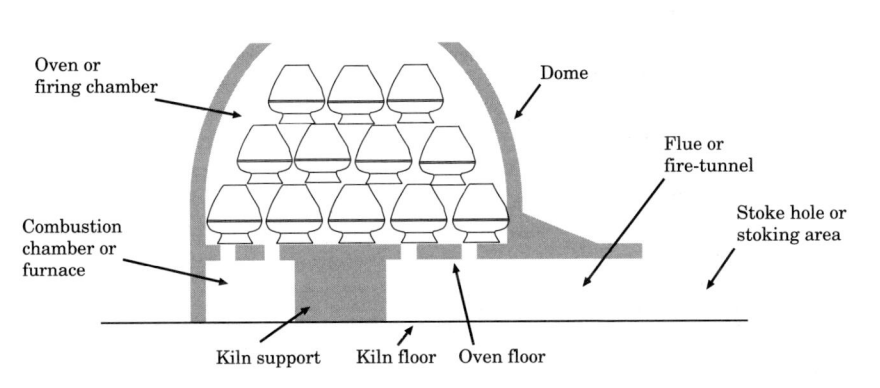

14 *The principal components of a pottery kiln*

becomes commonplace throughout the country, it is clear that clamp-fired pottery remains an important element of the industry. Clamp (or open or bonfire) firings leave relatively little trace in the archaeological record and have been only rarely identified in either the Roman or prehistoric periods (Swan 1984, 43-4). Spreads of ash and shallow scoops on some sites have been interpreted as the debris from open firings. Waster rates in such firings are often quite low, so large waste-heaps need not be expected, and the absence of wasters is not evidence that firing has not taken place.

When we turn to the more sophisticated kiln structures (**14**), two distinct strains can be distinguished within those of the early Roman period. Firstly, there was an indigenous tradition of kiln construction, with its roots in the pre-conquest period. Such kilns were typically surface-built or in shallow scoops, with impermanent walls, probably largely constructed of turves with a thin clay lining. Within the firing chamber was a temporary raised floor made from prefabricated fired-clay pedestals, kiln bars, props, perforated plates and other elements. Such kilns (generally referred to as La Tène III or Belgic) have been recorded at a number of sites across southeast England, but there is a particular cluster in the Nene valley which has been studied in some detail (P. J. Woods 1974). The earliest seem to date from the early first century AD, but the style flourished into the Roman period. The use of removable bars continued through the second century, but semi-permanent arrangements of bars plastered into a permanent central circular pedestal had developed by the beginning of the second century AD. The style continued in use until the end of the Roman period.

Secondly, there are the large square or rectangular kilns with permanent raised oven-floors, supported on lateral pilasters. These date to the middle of the first century AD and are known from a few sites in the south-east – Colchester kilns 23, 26 and 34, Morley St Peter and Caistor St Edmund (Norfolk) and Little Munden (Herts). The pottery made in these kilns clearly marks their users out as immigrants from Gaul or the Rhineland, where the form of these kilns can also be paralleled (Swan 1984, 83-5). In addition to these square kilns, there are two new post-conquest types of circular or oval kiln; some (like their square cousins) had lateral pilasters, and others had tongue-supports. The former had relatively little long-term impact on kiln technology in the province, but kilns with tongue-supports were adopted by a number of the major industries (e.g. the Verulamium region, the Nene Valley, Colchester, Mancetter/Hartshill) and remained in use until the end of the Roman period.

Another important type is the single-chambered structure without a true floor but with a combined furnace and pottery chamber (Swan 1984, 113-20). The pottery to be fired was supported directly on temporary props, or wasters from previous firings, without any intervening floor. There are variants with inbuilt platforms or central pedestals, and they may have either a single or twin (opposing) flues.

Within these broad categories, Romano-British kilns vary considerably in the details of their construction. However, certain distinct regional categories can be distinguished that may be described as regional traditions. Some specialist types are particularly characteristic of one of the larger pottery industries, while others are shared between a number of smaller sites within an area. These regional traditions give us the possibility of tracing relationships between groups of potters and industries through the relationships between kiln types. Technology, including kiln construction and operation, is just as much a part of the cultural heritage of a potter as the forms and fabrics that are produced, and the development of kilns is likewise subject to outside influence and change. In a number of cases we can identify an intrusive kiln type in an industry which can be equated with the movement of potters from another workshop. This may be either from a continental industry (for example, the samian kiln at Colchester: Hull 1963) or a movement within the province (e.g. potters from the Verulamium region and Oxfordshire industries moving to Mancetter, War.: Swan 1984, 98–101; K. F. Hartley 1973a).

Finally, we should not forget the other tools and equipment on the production site, in addition to the kiln. Many sites have revealed traces of pits, ditches and other features which may have been for the preparation of clay or temper. Wheel pivots are a rare item, but are occasionally found. Small bone or metal tools for the forming, shaping or finishing of pottery should always be looked for, although the rather uninspiring collection of pieces of twisted metal and wire used by modern potters would doubtless not be recognized for what they are if recovered from an archaeological site.

The distribution of Romano-British kiln sites

The overall distribution of known pottery kilns is illustrated in **15**. The majority of sites are found south and east of a line from the Severn estuary to York. A number of factors are likely to be responsible, at least in part, for the location of pottery kilns. The distribution of raw materials will have some influence, although clays suitable for potting can be found in most areas of the country. However, social and economic factors undoubtedly influence location as well. The influence of the changing military situation in the north of England and Scotland during the Hadrianic and later period – with the stabilization of the frontier on the Tyne–Solway line, may have affected the fortunes of industries further south. During the Flavian–Trajanic period the kilns at Brockley Hill (between London and St Albans) had been a major supplier of mortaria to sites in the north, but during the Hadrianic period new workshops in the Midlands (e.g. Mancetter/Hartshill in Warwickshire) were set up which began to exploit the northern markets effectively. The process of supplying the military establishments of the north from forward suppliers rather than industries to the south culminated in the fourth century with almost all pottery being supplied from kilns in Yorkshire (Gillam 1973).

A further factor, operating at a more local level, is the changing relationship between pottery industries, towns and the rural economy. During the first and second centuries a high proportion of pottery kilns were located within a relatively short distance of towns, but these decline in number in the fourth century, when many of the most successful producers are in the countryside. The pottery industry was becoming increasingly ruralized. The growing competition for timber resources in the vicinity of towns may have been part of the cause of this phenomenon (Fulford 1977a, 307), but there are examples in the ethnographic literature of substantial pottery industries which rely on a mixture of coppiced wood and the waste from agricultural operations as fuel. An alternative explanation is that a production site located equidistant from two or more towns had simultaneous access to the marketing networks of all of them, and this advantage outweighed any increased costs of transport (ibid., 308). It has also been suggested that there was a general contrast between economic growth in the early Empire, which was centred on the towns, and the late Empire, when it was more decentralized (Millett 1990, 148) and pottery production is reflecting a more general trend. The rural industries of the later Roman period may be situated at the boundaries between adjacent *civitas* (ibid., 166,

fig. 68) in order to exploit the marketing systems attached to both (**16**).

Production assemblages

The final aspect of the kiln assemblage is the pottery itself. The range of forms and fabrics which are produced together can be described as the production assemblage. The final arbiter of the relationship between fabrics that have been defined macroscopically, or by some other means, at a consumption site will often be their discovery together in a production assemblage. The successive phases of a production assemblage will illustrate influence from other styles, either through the migration of potters, or the copying of imports or other widely traded types.

The often enormous quantity of pottery from the excavation of a kiln site is both the problem and the potential. The processing of a large group of material is inevitably time consuming, and there are few short-cuts to be had. The report should aim to produce a summary of the wares and types produced (or perhaps we should say those that became wasters), with data on the proportions of the different forms and their dimensions. These provide the fixed points against which a site assemblage can be judged. A kiln group is the nearest we shall ever get to those responsible for the raw material of our study – the potters.

2.3 TYPOLOGY

Shape is obviously a key element of the study of pottery. Clay is a uniquely tactile and malleable medium, and in the hands of a competent craftsman is capable of taking and holding a bewildering variety of forms. Anyone who has stood and watched a potter working at the wheel will see a sequence of shapes appear and disappear in rapid succession. Centuries of typological progression in the curve of a rim or the angle of a shoulder can pass by in seconds with the slightest changes in pressure and position of the potter's fingers.

Yet the archaeological study of pottery depends on the fact that, even though faced with this vast range of possibilities, a potter will nevertheless tend to reproduce a limited range of forms with remarkable accuracy. In common with many other simple crafts and technologies, potters will follow the recipes (for clay, slip or fuel mixes) and procedure (for forming, decoration and firing) that have been passed down to them and that they, in turn, pass on to their successors. In a pre-scientific age, the traditional descriptions of a manufacturing process may be surrounded by semi-mystical explanations of the behaviour of materials. Most craftsmen do not take the risks involved in experimenting with their manufacturing processes and the resultant conservatism is reflected in the archaeological record as the long-lived ceramic traditions that we can see. These cover not only major features of the overall form, but lesser details such as the shape and finish of

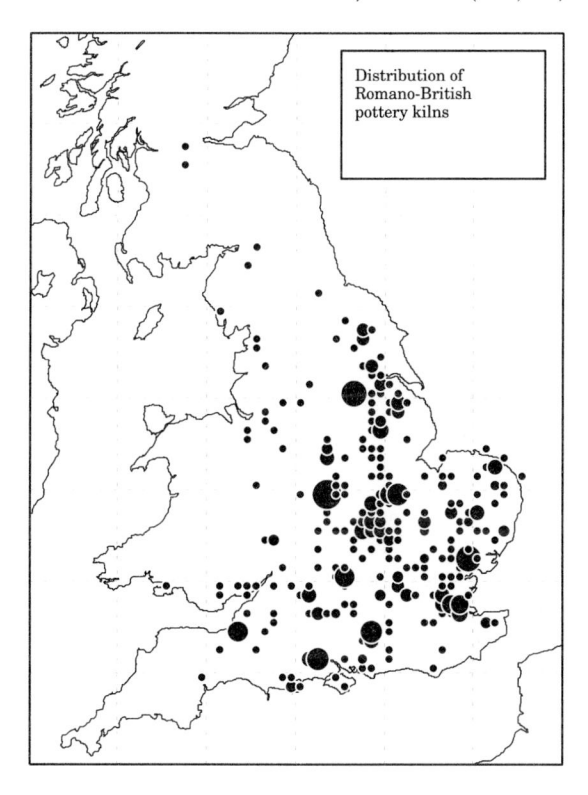

15 *The distribution of Romano-British pottery kilns*

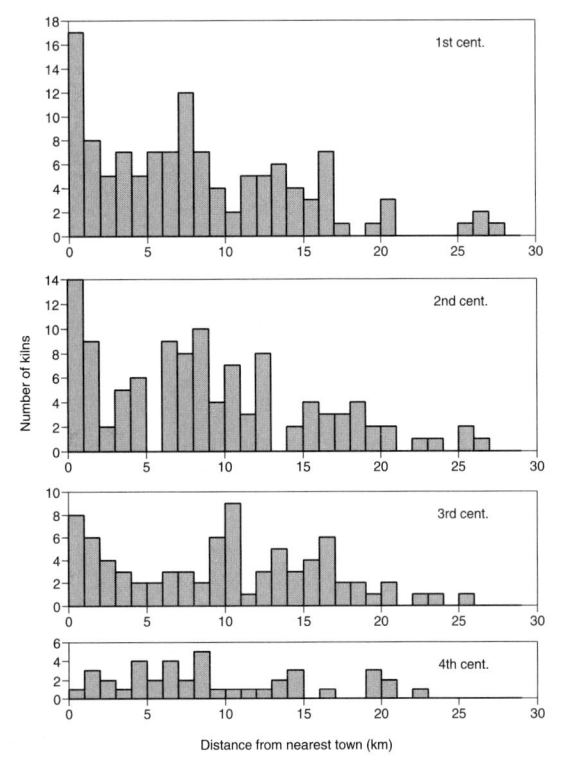

16 *Ruralization of the pottery industry (after Millett)*

a rim or a cordon or a decorative technique.

In Roman archaeology, the principal approach to pottery shape has been through the publication of a type-series. Historically we can trace most of this back to Dragendorff's original terra sigillata series of 1895. The process behind the creation of such a series is generally left unstated, but it is a grouping together of similar items judged on a number of criteria assessed simultaneously, and their separation from dissimilar groups. The groups thus formed might be thought to relate in some way to the groupings the original maker or users of the vessels would have recognized, and so serve as a suitable foundation to base a study of, for instance, pottery function.

On the other hand, the study of pottery by modern ethnographers often reveals that the classifications devised by archaeologists take insufficient account of criteria that the makers or users of the pottery consider to be important. This relates to the more general problem of the identification of the function of pottery. Nevertheless, the conventional type-series remains the basis of most studies of Roman pottery. Some are based around the material from a single site or region (such as the *Camulodunum* series or Gillam's 1957 type-series for pottery from northern Britain), or cover material of a single fabric or ware (e.g. the New Forest and Oxfordshire series). Types are used to summarize the ceramic assemblage from a site, enable comparison within the site (between features) and between sites, and as a series of hooks on which other data may be hung.

Alternatives to the traditional type-series
The traditional type-series is not the only approach to the classification of shape. A number of mathematical or geometric techniques have been employed in the description of pottery shape, although it cannot be claimed that any of these has achieved any notable success in the field of Roman ceramics (summary in Orton, Tyers and Vince 1993, 155–62). Traditional types are usually not simply descriptions of shape. Decoration, finish and fabric have some part to play, and in this respect the mathematical approaches to shape are only addressing part of the problem. A further problem with the description of archaeological pottery, which many of the simpler geometrical or mathematical techniques fail to cater for, is sherd material. A classification based on ratio measurement, for instance where a bowl is defined as a vessel whose height is more than one-third of, but not greater than, its diameter, cannot be applied where only the rim is present and the height/diameter ratio cannot be calculated. This would not be a problem if each rim type was exclusive to a single form, for the type could be defined on the basis of the complete examples. Alas this is not the case, for many potters build vessels from a kit of 'reusable' parts, such that the same rim form may appear on vessels with quite different proportions.

Techniques which are more suitable for dealing with sherd material do exist, such as the 'envelope' and 'two-curve' systems (Orton, Tyers and Vince 1993, 158, 162–3). Neither has been widely employed, but in some specialized circumstances may be the only solution to a problem. For example, data might be required on the shapes and sizes of the vessels represented in an assemblage where the rim forms give no clues. The data which result are not a substitute for the conventional type-series, but rather an alternative view of the same material.

There have been experiments on computer-aided classification of pottery shapes. A system that attempts to recognize amphora shapes from drawings by breaking the image down into its constituent parts and comparing it with a database of descriptions is described by P. H. Lewis and Goodson (1991). Despite all the undoubted ingenuity of such a tool, it may be reasonable to ask if such systems would ever have much practical application in the field. The real problems with ceramic typologies are perhaps rather less the assigning of new specimens to existing types, and rather more what we are going to do with the data once we have collected them.

2.4   THE ANALYSIS OF CLAY
The study of the fired clay body of the pot has a long history in Romano-British ceramics. Thomas Wright, in his account of Roman Wroxeter, records the experiments of one Dr Henry

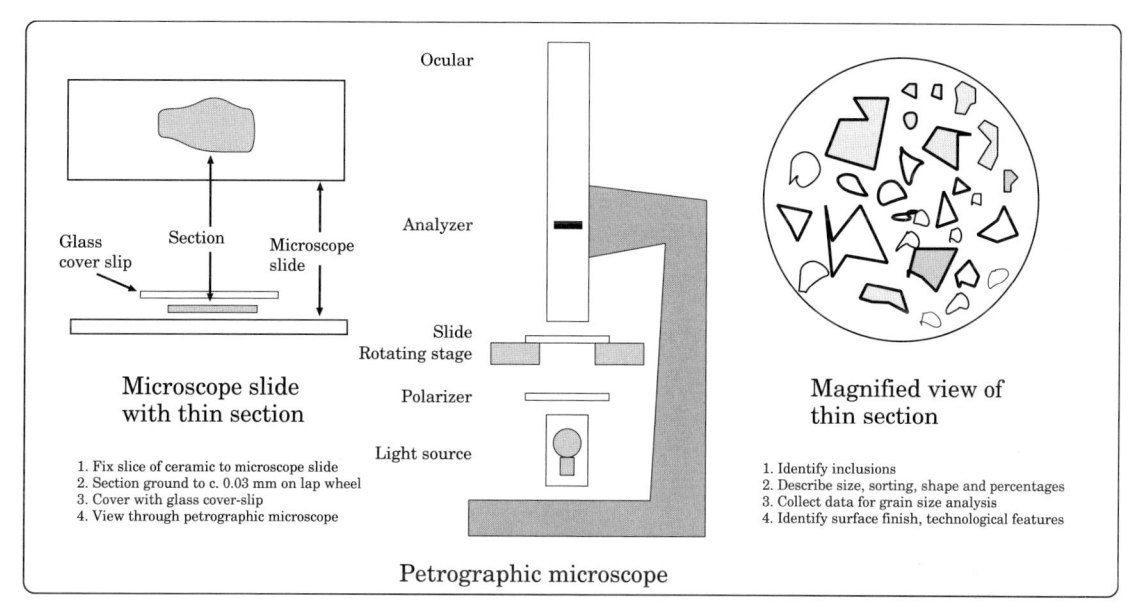

17 Thin-section analysis

Johnson who demonstrated that the Roman pottery from the site was manufactured from the local Broseley clay (T. Wright 1872), then used for the manufacture of clay tobacco pipes. In a passage in the foreword to *Excavations in Cranborne Chase* (1892), Pitt Rivers described the geological basis of pottery studies. The techniques that had been applied so successfully during the nineteenth century in unravelling the geological stratigraphy of the country could, he asserted, equally well be applied to the study of the clays and rock fragments in pottery, with the aim of identifying sources and trade routes.

However, this approach did not find much support among most students of Roman pottery in the first decades of the twentieth century. The work of Bushe-Fox, May and others was essentially typological and any assessment of fabric is generally confined to some broad technological groupings such as red-gloss wares or grey-fired wares. Even those labels that could, in theory, have been attached to the products of a particular locality, such as Castor, New Forest and Upchurch ware, were being used (if at all) as stylistic categories, rather than descriptions of a fabric. The rise in the number of kiln-site excavations served to underline the regional character of Romano-British pottery, particularly of coarse wares. From the 1970s, the effect of an approach explicitly based on geological techniques coincided with the need to process the increasing quantities of pottery from large-scale excavations. In 1977, D. P. S. Peacock drew together all these threads and laid out a manifesto describing an approach to the processing of pottery based on a hierarchy of investigative procedures (Peacock 1977a). The three levels in this system are (1) physical examination of the hand specimen, (2) petrological examination and (3) compositional analysis.

The aim of the primary visual sorting of the material is to divide the sherds into a series of fabrics, and provide a description of each fabric rather than descriptions of each vessel, which had been the general practice in the past. Petrological study is generally considered as a second-stage tool to answer specific questions that are thrown up by the primary visual classification, such as the identity of a particular inclusion. In thin-section analysis the minerals present are identified and the samples are grouped together on the basis of the inclusions (17). In some cases the identification of a particular mineral or rock type (however sparse) may be sufficient to assign a vessel to a source region, such as limestone from the Malvern hills or gabbro from the Lizard peninsula. Even a more general identification, such as a fresh granite inclusion in an area of sedimentary geology, may suggest that the fabric is an import to a region rather than a local product.

However, many fabrics, and in the particular case of Romano-British coarse pottery this includes many of the commoner wares from southern and eastern Britain, do not contain such exotic minerals, but are dominated by quartz sand. These can be studied in thin-section using the technique of textural analysis (Darvill and Timby 1982). The dimensions, shape and roundness of a randomly selected sample of sand grains are measured on each slide and the results compared with the data from other specimens, perhaps simply by plotting cumulative frequency curves or with more sophisticated statistical procedures. Textural analysis has been applied to a number of different types of Romano-British pottery, and some results have been encouraging (Timby 1987).

A thin-section may also be of value in the description of the manufacturing technology of a vessel. Sometimes it is possible to distinguish between hand-formed and wheel-thrown wares in thin-section because of the alignment of the

18 Heavy mineral analysis

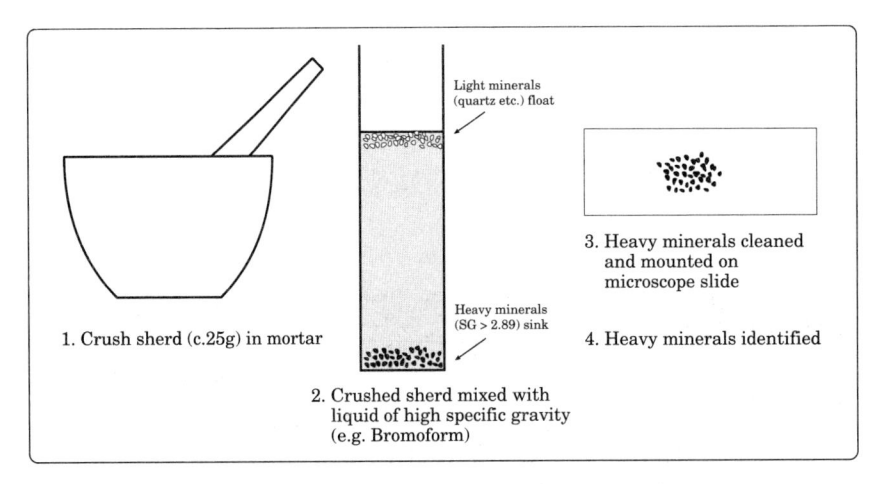

inclusions (A. J. Woods 1984). Surface finishes such as slips may, in some cases, be better seen in the thin-section than the hand specimen.

Another geological-derived technique that is suitable for dealing with quartz-tempered wares is heavy mineral analysis (Peacock 1967b), which had been used intermittently since the 1930s (Oakley 1933). This technique (18) does not attempt to characterize the vast number of quartz grains that are present in the temper, but concentrates instead on the very small number of grains of heavy minerals such as tourmaline and zircon that are a natural constituent of most sands. The classic application of this technique to Romano-British pottery is Williams' study of BB1 (D. F. Williams 1977). He demonstrated that the tourmaline-rich sands of BB1 were likely to be derived from the Tertiary sands of the Purbeck region.

Both textural analysis and heavy mineral analysis are time-consuming, requiring many hundreds or thousands of individual identifications or measurements during the course of the average project. The identification of the major mineral or rock fragments in a thin-section, in contrast, is a relatively straightforward task, well supported by accessible handbooks and guides. It is the natural extension of the visual identification of the minerals in the hand specimen.

The last of the three levels of fabric study is the compositional analysis (also known as elemental analysis or chemical analysis). There are several techniques available, such as Neutron Activation Analysis (NAA) and X-ray Fluorescence (XRF), but the underlying principles are similar in all cases. The chemical composition of the fabric is measured and expressed in percentages for the major elements present (and in ppm, parts-per-million, for the minor constituents). The measurement of a number of samples is usually compared statistically with samples of clay or pottery from known sources, to determine whether or not they can be the same. The final results are usually presented on a scatter diagram. The many practical difficulties surrounding sampling, measurements, contamination, accuracy, consistency and statistical treatments have been described elsewhere (for details: Orton, Tyers and Vince 1993, 144–51).

One example of the application of these techniques to Romano-British pottery is the examination of the fine colour-coated white-ware hunt cups of the type usually described as Castor ware (A. C. Anderson *et al.* 1982). Chemical analysis (in this case Atomic Absorption Spectrometry) suggested that a large proportion of this material from Britain was from the Köln industry rather than the Nene Valley. Within the relatively small Nene Valley group there was some discrimination between the products of the kilns at Stanground, on the one hand, and Water Newton, Sibson and Stibbington on the other (19).

Having successfully distinguished between groups of pottery, perhaps of differing source or date, on the basis of chemical analysis, the visually distinguishing criteria should then be identified so that the data can be used by others to make the same distinction in the hand specimen or under the

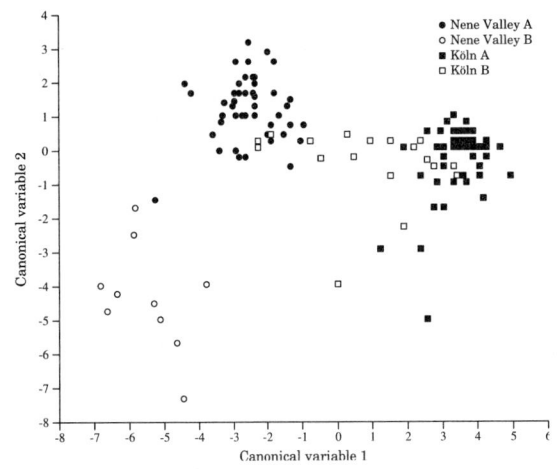

19 Discriminant analysis of Köln and Nene Valley sherds (after A. C. Anderson et al.*)*

Sources for the study of Roman pottery

binocular microscope. Such criteria will not always exist, and we should not expect them in all cases, but without this feedback the value of much chemical analysis will necessarily be limited.

Compositional analysis in its simplest and most common form does not take account of any of the physical structure of the fabric. The elemental composition is an average of the compositions of the clay body, and the inclusions, and it is not possible to translate the chemical analysis into any form of the visual description. There are some hybrid techniques such as the electron microscope, that allow the compositional analysis of a small area of a fabric, perhaps a single inclusion, or part of a composite inclusion, or just the clay body (Freestone 1982). Even with the growth in the availability of appropriate analytical techniques at research and commercial laboratories, the compositional analysis of pottery fabric will remain an area of specialized interest.

The study of fabric is not an end in itself but a means to an end. It is true that there is little more uninspiring to the non-specialist (and to many specialists) than long catalogues of obscure local fabric types, garnished liberally with Munsell codes and the dimensions of quartz grains. There is clearly a danger of losing sight of the overall structure of the assemblage, and its relevance in a local and regional context, behind a fog of minutiae.

Our increasing understanding of the raw materials of pottery – the clays and tempers – should be balanced with an increased awareness of the actions of the potters in creating the finished vessel. In regions with rather homogeneous geology the best clues to identifying the production of different areas may not be the details of the fabric itself but the finishes, surface treatments and other technological tricks used by the potters (Darling 1989). These two approaches are complementary, not alternatives.

2.5 EXPERIMENTAL ARCHAEOLOGY AND ETHNOGRAPHY

Both experimental archaeology and ethnographic analogy have had a role in the study of Roman pottery since the nineteenth century. When faced with a particular phenomenon in the archaeological material it has been natural either to perform

20 Experimental kiln firing at Highgate Wood (North London)

experiments to reproduce it or turn to the work of ethnographers or other writers for some suitable analogy in the pottery of another period or culture.

The topics that seem to have attracted most attention in these early works, almost to the exclusion of all others, were the colour of pottery and the identity of the various surface treatments. However, the concern for these topics in the case of Roman pottery was a mere side-show to the much longer running saga surrounding the technology of Greek red- and black-figure wares. The nineteenth-century literature is littered with discourses on the finish and firing of Greek pottery and numerous attempts at imitation.

The technology of red sigillata wares and some of the other categories of fine wares, it was realized, was comparable with that of its Greek predecessors. Thomas May's volume on the Silchester pottery (1916) begins with a description of the principal categories of ware and an explanation of their technology. His discussion drew on a wide range of sources including experiments with Bunsen burners and test-tubes to identify the chemical constituents of a coating, the refiring of sherds to demonstrate reversibility of the change in colour from red to black, Classical references to the use of pitch as a coating on wine jars, the same on contemporary Peruvian liqueur jars and the salt-glazes created by Japanese potters throwing seaweed into the kiln during firing. Some of this may read rather strangely now, such as his description of the black terra nigra finish as a coating of bitumen, but it does illustrate the diversity of evidence that could be drawn upon.

One aspect of experimental archaeology with a long connection with Romano-British pottery studies is experimental kiln firing (**20**). Edmund Artis, the excavator of Castor in the Nene valley in the 1820s, undertook kiln firing to test his hypotheses about their operation. He also demonstrated the reversibility of the change in colour from grey to light-coloured wares (Smith 1845, 4). A series of experiments in the 1960s (Bryant 1973) tackled such problems as firing times, fuel usage, the temperature in the firing chamber and waster rates.

A comparable body of data is available from the studies of pottery firings collected by ethnographers (Rye 1981, 102-3). Although this may not solve the particular problems associated with Roman kilns, it is likely to be more reliable in such areas as waster rates and fuel usage. The potters controlling these firings will be more familiar with the technology they are using then modern experimenters. The descriptions in the ethnographic literature of open or bonfire firings are particularly valuable. One aspect that is particularly striking is the enormous diversity of these operations, ranging from two or three pots fired in a shallow scoop in the ground, to many hundred or even thousands of vessels fired in large clamps. Such insights are lost from the archaeological record. The sites of open firing are only rarely identified, and yet are essential to our understanding of how these industries may have operated. The general organization of pottery workshops is often best explained by reference to those that were still operating in similar environments in the recent past. The detailed surveys by R. Hampe and A. Winter of pottery workshops around the Mediterranean in the 1950s and 1960s are the classic example of such studies, oft quoted by archaeologists searching for an explanation of the enigmatic features excavated on kiln sites (Hampe and Winter 1965).

Mode	Description
1 Household production	Occasional production for use within household. Typically by women. Simple technology.
2 Household industry	Production part-time, but more continuous or seasonal, for exchange. Typically by women. Simple technology.
3 Individual workshop	Production part-time, generally seasonal. Orientated towards markets. Usually men. Use of wheel and kiln common. Simple distribution mechanisms.
4 Nucleated workshop	Major economic activity. Extensive investment in technology (wheel, kiln, drying shed etc.). Some specialization within industry (throwers, assistants etc.). Marketing through middlemen. Often rurally situated as 'village industries' but also urban.
5 Manufactory	As nucleated workshop, but larger, with increasing investment, specialization with some assembly-line techniques.
6 Factory	As above, but employing mechanical power.
7 Estate production	Production on an estate for internal use. May assume commercial role once set up.
8 Military/official production	Production attached to military or other state authorities for official purposes.

Table 10 *Modes of pottery production (after Peacock)*

There have been attempts to analyse the broader picture of pottery production through ethnographic study and define a series of production systems which incorporate data on technology, economics and social structure. The use of ethnographic data as a means of investigating archaeological problems is usually referred to as *ethnoarchaeology*.

The book by D. P. S. Peacock, *Pottery in the Roman World*, takes an explicitly ethnoarchaeological approach to Roman ceramics (Peacock 1982). He organizes ceramic production into eight *modes*, based on a survey of recent and modern pottery manufacturing systems in Europe and elsewhere, and then proceeds to interpret the evidence from the Roman period against the background of these modes, suggesting possible social and economic correlates for the observed archaeological data.

Such a use of ethnographic data is not universally accepted, and there is a lively debate about the value of such cross-cultural generalizations and the particular role of ethnographic analogy in the interpretation of archaeological data (McVicar 1983). The social context of pottery production has been considered in detail by Arnold and others (e.g. Arnold 1985). It is clear that a great many factors must be brought into play to explain how and why pottery is produced in some societies, and why a production system shifts from one form to another. But it is equally clear that many of these factors will leave little or no archaeological trace, so we may be left with those technological and economic correlates considered by Peacock (**table 10**).

Rice considers Peacock's modes, and similar schemes developed by van der Leeuw and others (Rice 1987, 182–3). She makes the general point that most of these definitions include statements on both production and distribution and it may be preferable to separate these, and simplify the scheme down to two basic models, household and workshop, with rising levels of scale within both, but particularly the workshop model.

Griffiths and Greene (1983) suggest that modes 7 and 8 – estate and military production – are based on prior knowledge of the Roman economic system rather than growing out of ethnographic data by deductive reasoning. Thus the military mode is probably not a separate mode at all but a specialized case within the other modes. By grouping too many diverse phenomena under the military label, both here and in other contexts, we are losing important information about how military production and supply operated in the Roman world. Greene and Griffiths go on to suggest that the missing element in the discussion at this level is a consideration of the nature of the Roman economy, drawn from the literary and epigraphic sources (a topic tackled at greater length in Greene 1986). In this view, the archaeology of a historical period is inevitably hemmed in by that framework, and its relevance cannot be denied. This is serious stuff, and there are no easy answers. Here, we are delving deep into the foundations of Roman archaeology and its role as the handmaiden of history, or otherwise, and the relationships between archaeology and the other social sciences. Pottery, as ever, will be an important part of these discussions.

Despite these criticisms, the framework given by the modes is a useful overview of the pottery production system, providing pointers to the types of data that should be looked for, but it is a long way from being a predictive model. But it is clear from the criticisms outlined above that some would seek to bring more factors into the discussion, others less.

A rather specialized form of ethnography that can be applied to Roman pottery is reference to ancient literature. Roman writers are notoriously silent on the details of much that might be of interest to an archaeologist of the twentieth century; in particular the whole area of the crafts, and the lives of manual labourers and traders is sparsely covered. Roman literature was largely written by and for a restricted segment at the top of society and is dominated by the doings of the great and the good. A work such as Pliny's *Natural History* has relatively little to say on the subject of pottery, although he does give us a list of the principal high-quality wares known in his day (*Natural History*, XXXV, 12, 46). Beyond this, we have passages in the works of the agricultural writers describing the preparation of amphoras and other vessels as containers for wine, oil and other produce (e.g. Columella, *De Re Rustica*, 12.18.6, on coating amphoras with resin for transporting wine).

In summing up, we might suggest that good ethnographic studies of pottery production and use (e.g. Rye 1981; Rye and Evans 1976; Miller 1985; Barley 1994) should be essential bedtime reading for the student of Roman pottery. Similarly anyone with the opportunity to visit one of those countries around the Mediterranean where small pottery workshops still flourish should certainly pay them a visit, even if it means spending less time lying on the beach.

3 The role of pottery in Roman archaeology

Having described the tools that are available we shall now see how they are put to use in the service of Roman archaeology. Most archaeologists would probably agree that the major roles of pottery studies are in the fields of (1) chronology, (2) economics and (3) function or status. We shall also look briefly at the pottery as a source of information about the potters themselves.

3.1 POTTERY AS CHRONOLOGY

Pottery is not alone as a source of chronological information on archaeological sites, yet, for better or for worse, it has often come to take first place. A survey of the state of Romano-British pottery studies placed chronology at first place in the list of questions asked of the assemblage (at 83 per cent), beating the economic implications of the material into second place, at 57 per cent (Fulford and Huddleston 1991, 5–6). The underlying mechanism for the resolution of pottery dates, the dating cycle, is best illustrated by terra sigillata, indeed one-third of the publications in the 1991 survey used only samian dates.

Since Oswald and Pryce's study of 1920, terra sigillata has played a major role in dating most Romano-British sites of the first two centuries AD. The subtitle of their volume was '... *from a chronological standpoint*', and it is the chronological value of the evidence they bring together which is their main theme. Their *modus operandi* is made clear in the introduction (F. Oswald and Davies Pryce 1920, 2):

> The method, by means of which a chronological estimate of Sigillata evidence is arrived at, is based in its essentials on the determination of 'site-values'. Thus the exclusive or predominant occurrence of certain types on properly excavated sites, such as Haltern, Hofheim, Newstead and Niederbieber, which can be dated by external historical evidence, affords a valuable aid to the determination of the period and distribution of these particular forms of Sigillata. Light is also thrown in this way on these wares, as well as on the period when certain modes of decoration were in vogue.

So, in this scheme, it was the historically dated sites and closed assemblages that provided the framework for the chronology of terra sigillata. The type sites provide cross-sections of the material in circulation at one period, against which undated material can be compared.

The broad geographical spread of some wares, from Scotland to Italy in the case of La Graufesenque samian, increases the possibility that the stamp of a particular potter, or a vessel with a particular decorative style, will be recovered from one of the historically dated assemblages. If not the potter in question, then perhaps it will be one of his known associates, taking into account the evidence from the production sites, or a potter using the same decorative motifs. Much of the pleasure of studying samian ware is undoubtedly this recognition of the individuals operating behind the mute sherds; the spin-off is the prospect of data of chronological value.

To take just one short example to illustrate, the South Gaulish potter Modestus used a die reading OFMOD, which

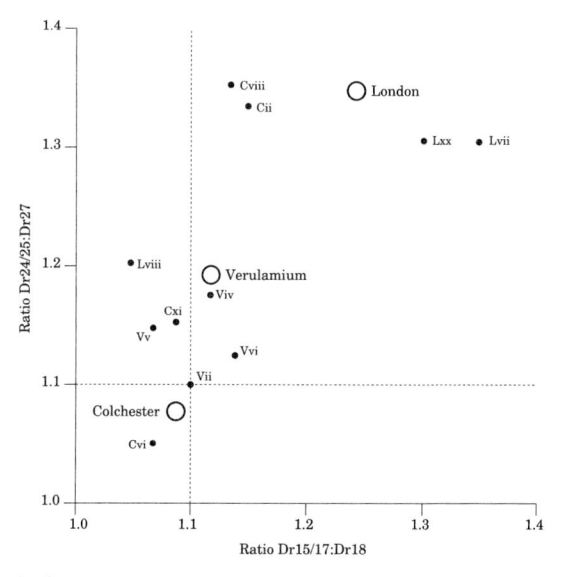

21 Samian plate and cup ratios in Boudiccan destruction horizons (after Millet)

at some time in its life was broken and had the ends filed off diagonally, to give the reading /OFMOI/. The complete version is found on cups in deposits below the Boudiccan destruction horizon (AD 61) in Colchester, but the amended version of the die is found on vessels from forts founded in the early Flavian period in Scotland (that is from the early AD 70s; B. R. Hartley 1972a, 224, S16). So the die may have been used over the period of a decade or so, and was perhaps remodelled some time in the AD 60s.

Of course there are limitations on the refinement of such dates. While we might prefer to give dates to the period of manufacture of an industry or a potter, in fact we are collating the evidence for their period of deposition. This is a product of their dates of manufacture, plus some undetermined interval while the vessel was in use. We can see the effect of this when we look at the composition of destruction assemblages, such as the Boudiccan levels in London, Colchester and Verulamium, studied in detail by M. Millet (1987). Here the material whose lifespan has been 'prematurely terminated' by the actions of Boudicca and her followers is 'later' in character than that from contemporary rubbish deposits, where the pottery has lived through its allotted span. There are also differences between the assemblages from the three cities, with the London material being consistently 'later' than the other two. This may be explained by the slightly later foundation of London, and hence a lower proportion of residual and 'heirloom' material (**21**).

The key sites and assemblages remain at the heart of the chronology built up by this method, and of course we must be aware of the consequences of any change in their chronology. Thus a reassessment of the abandonment of the Augustan fortress at Haltern in Germany (down from AD 16 to AD 9) has consequences for the dating of the initial occupation at Camulodunum (Sealey 1985, 108). The redating of Haltern affects the dating of other types of pottery found there, which in turn has repercussions on the dating of other sites where those same types are found, and so on all the way down the line. To keep track of this web of interconnections we use the major type-series which serve as labels to transfer packets of chronological data from one site to another.

However, the apparent simplicity of these schemes is disrupted when we recognize that several producers may be responsible for a particular group of pottery where only one had originally been recognized. The discovery, by chemical analysis, that 50 per cent of the 'Italian' sigillata from Haltern was in fact from Lyon (and a mere 10 per cent from Arezzo) has thrown several spanners in the works. How can we be sure that these widely separated workshops were all producing pottery of the same form at the same time? Indeed we cannot now be certain which parts of the typological diversity of the ware are due to chronology and which a reflection of the idiosyncrasies of a particular workshop (Ettlinger *et al.* 1990, 1–2).

What is true for the fine-ware industries is no less true of coarse wares. Few of these have anything like the geographical spread of samian, and generally we have to set up a secondary regional framework. Contexts dated initially by samian ware or coinage in the conventional way provide dates for the local coarse wares, which may in turn provide dates for another assemblage. Such sequences will be of value for the immediate locality, but perhaps not beyond its boundaries. It is clear, however, that many coarse wares do not develop typologically, in a regular, even, fashion from one decade to the next. In some cases once a form that is fit for its purpose is hit upon, it will remain static for many decades, if not centuries (Loughlin 1977, 90). Thus on a regional scale a more valuable guide to chronology may not be the typology of the individual vessels in an assemblage, but rather the proportions of pottery of different types and from different sources. For this we need firstly a method of quantifying the pottery in a series of assemblages and secondly some system for comparing them.

One approach is to define a series of ceramic phases on the basis of the wares that are present and their relative proportions. The classic example of this approach is C. Going's analysis of the pottery from Chelmsford (Essex), where eight phases spanning the Roman period are identified. Where the supply situation in each phase is illustrated (as in the Chelmsford study) by maps showing the sources supplying the site, then the relationship between chronology, pottery supply and the economy is made explicit.

Quantification, mechanical ordering and chronology

The principal mechanical technique for ordering assemblages and types is seriation (Kendall 1971). If we visualize our data as a table with, for example, contexts as rows and types as columns, then we can shuffle the order of both so that the contexts (that is rows) with a similar spread of types (i.e. columns) are brought together, while simultaneously ordering the columns to bring together types that appear in similar groups of contexts. With small tables a reasonable seriation may be

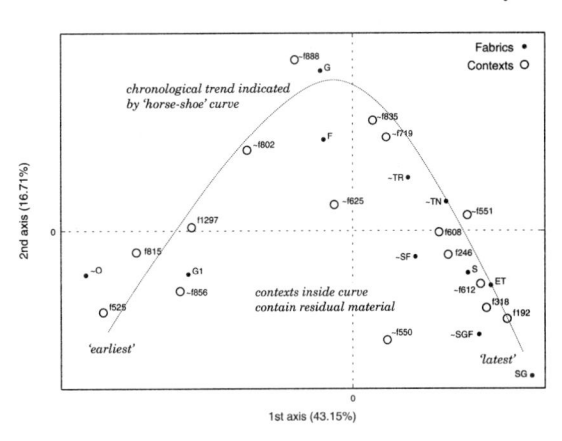

22 Analysis of ceramic assemblages using pie-slice

accomplished by physically shuffling strips of paper (Doran and Hodson 1975), but with larger samples the number of possible permutations rises quickly to the point where some mechanical (i.e. computerized) ordering is necessary. There are several computer programs available which perform seriation, often written for or by archaeologists, as the procedure is not part of most commercial statistics packages (Fletcher and Lock 1991).

The types to be ordered should follow the general pattern of a period of rise in usage, up to a maximum, followed by a decline (Orton, Tyers and Vince 1993, 191). Types which are more or less constant across all contexts add little to the picture and are best eliminated; types with bimodal distributions – that is two periods of abundance separated by a deep trough – will disrupt the ordering procedure and are best eliminated. Seriation is not capable of giving absolute dates to any point in the ordering; it is even up to the interpreter of the output to decide which direction the contexts have been ordered for the earliest contexts may be at either the 'top' or 'bottom' of the final table. Careful inspection of the seriated output will sometimes identify features other than chronology that are of interest. For instance, contexts with residual material will show a long tail of earlier types stretching away from the leading edge of the curve.

Other mechanical methods of ordering contexts have been developed. The Pie-slice package (Orton and Tyers 1990; Orton, Tyers and Vince 1993, 175–7) tries to tackle the general problems of comparing between assemblages, and chronology is likely to be among the principal causes of any differences. The procedure groups together the contexts and types which (as in seriation) are held in the rows and columns of a table, but then passes the result to a correspondence analysis routine for analysis and display.

In the plot (**22**) a chronological trend should be apparent in a 'horseshoe' shaped curve; it is for the observer to identify both the route of the curve, and its earliest and latest ends. Deviations from the curve are also of value. A context plotted on the inside of the curve may contain residual material. It is drawing the ends of the curve together because it includes types from points all along the length. Similarly a type on the inside of the curve may be an indicator that it is of poor chronological value – it is drawing together the ends of the curve because it is present in contexts all along its length.

Although this seems to have taken us a long way from the beginning of our discussion of chronology, the underlying principles have not altered. We are still attempting to compare assemblages, perhaps more rigorously than before, and with the aim of extracting information on topics other than chronology.

Seriation case study

As an example of a seriation we shall look at Gillam's classic 1957 paper on '*Types of Roman coarse pottery vessels in northern Britain*'. Gillam defined 350 types and recorded their occurrence in 134 key assemblages. Thus we start with a 134 by 350 data table. Seriation methods are available for working with both fully numerical data and simpler presence/absence data. Gillam's data records only the presence of a type in a particular assemblage, so a relatively simple seriation technique will be used (Duncan *et al.* 1988). We can envisage the cells of the table holding ones, if the type occurs in the group, and zeros otherwise. We first eliminate types and contexts with less than three occurrences. These add little to the data set and by removing them we reduce it to more manageable proportions (90 by 134).

The early part of the seriation covering the first and second centuries is illustrated in **23**. We can see that the first major change in the sequence is about one-third of the way down the table (the Stanegate forts of Chesterholm and Haltwhistle Burn). Many of the earlier (Flavian–Trajanic) types are restricted to the sites above that line and there are a number of new introductions at this point, including black-burnished wares. Many of the groups in the next ten lines or so are turrets and milecastles on Hadrian's Wall. It is notable from the sequence of types at this point that many of the vessels in these assemblages are cooking pots (e.g. Gillam types 116–25) and they contain relatively little 'heirloom' or residual material. The next cluster of new introductions is two-thirds of the way down, with BB2 jars (types 139 & 142) and a number of new mortarium forms (types 245, 248, 253, 267).

A mechanical seriation such as this provides only part of the answer. It is but one of the tools available for the ceramicist seeking to put some order into the material and should be used alongside the analysis of quantified data and conventional chronological assessments.

3.2 POTTERY AND ECONOMICS

Pottery production requires both resources – land, water, clay, fuel and labour – and some outlet for the finished products, and so here we must delve into the realm of the Roman economy. The character of the Classical economy is a subject of lively controversy among economic historians. There are excellent descriptions of the state of play by Greene (1986) and Peacock (1982) and the roots of this debate need only be summarized here.

On the one hand we have a view that the Roman economy was essentially primitive, lacking concepts of efficiency and economy of scale, and where commercial activity was largely confined to premium goods of high status and low volume. Conspicuous consumption – 'a veritable potlach of architecture, art and cuisine' (Gillam and Greene 1981, 5) – was a tool of the aristocratic elements of society to maintain their status and power. Wealth was generally accumulated by taking or inheriting it from someone else rather than, for instance, investment in more efficient production. The role of the State was limited to extracting resources, in the form

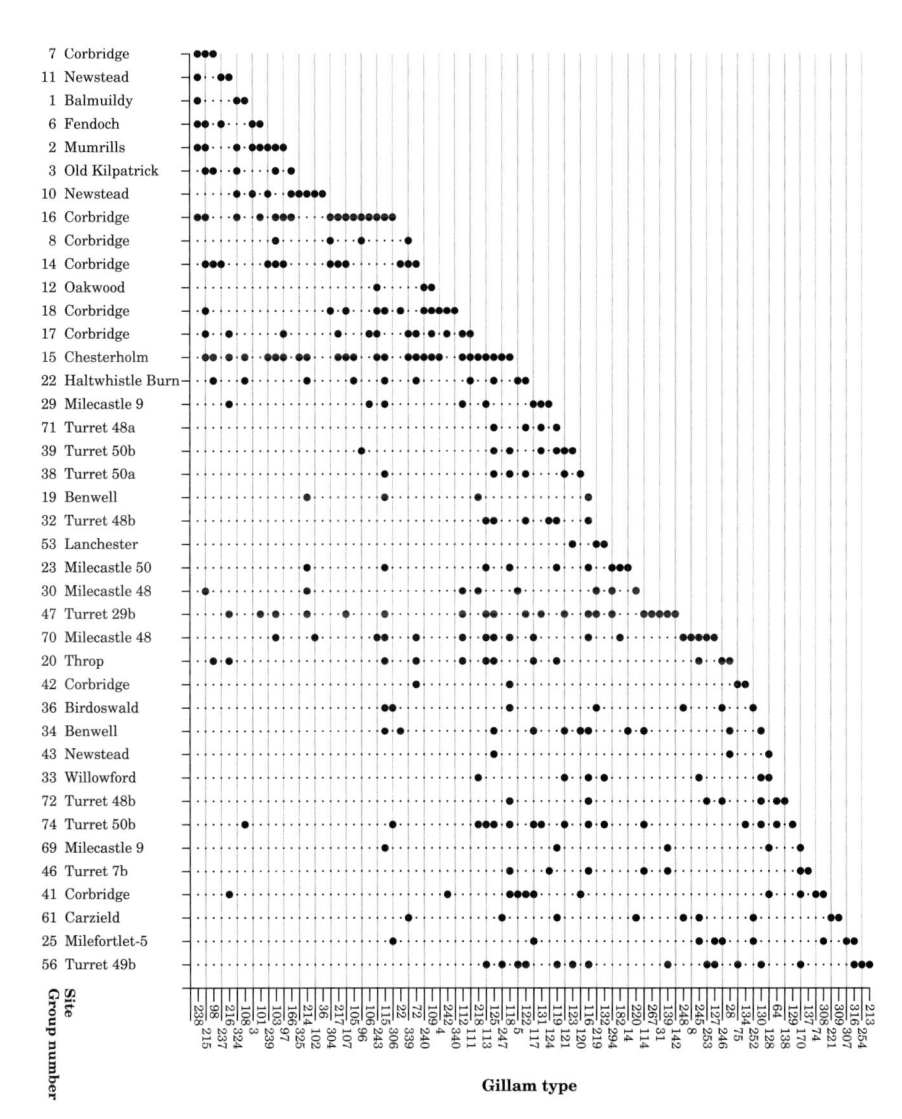

23 Seriation of Gillam's types

The role of pottery in Roman archaeology

of taxes, but it did not intervene to promote production or trade. The vast majority of the population was largely self-sufficient.

The contrary view is that the self-regulating market had a more significant role in the Roman economy. A wider range of goods was distributed to sites of low status and the monetized economy extended well beyond the cities into the countryside. The effect of taxation and rents (whatever its declared purpose) was to draw the peasantry into a market system by obliging them to generate a surplus.

Most economies are not exclusively one thing or the other and there is a fair amount of common ground between these two views. Low-level economic transaction in small denomination bronze coinage may have been essentially 'piggy-backed' on the more important purpose (from the State's point of view) of tax-collection. Yet it may have been enough to generate movements of goods traceable in the archaeological record over both short and long distances. Few markets are totally unconstrained, and in the Roman Empire reciprocal or redistributive process of the classic substantivist type may have operated alongside and partially overlapping with activities oriented towards markets.

We should also bear in mind the size and diversity of the Roman Empire. We should not expect all regions to behave in precisely the same way, since the underlying factors such as the proportion of free labour in the system may have been quite different. The world seen by the inhabitants of Rome, or Pompeii, or Antioch, need not have been identical to that seen by their contemporaries in London or Cologne.

The contribution of pottery studies

Our understanding of the workings of the Classical economy

39

is deeply relevant to our interpretation of the evidence of pottery production and distribution. But additionally pottery (and other artefact studies) should have something to contribute on their own account. Answers to many of the questions posed by economic historians require numerical data to be extracted from the archaeological record (Duncan-Jones 1982). The interest in pottery quantification since the 1960s has been inspired, at least in part, by these needs.

Even though it is evident from many studies that some pottery was widely distributed, it is not quite clear how significant this was, in terms of volume and value, and what interpretation we may place on it. On the one hand it may be that the pottery trade was economically significant and thus worthy of study in its own right; on the other, it may be that pottery was only a minor item of trade, and thus not worthy of much attention, beyond the rather introspective reason that it is telling us about the trade in pottery.

At first sight the latter might seem to be the case, for pottery (other than amphoras) is only rarely a significant part of the cargo of wrecks in the Mediterranean. Amphoras with their contents, in contrast, were regularly the principal (often the only) cargo and seem to have been a major item of trade. The link is that the minor pottery types in a cargo are parasitic on the mechanisms set up for the amphora trade. Thus in Britain, for instance, we have imports of a few fine pottery cups and beakers from Baetica, in southern Spain. This is the source area of the Dressel 20 olive-oil amphora, and it is probably the amphoras that are dragging the Baetican fine wares along in their wake across Europe. We can go a step further and suggest that the distributions of other pottery types (even when not associated with amphoras) may be indicating the general directions and flows of trade in other items, now disappeared, such as foodstuffs or other raw materials. In this view, pottery serves as an indestructible *marker* or index of the whole trading system, and other traffic flows, and is thus of considerable importance. There is some support for this in Fulford's study of the movements in goods around the North Sea in the medieval period. The historically attested trade in raw materials that have now disappeared from the archaeological record, such as wool or foodstuffs, seems to be tracked by the movements of pottery types, which do survive (Fulford 1978). Similarly, the Saintonge jugs from the Bordeaux region found in England in the fourteenth century are a reflection of not only the more significant trade in wine and salt, but also the political links with the region.

Some of the potential mechanisms behind the movements of goods within the province may be illustrated by the letters from the Roman fort at *Vindolanda* (Chesterholm, Northumberland). The exceptional environmental conditions at this site have preserved numerous wooden writing-tablets upon which the text can still be read. One letter (dating to between AD 105 and 125) records the business and financial dealings of two individuals, Candidus and Octavius, relating to the delivery of sinew, cereals and hides to Vindolanda from sites further south (the hides are to be sent from Catterick in Yorkshire). Although none of the items referred to in this example are pots, or need be contained in pots, we can envisage that dealings such as these may have led to the movement of ceramics around the country (Bowman *et al.* 1990).

It is not only goods (ceramic or otherwise) that move through such systems, but people and ideas as well. Trade with an area may also indicate the movements of individuals, such as craftsmen. Thus the trade in fine colour-coated wares through the Rhineland ports to Britain in the first century AD is followed in the second century by the movement of potters from the workshops of the Rhine and Mosel to sites in eastern England.

Economic fluctuations

In addition to these questions of trade and distribution, there are other broadly economic questions that can be tackled by the data in the archaeological record. We can take as an example the study by G. D. Marsh of the supply of samian ware to London (1981). The distribution of dated samian ware on a site had generally been assumed to be a product of the history of the site (e.g. Cunliffe 1968, 146–7), and periods of intense occupation would be represented by peaks in the samian distribution, and periods of low occupation by troughs. This is the implicit assumption that lay behind most work in samian since Dragendorff. However, data from sites in Britain with apparently rather different histories all showed similar patterns in the distribution of dated samian – a strongly bimodal pattern with peaks in the early Flavian period (*c.* AD 70–80) and the middle of the second century (*c.* AD 160–70), and a low point in the decade AD 130–40. When the net was cast wider and data from many other sites in western Europe incorporated, then again the bimodal pattern was found. These curves (known colloquially as Marsh curves) are now a regular feature of larger samian reports (**24**).

Thus, apart from obvious boundary effects – where a site was founded or abandoned within the period of supply – the overall pattern of samian supply measured by the distribution of dated samian remained the same. It could be argued that there are faults in the dating of samian, in other words, the distribution patterns should be 'flat' but are distorted due to some erroneous clustering of dates. It could be that rate of stamping varies from one period to another, but against this the pattern is present in the distribution of decorated wares as well. The favoured explanation currently is the economic one, namely that the pattern is real and represents rises and falls in the amount of samian in circulation.

This by itself is of considerable importance. The chronological distribution of samian in a site assemblage must be 'weighted' with a calibration curve such as that published by Marsh (1981, 215) to enable it to be used as a chronological tool. In crude terms a sherd of samian of the Trajanic period

The role of pottery in Roman archaeology

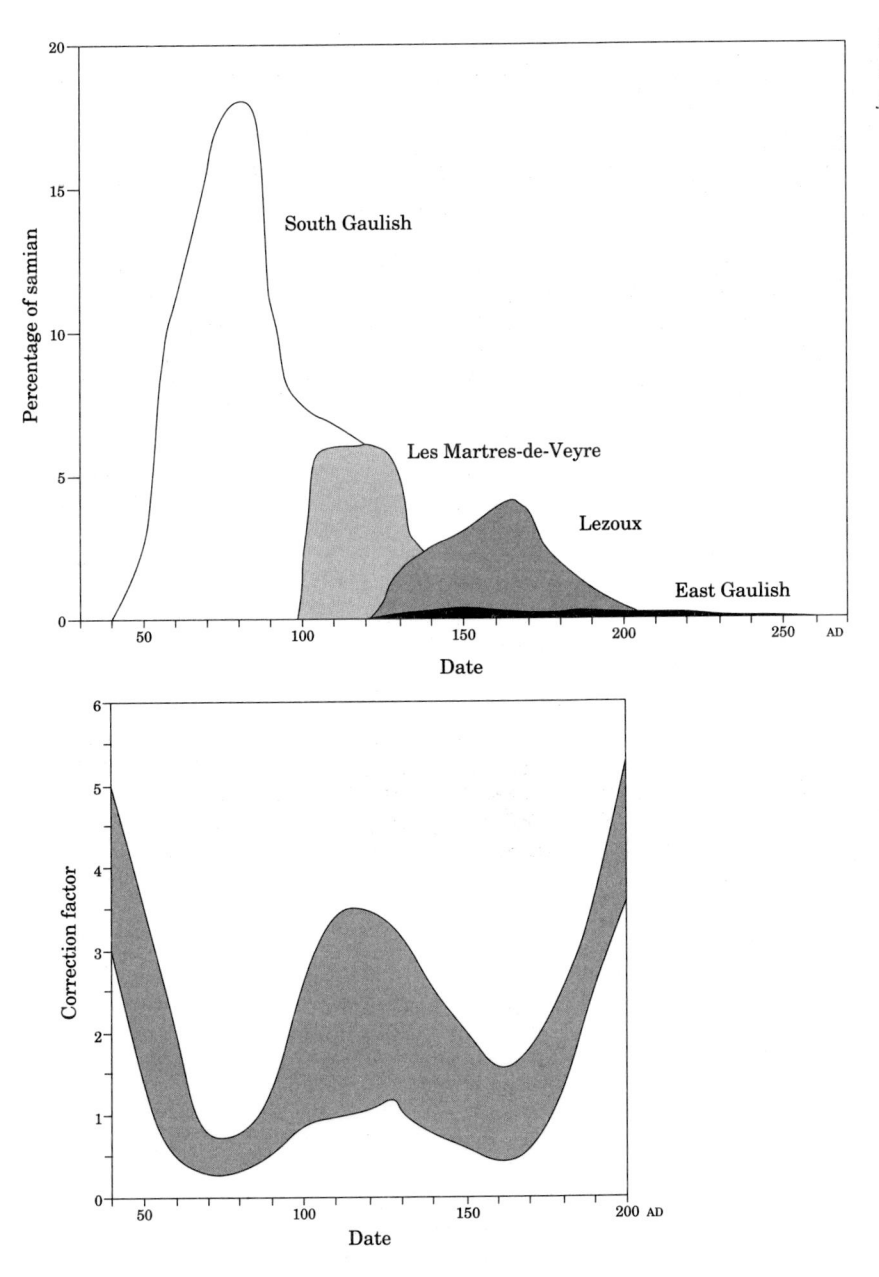

24 *Samian supply to London and samian calibration curve for Britain (after Marsh)*

has the same value as three of the early Flavian period, and between one and a half and three times the value of a sherd of the period AD 150–60. This is of particular importance in the interpretation of samian lists to determine if there are breaks in the occupation (ibid., 216), or in the analysis of field-survey data where information is often being gathered about the intensity of occupation prior to some decision about the advisability and location of further investigation (Haselgrove 1985, 26–7).

The further, and obvious, question to be asked is whether the bimodal distribution is some phenomenon confined to the samian industry, perhaps shared with other fine-ware industries, or can it be extended to the production of other pottery, other artefacts, and even beyond. This is the view taken by C. Going (1992), who suggests that the fluctuations seen in the samian curve may be part of a longer series of cycles that should be extended back into the earlier first century AD and forward into the third and fourth centuries, and indeed beyond.

Part of Going's evidence for these fluctuations are the dates of the expansions and declines of Romano-British pottery

The role of pottery in Roman archaeology

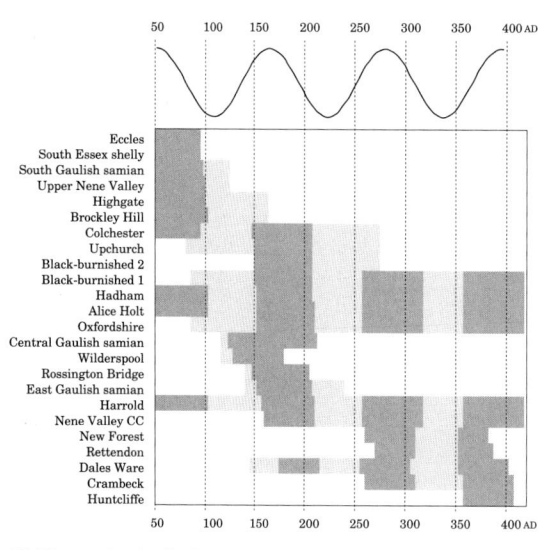

25 Fluctuation in the Roman pottery industry (after Going)

industries. These may suggest that synchronous changes across them all took place on an approximately 50–60-year cycle (**25**). The intervening troughs, in this scheme, represent periods when pottery is in relatively short supply, and typological development is relatively stagnant. Through careful quantitative analysis it may be possible to recognize changes in the behaviour of ceramics, such as periods when pottery is in use for a longer time and the stock of new pots is not being replenished, and this is where further investigation will undoubtedly concentrate. The implications of these fluctuations are as important for archaeological chronology as they are for the study of the economy. Pottery dating in the troughs will be affected by the extended use of pottery types from the preceding peak and, combined with the difficulties of a static typology, such deposits may not be recognized for what they really are.

We are a long way from understanding the roots of such fluctuations, whether in the samian industry or elsewhere. A 50–60-year cycle squares quite well with the periodicity of an economic cycle recognized in the data from more recent periods – the Kondratieff cycle – and Going describes the possible combined effects of this and other longer-term waves during the Roman period (1992, 108–10).

3.3 POTTERY AND FUNCTION

In addition to their value to the modern archaeologist as a chronological marker and their role in economic activity, pots are, in the broadest sense, tools. They were used to perform a function, and often several functions, simultaneously or sequentially. Some of these leave traces that can be identified. Function comes in several guises. Firstly, there is the function of individual vessels. Thus, an amphora has a function as a transport container for wine, the flagon is its temporary container, the samian cup is for drinking it at the table. Then there is the function of assemblages of pottery. The proportions of different types of pottery in an assemblage, or the way that they have been used, may reflect the activities that created the assemblage. Finally, there is the rather diverse area of the social function of pottery, the aspect of ceramic studies that is much beloved of anthropologists and ethnographers, but notoriously difficult to apply to archaeological material.

Put at its simplest we would expect that the range of pottery types in use in a kitchen, where food is being prepared or cooked, would be different from the range in use where food is being consumed. If we were allowed to wander through the rooms making an inventory of all the pots we find, as the modern ethnographer might do, this would be relatively simple. The question for the archaeological ceramicist is whether any sign of these patterns remains in the rubbish-pits outside the back door.

Individual vessel function

The inherent physical characteristics of a vessel may be an indicator of its original function, or at least indicate which functions are more or less likely. Thus large vessels with handles and narrow mouths are more suitable for corking and sealing and transporting with contents, than a shallow bowl. A summary of principal vessel functions and their possible physical correlates is given by Howard (1981, table 1.1). We can use these as pointers to the possible functions of Roman vessels, to be tested against further data.

One source of information on the function of Roman vessels are the Latin names that were given to them (Hilgers 1969). Many vessel names are rather nondescript, the equivalent of our 'bowl' or 'jar', and like their English counterparts hold little information of functional value. More rarely a particular vessel type in the Classical literature may be equated with one of our archaeological recognizable wares. Several of the recipes in the books of Apicius prescribe the use of a vessel called a *cumana*, which other sources tell us was a red-coloured plate or dish, from Cumae in the Bay of Naples. Pucci suggests that this may be equated with Pompeian-Red ware fabric 1, which has the correct physical characteristics and originates in this region (1975).

Graffiti on vessels occasionally give a name to the form. A good example is a pre-firing graffito from Usk (Gwent) with the text PE]LVEIS CONTUB(E)RNIO MESSORIS, 'a mixing bowl for the barrack room of Messor'. The text is on what we would now call a mortarium, and shows that one of the Latin names for the form was *pelvis* (*RIB* ii.6, 2496.3; Collingwood *et al.* 1994). This name, in turn, is common in Apicius, where there are instructions to pound various mixtures in such a bowl. Graffiti go beyond simple names to interesting insights into how pots were used. There are numerous examples, and we shall just pick out a few here to illustrate the range. A pot that was to be filled was often weighed before and after to record the quantity that the vessel contained, and these values may be recorded on the pot. A flagon from Chesterholm has the inscription T(ESTA) P(ONDO) VIII S(EMIS) P(LENA) P(ONDO) XXXXIII S(EMIS), 'vessel 8½ (Roman) pounds, filled 43½ pounds' (*Britannia*, 17 [1986], 454, d). Such 'tare and weight' texts are common on amphoras.

Sometimes the inscription records not only the quantity but also the contents: MEL P(ONDO) XXIIII, 'Honey 24 pounds' on a grey-ware storage jar from Southwark (*Britannia*, 6 [1975], 288, no. 24). There is a cluster of at least a dozen inscriptions mentioning honey on a form of jar with two small handles just below the rim, from sites in Germany and Britain (May 1911, 22–3). This form is now regularly referred to in the archaeological literature as a honey-pot (or Honigtöpf), although the storage of honey was unlikely to have been its only (or even major) function. We are sometimes told who measured the capacity of a vessel. NICERIVS M VIII, 'Nicerius measured this at eight (urnae)' on a large storage jar from Winchester (*Britannia*, 8 [1977], 441, no. 85). Eight urnae are the equivalent of 105 litres, and when reconstructed this jar indeed had a capacity of 107.6 litres. Some graffiti are more mysterious. A jar from Chesterholm has the inscription CORS MDCCCLXXXIIII. This seems to be the count of 1,884 of something small and presumably reasonably valuable into the jar (*Britannia*, 19 [1988], 503, 79). Some inscriptions that mention contents and quantities may be sealed samples that were sent with larger cargoes to verify they had not been adulterated *en route*, a practice attested with grain shipments in Egypt (N. Lewis and Reinhold 1966, 141–2, with refs) and Gaul (Liou and Morel 1977).

Many of the uses to which pottery vessels are subjected will leave traces on the sherds. One clear example in Romano-British ceramics is the BB1 cooking pot which frequently has significant white or pale grey deposits on the inside. This looks for all the world like the fur on the inside of a kettle, perhaps suggesting that these pots were used regularly for boiling water. Other visible deposits are noted occasionally in the literature, such as the location of sooting marks on the outside of a pot which show how the vessel was used over a fire. But it is unlikely that this type of information is systematically and comprehensively collected.

In addition to these visible deposits, it is known that pots will absorb invisibly many organic substances into the body of the fabric. These traces can be extracted, using solvents, and identified using standard analytical techniques such as gas chromatography (Orton, Tyers and Vince 1993, 224–5). The final result of this endeavour is usually a list of complex organic molecules, such as fatty acids, which are the building blocks of the original compounds. From the list it may be possible to reconstruct some of the original substances in recognizable terms such as olive-oil or mutton fat. Of course, few pots come into contact with only a single substance during their lifetime, and there are also potential problems with contamination from compounds in the soil. The most promising results with Roman vessels have probably been with amphoras, and particularly the resins and tars that were used to seal their inner surfaces prior to filling, as recorded by the ancient agronomists. To exploit fully the potential of this technique it will probably be necessary to organize a systematic survey of such residues from a single site. Only then will it be possible to distinguish significant data from the general background noise.

Chemical residues are not the only traces left on pots. Many actions on the vessel during its lifetime are likely to leave abrasion or wear-marks. Some shallow dishes show scraping around the edges as if a pie has been loosened from the wall of the pot with a flexible blade. Plates sometimes have scoring lines on the base where a knife has been drawn repeatedly across them. The cumulative value of such data will be the classification of pottery according to use.

The function of assemblages

The individual vessels in the assemblage will each have had a function, but the composition of the assemblage, the balance of the different vessel types, will reflect the totality of functions that were taking place on the site. The usual method of comparing function is to divide the assemblage into broad functional categories – jar, bowl, flagon, beaker etc. – and proceed from there. These categories are likely to be combinations of the types that have been defined for chronological or other purposes, and will cut across the divisions of fabric. There are certain long-term trends in the composition of Romano-British pottery assemblages, which provide the background against which any differences between contemporary assemblages must be judged.

Summaries of the functional composition of sequences of assemblages have been published from a few sites. We shall here look at those from Caernarfon (Roman *Segontium*: Casey 1993) and Chelmsford (Going 1987). Both of these sequences cover most of the Roman period, from the mid-first century until the end of the fourth. The principal functional trends in the assemblages are illustrated by the bar charts in **26**.

Some of the differences between the two sites are clear. The Segontium assemblage is notably lacking in fine wares, and particularly beakers. These form *c*. 15 per cent of the Chelmsford group in the first century AD. Cups, on the other hand, are more common at Segontium (over 15 per cent until the mid-second century), while they never rise above 5 per cent at Chelmsford. Interesting contrasts can also be seen in the proportions and chronological distributions of the dishes, jars and bowls.

It might be tempting to see the Chelmsford pattern, with its high percentages of both beakers and jars, as essentially a continuation from the pattern of ceramic usage from the pre-conquest period in south-eastern England, contrasted with a Roman military pattern at Segontium, with high percentages

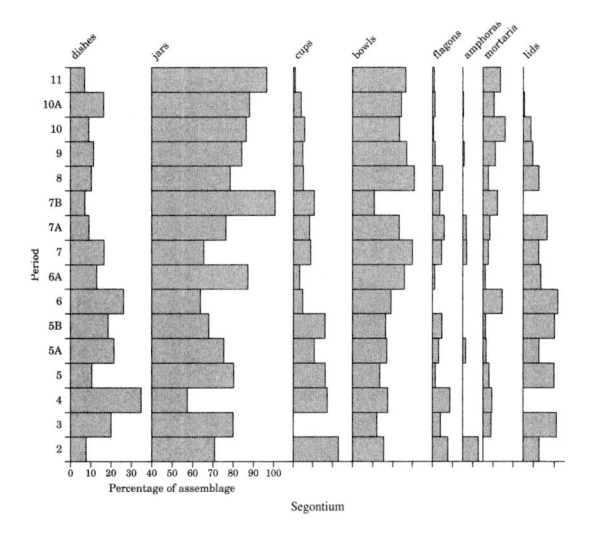

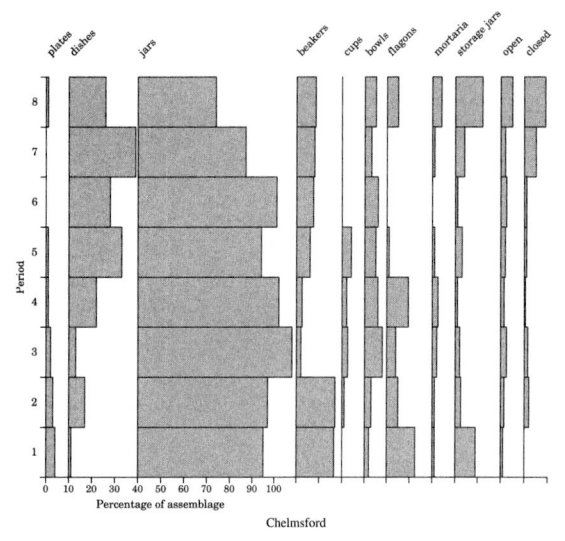

26 Functional analysis of pottery from Segontium and Chelmsford

of bowls, cups and dishes. Flagons and mortaria, which have traditionally been thought of as one of the hallmarks of the Romanized assemblage, do not seem to be that significant in this case. One question that must be addressed is just how real these patterns are, and how much they reflect divergences in the recording and classification systems in use on the two sites. There is at least a suspicion that some of the vessels classed as jars at Segontium would have been described as beakers at Chelmsford (e.g Segontium no. 84, a barbotine-decorated poppy-head 'beaker'). The pattern in the cups is not affected by this and would seem to be a real difference between the assemblages. There is clearly much potential for this type of comparison, but a necessary precursor for any intersite functional analysis is a consistent classification sys-tem. The developments of the last decade have made it possible to compare the data on fabrics and wares across sites with reasonable confidence. The same should be true for forms.

Sometimes the patterns in a ceramic assemblage are relatively easy to interpret. The pottery from the drain leading out of the *frigidarium* of the Roman baths at Caerleon was largely composed of sherds from small containers, dishes and bowls, such as might be suitable for prepared foodstuffs, and cups and beakers for drinking (up to 45 per cent in the main drain fill). The material was derived from the baths, where eating and drinking must have been regularly taking place (Zienkiewicz 1986, 20). The associated assemblage of bones and shells clearly illustrated the types of light, portable snacks that were favoured by the bathers. Sometimes the presence of an unusual pottery type in large numbers marks out an assemblage. The material from the Roman temple at Lamyatt Beacon (Somerset) includes large numbers of miniature vessels which, in this case at least, seem to be votive offerings (Leech 1986).

But it is not always enough simply to compare the forms present. The usual pattern is that different groups of potters (represented as wares) will produce different ranges of forms, so a change in the proportion of wares may result in differences in the proportions of forms. Some statistical techniques will allow the analyst to distinguish between a difference in the forms that is dependent on a change in the proportion of wares, from the situation where the changes in form are independent of the wares. There is also the question of whether a pottery type will have the same function in all circumstances. Depending on economic and social circumstances, the same vessel type may be used for different purposes. So, it is not enough just to count up the types present, but it is also necessary to look at use and wear-marks (as discussed above) for evidence that pottery is being used in the same way.

Again the study of graffiti on pots provides us with some interesting data on the functional content of assemblages. A paper by Evans (1987) considers the graffiti on pots reported in four of the annual summaries in the journal *Britannia*. This is a complex data set, with information (of varying quality) on the type of site (fort, *vicus*, *civitas*, capital, small town, villa, rural), date, geographical region, pottery type (fine ware or coarse ware), form (bowl, storage jar, jar, beaker, dish, flagon, lid, mortarium, amphora and other) and the class of graffiti (personal name, number, contents, other). This data is a valuable insight into the spread of literacy in the province (as Evans discusses) and also shows us how the pottery was viewed by its users. Some pottery was evidently worth labelling with your name, suggesting that it was both considered as personal property and likely to wander off if not protected. We shall look at just three of these variables – the type of site, the form of the vessel and the class of graffiti (**table 11**).

The graffiti are dominated by personal names (73 per cent), but storage jars have a high proportion of 'other'

The role of pottery in Roman archaeology

	Personal Names	Numbers	Contents	Others	n
Bowl	91	6	0	3	78
Storage jar	16	21	5	58	19
Jar	71	13	0	16	45
Beaker	78	12	0	10	59
Dish	82	9	0	9	57
Flagon	58	8	8	25	12
Lid	100	0	0	0	1
Mortarium	70	20	0	10	10
Amphora	42	38	13	8	24
Other	100	0	0	0	4

Table 11 *The distribution of graffiti by type of vessel (after Evans)*

(mostly capacity measures) and amphoras record numbers and contents. The distribution of the pottery types with graffiti across the sites (shown in **27**) is the result of a correspondence analysis.

The major contribution to the first axis (left to right) are bowls and amphoras on fort and *vicus* sites (left) against jars and storage jars on villas and rural sites (right). In the second axis (top to bottom) are mortaria and jars on rural sites (top), contrasted with beakers and dishes on villas and small towns (bottom). The composition of the pottery assemblage with graffiti varies significantly from one type of site to another. What is not quite so clear is whether it is the frequency of graffiti that is varying between sites, or whether it is the range of pottery in use that is fluctuating. It is likely to be a combination of these two factors.

It is perhaps appropriate to reiterate that many of the questions raised above require that large assemblages of pottery are compared, and the differences highlighted. If we are concerned with looking for differences in usage between sites, then we need to compare the wear-patterns, use-marks and so on, of the same pottery types across sites of different character – not compare different pottery types which because of their physical characteristics may bear quite different marks even under the same conditions of use. In the British context, the common amphoras and samian wares and some of the major coarse wares such as BB1 have precisely these characteristics. They are widely distributed in time and space, and appear on sites of many different types – both military and civilian, urban and rural, high and low status. Differences in the usage and function of such vessels between sites is significant and worthy of attention.

Anyone who has worked with pottery for any length of time will be aware of the storage problems that come with large assemblages. There is constant pressure from managers, museum curators and others to reduce the resources necessary

on storing and curating such material, and one procedure commonly suggested is the discard of substantial parts of the assemblage, after they have been studied. In the worst case the entire assemblage may be discarded, but often some sort of partial discard is suggested. It is unfortunate that the usual victims suggested for this treatment are precisely those pottery types – amphoras and common coarse wares – that are likely to be of greatest use in the intersite comparison of pottery usage, site formation and similar problems. Currently we have neither the descriptive language nor the appropriate analytical tools for recording and processing this type of information. So if the discard of common wares was carried out to any great extent now, there is the real danger of eliminating any possibility of cross-site comparisons in the future.

3.4 POTTERY AND POTTERS

The finished products of the pottery industry can, as we have seen, be used to shed light on such questions as the chronology of a site, or the nature of long-distance trade or regional distribution patterns. But additionally we should use the pottery data to investigate the industry itself, and address such questions as who were the potters and how did they relate to their craft, their customers and the many social, artistic and economic influences that swirled around them.

Further, because its product is so visible, pottery production has been studied in more detail than other contemporary industries. Does our knowledge of the pottery industry have any relevance to the understanding of the activities of these other, less visible, craftsmen? We have relatively few texts or inscriptions from the Roman period which illustrate the life of the potter, or indeed any other craftsmen. There are a few gravestones from sites in Gaul, but potters were evidently not in that part of the population that regularly set up inscriptions.

One source of information on the potters operating in Britain, at least during the first and second centuries AD, are the names recorded on mortarium stamps (A. Birley 1979, 131–6). Latin personal names contain important clues about the origins and status of an individual. A Roman citizen would have, and generally used, a three-part name, the *tria nomina* (e.g. Gaius Julius Caesar). Freedmen (i.e. ex-slaves) would usually take the first two names of their patron, and add a third name, a *cognomen*, of their own. Some *cognomina* are from good Latin roots, but others are adapted from Celtic personal names.

A number of the potters making mortaria in Britain (or operating in northern Gaul but supplying Britain on a large scale) were evidently citizens. A group of five with the names Sextus Valerius, but different *cognomina*, all operated out of Colchester during the first century AD. They are likely to have been the freedmen of a single individual. Also a citizen was G Attius Marinus, who started his career at Colchester

The role of pottery in Roman archaeology

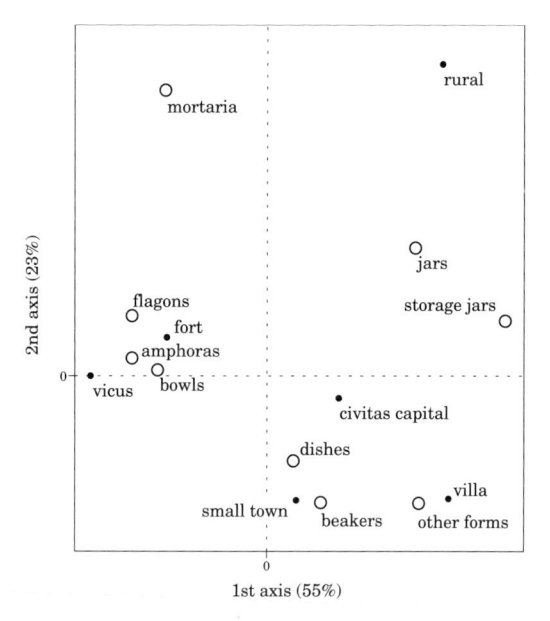

27 Graffiti usage on Romano-British sites

but moved on to the St Albans region and then to the Midlands. Many of these individuals migrated into the new province, probably from Gaul, during the first century AD.

The most prolific wielder of the mortarium die in Britain, Albinus, may have started at Colchester but soon moved to the St Albans region. A later potter in the same workshops, Matugenus, records himself as the son of Albinus. There are a few other father–son relationships recorded on mortaria (such as Brariatus and Vacasatus, who operated in Gallia Belgica), and this would doubtless have been one of the principal methods by which the craft was passed on from one hand to another. Interestingly, Albinus is a good Latin name, but Matugenus is strongly Celtic – it means 'son of the bear'. One wonders how many of the potters with Celtic names operating from the later first century AD are the sons of the potters with Latin names of the previous generation.

It seems likely that potters like Albinus were operating for the whole of their working lifetime. However, a number of mortarium potters are only known from one or two stamps, sometimes only from the kiln site. Perhaps their mortarium-stamping career was short compared to the total working life of a potter. On the other hand, some potters may only have operated for a season or two. There is a wall graffito from Pompeii that contains a short text that may be relevant here. An unnamed individual is being mocked for his numerous career changes, and failings. 'You have failed eight times, but you could well fail sixteen times. You have been a publican, you have had a shop that sold vases, you have been a grocer, a baker, a farmer; afterwards you sold small bronze objects and then became a second-hand dealer; now you make jars ...'. (*CIL* IV, 10150; Baldi 1964; translation in Varone 1992, 31).

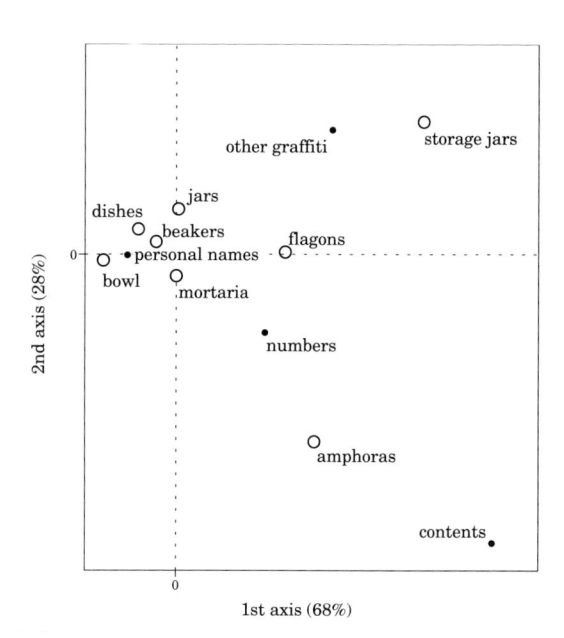

Evidently for some individuals potting was only one of a number of possible sources of employment.

Life on the kiln sites

The features that have naturally received most attention on kiln sites are the kilns themselves and the pottery assemblages associated with them. Small buildings that seem to have been used as workshops have been excavated on several sites. Some contain troughs or pits, perhaps for the storage and preparation of clay. Sockets for the placement of wheels have been tentatively identified in a few cases (Swan 1984, 46–7 for summary). Doubtless many workshops were extremely ephemeral and we should not expect traces to survive in the archaeological record. The physical conditions around the workshops and kilns were probably not unlike those found in modern pottery workshops. There is evidence that whole family groups were present on some sites. At the Highgate Wood kiln site (North London) the bone assemblage includes skull fragments from a young child.

The range of activities that was taking place on kiln sites can be deduced from our knowledge of the pottery manufacturing cycle, but there is more direct evidence as well. Excavations on the South Gaulish samian kiln site of La Graufesenque has yielded a number of graffiti, written with a stylus into the clay on an unfired pot, which illustrate different aspects of the manufacturing system (Marichal 1988). Most are tallies listing types of pots, and the numbers that have been made over some period of time. Some seem to be records of kiln firings. One, however, lists the month's activities of the slaves of Atelia, from 22 July to 23 August. Five individuals are mentioned, some of whom were off the site for various periods while others were preparing clay or cutting wood. We can expect that a similar organization was present at some of the larger Romano-British kiln sites.

Most pottery production in Britain (and elsewhere in the northern provinces) is likely to have been seasonal, because of the difficulties of drying the pots during the winter months. Some evidence of this comes from the tile industry which would have required rather similar conditions, and pottery and tiles were sometimes made on the same site. The broad flat surface of the unfired tile is a rather more inviting surface to the potential graffiti artiste than a pot, and pre-firing marks, batch-marks and inscriptions are often found. Some are tallies recording the number of tiles made in a day – the counts cluster intriguingly around 220 – while others record the calendar date. The latter span the summer months, up to 26 September, but apparently no later (Brodribb 1987, 130–1).

Pre-firing graffiti are relatively uncommon on pottery. There are some that can be interpreted as batch-marks, such as the south Essex 'graffito jars' (M. U. Jones 1972) or the products of kilns in Sussex (Cunliffe 1971, types 313–4). Occasionally the potter records his name, such as CA]PITO.F 'Capitus made this', on a flagon from Cirencester; VITALIS on a beaker from Rushden and the flamboyantly named THAMESUBUGUS on a mortarium from the Churchill hospital kilns, Oxford (*Britannia*, 5 [1974], 468, no. 50; 3 [1972], 359, no. 39; 8 [1977], 440, no. 77).

In sigillata industries many individuals moved from one production site to another during their career. In some cases several workshops seem to have been open simultaneously, such as the Ateius firm, which produced Italian-type sigillata at both Arezzo and Lyon. Ateius ran different slaves at the two sites, as is shown by the name stamps. Some system of master/apprentice pairing was probably commonplace in the pottery industry (and most other crafts) although it is only rarely discernible in the ceramics.

Relationship with other industries

We have some evidence of the relationship between pottery production and other crafts. The pottery industry on the Upchurch Marshes seems to have been closely associated with salt workings, and the large storage jars from this area may have served as transport-containers for this product (Atlas NKSH). The grits on mortaria from several sources, including the Nene valley and Lincolnshire (Atlas NVMO, LIMO) have been identified as iron silicate slag, which suggests some reasonably close association with the iron-working industry.

The works depots associated with some early military sites are a rather special case, but pottery production was here often juxtaposed with iron smelting, bronze-working and numerous other activities (such as timber and leather preparation) whose traces do not remain. In urban settings it may be that areas outside the settlements were occupied by a number of industries, including potteries. These areas may have been set aside for these workshops or simply sanctified by usage. We can see this today in the roads leading away from towns in India or North Africa which are occupied by small workshops of all types, in close proximity.

4 A short history of Roman pottery in Britain

4.1 ROMAN POTTERY IN PRE-ROMAN BRITAIN

For over a century before the Claudian invasion – the event that marks the official beginning of the Roman occupation of Britain – these islands had been subject to influence from the Roman world. At one end of the spectrum, we have the direct military involvement of Rome in British affairs – Julius Caesar's expeditions into Kent and the Lower Thames valley as part of his Gallic campaigns – while at other times the links were diplomatic. The century from Caesar to Claudius saw Rome employing the usual techniques of patronage and protection to extend her influence over events in Britain. Our current purpose is to examine the evidence of pottery against the backdrop of these events and, where appropriate, draw parallels between the developments in Britain and those of Gaul.

Marseille and amphoras

Since the foundation of the Greek colony at Massilia (modern Marseille), traditionally dated to 600 BC, objects of Mediterranean manufacture had circulated widely in the interior of Gaul. The Massiolite Greeks were probably responsible for the introduction of those two essentials of the Mediterranean life-style, the vine and the olive, to southern France. Certainly amphoras for the transport of wine and all the apparatus associated with its consumption – cups, jugs and mixing bowls – are prominent among the imports from the Greek world found on sites in the interior of Gaul (P. S. Wells 1980).

The production of amphoras in southern France, presumably for filling with the new local vintages, commenced at some time in the sixth century BC. These distinctive micaceous Massiolite amphoras are found widely in southern France and up the Rhône valley, and stand at the head of a long line of Gaulish amphora production (Bats 1990) (28).

Wheel-thrown grey wares in the style of Phocaea – the homeland of the colonists of Massilia – and other pottery types with Greek prototypes were also made in southern France but were less widely distributed. Although Marseille seems to be the entry point for much of this technology, it also appears in the trading posts and 'sub-colonies' set up along the southern French coast and into the lower Rhône valley.

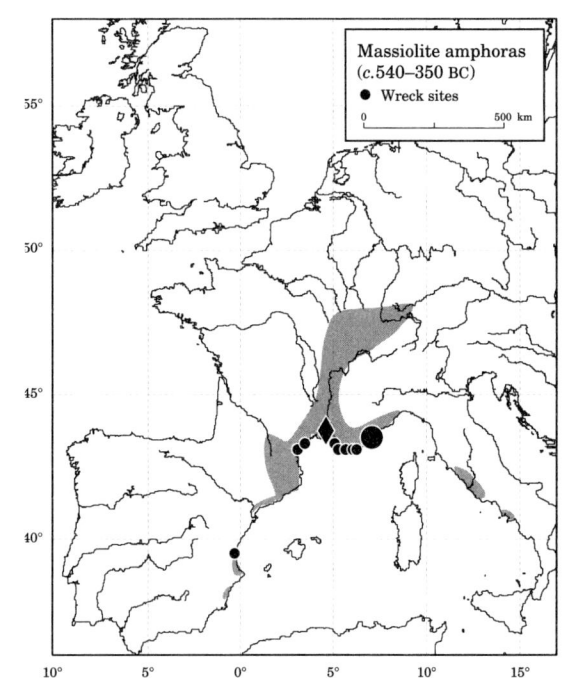

28 Distribution of Massiolite amphoras, c. 540–350 BC

Beyond, into central France and Germany, there are signs of influence from the Greek culture of southern France. The earliest wheel-thrown pottery from Central Europe, such as the sixth-century BC material from Heuneburg in southern Germany, suggests some familiarity with the ceramic technology of southern France (P. S. Wells 1980, 59). This was probably transmitted directly from one potter to another, either in one of the Greek settlements of the south, or by a Greek potter (or one who had been trained by them) moving to south Germany to operate. The Heuneburg site has also yielded amphoras and Attic painted wares, and the unusual construction of the wall of the settlement, which employed sun-dried clay bricks, suggests the presence of other Greek-influenced craftsmen on the site. Such developments are very much the exception, however. In many of the hill-forts of southern France, indigenous ceramic traditions continued to flourish, apparently unaffected by the more advanced technology of the potters operating in the Greek cities of the coast.

The wine trade in the late Republic

But we must return to amphoras and the wine trade for the rest of our story. Alongside the locally produced Massiolite amphoras, there was some importation into southern France during the sixth century BC of Etruscan amphoras and their accompanying black 'bucchero' tablewares. Some of these vessels may even predate the founding of Massilia, and there are a few wrecks along the south French coast as evidence of this early trade with Italy (e.g. Parker 1992, no. 183).

During the third century BC the intensity of the Italian trade seems to pick up. Wine is exported in new amphora types, particularly the Graeco-Italic type – a large robust pear-shaped vessel which was the typological starting point for the most important series of Italian amphora types of the late Republican period. The earliest specimens of these Graeco-Italic amphoras at Manching – the great Celtic *oppidum* in south Germany – may date to *c.* 200 BC (Will 1987). They are certainly common in the south of France at this time, and examples of similar date may yet be identified in central and northern Gaul. By 150 BC a new form had developed: a tall vessel with a cylindrical body and triangular rim, known as the Dressel 1A. This form has a wide, but uneven, distribution in Gaul, and is the first in our narrative to be found in Britain (Atlas DR1).

The history of the Italian wine trade is one of the clearest examples of the contribution that archaeology can make to our understanding of Roman economic history. The mass of sherds of Italian amphoras recovered from sites throughout Gaul bring to life the passages in the ancient texts referring to the trade. We can start with the wrecks on the southern French coast. Some of these vessels were very large indeed. It has been estimated that the Madrague de Giens ship carried 400 tons of cargo, including 6000–7000 amphoras, while the vessel wrecked at Albenga may have carried almost twice this number (Parker 1992, nos. 616, 28). It is clear from this and a score of other finds that Italian wine amphoras were a major cargo item in these ships. They are not mere fillers, and were considered valuable enough for attempts to be made at salvage on wreck sites in shallow waters.

We do not know what proportion of the amphoras arriving in Gaul were for consumption in the cities of the south – the area was under effective Roman control from *c.* 121 BC – and how many were destined for the interior. One estimate (admittedly based on the thinnest of data) is that over forty million may have been imported in Gaul in the century or so that the Dressel 1 type lasted (Tchernia 1986). It seems that the Gaulish river system – much praised by Strabo and other writers – was employed as far as possible for their transportation. There are two routes from southern Gaul, north and west

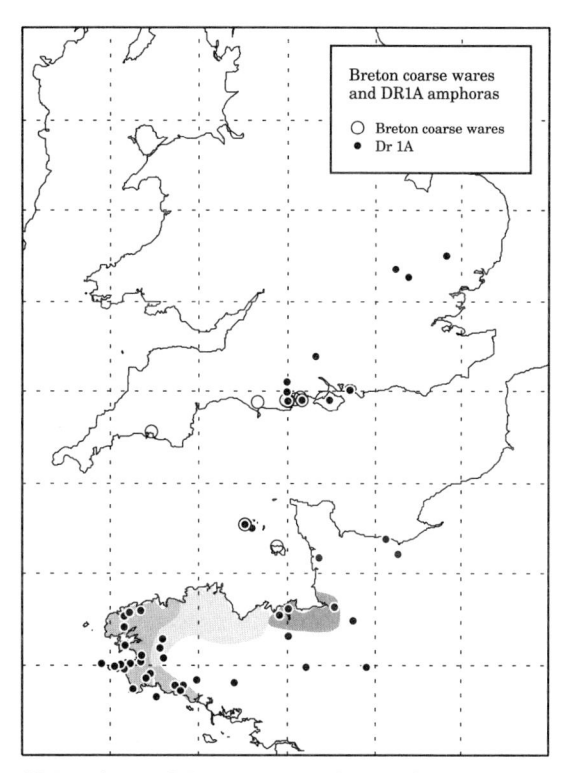

29 *Distribution of Breton pottery and Dressel 1A amphoras in Britain, c. 100–50 BC*

towards the Atlantic and Channel coasts. The route from Narbonne across the 'Gaulish isthmus' via Toulouse to Bordeaux was certainly used to carry amphoras. There are many hundreds of these vessels in the huge funerary pits that have been excavated in the Toulouse area. From the Garonne estuary, the route north to Brittany lay open. The second route from the Mediterranean is up the Rhône valley. The very large numbers of amphoras at sites such as Lyon, Châlons-sur-Saône and Tournus suggest that these were some of the transhipment points for the traffic on the Rhône–Saône river system. Here vessels would be unloaded from barges and carried thence by wagon, as the Greek writer Diodorus Siculus describes (*Histories*, 5, 26, 3). From here it was but a short overland step to the headwaters of the Seine and Loire, where the jars could take to the water again. We can again trace the routes taken by the concentrations on sites along the Loire valley and on into Brittany (Galliou 1982, 17–25).

It was from the north coast of the Breton peninsula that the boats for Britain set sail. They carried not only the Italian amphoras but also local coarse wares from northern Brittany. The key British site for our understanding of this trade is Hengistbury Head (Dorset), on the promontory on the southern side of Christchurch harbour. The site was first investigated in detail by J. P. Bushe-Fox in 1911–12, who published a report which includes a type-series for the pottery (1915). Further excavations in 1979–86 have led to a complete reassessment of the site and the material, with a report on the important amphora assemblage by D. F. Williams (Cunliffe 1987). The amphoras include some thirty specimens of the Dressel 1A form, and perhaps six examples of the slightly later Dressel 1B. The coarse wares include three distinctive fabrics from Brittany, which originate along the north and west of the peninsula (**29, table 12**).

Form	By weight		By sherd count	
	g	%	n	%
Dressel 1A	8584	8.4	69	5
Dressel 1B	1489	1.5	8	0.6
Dressel 1sp	59492	58.1	942	68.9
Pascual 1	3677	3.6	43	3.1
Dressel 2–4	746	0.7	15	1.1
Dressel 20	24960	24.4	229	16.8
Haltern 70	1807	1.8	35	2.6
Cam. 186sp	125	0.1	1	0.1
Unassigned	1448	1.4	25	1.8
	102328		1367	

Table 12 *Amphoras from Hengistbury Head (Dorset)*

Both the Italian amphoras and the Breton coarse wares are found beyond the immediate environs of Hengistbury Head, principally inland into Wessex, north towards the Severn estuary and westwards along the coast of the south-west peninsula. The historical context for this material may be given by a passage in Caesar's *Gallic War*, where he describes the ships of the Veneti (one of the tribes of Brittany) travelling regularly to and from Britain (*Gallic War* 3, 8) and Strabo notes their use of an emporium in Britain (*Geography*, 4, 5, 1). It has been suggested that Hengistbury served as a port-of-trade through which most of the interaction between Britain and the continent was channelled. The amphora assemblage suggests that these contacts had begun by *c.* 100 BC.

When looking at the simple list of amphora sherds from Hengistbury we should remember that each of these vessels has been carried by boat, horse and wagon across Gaul, from the ports of the south to those of the Channel coast. It is certain that Roman traders were involved in this trade – Roman citizens had, in theory at least, a legal monopoly – but we do not know how far their influence stretched along the route, and how much was carried out by intermediaries. All the effort involved in the transport would have been by Gauls, whatever the case. The Gaulish appetite for the fruit of the vine is noted by many ancient authors. The predilection for drinking undiluted wine which is constantly referred to, would have been considered very low behaviour to the sophisticated Roman reveller.

An episode in the writings of Diodorus Siculus where he relates the exchange of a Gaulish slave for an amphora of wine suggests the slightly bizarre transactions that may have resulted in the amphora distribution we now see. The distribution of Italian amphoras in south-west Britain may, however, suggest some relationship with the trade in Cornish tin which seems to be a constant feature of the relationship between Britain and Europe throughout much of later prehistory and beyond (Potter and Johns 1992, 13–15).

Italian amphoras were not the only pottery types travelling along the rivers and roads of Gaul. The wrecks along the coast of Provence show that black-gloss Campanian tablewares were imported in some quantity alongside the wine jars, and there are smaller numbers of coarse wares, mortaria and fine thin-walled beakers from Italy (see for instance the assemblage in the Madrague de Giens wreck: summary in Parker 1992, no. 616, with refs). Campanian wares are transported with the amphoras at least as far as central France, although not in large quantities (Morel 1978). They do not apparently reach northern Gaul or Britain. Coarse wares of Italian type (which could either be imports or products of the Romanized cities of Provence) also travel north into the interior of Gaul. A group from Les Aulnes du Canada, near Beauvais (Oise), and only 60 miles or so from the Channel coast, includes Dressel 1A amphoras, flagons and mortaria of Italian form, and micaceous coarse-ware jars from central Gaul which had been picked up *en route* as the amphoras moved north through Gaul (Woimant 1983). Such assemblages demonstrate the wide circulation of objects and, by implication, people and ideas, across Gaul before the mid-first century BC. Britain may have lain at the far end of this system, but would nevertheless have been affected by it.

After the Gallic wars, the importation of Italian wines into Britain continued, but rather than the south-west, the principal destinations now lay in the south-east of Britain. The break is not clear-cut, for there are specimens of the earlier Dressel 1A type from Essex and Hertfordshire, and, conversely, examples of the Dressel 1B from Hengistbury and elsewhere in the south-west, but the general shift in the focus of the amphoras seems clear (**table 13**).

Region	Settlement	Funerary	Other
Hants/Dorset	18	0	3
Herts./Essex	14	17	0

Table 13 *The archaeological contexts of Dressel 1 amphoras in Britain*

The role played by these vessels in the two regions also differs. While the amphoras of the south-west and central-southern England are found on occupation sites, those in the south-east are particularly associated with funerary assemblages (Fitzpatrick 1985). The sequence of rich burials in eastern England, named Welwyn graves after one of their number, commences towards the mid-first century BC. The earliest contain local coarse wares, a group of Dressel 1B amphoras and imported Italian metal vessels such as cups, jugs and pans. The assemblages from the later, Augustan, graves are more diverse. Alongside Italian amphoras, there are Spanish vessels (containers for wine and *garum*), and a range of fine-ware cups, plates and flagons of types that will be discussed in more detail below. The associated local coarse wares now betray the influence of imported forms for they include copies of metal jugs and flagons and imported pottery types (Stead 1967; Rodwell 1976). Graves of the Welwyn type are also found across northern Gaul (Collis 1977). The general sequence of metal wares, amphoras and other pottery types mirrors that in Britain, again emphasizing the similarity of the underlying culture in these regions, despite their differing political status.

Augustan pottery in Britain and Gaul

After the Gallic wars and the interruptions of the Civil War, Gaul was brought under Roman administration. The next major archaeological horizon are the sites in Germany associated with the campaigns across the Rhine, which started in earnest in 12 BC (C. Wells 1972). This 'fortress horizon' is a key point in the early history of both Gaulish and British pottery. Three phenomena associated with these fortress assemblages require discussion.

Firstly, there is the appearance of terra sigillata from Italian workshops, principally Arezzo. The new red-gloss wares had developed shortly after the middle of the first century BC, influenced in part by the pre-existing Campanian black-gloss industries of Etruria. The earliest exports from Italy – dating from *c*. 30 BC – are largely confined to Provence and north-east Spain, and this is followed shortly by the founding of provincial workshops in both areas (Ettlinger *et al.* 1990, 20–2). These seem to have been short-lived, and the major expansion of the distribution of sigillata wares dates to a decade later, and the founding of the Rhine fortresses. Potters from Arezzo moved into Gaul, to Lyon, and set up workshops there to serve, successfully, these new markets. Outside those sites with clear military connections, sigillata remains uncommon across Gaul until the later Augustan or Tiberian period (by which time the principal source is south Gaul rather than Lyon or Italy).

The second feature of the fortress assemblage is the appearance of coarse-ware assemblages of flagons, jars, bowls and mortaria; forms whose ultimate origins lie in Italy and the Mediterranean world. The background to these fortress styles is described fully by K. T. Greene (in Manning 1993). It is clear that these industries are not transplanted directly from, say, Italy to the Rhineland factories. Some of the potters produce forms that betray influence from the indigenous Gaulish styles. We should envisage a period of cross-fertilization in areas such as the Rhône valley in the decades between Caesar and Augustus, whence the potters moved to the Rhineland to serve the new military bases. Similar 'Italian-derived' assemblages are found at other sites in Gaul. A large group of particularly early sigillata from Amiens, in the Somme valley, dated to *c*. 20–15 BC, is associated with a coarse-ware assemblage of distinctly Italian character (Massy and Molière 1979). Such groups seem to be the exception at the moment, and appear as islands in a sea of indigenous Gaulish pottery. Nevertheless, the roots of the Romano-Gaulish styles of the mid-first century AD – and hence some of the potters who moved to Britain in the Claudio-Neronian period – lie here, in the interplay of Italian/Mediterranean and indigenous styles.

The third and final element in the fortress assemblages are the fine wares from industries in northern and central Gaul, including the so-called Gallo-Belgic wares. These red-and-black wares, plates, cups and beakers are one representative of a broader style, which is found throughout north, central and western Gaul, and has roots going back into the pre-Augustan period. Local copies of Campanian-ware plates and cups are common in southern France in a variety of fabrics throughout the first century BC. Similar forms are also assimilated into some of the indigenous coarse-ware industries of central and western Gaul, and are far more abundant there than the imported Campanian originals. The addition of forms and techniques apparently derived from sigillata, such as red colour and the use of potters' name-stamps to the mix resulted in the diverse fine-ware industries of the Augustan period. Northern Gaulish production seems to be concentrated in two areas, the Vesle valley near Rheims and the Mosel valley near Trier. Products of these centres circulated widely in north-east Gaul during the Augustan period, and there is export to Britain. As with other early imports the British distribution is limited to a relatively small number of sites in the south and east of the country, and we do not see much penetration of these wares until the Claudian period (**30**).

Nevertheless, there is importation into Britain of wares from an increasing number of continental sources from the beginning of the Augustan period. There are a handful of sigillata vessels that should be dated to about 20 BC, and the first vessels in the terra nigra and terra rubra fabrics of northern Gaul should be placed in the following decade. The assemblage from the burial at Welwyn Garden City (Stead 1967) includes plates and large flagons in a fine micaceous ware that originates in central France, probably in the middle Loire valley (perhaps near Orléans). Mica-dusted jars from the same source have been identified on other sites in both the south and the east of the country. At Skeleton Green (Herts.) they were recovered from a large early pit associated with Augustan

A short history of Roman pottery in Britain

Type	Function	Source	ATLAS
Dressel 1A amphoras	Container	Italy	DR1
Dressel 1B amphoras	Container	Italy	DR1
Spanish amphoras	Container	Spain	SALA
Italian sigillata	Tableware	Italy	ITTS
Lyon sigillata	Tableware	Central Gaul	ITTS
South Gaulish sigillata	Tableware	South Gaul	SGTS
Terra rubra / Terra nigra	Tableware	North Gaul	TRTN
North Gaulish white wares	Tableware	North Gaul	
Central Gaulish micaceous plates	Tableware	Central Gaul	CGSF
Central Gaulish micaceous flagons	Container?	Central Gaul	CGSF
Central Gaulish coarse wares	Container?	Central Gaul	CGMW

Table 14 *Principal pottery imports into pre-Roman Britain*

sigillata and north Gaulish wares (Partridge 1981, 99–103). Contact with central Gaul is also indicated by the moulded rim jars in a distinctive coarse micaceous granite-tempered fabric (*Camulodunum* type 262) which originate in Burgundy, on the northern edge of the Massif Central (Tyers (forthcoming) a). These vessels are, like the amphoras, probably a container rather than a tableware. Other imports during the Augustan and Tiberian periods from northern Gaul include flagons, beakers and even the occasional mortarium in fine white fabrics.

The sequence of amphora imports into Britain advances in harmony with the Gaulish evidence. From the Augustan period Spanish products – wine, preserved fish products, *defrutum* syrup and olive-oil – are increasingly exported in large numbers from the Spanish provinces, particularly Baetica (southern Spain). We have all of these types in Britain, both on occupation sites and in the later Welwyn-type graves (Sealey 1985, 148–51). The tastes of those in Britain who had access to these vessels, or more precisely their contents, evidently went beyond the immediate attractions of wine to more exotic commodities. Some of these, such as the olive-oil and the various grades of fish-sauce (*liquamen* and *garum*) might suggest some familiarity with Romanized culinary techniques and recipes, just as the imported cups and platters suggest the assimilation of Romanized habits at the table. In the recipes of Apicius, over 350 of the *c.* 480 preparations include *garum* as an ingredient (Blanc and Nercessian 1992, 216). The three Beltrán III amphoras in the burial at Mount Bures would have contained some 45 litres of fish-sauce, or the equivalent of some 300 bottles of Lea & Perrins Worcestershire sauce (**table 14**).

4.2 THE LATE IRON AGE POTTERY OF BRITAIN

Alongside, and overwhelmingly more abundant than the imports described above, are the products of the indigenous pottery industries. Much of the discussion of Late Iron Age coarse pottery in south-east Britain, and most other aspects of contemporary culture, had traditionally revolved around the possibility of distinguishing material that can be linked with immigrants from northern Gaul. The movement of peoples into southern England from an area known as *Belgium* is specifically noted in a passage in Caesar's *Gallic Wars*, but the extent, date, nature and destination of any such immigration is unknown. Furthermore, an identifiable group of objects or settlements that can be linked with any such event remains elusive, despite much ingenuity in their interpretation. The general

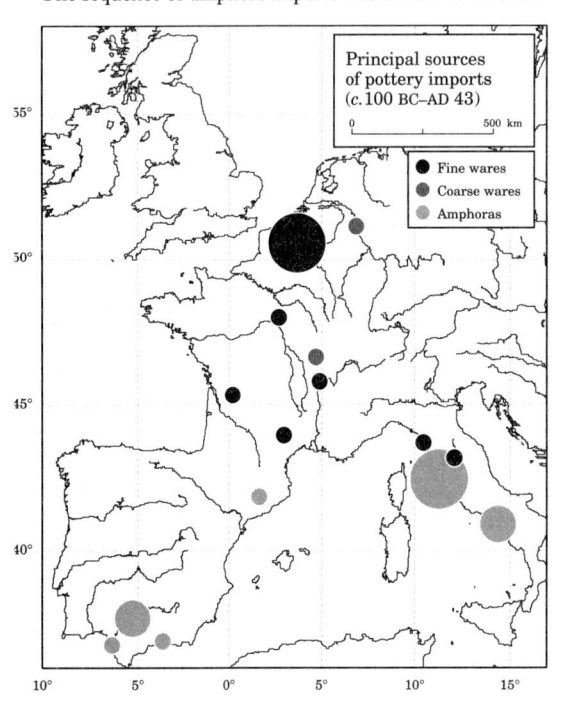

30 *Sources of pottery imports to Britain, c. 100 BC–AD 43*

drift of opinion since the 1970s has been away from a Belgic invasion as an explanation of change in Late Iron Age Britain.

Nevertheless, despite regular protests about 'Belgic' ('the word ... should be banned from archaeological literature': Stead 1967) the term remains in widespread use as a shorthand description of the pottery styles current across south-east England in the decades either side of the conquest. The term 'Aylesford–Swarling style' (named after two cemeteries in Kent) has also been widely used.

We can distinguish a number of distinct regional styles or zones within south-east England, linked together by certain elements of shared technology and typology. There are two common threads of particular note: firstly the common use of grog-tempering and secondly the use of the fast wheel for forming pottery. Both have often been taken to be synonymous with the 'Belgic' pottery style, although this is somewhat of an oversimplification. In an exhaustive survey of Late Iron Age pottery in south-east England, I. Thompson distinguishes nine major style zones. These are based primarily on the associations between grog-tempered wares and the fabric types (e.g. shell, sand or flint-gritted wares), and distinct regional typological groupings (Thompson 1982, 8–17).

In contrast to the pottery of the Roman period that we shall be discussing below, there are very few recognized kiln assemblages for the pre-conquest period. The petrology of the grog-tempered wares also seems to be relatively uniform across the entire region (ibid. 20), although other more sophisticated analytical techniques may be more appropriate to characterize such fabrics. Thus, in general, we cannot describe the pre-Roman pottery assemblages in terms of sources and distributions. Each zone is likely to be the product of a number of production sites or areas, which may either produce the entire range of types found within a zone or a sub-set of fabrics or forms.

Although this is not the appropriate place to describe the minutiae of pre-conquest pottery assemblages, we shall look at the evidence from two areas which are particularly relevant to the later chapters of our story.

Late Iron Age pottery in Hertfordshire and the Chilterns

The pottery from sites in the Vale of St Albans and along the Chiltern Hills provides one of the clearest sequences of Late Iron Age pottery in the south-east. The material from the graves and cemeteries is balanced by the assemblages from a number of occupation sites, culminating in the material from the Roman levels at sites such as *Verulamium* (St Albans).

The richest Welwyn-type burials in the region give us a valuable, if somewhat biased, insight into the pottery types. The earliest phase is represented by a burial from Baldock. Here the grave includes two wooden iron-bound buckets, iron fire-dogs, and bronze pans and cauldrons, but only a single pot – a Dressel 1A. This form is known from a number of sites in Hertfordshire and Essex (Fitzpatrick 1985, nos. 30, 31b, 31d; D. F. Williams 1990), although, as outlined above, it is more typical of the amphora assemblages of the south-west. A Dressel 1A would conventionally be dated to the pre-Caesarian period but in a group from Stanstead in Essex there are specimens associated with the Dressel 1B and perhaps the Dressel 2–4, suggesting a later date for their deposition. It will be interesting to watch how the evidence accumulates on the dating and character of this early contact between the south-east of England and the Roman world.

There is a series of Welwyn-type burials which include Dressel 1B amphoras, such as those from Welwyn itself and nearby Welwyn Garden City. In addition to the amphoras, the graves include Italian silver two-handled cups and bronze jugs and pans (Stead 1967). The group of pottery from the burial at Welwyn Garden City includes 36 pots of a wide range of types, in addition to five Dressel 1B amphoras (Stead 1967, hereafter WGC). Three of the vessels are imports from central Gaul – two platters and a flagon in a micaceous fabric, probably from the middle Loire valley (WGC nos. 29, 30 and 36). The remainder are in grey or orange grog-tempered fabrics, most with finely burnished surfaces and wheel-thrown. Although no precise source is known for this material it is probable that it is all from a single, reasonably local, workshop. There are seven pedestal-urns in the grave. One of these (WGC no. 3) is of a type known from a number of sites in Hertfordshire, Bedfordshire and Cambridgeshire including three specimens from the burials at Welwyn itself (Thompson 1982, type A1). These urns all share the same features – a short, wide neck, usually with a simple bead at the lip but without a neck cordon, and an elegant pear-shaped body which curves out towards the foot (similar to **31**, 1–2).

The storage, preparation and consumption of wine is a theme linking much of the material in the Welwyn-type burials, most notably the Italian amphoras and silver and bronze vessels. The WGC coarse-pottery assemblage includes three locally made, two-handled flagons (WGC nos. 33–5) in orange-fired ware, in addition to the one imported flagon noted previously – clearly all prompted by the need for vessels to store and serve liquids. The grog-tempered cups and beakers (with or without feet) could function as drinking vessels. The coarse ware from Welwyn Garden City represents the earliest definable horizon in the burials north of the Thames, but the wide range of pottery, some perhaps already showing the influence of imported fine wares from Gaul, is the product of a mature potting tradition. There is no hesitancy or unfamiliarity with the materials and techniques and the fine, flowing curves of the pedestal urns, in particular, would be products of a high standard of potting at any period. The origins of this industry presumably lie some time before the Welwyn Garden City burial, but this cannot be defined with any greater precision at present.

A short history of Roman pottery in Britain

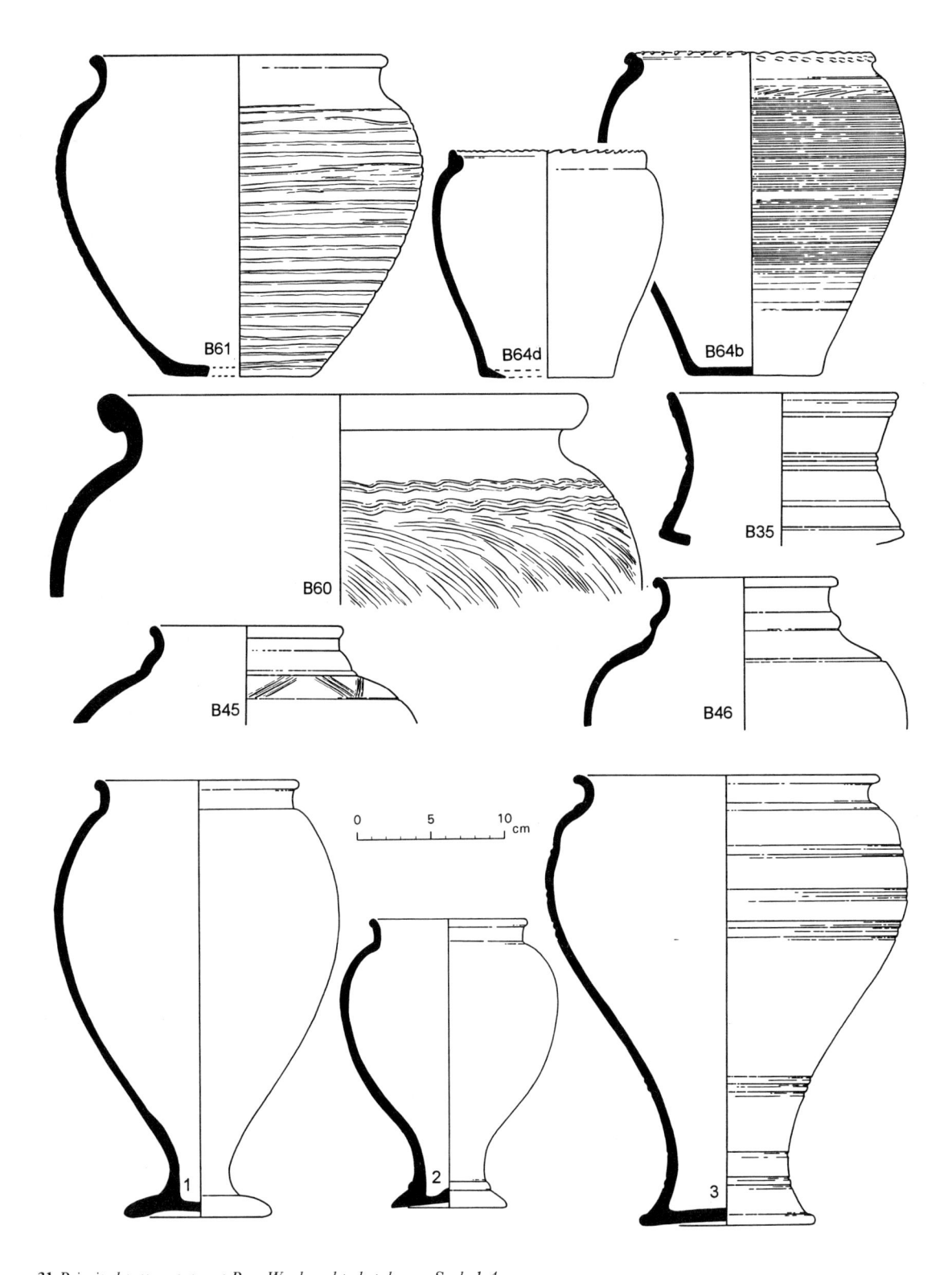

31 Principal pottery types at Prae Wood, and pedestal urns. Scale 1:4

A short history of Roman pottery in Britain

Domestic assemblages

The pottery from the Prae Wood excavations of 1930–6 (Wheeler and Wheeler 1936) provides a suitable starting point for our discussion of the latest phase of pre-Roman pottery in Hertfordshire. The large group of pottery from the Wheelers' group B (associated with a little Arretine, terra nigra and terra rubra) illustrates the range of coarse wares current during the Tiberio-Claudian period. Representatives of the important types are illustrated in **31**.

Puddlehill type	Prae Wood type	Total	Description
1	61	400	necked jars, some 'furrowed'
2	64	279	ledge-rim jars
3	-	74	storage jar
4	46	67	tall, cordoned jars
5	55	3	ledge rim ? bowls
6	60	45	large storage jars
7	66	23	simple bead-rims
8	69	21	'ill-defined' necked jars
9	-	5	butt-beakers
10	35	11	'tazze' types
11	-	6	platters/lids
12	42	9	bowls?
13	44	9	jars with corrugated necks
14	67	7	jars with incised decoration
		959	Total

Table 15 *Late Iron Age coarse-ware assemblage at Puddlehill (Beds.)*

The type B61 combed jars are the most distinctive element of the latest phases of Late Iron Age pottery in Hertfordshire. The ledge-rim jar is its principal companion, although here at Prae Wood it is not particularly common. At Puddlehill, Bedfordshire (Matthews 1976), both types are abundant, as **table 15** shows. Several points emerge from this group. Firstly there is the general orientation of the coarse-ware assemblage towards jars, in particular the simple necked jars, furrowed jars and ledge-rim jars. Shallower and more open vessels, such as bowls and dishes, are sparse. Secondly there is the very small proportion of the assemblage that is made up of finer wheel-thrown vessels such as the cordoned jars or 'tazze' (e.g. types 4 and 10) – types that have generally been considered to be 'typically Belgic' due to their abundance in the grave groups. Finally there is the very small number of butt-beakers and platters derived from or influenced by Gallo-Belgic wares (about 1 per cent here). This pattern is reflected in other Late Iron Age assemblages in the zone, and suggests that a group of pottery would have to be of a considerable size before the absence of Gallo-Belgic wares, their imitations and derivations, becomes statistically valid, and therefore of chronological value.

A range of influences may have impinged upon the finer end of the pottery assemblage during the first century BC. One area of overlap is with rare vessels made in shale. Tall, shale pedestal vases with grooving or cordons on the body are found on several sites in Hertfordshire, particularly in burials (e.g. Kennett 1977, fig. 1 – from Harpenden). It is suggested that these vases may have been made from a local shale which outcrops at a number of places along the Bedfordshire greensand ridge. Other shale vessels include a number of fine tazze which closely match their pottery counterparts (e.g. Kennett 1977, fig. 4; Birchall 1965, fig. 26, 214; compare Stead 1967, no. 18). The possibility of some cross-fertilization of ideas between the potters and shaleworkers cannot be ignored, and the same forms may also have been made in wood, which would have required similar manufacturing techniques to shale.

Other sources of influences from the Augustan period are the imports of plates, cups and beakers from the Gallo-Belgic industries of northern Gaul. Imitations in local grog-tempered wares seem to follow shortly after the earliest imports, and on many sites they are more abundant than the originals. A particular feature of the grog-tempered Gallo-Belgic copies is the use of an orange- or red-fired fabric. The colour is caused by oxidized firing conditions and the fabrics seem otherwise identical to the grey wares. The technique goes back at least as far as the Welwyn Garden City grave group which contains several flagons or jugs in an orange-fired fabric. These seem to be influenced by bronze originals, suggesting that the orange fabric is not confined to copies of Gallo-Belgic wares, but is a technique applied to finer vessels inspired by a variety of originals. Thus we can see the willingness of British potters to take, adapt and blend shapes and techniques from many sources – a process that continues vigorously during the Roman period.

The post-conquest history of the Hertfordshire pottery industry is not a topic for this chapter. However, there is very little doubt that the descendants of the rilled jar (Prae Wood type B61) and the ledge-rim jar (type B64) were produced throughout the Roman period, and emerge as important players on the scene at the end of the fourth century AD (see 4.6).

Southern-central England

The Late Iron Age pottery of southern-central England, broadly those counties south-west of the Thames valley, seems to develop under influences that are quite different to those felt north of the Thames and in Kent. The pottery from this region is usually excluded from the Aylesford–Swarling style, although it has been sometimes described as 'western Belgic' or, more recently, Atrebatic.

There are two contributory elements to the development of the pottery traditions south of the Thames in the pre-conquest period. Firstly there is the influence of the imported Gaulish coarse pottery, and secondly the developments of the indigenous Iron Age 'saucepan pot' tradition. The role of Hengistbury Head in the history of the trade in Italian wines into Britain has been described above. Wheel-thrown coarseware jars and bowls made by potters in Brittany from micaceous clays (derived from the granites of the Armorican peninsula) occur in some numbers at Hengistbury Head. Like the amphoras they are found inland from the site, north into Gloucestershire, west along the coast of Devon and Cornwall, and north-east into the Hampshire basin. It is also probable that versions of the imported vessels were produced in the Hengistbury area, perhaps by immigrant Breton potters (Cunliffe 1987, 211, 342). Thus the first phase of the development of the Late Iron Age potting style of southern England is marked by the importation of pottery from Brittany and Normandy, and the arrival of potters versed in the use of the fast wheel. The later history of the industry is largely the story of the interaction between these imported styles and the indigenous traditions.

The next stage can be seen in a small group from Ufton Nervet in Berkshire (Manning 1974). The material from Pit H at this site can be divided into two groups on the basis of fabric, form and technology. The necked jars with finely moulded rims and cordons are wheel-thrown in lumpy, grey-brown or black fabric, finely burnished over the rim and exterior surface. The remainder of the group are in coarse black or dark grey-brown fabrics with prominent flint tempering; all are hand-formed. The surface burnishing, where present, is uneven. The flint tempered vessels fall into the Middle Iron Age 'saucepan pot continuum' (Cunliffe 1974, 78) but here they are associated with products of another industry producing wheel-thrown wares (see **35**).

The Ufton Nervet group represents a stage when the influence of potters using the wheel was being felt widely in southern England, but alongside residual elements of Middle Iron Age potting. It is difficult to give absolute dates to this phase. The two traditions may have run in parallel for several generations, but on the eve of the Roman conquest we find potters across the region producing both bead-rim jars and necked jars in the same wares. This merged tradition forms the starting-point for most of the early Romano-British coarse wares across a broad swathe of southern England, from Surrey and Hampshire to the Severn estuary. We shall follow the fate of these industries through and beyond the conquest in the next chapters.

4.3   THE CLAUDIO-NERONIAN PERIOD
The conquest
The Claudian invasion forces when on active campaign would have had little need for (or access to) pottery supplies. Metal pans and cooking vessels, such as those illustrated on the later Trajan's Column (Lepper and Frere 1988, pl. 80) must have served many of their needs. The occasional amphora sherds recovered from the otherwise barren temporary marching camps of all periods suggest that the fruit of the vine or olive could not be completely dispensed with, even in the hazardous circumstances of a military campaign. We might also expect to find pottery vessels among the personal possessions of individual soldiers. These baggage items may have been acquired at their original home bases, points of embarkation or in transit. But it is hard to distinguish such personal possessions in the ceramic assemblage, and more difficult still to infer anything from them.

Archaeological assemblages of the immediate conquest period are difficult to identify with confidence, and precise ceramic chronology during the first decade is elusive. In most regions the stratigraphy does not exist to enable us to distinguish an assemblage of, say, AD 35 from one of AD 50. One consequence of this has been the tendency for a compression of developments into the first decade of the occupation. Wares that are found in undoubted early Roman contexts – associated with Claudian coins or samian or in military bases – have tended to be considered as developments of the Roman period. When the same wares are found in isolation they are nevertheless dated to the Claudian period. Thus many of the principal coarse wares of the later first century AD are deemed to have their origins 'at the conquest', but there are voids in the preceding decades. They seem to spring into life, as it were, fully formed, but without any obvious antecedents.

We shall look at the developments in the Claudio-Neronian period in three parts: (1) the sequence of imports; (2) the appearance of Romanized industries; (3) the developments in the indigenous industries.

Imports
The Claudian period marks the beginning of massive imports of La Graufesenque sigillata. The number of vessels from this source that need be dated earlier (to the Tiberian period) is small indeed, and some at least are from sites which are Roman foundations and may have been baggage items of the Claudian period. The Tiberian period coincides with one of the periodic low points in the distribution of samian on sites in Gaul and Germany, which should, in theory, have had access to ready supplies. The absence of larger assemblages from Britain may be more a product of the fluctuations of the samian industry, as described by Marsh (1981), than anything else. The full range of samian, both plain and decorated, was imported during the Claudian period, but what is less certain is the penetration of the ware into, for instance, rural areas, or native sites. Lack of quantified data makes any direct comparison difficult in many regions, but it is likely that samian, and many of the other imports described below, had a limited distribution outside urban and military sites, or sites situated along roads or major supply routes (Pollard 1988, 47).

A short history of Roman pottery in Britain

Alongside sigillata, a wide range of fine wares was imported (table 16). Pre-eminent were the fine hemispherical cups in Lyon ware, whose expansion in production and distribution in the Claudian period seems to coincide with the opening of the British market. Fine cups and beakers from a number of other sources also appear in smaller numbers during the pre-Flavian period. Among these, the golden-brown Spanish cups and beakers are perhaps the most striking. However, the dominance of Lyon in this trade, despite the presence of producers closer to hand, emphasizes the importance of this route north through Gaul to the Rhineland and Britain (Greene 1979, 141–2). Another new class to appear in the Claudian period in Britain are the Pompeian-Red wares. These dishes with their distinctive 'non-stick' red surfaces come from a number of sources, including Italy and Central Gaul (Atlas PRW1, PRW2, PRW3).

Source	Total sites	Proximity to Britain	ATLAS
1 Lyon	203	3	LYON
2 Spain	18	6	SPAN
3 North Italy	8	5	–
4 Central Gaul	6	2	CGCC
5 South Gaul	5	4	SGCC
6 Lower Rhineland	3	1	–
7 South or central Italy	2	7	–

Table 16 *Pre-Flavian fine-ware imports to Britain (after Greene)*

The contrast between the amphora imports of the pre-Claudian and Claudio-Neronian periods now seems less marked than was once the case. Spanish fish-products, Baetican oil and Italian wine had all been imported from the Augustan period (in some cases earlier), and all continue into the Claudian period and beyond. The Catalan Pascual 1 type is largely a pre-conquest import in Britain and, conversely, the Rhodian wine amphoras, Gaulish wine amphoras and the Cam 189 'carrot' amphoras seem to be almost exclusively post-conquest. In the case of the Rhodian-style amphoras it is probable that they were exacted from the island of Rhodes itself in part punishment for misdemeanours in the early Claudian period, and in Britain and elsewhere in north-west Europe they are particularly associated with military sites (Sealey 1985, 133–4).

Within the amphora assemblage, the balance of types and sources shifts from one decade to another, and also from site to site. As with sigillata, the most diverse and most abundant assemblages are restricted to major urban sites and ports. The data from Sheepen, assembled by P. R. Sealey, give us a particularly clear insight into the amphora trade of the Claudio-Neronian period, and more importantly the details of the commodities carried (1985, 10-14). From these it can be seen that wines and olive-oil were the principal items in the amphora-borne trade (table 17).

Mortaria appear sporadically in pre-Claudian contexts (e.g. Partridge 1981, 196–7) but their numbers increase rapidly during the Claudio-Neronian period. Wall-sided mortaria were initially imported from northern Gaul, but small-scale production in Britain, perhaps at Colchester, may have commenced shortly after the conquest. However, imports continued to supply large parts of this market up until the end of the first century AD, particularly in coastal areas and in the north of the country. The major factories were located in northern France, but smaller numbers of vessels from central Gaul and the Rhineland made some contribution (**32, table 18**).

Form	Minimum number of vessels	Contents	Total volume (l)	ATLAS
Dressel 1	5	wine	120	DR1
Dressel 2–4	44	wine	1213	DR2–4
Rhodian	21	wine	285	RHOD
Haltern 70	8	defrutum syrup	240	H70
Dressel 20	21	olive-oil	1393	DR20
Beltrán I	16	fish-products	276	SALA
Beltrán IIa	1	fish-products	14	SALA
Beltrán I/IIa	4	fish-products	63	SALA
Cam 189 ('carrot')	7	palm fruit?		C189
Richborough 527	1			R527
Dressel 28	5	wine?		
Unidentified	2		–	
Total	135			

Table 17 *Amphoras and contents from 1970 excavations at Sheepen (after Sealey)*

57

A short history of Roman pottery in Britain

Source		ATLAS
Northern Gaul	France	NGMO
Eifel region	Germany	EIMO
Aoste	France	AOMO
Rhône valley	France	RVMO

Table 18 *Imported mortaria in pre-Flavian Britain*

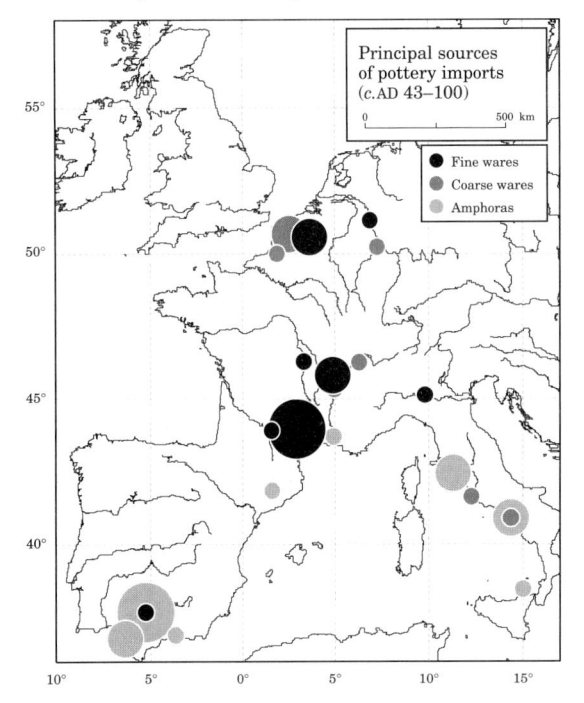

32 Sources of pottery imports to Britain, c. AD 43–100

Immigrant potters

The mortarium factories set up at Colchester and the Verulamium region during the AD 50s were only one facet of a more general process, whereby potters from the Continent set up workshops in Britain in the decades following the conquest. Two broad strains may be discerned in these new styles: firstly there are the Romanized, or Rhineland traditions, ultimately of Italian/Mediterranean descent, which are marked by assemblages of flagons, bowls, jars, mortaria and fine wares, often in light-coloured, oxidized wares. This Romanized potting style was fairly widespread, found along the length of the Rhine, and as increasing publication makes clear, in the towns of northern and central Gaul. The second group, apparently less common, employed Gaulish styles, often derived from or related to the Gallo-Belgic traditions of the north (**table 19**).

The classic investigation of the origins of immigrant potters is K. T. Greene's study of the pottery from the fortress of Usk (Gwent) (**33**). Greene identified two jar forms in the Usk assemblage, one with a series of cordons on the neck and the other with an angular shoulder (Usk types 12 and 13) derived from indigenous late La Tène ceramic styles, which became incorporated into the repertoire of the Romanizing potters in the Rhône valley or western Switzerland during the first century BC, whence the potter moved to Usk in the Neronian period (Greene in Manning 1993). The other types in the Usk assemblage include flagons, jars, bowls, mortaria and other types with their roots in the Italian/Mediterranean ceramic styles of the first century BC.

The context of these immigrant introductions varies. Some are clearly associated with military sites, such as the kilns outside the Longthorpe fortress or the Usk potter, while others are in rural or urban contexts and not apparently associated with military sites. Sometimes the kiln structure as much as the ceramic repertoire points to the exotic origins of a potter. The early square and rectangular kilns with lateral pilasters, which is a continental form, have been discussed above (p. 28). These are undoubtedly the handiwork of immigrant potters, as their pottery assemblages confirm. The assemblage from the Central Girls School site at Chichester contains butt-beakers, jars and platters in the Gallo-Belgic style; this and the unusual kiln structure (with twin-flue and pedestal) point to northern France as the probable area of origin of these potters (Down 1978; Swan 1984, 118).

A further point of interest in these early introduced assemblages is their association with British potting styles. In two cases, Corfe Mullen (Dorset) and Longthorpe (Northants), pottery of undoubted continental derivation is being made alongside pottery of British forms. The Longthorpe 'British' assemblage of ledge-rim jars, storage jars and rilled jars is derived from the styles of Northamptonshire or north Hertfordshire. The Corfe Mullen vessels are in the local Durotrigian style of everted-rim cooking pots with burnished lattice decoration on the body – but, bizarrely, they are wheel-thrown rather than in the native handmade tradition. Potters familiar with the techniques appropriate to handmade potting cannot immediately turn to the wheel and produce the same forms, even if they should wish to, and it is not immediately clear who was responsible for these vessels. Nevertheless these two cases show that during the Claudio-Neronian period there was the possibility of cross-fertilization between indigenous and Roman potting traditions – the seeds of the Romano-British style had been planted.

Several other processes can be identified within the native industries during the Claudio-Neronian period. One is the spread of the 'Belgic' style north into the Midlands. Potters familiar with cordoned jars and ledge-rim jars seem to move into regions which had been previously aceramic, or where earlier (i.e. 'non-Belgic') pottery styles had been current. This process may have started in the pre-conquest period, but con-

Site	Products and setting	Kiln type	Bibliography
Bricket Wood	Mortarium potter Oastrius	Square	Saunders and Havercroft 1977
Brockley Hill	Flagons, mortaria and coarse wares. Earliest assemblage from mortarium workshops		Castle 1973
Caistor-by-Norwich	Flagons and coarse wares	Square	Swan 1981
Canterbury	Flagons and grey wares of north Gaulish type		Pollard 1988
Chichester	Gallo-Belgic style	Twin-flue	Down 1978
Colchester	Flagons and coarse wares. Operating outside fortress	Square	Hull 1963, kiln 23
Corfe Mullen	Flagons and mortaria made alongside Durotrigian wares		Calkin 1935
Eccles	Flagons and coarse wares		Detsicas 1977
London	Sugar Loaf Court wasters, including flagons and mortaria		Chadburn and Tyers 1984
Longthorpe	Flagons and coarse wares made alongside indigenous coarse wares. Operating outside fortress		Dannell and Wild 1987
Rushden	Painted wares with some Gallo-Belgic features		P.J. Woods and Hastings 1984
Usk	Flagons and coarse wares. Operating outside fortress		Greene in Manning 1993

Table 19 *Immigrant potters operating in pre-Flavian Britain*

tinued through the first century, and, as we shall see later, had important influences on the development of later Romano-British pottery in the Midlands. This spread of the 'Belgic' style has often been claimed as another aspect of military potting with 'potters following the army' carrying the tradition north into previously aceramic areas.

The southern British industries

Across a broad swathe of England from Dorset and the Severn valley to Kent a series of major industries developed during the mid-first century AD which were to be major players during the later first century AD, and far beyond. In some cases, such as the Durotrigian/BB1 wares, the links with pre-conquest style are clear and there are direct lines of descent for most of the principal forms in the Claudian assemblage from the earlier first century AD. In others, such as Severn Valley wares, Savernake wares or Alice Holt-Farnham industry, the origins of the fabric lie shrouded in the mists of the 'conquest period'. Some would see the hand of the military as a major factor in the inception and consolidation of these wares – giving them the impetus to move on to be major producers in the later first century AD (Swan 1979; 1975). The addition of new forms such as flagons to an existing native repertoire has often been taken to be a sign of adaptation for a military market – but the additions of new forms, be they flagons or imitations of metal prototypes, is a feature of the British pottery industries in the south-east as far back as the Augustan period.

The origins of one of these wares, Severn Valley ware, have recently been considered in detail by J. R. Timby (1990) who suggests that we should be looking before the conquest for the roots of the industry. It may be that an origin at the same period should be sought for other wares in western and southern England. During this period, these assemblages are dominated by jars (usually both necked jars and bead-rim jars), but some produce more specialized regional forms, such as the Severn Valley ware tankard and carinated bowl.

Many Claudio-Neronian assemblages contain a wide range of locally produced fine wares. They are often in the broad Gallo-Belgic style – butt-beakers and plates – produced alongside a predominantly coarse-ware assemblage. Such a development continued the pattern that had been established before the conquest. The new fine wares imported from Gaul, Italy and elsewhere (e.g. samian, Lyon roughcast cups, Pompeian-Red ware platters) seem to have had relatively little impact on native potting at this period, although potters working in the Rhineland tradition occasionally took these as their prototypes (e.g. at Eccles, Usk, Longthorpe, Colchester).

Evidence of more specialized fine-ware production in

A short history of Roman pottery in Britain

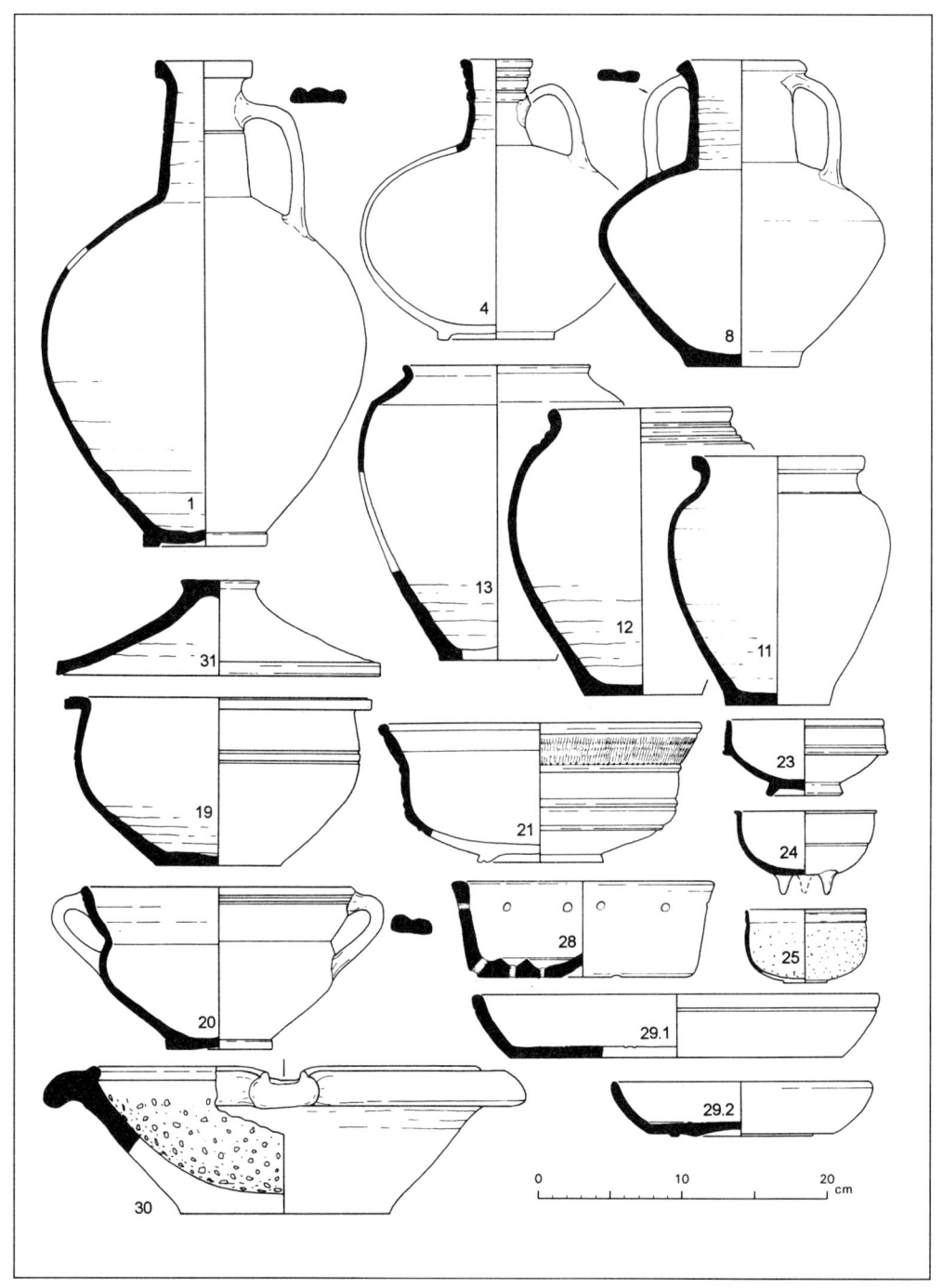

33 The coarse pottery assemblage made by immigrant potters at Usk (after Greene)

Britain comes in the form of the fine black or grey wares, often micaceous, generally ovoid or globular in shape with rouletted or barbotine decoration, that are found widely across southern England (e.g. Marsh and Tyers 1978, forms IIIB, IIIC) although they have not been studied in any detail. Vessels in the same general tradition can be seen in northern Gaul, particularly in Belgium and the lower Rhineland, and some of the earlier British specimens may be imports, but most are local. Some evidence of experimentation with more exotic potting technologies can also be seen. There are occasional vessels with mica-slipped finish that are likely to be indigenous products rather than imports, and a sherd of glazed ware in a local fabric from the rubbish–dump at Oare (Wilts.) seems to be of Claudian date (Swan 1975, fig. 5, 64).

4.4　FLAVIAN–TRAJANIC
Imports

The peak period for samian imports from the southern Gaulish factories, at least as measured by the chronological distribution of dated stamps and decorated pieces (Marsh 1981) falls into the years between AD 70 and 90. Thereafter, numbers seem to decline, a process which was not noticeably arrested by the substitution of the decaying La Graufesenque product by the better-quality vessels from the factories at Les Martres-de-Veyre, in Central Gaul, *c.* AD 100 (Atlas CGTS).

The sources and character of other classes of imports also changed during the Flavian period. The Lyon industry declined and disappeared rapidly – a process that might have been hastened by the military upheavals of AD 69 (Greene 1979, 17–8, 141) but also reflects in part a shift away from cups (the staple Lyon product) to beakers. The Flavian imports to Britain of fine colour-coated beakers are from Central Gaul and, from the end of the century, the lower Rhineland (Atlas CGCC, LRCC). Pompeian-Red ware platters from both Italy and Gaul continue to be imported in small numbers. Within the amphora assemblage, many of the types of the Claudio-Neronian period are still present, but there is a tendency for the proportion of the Baetican oil amphoras to increase with respect to the other types, a process that continues into the second century.

Mortaria

Mortaria continue to be imported from the factories of northern Gaul in some numbers, perhaps accompanied by some flagons, but the Flavian period sees the rise to prominence of the major British mortarium factory in the Brockley Hill/St Albans region (Atlas VRMO). The roots of this industry lie in the AD 50s, but with the opening of workshops by potters such as Albinus, the quantity and distribution of Verulamium-region mortaria both increase. Albinus – the most prolific stamper of mortaria in Britain – probably moved to an as yet unlocated workshop in the Brockley Hill or Bricket Wood area *c.* AD 60/65, after a short spell at another site, perhaps Colchester (Hartley in Frere and Wilkes 1989, 239). His mortaria have a wide distribution, covering Britain as far north as Inchtuthil – the fortress at the high-tide mark of Agricolan expansion in Scotland (Pitts and St Joseph 1985, 333, no. 92).

Indeed it is often suggested that the military markets in the north and Scotland were a major factor behind the development and success of the Verulamium industry. However of the 350 or so known stamps of Albinus, over 120 are from London

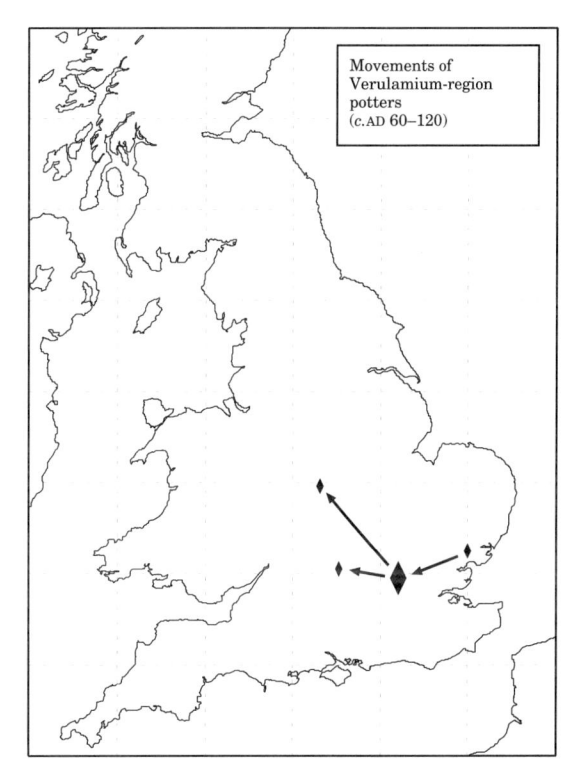

34 *Movements of Verulamium-region potters, c. AD 70–120*

and a further 60 from St Albans. The remainder are found on sites throughout the country, with no clear concentration on forts along the northern frontier, where his stamps occur in only small numbers (only 12 from Scotland). A similar pattern can be seen in the output of other Flavian–Trajanic potters at Brockley Hill. It is possible to debate the effect of the degree of investigation and excavation at these sites on the numbers of stamps which have been recovered, but it seems more likely that the local market (i.e. St Albans and London) is the bread-and-butter of these potters, rather than that in the north.

Many of the coarse-ware industries which had their origins in the pre-Flavian period continued to flourish. The Flavian–Trajanic period marks, for many, a period of consolidation. In London, for example, the potters of the Verulamium region are only one of a number of sources of flagons and related forms in oxidized fabrics which are present in the pre-Flavian period. But by the end of the first century over 95 per cent of the demand for these types in London is taken by these workshops, and the others have all but disappeared (Atlas VRW).

From the beginning of the second century, the Verulamium-region mortarium potters were setting up workshops in the Midlands. The movements of G. Attius Marinus are particularly instructive here. He had started his career at Colchester in the AD 80s, but had moved shortly thereafter to

61

A short history of Roman pottery in Britain

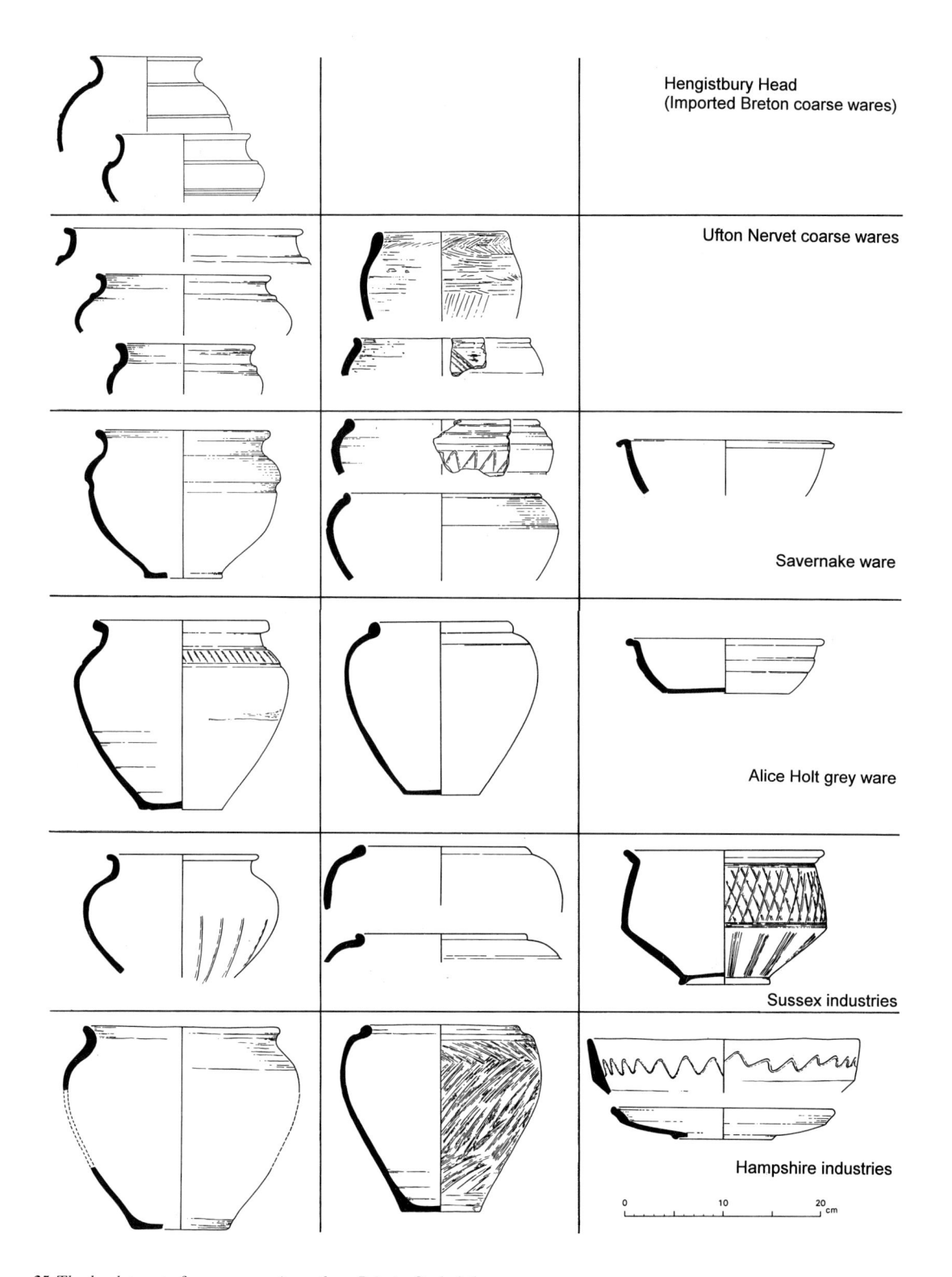

35 The development of coarse wares in southern Britain. Scale 1:6

A short history of Roman pottery in Britain

Brockley Hill. By about AD 100 he had a workshop at Mancetter, in Warwickshire, and the mortaria he made there are distributed in the Midlands and north (Atlas MHMO). Several other Verulamium-region potters moved to Mancetter during the period AD 100–20, and the early mortaria from these workshops are clearly influenced by the styles current in the Verulamium region. A similar process may be seen in the Oxfordshire potteries at the same time (Atlas OXMO). Here we do not have the evidence of the movement of a named mortarium potter such as at Mancetter, but the general typological similarity of the early mortaria, flagons and bowls suggests movement of potters from the Verulamium region. The mortarium stamps typical of the early Oxfordshire industry are illiterate trade-marks rather than name-stamps, and there is a similar trend towards the use of such marks in the Verulamium-region industry during the early second century.

Flagons, bowls and other Romanized forms were produced across northern England during the Flavian–Trajanic period, often (but not exclusively) associated with military sites, or in their wake. Although clearly related, there is a gradual drift away from the contemporary continental style seen at sites along the Rhine. In particular the ring-necked flagons on British sites are distinct from their continental cousins by the Flavian period, and the collared flagon seems to have a longer life in the Rhineland, and elsewhere in Gaul, than in Britain. Although there is probably some continued immigration during the later first century (such as the potters supplying the legionary base at Wroxeter: Darling 1977), suitable craftsmen could probably be found in and around towns of southern Britain by the Flavian period. The specialized case of the movement of mortarium potters to Mancetter and Oxfordshire from Verulamium demonstrates that such 'transfers of technology' did occur within the province (**34**).

Coarse wares

Within the industries which had their roots in indigenous potting styles – broadly the grey or darker-coloured fabrics – one particular phenomenon at this period is worthy of attention. As we have seen above, the British coarse-pottery assemblage of the Augustan–Tiberian period is dominated by the jar form.

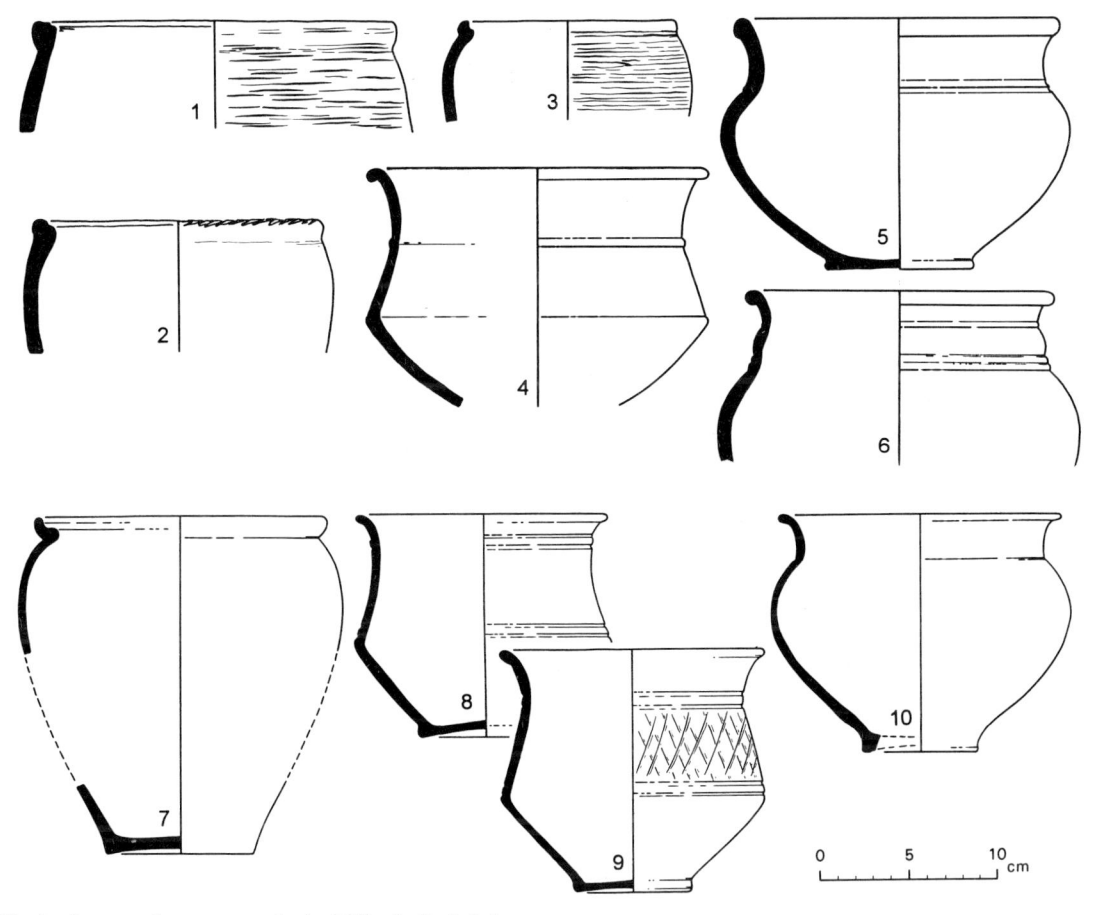

36 The development of coarse wares in the Midlands. Scale 1:4

A short history of Roman pottery in Britain

The Romanized assemblage introduced at the conquest certainly included jars, in large numbers, but the lower and more open bowl form is also a significant element. During the Neronian–Flavian period many of the indigenous industries started to produce bowls alongside their other types. We can only speculate about the nature of the changes in culinary habits that underlies this aspect of specialization in the ceramic repertoire. We do not know whether it is particularly associated with towns or also affected rural populations, but the comparison of quantified data might illuminate this point. Nevertheless, the process was sufficiently widespread to result in the addition of bowls to the repertoire of many of the indigenous coarse-ware industries of southern Britain. In many cases the Roman carinated bowl with a reeded rim was taken as a prototype. In the Durotrigian/BB1 industry of south-east Dorset (Atlas BB1) a plausible prototype for a bowl existed in the native repertoire in the carinated beaded-rim 'war cemetery' form, but the flat-rimmed bowl which developed during the Neronian period seems to be a native version of the bowls produced at Exeter and elsewhere in the south-west by potters trained in the Rhineland traditions (Holbrook and Bidwell 1991, 96–7).

Similar processes were taking place in the Highgate industry, which was a major supplier of coarse wares to London in the Flavian–Trajanic period. The typical Highgate bowl has a hooked rim, often marked by multiple grooves in the upper surface. A few specimens have three feet. In the Alice Holt industry the typical bowl has cordons half-way down the outer wall and grooves or mouldings at the rim (Atlas AHFA). In the Sussex area the bowls are sharply carinated with simple flanges at the rim. Despite their differing final appearances, the most likely point of departure for these vessels is the introduced Roman bowl form.

Thus, by the end of the first century AD we can see a recurrent pattern in the coarse-ware industries of southern Britain (35). Each industry produces its own suite of vessels which nevertheless conform to a common structure. Most frequently they include a necked jar, a bead-rim jar and a bowl. Within each industry or style the vessels may share common characteristics such as decoration.

In the south and east Midlands the dominant typological models are a combination of the cordoned jar, rilled cooking pot and ledge-rim jar – all ultimately derived from pre-Roman 'Belgic' prototypes (36). The production of these forms in shell-tempered wares in the industries of Bedfordshire and Northamptonshire continued, apparently uninterrupted, through this period. Further north the style was introduced into regions that had hitherto been largely aceramic, and harder sand-tempered fabrics were employed. By *c.* AD 100–20, ledge-rim jars in coarse sandy grey wares which can be considered as the prototypes of the later Derbyshire ware jar (Atlas DERBY) were being made in the kilns at Little Chester, Derby, alongside cordoned jars and bowls of loosely 'Belgic' ancestry (Brassington 1971). A similar combination can be seen in the lower Nene valley at the same period (Pryor 1984).

The third major style apparent in the coarse pottery of the Flavian–Trajanic period lies in western England. From the mid-first century orange Severn Valley wares had been produced in the Gloucester area (Atlas SVW). The repertoire is dominated by necked jars, narrow-mouthed jars, carinated jars and, characteristically if not abundantly, handled tankards. There is no common open bowl form in the ware, nor any influence from the ledge-rim jar industries of the east Midlands. The influence of this ware both by distribution and influence, can be seen in south Wales, up the Severn into the Cheshire Plain and into the west Midlands.

Fine wares

The Flavian period saw the introduction of a range of new fine-ware techniques and styles into Romano-British potting. These can be considered in three broad groups, although, as will be seen, there is some overlap between them.

Firstly, there are a number of attempts at the production of vessels which broadly follow the typology of sigillata prototypes. The most widespread of these are grouped together under the banner of London ware – a diverse collection of grey or black wares which include bowls copying the Drag 29 or 37 and decorated with compass-drawn incised, combed, stamped and rouletted decoration, or some combination of these (Atlas LOND). One major production centre for this material was certainly at London itself (Marsh 1978) although the distribution of its products is not clear – it may not be very extensive. Elsewhere, London-ware style vessels are made in small numbers alongside coarse wares, and in the same fabrics, rather than by specialized fine-ware producers.

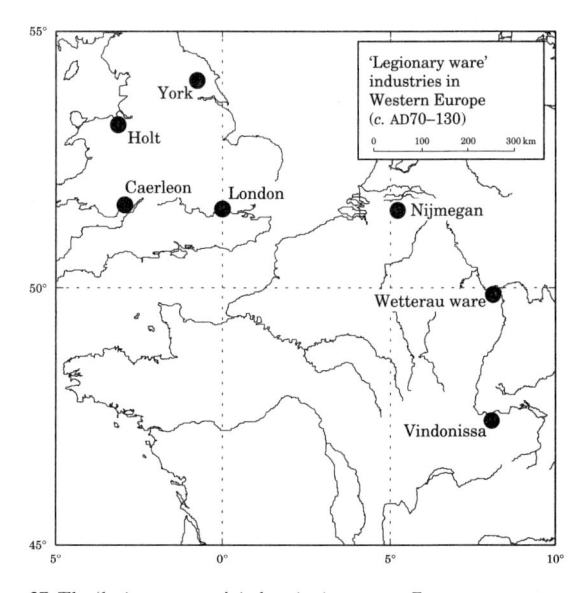

37 The 'legionary ware' industries in western Europe

A short history of Roman pottery in Britain

Technique	London	Holt/Chester	York	Caerleon
Oxidized & slipped	-	main technique	main technique	main technique
London ware	major technique	sherds	-	sherds
Mica-dusted	major technique	present	rare	rare
Eggshell ware	present	present	present	present
Marbling	present	-	(painted wares)	(mottled wares)
Lead-glazing	common	present	-	present
Stamping	-	present	present	present
Moulding	-	present	faceted	flagon
Barbotine	-	-	-	present
Imitation samian stamps	-	-	-	present
Lamps	moulds	present	present	mould

Table 20 *Techniques in 'legionary ware' industries in Britain (after Marsh)*

In addition to the bowl forms, London ware includes flasks, plates and cups, similarly decorated with combing or compass-drawn decoration. These are less clearly derived from sigillata prototypes and a general Gallo-Belgic feeling can be discerned. Vessels in the London-ware style were made at sites on the lower Rhine during the mid-first century AD, and some influence from these may have been responsible for the British production, although this requires further investigation.

Some vessels classed as London ware are decorated with simple circular or rosette stamps in addition to compass-drawn and incised motifs (Perrin 1990a). Bowls with more sophisticated block-stamped decoration, once known as 'stamped London ware' but now classed as London–Essex stamped wares (Atlas LEST) were made in the Little Hadham potteries in Hertfordshire, and achieved some success around the lower Thames basin during the Flavian–Hadrianic period. Some of the bowl forms seem to be influenced by samian prototypes but, as with standard London ware, there are other influences. Stamped wares of a wider range of forms are also found elsewhere in East Anglia and further north into Lincolnshire, where there is a distinct group known as Parisian wares (Rodwell 1978; Elsdon 1982).

Other influences from the Rhineland may be seen during the Flavian period. The poppy-head beaker, decorated with vertical panels of barbotine dots, seems to have its roots in a form of beaker current on the middle Rhine in the early Flavian period (Tyers 1978), although the precise mechanism behind its arrival in Britain is uncertain. We have no evidence for migrating potters, and in Britain the beakers seem to have attached themselves to coarse-ware industries, rather than to specialist fine-ware producers. Possibly related, at least in origin, is one of the rare glazed-ware industries of southern Britain. The south-eastern glazed-ware group (Atlas SEGL), perhaps manufactured in west London or north Surrey, includes some beakers with barbotine panel decoration, but more typical are bowls copying the samian forms Drag 30 and 37 decorated with vertical lines or circles in white barbotine under a green glaze. A very similar assemblage in grey ware is known from the middle Rhine (Heukemes 1964) but, as with the poppy-head beaker, the transfer mechanism – in this case including a change in technology – is unclear.

Another strain in the fine wares of this period comes from more exotic sources. Tablewares with unusual finishes such as red-slip coatings, marbling, mica-dusting, lead-glazing, and often in forms derived from glass and metalware, were initially recognized, in Britain, on sites associated with the legionary fortresses at Chester and Caerleon and hence were termed legionary wares. On the Continent similar assemblages are found at Nijmegan (Holland) and Vindonissa (Switzerland), both major legionary bases. The significance of these assemblages was recognized in a paper by Elisabeth Ettlinger in 1951, and developed further by K. T. Greene in 1977. Some of the plates and dishes in legionary wares, which had been considered as rather poor imitations of Gaulish sigillata, were in fact closely paralleled by vessels from the eastern, Greek, half of the Empire, and the whole assemblage (both forms and technology) seems to originate somewhere in that region. Greene illustrates material from the legionary wares of Britain, the Rhineland and Switzerland, and the lower Danube and the Aegean that demonstrates these links.

The suggestion is that these industries in the west were started by potters from the eastern Mediterranean. There is some direct evidence of the involvement of Greek-speaking personnel at the legionary pottery works at Holt, which supplied the fortress at Chester, and is one of the key 'legionary ware' sites in Britain. There are at least three graffiti in Greek characters on potsherds and tiles (Grimes 1930, 133–4, nos. 15, 32, 33; Greene 1977, 124); a pre-firing graffito in Neo-Punic script on a large sherd gives the name MA'QAR, perhaps suggesting the presence of an individual from North Africa

A short history of Roman pottery in Britain

(Grimes 1930, no. 26; Guillaume 1940). Greene suggests that slave labour from the east may have been responsible in part for the appearance of these industries at such diverse points around western Europe (1977, 125–8) (**37**).

Beyond the specifically military contexts of Holt, Caerleon and York, similar material is found at London (Marsh 1978) and elsewhere in southern Britain (Greene 1974) and northern Gaul (Tuffreau-Libre 1978). The appearance of the eastern styles at Vindonissa and Nijmegan should be dated to *c*. AD 70. The British industries seem to start nearer AD 100, and are also more diverse. At London the vessels in the eastern style are associated with the production of London ware which as we have seen has at least some roots in the Gallo-Belgic traditions of northern Gaul. The Holt assemblage lacks these elements, but otherwise shares many techniques and forms with London (Marsh 1978, 203). Perhaps industries such as that at London are 'second-generation' creations, developed from a blend of eastern and Gallo–Belgic elements in the Rhineland, and imported thence to Britain (**table 20**).

The initial impetus behind these long-distance movements of potters must be sought in the internal arrangements of pottery supply to the legionary bases. Part of the background may be the decline in the output of the South Gaulish sigillata industry, although this was probably not a serious factor until the later Flavian period, whereas the eastern styles had arrived a decade or so before this. At London, production of mica-dusted and other fine wares continued into the early second century – through the 'samian gap' – but the absolute numbers do not seem enough to compensate for any deficit in the samian supply.

The legionary-ware episode, as much as any of the imports now finding their way into Britain, demonstrates the wide range of influences impacting on Roman Britain in this period. Now fully integrated into the imperial system, the province is open to craftsmen and others from all parts of the Empire, and the student of pottery is obliged to cast a net far beyond the Channel to understand the development of the industry.

4.5 FROM HADRIAN TO SEVERUS

The visit of the Emperor Hadrian to Britain in AD 122 coincides with the decision to construct a permanent frontier – Hadrian's Wall – across Britain on the Tyne–Solway isthmus. The construction of the Wall, as well as being a remarkable feat of engineering, marked a major point in the development of the Romano-British pottery industry. The key player was the Durotrigian black-burnished industry of south-east Dorset.

Black-burnished wares

Cooking pots and bowls in this hard dense black fabric, with burnished lattice decoration, had been used at forts such as Exeter during the pre-Flavian period, and enjoyed some success across the south-west and south Wales during the later first and early second century AD (Atlas BB1). Dorset black-burnished wares were being supplied to sites on Hadrian's Wall during the Wall construction phase, by about AD 125, but are not present in Trajanic deposits there (Holbrook and Bidwell 1991, 93). Elsewhere in the province, we do not have the benefit of the historically dated sequence in the north, but most of the evidence points to an appearance of Durotrigian BB1 at about the same time. In London, BB1 appears, in small quantities, in levels that immediately precede the Hadrianic fire horizon, which Marsh suggests should be dated to *c*. AD 120–5 (1981, 222). The most satisfactory model is for the simultaneous appearance of BB1 across the province, both north and south, in the early Hadrianic period. Most discussions of the situation in the north invoke the activities of military quartermasters in the procurement of supplies for the garrisons. However, the involvement of Roman officialdom in the details of such matters is far from certain, and the activities of independent traders or merchants may be behind the success of BB1. The production area, in Dorset, is adjacent to the coast and the pottery may be 'piggy-backed' on the transport of other goods, such as agricultural produce, from southern Britain to the north. The more immediate reason behind the success of BB1 was its undoubted excellence as a cooking vessel. It may have been the Second Legion from Caerleon who first took BB1 to the north, when they were moved there during the Wall construction phase. They were familiar with the

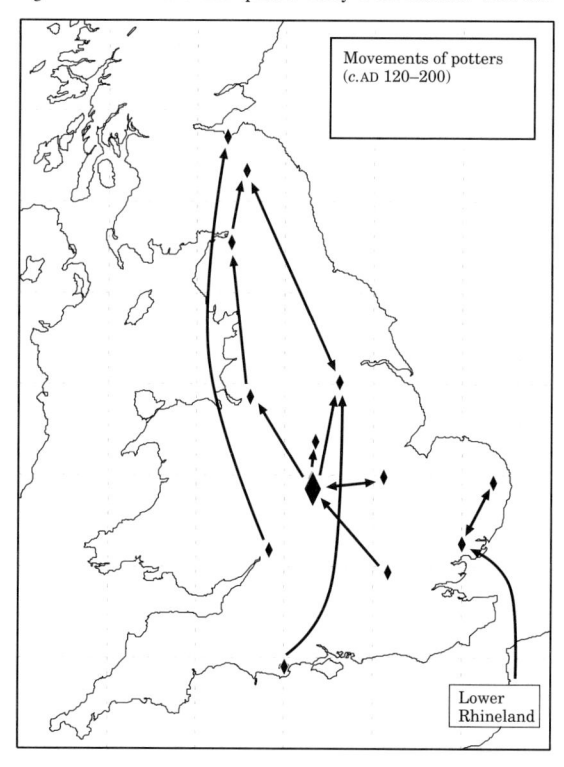

38 Movements of potters in Britain, c. AD 120–200

ware at their south Wales base during the Flavian–Trajanic period.

Just as important as the distribution of BB1 itself is the effect of the black-burnished style on pottery industries elsewhere in the province. Everted-rim jars and bowls modelled on BB1 prototypes are soon found around the Thames estuary and, where we have the benefit of well-dated sequences, it is obvious that they follow closely on the heels of the Dorset originals. The vessels are wheel-thrown, and seem to be grafted on to the region's existing grey-ware industries.

This is demonstrated particularly well by the sequence at the Highgate kiln site (Brown and Sheldon 1974). During the early second century AD, Highgate was a major supplier of grey wares to London and the surrounding settlements. Black-burnished style vessels were added to the existing Highgate repertoire during the Hadrianic period, and continue to be manufactured until the end of the industry in the Antonine period. The black-burnished style pots are wheel-thrown and white slipped – the normal Highgate techniques – but have burnished lattice decoration, and a fabric that is significantly coarser than the standard Highgate grey ware, produced by the addition of a coarse sand. Thus it seems that the demand the Highgate potters were responding to was not just a sudden preference for everted-rim cooking pots and dishes with burnished lattice decoration, but also for a fabric that was coarser and perhaps more resistant to temperature change. A similar process was taking place in other industries around the Thames estuary during the Hadrianic period. In the Upchurch industry of north Kent the jars in the black-burnished style were made in a fabric that had earlier been used for the manufacture of a local bowl form, although the dishes are in a slightly coarser ware (Monaghan 1987a, 223). Wheel-thrown black-burnished wares had largely displaced the handmade product of Dorset by the Antonine period in the south-east and for the remainder of the second century, BB1 remains relatively rare in the area.

A sub-set of the wheel-thrown material can be classed as BB2 (Atlas BB2). This term was first defined by Gillam in 1960 in his study of the pottery from Mumrills, on the Antonine Wall (Steer 1960). It is important to grasp that this classification was based on material recovered from a consumption site. When the term is applied to the south-east of England and to production sites, the clarity of the definition becomes obscured with material that is clearly related yet does not fall precisely within the limits of the ware as defined in the north. It is generally preferable to classify wares on material from production sites, not, as here, around a selection of pottery from one area transferred through trade and other mechanisms to another. It is thus not helpful to describe vessels from southern British production sites as 'imitations of BB2'. The results of heavy mineral analysis suggest that a number of sources participate in the supply of BB2 to the northern frontier during the Antonine period. One major source is likely to be at or near Colchester, but vessels from the potteries in north Kent are also found (D. F. Williams 1977; Monaghan 1987a, 211–13).

Towards the end of the century, the black-burnished style in the south-east developed new forms and decorative style. The everted-rim cooking pots tended to be taller, with narrower bases, and the burnished decoration – which was almost always a simple lattice in the mid-second century – became more diverse and varied. The pie-dish form tended to lose its decoration completely, and a series of finer-textured fabrics also appeared. These continued to be made in Kent and Essex, but sources further inland in Hertfordshire and Buckinghamshire are also known. Export to the north continued into the third century (e.g. Gillam types 225, 313). Jars derived from the earlier (pre-black-burnished) cordoned jars and ledge-rim jars are made alongside black-burnished wares at industries in Essex (e.g. at Mucking: M. U. Jones and Rodwell 1973). Some of the ledge-rim jars reached the north, where they are Gillam's type 151 (Bidwell 1985, 177–8).

A different mechanism for the spread of black-burnished style from Dorset to other parts of the country is shown by the material from Rossington Bridge, near Doncaster (Yorks.). In contrast to the south-eastern product, the Rossington Bridge material is hand-formed and probably fired in bonfires, both hallmarks of the original Durotrigian industry (Atlas RBBB1). The most likely explanation for this is the movement of potters from Dorset to Yorkshire. Production commenced in the early Antonine period, and Rossington Bridge BB1 had some limited success on the northern frontier – although the product is difficult to distinguish visually from the Dorset original.

The movement of the Durotrigian potters is but one of a series of contemporary migrations to Rossington Bridge. We have also the mortarium potter Sarrius from the Mancetter–Hartshill industry of Warwickshire (Atlas MHMO), and potters from Lincolnshire producing fine wares. There is the distinct impression of a deliberately planned collecting together of potters at a single location in about AD 140, and the relative proximity of the markets of the northern frontier is the most likely explanation. It is tempting to identify the driving force behind all this activity as Sarrius, who seems to have returned to Mancetter towards the end of his career, and may have run his Yorkshire and Warwickshire workshops in parallel in any case. However, rather than one of the potters it is perhaps more likely that some unnamed merchant or landowner was the instigator of the Rossington Bridge workshop.

There are hints that a similar arrangement may have been operating at Little Chester, Derby, some twenty or so years earlier. The Mancetter–Hartshill potter, Septuminus, worked there for a time. The coarse wares are in the ledge-rim jar/cordoned jar-style from the Midlands, and there are fine wares, including glazed wares, which may owe something to the legionary styles of the Flavian–Trajanic period. These two

A short history of Roman pottery in Britain

industries – Rossington Bridge and Little Chester – demonstrate how pottery styles from around the province were being thrown together during the early second century AD (**38**).

Fine wares

Another element in the mix was the new colour-coated industries. During the Flavian–Trajanic period fine colour-coated beakers had been imported from the Central Gaulish and Lower Rhineland industries (**41**). The latter area was probably the source of the potters who moved to Colchester at the beginning of the early second century AD. Bag-shaped beakers with roughcast and rouletted decoration, closely modelled on the Rhineland prototypes, were distributed from Colchester to sites around the Thames estuary, and from the middle of the second century, to the northern frontier (Atlas COLC). From the middle of the century a second wave of fine-ware producers appeared, again heavily influenced by the Rhineland industries. In the Nene valley an important colour-coated production was grafted on to the pre-existing grey-ware industry. Other smaller producers appeared in the eastern counties from the mid-second century on into the third (**table 21**).

Site	Date	RCHM gazetteer	ATLAS
Colchester	Early 2nd		COLC
Nene Valley	Mid 2nd		NVCC
South Carlton	Mid 2nd	466	
Great Casterton	Mid 2nd	576	

Table 21 *Colour-coated industries following Lower Rhineland traditions*

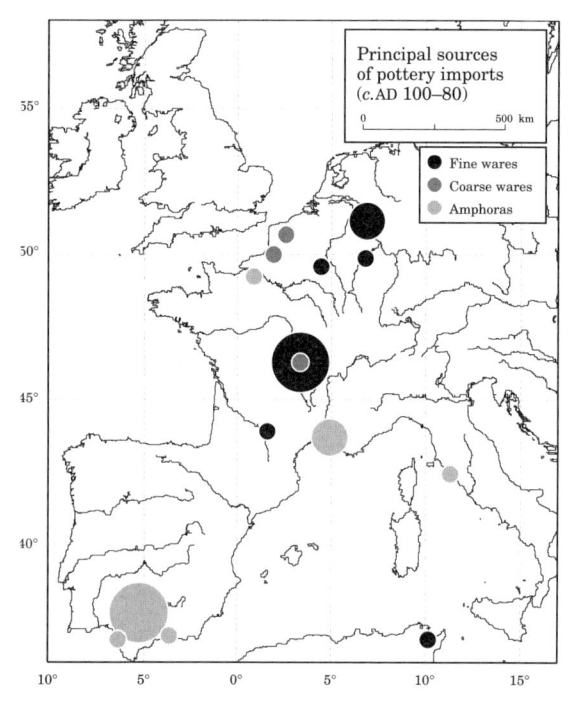

39 *Sources of pottery imports to Britain, c. AD 100–80*

Although all these industries were working in a similar tradition, ultimately traceable to the Rhineland colour-coated industries, it may be that some were in fact secondary industries, derived from Colchester or the Nene valley rather than set up directly by immigrant potters. The pottery industry at Colchester was also an important supplier of mortaria and some of the forms of the mid-second century and later seem

Site	Description	Bibliography
Moulds and other equipment		
York	Mould of Central Gaulish potter, X3	Hull 1963, 45
York	Mould fragment, with base included in mould	Hull 1963, 46
Littlemore (Oxon.)	Mould fragment for Drag 37	Young 1977b
Peterborough	Mould with incised decoration	Hull 1963, 46
London	Name-stamp of Cerialis	Hull 1963, 46
Moulded wares		
Wiltshire	Moulded cups (cf. Déch 74)	Swan 1977
Wiltshire	Moulded bowls (cf. Drag 30)	A. S. Anderson 1978
Great Casterton	Moulded bowls (cf. Drag 37)	Swan 1984, fiche 576
Samian workshops		
London/Pulborough	Aldgate–Pulborough potter	Simpson 1952; P.V. Webster 1975
Colchester	Colchester samian workshop	Hull 1963

Table 22 *Romano-British samian and other moulded wares*

A short history of Roman pottery in Britain

to be inspired by continental prototypes, again from the Rhineland (Atlas COMO).

The top of the heap, as far as the introduction of continental potting technology is concerned, are the British samian industries. The later first and second century saw a number of attempts at pottery manufacturing using moulds in Britain (**table 22**). One of these, the industry located in Wiltshire and making bowls loosely based on the Drag 30, achieved some moderate success during the Flavian period (A. S. Anderson 1978). But the two most significant attempts at British samian (rather than a moulded fine ware) are the work of the Aldgate–Pulborough potter and the Colchester industry.

The double-barrelled name of the Aldgate–Pulborough potter reflects some uncertainty about the location of the workshops. A single waster from Aldgate (London), discovered during excavations for the Metropolitan railway in 1882, initially suggested that they lay in or near London, but the discovery of moulds, decorated pieces and plain wares evidently by the same hand in the vicinity of Pulborough (Sussex) suggests that at least one workshop lay there (Simpson 1952; P. V. Webster 1975). There is an antique and possibly unreliable description of samian moulds discovered in the vicinity of St Paul's Cathedral during building work in the aftermath of the Great Fire (reproduced in Wheeler 1928, 140) but the relevance of this, if any, to the Aldgate waster is not known. Only one potter's name is known on the plain wares, G. Severian(us), but there may have been a number of craftsmen involved in the production. The Aldgate–Pulborough decorated wares make extensive use of the *surmoulage* technique, that is mouldings for the figure types are taken from finished bowls (in this case Central Gaulish bowls), rather than having access to 'original' *poinçons*. His work is known from a handful of sites in the south of the country and it seems to have been a short-lived experiment. The date of the bowls being copied places this in the period between AD 125 and 150 (Bennett 1978; Dickinson in Gurney 1986, 75).

Rather more is known of the Colchester industry, where the kiln, Colchester kiln 21, was excavated by M. R. Hull in 1933 (Atlas COTS). It had been partly demolished in antiquity, but sufficient remained to confirm its relationship with the sigillata kilns of the East Gaulish industries (Swan 1984, 92–4). The firing chamber was surrounded by vertical clay pipes, linked together with collars, to conduct the heat through the kiln. In the vicinity there were large numbers of mould fragments, the work of two mouldmakers, and much samian ware, both plain and decorated. Between ten and fifteen potters worked in the Colchester workshop, and both the style of their products and the previous career of some individuals, demonstrate links with the workshops of Sinzig and Trier. The close relationship between samian and other contemporary pottery types at Colchester is shown by the name-stamps of the samian potters Cunopectus and Acceptus iii on both mortaria and colour-coated beakers. The Colchester samian episode, which can be dated to *c*. AD 160–200/210, had rather limited success when compared with the contemporary manufacture of mortaria and colour-coated beakers, but there is a scatter of specimens across East Anglia.

Pottery supply on the Hadrianic–Antonine frontier

The garrisons on the northern frontier drew many of their supplies from sources further south. We have already seen that BB1 and BB2, from south-west and south-east England respectively, were major cooking wares. Fine wares were largely supplied by the sigillata industries of central Gaul, with some colour-coated beakers from Colchester. For quantified data on trade within the province we can look once more at the mortaria. The data from Inveresk is illustrated by the source map in **40**.

The major supplier is Colchester (Atlas COMO) and this is consistent on most sites in the north at this period. We can link this with the sourcing of black-burnished supplies from around the Thames estuary. Other major sources are Mancetter–Hartshill in the Midlands (Atlas MHMO), and the industries of the northern frontier zone, including the Corbridge area (Atlas CBMO), the Eden valley and somewhere in southern Scotland, perhaps near Newstead (K. F. Hartley 1976). Collectively this northern group now accounts for about a quarter of the mortaria in use, and shows how far the economic development of this region had progressed since the Flavian period.

Bar Hill form	Number of sherds	Hayes form	Description
1	143	23A	Round-based casserole
2	133	4B	Carinated dish
3	5	3C	Flanged dish
4	19	196	Lid
5	6	84	Bowl with sagging base
6	58		Wide-mouthed bowl
7	11		Plain-necked flagon
8	6		Small beaker
9	1		Mortarium
10	2	16	Small carinated dish
11	1	6	Shallow dish/plate

Table 23 *Bar Hill ware assemblage*

Some forts in Scotland were supplied by coarse wares from adjacent kilns. At Inveresk the potters produced vessels in a style including elements of Severn Valley ware, and they had probably moved to the north from somewhere in Gloucestershire or the west Midlands (G. D. Thomas 1989). At Cramond and Bar Hill a rather more exotic origin seems likely. Elements of the assemblage here suggest that the potters

A short history of Roman pottery in Britain

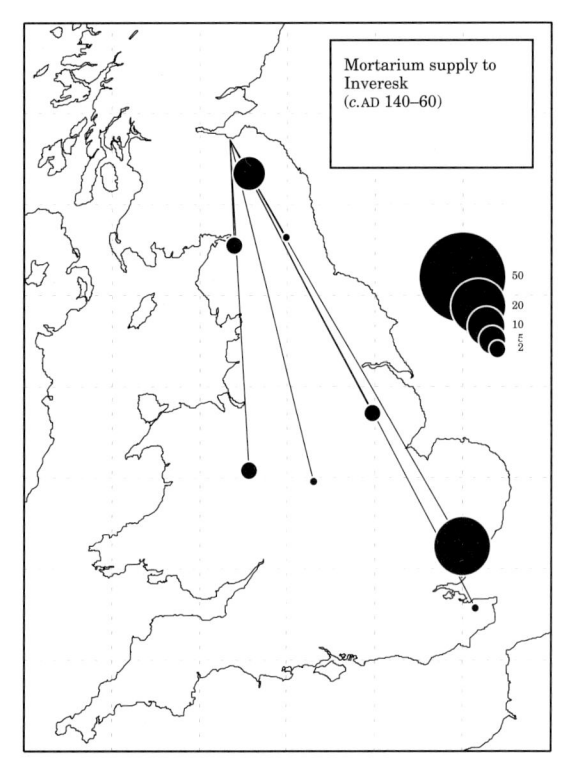

40 Mortarium supply to Rough Castle and Inveresk, c. AD 140–60

were familiar with the ceramic styles current around the western Mediterranean (Rae and Rae 1974; Ford, forthcoming; Keppie 1985) (**table 23**).

At Bar Hill, the bowls and some of the finer forms can be matched in the repertoire of North Africa wares (Hayes 1972) but the round-based casseroles in particular are of a type that is found more widely around the west Mediterranean basin (e.g. Pellecuer and Pomaredes 1991, from Languedoc). Cramond and Bar Hill are not the only sources of evidence of such potters in Britain. There are a few casseroles from other sites in the north (e.g. Gillam type 302) and perhaps also at Holt (Grimes 1930, fig. 74, 22) and Caerleon (Zienkiewicz 1986). The locally made Eboracum ware from York includes a casserole form (Perrin 1981, 59–60; Perrin 1990b, 265–6) and other forms and techniques that may have Mediterranean origins (Swan 1994).

So, on top of the layers of Gallo-Belgic, Rhineland and legionary wares we have another source of influence on the coarse wares of Britain. The key site is probably York, which was the headquarters for the campaigns of the Emperor Severus in the north from AD 208. It might be tempting to link these 'North African' forms with the presence of Severus (the 'African' emperor) and his entourage in York, but their appearance on the Antonine Wall would seem to pre-date this by several decades. It may also be too simplistic to think of these types as exclusively North African, for many have a wide distribution around the Mediterranean and we can see 'African' influence on the coarse wares of both Spain and Gaul during the later second century. Perhaps their arrival in Britain should be seen as part of this broader picture rather than linked with some particular historical event.

4.6 THE THIRD AND FOURTH CENTURIES

The third century has long been recognized as a problem in Romano-British ceramic studies (Hull 1963, 176–7). There are two views on the apparent 'invisibility' of third-century pottery, which can be paraphrased as follows: one is that the gap is a genuine phenomenon, reflecting a real drop in the quantity and variety of pottery; the second is that the problem is largely concerned with dating – types known to circulate during the later second century tend to get drawn back in date and, conversely, types that appear in levels of the later third century are pulled forward. If this is the problem, it can be remedied by stretching the surrounding material (chronologically) to cover the gap. There is also some evidence that the difficulty is more acute in southern Britain than in the north and west, perhaps suggesting that it is partly an artefact of the way the material is being approached.

There is evidence of continuity in the history of many coarse-ware industries. Many of the major wares of the later third century had their roots in the second century – BB1, Alice Holt, the Thames-side industries, Derbyshire ware, the

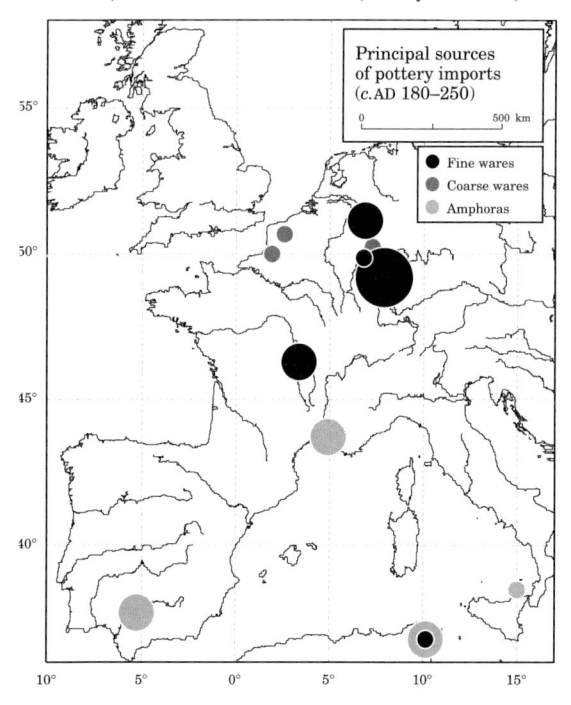

41 Sources of pottery imports to Britain, c. AD 180–250

Nene Valley industry, Severn Valley ware, the shelly industries of the Midlands, Mancetter–Hartshill – all these, and others, seem to work through the third-century gap.

Some recent developments in the study of the typology and dating of BB1 illustrate the type of adjustment that we might expect in third-century chronology. The general trends in the BB1 everted-rim cooking pot are reasonably clear. Compared with early second-century specimens, those of the later third and fourth century are narrower, with a tapering foot, the rim flares out from the shoulder at a greater angle and the decorative band narrows (covering less of the body of the vessel) and consequently the angle of the burnished lattice changes from acute, through a right angle, to obtuse. Gillam, in his 1957 types paper, gave a date of AD 270–340 to his form 145, the earliest with obtuse lattice. The most recent discussion of everted-rim jar chronology, drawing on data from Vindolanda (Northumberland) and Exeter suggests that the obtuse lattice had appeared by AD 225, and perhaps even a decade or so earlier (Bidwell 1985, 174–5).

The decline in samian exports from the Gaulish industries, a process that commenced in the later Antonine period, continued apace into the first decades of the third century. Unlike South and Central Gaulish sigillata, which were distributed across the whole province, East Gaulish wares are particularly concentrated in the south and east of the province (Atlas EGTS). The study of the latest East Gaulish evidence allows the material to be dated with increasing precision. It is clear that production continued into the AD 240s, but material of this date only appeared in Britain in any quantity on sites around the Thames estuary (Bird 1987).

One of the key groups of the early third century in Britain is the material from the London waterfront at New Fresh Wharf (masquerading as St Magnus House in the published report: B. Richardson 1986). Here, large groups of pottery were dumped in the backfill of a wooden quay structure. There is a sequence of dendrochronological dates from the massive quay timbers, suggesting that they were felled between AD 209 and 224. Thus at first sight, this might be an ideal assemblage to study the ceramics of the early third century. The pottery includes large groups of both Central and East Gaulish samian wares, accompanied by a rich and diverse range of other Gaulish and Rhineland imports, both fine and coarse wares, and Mediterranean amphoras, as well as Romano-British wares (**41**).

In her detailed study of the sigillata, J. Bird argues that the assemblage includes two shipment groups separated in date by half a century – the Central Gaulish material dating to *c.* AD 180 and an East Gaulish group of *c.* AD 235–45 (1986). If we accept this, the remainder of the material from the quay cannot be dated any more precisely than the same half-century and the group does not in fact have the potential suggested by the dendrochronological dates.

An alternative view of sigillata dating, proposed by A. King (1981), attempts to reconcile this disparity. He proposes that the chronology of the latest Central Gaulish samian from Lezoux, including the work of major potters such as Cinnamus, should be extended into the third century – well beyond their conventional terminal date of AD 175. This view currently receives little support from specialists on samian pottery (e.g. Bird 1986, 146, fn. 2), and there is no evidence for the reuse of old samian moulds in the Central Gaulish workshops, as is apparent at Trier and Rheinzabern for instance. We should undoubtedly be looking at the history of the New Fresh Wharf quay itself to explain the apparent discrepancies in the pottery dates. Anyone who saw the quay during excavation – under most difficult waterlogged conditions – might not be surprised that the stratigraphy and pottery dating have proved difficult to reconcile. It is to be hoped that further groups of the period AD 200–50 will be recovered which will clear up some of the difficulties surrounding the New Fresh Wharf group.

The end of samian and its aftermath

The end of East Gaulish terra sigillata exports did not, however, mark the end of this fine-ware style. The influence of the samian industry had been felt by other potters ever since the beginning of its history. Sometimes this had been marked merely by the production of a few samian forms alongside a predominantly coarse-ware assemblage, as at Usk in the Neronian period. In other cases the influence was deeper and longer-lasting, such as the early sigillata forms incorporated into the Gallo-Belgic industry during the Augustan period. During the second century a number of industries had sprung up in Gaul producing red-slip wares outside the conventional samian industries, but which loosely followed samian prototypes, and used simpler technology. Any decoration was generally stamped or in barbotine rather than moulded. One such was the *sigillée claire B* of the Rhône valley. Here were simple hemispherical bowls, loosely based on the Drag 37, and a range of cups, plates and flagons. The ware had some success from Lyon, south to the Mediterranean, and the style continued through into the fourth century AD.

Another industry with its roots firmly in samian was Argonne ware. Standard moulded samian had been produced at sites such as Lavoye, in the Argonne forest, from the middle of the second century AD, but by the end of the third century production had turned to bowls, again loosely modelled on the Drag 37, but decorated with a broad zone of roller-stamped decoration in place of the moulding (Atlas ARGO). Some of the earliest roller-stamped motifs echo the ovolo of the earlier moulded wares, but simple abstract or crosshatch patterns were favoured. Argonne ware continued in production up to the fourth century and enjoyed wide success across northern and eastern Gaul, with some export to Britain.

In Britain, the demise of the east Gaulish samian industry was followed shortly by the production of samian style red-slipped wares. The origins of the Oxfordshire industry (Atlas

A short history of Roman pottery in Britain

OXRS) have been studied in detail by Bird and Young (1981) who demonstrate that many of the earliest Oxfordshire forms are based closely on East Gaulish samian prototypes. This includes a number of forms that were rarely, if ever, imported to Britain, and the most likely explanation is the arrival of craftsmen familiar with the East Gaulish samian industry. What does not travel, however, is the technique of using moulds. From the beginning of the Oxfordshire industry the bowls were decorated directly with stamps.

Although dating at this period is (as we have seen) difficult, there is no reason to suppose that the beginning of Oxfordshire red-ware production much post-dates the end of East Gaulish exports, and a date in the AD 240s is most likely. What might be thought slightly curious is the choice of Oxfordshire for this industry rather than, for instance, Colchester – a site with a long history of contact with the East Gaulish and Rhineland industries and location of a previous attempt at samian production in Britain. Oxfordshire was the location of existing grey-ware and mortarium producers, the former of only local significance but the latter already achieving some success across southern Britain. With the benefit of twenty-twenty hindsight we can see that the choice was right, for the Oxfordshire industry ultimately gained a market far greater than anything that was ever to be achieved by Colchester.

Imports

With the collapse of samian, the quantity of pottery imported into Britain certainly declined, although a large number of sources is represented in the remaining trade (**42**). Fine wares from the post-sigillata industries of Gaul are represented by a little Argonne ware and *céramique à l'éponge*. The only coarse fabric of any significance is the *Eifelkeramik* of the Mayen region, near the Rhine. All these seem to be largely fourth century in Britain, and their distribution is almost confined to the south and south-east of the province (**table 24**).

Of the earlier amphora types, Spanish oil amphoras had declined from the beginning of the third century, but Gaulish wine amphoras remained common – perhaps the most common amphora type in some third-century levels. These were probably imported through the Rhineland and ports on the North Sea coast (Peacock 1978). Amphoras from elsewhere in the Mediterranean were certainly being imported during the third and fourth centuries, although there are very few large quantified assemblages which allow the progress of the different types and sources to be monitored. We might expect that the disappearance of Spanish olive-oil might be mirrored by a rise in imports from North Africa, as certainly seems to be the case in the Mediterranean. However, the number of African oil jars in Britain seems to be nothing like enough to compensate for the absence of the Spanish product, and the use of olive-oil must have declined during the later Roman period.

Fabric	Source of sites	Number	ATLAS
Fine wares			
Argonne ware	North Gaul	41	ARGO
Céramique à l'éponge	Aquitaine	36	EPON
German marbled wares	Rhineland	10	MARM
Coarse wares			
Mayen ware	East Gaul	60	EIFL
North Gaulish grey	Picardy/ Pas-de-Calais	–	NGGW
Amphoras			
Gauloise	Provence/ Languedoc	–	GAUL
North African	Tunisia/ Libya	–	NACA
Kapitän II ('Hollow foot')	Aegean	13	HOFA
B4 ('micaceous jars')	Asia Minor	20	B4
Dressel 30	Algeria	–	–
Campanian cylindrical	Campania	6	MRCA
Gaza amphoras	Gaza	4	–
Other eastern amphoras	East Mediterranean	–	–

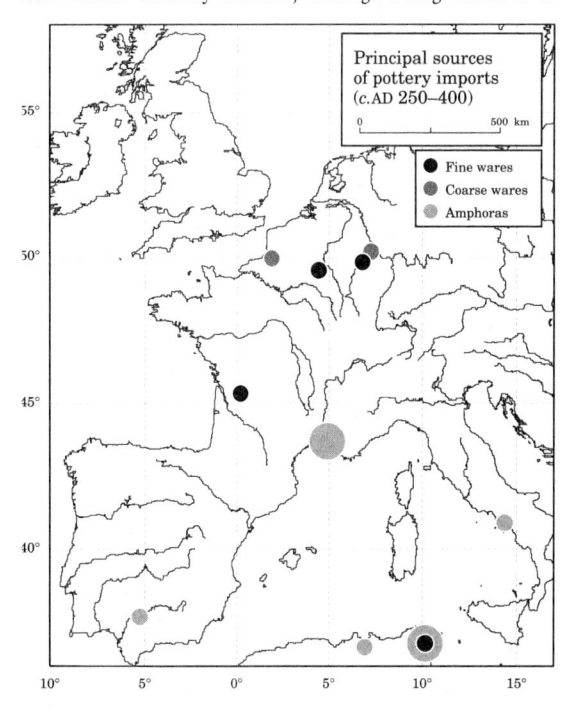

42 Sources of pottery imports to Britain, c. AD 250–400

Table 24 Types of pottery imported to Britain, c. AD 250–400

A short history of Roman pottery in Britain

Romano-British pottery on the Continent

The flip-side of the importation of pottery into the province at this period is the evidence for the export of Romano-British wares to the Continent. It has been recognized for some time that Romano-British pottery turns up on sites along the north French coast in some quantities (Fulford 1977b). Some of these vessels are the products of the major late Roman fine-ware industries – such as Oxfordshire and the New Forest – but the larger proportion are coarse wares. BB1 from Dorset is found in some quantity in Normandy and Brittany (Pilet 1987) and further east in the Pas-de-Calais and Flanders. Coarse wares from the south-east of England, such as the late BB2 of Essex and Kent, or the grey wares of the Alice Holt industry, are found with BB1 in third- and fourth-century levels at Boulogne. Boulogne was a naval base for the British fleet. Its British counterpart was Dover and coarse wares from northern Gaul can be identified in some numbers in the assemblages published from there (Philp 1981). We should probably consider the assemblages from these two sites together for the links between them are likely to be quite close, and it is probable that only the more obvious exports in either direction have been identified at present. Other sites associated with the fleet, such as the ironworking site at Beauport Park, Sussex have also yielded groups of north Gaulish grey wares and other unusual imports (Brodribb and Cleere 1988, 252-3). The immediate activities and supply lines to the fleet is certainly one mechanism behind the movement of pottery across the Channel during the third and fourth centuries, but there are others.

Good evidence of this comes from the wreck of a small cargo boat which sank in Guernsey harbour some time between AD 275 and 325 (Rule and Monaghan 1993). The small pottery assemblage is extremely diverse, and shows with startling clarity how wide a range of material could be brought together at one point, and could potentially at least come to rest almost anywhere along the north and west coasts of Gaul, or in Britain. The sources of the pottery in the wreck are listed in **table 25** and illustrated by the map (**43**). The Aquitanian fine ware, *céramique à l'éponge* is represented by two vessels. Its British mainland distribution of some forty sites is concentrated along the south and south-western coasts. One wonders how much of this arrived in small boats like the Guernsey wreck, and was taken ashore by the crew. The numbers of the different pottery types in the wreck may suggest that the vessel had a three-man crew; each of whom had, or at least used, a bowl, a jar and a large flagon, or reused amphora. The major cargo of the ship on this, its last trip, was half a ton of pitch-pine resin, and it was the conflagration of the latter that caused its demise. The pottery may be the markers of one of the routes of the vessel – perhaps between south-west France and Britain – but it is the pitch that is the principal item of trade. If it were not for the accidental destruction of the ship and its cargo, the pitch would probably have disappeared from the archaeological record. The pottery assemblage would have

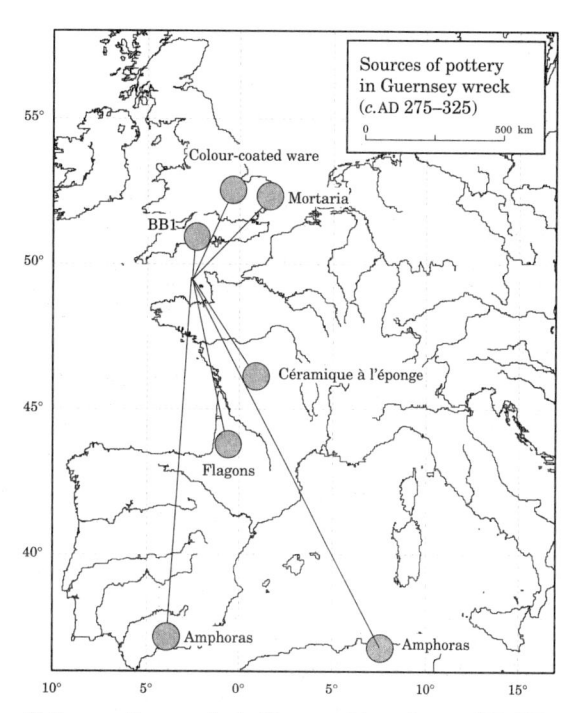

43 *Sources of pottery in the Guernsey shipwreck, c. AD 275–325*

Ware	Form		Source	ATLAS
Céramique à l'éponge	Bowl	Raimbault type VI	Aquitaine	EPON
Black burnished 1	Jar	Obtuse lattice	SW England	BB1
Black burnished 1	Bowl	Gillam 227/228	SW England	BB1
Dressel 30	Amphora		Algeria	
Almagro 55	Amphora		S Spain?	
Oxidized fabrics	Flagons		SW France?	
Nene Valley			E England	NVCC
East Anglian grey	Mortaria		E England	

Table 25 *Types of pottery in the Guernsey shipwreck, c. AD 275–325*

A short history of Roman pottery in Britain

dissolved into a few enigmatic points on our distribution maps, if ever the pots were finally taken ashore.

Fine wares

Red-slipped wares following samian prototypes were in production in the Oxfordshire industry by the AD 240s, and shortly after similar styles were being made in the Nene valley. A competitor to the Oxfordshire industry in southern Britain appeared in the New Forest, probably in the AD 260s (Atlas NFCC, NFMO). This was an independent development, perhaps founded by potters familiar with north-east Gaulish or Rhineland styles, and the ware is typologically distinguishable from the Oxfordshire product (Swan 1984, 109).

The distribution of Oxfordshire red-slipped wares expanded during the later third century, to cover much of the Thames valley, with extensions westward into the Severn plain. By *c.* AD 300 it was competing successfully with the New Forest potters along the south coast. This expansion was accompanied by migrations of Oxfordshire potters towards the margins of the distribution of the main factory. During the later third century 'Oxfordshire' red-slipped ware workshops were set up at Harston, Cambridgeshire, and also attached to the mortarium factory of Hartshill, Warwickshire (Bird and Young 1981, 303–9). The kiln used by these potters at Hartshill (Kiln G), has the typical tongue–support, corbels and solid clay floor of the Oxfordshire kilns (Swan 1984, 101), and is quite different to the form of the local tradition. Neither Harston nor Hartshill products are widely dispersed and both were short-lived. A later movement from Oxfordshire was responsible for the fourth-century Pevensey ware industry of Sussex, and there are other minor fabrics in south and western Britain which suggest the activities of Oxfordshire potters during this period (e.g. Zienkiewicz 1986, 58). The distinctive Oxfordshire kiln type was also used at several kiln sites in Berkshire and Buckinghamshire during the fourth century where grey wares were produced (Swan 1984, 104).

Mortaria

Mortaria from Oxfordshire have a wide distribution during the later third and fourth century, reaching from coast to coast across southern Britain (Atlas OXMO). The Mancetter–Hartshill industry remained in production throughout this period, and continued to be a major supplier to the north, where Oxfordshire products never reached. Other Midlands mortaria reached northern markets, such as those from the Nene valley, and there were also major producers in Yorkshire. At Cantley on the outskirts of Doncaster, production had started during the later second century, and included mortaria stamped by Virrinus, a potter working in the Mancetter–Hartshill style. Production continued into the third and fourth centuries, and mortaria from this site, now unstamped, are found at forts on the Wall and elsewhere in the north. Typologically they continued to resemble the

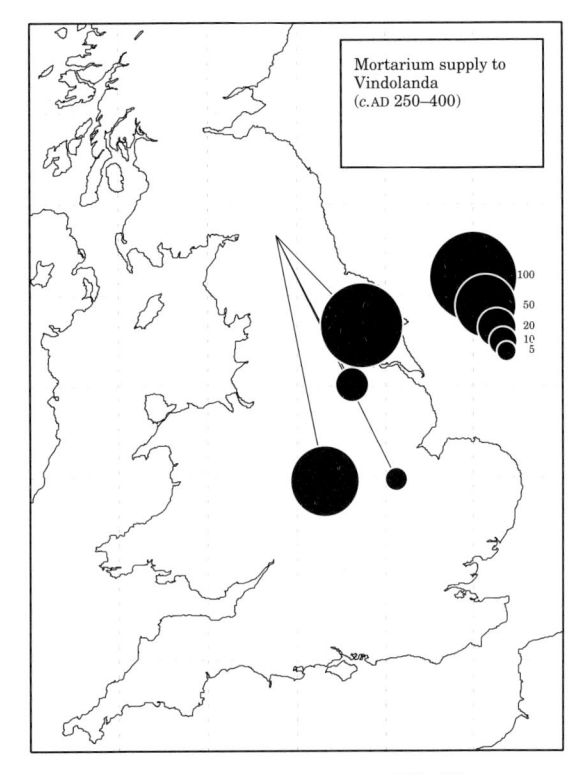

44 Mortarium supply to Vindolanda, c. AD 270–400

Midlands types.

The major new mortarium producer founded during the third century was at Crambeck, in Yorkshire (Atlas CRAM). Workshops set up here also made a limited range of red-slipped wares (of the standard post-sigillata shapes), a range of grey wares and light-coloured parchment wares. Stylistically, the industry seems to be an amalgam of different sources, but is not a transplant from one of the major southern British producers. The coarse-ware types may owe something to Lincolnshire. Crambeck mortaria are found in some numbers on Wall sites and across the north during the early fourth century (**44**).

Coarse wares

The history of the coarse-ware industry from the mid-third century can largely be written as the story of the rise to prominence of two pottery types: the everted-rim cooking pot and the flanged bowl. Both forms were developed by the Durotrigian potters of Dorset. The everted-rim jar had been the major jar form of the BB1 industry from the first century AD but the typological drift of the form had arrived at a shape that was relatively wide-mouthed, with a flaring rim and narrow decorated band, by the middle of the third century. The earlier BB1 pie-dish, with a short flat projecting rim, had been superseded by a form with a single groove marking the top of the rim during the early third century. The true conical

A short history of Roman pottery in Britain

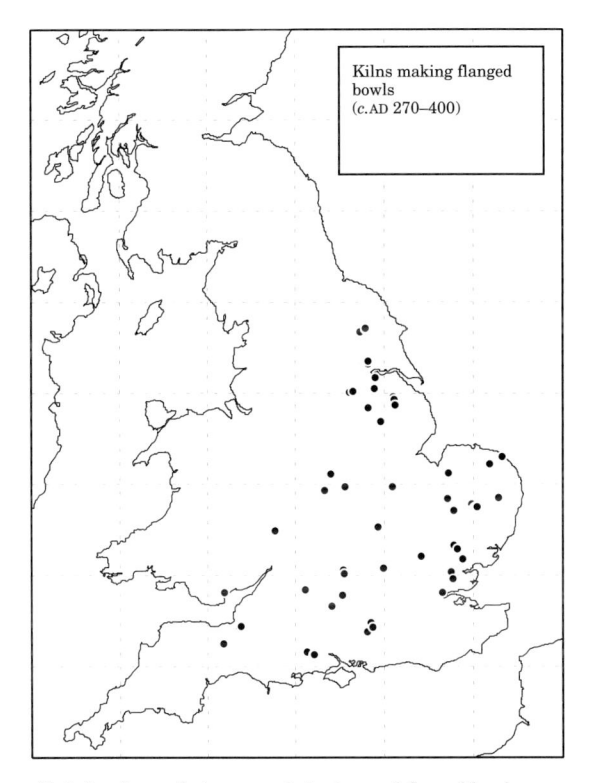

45 Industries producing everted-rim jars and flanged bowls, c. AD 270–400

flanged bowl, with the flange below the lip of the vessel which left the bead standing proud above, develops by c. AD 270, perhaps a decade or so earlier (Holbrook and Bidwell 1991, 98–9).

The everted-rim jar and flanged bowl proved almighty, not so much in the impact of the Durotrigian originals (although they did have a wide distribution into the fourth century), as in the effect on Britain's other coarse-ware industries. From the later third century onwards most existing industries adopted the everted-rim jar/flanged bowl combination into their repertoire, in some cases displacing the pre-existing jar and bowl forms, in others, produced alongside them. Where new industries were founded during the fourth century they invariably produced versions of these forms (**45**).

Some, such as the Thames-side industries of Kent and Essex which had already accommodated an adaptation of BB1 forms during the second century, succumbed a second time. The Alice Holt industry, which had been largely immune to the earlier advent of black-burnished wares, adopted flanged bowls and everted-rim jars. The coarse-ware producers attached to the major colour-coated industries – Nene valley and Oxfordshire – adopted the forms. This remarkable sweeping away of the opposition would in another context be interpreted as some form of cultural hegemony on the part of the inhabitants of Dorset. It results in a greater degree of homogeneity (some might say dullness) in the character of the ceramic repertoire than had been seen previously. This feeling is reinforced by the activities of the major fine-ware producers, who distributed their products (often again very similar) over large stretches of the province.

As in any case where near universality is the first impression, it is instructive to look again for the differences, and in this case it is resistance to the dominant typological combination. In the Midlands and north, several distinctive jar forms circulated during the third century that owe nothing to the black-burnished everted-rim jar. Derbyshire ware, with its distinctive bell-shaped mouth, had its widest circulation during the third century (Atlas DERBY). The most likely origin of this shape are the ledge-rim jars of south-east Midlands introduced into Derbyshire during the later Flavian period (see p. 64). The Dales ware jar of north Lincolnshire again seems to owe nothing to the Durotrigian forms, indeed it may have rather exotic origins, distantly related to the Mediterranean-influenced potters of York (Atlas DALES). In the south, the shelly industries of Bedfordshire continued to produce necked jars with horizontal rilling on the body, derived from indigenous forms. These were to become important from the middle of the fourth century, when the industry underwent a massive expansion (Atlas LRSH).

Romano-Saxon wares

This is an appropriate point to touch on the problem of *Romano-Saxon* pottery. The term was first coined by J. N. L. Myres in 1944, and the general line of argument about this material can be traced through a series of papers from the 1950s onwards (Myres 1956; Myres 1969; Gillam 1979; Roberts 1982; Myres 1986, 89–96). The name was applied to 'a class of hybrid... pottery combining Romano-British mass-production methods with decoration of a Saxon kind'; in short, kiln-fired wheel-thrown wares decorated with grooves, bosses, depressions and dimples that were considered to be reminiscent of the Anglo-Saxon style. The largely East Anglian distribution of such wares – coinciding with areas of known early Anglo-Saxon settlement – reinforced the view that the material was produced by Romano-British potters in response to the tastes of Anglo-Saxon settlers in eastern England. The material turns up in otherwise purely Romano-British contexts of the fourth century and was considered to be evidence of a 'hidden' population of Anglo-Saxon settlers in eastern England during this period – somewhat before the previously accepted dates for their arrival.

The supposed Saxon character of the Romano-Saxon decorative style was questioned by J. P. Gillam (1979) who pointed to earlier Roman pottery types that carried the same motifs. It also became clear that the particular Anglo-Saxon decorative styles were too late – from the end of the fifth century – to serve as potential prototypes for Romano-British potters of the fourth century. Such similarity as did exist between late Roman and Saxon decorative motifs could be explained by

A short history of Roman pottery in Britain

their common influence from the decoration on late Roman metalwork and glassware.

A high proportion of the known Romano-Saxon material is now considered to be the product of the kilns at Hadham on the Hertfordshire–Essex border (Atlas HARS). This industry produced a range of orange- and grey- slipped and burnished wares from the mid-third century. Some vessels are in the standard late Roman red-slipped (post-sigillata) tradition and there is a distinctive range of flagons. Others are decorated with combinations of bosses, dimples or stamps, or other more sophisticated techniques including moulded and appliqué animals and human faces. Once we remove the Hadham products from the corpus of Romano-Saxon vessels, what are we left with? Some are the products of smaller regional kilns – such as those at Chelmsford, Inworth and Thurrock, in Essex (Swan 1984, nos. 272, 292, 303) – which are perhaps directly influenced by the Hadham potters. Vessels in the Romano-Saxon style also formed a small part of the output of other major fine-ware industries such as those in the Nene valley.

There is no evidence for any ethnic connection in the flowering of the Romano-Saxon style and it should be seen as a facet of late Roman fine wares. We could point to the vogue for highly decorated stamped wares across much the same area of eastern England during the second century as an earlier parallel for a regional fine-ware style – and some of these were also from Hadham (Atlas LEST).

Germanic pottery in Britain

The removal of the Romano-Saxon concept from the scene does not mean that there is no evidence of Germanic pottery styles in Britain during the Roman period. On the contrary there is at least one example where it seems tolerably clear that pottery styles from outside the Empire – or at least from the margins of it – were carried to Britain by a Germanic population. Among the pottery from the Hadrian's Wall forts of Housesteads, Chesterholm and Birdoswald there is a quantity of coarse handmade ware with finely burnished black exteriors and characteristic angular rim forms. This material – labelled Housesteads ware – shows close parallels with material from the Frisian Islands of north Germany and the Netherlands (Jobey 1979, following up a suggestion by Gillam). Two military units with German names are recorded from altar inscriptions in the Housesteads area during the third century AD: the *Numerus Hnaudifridi*, Nottfried's unit, and the *Cuneus Frisiorum*, the cuneus of Frisians; both *numerus* and *cuneus* are descriptions of units of the late Roman army. The probable area of origin of these troops coincides with the region identified as the source of the Housesteads ware style. The picture is not perfectly cut-and-dried, for there are some slight discrepancies between the dating of the Housesteads ware sherds on the various sites, and the relationship with the continental material, while close, is not exact. Nevertheless it seems reasonably clear that a group of Germans, almost certainly from the boundaries of the Empire, and part of a military force, were settled enough on Britain's northern frontier to turn their hand to pottery making (**46**).

The interesting question that arises is who, precisely, was making the pots. Two possibilities spring to mind. One is that the soldiers themselves were responsible for this material. The forming and firing of hand-formed pottery is not a skill that is

46 The origins of Housesteads ware

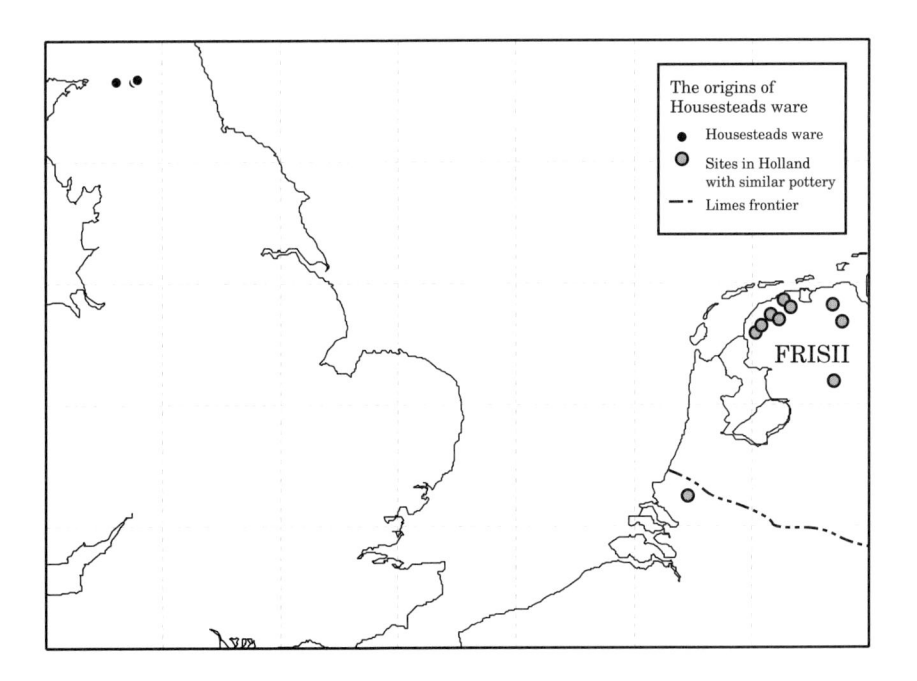

acquired by mere observation, but pottery manufacture may have been a normal male role. The picture of the rough, tough soldiers spending wet afternoons making pots may not ring quite true, and ethnographic studies suggest that the production of hand-formed pots for domestic use is frequently (but not universally) the female preserve. The possibility that Housesteads ware represents the activities of Germanic women rather than men should be considered, and the presence of complete family groups, men, women and by implication children, at this date in Britain may be important for the interpretation of the references to German soldiers serving in the Roman army. While adequate local pottery supplies were available at Housesteads and the other sites where these wares are found, it may be that these special handmade wares were deemed necessary for the preparation of some traditional recipes. In the modern world, the survival of traditional pottery manufacturing may only be supported by its continued use as an adjunct to traditional food preparations, where the taste or other desirable culinary benefits of using traditional pots is considered important (Arnold 1985, 139).

4.7 THE END OF ROMAN POTTERY IN BRITAIN
The final flourish

From c. AD 350 there are new developments in the Romano-British pottery industry which form the backdrop to the final decline of the early fifth century (**table 26**). Amongst the large-scale producers of the earlier period there seems to have been a reduction in the number of forms and a simultaneous decline in the range and extent of decorative techniques (Fulford 1979, 121–2). In the Oxfordshire potteries, for instance, no significant additions to the range of forms and decoration were made from about AD 350 (Young 1977b, 240). In the New Forest industry few new forms were introduced after the middle of the century – rather the repertoire was shrinking and production was in decline throughout this period (Fulford 1975a, 116). This phenomenon was evidently not universal. Some industries, such as Much Hadham, extended their range at this time (Going 1992, 101), but many concentrated more and more on the black-burnished derived jar and bowl types. Alongside this retreat to a simpler and less elaborately decorated suite of vessels is a marked change in the distribution of products from many industries. Oxfordshire mortaria had been used on sites around the Thames estuary since the second century, but the red-slipped wares were relatively uncommon there until the mid-fourth century, after which they take an increasing share of the market (Pollard 1988, 138–40; Going 1987, 118). A similar process was taking place at the western limits of the Oxfordshire distribution and along the south coast, where Oxfordshire wares displaced New Forest wares at sites such as Portchester (Fulford 1975b, 285–6).

We can identify a similar late flourish in the coarse-ware industries. The expansion of distribution of the shell-tempered industry of the south-east Midlands is dramatic (Atlas LRSH). This style had a long history, stretching in an unbroken line back into the first century AD and the Late Iron Age (see p. 55). Until c. AD 350, or a decade or so later, the ware had a relatively limited, local distribution, but thereafter, the distinctive jars with horizontally rilled surfaces are found across southern Britain, from Wales to East Anglia. Although they remain most abundant in their homeland, they form significant proportions of assemblages in both the west (e.g. 5 per cent at Bath: Cunliffe and Davenport 1985) and the east (10 per cent at Canterbury: Pollard 1988, 243) by the late fourth century.

Industry	ATLAS
Alice Holt – Farnham	AHFA
East Yorkshire (Crambeck/Knapton)	CRAM
Late Roman grog-tempered wares (Hants/Sussex/Kent)	LRGR
Mancetter–Hartshill	MHMO
Much Hadham	HARS
New Forest	NFCC NFMO
Oxfordshire	OXRS OXMO
South-east Dorset	BB1
South-east Midlands shell-tempered	LRSH

Table 26 *Major late Romano-British industries*

A related phenomenon is the appearance of imitations of the principal shell-tempered form in other fabrics. Potters in the Alice Holt Forest adopted the rilled jar and developed a coarse buff-coloured fabric (Portchester fabric D) (Atlas PORD) for its production, while continuing to use their fine-textured grey sandy wares for other forms. Portchester fabric D enjoyed some success in the south-east counties (Kent, Surrey and Sussex) during the later fourth century and, with the Midlands shelly wares, is one of the hallmarks of the latest groups in the London area. Jars which were apparently influenced by the shell-tempered wares appear elsewhere in southern Britain. Late in the sequence at Bath there is a coarse grey or red-brown sandy fabric, apparently of local origin, which copies the hooked-rim, rilled jars of the Midlands (Cunliffe and Davenport 1985, fabric 10.1). There are certain echoes here of the behaviour of BB1 during the second century – a rapid expansion in distribution followed by local imitation of both form and fabric. One wonders what might have happened if this development had not been curtailed by the events of the early fifth century.

Other southern industries also expanded at this period. Jars, and particularly larger storage jars, from the Alice Holt potteries (Atlas AHFA) have been identified from the latest levels of many Roman settlements across southern Britain, extending north of the Thames into the Midlands and into the west, suggesting some expansion in distribution towards the end of the century (Lyne and Jefferies 1979, fig. 50). In eastern England, the Nene Valley industry distributed its new range of 'colour-coated coarse wares' (inevitably influenced by the black-burnished style) across the southern part of the country by the end of the century (Atlas NVCC).

In northern Britain the later fourth century saw the rise of the potteries of east Yorkshire, and they supplied the majority of the pottery along the Wall by the end of the century. The potteries at Crambeck and other sites in the vicinity of the fort at Malton (Atlas CRAM) produced a complete range of grey wares, parchment wares (including mortaria) and red-slipped wares. Coarse shell-gritted Huntcliff wares, probably from the same area, became the principal cooking pot in the latest Roman levels on sites across the north. The particular success of the east Yorkshire potters may be linked with some form of new marketing arrangement with the quartermasters of the northern armies, but against the background of developments in the south we may see that an expansion at this period is almost the norm for any industry that was a going concern, rather than the exception prompted by military contracts.

Another aspect of the later fourth century was the appearance (or more strictly the reappearance) in some regions of hand-formed wares (Atlas LRGR). In Sussex the production of simple grog-tempered wares extended, again in an unbroken line, back to the pre-conquest period, but we witness a period of increased popularity from the mid-fourth century (C. M. Green 1980a). In common with most contemporary industries the late repertoire was heavily influenced by black-burnished prototypes. In east Kent, the latter half of the fourth century saw the rise of such wares to a point of almost total dominance of the coarse-ware assemblage. The latest deposits from sites such as Canterbury and Wye include little more than hand-formed grog-tempered wares (up to 70 per cent), Midlands shell-tempered wares, Portchester D, and a light garnish of Oxfordshire red-slipped wares and mortaria, and colour-coated wares from the Nene valley (Pollard 1988, 243). Heavy-mineral analysis of the late Roman grog-tempered wares from Portchester (Fulford 1975b, 286–92) suggests that they were supplied from three or four sources – not from a multiplicity of small 'household' producers. Despite their simpler technology, these wares are the work of potters working well within the norms of standard late Roman pottery rather than some crude reflection of sub-Roman degeneration.

The result of all these changes seems to have been the concentration on a smaller simpler repertoire that was often distributed over larger areas. The reduction in decoration seen on many types during the fourth century will have reduced the time taken on each vessel, which might indicate there was a need for faster and larger-scale production. What is not so clear is whether the surviving large producers were competing for a smaller and shrinking market, or an expanding one. However, the net result across much of the country was that while there may have been several potential sources for each class of ware (such as mortaria or cooking pots) in each region, there often was not very much to differentiate between them.

The fifth century

There are three interrelated topics that must be addressed by the study of the pottery of the very end of the Roman period. Firstly, there is the date when the earliest Germanic pottery appears in England; secondly, the date at which the Roman pottery industry ceases to operate and the circumstances of its collapse, and finally, there is the question of how long Roman pottery might remain in use, after it is no longer being manufactured.

The date at which the earliest Germanic pottery appears in England has been the subject of varying interpretations over the years. The view of J. N. L. Myres, expressed most forcefully in the report on the cemeteries at Caistor-by-Norwich (Myres and Green 1973), was that Germanic pottery was present in East Anglia from as early as the third century AD. The long period of overlap indicated by such a date was in part supported by the suggestion that 'Romano-Saxon' wares were produced for the use of a population with Germanic tastes in decoration. The basis of the early date for these wares from Caistor and elsewhere – principally a series of links between very long-lived forms and rather imperfectly dated continental sequences – has now been questioned, and the Romano-Saxon wares seem more at home as a standard, if highly decorated, late Roman fine ware. A recent assessment of the early Saxon pottery from the site of Mucking, beside the Thames in Essex, places the earliest settlement in the period AD 420–50, and there seems to be little indication from elsewhere of any Saxon pottery that predates this (Hamerow 1993).

After AD 402 no new bronze coinage was shipped into Britain, and, unlike earlier periods of shortage of official coinage, no attempts were made at local counterfeiting (Esmonde Cleary 1989, 140). Some commentators suggest that this lack of interest in covering the shortfall in official supplies suggests a reduction in the scale of economic activity, or perhaps the massive coinage imports of the previous period had built up a sufficient stock in circulation to cover all needs. Whatever the case, the dearth of new bronze after AD 402 has a direct follow-through into a rather insecure archaeological chronology after that date.

However, at many sites we can recognize sequences of stratigraphy after the latest coins, and sometimes these are quite extensive. One approach to the construction of an archaeological framework for such levels is what might be termed 'stratigraphic analogy'. Thus, if the post-coin stratigraphy consists of a series of worn cobbled floors, or a sequence of repairs and refurbishment of a road, then it may be possible to calculate the time-spans covered by examining similar activities in earlier, but more tightly dated sequences from elsewhere on the same or a similar site.

One sequence that has been examined by such methods is from the temple precinct at Bath. The stratigraphic evidence is described and discussed by Cunliffe and Davenport (1985) and is conveniently summarized by Esmonde Cleary (1989, 155–7). The key sequence is a series of six levels of cobbling (phases 5a–5f) separated by accumulations of earth, and the whole block sealed above and below from contamination and residual material. The lowest level (5a) seals a coin of Constans (AD 347–8), and level 5c, one of Theodosius (AD 388–402). The extrapolated chronology of this sequence, leaving adequate time for each accumulation and reflooring, places the end well into the fifth century ('perhaps even into the early sixth'), with consequent significant implications for the later Roman pottery it contains (Cunliffe and Davenport 1985, 74–5).

The pottery report (by C. J. Young and S. Green) takes a rather different line. They prefer a shorter chronology, perhaps terminating no later than the AD 410s. The pottery in the levels with the latest coin (5c) is, within the limits of our knowledge, what might be expected from a late fourth-century group. It includes shelly wares from the Midlands and a range of late Oxfordshire red-slipped products. The next two phases (5d–e) contain more shelly wares and a local imitation in a buff sandy ware. Thus there are clearly potters capable of copying new styles and forms, and considering it worthwhile to do so. Through phases 5c–5e the proportion of BB1 is declining, but a range of new late types appears in the last phase. The known expansion of the south-east Midlands shelly wares at the end of the fourth century, and the retreat of BB1, are clearly being reflected in this group. Although there are clearly changes in the proportions of wares right up to the latest levels this need not imply a dynamic pottery industry responding to demand. The differences in proportions could equally well be the effect of the differing lifespans of the pottery types, with the assemblage in the successive phases representing the 'decay curve' of a shrinking base population. It may be possible to test this by assessing the brokenness of the assemblage (Going 1992). Alternatives to the stratigraphic analogy approach are, unfortunately, thin on the ground. Datable imports are of little help. Many of the amphora types that are known to circulate in the Mediterranean through the fifth century, and reappear briefly in western Britain in the early sixth century (see p. 81), have long pedigrees stretching back into the fourth or even third centuries AD (Atlas B4, NACA).

We can now look at the question of how long Roman pottery remained in use into the fifth century. This has been examined on a number of Saxon sites in eastern England. The problem is to try and distinguish material that might have been in use alongside Saxon pottery from a normal assemblage of residual Roman pottery, incorporated into later levels. At West Stow (Suffolk) and Heybridge (Essex) the assemblages of Roman pottery from the infill of Saxon *Grubenhäuser* seem to be significantly different from a standard late Roman group, both in terms of the range of fabrics and the types of sherds. At West Stow no less than 77 per cent of the Roman pottery was either Oxfordshire slipped wares or Nene Valley colour-coated wares. The comparable figures from stratified late Roman assemblages at local sites was only 20 per cent. The West Stow assemblages were also dominated by 'significant' sherds, that is rims, bases or decorated pieces (West 1985). At Heybridge there was a similar pattern, with high proportions of Oxfordshire slipped wares from Saxon *Grubenhäuser* (Drury and Wickenden 1982). At the Pennyland site, Milton Keynes, the range of wares in the Saxon levels again differed from that on late Roman sites in the region, with a bias towards lighter-coloured and/or finer-textured sherds. However there was no clear preference towards rim and base sherds in this group (R. J. Williams 1993, 244–5) and it is suggested that whole vessels may have been introduced to the site. In contrast, the picture at Mucking (Essex) is inconclusive with no clear evidence for the selection of Roman pottery in Saxon levels (Going in Hamerow 1993, 71–2). So in some cases it seems that Saxons were picking up brighter, finer or more interesting sherds from Roman sites, and perhaps occasionally complete vessels (**table 27**).

Site	Rim sherds	Base sherds (percentages)	Body sherds
Roman			
Milton Keynes	15	8	77
Icklingham	22	8	70
Saxon			
Pennyland	29	11	58
West Stow	19	44	37

Table 27 *Comparison of sherd types of Roman material from Roman and Saxon contexts*

The possible reuse of Roman pottery during the post-Roman period is also relevant to the interpretation of material from elsewhere in the country. At Cadbury-Congresbury, Somerset, there is a substantial collection of Roman pottery and other artefacts from a reused hilltop settlement, occupied during the fifth and sixth centuries AD, by a sub-Roman (British) population. Roman material there, it is argued, is not the residue of occupation on the hill during the first to fourth century AD, but rather was carried to the site during the post-Roman period 'at a time when such artefacts were scarce, no longer manufactured and unlikely to be replaced' (Rahtz *et al.*

1992, 228). Some of these objects may have been in the personal possession of the individuals who moved to the hilltop, but others were perhaps robbed from known Roman sites, such as cemeteries, for reuse during the post-Roman period. In addition to this Romano-British material these levels include a few amphoras and fine wares that were imported during the fifth and sixth centuries (which we shall discuss in more detail below), but the only pottery that may have been made on or near the site in the post-Roman period is a rather poor handmade chaff-tempered ware, barely distinguishable technologically from the Iron Age fabrics of the area, but with one or two pieces showing a distant typological echo of late Roman forms.

Some writers prefer to base their date for the demise of the Romano-British pottery industry on the dating of the general collapse of the economy and other aspects of the Romano-British life-style (such as the towns) which were supporting the ceramics industry. Using this method, it has been suggested that the industry had disappeared as a recognizable entity by *c.* AD 420 or 430 (Esmonde Cleary 1989, 144). While such estimates are the best that we have at the moment, they make the assumption that the activities of the major pottery industries were dependent on and to some extent the product of a coin-using economy. The link may not in fact have been very strong. Coin usage in rural areas may have been declining during the later fourth century, when pottery distributions were still extensive, and in some cases increasing. The major late Roman industries may have been located to exploit the adjacent *civitas* networks (Millett 1990) and part of the distribution mechanisms may have been outside the coin using economy.

The products of smaller local industries (rural or urban) may likewise have been distributed using embedded networks within a *civitas*, outside the coin-using system. There is no evidence at present that smaller local industries survived in any significant degree beyond the end of the life of the major producers, although such assemblages might be difficult to identify, if they existed. Given these possibilities, the absence of coinage *per se*, or any other single factor such as the loss of urban markets, may not be sufficient to explain the end of the industry.

A broader social collapse must be the underlying cause. It is notable that there is apparently no typological or technological influence from the Romano-British pottery industries of the fourth century on pagan Saxon pottery. Even the simpler handmade wares of the later Roman period – such as the grog-tempered fabrics of south-east England – do not seem to have continued through into the Saxon period. Although such fabrics share many of the technological characteristics of Saxon pottery – hand-formed and open firings – they are evidently not the products of household industries, and they did not continue in production across into the fifth century (Pollard 1988, 160–1).

The pottery of post-Roman Gaul

We could instructively compare the situation in England with that apparent in post-Roman Gaul. Across much of France and the Rhineland the Romanized pottery styles – and in many cases the industries themselves – continued across the political upheavals of the fifth and sixth centuries and provided the foundation of the pottery industries of early post-Roman France. For example, the production in the Mayen region, exploiting the coarse high-firing clays of the Eifel mountains, continued through the fifth to seventh centuries to re-emerge as a major source of pottery for the Rhineland in the eighth century. Some of the forms of the later industry (including single-handled flagons and moulded-rim jars) seem to be the descendants of the late Roman forms (Redknap 1988). Elsewhere across northern Gaul similar continuity of style can be observed in some coarse-ware industries. The wheel-thrown, high-fired coarse pottery of the Frankish period – collectively termed Romano-Frankish – owes much in both technology and typology to its late Roman precursors.

In fine wares too, the ultimate descendants of the sigillata industries of the early Empire were widely distributed across south and western France during the fifth to seventh centuries. Known collectively as *dérivées de sigillée paléochrétienne* or DSP these wares are marked by combinations of stamped and rouletted decorations on bowls, plates and jars. Both grey and orange versions were produced and there were a number of distinct regional groupings of both form and fabric, suggesting production at several centres. The echoes of the arrangement of the major regional late Roman industries are clear. As we shall see below (p. 81), a little of this material is carried from western France to Britain during the sixth century, but for the moment we should note the continuity of late Roman styles through into the post-Roman period. The grey DSP of Aquitaine was indeed generally referred to as Visigothic ware, for this region had passed into effective Visigothic control in AD 419.

Returning to Britain, the absence of such continuity in the Romano-British pottery industry need not imply that the late-Roman population itself had disappeared. Their presence is apparent in the sparse historical record, but they are not making pots.

4.8 BYZANTIUM AND THE WESTERN SEAWAYS

An interesting postscript to the history of Roman pottery in Britain is the importation of pottery of the late fifth and sixth centuries to sites in western Britain. This material was first identified in the 1940s at Tintagel in Cornwall, but small numbers of these vessels are now also known from sites in the south-west, Wales and around the south and east coasts of Ireland and western Scotland (C. Thomas 1981; Campbell in Edwards and Lane 1988). Most of these sites have yielded only a few sherds, perhaps representing a single vessel, though the assemblages from Dinas Powys (Glamorgan) and Cadbury-Congresbury (Avon) are more substantial. Tintagel is by far the largest group with many hundreds of sherds (**table 28, 47**).

The material in question comprises amphoras (generally in very micaceous fabrics or with rilled surfaces), fine red tablewares, some with stamped decoration, fine grey wares (also stamped) and wheel-thrown grey wares. The original alphabetical classification based on this material (British A, B, D, E) remains a convenient shorthand particularly for some of the amphora categories, but has been replaced in part by classifications devised to cover the same material on Mediterranean sites.

This material can be considered in two parts. The first suggests contact with the Mediterranean via the Straits of Gibraltar, and this is responsible for the amphoras and fine red-slipped wares. The origins of most of the amphoras is reasonably clear. The Bv is a Tunisian oil amphora, but the majority (Bi, Bii, Biv) are from the north-east Mediterranean – Asia Minor, the Aegean and Greece. The tablewares are from two sources: Ai, the most common, is Phocaean red-slipped ware (Atlas PRSW) from western Asia Minor, but the remainder, Aii, is North African (Atlas NARS). Some of these pottery types have roots stretching back into the late Roman period, and indeed even earlier. North African red-slip wares appear sporadically in Britain from the first century AD, and African amphoras from the middle of the second. Micaceous amphoras of the Biv variety were imported sporadically during the third and fourth centuries. The stamps on some of the PRSW dishes include crosses and other Christian motifs.

This imported assemblage is particularly interesting on a number of counts. The range of amphora and fine-ware types is not, as might have been thought, a representative selection of the principal wares circulating in the west Mediterranean, which would have been dominated by African wares. Rather, the strongly north-east Mediterranean character of the amphora and fine-ware assemblage suggests a more direct interest from Byzantium, the modern Istanbul (Fulford 1989). The principal PRSW form in the British assemblage (Hayes form 3) has an extensive distribution around the west Mediterranean, and the British specimens can be seen as the 'bow wave' of trade from the east, probably dated between AD 475 and 550. In Britain this may only represent one or two visits, with a ship coast-hopping from one harbour to another.

The British material of this phase is not entirely isolated. There is a growing body of comparable data from Brittany and the Channel Islands, and PRSW is a notable element of the assemblage at Conimbriga on the Portuguese coast, perhaps indicating the route taken by the boats from Byzantium. On this model, the African and perhaps the Aquitanian grey wares, would have been picked up *en route* to Britain, but it is the PRSW and north-east Mediterranean amphoras that betray their origin. Fulford points to the tin of the south-west as a motive force behind these contacts (1989, 4-5) and places them in the historical context of the contacts between the Byzantine world and Britain indicated by the written sources.

The second phase overlaps geographically and chronologically with the first, but is generally later, and has a wider distribution in Ireland and western Scotland. It can be seen as a continuation of the contacts between Britain and France along the western seaways, which was seen in the third and fourth centuries with the cross-Channel distributions of Aquitanian *céramique à l'éponge* and south-western (British) BB1. The principal ware marking this zone of contact is the

Class	Number of vessels	Source	Name	Contents	ATLAS
Table wares					
Ai	46	Asia Minor, Phocaea	Phocaean red-slipped	-	PRSW
Aii	16	Tunisia	African red-slipped	-	NARS
Amphoras					
Bi	41	Aegean/Black Sea	Late Roman 2	wine?	
Bii	62	Cilicia/Antioch	Late Roman 1	oil	
Biv	9	Asia Minor, Sardis?	B4	oil?	B4
Bv	3	Tunisia	African cylindrical	oil	NACA
Grey wares					
D	21	Gaul, Aquitaine	DSP	-	
E	144	Gaul (?western)	E-ware	-	EWARE

Table 28 *Types of imported pottery in western Britain*, c. AD 475-550 *(after Thomas)*

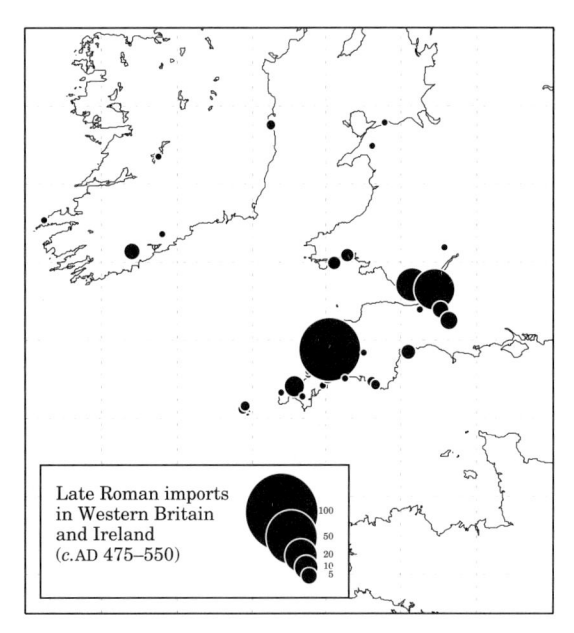

A short history of Roman pottery in Britain

47 *Distribution of imported pottery in western Britain c. AD 475-550*

enigmatic class E (Peacock and Thomas 1967; Campbell 1984, with comments by Peacock and Hodges). Thomas (C. Thomas 1990, 2) has reasserted the 'continuing Gallo-Roman character' of class E (Atlas EWARE). The group is sufficiently uniform in texture to imply a source that is no more diffuse 'than one group of commercial potters and kilns in a restricted locality'. Unfortunately this locality still eludes us, although somewhere in the basin of the two major rivers of western France, the Gironde and the Loire, seems to be the strongest candidate. There must be a strong possibility that production at this site (or sites) is continuous from the late Roman period, when plausible prototypes are in circulation, into the seventh century AD. As with earlier pottery distributions, this one may have piggy-backed on the transport of some other commodity; a trade in wine in casks or barrels between France and the Celtic west is attested in the documentary sources (ibid., 17). On the Cornish sites where Class E is found the only local ceramics are simple dishes and cooking pots in a handmade grass-marked ware. There is no sign of any residual Romano-British potting here.

To the reader of a history of Roman pottery in Britain a certain feeling of *déjà vu* may be excused. Here at the trailing edge of history we again have contact between the Mediterranean and the tin-rich lands of south-west Britain, marked by amphoras carrying the fruits of Classical civilization to the cold lands of the north. As Thomas points out, the still mysterious site on the remote headland of Tintagel must hold the key to this part of the story. But there the analogy must end, for the worlds inhabited by the imbiber of Italian wines at Hengistbury Head and the users of the oils and wines of the exotic east at Tintagel were separated by far more than just the intervening centuries.

PART TWO

Atlas and guide to Roman pottery in Britain

The subject of ancient pottery discovered in this country would of itself, if fully treated on, make a volume; for it has a very wide range, and would embrace numerous classes and an almost infinity of types.

Charles Roach Smith, 1855

INTRODUCTION TO THE ATLAS

Each ware is described in a consistent format, and accompanied by illustrations and a map showing the distribution of the ware in Britain and, where appropriate, the continental distribution. The types for inclusion in the Atlas have been chosen principally to illustrate the arguments and themes marshalled in the main text. The 1992 issue of the Roman Pottery Bibliography in the *Journal of Roman Pottery Studies* lists some 279 recognized pottery types or classes. Many of these will be locally abundant and significant, but perhaps very limited in their distribution. Some wares such as these have been included in the Atlas, but most will be wares of either national or regional significance.

There is no standard sequence for presentation of ceramic types in a report, but the ordering here seeks to balance the needs of grouping together physically similar wares with grouping together vessels by source, function or date.

Amphoras	p.85
Terra sigillata	p.105
Mortaria	p.116
Imported wares	p.135
Romano-British fine wares	p.166
Romano-British coarse wares	p.180

Each section is headed by an introduction to the group. Cross-referencing within the Atlas, and from the main text to the appropriate Atlas entries, is facilitated by the use of

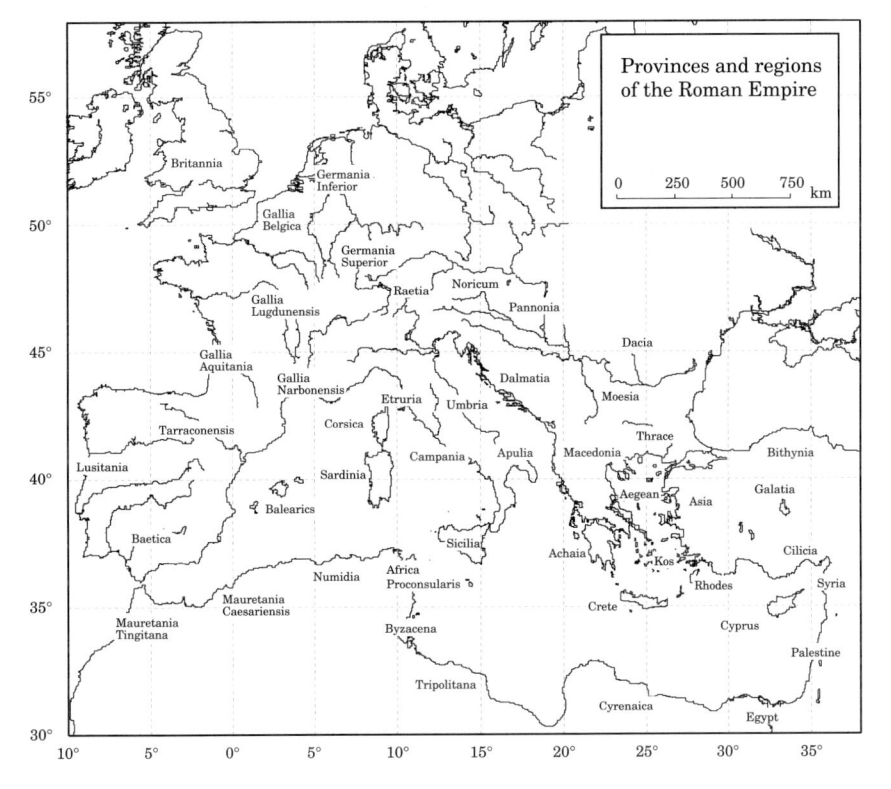

48 *Provinces and regions of the Roman Empire*

Atlas and guide to Roman pottery in Britain

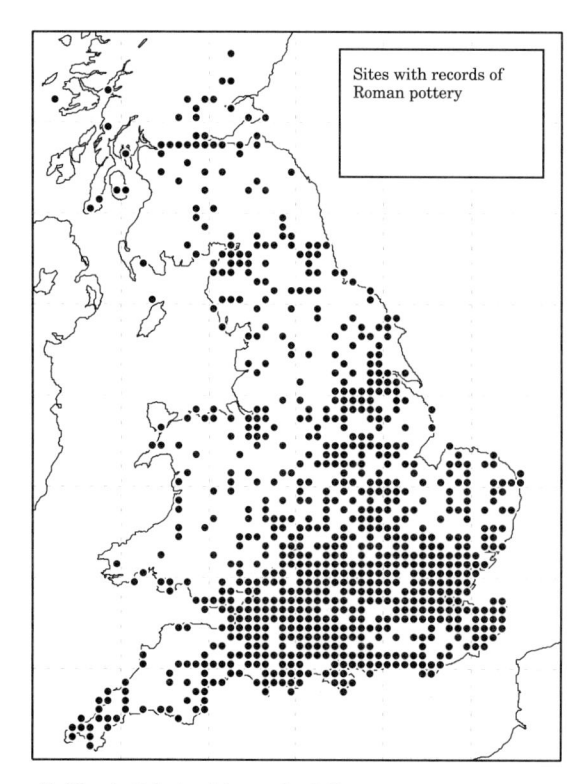

49 Sites in Britain with records of Roman pottery

simple three or four character codes.

Fabric and technology

A description of the principal ware(s), where possible following the conventions set out in Orton, Tyers and Vince (1993, 231–42). Munsell colours refer to the *Munsell Soil Color Chart* (Munsell Color Company 1975).

These descriptions are compiled from numerous sources, including first-hand observation, where possible. The precise fabric descriptions published by J. R. Timby (in Hurst 1985), P. Bidwell and N. Holbrook (1991), P. T. Marney (1989), C. J. Going (1987) and the Department of Urban Archaeology of the Museum of London (C. M. Green 1980b; B. Richardson 1986) have proved particularly valuable for cross-referencing and confirmation of details.

Forms

The principal forms in the ware(s), referenced to illustrations.

Stamps

Location and character, where present. Lists of the principal potters' stamps on mortaria and their dating are included here.

Average capacity

Where appropriate, particularly for amphoras.

Chronology

The dates of production, and date of distribution in Britain. This is summarized on a vertical bar-chart, which is usually adjacent to the first map.

Source

Where known, and usually indicated on the maps with a diamond. Many imported pottery types are conventionally referred to by the name of the Roman province where they were produced (**48**).

Principal contents

Where appropriate, particularly for amphoras.

Distribution

The distribution maps are compiled almost entirely from published sources, and while they do not claim to be complete they should give a reasonable indication of the distribution of most wares. Where the distribution is likely to be particularly

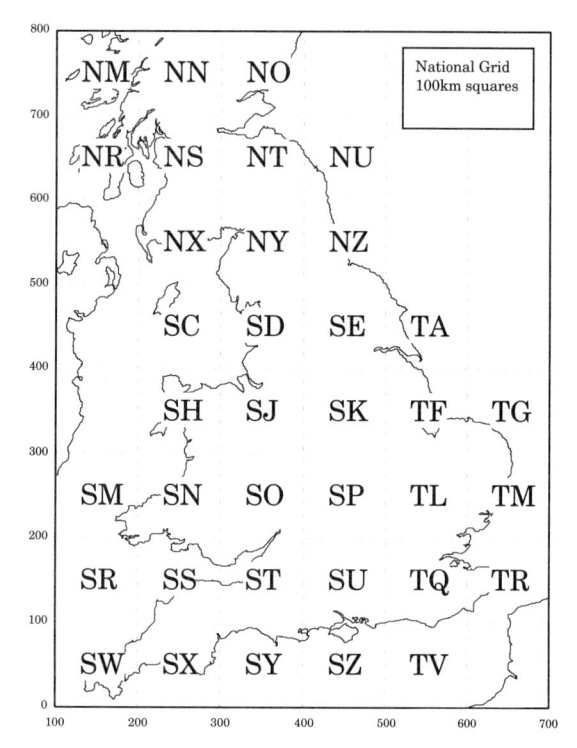

50 Letter codes for 100km National Grid squares

incomplete (due to mis-identifications or poor recording) this is noted.

The principal sources for the British distribution maps are:

1. Detailed studies of major industries (e.g. Fulford 1975a; Young 1977b; Lyne and Jefferies 1979; Wilson 1989).

2. Regional surveys such as that by Pollard (1988) or studies of urban assemblages that incorporate significant data on their regional background (e.g. Holbrook and Bidwell 1991, on Exeter and the south-west).

3. The lists of pottery types in the Roman Pottery Bibliography, published in the *Journal of Roman*

Pottery Studies, vols 1–5 (1986–92) – with corrections and additions.

4. The distributions of mortarium stamps reported by K. F. Hartley in numerous published studies (e.g. 1984).
5. Lists of pottery types compiled from other published sources.

On the British maps, one point usually represents a single site where the ware is recorded. Some very dense distributions are reduced to a smoothed 10km grid, where one point represents one or more sites within a 10km grid square. In a few cases where reliable quantified data is available this is shown as circles of different diameters, centered over the location of the site. The British distribution maps should be read in conjunction with **49**, which illustrates the distribution of records of pottery of all types, and indicates areas where records of pottery (and in some cases Roman sites) are sparse. The grid on the maps represents the 100km squares of the Ordnance Survey National Grid (**50**).
The mechanics of the compilation of these maps is described in Appendix 3.

Aliases
Aliases to the ware in some of the principal published fabric series. Further details and discussion of the ware will often be found in these sources.

Bibliography
A brief annotated bibliography.

Abbreviations in the Atlas

Cam 00 Vessel-form numbers in C. F. C. Hawkes and Hull 1947.
Gillam 00 Vessel-type numbers in Gillam 1957.
RCHM gazetteer F000 Gazetteer entries (fiche frame number) in Swan 1984.

Alias references

Augst	Martin-Kilcher 1994
Bath	Cunliffe and Davenport 1985
Caersws	Britnell 1989
Caister-on-sea	Darling 1993
Carlisle	McCarthy 1990
Chelmsford	Going 1987
Chesterfield	Ellis 1989
Chichester	Down 1989
Cirencester	Rigby 1982
Colchester	Symonds and Wade – forthcoming
Doncaster	Buckland and Magilton 1986
Dorchester	Woodward *et al.* 1993
Exeter	Holbrook and Bidwell 1991
Gestingthorpe	Draper 1985
Gloucester	Hurst 1985
Great Chesterford	Draper 1986
Keay	Keay 1984
Kent	Pollard 1988
King Harry Lane	Stead and Rigby 1989
Leicester	Leicester fabric type series – forthcoming
Lullingstone	Pollard 1987
Milton Keynes	Marney 1989
Old Penrith	Austen 1991
Portchester	Fulford 1975b
Peacock and Williams	Peacock and Williams 1986
Rough Castle	MacIvor *et al.* 1981
Sheepen	Niblett 1985
Sidbury	Darlington and Evans 1992
Silchester	J. R. Timby – forthcoming
British (Tintagel)	C. Thomas 1981
Towcester	Brown and Woodfield 1983
Usk	Manning 1993

AMPHORAS

Amphoras are pottery containers which were used for storage and transport in the Greek and Roman world (**51**). Their importance to the original users was their contents, and to the archaeologist they offer a direct reflection of the large-scale movement of goods, principally foodstuffs, in the ancient world. While many are large, two-handled and with a rounded or spiked foot, there are exceptions to all these rules, and 'amphora' is not a typological category, but rather a functional grouping, and should be confined to vessels that have been stoppered, sealed and transported with contents. Anything else is a flagon, however large and however much it resembles one of the known amphora forms.

Long lists have been published compiled of the many commodities that have been recorded as the contents of amphoras (Callender 1965, 37–41) but these should not obscure the fact that it is the bulk movement of wine and olive-oil that is responsible for most amphoras recovered from archaeological sites. Other preserved grape, olive and fish products are of lesser significance, and the more exotic fruits, vegetables and non-food items encountered can never have been of more than minor interest.

The shifting patterns of amphora supply from different regions – and hence the trade in the commodities they contain – are an invaluable resource for the study of Classical agriculture. The successive rise and fall of production and export from Italy, Iberia and the African provinces are reflected in amphora assemblages throughout the Empire.

The principal mechanism behind the movement of these amphoras was shipping, and the archaeological benefit of this is the recovery of many amphora cargoes from wrecks around the Mediterranean basin, and more rarely in northern waters. Indeed it is often a spread of amphora sherds on the sea-bed

AMPHORAS

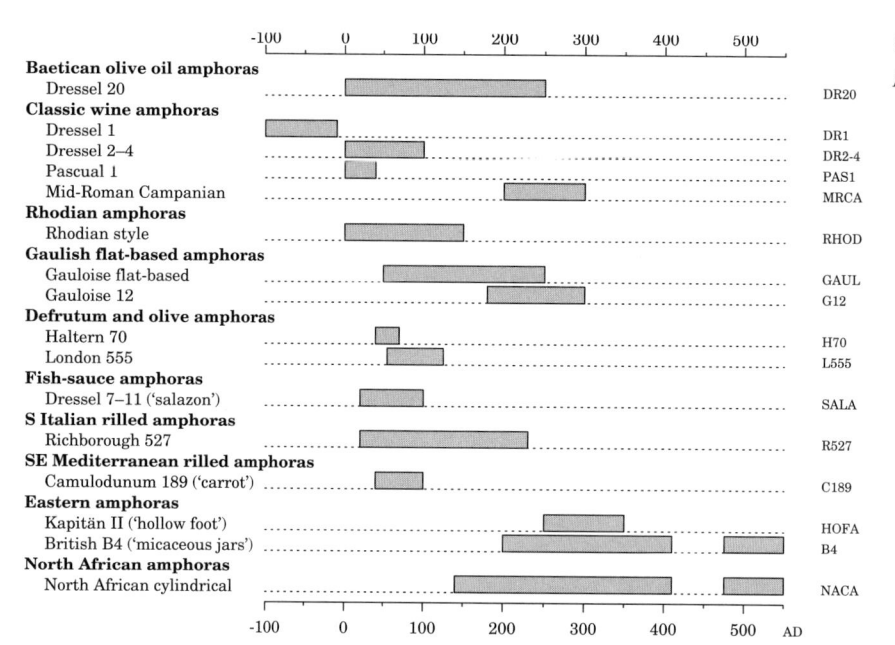

51 Amphoras: dating of principal classes

Forms

There is no unified typological series covering all amphora forms, and the standard labels are drawn from a combination of Dressel's 1899 typology, vessels from site-based typologies (Haltern, *Camulodunum*, Carthage etc.) and the typologies developed for amphoras from particular sources (e.g. *Beltrán* for Spanish amphoras, *Gauloise* for Gaulish, the *Africana* or *Tripolitana* series for North African material). The same form may be referred to under different names by different authors, following regional traditions or personal tastes. A concordance of the principal classification schemes has been drawn up by Peacock and Williams (1986, 218–21). The petrology of amphora fabrics demonstrates that some classes were produced simultaneously in many regions, and some exported types became widely copied. The complete identification of a vessel must take account of both fabric and form.

Some recently identified amphora categories have been named after a published specimen in an existing type-series or site report (e.g. Richborough 527, Kingsholm 117). This must be preferable to appending *similis* to the label for some pre-existing amphora class (hence Haltern 70 *similis* or Dressel 20 *similis*), which seems to be a recipe for chaos.

Fabric and technology

Most early work on amphoras tended to concentrate on the form of the vessel, with any fabric description confined to a simple note of colour. The detailed petrological description of fabrics is now central to the study of amphoras and much recent work has concentrated on this aspect of the material.

Stamps, graffiti and dipinti

Stamps and *dipinti* – painted inscriptions on the vessel surface – are key elements of amphora studies and many large *corpora* have been published, starting with the catalogues in the *Corpus Inscriptionum Latinarum* of the 19th cent. Stamps are used to trace the products of particular workshops or production areas and they can be dated, although rarely with as much precision as samian stamps.

Painted inscriptions have been studied in great detail and contain much information on the contents, shipping and marketing of amphoras. These inscriptions are often very faint and may only be visible under specialized lighting conditions, but their presence should always be considered when studying (or cleaning) collections of amphora sherds. A description of the forty-four *dipinti* on amphoras from Britain found down to the end of 1986 has been published in *The Roman Inscriptions of Britain* volume 2, fascicule 6 (Collingwood, et al. 1994) as *RIB* 2492. No less that seventeen of these (38%) are from excavations in London, perhaps a consequence of the extensive waterlogged deposits along the Thames waterfront and in the Walbrook valley. Pre- and post-firing graffiti on amphoras in Britain are catalogued as RIB 2493 and 2494.

The capacity of amphoras

The capacity of any complete amphora should be measured and recorded. These figures are of great value in calculating the quantities of the foodstuffs represented by the sherds in an assemblage, and it is also evident that many amphora types were produced in multiples of one of the standard Roman units of volume. The *modius*, although normally a dry measure, was commonly used to record the volume of amphoras in the western Empire. It is roughly equivalent to two imperial gallons. The graffiti and dipinti referred to above often record the volume of the amphora in *modii* and a smaller unit, the *sextarius* – approximately a pint. The Latin word *amphora* is also a unit of volume, used to describe the capacity of shipping. In the eastern Empire the system is complicated by the use of local systems of measures. Some amphoras seem to be multiples of the *choe*, equivalent to the Roman *congius* (**table 29**).

Measure		Volume
sextarius		0.547l
congius	= 6 sextarii	3.28l
modius	= 16 sextarii	8.75l
amphora	= 3 modii	26.26l

Table 29 *Roman measures of capacity*

Bibliography.
The bibliography of amphora studies is extensive, and fast expanding to rival that on samian wares. For general introductions to theory and practice of 'amphorology': Peacock and Williams 1986; Laubenheimer 1990a; Sealey 1985; Grace 1961; brief descriptions of principal types, with fabrics, dating and distribution maps: Peacock and Williams 1986; Sciallano and Sibella 1991; more obscure varieties of the later Roman period and eastern provinces are covered by Riley 1979; Keay 1984. The earlier studies by Callender 1965 and Beltrán Lloris 1970 remain valuable.

The most thorough studies of the principal amphora types circulating in the north-western Roman provinces, including Britain, will be found in the thoroughly researched catalogues of the material from Augst (Switzerland) by Stefanie Martin-Kilcher (1987; 1994). These lavishly produced volumes cover all aspects of the typology, chronology and economic significance of the Augst amphora assemblage, and include a splendid set of colour photographs of the principal fabrics (cross-referenced here as *Augst* TG 00).

F. Laubenheimer has compiled an annotated amphora bibliography, published in the *Bibliographies Thématiques en Archéologie* series (Laubenheimer 1991). M.-B. Carre (1992) describes a database system holding records of amphora stamps developed at the University of Aix-en-Provence which, it is intended, can be distributed on computer disks.

Reports from the *Ancient Monuments Laboratory* in London by D. F. Williams and others contain interim assessments of important collections of amphoras from sites in Britain, prior to the publication of the final site reports.

The track of amphora studies through the 1970s and 1980s can be followed through a series of conference proceedings, published in the *Collection de l'École Française de Rome* and elsewhere as Baldacci *et al*. 1972; Vallet 1977; Badalona 1987; Lenoir *et al*. 1989; Laubenheimer, (ed) 1992). The catalogue of Roman shipwrecks compiled by Parker (1992) contains a wealth of data on the transport and distribution of amphoras. For scientific analyses of residues on amphoras see Heron and Pollard 1988; Rothschild-Boros 1981. Examples of the application of amphora data to economic history will be found in

Sealey 1985, 113–51; Garnsey *et al*. 1983; Tchernia 1986; Fulford 1987; the papers by Carandini, Morel, Tchernia and Whittaker in Lenoir *et al*. 1989, 505–39 give vent to some of the major themes and problems.

In the Atlas pages the ordering of amphora classes follows the Augst type-series (Martin-Kilcher 1987; 1994).

Dressel 20 amphoras and allied types

Forms. The Dressel 20 is a large globular form, with two handles and thickened, rounded or angular rim, concave internally. A distinctive 'plug' of clay seals the base of the vessel. The Augustan precursor of the Dressel 20 – the Oberaden 83 – has an ovoid body, a more prominent, pointed spike and is of less massive construction. The successor form – the Dressel 23 – is smaller and has a more pointed base. The rim shape develops from more rounded forms in the 1st cent. to more angular forms in the 3rd cent. (**52**). Commonly stamped, most often on the summit of the handle, but occasionally on the neck or body.

Painted inscriptions (*tituli picti*) may be found on the shoulder (between the handles) and there are occasional pre-firing graffiti, some with consular dates (*RIB* ii. 6, 2493.1–11: Collingwood, *et al*. 1994) which show the date of manufacture.
Fabric and technology. Thick, coarse sandy fabric with irregular fracture, tending to laminate; variable in colour, but generally with buff (e.g. 7.5YR 7/4) or grey core with darker margins and yellow or off-white surfaces. Abundant coarse white and multi-coloured inclusions of quartz, limestone feldspar and composite rock fragments, slightly micaceous. Deep, but uneven wheel-marks on the internal surface. Later examples tend to be red in colour, harder and white-slipped. (*Augst* TG 1–11).
Average capacity. Average 60-5l, but ranging from 40l to 80l. Post-firing graffiti on the rim or handle may record the volumes of the empty vessel in *modii* and *sextarii* (see discussion in *RIB ii*. 6, 2494). Most record volumes between 7 and 8 *modii* (i.e. 61–70l).
Chronology. Oberaden 83 form found in small quantities on Augustan sites in Britain, but the classic Dressel 20 form is present on a few sites from Claudian period. Widespread on post-conquest sites, up to the mid-3rd cent. Production ceases by *c*. AD 260, but succeeded by the smaller Dressel 23 form (up to mid-4th cent.). The proportion of Dressel 20s in the British amphora assemblage reaches a peak in Antonine period (D. F. Williams and Peacock 1983).
Source. The Guadalquivir valley in southern Spain (the Roman province of Baetica), between the cities of Cordoba and Seville. The extensive surveys by Ponsich (1974; 1979; 1991) describe the evidence from the production sites.
Principal contents. Principally olive-oil; occasionally preserved olives (Sealey 1985, 74).
Distribution. Widespread around the western Mediterranean. Large numbers exported to Rome during the 2nd cent. AD

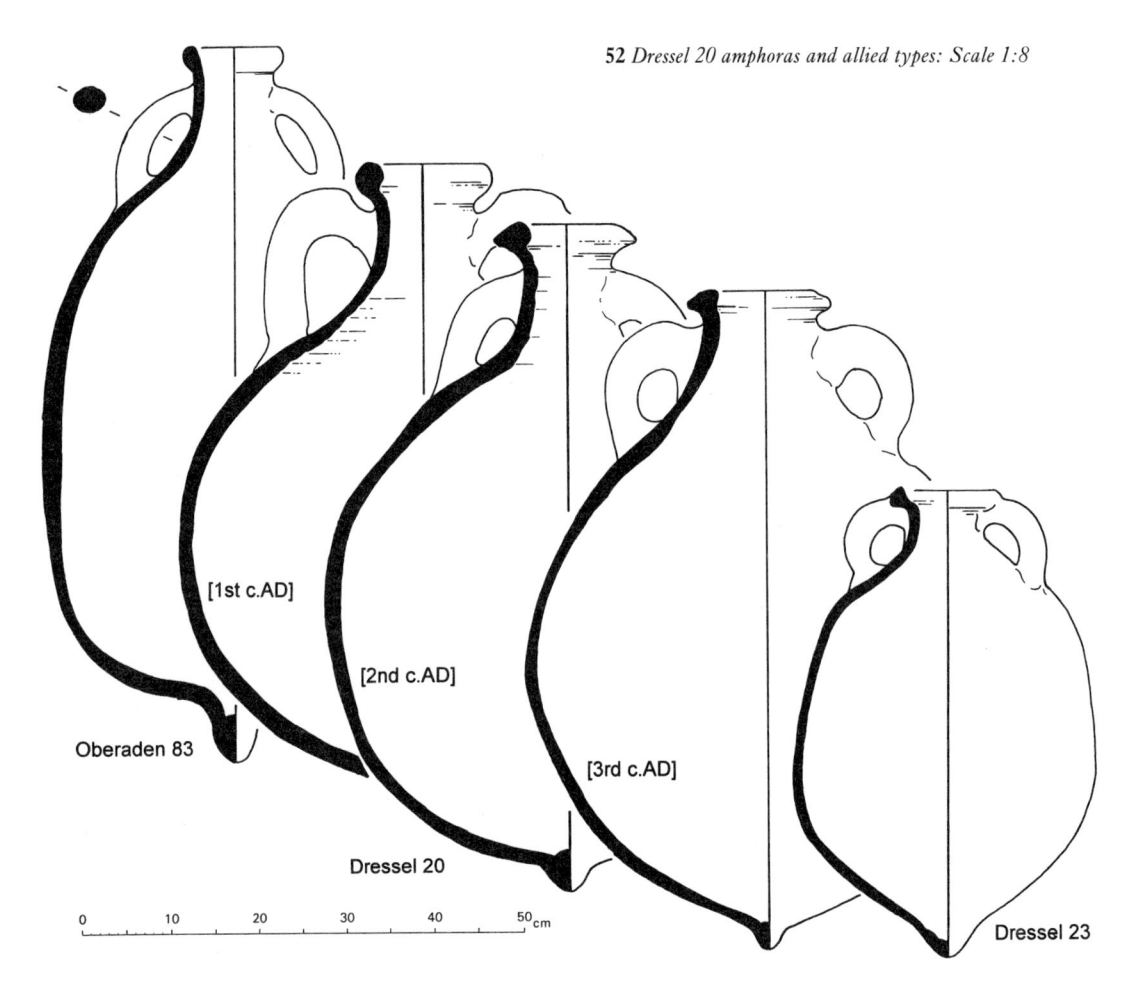

Dressel 20 / AMPHORAS

52 Dressel 20 amphoras and allied types: Scale 1:8

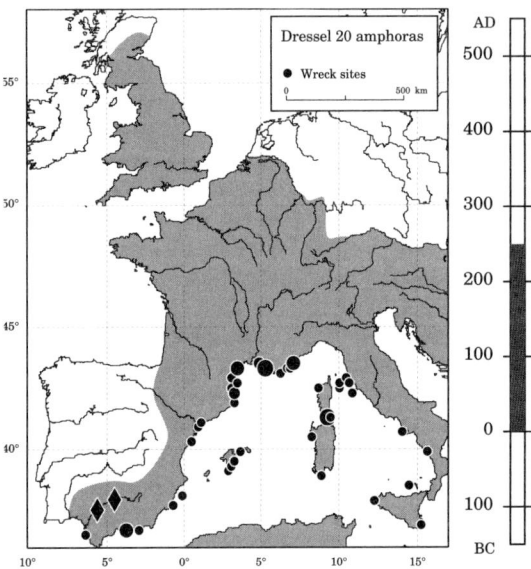

53 Dressel 20 amphoras and allied types: overall distribution

where the broken vessels form the Monte Testaccio. In the northern provinces, distribution seems to follow the Rhône–Rhine system (53), thence to Britain, where widespread.

Aliases. *Augst* class 1. *Carlisle* fabric 162. *Chelmsford* fabric 55. *Cirencester* fabric 40. *Colchester* fabric AJ. *Gloucester* fabric TF10A. *Keay* fabrics 10-13. *Leicester* fabric AM9. *Lullingstone* fabric 79. *Milton Keynes* fabric 22. *Peacock and Williams* classes 24 (Oberaden 83, Haltern 71, Dressel 25), 25 (Dressel 20, Beltrán V, Ostia I, Callender 2) and 26 (Dressel 23, Keay XIII). *Sidbury* fabric 42.1.

Bibliography. The most complete general discussion is Martin-Kilcher 1987, with an analysis of typology, fabrics, sources and dating. There are numerous shipwrecks (Parker 1992). The literature on the stamps is scattered. Callender's (1965) extensive survey should be used in conjunction with more recent works; the stamps from the production sites are indexed by Ponsich 1991, 267–70. Modern approaches attempt to study production and trade patterns through the stamps e.g. Remesal Rodríguez 1986; Remesal Rodríguez 1982. For Monte Testaccio: Rodríguez Almeida 1984. On the

tituli picti: Rodríguez Almeida 1989.
See also H70

Dressel 1 amphoras

Forms. Cylindrical amphora with angular shoulders and long straight handles, generally oval in section (**54**). There are two sub-categories:

DR1A Short triangular rim with short spike.

DR1B Collared rim with longer, slightly flared, spike. Commonly stamped on rim or neck; generally small square or rectangular stamps with one or two letters or symbols.

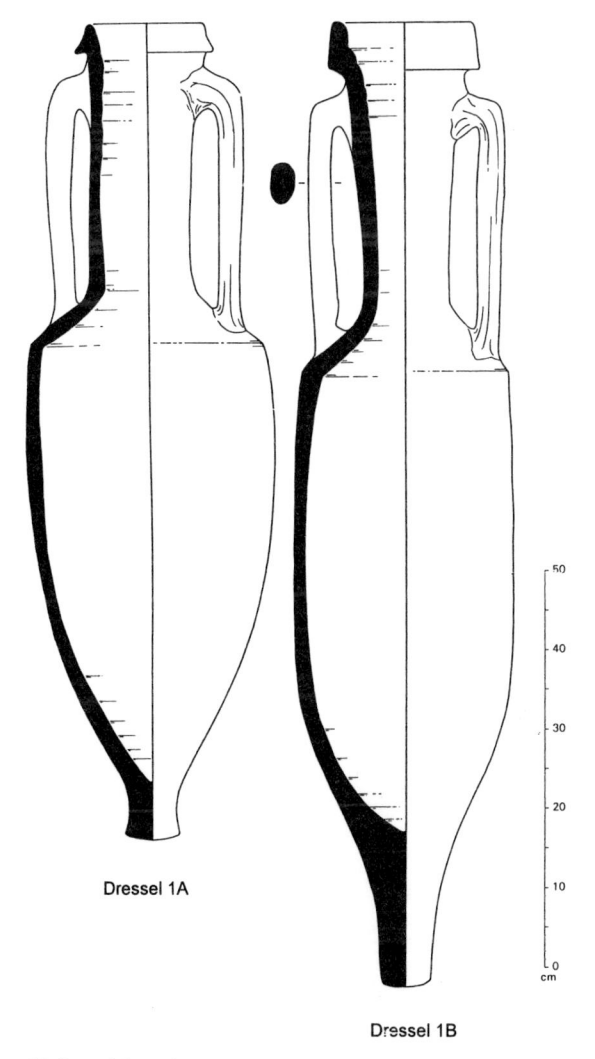

54 Dressel 1 amphoras

Fabric and technology. Peacock (1971) defines three fabrics. Fabric 1 is the product of a wide geographical region and varies in detail; generally red or light red with a white or cream slip, hard, with inclusions of quartz, feldspar, and occasional black grains and composite rock fragments. The most characteristic (fabric 2) ware is dark brick-red (10R 6/8) with white or off-white slipped surfaces (10YR 7/1 or 8/2) abundantly tempered with distinctive 'black sand' (identified as green augite). This 'black sand' fabric is shared by Pompeian-Red ware 1 (*PRW1*) Dressel 2–4 amphoras and other coarse wares, e.g. *Cam* 139 and seems to be a product of the Pompeii–Herculaneum region (*Augst* TG 12–13).

Average capacity. 24l.

Chronology. The conventional dates for the production of the Dressel 1A amphora is pre-Caesarian (i.e. pre-50 BC), with the Dressel 1B type appearing shortly before the middle of the 1st cent. BC. However, it has been argued that this chronology is too late and that the Dressel 1A is essentially a product of the 2nd cent. BC (Parker 1992, 32). The Dressel 1B was produced until *c*. 10 BC; the date of the latest *tituli picti* on the form is 13 BC. The British assemblage includes both the Dressel 1A and 1B variants.

Source. Italy, principally Etruria, Latium and Campania, where numerous kiln sites recorded. The Dressel 1B form is also produced in different wares in small quantities in Provence and the Rhône valley (Laubenheimer, Odiot and Leclère 1989; Sabir *et al*. 1983) but the distribution of these vessels is not known.

Principal contents. Principally wine, including some of the most celebrated *crus* of antiquity, such as Falernian and Caecuban. A minority carried *defrutum*, olives, nuts and other products. The contents may be recorded on painted inscriptions on the amphoras.

Distribution. Extensive distribution around the western

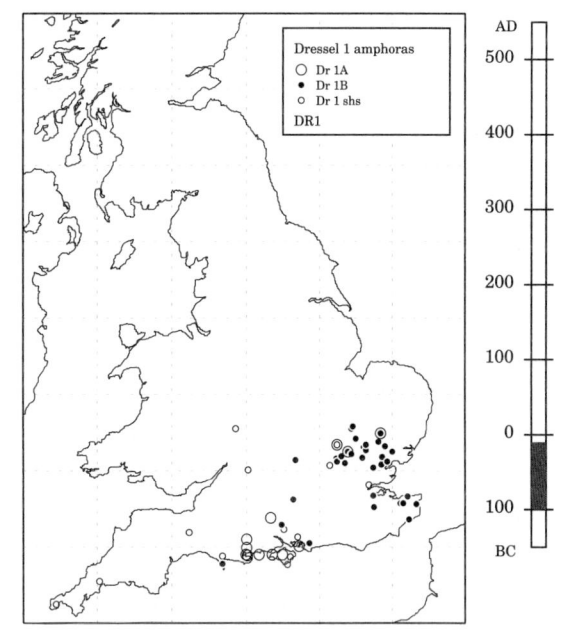

55 Dressel 1 amphoras: British distribution

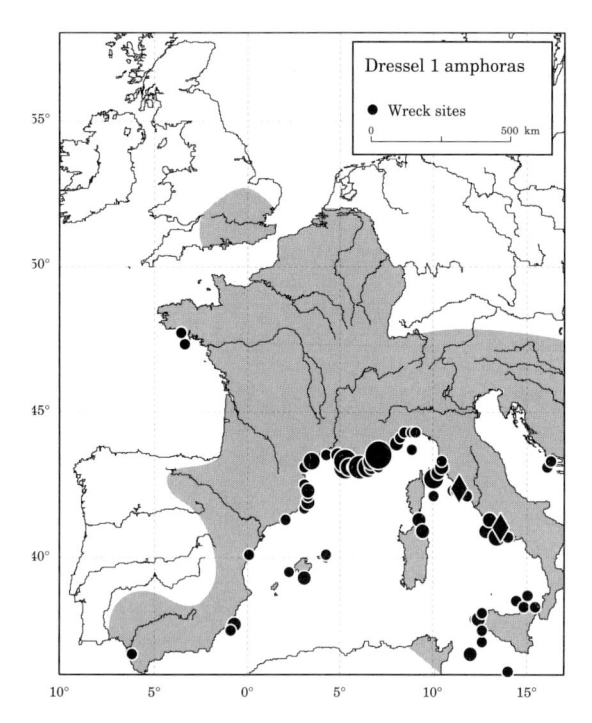

Dressel 2–4 / AMPHORAS

56 Dressel 1 amphoras: overall distribution

Mediterranean; very large number of wrecks carrying these amphoras, particularly along the coast of Provence and Liguria (Parker 1992, fig. 8). In Gaul, abundant in the Rhône–Saône valley system, and widespread (but thin) on 1st-cent. BC sites in the north and west. A few examples on Augustan military sites along the Rhine and in Switzerland. The British distribution is in two parts: the south-west (Dorset, Hampshire) and south-east (Kent, Essex, Hertfordshire). The DR1A is more common in the south-west, rarer in south-east **(55, 56)**.
Aliases. Augst class 3. *Peacock and Williams* classes 3 (Dressel 1A, Ostia XX) and 4 (Dressel 1B, Ostia XX, *Cam* 181, Callender 1).
Bibliography. An extensive literature. Sealey (1985, 21–6) gives a thorough survey, with references. For the petrology and sources: Peacock 1971; Hesnard *et al.* 1989. For the Gaulish and British distribution: Galliou 1982; Fitzpatrick 1985. The Bibracte collection of Dressel 1 stamps (one of the largest outside the Mediterranean) is reported in Laubenheimer and Rodriguez 1991.
See also DR2-4 MRCA PRW1

Dressel 2–4 amphoras

Forms. Cylindrical amphora with long bifid handles (composed of two rods), with small beaded lip and distinct carinated shoulder **(58)**. Occasionally stamped near the base, or on the neck or handle. The form is derived from a prototype distributed from the island of Kos, hence referred to colloquially as Koan amphoras.

Fabric and technology. Very varied, due to their widespread production (see below). There are examples in the distinctive fabrics of both the Italian Dressel 1 (including the Campanian 'black sand' fabric) and the Catalan Pascual 1.
Average capacity. 26–34 l.
Chronology. Production from the later 1st cent. BC through to the end of the 1st cent. AD, and probably beyond. Imports in pre-conquest deposits in Britain, but most common on early Roman sites.
Source. One of the most widely produced amphora types; made in Italy (Peacock 1977b; Hesnard *et al.* 1989), where it was produced on the same sites as the Dressel 1, Catalonia (Keay and Jones 1982), Baetica (Sealey 1985, 37, 42), central and southern France (Laubenheimer 1989, 118–23; Meffre and Meffre 1992), Lyon (Dangréaux, *et al.* 1992, type 2), western Switzerland (Martin-Kilcher 1994, 342–4), the eastern Mediterranean (Empereur and Picon 1989) and Britain, at Brockley Hill (Castle 1978; Sealey 1985, 128–30).
Principal contents. Principally wine, but occasionally *defrutum*, fish-based sauces, olive-oil and dates.
Distribution. Widespread in the western provinces. The distribution of the principal sources remains to be studied, but both Italian and Spanish products are found widely **(57)**.
Aliases. Augst class 5. *Carlisle* fabric 151. *Cirencester* fabric 39. *Gloucester* fabric TF10G. *Peacock and Williams* class 10 (Graeco-Roman, Koan, Ostia LI, *Cam* 182–183, Callender 2, Benghazi ER4). *Sidbury* fabric 42.2.
Bibliography. Sealey 1985, 27–50; Martin-Kilcher 1994, 337–46.
See also MRCA

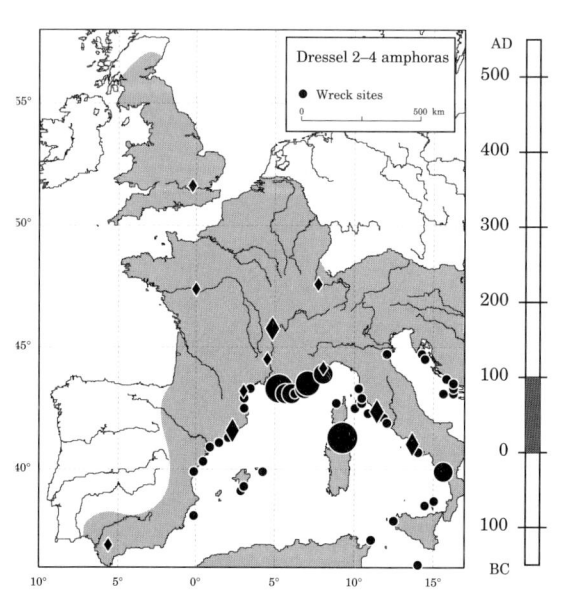

57 Dressel 2–4 amphoras: overall distribution

Mid-Roman Campanian / AMPHORAS

58 *Dressel 2-4 amphoras: Scale 1:8*

Camulodunum 183C

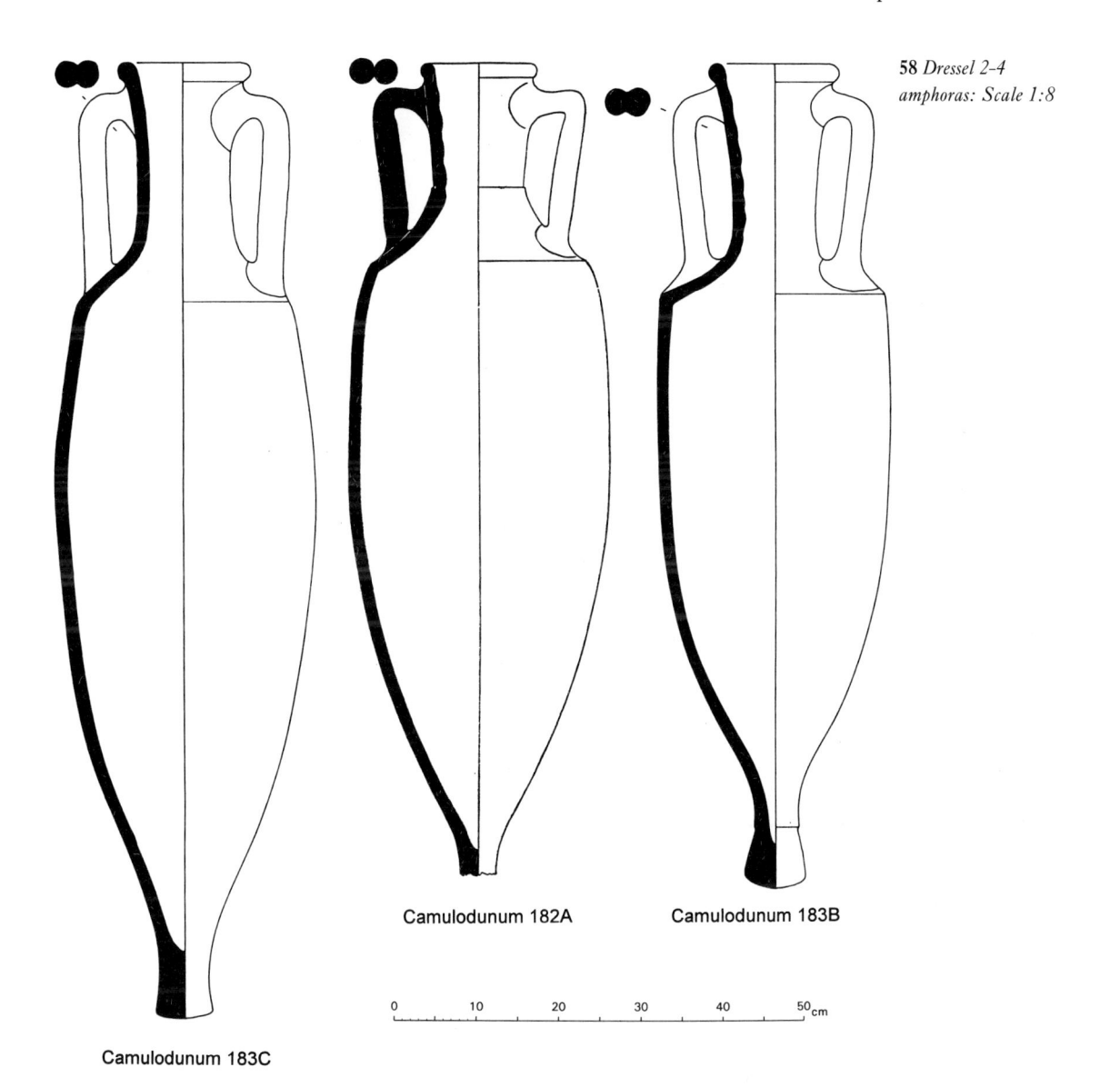

Camulodunum 182A

Camulodunum 183B

Mid-Roman Campanian

Mid-Roman Campanian amphoras
Forms. Cylindrical amphora, recalling the form of the Dressel 2–4, but with oval or round-sectioned handles and characteristic almond-shaped rim; solid spike (**59**).
Fabric and technology. Several fabrics, including the 'black-sand' fabric as on DR1 and DR2–4 amphoras and PRW1.
Chronology. Later 2nd and 3rd cent. AD.
Source. Campania, probably from the Bay of Naples.
Principal contents. Wine.
Distribution. Principally Italy, but a few from the Rhône valley, the Rhineland and Britain (**60**). This type has only recently been recognized and in the past may have been conflated with earlier Campanian amphoras in the same wares.

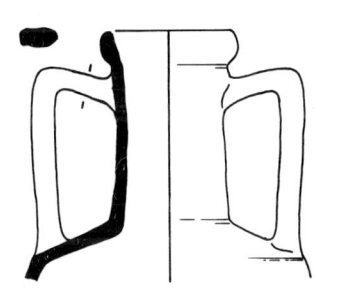

59 *Mid-Roman Campanian amphoras: Scale 1:8*

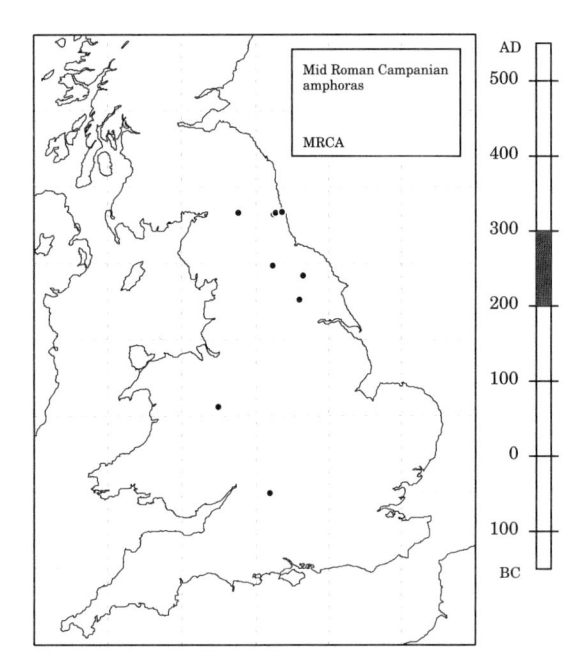

Pascual 1 / AMPHORAS

60 Mid-Roman Campanian amphoras: British distribution

Bibliography. Arthur and Williams 1992; Martin-Kilcher 1994, 339–40.
See also. DR1 DR2–4

Pascual 1 amphoras
Forms. Cylindrical amphora with distinctive tall vertical rim, rounded handles with narrow groove on outer face, cylindrical

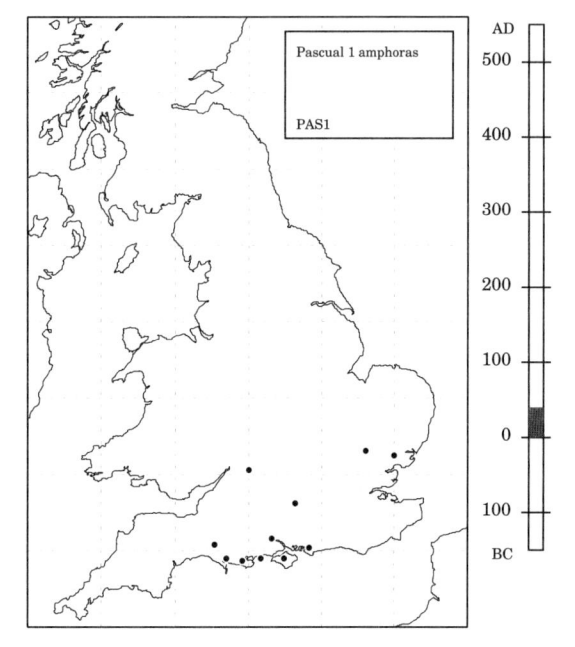

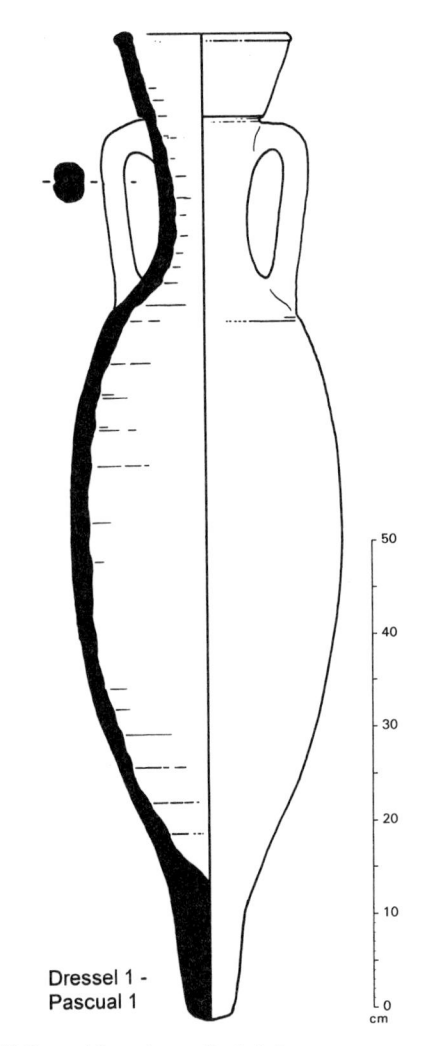

62 Pascual 1 amphoras: Scale 1:8

neck, ovoid body and solid spike (**62**). Regularly stamped on rim or near foot.

Fabric and technology. There are two fabrics:
1. Hard dark-red or red-brown fabric (10R 4/4 to 4/6) with large white quartz and feldspar inclusions; slightly micaceous with occasional composite rock (granite) fragments. (Augst TG 18).
2. Soft cream or off-white fabric (7.5YR 8/2 to 7/4) with white quartz and feldspar inclusions.

Average capacity. 22l.

Chronology. The majority of the British examples are from late Augustan–Tiberian contexts, although production may continue into the later 1st cent. AD.

Source. Catalonia, where there are kilns in the vicinity of Barcelona (Keay and Jones 1982). Some small-scale production of the form in southern Gaul (Laubenheimer 1985,

61 Pascual 1 amphoras: British distribution

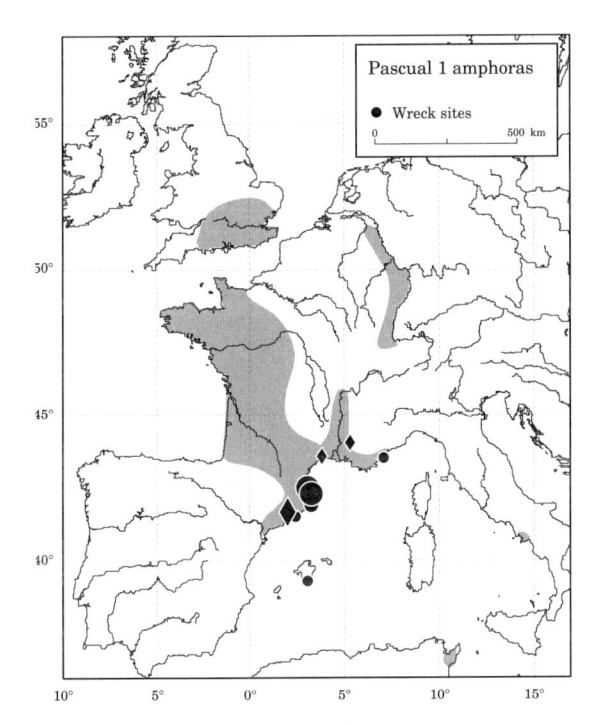

63 Pascual 1 amphoras: overall distribution

312–15; Meffre and Meffre 1992, fig. 7, 2), in different wares.
Principal contents. The Catalan examples probably contain Layetanian wine.
Distribution. Widespread, but thinly spread in Spain, Gaul and Rhineland; only a few examples in southern Britain (D. F. Williams 1981a; Williams in Woodward 1987, 79). The type is particularly common along the Narbonne–Toulouse–Bordeaux route and in western France – see the distribution of the stamps of M. PORCIUS (Comas Solà 1991, 344, fig. 15). There are a number of wrecks containing this type along the coasts of Catalonia and Languedoc (Parker 1992, fig. 10) (**61, 63**).
Aliases. *Augst* class 4. *Peacock and Williams* class 6.
Bibliography. Pascual Guasch 1977; Miró 1987; Comas Solà 1987; Comas Solà 1991.

Rhodian (Camulodunum 184) amphoras

Forms. Long tapering body, terminated in a solid spike; cylindrical neck with small beaded rim and single rod handles, of circular cross-section which rise to a distinctive peak (**64**).
Fabric and technology. Peacock (1977c, 266–70) defines six fabrics, of which nos. 1 and 2 are most important:
1. Fine reddish-pink (5YR 7/6) with thin pale slip; sparse inclusions of medium red-brown particles and larger angular fragments of white limestone (Augst TG 48–9).
2. Creamy-yellow (10YR 8/4) with large limestone inclusions, but usually with soft, pitted surface where these have flaked (Augst TG 50).

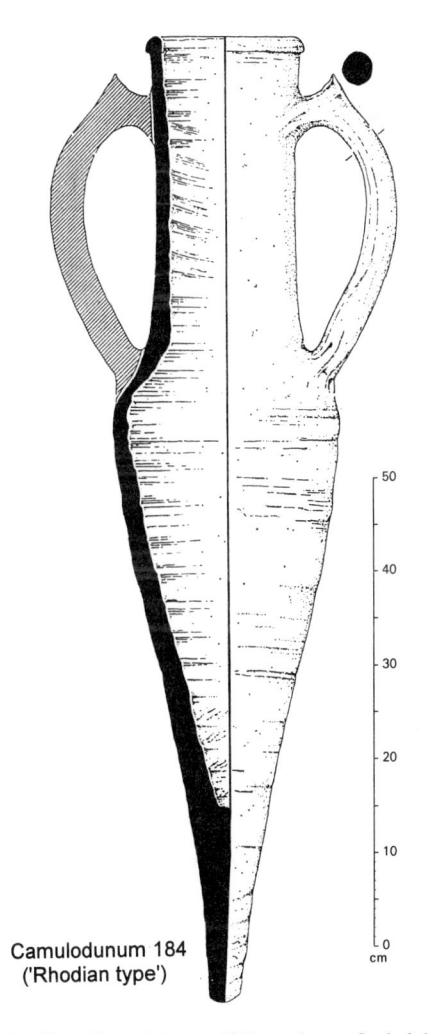

Camulodunum 184 ('Rhodian type')

64 Rhodian (Camulodunum 184) amphoras: Scale 1:8

The other wares are generally light or red coloured, but vary in their details.
Average capacity. Principally 25-26l, but some half-size vessels, including the *Cam* 184 type specimen with a capacity of 13.6l.
Chronology. The form was produced from the Republican period until the 2nd cent. AD. Some Augustan–Tiberian specimens from Gaul and the Rhineland, but imported into Britain from the Claudio-Neronian period. Importation continues until the mid-2nd cent. Perhaps particularly common on military sites (on the significance of which see Sealey 1985, 133–5).
Source. Several sources, including the island of Rhodes (fabric 1), the Cnidian peninsula (fabric 2?). Others probably from the Aegean region and Crete.
Principal contents. Principally wine; also figs and honey.
Distribution. Wide distribution in eastern and western

Gaulish / AMPHORAS

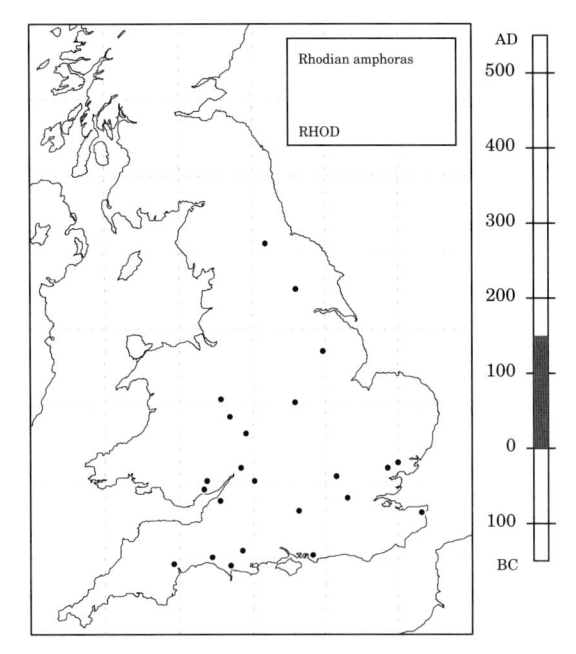

65 *Rhodian (Camulodunum 184) amphoras: British distribution*

Mediterranean, along the Rhine and Britain (**65**).
Aliases. *Augst* class 6. *Cirencester* fabrics 38A and 38B. *Gloucester* fabric TF10D. JRPS bibliography fabric arh. *Leicester* fabric AM10. *Peacock and Williams* class 9 (Ostia LXV, *Cam* 184, Callender 7). *Sidbury* fabric 42.4.
Bibliography. On petrology and British distribution: Peacock 1977c; also Sealey 1985, 51–8; Martin-Kilcher 1994, 348.
Notes. A related form, the Dressel 43, is smaller and thinner walled than the *Cam* 184, has a bulging rather than cylindrical neck, and a collared rim. This has been recorded in small numbers from Britain (Sealey 1985, 51; Martin-Kilcher 1994, 350).

Gaulish amphoras

The wide range of amphora types produced within the confines of Roman Gaul have been studied by F. Laubenheimer in a series of papers (e.g. 1985; 1989; 1990a, 77–110). Her *Gauloise* type-series covers the principal regional types. In addition there are Gaulish renderings of both Iberian and Italian prototypes (**table 30**).

Flat-based amphoras of types G1, G3, G4 and G5 are the most characteristic Gaulish products and are considered as a group below; the furrowed-rim G12 is described separately. The Gaulish versions of the Dressel 1, 2–4, 7–11 and Pascual 1 are discussed with their non-Gaulish counterparts.

There is increasing evidence for the production of other amphora types in Gaul, often in the same workshops as the commoner *Gauloise* types. Although many of these types may only have small-scale distributions the possibility of occasional imports to Britain must be considered. Possible Lyon amphoras (Dangréaux, *et al*. 1992) have been identified in London, and a Dressel 16 amphora with a painted inscription recording the contents as *liquamen* – a fish-sauce – from Antibes, and containing fish-head bones, box and iris seeds, has been recovered from Southwark. This vessel was apparently produced in the region of Fréjus (*RIB* ii.6, 2492.24; Laubenheimer, Gebara and Beraud 1992).

Type	Base	Description	ATLAS
Gauloise amphora types			
1	flat	flaring collared rim	GAUL
2	flat	rim with 'double external inflexion'	
3	flat	rim with 'double projection'	GAUL
4	flat	prominent half-rounded rim	GAUL
5	flat	flattened projecting rim	GAUL
6	flat	flared rounded rim	
7	flat	recurved collar	
8	flat	grooved collar	
9	flat	tall flaring collar	
10	pointed	rounded rim	
11	pointed	small conical amphora with concave neck	
12	flat	furrowed on top of rim	G12

Equivalent			ATLAS
Gaulish amphoras based on imported models			
Dressel 1			DR1
Pascual 1			PAS1
Dressel 2–4			DR2–4
Dressel 7–11			SALA

Table 30 *Typology of Gaulish amphoras (after Laubenheimer)*

Gauloise flat-based amphoras

Forms. Of the ten forms of flat-based *Gauloise* amphora types defined by Laubenheimer, at least five can be recognized in Britain (**66**). The furrowed-rim amphora of northern Gaul, *Gauloise* 12, is reported separately (G12) – the remainder are dealt with here. They are distinguishable by body form and rim shape:

G1 Flaring collar rim with short strap handles, usually with two grooves; spherical body with wide base.
G3 Thickened rim with distinct moulded collar below the lip and short flat handles; tapering body with narrow foot.
G4 Thick rounded rim and short flat handles with a

Gauloise flat-based / AMPHORAS

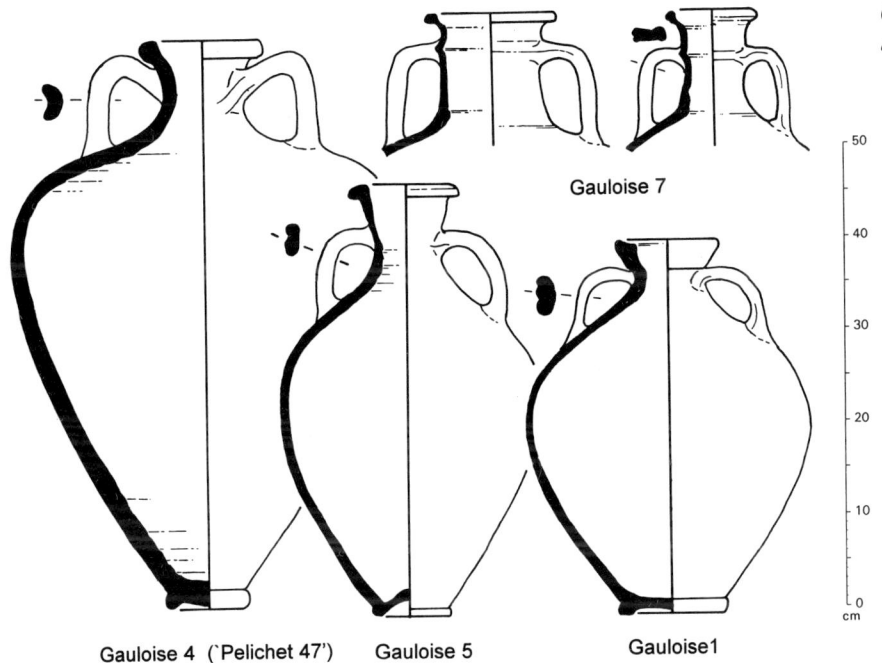

66 *Gauloise flat-based amphoras: Scale 1:8*

central groove; broad-shouldered body tapering to a narrow foot. The most common *Gauloise* type.

G5 Flattened projecting rim with relatively tall narrow neck; body shape as Gauloise 4.

Fabric and technology. Although produced at a large number of kilns, most fabrics are fine and reasonably hard, pale buff (e.g. 10YR 9/4) with fine inclusions of limestone, quartz and rock fragments; they tend to be rather micaceous. The surfaces can have a rather open finish that has been described as 'stretched dough'. Marks of cloth strips wrapped around the lower body may be visible – these would have supported the wet clay during manufacturing. A coarser fabric, *Gauloise sableuse*, has more abundant and larger inclusions and is particularly characteristic of the earlier specimens of Gauloise 1 from the lower Rhône valley. The variety of fabrics and their possible sources are described by Martin-Kilcher (*Augst* TG 22–36).

Stamps. Many examples (particularly of G1 and G4) are stamped across the shoulder or neck (catalogue of stamps in Laubenheimer 1985, 413–44).

Average capacity. From 26l and 37l (for G1 and G4). Post-firing graffiti on the handle or shoulder may record the volumes of the empty vessel in *modii* and *sextarii* (see discussion in Martin-Kilcher 1994, 368–9).

Chronology. Production commences in the lower Rhône valley during the early 1st cent. AD, with the G1 (perhaps based on earlier Massiolite prototypes). The G4 develops during the later 1st cent. AD and continues to be produced and exported throughout the 2nd and into the 3rd cent.

Source. Numerous kilns are known throughout *Gallia Narbonensis*, and this region is the source of most specimens. Flat-based amphoras were also produced at sites in Burgundy, the Loire valley, eastern Gaul (e.g. Baudoux 1992, fig. 7) and the Bordeaux region (Berthault 1992). The Marseille flat-based amphoras of the Roman period, in a characteristic highly micaceous fabric are described by Bertucchi (1992, 111–24, variants 6–7). Some Marseille name-stamps are in Greek characters.

Principal contents. Wine is the principal content attested on *tituli picti*.

Distribution. G4 amphoras were widely distributed in Gaul, the Rhineland and Britain, and were also exported to Italy and elsewhere around the Mediterranean – including some in the east. The Rhône–Rhine axis seems to have been the principal route to the north and a series of bas-reliefs and sculptures along this line figure *Gauloise* amphoras on barges and ships, where they are often depicted protected by wickerwork. In Britain *Gauloise* amphoras are found from the Flavian period (e.g. Fitzpatrick 1992, 181) and throughout 2nd and 3rd cent (**67, 68**).

Aliases. *Augst* classes 10, 11, 12 and 13. *Carlisle* fabric 188. *Chelmsford* fabric 56. *Chesterfield* fabric 27. *Cirencester* fabric 35. *Great Chesterford* fabric 27. *Leicester* fabrics AM12 and AM13. *Peacock and Williams* classes 27 (Gauloise 4, Pélichet 47, Ostia LX, Callender 10, Niederbieber 76), 28 (Gauloise 1), 29 (Gauloise 3) and 30 (Gauloise 5).

Bibliography. The principal study is Laubenheimer 1985; see also Laubenheimer 1989; Laubenheimer 1990a; Martin-Kilcher 1994, 358–76. The kilns at Sallèles d'Aude (12km north of Narbonne) have been reported in most detail

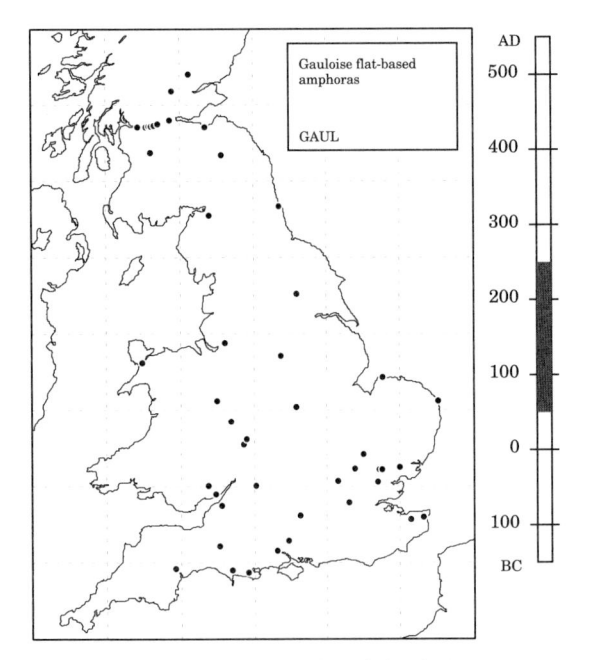

Gauloise 12 / AMPHORAS

67 Gauloise flat-based amphoras: British distribution

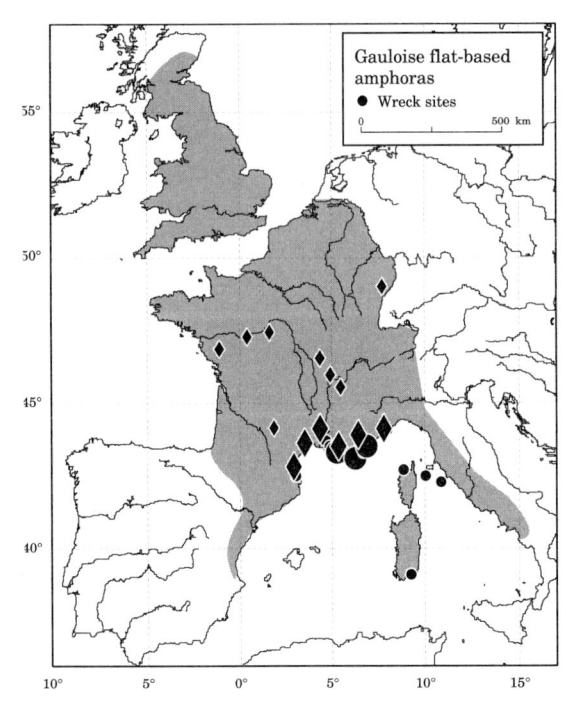

68 Gauloise flat-based amphoras: overall distribution

Gaulish products were also exported. Laubenheimer has drawn attention to a vessel from London stamped ABDUCIVSF which seems to be a product of the kilns at Gueugnon in Burgundy (Laubenheimer and Notet 1986, 439, fig. 7, 4). As further production sites outside southern Gaul are discovered it is likely that their products will be recognized in Britain.
See also. G12

Gauloise 12 amphoras

Forms. Flat-based globular vessel with a distinctive thickened rim, with multiple grooves on the upper surface. Often decorated with horizontal bands of combed wavy lines on the upper body (69).

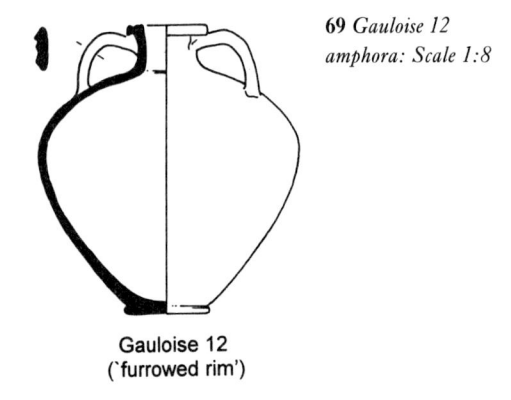

69 Gauloise 12 amphora: Scale 1:8

Gauloise 12 ('furrowed rim')

Fabric and technology. Fine sandy red or yellow fabrics.
Average capacity. Apparently produced in three sizes, averaging

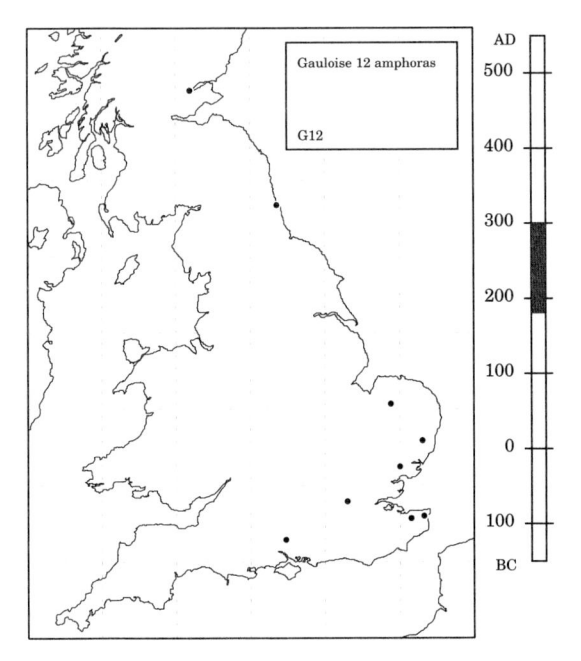

(Laubenheimer 1990b); the site is preserved under cover, with a museum. On the British distribution: Peacock 1978.
Notes. Although southern Gaul, Narbonnaise, is the principal source of flat-based amphoras in Britain, some of the central

70 Gauloise 12 amphoras: British distribution

6.4l, 14.5l (the most common) and 40.6l.
Chronology. Later 2nd–3rd cent. AD.
Source. Probably Normandy, on distributional grounds.
Principal contents. Unknown, but inner surface coated with resin (Formenti in Laubenheimer and Lequoy 1992, 91–2).
Distribution. Normandy, and southern and eastern Britain, as far as Carpow in Scotland (Fitzpatrick 1992) (**70**).
Aliases. Peacock and Williams class 55 (furrowed rim).
Bibliography. Laubenheimer and Lequoy 1992.
See also. GAUL

Haltern 70 amphoras

Forms. Cylindrical amphora with collared rim, oval handles with deep vertical groove and solid conical spike (**71**). Rarely stamped; but a few Haltern 70 stamps can be paralleled on Dressel 20, suggesting production in the same workshops.

Fabric and technology. Similar to the fabric of the early Baetican oil amphoras (*Augst* TG 1–3). Body sherds not always distinguishable.

Average capacity. 30l.

Chronology. Present in Augustan contexts (e.g. Haltern) but post-conquest in Britain, up to *c.* AD 70.

Source. The Guadalquivir valley (as Dressel 20s).

Principal contents. Several painted inscriptions record *defrutum* or olives preserved in *defrutum* as the contents of the Haltern 70. Although this much is clear, there is some dispute about whether *defrutum* should be considered as a wine or a non-alcoholic sweet syrup (the current view is summarized by Sealey 1985, 62–3).

Distribution. Widespread, but relatively sparse, around western Mediterranean (Colls *et al.* 1977, 36–8); in Gaul and Germany particularly common along the Rhône-Rhine axis, but also in western France (e.g. Siraudeau 1988, 183–4) and Britain (**72**).

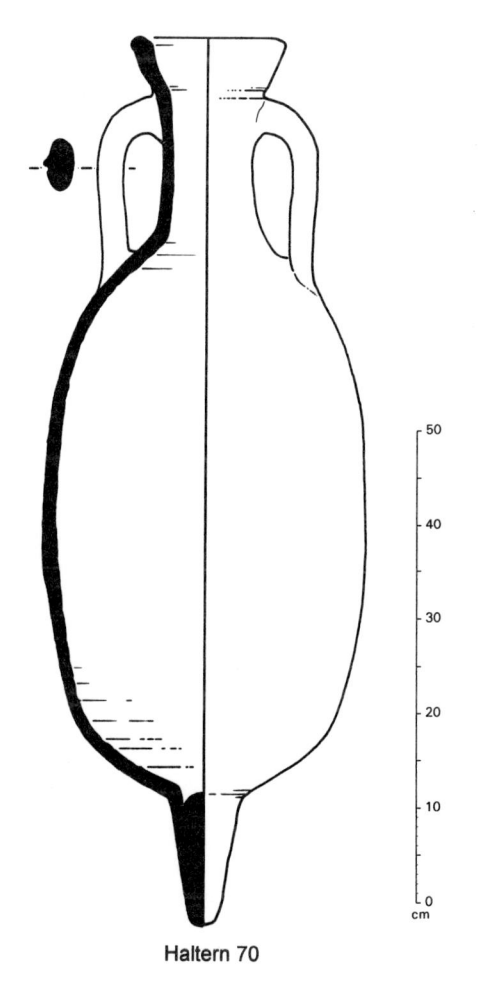

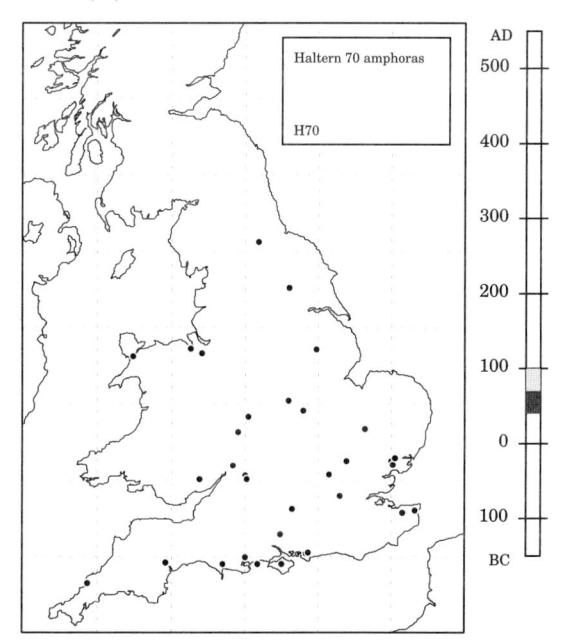

71 *Haltern 70 amphora: Scale 1:8*

72 *Haltern 70 amphoras: British distribution*

Aliases. *Augst* class 19. *Peacock and Williams* class 15 (*Cam* 185A, Callender 9).

Bibliography. Colls *et al.* 1977, 33–8 is first major discussion of the type; also Sealey 1985, 59–66. On the identity of *defrutum* see Parker and Price 1981; for the contrary view, van der Werff 1984, 380–1, with refs.

See also. DR20 L555

London 555 amphoras

Forms. Slim cylindrical amphora with deep groove just below the rim, oval handles with deep vertical groove and solid conical spike (**73**).

Fabric and technology. A range of fabrics – most hard, fine

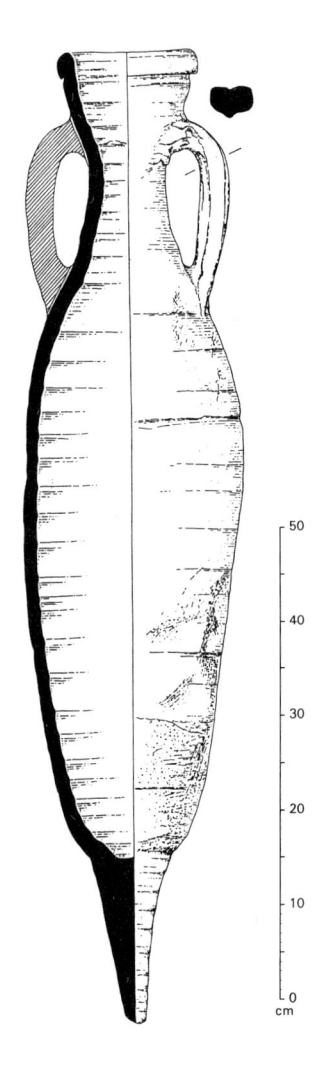

Dressel 7-11 'salazon'/AMPHORAS

tions indicate Baetica as one source. The first reports of the type from France, where it is classed as Haltern 70 *similis* (Desbat 1987, 408), concurred with this view although subsequent petrological work favoured a source in the Rhône valley, specifically in the Lyon region (Dangréaux and Desbat 1988). The form does not appear in a more recent assessment of Lyon amphora production (Dangréaux, *et al*. 1992). Martin-Kilcher distinguishes a rare Haltern 70 *similis* form, *Augst* 20, from the London 555, *Augst* 21. The former are assigned to the Lyon region or the middle Rhône – the latter to southern Gaul or the southern Rhône valley.

Principal contents. Several *dipinti* refer to olives, some preserved in dulcia or *defrutum* syrup; a complete example recovered from the sea at Pan Sand (off north Kent) contained 6206 olive stones (photograph in Milne 1985, fig. 64).

Distribution. Not common, but increasing recognition of the type will extend the distribution map (**74**).

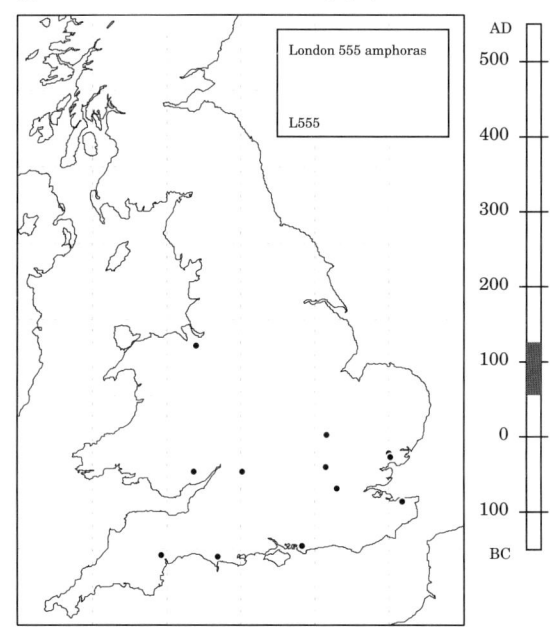

73 *London 555 amphora: Scale 1:8*

London 555

textured, perhaps with powdery surface; from creamy-buff, through to orange-red, or pink (perhaps with thin creamy wash); inclusions variable – some fine quartz (may be abundant) with scatter of larger quartzite, feldspar and composite rock fragments, set in lime-rich, slightly micaceous matrix; many specimens have a 'roughcasting' of coarse mixed sand applied, by hand, to areas around the base and neck. A few examples with abundant coarser inclusions, grey or grey-brown, resemble typical Baetican fabric of Dressel 20 and Haltern 70.

Average capacity. 13l.
Chronology. *c*. AD 55–130.
Source. Typology of the form suggests derivation from Haltern 70 and both fabric and palaeography of the inscrip-

74 *London 555 amphoras: British distribution*

Aliases. *Augst* class 21. *Peacock and Williams* class 59.
Bibliography. Sealey and Tyers 1989; Martin-Kilcher 1994, 391–2.
See also. H70

Dressel 7-11 'salazon' amphoras

Forms. A diverse series of forms, encompassing Dressel forms 7–11 and 38–9, Beltrán forms I–II and *Cam* 186. The typology of the class is discussed by Sealey (1985, 77–80). The principal shared characteristics are a flared mouth (perhaps with a hooked rim), a bulbous body and, commonly, a long hollow spike; handles are generally flattened ovals, sharply folded back to meet the body below the rim (**75**). Rarely stamped, but *tituli picti* common on neck, between the handles.

Fabric and technology. A range of pale-coloured (cream, off-white, pink and yellow) fabrics with darker cores; generally soft, powdery surfaces, perhaps with a thin slip or wash. Inclusions generally fine, but some with occasional large red inclusions. This last variant may be a particular product of the Cadiz region. (*Augst* TG 18–20, 58–62).

Average capacity. Variable, perhaps two sizes: 14–18l and 27–33l.

Chronology. Manufactured from late 1st cent. BC to the early 2nd cent. AD. Possibly some pre-conquest importation into Britain.

Source. Principally the southern Iberian coast, where several kiln sites are known and factories for fish products are located. Also some production on the Catalan and Provence coasts (Laubenheimer 1985, 318–9). The manufacture of variants of Dressel 9 and 10 has been reported at Lyon (Dangréaux *et al.* 1992, type 3) – these are represented by Augst 31-32.

Principal contents. The *tituli picti* principally record fish-sauces and salted fish; occasionally *defrutum* and wine. Bones of species such as Spanish mackerel carried in these amphoras are sometimes recovered from wrecks and other sites. The contents of the Lyonnaise production seems also to have been *garum*, despite inland location (Martin-Kilcher 1990).

Distribution. Widespread around the western Mediterranean, where there are numerous wrecks (Parker 1992, fig. 9) and throughout the northern provinces, including Britain, where the distinctive Cadiz fabric has been widely recognized (**76**).

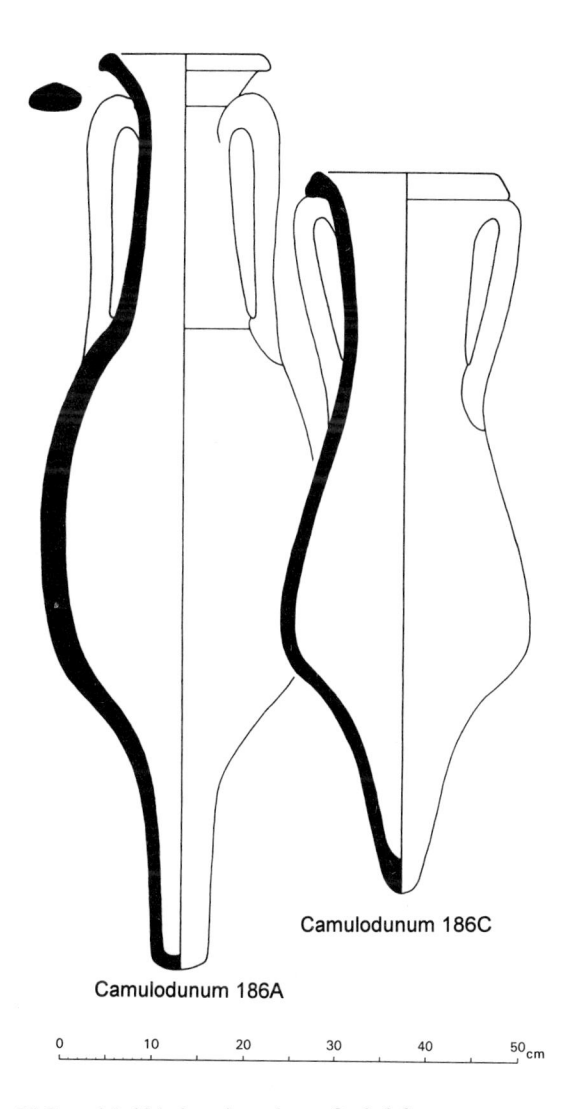

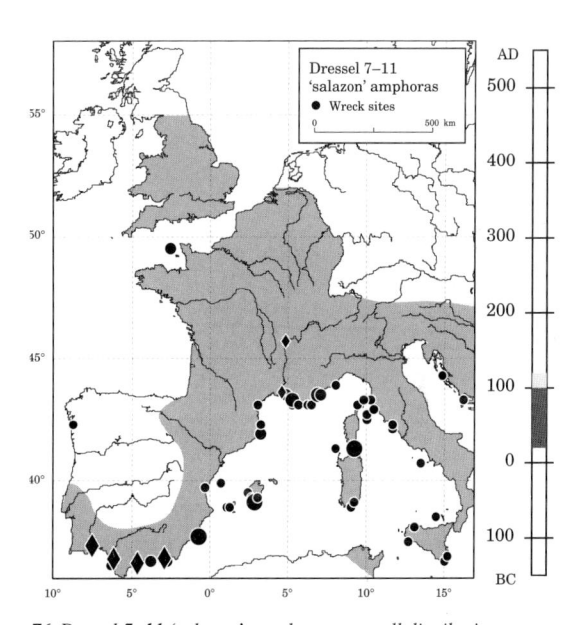

75 Dressel 7–11 'salazon' amphoras: Scale 1:8

76 Dressel 7–11 'salazon' amphoras: overall distribution

Aliases. Augst classes 22, 23a.b, 24, 25, 26 and 27. *Leicester* fabric AM7. *Peacock and Williams* classes 16 (Dressel 7–11, Beltrán I, Paunier 435), 17 (Beltrán I, *Cam* 186A, Schöne-Mau VII), 18 (Dressel 38, Beltrán IIA, Ostia LXIII, *Cam* 186C, Pélichet 46, Callender 6) and 19 (Beltrán IIB, Ostia LVIII).

Bibliography. Beltrán Lloris 1970; Peacock 1974; Martin-Kilcher 1994, 393–409.

Richborough 527 amphoras

Forms. A cylindrical amphora with thick rounded (almond-shaped) rim, two small loop handles and a short sloping neck; shallow horizontal rilling on the body above a solid spike or

Richborough 527/AMPHORAS

button-shaped foot (77). Borgard and Gateau define several sub-categories of *amphores canneleés* which include the R527 and allied types (Borgard and Gateau 1991).

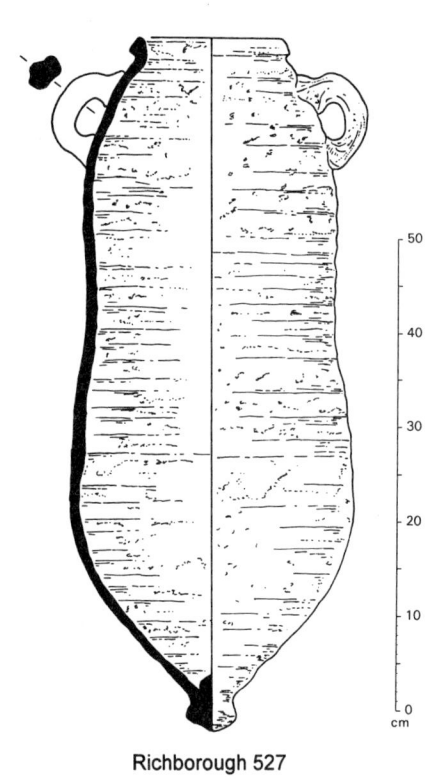

77 Richborough 527 amphora: Scale 1:8

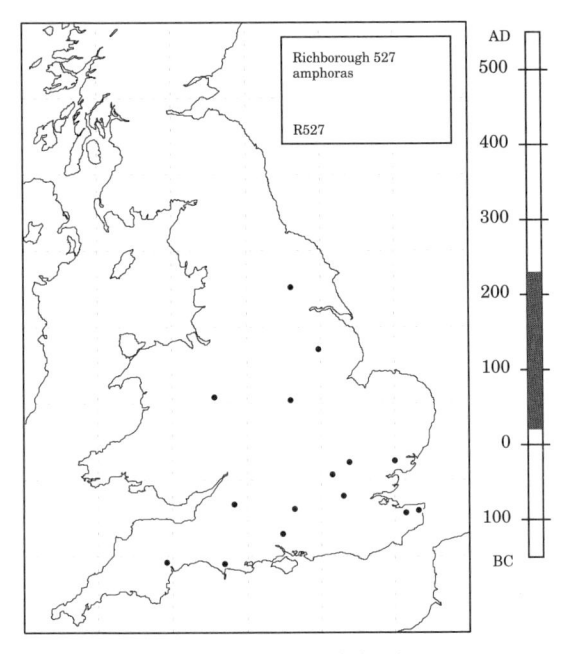

78 Richborough 527 amphoras: British distribution

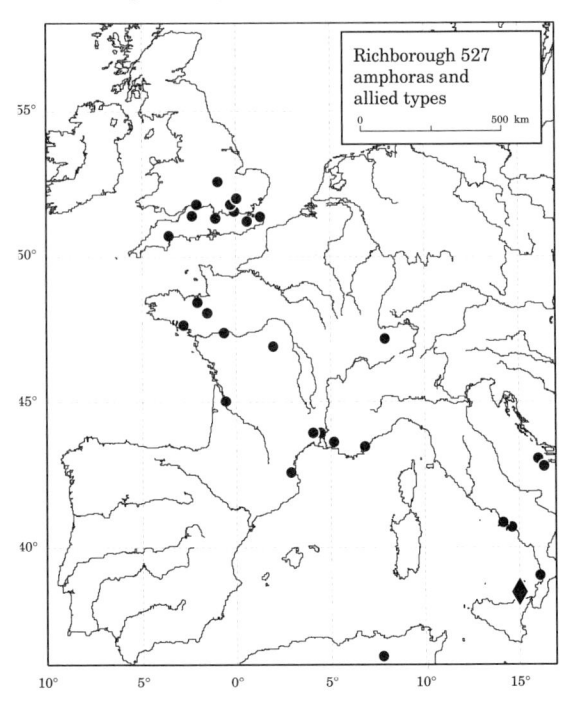

79 Richborough 527 amphoras: overall distribution

Fabric and technology. The fabric described by Peacock (1977c) is hard and rough with lumpy cracked surfaces, generally greenish-grey or pink (5YR 7/2 to 8/4) in colour; distinctive abundant volcanic inclusions, particularly large rounded 'lapilli' of colourless volcanic glass. The petrology indicates a source in an area of recent vulcanism and clay formations of marine origin (*Augst* TG 66).

Stamps. Some examples have small circular stamps on the upper body.

Chronology. Some of the vessels from Provence discussed by Borgard and Gateau, which are taller and slimmer than the British R527 specimens, date to the 1st cent. BC. The majority of those from western France (Brittany and the Loire valley) seem to be mid–later 1st cent. AD. British examples range from pre-conquest (Skeleton Green) through to later 2nd or early 3rd cent. AD (New Fresh Wharf, London). The material described by Arthur from Campania is largely 3rd cent. AD.

Source. Probably the Eolie islands (off the north-east corner of Sicily), where kiln-waste has been discovered near Lipari.

Principal contents. Unknown, but suggestions include fruit, capers and alum.

Distribution. Vessels claimed as R527 are recorded from Britain, western France, Provence and Italy. There is a single

sherd from Lambaesis (Algeria), in the same fabric as those from London. Parker records R527 from two wrecks on the Dalmatian coast (Parker 1992, no. 775, with Italian material, and 1124) (78, 79).
Aliases. *Augst* class 42. *JRPS bibliography* fabric r527. *Leicester* fabric AM16. *Peacock and Williams* class 13.
Bibliography. The original definition of the type is in Peacock 1977c. The situation thereafter is summarized by Sealey 1985, who records Peacock's suggestion that the type comes from the Massif Central. This was followed up in André 1989. The possibility of an Italian (Campanian?) origin is raised in Arthur 1989, but French reports continued to press the case for a Gaulish source, on the grounds of the large number of specimens (Borgard and Gateau 1991). For the Lipari kiln material and speculation on contents: Cavalier 1994; Borgard 1994.

Camulodunum 189 ('carrot') amphoras

Forms. Small conical amphora with horizontal rilling covering the outer surface (hence 'carrot'); two small loop handles just below the rim. On many examples the rilling is angular and formed with a square cut tool (**80**).

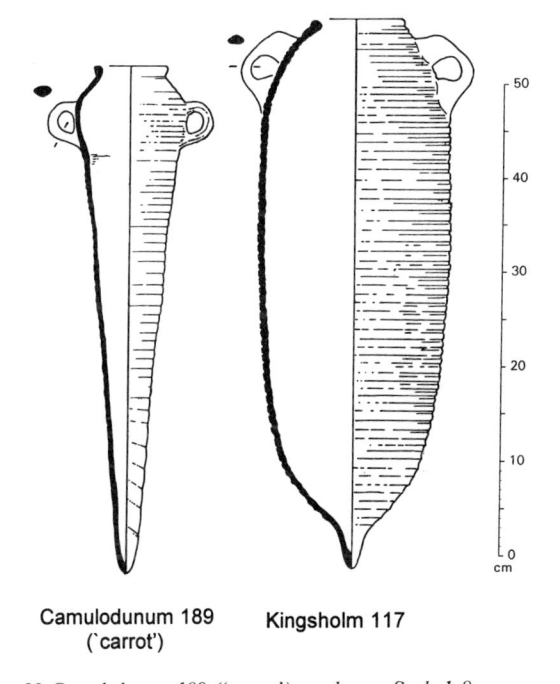

80 *Camulodunum 189 ('carrot') amphoras: Scale 1:8*

Fabric and technology. Hard, red-brown or brick-red (2.5YR 6/8 or 10YR 4/6) sandy fabric, sometimes with a grey core; some vessels are finer textured and may have a thin pale yellow slip (*Augst* TG 68). Analysis of sand temper suggests source in a desert region (Shackley 1975, 57–9).
Average capacity. 2–3l.

Chronology. Augustan at Oberaden, but post-conquest in Britain, up to *c.* AD 100.
Principal contents. A *dipinto* from Carlisle, apparently on a vessel of this form, reads KOYK in Greek letters, an abbreviated reference to κουκια, the fruit of the doum palm (*Hyphaene thebaica*). Other varieties of dried fruits, such as dates, may also have been carried.
Source. The south-east Mediterranean, perhaps Egypt.
Distribution. Despite probable eastern origin, the majority of published examples are from the western Empire, particularly from Rhineland and Britain, and often on military sites. Also recorded from the Rhône valley, Italy and Algeria (**81**).

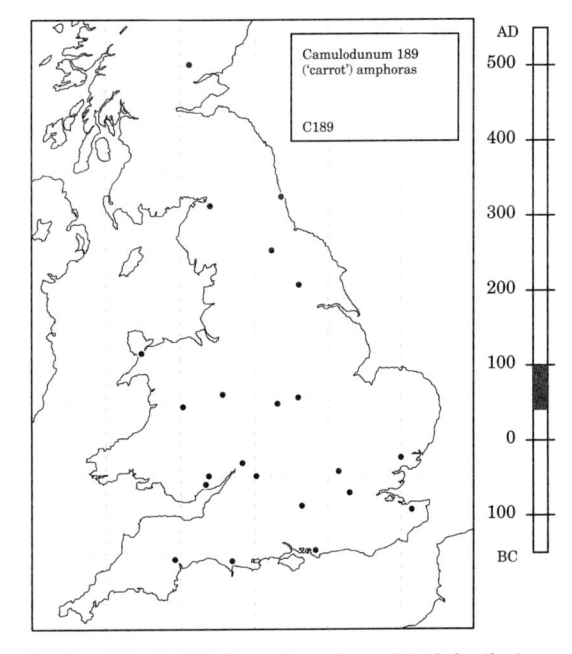

81 *Camulodunum 189 ('carrot') amphoras: British distribution*

Aliases. *Augst* class 44. *Cirencester* fabric 47. *Gloucester* fabric TF10F. *JRPS bibliography* fabric cta. *Leicester* fabric AM18. *Peacock and Williams* class 12 (Carrot, Schöne-Mau XV).
Bibliography. Reusch 1970; Sealey 1985, 87–90. On contents and origin: Tomlin 1992.
Notes. A related form, the *Kingsholm* 117 (*Augst* class 45. *Gloucester* fabric TF10F. *Peacock and Williams* class 65.) has a similar fabric to C189, but larger body diameter; probably indistinguishable in small sherds. This type has been identified on a few sites in Britain and there are examples from two wrecks on the Provence coast (Parker 1992, nos. 374, 1174). One of these contained dates. Martin-Kilcher describes several further minor forms of rilled amphora in the same ware (*Augst* forms 46–7).

Kapitän II ('Hollow foot') amphoras

Forms. Tall conical neck, tapering towards a simple thickened

British B4 ('micaceous jars')/AMPHORAS

rim, with a sharp flange just below the lip; tapering conical body ending in a short hollow tubular foot, with light grooves on the exterior. Broad, thick, steeply arching handles, with slight raised ridge on the outer face (82).

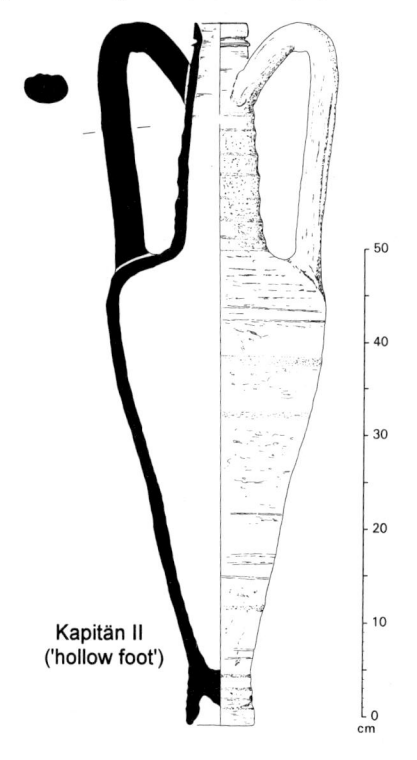

82 Kapitän II ('Hollow foot') amphoras: Scale 1:8

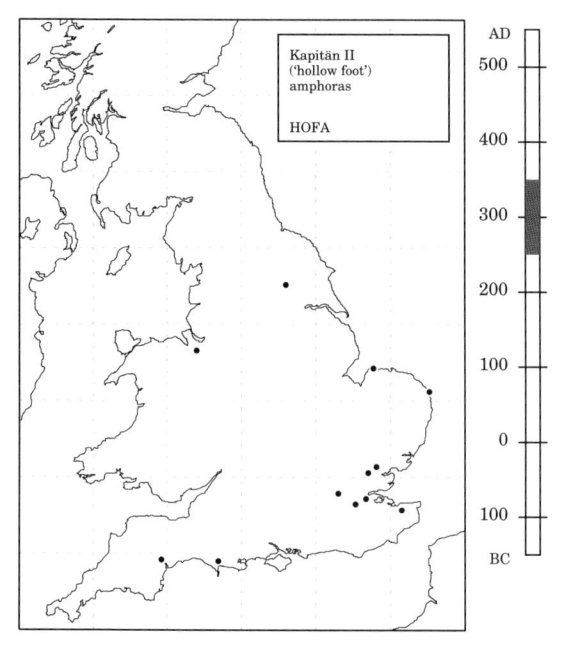

83 Kapitän II ('Hollow foot') amphoras: British distribution

Fabric and technology. Distinctive hard, rough orange-red (2.5YR 5/8) fabric with grey core (particularly in the handles); moderate quantities of large white quartz grains and occasional red-brown sandstone fragments.
Chronology. From late 2nd to late 4th cent. with little apparent typological change, but most date from later 3rd and 4th cent.
Source. Probably the Aegean region.
Principal contents. Unknown.
Distribution. Extensive distribution in the eastern Mediterranean, around the Black Sea and along the lower Danube. Less common in the west, but there are examples in at least one wreck off the French coast (Parker 1992, no. 76) and the type occurs sporadically in southern Gaul, the Rhineland and Britain (83).
Aliases. Augst class 54. *Chelmsford* fabric 59. *JRPS bibliography* fabric ahf. *Keay* fabric 22. *Lullingstone* fabric 80. *Peacock and Williams* class 47 (Ostia VI, Kapitän II, Kuzmanov VII, Niederbieber 77, Zeest 79, Benghazi MR7).
Bibliography. For distribution and chronology: Riley 1979, 189–93; for petrology: Peacock 1977d, 297.

British B4 amphoras ('micaceous jars')

Forms. A long slender amphora with high rounded shoulder, tapering foot and narrow neck; one or two tight strap handles

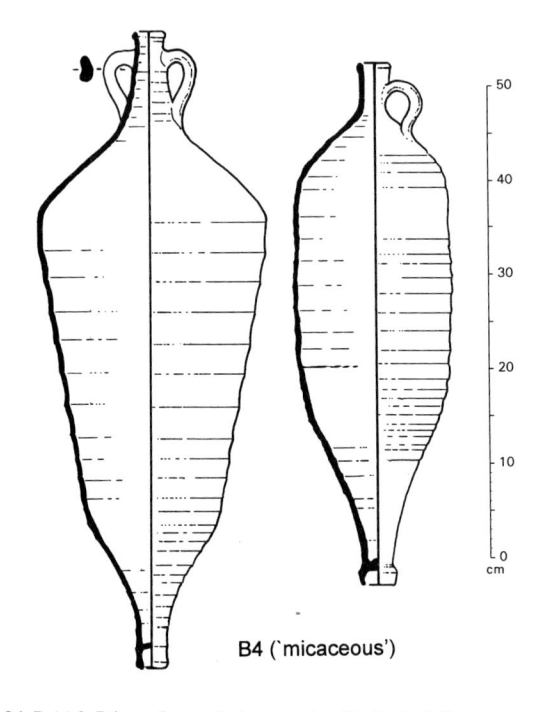

84 British B4 amphoras ('micaceous jars'): Scale 1:8

British B4 ('micaceous jars')/AMPHORAS

below small beaded rim; broad horizontal ribbing often visible over the lower body (84). Some of the earlier examples have two- or three-character graffiti in Greek characters on the shoulder below the lower handle attachment which can be interpreted as dates based on the Actian calendar, commencing in 31 BC (Lang 1955).

Fabric and technology. Friable, with laminar fracture, but smooth surfaces, sometimes almost soapy to the touch; red-brown (2.5YR 5/4 to 5YR 5/4) with golden-brown surfaces; abundantly micaceous fabric, with some quartz and other fine inclusions. Patchy creamy-yellow slip on external surface of some examples *(Augst TG 71)*.

Average capacity. c. 6.5l in 2nd cent. AD. Later examples can be larger.

Chronology. A very long-lived type, appearing in later 1st cent. (one-handled) – dated graffiti range from AD 74 to 158. Two-handled from later 4th cent., and continuing to end of 6th. Distribution covers Italy (Ostia) and Provence by mid-2nd cent. Many British examples are from 3rd/4th cent., but a few earlier; also *c.* AD 475–550 in western Britain. Featureless sherds only datable by context.

Source. Petrology and distribution suggests western Asia Minor, perhaps the region of Sardis.

Principal contents. Not certain. They are often described as 'water jars', and some analyses have identified oil residues (Rothschild-Boros 1981) but Martin-Kilcher suggests that wine was the most likely contents (1994, 440–1).

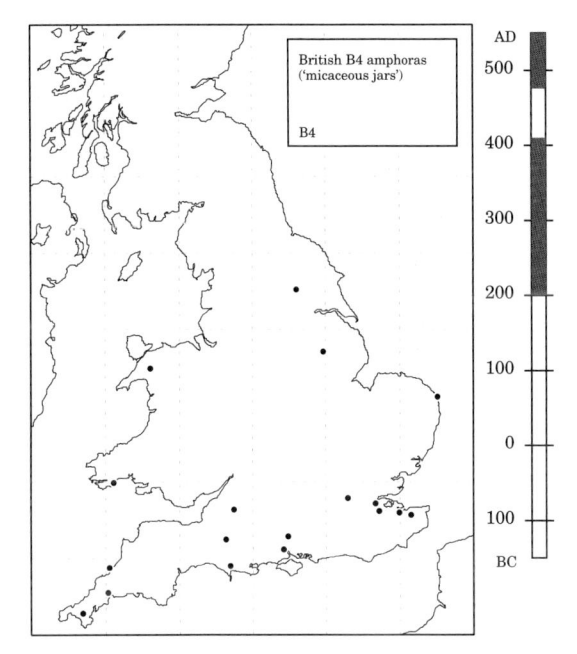

Distribution. Extensively around eastern and western Mediterranean, but never abundant and not common on

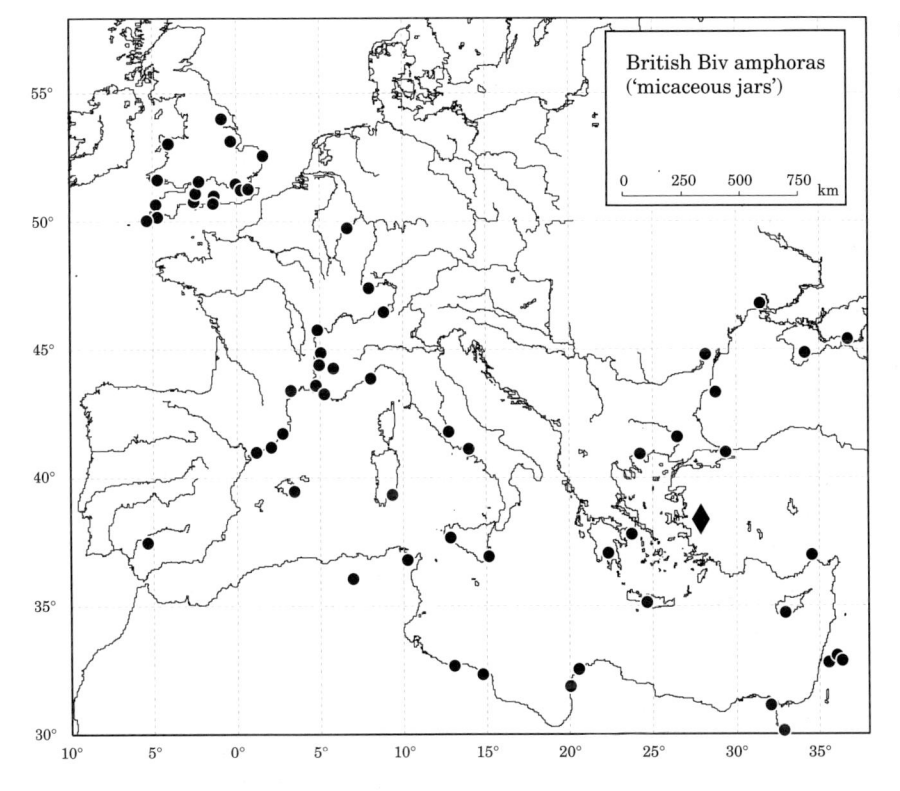

85 *British B4 amphoras ('micaceous jars'): British distribution*

86 *British B4 amphoras ('micaceous jars'): overall distribution*

North African cylindrical/AMPHORAS

wreck sites (Parker 1992, no. 499) perhaps suggesting that not transported in large numbers as other amphoras (**85, 86**).
Aliases. *Augst* class 55. *Keay* fabric 17. *Peacock and Williams* class 45 (Ballana 13a, Kuzmanov VIII, Scorpan 5, Carthage LR3, Benghazi LR10).
Bibliography. For summary: Tomber and Williams 1986; distribution in Riley 1979; C. Thomas 1981; post-Roman importation: Fulford 1989.
See also. PRSW

North African cylindrical amphoras

Forms. Cylindrical amphora with short straight neck, small thickened or rounded rim and sharply bent handles; long body with short spike, which may be either hollow (Africana I) or solid, with slightly bulging profile (Africana II) (**88**). Occasionally stamped on the neck.
Fabric and technology. Hard, red (2.5YR 6/6) fabric with darker (perhaps black) surfaces covered with a thin white 'wash', apparently the result of brushing saline water on the unfired vessel (Peacock 1984); moderate or abundant fine quartz and white limestone inclusions, some showing reaction rims (*Augst* TG 76-7).
Average capacity. c. 60l (for the Africana Grande).
Chronology. Produced from the early 2nd cent. until at least the late 4th cent. Imports into Britain commence by the mid-2nd cent., but most commonly in the 3rd and 4th cent. Some importation into western Britain in post-Roman period.
Source. Central Tunisia, the Roman province of Byzacena (hence sometimes known as Byzacena amphoras).
Principal contents. Principally olive-oil, but also fish-sauces.

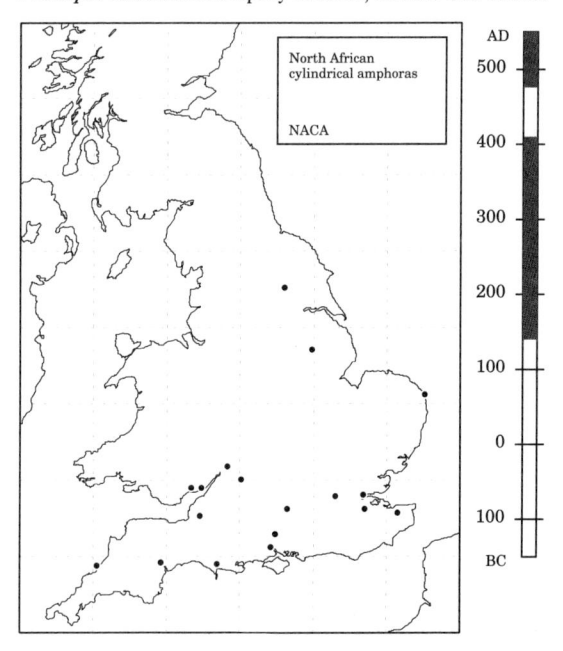

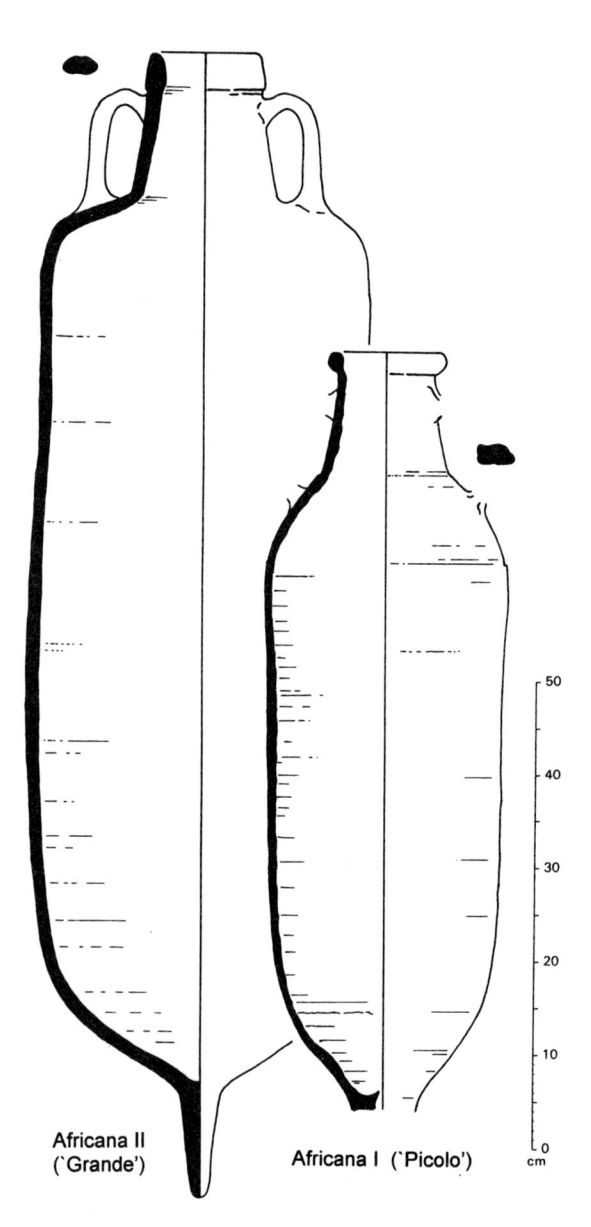

88 North African cylindrical amphoras: Scale 1:8

Distribution. Widespread around the western Mediterranean, where there are a number of wrecks (Parker 1992, fig. 14); patchy distribution in the northern provinces, where very few have been identified in Gaul, but increasing numbers from Britain (**87, 89**).
Aliases. *Augst* classes 65 and 66. *JRPS bibliography* fabric ana. *Keay* fabrics 1–2 (Northern Tunisia) and 3 (Central Tunisian). *Peacock and Williams* classes 33 (Africana I – Piccolo, Beltrán 57, Ostia IV, Keay III) and 34 (Africana II – Grande, Beltrán 56, Ostia III, Keay IV–VII). British

87 North African cylindrical amphoras: British distribution

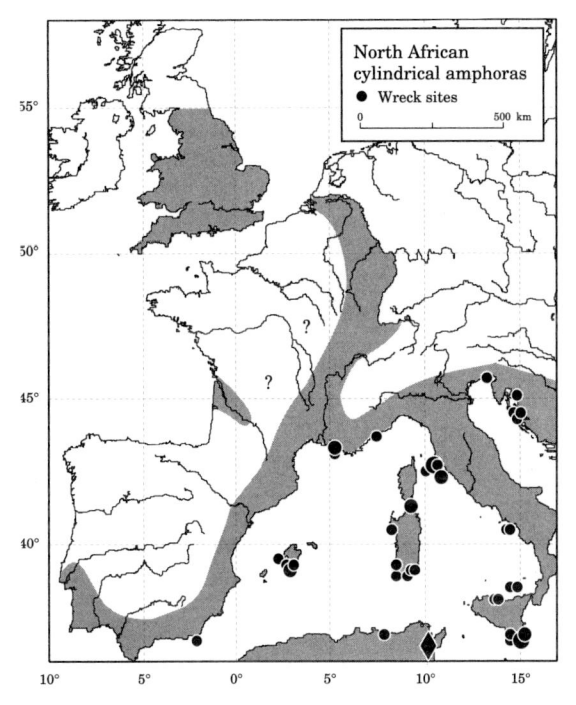

89 *North African cylindrical amphoras: overall distribution*

(Tintagel) class Bv.
Bibliography. Peacock 1977c, 270–2.
See also. NARS

TERRA SIGILLATA OR SAMIAN WARES

The red-gloss wares, known collectively as samian wares or *terra sigillata* – both terms are misnomers – are the classic fine wares of the early Roman period, familiar to any visitor to a museum or excavation with finds of this period. Their study has a long and brilliant history, and has traditionally overshadowed that of more humble wares.

Source. The earliest sigillata wares, including the pre-conquest imports to Britain, are from Italian workshops, but the most important sources for the Roman period are, successively, the factories of South, Central and Eastern Gaul. A small workshop operated out of Colchester during the Antonine period (**90**). These are described separately in the following Atlas entries:

ITTS	Italian-type sigillata
SGTS	South Gaulish (La Graufesenque)
MOTS	South Gaulish (Montans)
CGTS	Central Gaulish
EGTS	East Gaulish
COTS	Colchester

Forms. The standard sigillata type-series originates in Dragendorff's 1895 paper (**table 31**). He defined 55 types, and the series was extended by Déchelette, Knorr and Walters, who all added new forms to the end of the existing sequence. References to other common types are taken from the publications of Ritterling and Curle. These forms duplicate numbers in the main series, but are quite different – a Dragendorff 15 is not the same as a Curle 15. To avoid any potential confusion it is often preferable to use both the name of the type-series and the type number. The type-series is usually referred to by abbreviations (e.g. Drag or Dr, De or Déch, Kn, Wa, Cu, Ritt), particularly in the detailed listings of samian assemblages found in some published reports and much unpublished archive data.

Series		Types
Main series		
Dragendorff	Dr Drag	1-55
Déchelette	De Déch	56-77
Knorr	Kn	78
Walters	Wa	79-82
Additional forms		
Ritterling	Ritt	8 9 12 13
Curle	Cu	11 15 21 23
East Gaulish wares		
Ludowici	Lud	
Italian-type wares		
Loeschcke/Haltern	Ha	1-17
Conspectus	Consp.	1-54

Table 31 *Principal terra sigillata type-series*

Some extensions to the standard types are widely understood. There are transitional forms such as the Drag 15/17 or Drag 18/31, and the suffix R indicates a form with a rouletted band, either inside a plate or dish (e.g. Drag 18R, Drag 15/17R) or more rarely on a bowl, normally moulded, where the decoration has been replaced by rouletting (e.g. Drag 37R). The Drag 27g has a groove on the outer face of the footring, and the Drag 33a has a moulding at the junction of the wall and base (B. R. Hartley 1972a, 216).

The type-series developed by Ludowici for the material from his excavations at the major East Gaulish workshops at Rheinzabern partly overlaps with the standard series. Unlike the latter, however, Ludowici's classification is not a numbered sequence but a series of letter codes (e.g. Sd, Tg), where the initial letter is the abbreviation of the German name of the form (*Schüssel, Teller* etc). References to further rare East Gaulish forms are taken from other publications (Bird 1995).

Early Italian ('Arretine') wares have traditionally been classified using the typology developed by Loeschcke in 1909 for the material from Haltern (Loeschcke 1909), which again overlaps with Dragendorff's forms. A more recent study of Italian

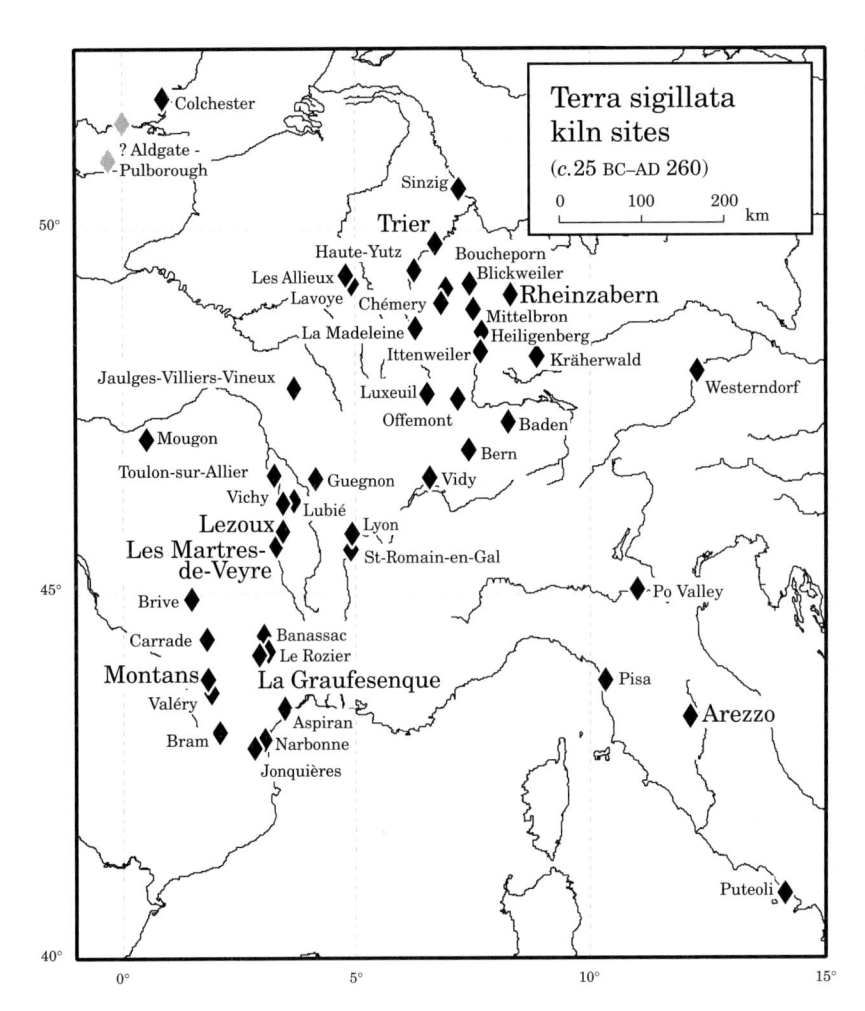

90 Terra sigillata kiln sites, 20 BC–AD 260

sigillata proposes a new classification (the *Conspectus*: Ettlinger et al. 1990), which is likely to become widely used.

The multiplicity of reference numbers can tend to obscure the structure of the samian typology. Many forms can be grouped together into sets, particularly matching pairs of cups and plates such as Drag 46 (cup) and Curle 15 (plate). This is often the easiest way of understanding the development of samian types.

Stamps. Stamps on sigillata serve several purposes. Many were probably used as control-marks within and between workshops and to distinguish batches of pottery in communal firings. Larger stamps on decorated wares may have been used as 'advertisements'.

Plain wares, when stamped, have marks on the interior of the vessel, usually central, but radial on some of the earliest Italian wares. The rate of stamping varies between forms and some of the rarer types (e.g. Drag 35 and 36) are only rarely stamped.

Decorated wares may have more than one stamp on the same vessel, and in different locations. There may be stamps within the decoration – which were originally stamped into the mould – giving the names of mouldmakers. Related to these are the signatures of the mouldmakers written in the mould with a stylus, usually in a cursive script. These were usually placed towards the bottom of the bowl, and are thus obscured by later stages of the manufacturing processes, such as the addition of the footring. Small stamps (sometimes the same as those on the plain wares) on the interior of the vessel, or on the exterior near the rim or base are the marks of the potters or bowl-finishers. These often give a different name to that of the mouldmaker.

These abbreviations are common on stamps:

OF OFIC OFFIC	*officina*	workshop of ..
F FE FEC	*fecit*	.. made [this]
M MA MAN	*manu*	by the hand of ..

Work on a major new Index of samian stamps has been in progress for some years at the University of Leeds, led by B. R.

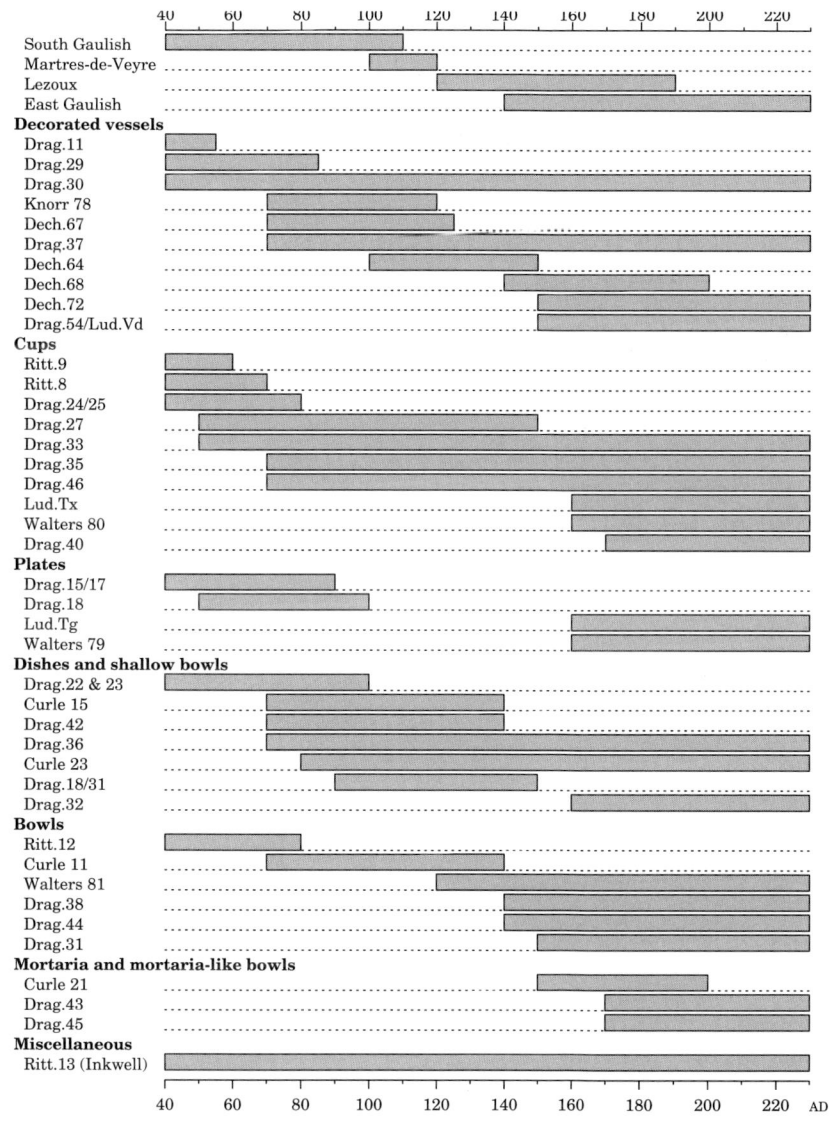

91 *Terra sigillata or samian wares: dating of principal forms*

Hartley and B. M. Dickinson. The provisional die numbers from the Leeds Index have been used extensively in samian reports in Britain since the 1970s. They are in two parts, usually written as Ia or 1a. The numeral refers to the reading, the letter to the precise die giving that reading. A broken die has the suffix ' (e.g.1a'). The Leeds Index will be an immensely valuable tool for sigillata studies, not only for an improved chronology of potters and dies but also for the insights into the connections between the workshops (e.g. B. R. Hartley 1977).

Chronology. Dating will depend on a combination of fabric, form and (where present) the decoration and stamps. Some forms have a long life and are produced successively in the major centres, while others may have a more limited lifespan. The major forms commonly found in Britain are illustrated in **92–94**, with their broad dates in **91**.

Bibliography. The bibliography of samian ware is notoriously vast and scattered. Basic introductions can be found in B. R. Hartley 1969; Johns 1971; Bulmer 1980; De la Bédoyère 1988; most of these contain photographs of the principal forms and decorative types, some in colour. A more complete guide to the practicalities of the identification and study of form, fabric and decoration is P.V. Webster 1996. Illustrations of some of the more obscure forms are still most readily accessible in the pages of *Oswald and Pryce* (F. Oswald and Davies Pryce 1920) and two papers by Stanfield (1929; 1936). A series of classic publications, starting with the works of Déchelette, Knorr and Hermet, remain fundamental to the study of decorated wares. Further bibliographic references will be found in the appropriate Atlas entries.

TERRA SIGILLATA

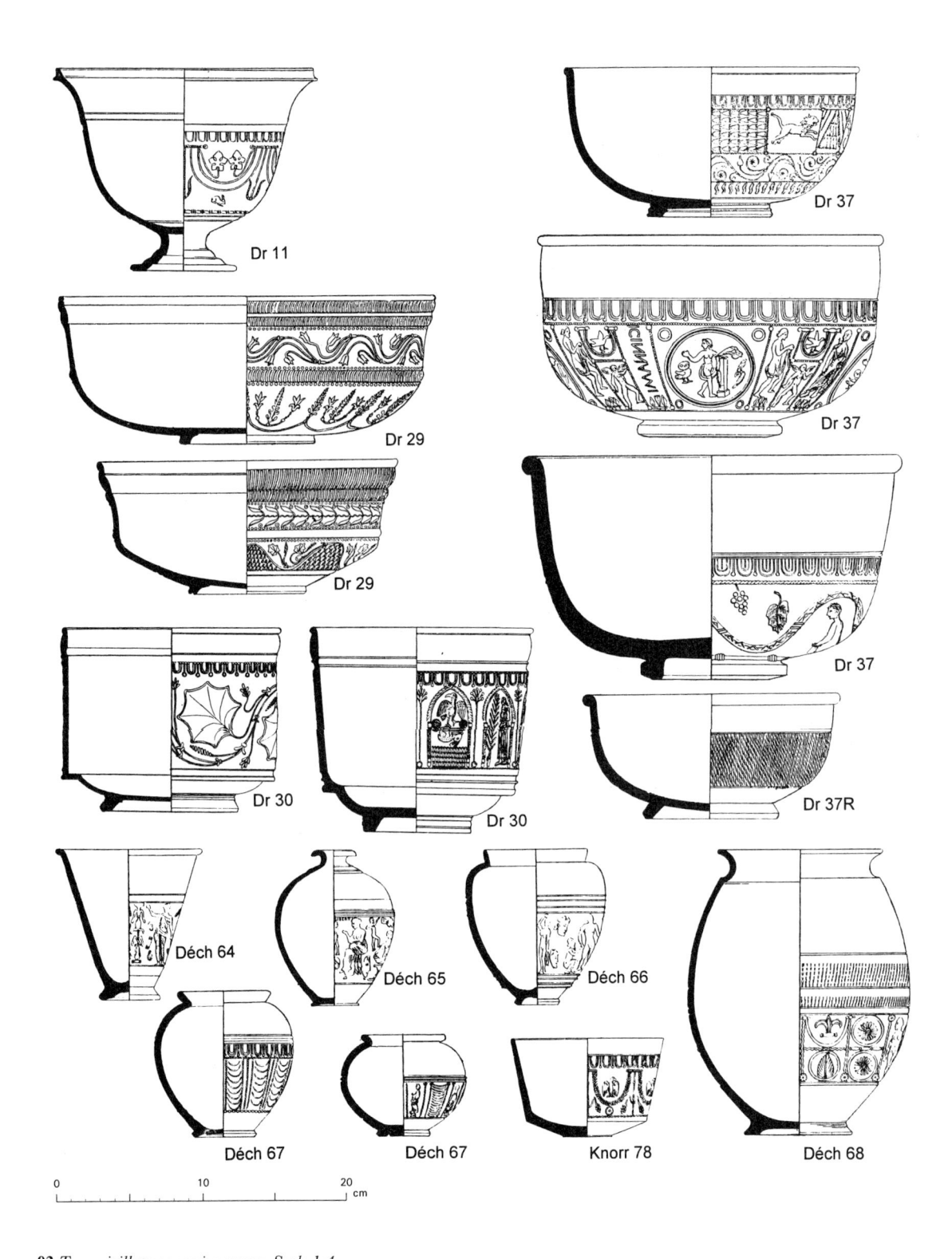

92 *Terra sigillata or samian wares: Scale 1:4*

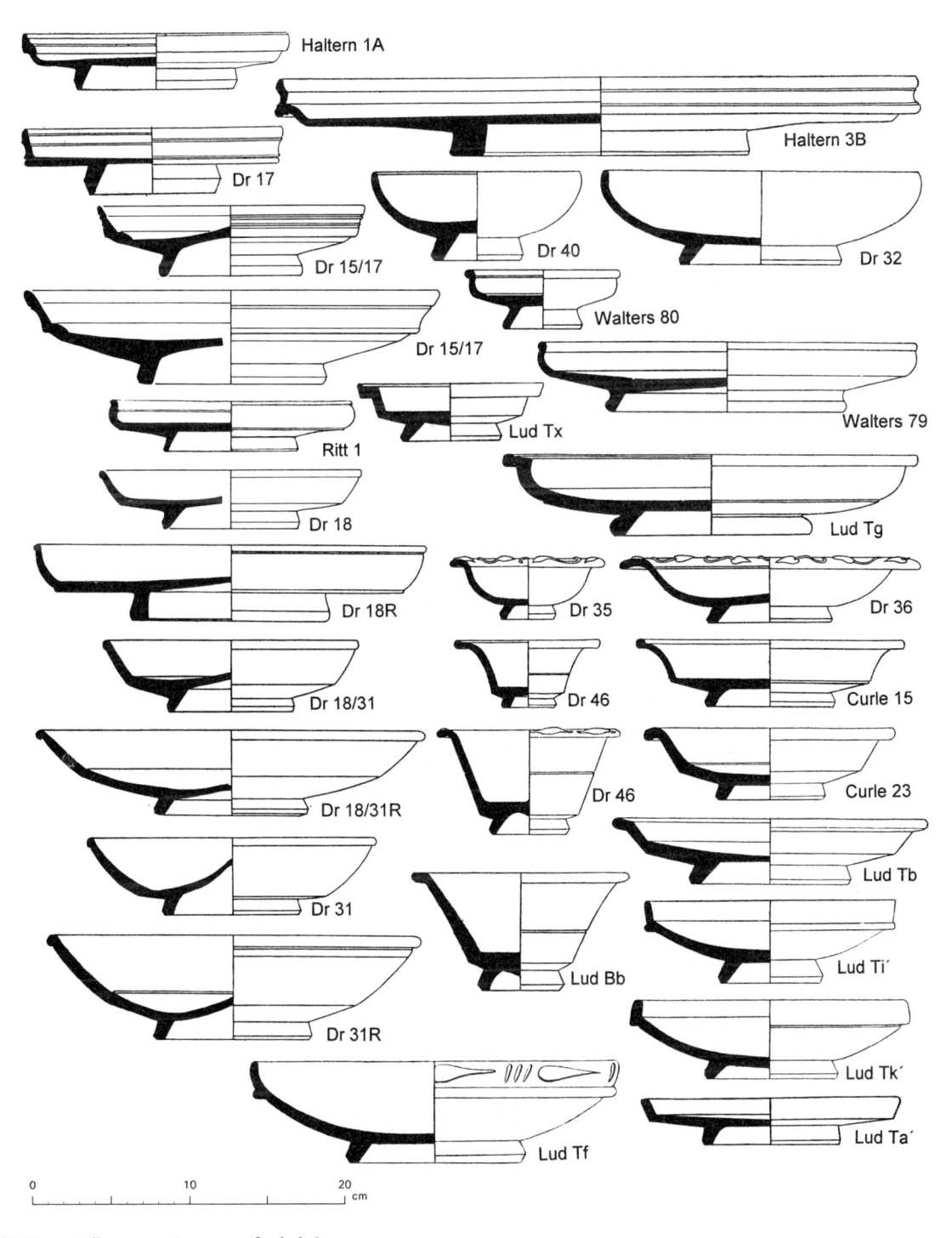

93 *Terra sigillata or samian wares: Scale 1:4*

TERRA SIGILLATA

94 *Terra sigillata or samian wares: Scale 1:4*

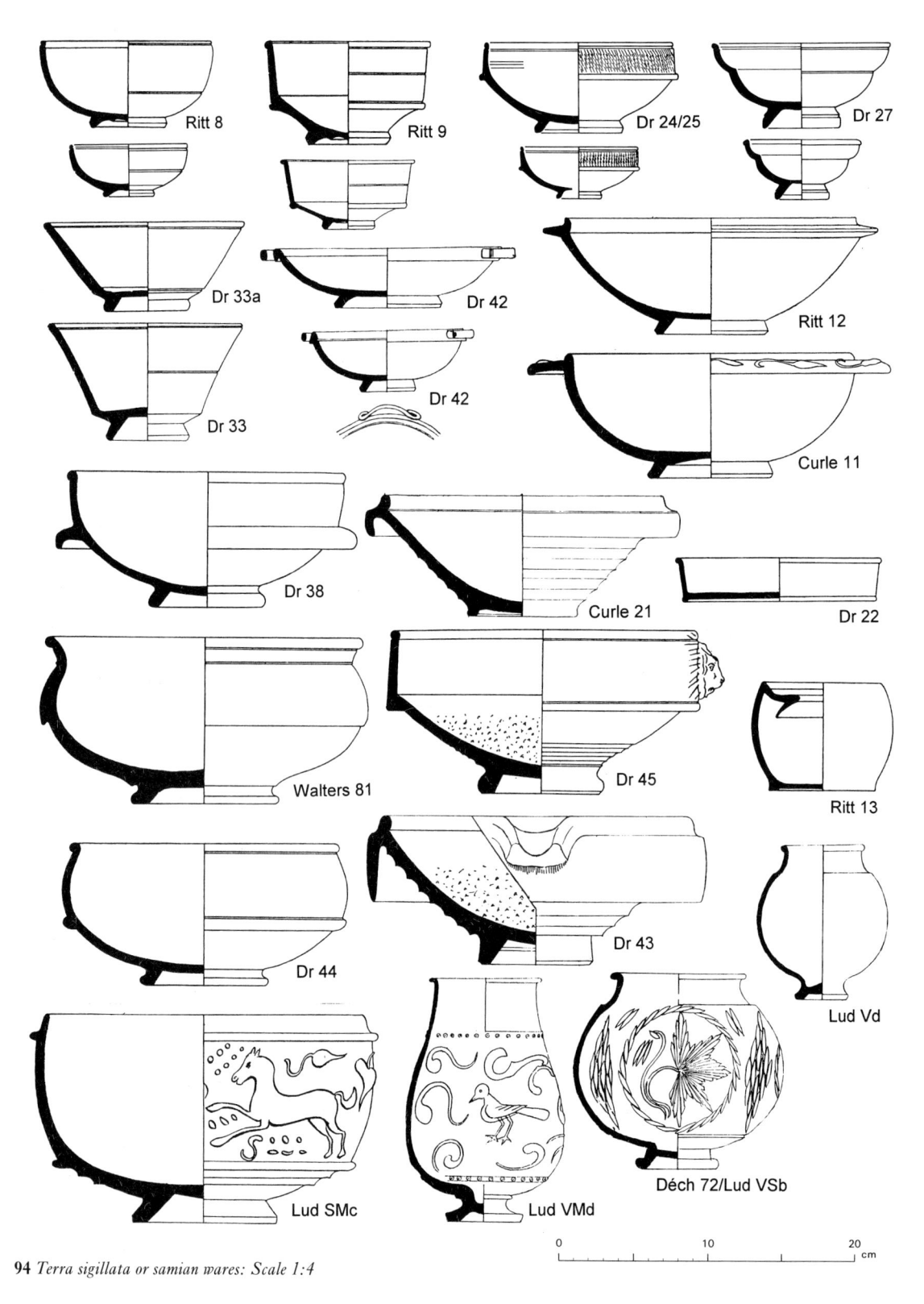

Italian-type ('Arretine')/ TERRA SIGILLATA

In the Atlas pages the wares are ordered chronologically.

Italian-type ('Arretine') sigillata
The workshops at Arezzo (Etruria) had long been considered to be the only significant source of 'Arretine' ware. The discovery of kilns producing apparently identical material at Lyon in 1966 demonstrated the existence of branch-workshops, some initiated by Arezzo potters. Subsequent application of chemical provenancing techniques to the assemblage from the Augustan legionary fortress of Haltern in Germany (the 'type site' for Loeschcke's classic study of 'Italian' sigillata) has shown that 50% is from the La Muette workshop at Lyon, 30% from Pisa and only 10% definitely from Arezzo. Sigillata studies are currently in a state of flux, with the discovery of new and previously unexpected sources, and it is proposed that the term 'Italian-type' be employed for any material (of whatever source) whose appearance closely resembles that of the Arezzo workshops (Ettlinger *et al.* 1990, 1).

Fabric and technology. Identification of sources of 'Italian-type' sigillata fabrics is a specialized task, which may be assisted by petrological and chemical analysis. Classic Arezzo ware is a hard, smooth-textured orange-brown (2.5YR 5/8) fabric with conchoidal fracture. Slip bright glossy red (10R 4/8); clean matrix includes only a few white flecks (<0.1mm) and occasional voids. Lyon fabric varies somewhat, but generally hard, smooth-textured light red-brown fabric (5YR 7/6, 6/6) with dull red-brown slip (10YR 4/8); finely irregular fracture with abundant fine white flecks, sparser red flecks, a little fine quartz sand (all <0.1mm) and a scatter of elongated voids (up to 0.2mm).

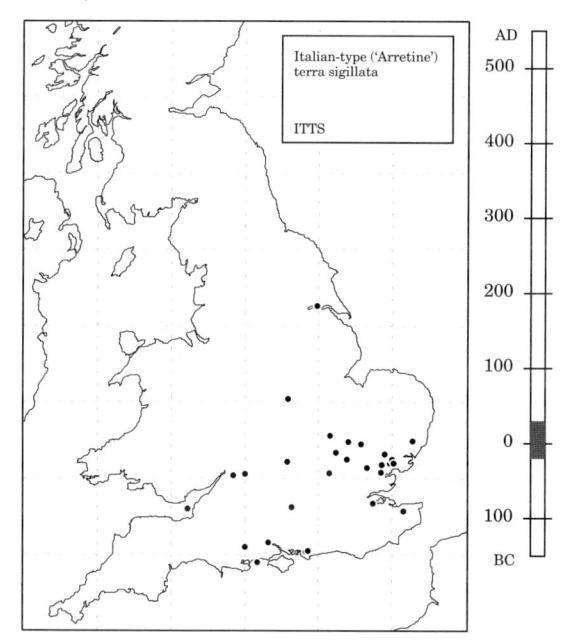

95 *Italian-type ('Arretine') sigillata: British distribution*

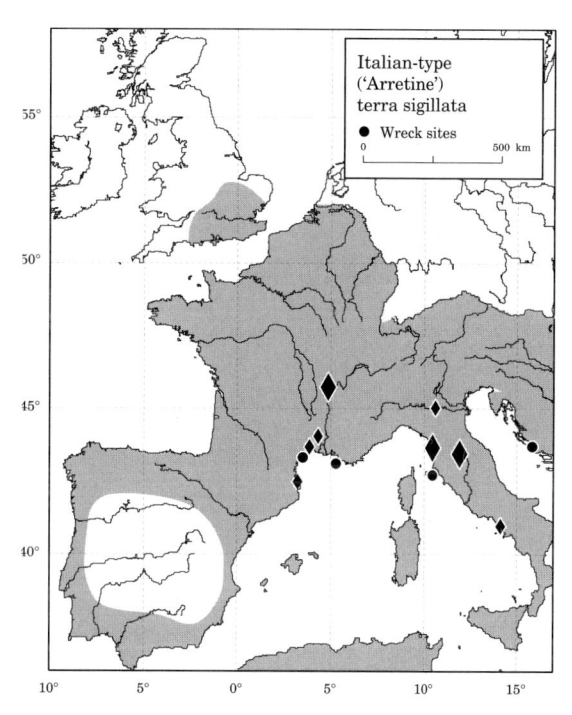

96 *Italian-type ('Arretine') sigillata: overall distribution*

Chronology. Production at Arezzo from *c.* 45 BC, of both red- and black-slipped wares; some provincial workshops opened by *c.* 35/30 BC, with production at Lyon from *c.* 15 BC. Earliest imports to Britain include platters with radial stamps, which should date to *c.* 20 BC (e.g. Wickenden 1986, 53, fig. 26, 9), but the bulk of the British assemblage can be matched at Haltern (*c.* 5 BC–AD 9) rather than at earlier sites. Decline during Tiberian period, and very rare on conquest-period, Claudian sites.

Source. Principal Italian factories at Arezzo, Pisa and Puteoli; provincial workshops located in north-east Spain, southern France and Lyon. The British assemblage certainly includes many pieces from Arezzo, but a few vessels from Lyon, Puteoli and Pisa workshops have also been identified (D. F. Williams and Dannell 1978, 9).

Distribution. Widely distributed around the western Mediterranean basin, and beyond, in the eastern provinces. In Gaul, common in Languedoc and Provence, along the Rhône/Saône river systems and in the Rhineland, particularly in Augustan military assemblages; outside this region generally less abundant, but increasing publication demonstrates a presence throughout Gaul. In Britain, central-southern Britain and the south-east, particularly Essex and Herts (**95, 96**).

Aliases. *JRPS bibliography* fabrics arr and its. *Silchester* fabric E1.

Bibliography. Fundamental study now Ettlinger *et al.* 1990; for stamps: Oxé and Comfort 1968. A new computerized corpus of stamps is under development: Kenrick 1994. On British

111

South Gaulish (La Graufesenque)/TERRA SIGILLATA

material: C. F. C. Hawkes and Hull 1947; Rodwell 1976; Dannell in Cunliffe 1971; Dannell in Partridge 1981; Hartley and Williams in Potter and Trow 1988; for petrology: D. F. Williams and Dannell 1978; D. F. Williams 1981b; Jefferson, Dannell and Williams 1981.

South Gaulish (La Graufesenque) terra sigillata

Fabric and technology. Hard, smooth-surfaced fabric with conchoidal or slightly laminar fracture; pinkish-brown (10R 5–6/8, sometimes 10R 5/10) typically with glossy red slip (10R 5/8 or darker, 2.5YR 4/6) covering the entire vessel, except interior of enclosed vessels. Earliest specimens in Britain (Tiberio-Claudian) lack high gloss of classic ware and are duller in appearance. Very abundant inclusions of finely divided limestone, usually under 0.1mm in diameter but occasionally up to 0.5mm, or in longer streaks; occasional fragments of rounded quartzite (up to 0.5mm diameter) in the paste and the underside of footrings. A distinctive variant of the ware has a yellow slip (2.5Y 7/4) marbled with red streaks.

Stamps. Although *c.* 600 potters are known to have operated at La Graufesenque the assemblage in Britain is often dominated by a small number of firms, particularly Aquitanus, Bassus, Calvus, Crestio, Frontinus, Germanus, Licinus, Modestus, Murranus, Niger, Pass(i)enus, Patricius, Primus, Rufinus, Secundus, Severus, Virilis and Vitalis.

Chronology. Production at La Graufesenque commences in the late Augustan period, and there may be some Tiberian exports to Britain, but the period of the major export is *c.* AD 40–100. Local production continues up to at least *c.* AD 200.

Source. La Graufesenque (Aveyron), on the outskirts of Millau.

Distribution. Extensive around western Mediterranean, including Italy and North Africa, Gaul, Rhineland and Danube provinces, and Britain. Also a wide scatter in eastern provinces, and beyond as far as the Sudan and India (**97**).

The marbled variant dates to *c.* AD 40–75 and is uncommon in Britain – rarely more than a sherd or two in even large collections – but is far more prominent in assemblages around the Mediterranean (Rogers 1981).

Aliases. Colchester fabric SG. *JRPS bibliography* fabric sts. Kent fine fabric 20a. Silchester fabric E3.

Bibliography. Bémont, Vernhet and Beck 1987 and Bémont and Jacob 1986, 96–103 give summaries of production at La Graufesenque. The papers presented at the SFECAG conference at Millau in 1994 (Rivet 1994) illustrate some new developments in *sigillata* studies, such as the use of statistical techniques to investigate the relationships between potters within a workshop or the links between potters and consumers.

The important series of pre-firing graffiti from La Graufesenque are reported by Marichal 1988. South Gaulish decorated wares are covered by Knorr 1919; Knorr 1952; Hermet 1934; with important collections published by D. Atkinson 1914 (the Pompeii hoard); Hull 1958; C. F. C. Hawkes and Hull 1947; Curle 1911; Dannell in Cunliffe 1971; Manning 1993.

South Gaulish (Montans) terra sigillata

Fabric and technology. Hard, fine-textured, with slightly irregular fracture; distinguished by pale brown fabric (e.g. 10YR 8/4) with matt brownish-red slip (2.5YR 5/6).

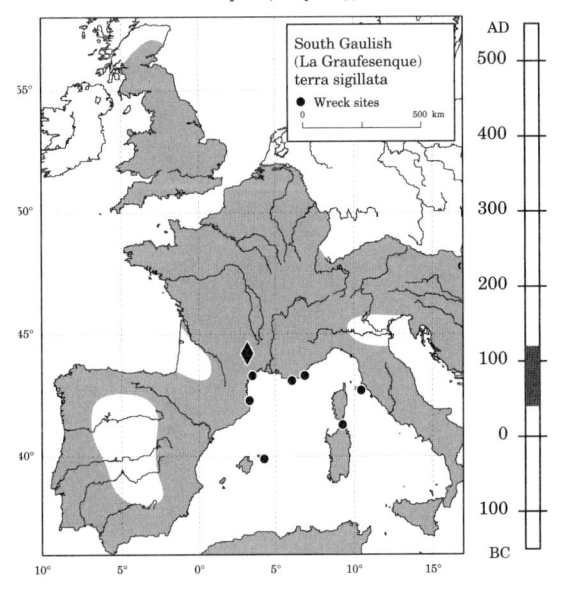

97 South Gaulish (La Graufesenque) terra sigillata: overall distribution

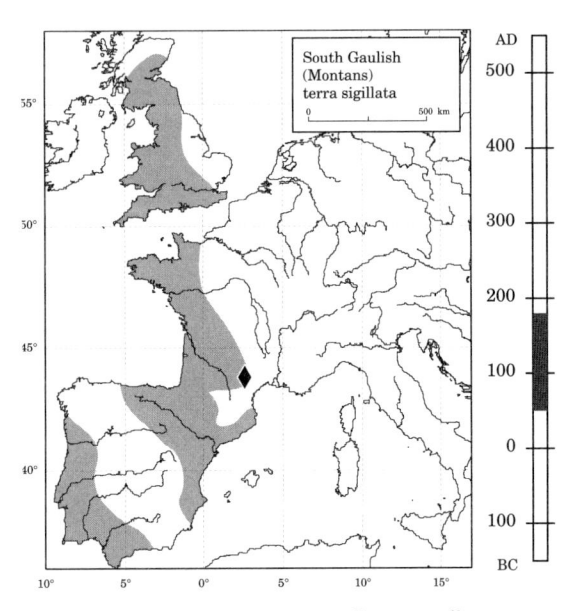

98 South Gaulish (Montans) terra sigillata: overall distribution

Inclusions of abundant fine red iron ore and sparse quartz and mica.
Chronology. Manufacture commences in Augustan period; plain and decorated wares exported to Britain from Neronian period until end of production in late Antonine period. In London, most is probably Flavian/Trajanic, but includes cache of nine stamped vessels from 'second fire' levels (Marsh 1981, 200–1).
Source. Montans (Tarn), in Aquitaine.
Distribution. A predominantly western French distribution, with extension into northern Spain; wide but thin distribution in Britain, as far as northern frontier (B. R. Hartley 1972b, 42–5), but rarely more than a few sherds on most sites (**98**).
Aliases. *Colchester* fabric MT.
Bibliography. Bémont and Jacob 1986, 58–71. Some of the British material is described in Simpson 1976.
See also. SGTS

Central Gaulish terra sigillata

The two principal Central Gaulish sigillata producers, Les Martres-de-Veyre and Lezoux (near Clermont-Ferrand) were the main samian exporters to Britain for most of the 2nd cent. The earlier product of Lezoux, in a distinctive micaceous fabric, was also exported in small quantities.

Fabric and technology. Les Martres-de-Veyre: Very hard, high-fired fabric (sherds ring when knocked together) with conchoidal fracture; bright orange-red or red (2.5YR 5/6) with 'satin' gloss slip (2.5YR 4/6) on all surfaces, sometimes marred with finger-marks and other blemishes near rim and base; abundant very fine limestone flecks (visible under x20 lens), with sparser red iron ore, quartz and a little mica.

Micaceous Lezoux ware: Slightly laminar fracture, often with numerous horizontal voids; reddish-yellow (5YR 5/6 to 5YR 6/3) with porous red or reddish-brown slip (e.g 2.5YR 3/6 or 5/6) which may appear thin; distinctive abundant fine mica, with some fine quartz sand, red iron ores and rounded limestone particles. Plain wares normally fairly hard fired, but decorated ware tends to be softer with flaking slip – Dannell's description as 'mica filled digestive biscuit' (1977, 231) is particularly apt.

Standard Lezoux fabric: Hard fabric with finely irregular fracture; brown or orange-brown (2.5YR 4/8 or 4/6) matrix and relatively dull slip; some fine mica visible in matrix (but significantly less than in the earlier fabric), with fine quartz sand, sparse limestone and red iron ores.

Chronology. Production at Lezoux commences in Augustan–Tiberian period and micaceous Lezoux fabric exported to Britain *c.* AD 50–120; main phase of production from *c.* AD 120 until later 2nd cent. Significant export from Les Martres-de-Veyre almost confined to AD 100–25, with exception of potter Cettus (*c.* AD 135–65).

Distribution. Early Lezoux wares are common in 1st-cent. AD assemblages along the Loire and in Brittany; thence to Britain, where more common in south and west (Boon 1967; Dannell in Cunliffe 1971, 266–7). Martres and later Lezoux wares have wide distribution through northern and eastern Gaul, the Rhineland and into Danube provinces; in Britain, abundant throughout (B. R. Hartley 1972b, 28) (**99**).

Aliases. *Colchester* fabric CG/LZ. *JRPS bibliography* fabric cts. *Kent* fine fabric 3d. *Silchester* fabric E4.

Bibliography. Bémont and Jacob 1986, 137–64, with refs. Lezoux production summarized in: Bet, Gangloff and Vertet 1987; for decorated wares: Stanfield and Simpson 1958 revised as Stanfield and Simpson 1990; Terrisse 1968; Rogers 1974; for figure types: Déchelette 1904; F. Oswald 1936; for dating of major potters, particularly Cinnamus: B. R. Hartley 1972b; Simpson and Rogers 1969; for an alternative view see King 1981.

See also. CGBL CGGW

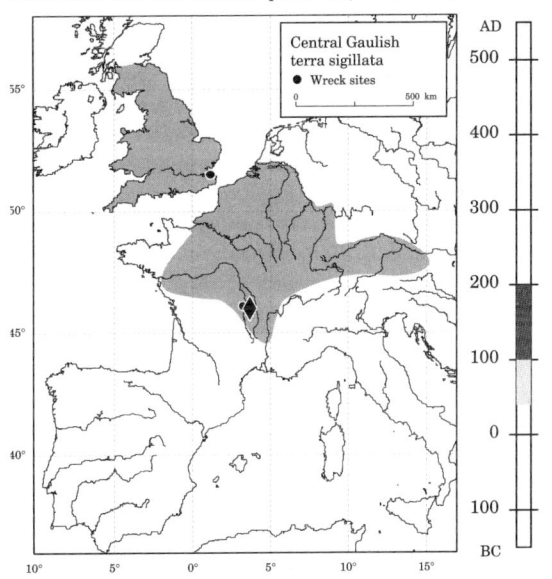

99 *Central Gaulish terra sigillata: overall distribution*

East Gaulish terra sigillata

Fabric and technology. Details of fabrics and finish vary with precise source and date. The products of major kilns are described below, but there are vessels on the British list from a number of other sources.

Trier: Products of Antonine period and early 3rd cent. resemble contemporary Lezoux ware in both colour and quality, but lack the distinct mica and may be densely chalk-filled, especially on larger forms. Later wares (of early to mid-3rd cent.) are pale, often pink or yellowish with relatively coarse thick fabric and uneven, rough-textured orange-red slip.

Rheinzabern: Earlier ware (Antonine to early 3rd cent.) is generally red or orange-red with sparse inclusions and faint swirl-marks in the slip. By mid-3rd cent. a coarser, thick pale red or yellowish fabric with a thin, slightly glossy light-orange slip.

Argonne: Tend to be rather orange or orange-red in colour with a pinkish core and a fine gloss (very similar to the later roller-stamped products of the region: see ARGO).

Chronology. Production established by mid-1st cent. and increasing from *c.* AD 80. Significant export to Britain from *c.* AD 120 until 260. Products of La Madeleine, Heiligenberg, Blickweiler, Chémery and other small sites were imported during Hadrianic and early Antonine periods (Marsh 1981, 181; B. R. Hartley 1972b, 31), and some Argonne wares from *c.* AD 150 until 200, but Rheinzabern and Trier dominate from later 2nd cent. The study (and dating) of the latest decorated wares from both Trier and Rheinzabern is slightly complicated by the reuse of moulds from earlier phases of production on these sites, although these should be distinguishable from the earlier products by their fabric and details of form, such as the tall flaring rims and thick square footrings.

Source. Eastern Gaul; with major kiln sites in the Argonne Forest, through the Moselle region and into Rhine valley.

Distribution. Rhineland, eastern Gaul and Danube provinces; in Britain, throughout, but sparser in west, with largest assemblages from south-east (**100**).

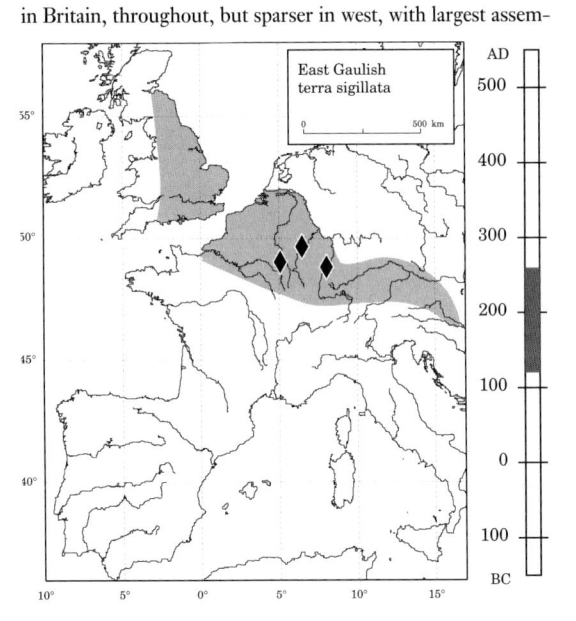

100 *East Gaulish terra sigillata: overall distribution*

Aliases. Colchester fabric EG. *JRPS bibliography* fabric ets. *Kent* fine fabric 5c.

Bibliography. Bémont and Jacob 1986, 195–263, with refs. For earlier production sites and dating: Lutz 1966; Lutz 1975; for Rheinzabern: Ludowici 1927; Ludowici and Ricken 1948; Ricken and Fischer 1963; Bittner 1986; for Trier: Huld-Zetsche 1971a; 1971b; 1972; 1993; the important 'shipment' group of East Gaulish material from New Fresh Wharf, London is described in Bird 1986; for a valuable summary of Rheinzabern and Trier wares in Britain: Bird 1995.

See also. MOSL ARGO

Colchester terra sigillata

M. R. Hull, in his final report on the Colchester samian kilns, recognized the difficulties in distinguishing the local products from imported material in the vicinity of the kilns. Subsequent analyses of the material have confirmed these problems and the precise extent of the samian production at Colchester remains unclear.

Fabric and technology. At its best, Colchester sigillata fabric is indistinguishable from East Gaulish products; generally red-brown core with a good brown or yellow-brown slip; fine-textured matrix with occasional larger white (chalk?) inclusions.

Decorated wares. Hull distinguished three decorative styles in fragments and moulds from the area of the kiln, referred to as Potters A, B and C. A and B are represented by both moulds and decorated fragments and are undoubtedly Colchester products. Potter C is represented by decorated sherds only (no moulds), and is unlikely to be a Colchester product; it is most probably from the workshops at Sinzig. A further rare style, tentatively identified by Hull as Potter D, is also likely to be from an East Gaulish workshop, perhaps Trier (Simpson 1982).

Stamps. Hull's original list of probable/possible Colchester potters has been whittled down (using kiln site evidence and chemical analysis) to a more restricted workforce (**table 32**).

Potter	Comment	
ACCEPTUS ii	Stamped COLC & COMO	
AMANDINUS		
CINTUGNATUS		
CUNOPECTUS	Stamped COLC & COMO	C
GABRUS ii		C
LATINUS iii		S
LIPUCA	← Sinzig ← La Madeleine?	S
T. LITTERA		
LITUGENUS iv	Stamped COMO (?)	C
MATUACUS		
MICCIO vii	← Sinzig	S
MINUSO ii	← (Sinzig?) ← Trier	C
REGU ..		
SENILIS iv		C

Results of chemical analysis: S = Sinzig, C = Colchester

Table 32 *Colchester sigillata potters*

Acceptus and Cunopectus are certainly Colchester potters – their stamps are also found on local mortaria and colour-coated

Colchester/TERRA SIGILLATA

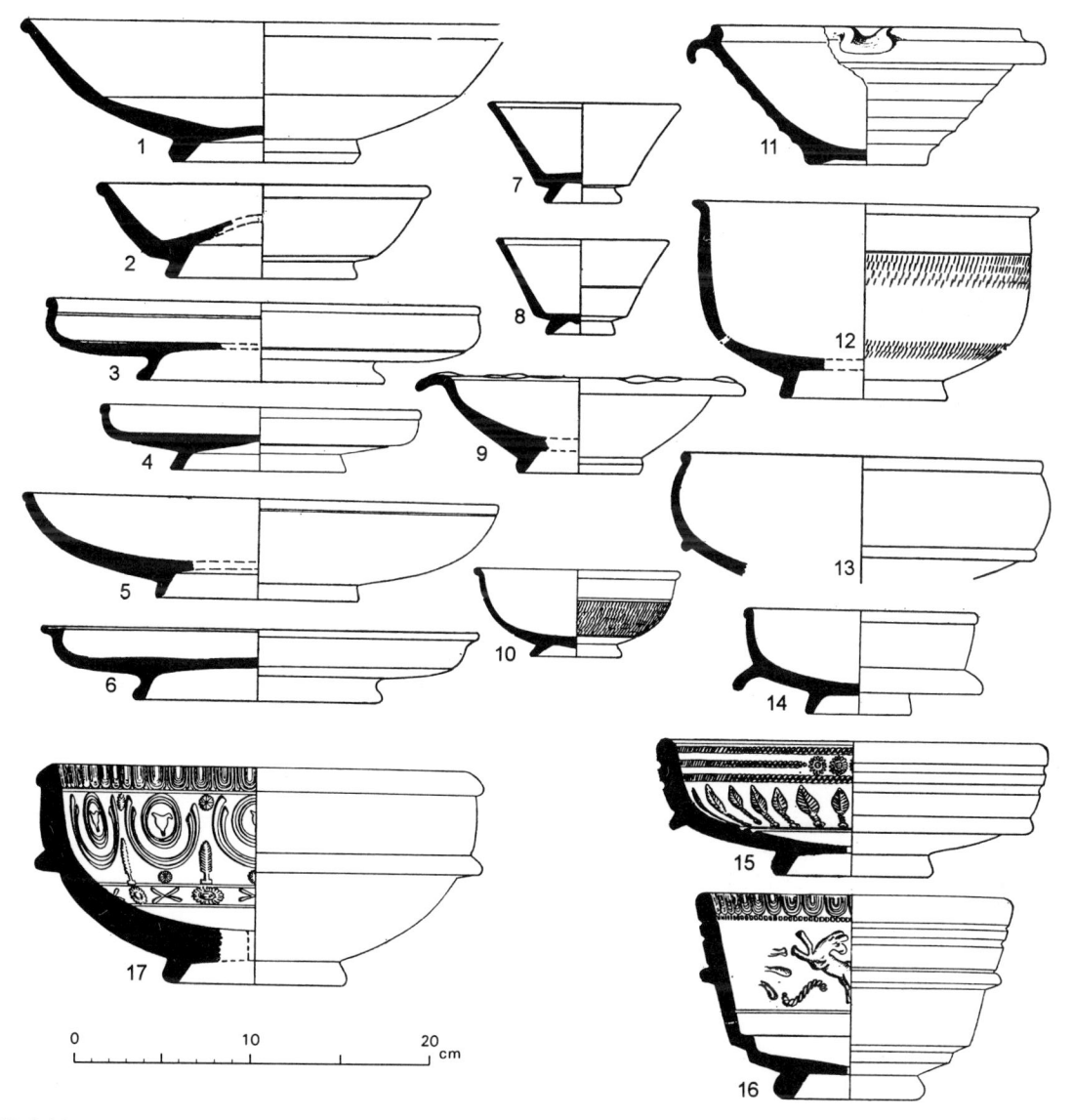

101 Colchester terra sigillata: Scale 1:4

wares. The potters Lipuca, Miccio and Minuso are thought to have worked in the workshops at Sinzig, Trier and elsewhere, before their move to Colchester. However, the chemical analyses reported by Storey *et al.* (1989) suggest that some sherds from Colchester stamped by Latinus, Lipuca and Miccio should be classed as Sinzig products rather than Colchester (these are marked S in table **32** – vessels stamped by potters marked C were confirmed as Colchester products). It is evident that the precise careers of some of these individuals is not yet fully understood.

Forms. Allowing for the difficulties in identification, the production seems to cover the full range of contemporary east Gaulish sigillata shapes: Drag 30, 37, 18/31 (common), 27, 31, 32, 33 (common), 35/36, 38, 40, 44, 45; Curle 15, 21; Walters 79–81; Lud. Sb, Ty, Tq (**101**).

Chronology. *c*. AD 155–80.

Source. Colchester kiln 21.

Distribution. Rare at Colchester; otherwise restricted to East Anglia, but rarely more than a few sherds on a site (distribution in Rodwell 1982), with an outlier at Newstead (but see Bird in C. Green 1977, 60). Some identifications may need reassessment in the light of furthur analysis (**102**).

Aliases. *Colchester* fabric CO. *JRPS bibliography* fabric cls.

Bibliography. Hull 1963, 43–90; for the kiln structure and its

115

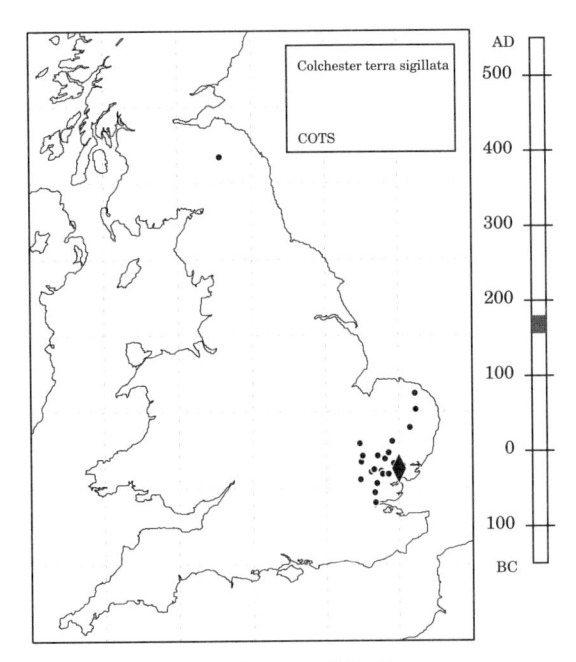

102 Colchester terra sigillata: overall distribution

affinities: RCHM *gazetteer* 92–4, F280; on Potter C and the Sinzig connection: Simpson 1982; Storey *et al.* 1989. Rodwell (1982) suggests that the Potter C bowls may be products of Colchester, but made in moulds imported from Sinzig, rather than imports themselves. On the wanderings of the plain-ware potters: B. R. Hartley 1977. The interconnections and dating of the East Gaulish workshops where some Colchester potters originated are summarized by Huld-Zetsche (in Bémont and Jacob 1986).

See also. EGTS COMO COLC

MORTARIA

Mortaria are bowl-shaped vessels with a prominent hooked flange or vertical 'wall-sided' rim. They often have a spout formed in the rim, and grit embedded in the inner surface. The form suggests use as a grinding and mixing bowl, and many examples show significant wear on the inner surface suggesting a heavy grinding action. Pounding or crushing is a part of the initial preparation of many ingredients, and the use of a vessel called a *mortarium* or *pelvis* for this purpose is recorded in the Roman agricultural texts and recipe books, and occasionally in graffiti on the vessels themselves (R. P. Wright *et al.* 1976, 391, fn. 85).

Vessels recognizable as mortaria were produced in Italy from at least the 3rd cent. BC, whence examples were exported to sites around the Mediterranean littoral, alongside other Italian amphoras and coarse wares. There was increased production in central and northern Gaul and along the Rhine frontier from the Augustan period, and the form is a key part of the 'Romanized' ceramic assemblages typical of the earliest military sites of this region. A few examples were imported into Britain from northern Gaul during the pre-conquest period.

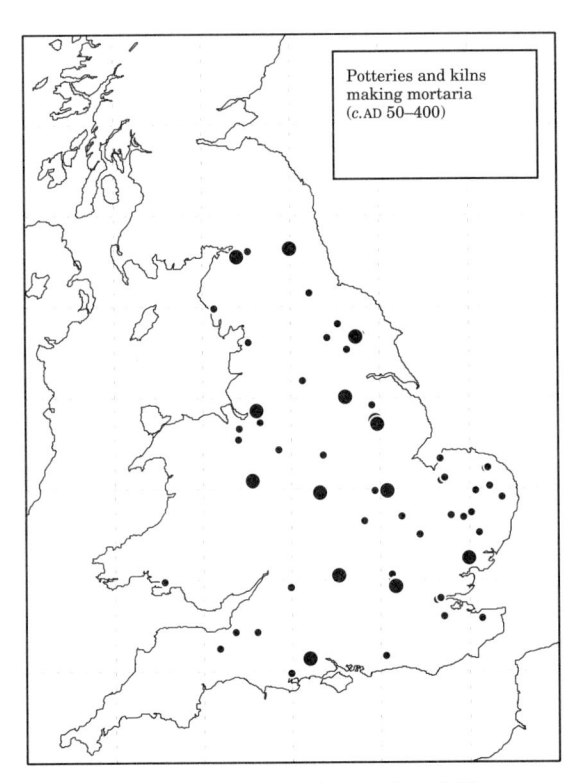

103 Romano-British mortaria: major potteries and kilns

The earliest British mortaria are of the wall-sided form (these were both imported and locally produced) but from the mid-1st cent. AD flanged forms become almost universal. A number of factories in Gaul supplied many mortaria to Britain in the pre-Flavian period – some were located in areas or on routes used for the shipment of other goods. Large-scale production in Britain started in the AD 50s when important factories were founded in the London/St Albans area, in Colchester and probably in Kent. Some of the earliest potters in Britain were certainly immigrants from Gaul. Production in factories in the Midlands and north started in the early 2nd cent. During the later Roman period, mortaria form part of the output of the major industries such as those in Oxfordshire and at Crambeck, alongside colour-coated wares and coarse wares. The later forms include flanged, hammer-headed and wall-sided types.

Mortaria also form a part of the samian repertoire, particularly the wall-sided Drag 45, of the Antonine to early 3rd cent. AD. These vessels, and late Roman examples in fine colour-coated 'tableware' fabrics, suggest that some grinding/mixing food preparation was carried out at the table as well as in the confines of the kitchen.

Forms. There is no unified type-series for mortaria in Britain,

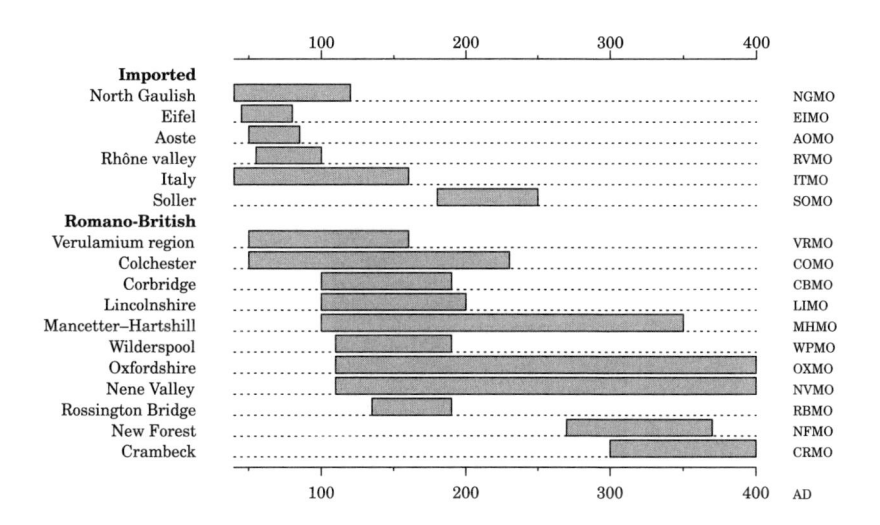

104 *Mortaria: dating of principal industries*

Industry		Code
Imported		
North Gaulish		NGMO
Eifel		EIMO
Aoste		AOMO
Rhône valley		RVMO
Italy		ITMO
Soller		SOMO
Romano-British		
Verulamium region		VRMO
Colchester		COMO
Corbridge		CBMO
Lincolnshire		LIMO
Mancetter–Hartshill		MHMO
Wilderspool		WPMO
Oxfordshire		OXMO
Nene Valley		NVMO
Rossington Bridge		RBMO
New Forest		NFMO
Crambeck		CRMO

but many of the more common forms will be found among Gillam's 1957 *Types* or in Bushe-Fox's *Wroxeter* mortarium typology (Bushe-Fox 1913a, 76–80). Detailed study of Romano-British mortaria over many years has defined the major centres of production, their typology, chronology and distribution. It is now common practice in British excavation reports to assign a vessel to a fabric group (and hence usually a source). The typologies developed for some later Roman industries such as the Oxford industry incorporate a mortarium type-series, but there are no definitive studies of many of the most important earlier factories.

Stamps. From c. AD 50 to 200 many mortarium potters stamped their wares with a name-stamp. Over 200 named potters are known to have operated in Britain, and indeed the stamping of mortaria seems to have been rather more common in Britain than in other western provinces. The stamps are usually on the rim near the spout, and it is common in some workshops for a second stamp (a *counterstamp*) to be placed opposite the first. Mortarium stamps are a most important resource for the study of the development of the industry, having much of the same potential as samian stamps. Some of the most prolific mortarium potters are represented by many hundreds of stamped vessels, while others may have only one or two. By comparing stamp readings, dies and fabrics it is possible to identify potters that moved from one workshop to another. The general framework of chronology and relationships between workshops gained from the study of mortaria is of great value to other Romano-British wares.

In the tables listing the principal potters these symbols are used to show migration:

  ← migration from ...
  → migration to ...
  ↔ also worked at ... but sequence uncertain

Source. While many local potters produced a few mortaria among their output, some large industries were clearly specialists and the mortaria are often the most widely distributed of their products. The location of the major mortarium factories is shown in **103**, and their period of production in **104**.

Bibliography. Romano-British mortaria are studied in a series of papers by K. F. Hartley (e.g. K. F. Hartley and Richards 1965; K. F. Hartley 1973b) and many reports on individual stamps are incorporated in site reports. The pre-conquest and Claudian types are described in: Partridge 1981, 196; Niblett 1985, 96 – the detail of this important report unfortunately in microfiche. On the function and status of mortaria: Baatz 1977; for Classical references: Hilgers 1969, 226–8 (*mortarium*), 248–9 (*pelvis*), 68, 73; for graffiti and other inscriptions on mortaria from Britain: *RIB ii.* 6, 2495–7.

In the Atlas pages the mortaria are ordered alphabetically.

Aoste mortaria

Fabric and technology. Hard, smooth, fine-textured cream-coloured (10YR 8/2 to 5Y 8/2) fabric with conchoidal fracture; abundant fine quartz and white limestone and sparse red and black particles and mica. Gritted with abundant milky quartz on lower internal surface. Wheel-thrown.

Forms. Mortaria. Most characteristic form has relatively small diameter, deep thin curving flange, and finely moulded spout, *Gillam 236*, but other hooked flange forms also produced (**105**).

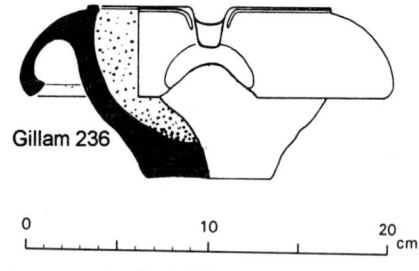

105 *Aoste mortaria: Scale 1:4*

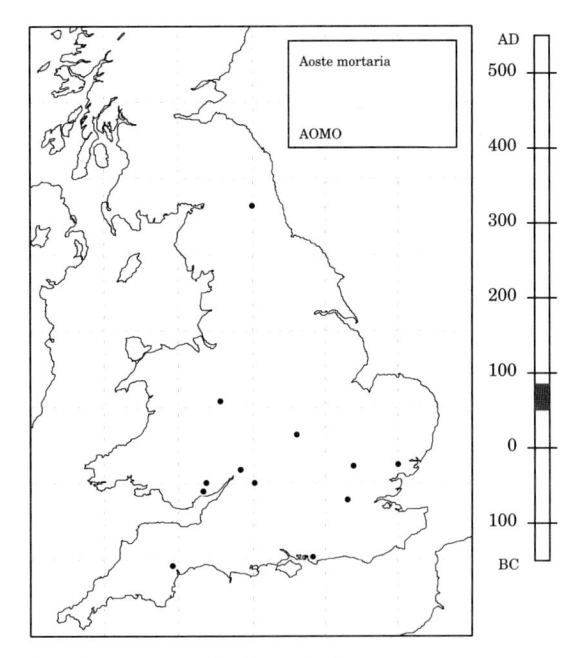

Corbridge/MORTARIA

106 *Aoste mortaria: British distribution*

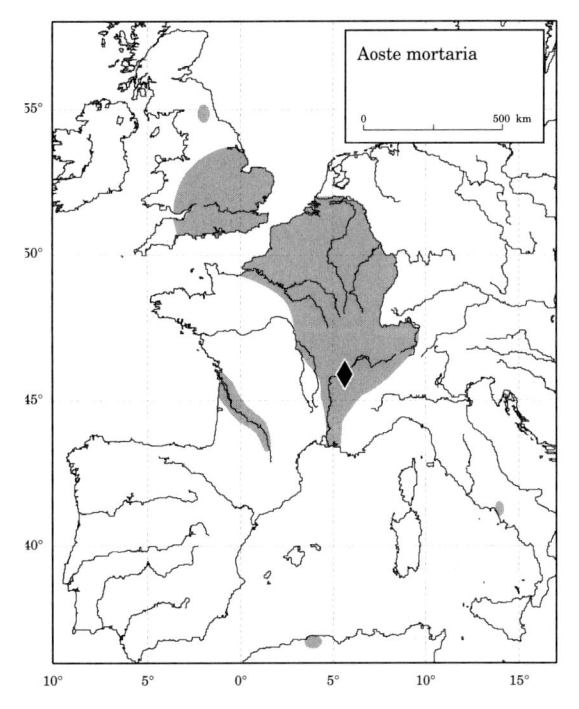

107 *Aoste mortaria: overall distribution*

Stamps. Stamped across the flange. Three potters are known: G. Atisius Gratus, G. Atisius Sabinus and L. Atisius Secundus.
Chronology. AD 50–85.

Source. Aoste (Isère).
Distribution. Most abundant in the Saône valley, Isère and western Switzerland. A scatter along the Rhône valley, the Rhineland, through western and northern France; occasional in Britain (**106, 107**).
Aliases. *Cirencester* fabric 69. *Exeter* mortarium fabric FC22. *Gloucester* fabric TF9Z. *JRPS bibliography* fabric aom. *Sheepen* mortarium fabric 18. *Usk* mortarium fabric 7.
Bibliography. K. F. Hartley 1973b, 46; for the kiln site: Laroche 1987.
Notes. The characteristic deep-flanged Aoste mortarium form was occasionally produced in the north Gaulish mortarium factories (NGMO), and perhaps in the Verulamium region (VRMO). This may indicate the migration of potters from Aoste.

Corbridge mortaria

Fabric and technology. Fine-textured with slightly rough surfaces, varying from creamy-grey to pale orange or brown; inclusions of ill-sorted quartz and some rounded red-brown particles; quartz and black and red-brown sandstone trituration grit. Wheel-thrown.
Forms. Mortaria with bead and roll flange (**108**). Gillam 242, 243, 256, 264, 266, 267.
Stamps. Several potters can be assigned to the Corbridge region on distributional grounds (**table 33**).

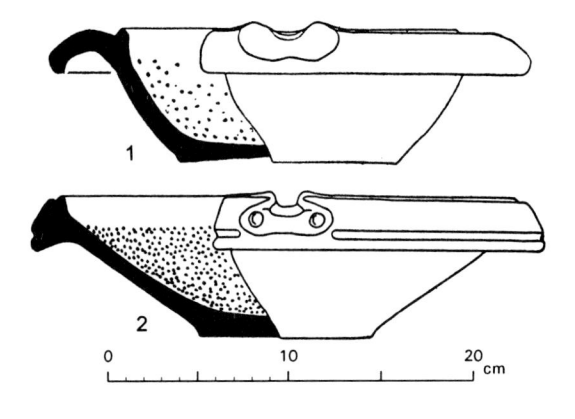

108 *Corbridge mortaria: Scale 1:4*

Chronology. 2nd cent.
Source. Corbridge.
Distribution. Principally Corbridge (where there are large numbers), with small numbers from elsewhere in the northern frontier zone, including the Antonine Wall (**109**).
Aliases. *JRPS bibliography* fabric cbm. *Rough Castle* mortarium fabric 3.
Bibliography. The principal potters are discussed in Bishop and Dore 1989, 265–6; MacIvor, Thomas and Breeze 1981, 258–9.

Colchester/MORTARIA

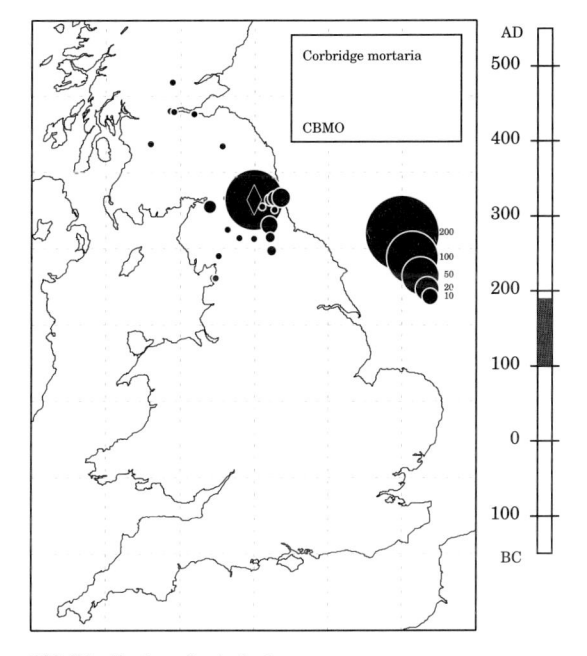

109 *Distribution of principal potters*

Potter	Date
ANAUS	120–60
BELLICUS	155–85
MARCUS (?)	120–60
MATUTINUS	120–60
SATURNINUS	100–30
SULLONIAC[or N]US	100–40

Table 33 *Principal Corbridge mortarium potters*

Colchester mortaria

Mortaria were produced at Colchester from *c.* AD 50/55, but until the mid-2nd cent. the industry was relatively small scale. Some Colchester potters moved to the Verulamium region during the 1st cent. (see VRMO). From *c.* AD 140 production expanded, influenced by potters from the Rhineland who developed colour-coated and sigillata in the same workshops. Only the 2nd-cent. Colchester mortaria are considered here.

Fabric and technology. Fine-textured cream or creamy-yellow fabric with some fine quartz, flint and red-brown ironstone tempering; gritted with quartz and flint.

Forms. Mortaria; several varieties, including hooked flange,

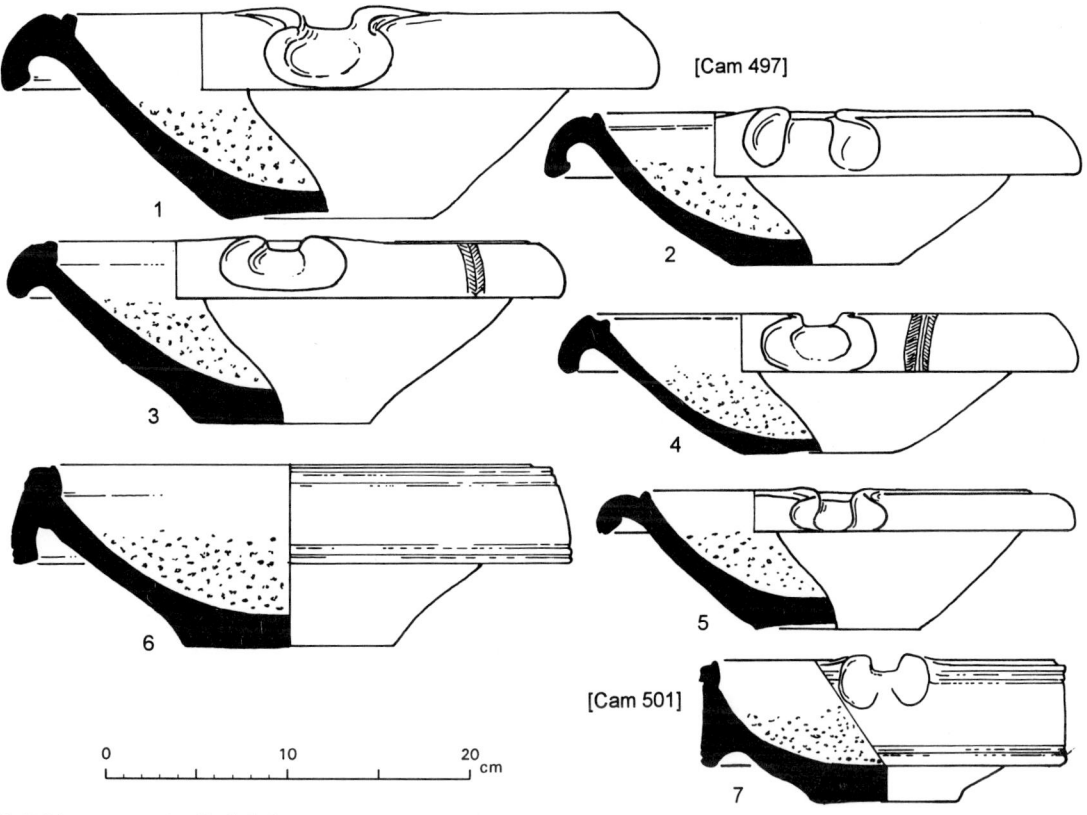

110 *Colchester mortaria: Scale 1:4*

119

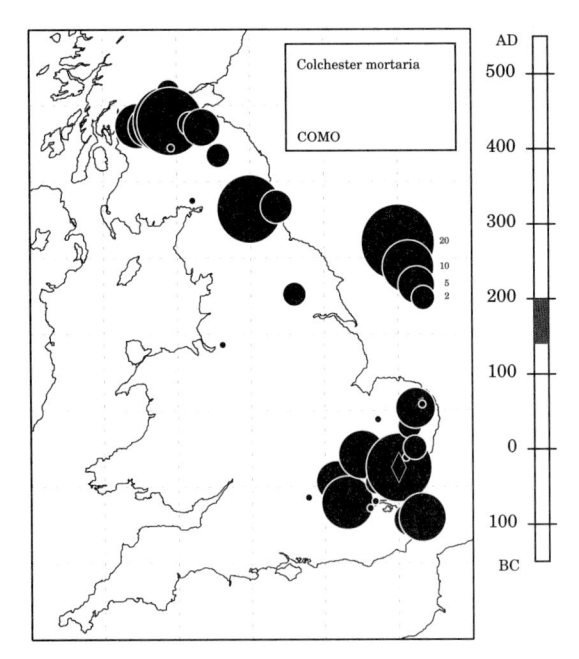

Eifel region/MORTARIA

111 Mortaria: distribution of stamps of principal potters, AD 140–200

deep vertical flange and short stubby flange with a narrow bead (e.g. Colchester forms 497, 498, 501. *Gillam* 263, 265) (110).
Stamps. Several named potters; also herringbone stamps, which are particularly characteristic of Colchester mortaria (**table 34**).

Potter	Date	
ACCEPTUS	140–90	also stamped COTS
AMMINUS	140–90	
BARO	140–90	→ RBMO?
CUNOPECTUS	160–200	also stamped COTS
DUBITATUS	140–80	
LITUGENUS	140–80	
MARIAUS	140–90	
MARTINUS	140–90	
MESSOR	140–80	
REGALIS	160–200	↔ Ellingham (Norfolk)

Table 34 *Principal Colchester mortarium potters, AD 140–200*

Chronology. AD 140–200; the herringbone stamps generally AD 140–70/80.
Source. Principally Colchester, but similar fabrics also produced elsewhere in East Anglia and perhaps Kent. One Colchester potter, Regalis, also had workshops at Ellingham (Norfolk) and two, Cunopectus and Acceptus, stamped both mortaria and sigillata at Colchester.

Distribution. South-east England (East Anglia and Kent), northern England and Scotland. Colchester was a major supplier to forts on the Antonine frontier (55 per cent at Rough Castle; 45 per cent at Inveresk) (111).
Aliases. Caister-on-sea fabric COLCH. *Chesterfield* fabrics m14 and m15. *Colchester* fabric TZ. *Gestingthorpe* mortarium fabrics A-G. *Great Chesterford* mortarium fabrics 14–15. *JRPS bibliography* fabric clm. *Rough Castle* mortarium fabric 2.
Bibliography. On the kilns: Hull 1963; *RCHM* gazetteer 92–5, F273-88; for overall distribution: K. F. Hartley 1973b; for Scottish distribution: Hartley in MacIvor, Thomas and Breeze 1981, 261–6.
See also. COTS COLC

Eifel region mortaria
Fabric and technology. Hard, rough unevenly mixed creamy-yellow (10YR 8/2) fabric with abundant red-brown inclusions of fine-textured sandstone, siltstone and clay pellets; wheel-thrown.
Forms. Mortarium with distinctive short thick flange and barely projecting spout. Cam 194 (112).

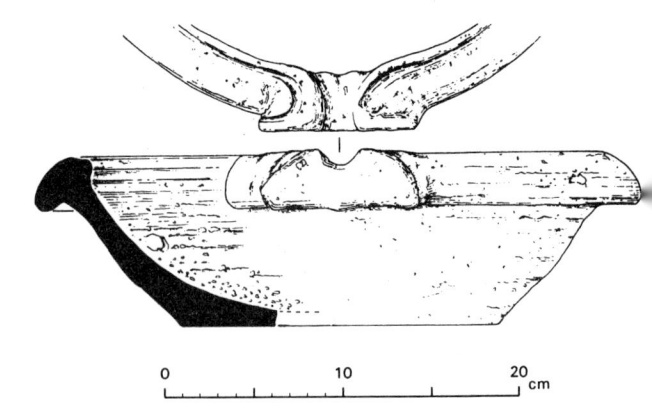

112 Eifel region mortaria: Scale 1:4

Chronology. Pre-Flavian.
Source. Probably the Eifel region of Germany (Williams in Manning 1993, 424). Hawkes and Hull note that the *Camulodunum* specimens are in a similar clay to those from Hofheim (C. F. C. Hawkes and Hull 1947, 254).
Distribution. Continental distribution not known, but probably lower and middle Rhine; occasional in Britain on pre-Flavian sites (113).
Aliases. Exeter mortarium fabric FC19. *JRPS bibliography* fabric mem. *Sheepen* mortarium fabrics 4-5. *Usk* mortarium fabric 5.
Bibliography. Hartley in Manning 1993, 398, imp2.
See also. MAYN SOMO

Italian/MORTARIA

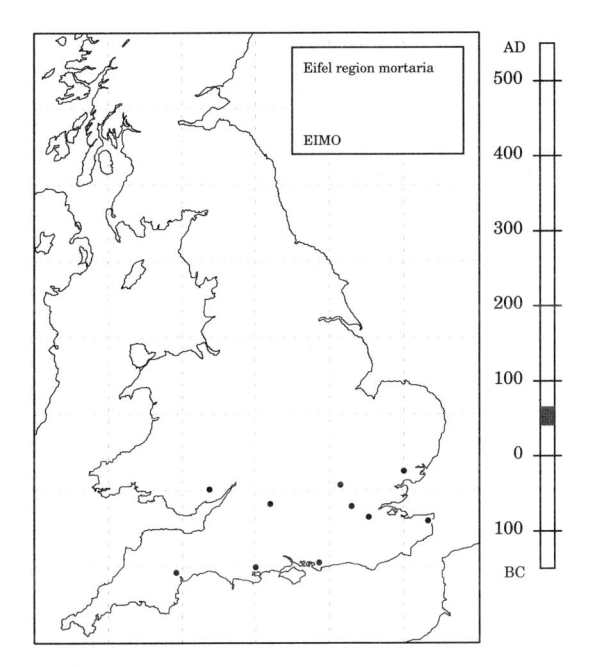

113 Eifel region mortaria: British distribution

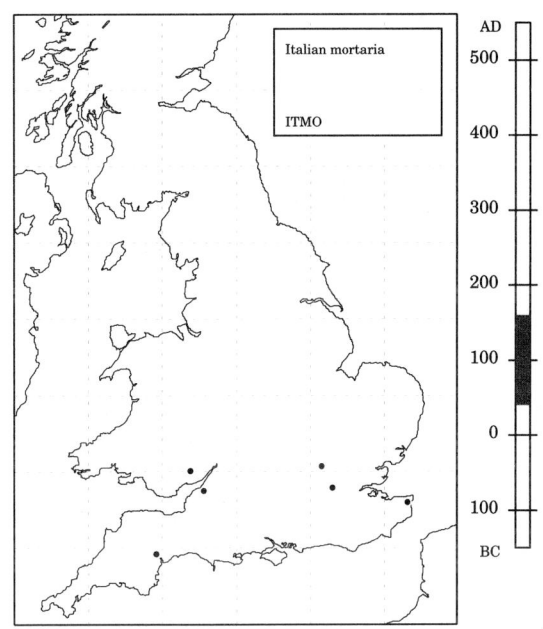

115 Italian mortaria: British distribution

Italian mortaria

Fabric and technology. Several fabrics, but generally hard, rough textured, light brown (10YR 6/3) or creamy-pink (e.g. 7YR 8/2) with irregular fracture; abundant brown and red inclusions including lava, volcanic glass, feldspar and quartz, with some dark mica. Wheel-thrown.

Forms. Large, heavy mortaria with flat base and wide plain flange. The rim on earlier (1st-cent. AD) examples is more down-turned than on later specimens. Perhaps made in two sizes in the 1st cent. AD – *c.* 42 and *c.* 49cm diameter (Joncheroy 1972, 22) (**114**).

Stamps. Stamped across the rim, on both sides of the spout, and sometimes elsewhere; up to 3 lines long and recording estate name or *tria nomina* of owner or manager, and occasionally a consular date. Some estate owners are historically attested individuals (including members of the imperial household or senatorial classes) whose dates are known from other sources.

Chronology. Principally AD 40–160.

Source. Central Italy, particularly the Rome region, but also

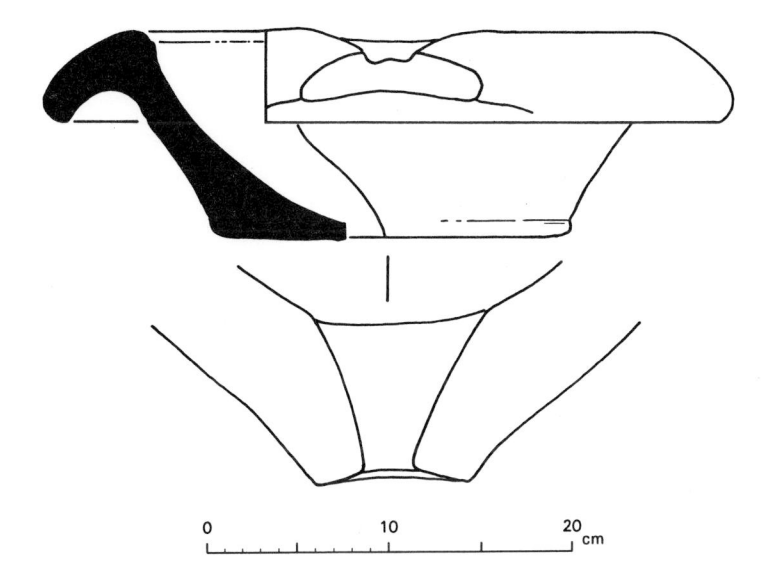

114 Italian mortaria: Scale 1:4

121

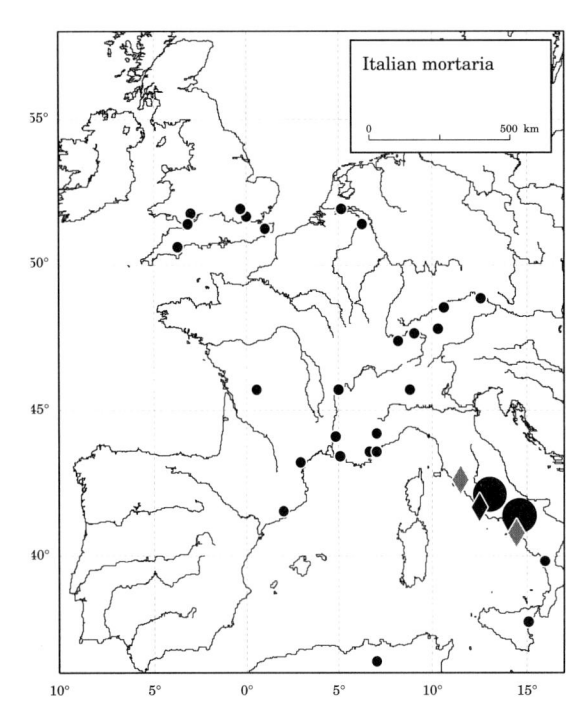

116 Italian mortaria: overall distribution

Etruria and Campania. Some made in the same workshops as building material, dolia, clay baths, sarcophagi, etc.
Distribution. Principally Italy, but a scatter around the western and eastern Mediterranean (Riley 1979, 295–6) and across the northern provinces; occasional in Britain. Bricks and tile from the Italian brickyards served as ballast in some shipping from Italy. Italian mortaria are also found in wrecks, sometimes as a major item in the cargo (e.g. Parker 1992, nos. 98, 374, 470) (**115, 116**).
Aliases. *Exeter* mortarium fabric FC20. *Usk* mortarium fabric 6.
Bibliography. K. F. Hartley 1973b; 1973c. For stamps: Steinby 1978.

Lincolnshire mortaria

Fabric and technology. Usually hard, slightly rough fabric, varying from creamy-white (2.5YR 7/4 to 10YR 8/2) through to pink, often with a yellow or darker slip; fine quartz inclusions, slightly micaceous; gritted with ill-sorted quartz, red and black iron silicate slags and some flint. Vitalis mortaria from Technical College kiln are in a coarser, granular white fabric. Wheel-thrown.
Forms. Mortaria, with bead and roll rim or high bead and small flange, including *Gillam* 258 (**117**).
Chronology. 2nd cent.
Source. Kilns at the Lincoln Technical College site and at South Carlton.
Stamps. In addition to those represented at the kiln sites,

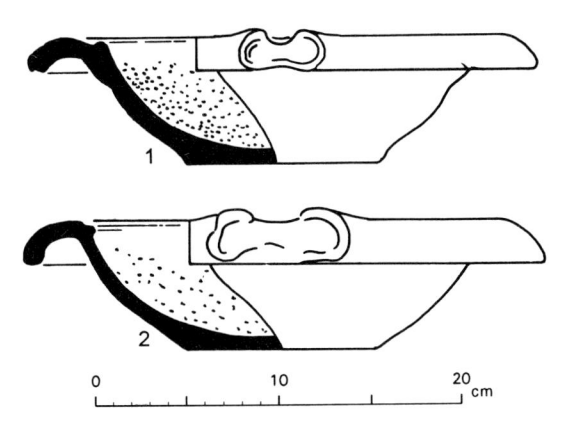

117 Lincolnshire mortaria: Scale 1:4

other potters can be assigned to a Lincolnshire source on fabric or distribution (**table 35**).
Distribution. East Midlands, northern England, and the Scottish frontier (**118**).
Aliases. *Carlisle* fabric 616. *Doncaster* mortarium fabric 10. *JRPS bibliography* fabric llm.
Bibliography. *RCHM* gazetteer F454, F466; stamps of the principal potters described in Darling 1984, 69–73; Stead 1976, 116–26.
Notes. At South Carlton, mortaria were manufactured alongside flagons and other coarse wares (some with stamped and painted decoration) and colour-coated roughcast beakers. This combination suggests that the potters migrated from one of the established industries of south-east England or northern Gaul.

Name	Date	Source
AESICO	140–70	SC?
ATEPACIUS	100–50	TC
BIL[I]CEDO	140–90	SC?
BISO	120–50?	TC
CRICO	140–80	SC
CUPITUS	140–70	SC
DECANIUS	110–60	
MARTIC	100–25	
Q. IUSTIUS CICO	100–40	
Q. IUSTIUS CRESCENS	100–40	
SENICO	140–200	
VITALIS i	90–115	TC
VOROLAS	140–200	SC

Sources: SC = South Carlton, TC = Lincoln Technical College

Table 35 *Principal Lincolnshire mortarium potters*

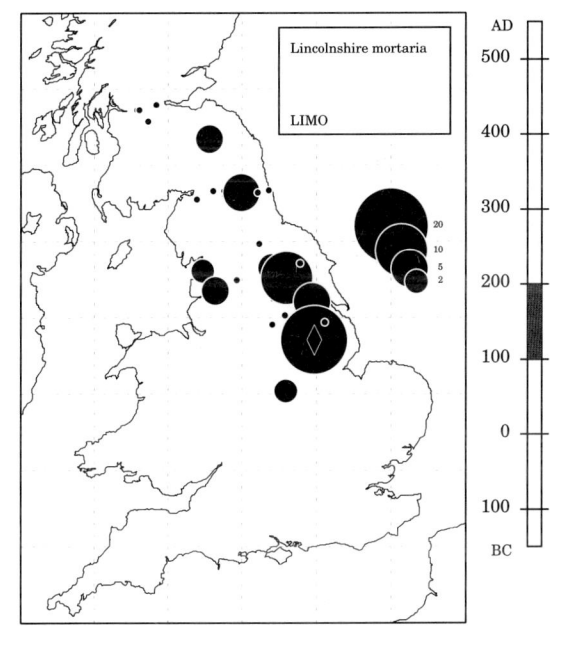

118 *Lincolnshire mortaria: overall distribution*

Mancetter-Hartshill mortaria

Fabric and technology. Fine-textured fabric, often very hard; creamy-white, perhaps with pink or grey core, occasionally with a pale-brown wash; inclusions of fine quartz and occasional red-brown and white particles; gritted with either quartz and red-brown sandstone (on earlier specimens), or abundant red-brown or black angular grits (including ironstone or slag). Wheel-thrown.

Forms. Mortaria. The earliest resemble contemporary products of the Verulamium-region industry with a hooked flange, later a smaller flange and higher bead. From *c.* AD 160 a new hammerhead style developed. Some painted with simple geometric patterns during 3rd cent. (**119**). *Gillam* 242, 253, 254, 257, 259, 261.

Stamps. The chronological distribution of the principal named potters is shown in **121**.

Chronology. From *c.* AD 100; some potters migrated from the Verulamium region industry (G. Attius Marinus, Doccas, Nidus) at this time. In some cases the same die occurs on both VRMO and MHMO products. From the mid-2nd cent. some MHMO potters moved north to workshops in Yorkshire (e.g. Sarrius). Stamping ceased at end of 2nd cent. but production continued into 4th cent (**table 36**).

Source. Around Mancetter and Hartshill, on the Warwickshire/Leicestershire border, where many kilns have been recorded and excavated. Painted wares, grey wares and other cooking wares produced alongside mortaria.

Distribution. Extensive in the Midlands and north between mid-2nd and early 4th cent. (Bidwell 1985, 183). The distribution of stamps of the principal 2nd-cent. AD potters is shown in **120**.

Potter	Date	
BONOXUS	120–60	
BRUSCIUS	140–70	
CANDIDUS ii	100–40	
CEVANOS	100–30	
CICRO | CICRUS	130–60	
COERTUTINUS	100–40	
DOBALLUS	140–80	↔ NVMO?
DOCCAS	100–25	← VRMO
ERUCANUS	100–30	
G. ATTIUS MARINUS	100–30	← VRMO ← COMO
GRATINUS	130–65	
ICOTAGUS	130–60	
IUNIUS ii	150–85	
IUNIUS LOCCIUS	135–65	
LOCCIUS PRO...	130–65	
LOCCIUS VIBIUS	135–65	
MAURIUS	150–85	
MINOMELUS	135–65	
MOCO | MOCUS	100–35	
MOSSIUS	145–85	
NANIECO	135–65	→ WPMO
NIDUS	120–40	← VRMO
RUICCO | RUTICO	150–85	
SARRIUS	135–70	→ RBMO
SENNIUS	160–85	
SEPTUMINUS	100–30	← Little Chester
SIMILIS	135–70	→ NVMO
SURUS	100–30	
VICTOR	100–30	↔ Little Chester?
VITALIS iv	115–45	

Table 36 *Principal Mancetter-Hartshill mortarium potters,* AD *100–85*

Aliases. *Caersws* mortarium fabric 5. *Carlisle* fabric 624. *Chesterfield* fabric m18. *Colchester* fabric TM. *Doncaster* mortarium fabric 11. *Exeter* mortarium fabric FB4. *Gloucester* fabric TF9D. *Great Chesterford* mortarium fabric 18. *JRPS bibliography* fabric mhm. *Kent* mortarium fabric 6. *Leicester* fabric MO4. *Lullingstone* fabric 43. *Milton Keynes* fabric 4c. *Old Penrith* fabric 109. *Rough Castle* mortarium fabric 1. *Sidbury* fabric 32. *Towcester* mortarium fabric 12. *Usk* mortarium fabric 17.

Bibliography. For the kilns: *RCHM gazetteer* 98–101, F636–53; K. F. Hartley 1973a; there is no complete published catalogue of stamps, but most of the principal potters are reported in MacIvor, Thomas and Breeze 1981; Buckland and Magilton 1986; Robertson 1975.

Mancetter-Hartshill/MORTARIA

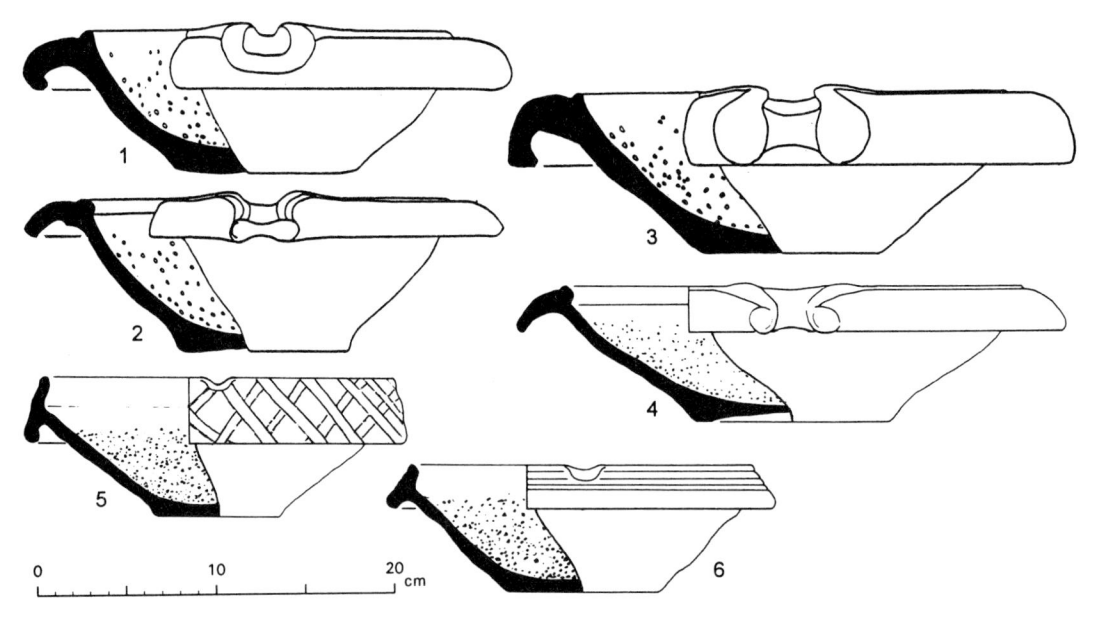

119 Mancetter-Hartshill mortaria: Scale 1:4

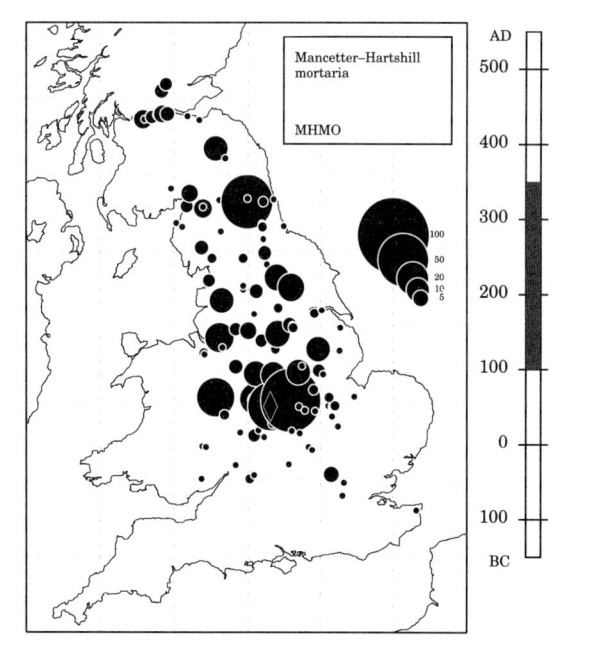

120 Mancetter-Hartshill mortaria: distribution of stamps of principal potters

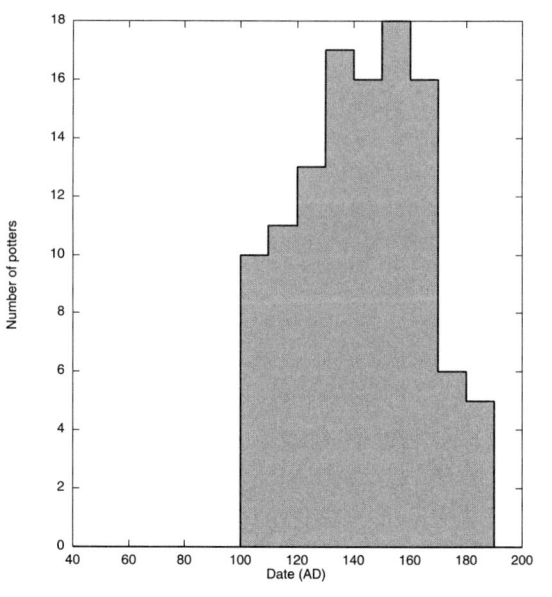

121 Dates of principal Mancetter-Hartshill mortarium potters, AD 100–85

New Forest mortaria

Fabric and technology. Hard sandy fabric; white or off-white, rarely with pale grey core; abundant well-sorted quartz sand temper with occasional red-brown or grey flint inclusions; trituration grit of quartz, flint, brown sandstone and other red-brown material. Wheel-thrown.

Forms. Mortaria, with bead and flange. Fulford defines six mortarium types (forms 102–7) in this ware, some decorated with incised wavy-lines on the flange (**122**).

Chronology. c. AD 260–370.

Source. The New Forest industry.

Distribution. Principally central-southern England, with a thin scatter beyond (**123**).

Aliases. Bath fabric 2.4. Colchester fabric TH. Exeter mortarium fabrics FB5 and FB6. *JRPS bibliography* fabric nfm. Fulford (1975a) fabric 2a.

Bibliography. Fulford 1975a, 74–9, 123. RCHM gazetteer 108–9, F322–41, F344.

Notes. Mortaria in slipped wares, including forms derived from the samian prototypes Drag 44 and 45, were also produced in the New Forest industry (Fulford 1975a, types 78–81).

See also. NFCC

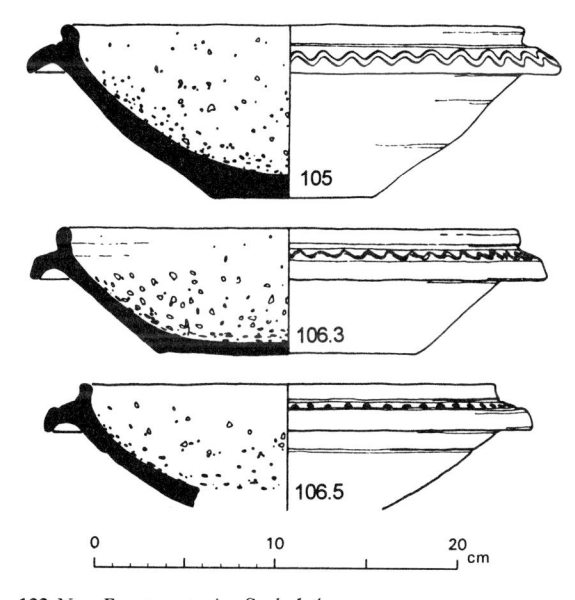

122 *New Forest mortaria: Scale 1:4*

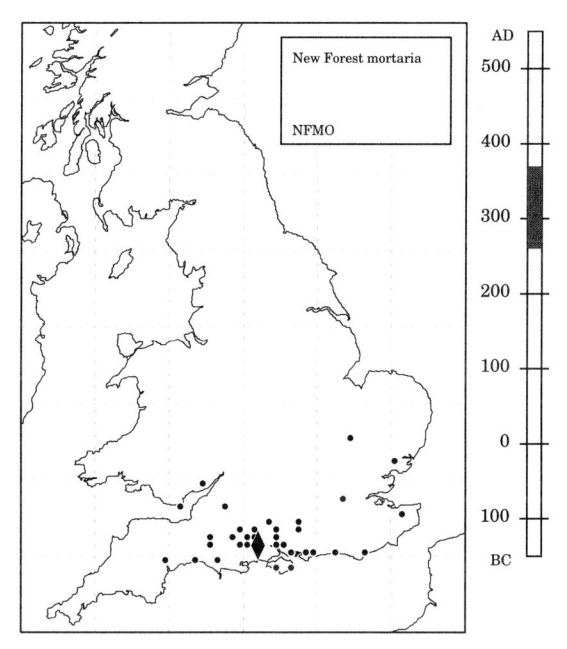

123 *New Forest mortaria: overall distribution*

North Gaulish (Pas-de-Calais) mortaria

Fabric and technology. A range of fine-textured calcareous fabrics with clean or conchoidal fracture, varying from cream or light grey, through yellow-buff to light brown (but commonly staining to dark grey or brown in water-lain or organic deposits); inclusions of fine quartz, iron-rich and clay pellets and chalky particles, occasional larger rounded ironstone or clay pellets, slightly micaceous. Wheel-thrown. Gritted internally with crushed flint and coarse quartz.

Forms. These mortaria have been divided into two groups (I and II) by K. F. Hartley (1977) and there are three varieties of rim form:

Rim	Flange	Group
1	strongly hooked	I (typical)
2	deep	I (rare)
3	broad flat	II (typical)

The rare deep-flanged form (rim type 2) is derived from the form typical of the Aoste potters (AOMO) but can be linked with the north Gaulish mortaria group because of fabric, distribution and a number of stamped vessels. The similarity suggests that potters trained at Aoste or otherwise familiar with the Aoste production moved to northern Gaul. The more typical group I rim form (rim type 1) also has similarities with Central Gaulish mortaria forms (RVMO), with which it has been conflated in some records.

The typical group II form (rim type 3) is equivalent to *Gillam* 238 (**124**).

Stamps. Both group I and II products are stamped and at least 30 named potters are known. The principal potters are Q. Valerius Se..., (group I) and Q. Valerius Veranius (group II) (**table 37**).

North Gaulish (Pas-de-Calais)/MORTARIA

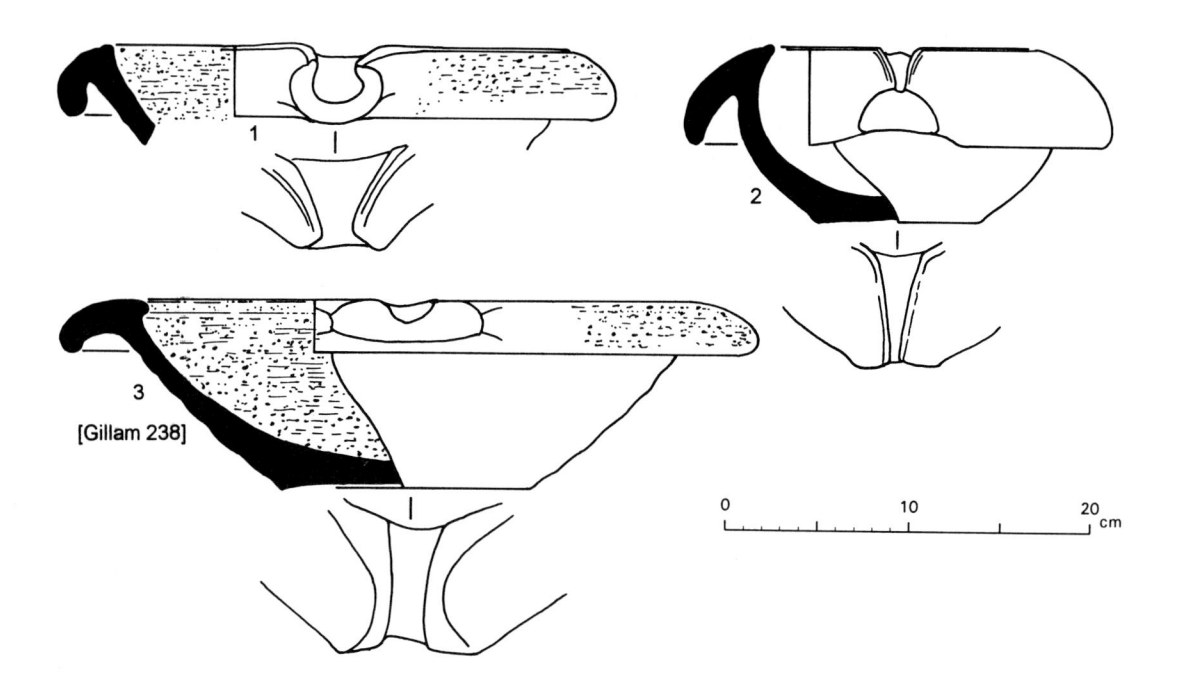

124 *North Gaulish (Pas-de-Calais) mortaria: Scale 1:4*

Chronology. Mainly *c.* AD 55–100, with some 2nd-cent. examples.

Distribution. Northern France, western Belgium and Britain. The distribution of stamps in Britain is shown in **125**; most common in Kent and around the Thames estuary (particularly Richborough, London and Colchester).

Source. Q. Valerius Veranius had workshops at Bavai (Belgium), but these products are not known in Britain. The location of his later workshops, and those of the other potters making these types, are not known, but the distribution suggests either northern France or south-eastern Britain. On several grounds the former seems most likely. The name of the workshops of Q. Valerius Veranius are recorded on some dies as DOGAERIA or DOCAERIA (Cunliffe 1971, 174)

Aliases. *Caersws* mortarium fabric 7. *Carlisle* fabric 613. *Chichester* mortarium fabrics 13–14. *Cirencester* fabrics 67 and 68. *Doncaster* mortarium fabric 14. *Dorchester* fabrics 42N and 42O. *Exeter* mortarium fabrics FC2–FC5. Gloucester fabrics TF9AB, TF9AC and TF9C. *JRPS bibliography* fabric ngm. *Kent* mortarium fabric 11a. *Leicester* fabric MO15. *Lullingstone* fabric 37. *Old Penrith* fabric 114. *Sidbury* fabric 36.2. *Usk* mortarium fabrics 1, 2, 3 and 4.

Bibliography. Lists of potters and stamp catalogue in K. F. Hartley 1977; more recent discussions in Holbrook and Bidwell 1991, 189–90, 198 and Manning 1993, 390, 398.

Notes. Flagons with a strongly marked, undercut collar and a groove on the outer lip (a 'pulley rim') in the same fabric as group I and II mortaria have been noted on a number of British sites – London (C. M. Green 1980b, fig. 21, 40–3), Exeter (Holbrook and Bidwell 1991, fabric 440, fig. 50, 1.1) and in the north at Corbridge, Camelon and Hayton (P. V. Webster 1977). Similar forms on other sites (e.g. Bushe-Fox

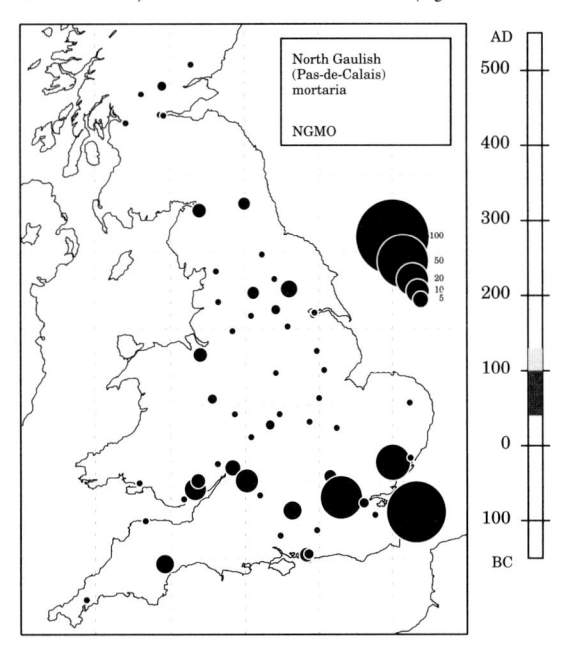

125 *North Gaulish (Pas-de-Calais) mortaria: distribution of stamps of principal potters*

1926, nos. 37, 39; Bushe-Fox 1928, no. 199; Down 1989, 117, fig. 16.1, 24–31) may be related. Identical flagons are recorded from Boulogne (Seillier and Thoen 1978, fig. 5) and were produced at a small kiln site at Bourlon, between Cambrai and Arras (Tuffreau-Libre 1976), alongside group II mortaria, strengthening the case for the production of both the mortaria and flagons in northern France, and perhaps particularly in the Pas-de-Calais. Early imports of north Gaulish grey wares (NGGW) from the same region may be related.
See also. NGGW

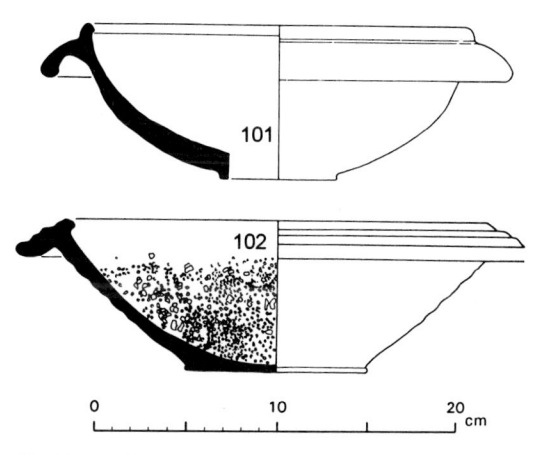

126 Nene Valley mortaria: Scale 1:4

Potter	Date	Group
BIIJI	55–85	I
BORIEDO	65–100	II
BUC[C]US	55–85	I
C. IUL[IUS] PRI[VATUS]	65–100	II
CACUMATTUS	65–100	II
CAVARIUS	70–100	II
FRONTO	55–85	I
GRACILIS	65–100	II
LITUGENUS ii	65–100	II
LOSSA	65–100	II
MOTTIUS BOLLIUS	65–100	II
ORBISSA	65–100	II
ORGILUS	55–85	II
PAULLUS	55–85	I
PRASSO	65–100	II
Q. VALERIUS ESUNERTUS	65–100	II
Q. VALERIUS SE...	55–85	I
Q. VALERIUS SURIACUS	65–100	II
Q. VALERIUS VERANIUS	65–100	II ← Bavai
SUMMACUS	55–85	I
T. IU[LIUS] AF[ER]	65–100	II
VASSONUS	65–100	II

Table 37 *Principal North Gaulish mortarium potters*

Potter	Date	
CAMULACUS iii	130–60	
CUNOARDA	130–80	
DOBALLUS	140–80	←MHMO?
VEDIACUS	140–80	
VIATOR	110–45	

Table 38 *Principal Nene Valley mortarium potters, AD 110–80*

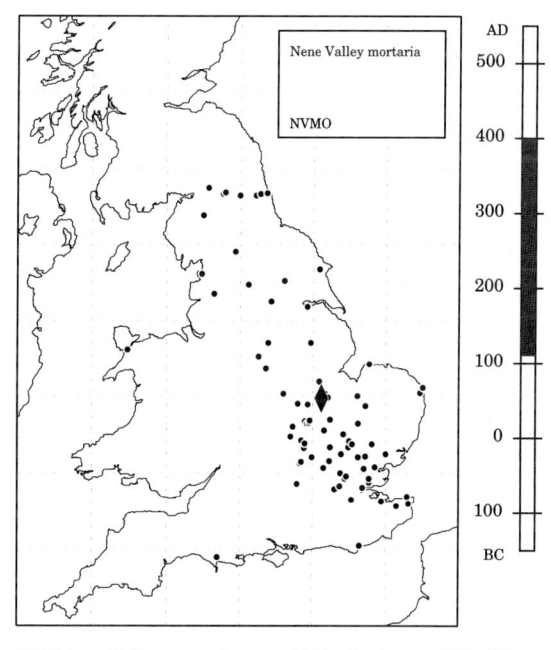

Nene Valley mortaria

Fabric and technology. Hard, off-white fabric with light grey or pink core, often a brown or yellowish slip; inclusions of fine red-brown and black particles and variable amounts of quartz. Gritted with abundant crushed dark grey or black iron silicate slag. Wheel-thrown.

Forms. Mortaria, with flange and high bead or reeded rim (126).

Stamps. During the 2nd cent. there are a few named potters, but stamping ceases by *c.* AD 180 (**table 38**).

127 Nene Valley mortaria: overall distribution, AD 100–400

Nene Valley/MORTARIA

Chronology. Earliest mortaria date to *c.* AD 110, and production continues into 4th cent.

Source. The Castor-Stibbington area in the lower Nene valley. The stamps of Cunoarda read CUNOARDA [FECIT] VICO DUROBRI[VIS] and a painted inscription on another mortarium reads SENNIANVS DUROBRIVIS VRI[..] (RIB ii.6, 2495.1; Howe, Perrin and Mackreth 1980, 3).

Distribution. Eastern England, as far as the northern frontier, but abundant in the east Midlands and a major source for East Anglia during 3rd–4th cent (Darling 1993, 202–3) (**127**).

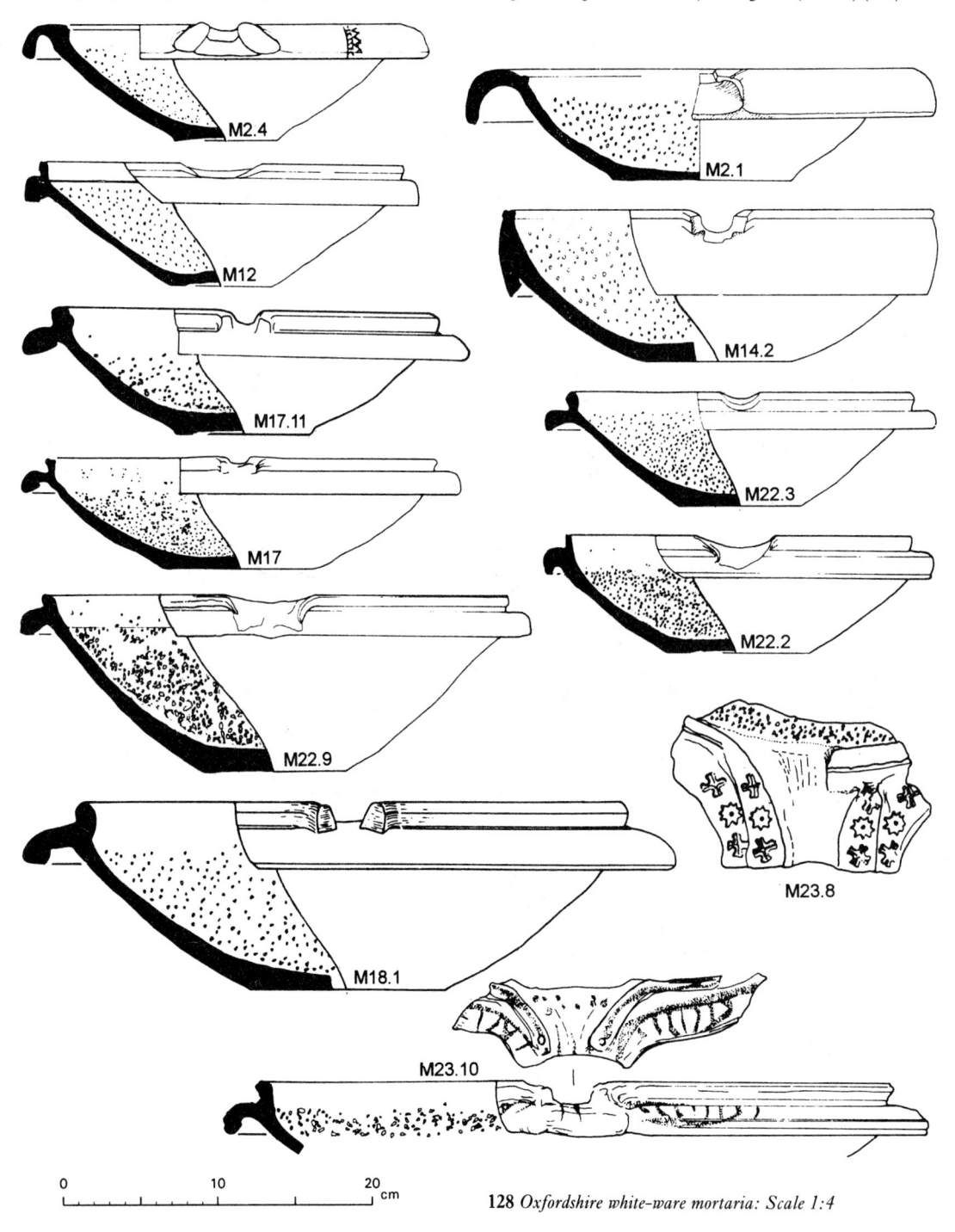

128 *Oxfordshire white-ware mortaria: Scale 1:4*

Oxfordshire white/MORTARIA

Aliases. Chelmsford fabric 24. *Chesterfield* fabric m17. Colchester fabrics TE and TF. *Gestingthorpe* mortarium fabrics K–L. Great *Chesterford* mortarium fabrics 16 and 17. *JRPS bibliography* fabric nvm. *Kent* mortarium fabric 8. *Leicester* fabric MO6. *Lullingstone* fabric 42. *Milton Keynes* fabric 4f. *Towcester* mortarium fabric 8b.
Bibliography. RCHM *gazetteer* 95–7, F366–86; production summarized in Howe, Perrin and Mackreth 1980.
See also. NVCC

Oxfordshire white-ware mortaria

Fabric and technology. Hard, fairly fine-textured fabric; white, or cream, sometimes darker (light brownish-cream, with a pink core or with a cream to buff slip; some earlier fabrics contain abundant translucent quartz sand but most have a little red-stained quartz and occasional larger red and black inclusions; trituration grit invariably rounded translucent or transparent quartz – pink, black, white or brown. Wheel-thrown.
Forms. Mortaria, principally with bead and flange, but some wall-sided. Young defines 23 types (M1–M23) which cover the range (Young 1977b, 56–79). Grooving on rim or flange common on later types (M17, M18, M22). Simple rosette, star or cross stamps on rare later 4th-cent. type, M23; occasional red-painted decoration during 4th cent (**128**).
Stamps. Stamps or marks used during 2nd cent. but never common; principal named potter is Vossullus (*c.* AD 140–200). A pre-firing graffito from the Churchill Hospital site records a potter named Thamesubugus (*RIB* ii. 6, 2496.4).
Chronology. Production from *c.* AD 100 until late 4th cent. The earliest forms of mortaria, and other early Oxfordshire products such as flagons, resemble those of the Verulamium-region industry (VRMO) and production may originate with migrants from that area.
Source. The Oxfordshire potteries.
Distribution. Second cent. distribution largely confined to Oxfordshire and surrounding counties. Expansion from early or mid-3rd cent. into London basin and Kent and (during 4th.) East Anglia and south-west. A scatter in Wales and the north (**129**).
Aliases. Bath fabric 2.1. *Caister-on-sea* fabric MOOX. Chelmsford fabric 25. *Chesterfield* fabrics m1 and m2. *Chichester* mortarium fabric 1. Colchester fabrics TK and TN. *Dorchester* fabric 19. *Exeter* mortarium fabric FB1. *Gestingthorpe* mortarium fabric P. *Gloucester* fabrics TF9A and TF9W. Great *Chesterford* mortarium fabric 1. *JRPS bibliography* fabrics oxm, oxwm and oxw mort. *Kent* mortarium fabrics 9a and 9b. Leicester fabric MO1. *Lullingstone* fabric 35. *Milton Keynes* fabrics 4a, 4ba and 4ag. *Old Penrith* fabric 112. *Sidbury* fabric 33. *Towcester* mortarium fabric 6. *Usk* mortarium fabric 15.
Bibliography. Young 1977b; for stamps K. F. Hartley and

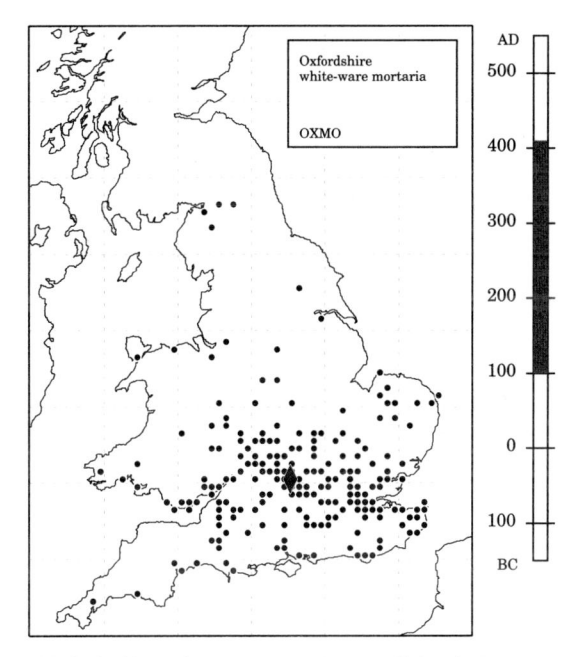

129 *Oxfordshire white-ware mortaria: overall distribution,* AD *100–400*

Richards 1965, 37; L. S. Green 1983; *RCHM gazetteer* 102–4, F561–73.
Notes. The Oxfordshire industry also produced mortaria in red-slipped and white-slipped fabrics.
See also. OXRS

Rossington Bridge mortaria

Fabric and technology. Hard, sandy fabric, usually orange-brown with grey core; abundant quartz sand tempering, with occasional red-brown and grey particles; mixed trituration grit, including haematite, quartz, and some flint and brown sandstone.
Forms. Mortaria with bead and rolled flange (**130**).

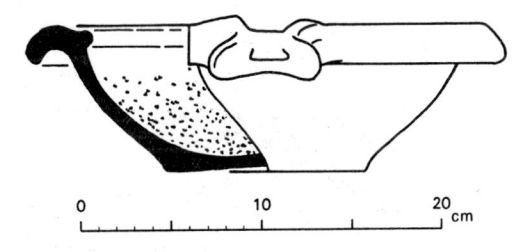

130 *Rossington Bridge mortaria: Scale 1:4*

Stamps. The principal Rossington Bridge potter is Sarrius, who had earlier worked at Mancetter-Hartshill. Some Rossington Bridge mortaria are stamped jointly by Sarrius and either Setibogius or Secundua. The latest work of Sarrius seems to be at Mancetter-Hartshill, so the Rossington Bridge

Rhône valley/MORTARIA

production may have closed down during his lifetime. The potter Baro may be related to the Baro of the Colchester workshops (**table 39**).

Chronology. Antonine.

Source. Rossington Bridge, near Doncaster.

Distribution. Northern Britain, including the Antonine Wall (**131**).

Aliases. Doncaster mortarium fabric 1. *JRPS bibliography* fabric rsm.

Bibliography. For the kilns see Swan 1984; discussions of Sarrius in MacIvor, Thomas and Breeze 1981, 260; Buckland and Magilton 1986, 148.

Notes. Some links with nearby site of Cantley, where production continues through 3rd and 4th cent (Bidwell 1985, 184). Other products of Rossington Bridge include a variety of BB1 (RBBB1) and Parisian wares.

See also. RBBB1

Potter	Date	
BARO	140–90	← COMO ?
SARRIUS	135–70	← MHMO
SECUNDUA	140–70	
SETIBOGIUS	140–70	

Table 39 *Principal Rossington Bridge mortarium potters*

Rhône valley mortaria

Fabric and technology. Hard, fine-textured fabric with smooth or conchoidal texture; generally cream (10YR 9/4) or pink-orange (7.5YR 8/4); abundant ill-sorted quartz and composite granitic rock fragments (up to 3mm) in a micaceous matrix; trituration grits of coarse quartz sand. Large flakes of gold or red-brown mica visible in surfaces. Wheel-thrown. In poor soil conditions the surface may become soft and powdery, leaving the coarser inclusions protruding.

Forms. Mortaria, with bead and hooked flange. The inner surface is scored horizontally by the trituration grits (**132**).

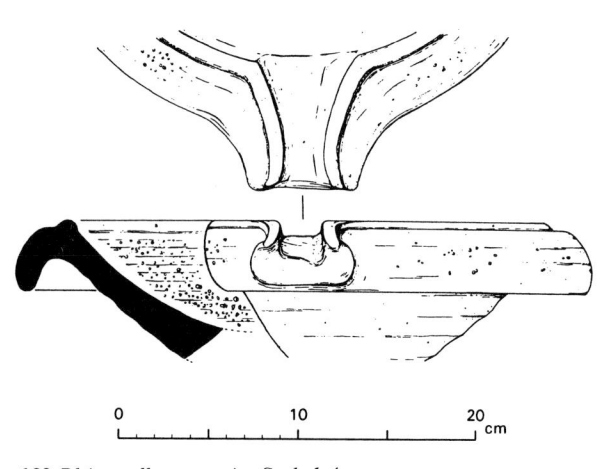

132 *Rhône valley mortaria: Scale 1:4*

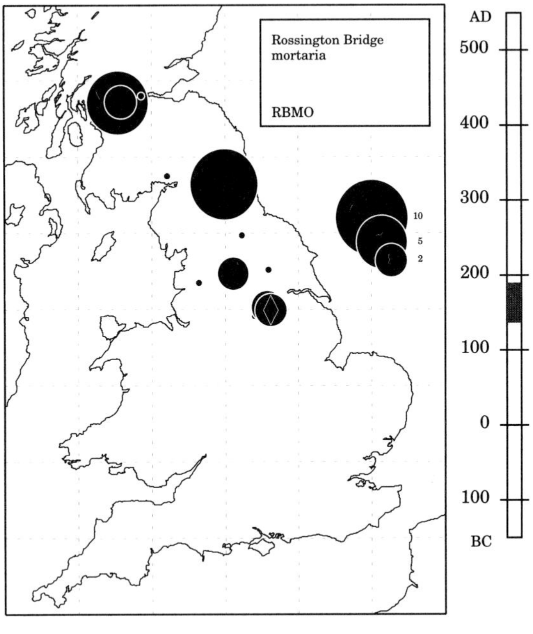

131 *Rossington Bridge mortaria: overall distribution*

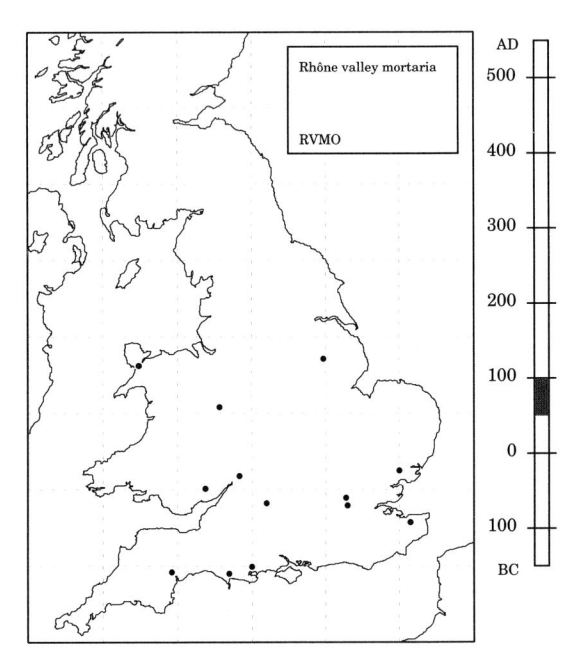

133 *Rhône valley mortaria: British distribution*

Chronology. From *c.* AD 50 to early 2nd cent.
Source. Probably from the Rhône valley, in the Lyon-Vienne region. The petrology of some British specimens can be matched by examples from St Romain-en-Gal (nr. Vienne), the location of many pottery workshops.
Distribution. Only sparse records from Britain, due to conflation with North Gaulish mortaria (NGMO) group I in older reports. In London, moderate numbers in pre-Flavian contexts. Distribution in Gaul uncertain, but there is one specimen from Orléans, on the Loire, and a few from Valence (south of Vienne) (133).
Aliases. Dorchester fabrics 42S and 42X. *Exeter* mortarium fabrics FC6-FC11. *Gloucester* fabric TF9AA. *Sheepen* mortarium fabrics 14–16. *Usk* mortarium fabrics 13 and 14.
Bibliography. Tyers (forthcoming) b.

Soller mortaria

Fabric and technology. Hard, fine-textured fabric, creamy-yellow in colour with pink core with large white trituration grits.
Forms. Mortaria, either wall-sided or with thick heavy flat flange (134).
Stamps. Some vessels with large flange are stamped by Verecundus (AD 150–200); his products are notable for their large diameter (at *c.* 75cm, twice the size of an 'average' mortarium) and he leaves thumb impressions near the stamp and on the end of the spout.
Chronology. AD 150–220.
Source. Kilns excavated at Soller, Kreis Düren (30km SE of Köln).
Distribution. The lower Rhineland and Britain, where they have a thin but widespread distribution. Several examples from waterfront deposits at St Magnus House, London (B. Richardson 1986, 111) (135, 136).

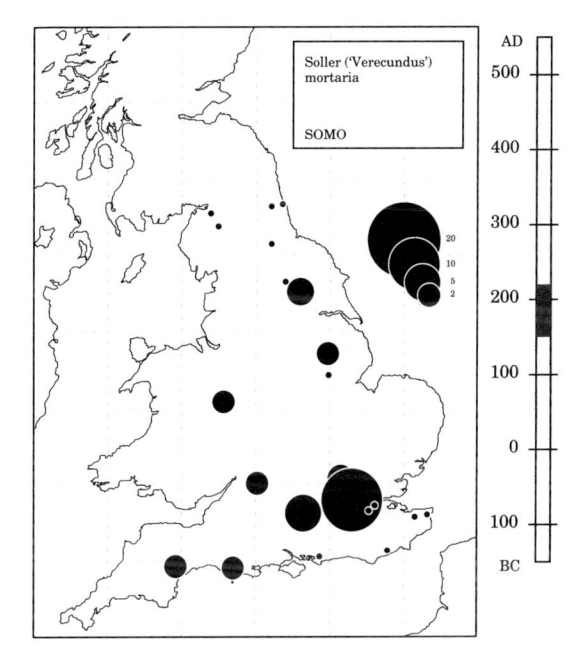

135 Soller mortaria: British distribution

Aliases. Carlisle fabric 618. *Chichester* mortarium fabric 24. *Dorchester* fabric 42G. *Exeter* mortarium fabric FC18. *JRPS* bibliography fabric slm. *Lullingstone* fabric 38. *Old Penrith* fabric 116.
Bibliography. For the kilns see Haupt 1984, with a note by K. F. Hartley on Verecundus.
Notes. More conventionally sized mortaria from other Rhineland sources have also been recognized in Britain, e.g. *Caister-on-sea* fabric RHINE. *Dorchester* fabrics 42H and 42R. *Lullingstone* fabrics 39, 40 and 41.

134 Soller mortaria: Scale 1:6

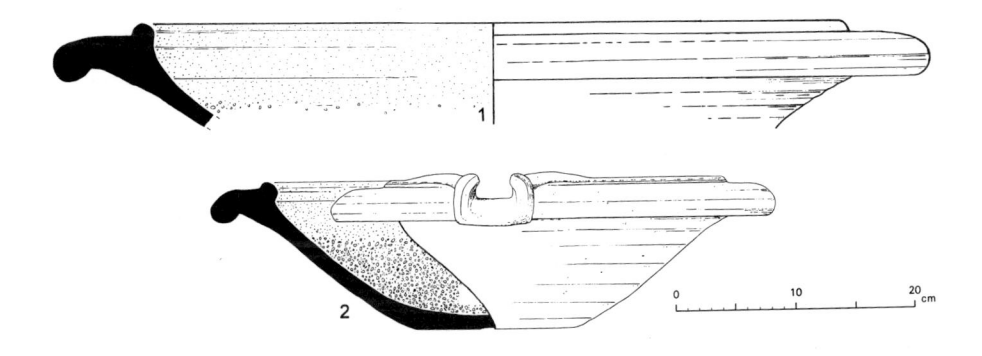

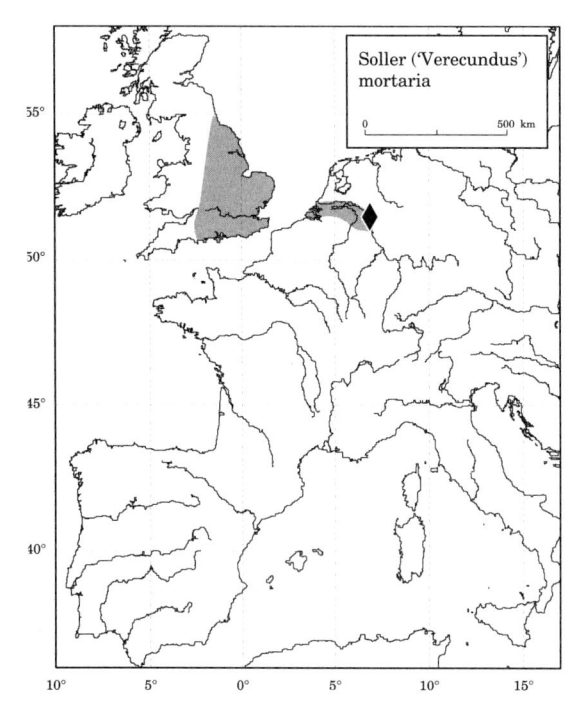

Verulamium-region/MORTARIA

136 Soller mortaria: overall distribution

Potter	Date	
ALBANUS	60–90	
ALBINUS	60–90	← COMO? LUGDUNUM potter
BRUC[C]IUS	80–120	
CANDIDUS	90–125	
CASTUS	100–40	
DEVALUS	70–100	
DOCCAS	85–110	→ MHMO
DOINUS	70–110	
DRICCIUS	100–45	
G. ATTIUS MARINUS	100–10	← COMO → MHMO
GISSUS	90–140	
JUNIUS	100–40	
L. ARRIUS CALUDUS	65–95	
LALLAIUS	80–125	
MARINUS	80–125	
MARTINUS	100–40	
MATUGENUS	80–125	Son of ALBINUS
MELUS i	95–135	
MERTUCUS	110–50	
MORICAMULUS	70–110	
MORINA	70–130	
NIDUS	100–20	→ MHMO
NSRO	120–45	
OASTRIUS	55–80	LUGDUNUM potter
OVIDUS	110–40	
Q. RUTILIUS RIPANUS	55–90	LUGDUNUM potter
RAMOTUS	65–95	
ROA	110–40	
S. VALERIUS IV..	55–90	← COMO
SATURNINUS i	105–40	
SECUNDUS	55–90	
SOLLUS	60–100	
TMH	120–45	← COMO
VIDEX	85–140	

Table 40 *Principal Verulamium-region mortarium potters*

Verulamium-region mortaria

Fabric and technology. Hard, granular fabric, which is rough to the touch but with a slightly laminar fracture; usually white or cream (e.g. 2.5YR 5/0 to 9/0 or 10YR 9/1) but sometimes more orange or buff, with pink or black core in thickest parts. Characteristic abundant inclusions of well-sorted quartz with sparser red ironstone inclusions set in a fine matrix. Gritted on the interior, and over the flange on some, with flint and coarse quartz. For other products of the Verulamium-region industries see VRW.

Forms. Mortaria. A wide variety of rim forms occur, and some variants can be assigned to individual potters or workshops. There is a progression from forms with a deeply hooked flange, through to those with a higher bead and shorter flange (137). *Gillam* 240.

Stamps. Often stamped, sometimes with a name stamp on one side of the flange and a counterstamp (e.g. FECIT) on the other. Stamps of over 50 named potters are known, and there are additional illiterate stamps or marks (138, table 40). Some potters are represented by many hundreds of specimens (e.g. Albinus – the most prolific, Matugenus, Doinus) while others by only a single example, perhaps only from one of the known kiln sites. The counterstamps of three potters (Albinus, Oastrius, Q. Rutilius Ripanus) record a place name, LUGDUNUM or LUGUDUNUM, which may refer to Bricket Wood (Herts.).

Some VRMO potters migrated to the region from elsewhere, principally Colchester (G. Attius Marinus, T.M.H, possibly Sex. Valerius Iu.., Aprilis, Severus and Albinus), and some later moved away to set up workshops in the Mancetter-Hartshill complex (G. Attius Marinus again, Doccas and Nidus). Family potting traditions are indicated by Matugenus, who records that he is the son of Albinus on some stamps.

An interesting sidelight on mortarium production in the Verulamium region is provided by a few specimens in this ware stamped with dies that were used more commonly as official tile-stamps. These read P.P.BR.LON or P.PR.BR, which can be interpreted as *p(rocuratores) p(rovinciae) Bri(tanniae)*

Verulamium-region/MORTARIA

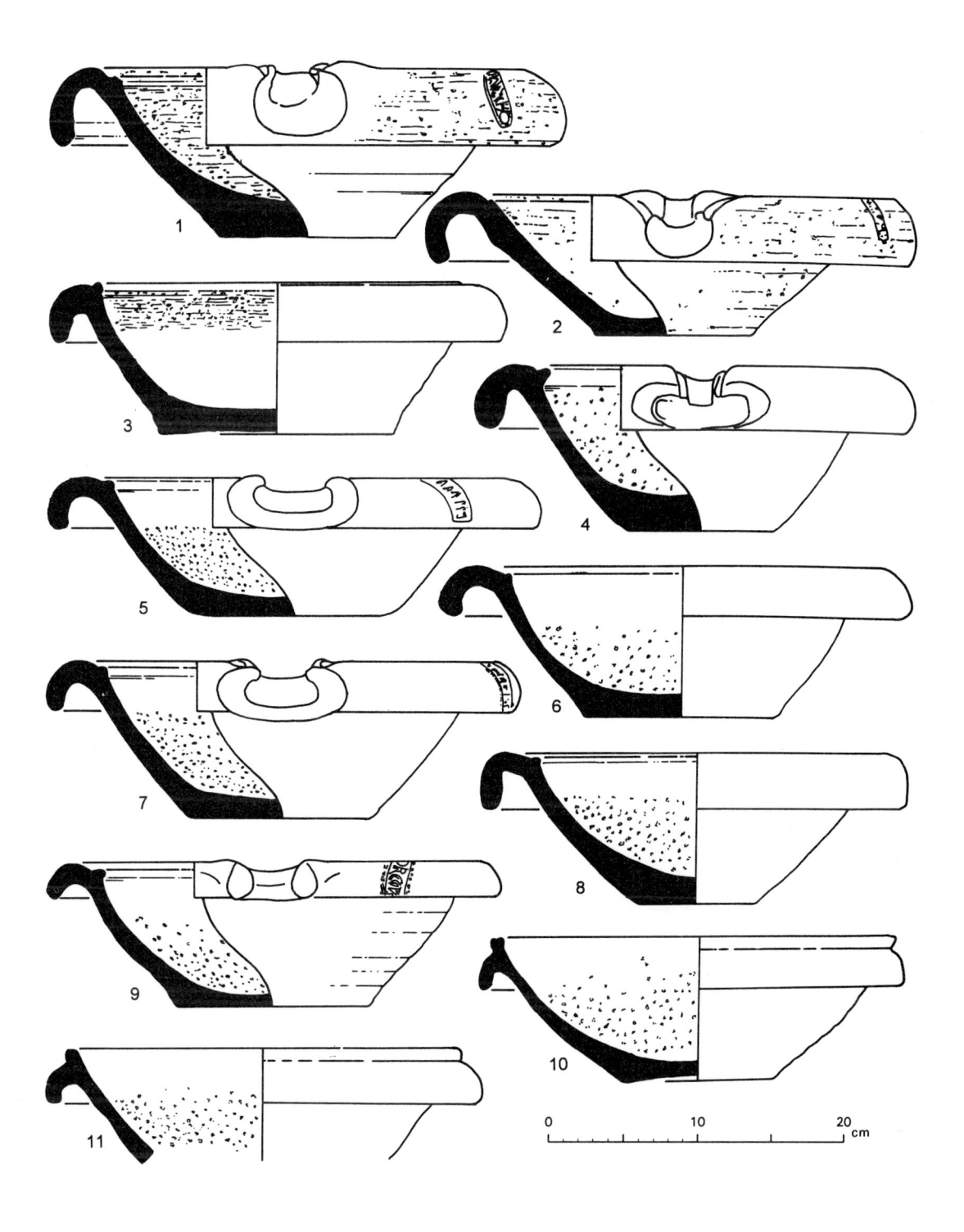

137 *Verulamium-region mortaria: Scale 1:4*

Wilderspool/MORTARIA

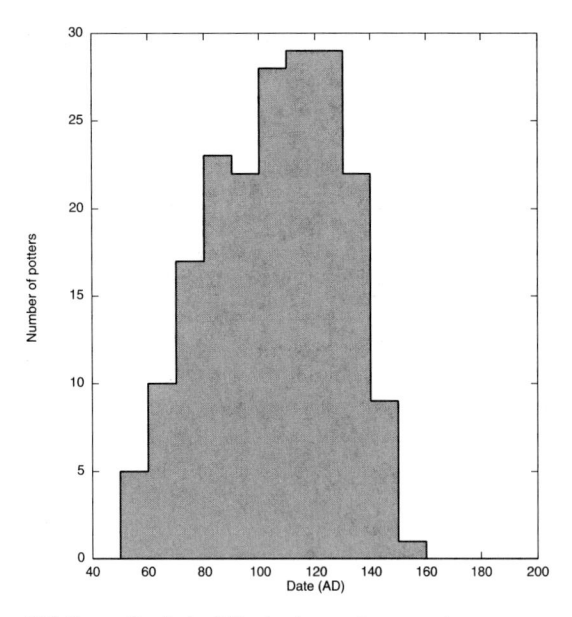

138 *Dates of principal Verulamium-region mortarium potters*

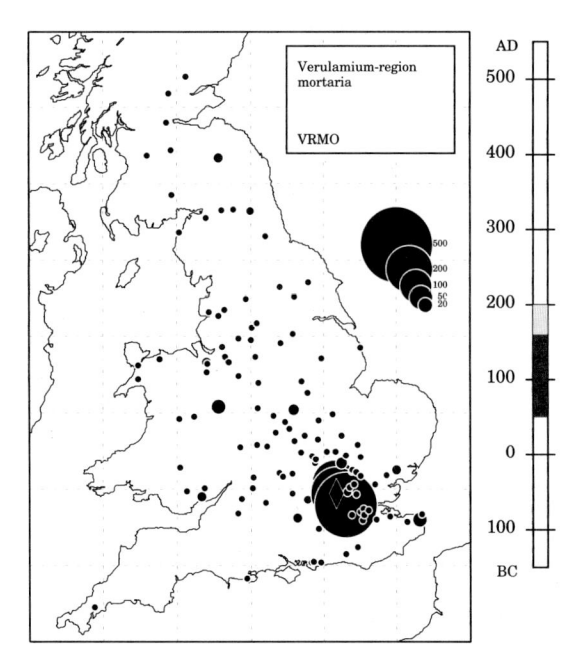

139 *Verulamium-region mortaria: distribution of stamps of principal potters*

[Lon(dini)] – 'The procurators of the province of Britain [at London]' (*RIB* ii.5, 2485; Collingwood, *et al.* 1993, 30).
Chronology. Production commenced before the Boudiccan revolt (*c.* AD 50/55), and mortaria were stamped until *c.* AD 155/160. Production continued on a smaller local scale until *c.* AD 200.
Source. Between St Albans (Verulamium) and London, near Watling Street. Kilns known at Brockley Hill, Radlett, Bricket Wood and on the outskirts of Verulamium itself.
Distribution. Mortaria have a wide distribution across Britain, including Scottish forts and the Hadrianic frontier, but largest concentrations are at London and St Albans, each with many hundreds of stamps (**139**).
Aliases. *Caersws* mortarium fabric 1. *Caister-on-sea* fabric VERUL. *Carlisle* fabrics 620 and 621. *Chesterfield* fabrics m3, m4 and m5. *Chichester* mortarium fabric 4. *Cirencester* fabric 72. *Colchester* fabric TD. *Doncaster* mortarium fabric 12. *Exeter* mortarium fabric FB34. *Gestingthorpe* mortarium fabric J. *Gloucester* fabric TF9F. *Great Chesterford* mortarium fabrics 3–5. *JRPS bibliography* fabric vrm. *Kent* mortarium fabric 1. *Leicester* fabrics MO7 and MO10. *Milton Keynes* fabric 4g. *Old Penrith* fabric 108. *Sheepen* mortarium fabric 28. *Sidbury* fabric 35. *Towcester* mortarium fabric 5. *Usk* mortarium fabric 18.
Bibliography. For the kiln sites: *RCHM gazetteer* 97–8, F354–5, F359–62, F475–80; summary of the industry in Marsh and Tyers 1978. There is no complete published catalogue of stamps, but the most common are reported in the large collection from Verulamium (K. F. Hartley 1984). For the LUGDUNUM group: Saunders and Havercroft 1977.
See also. VRW

Wilderspool mortaria
Fabric and technology. Fairly sandy fabrics with abundant quartz inclusions, varying from pink through to orange-brown, often with a blue-grey core; multi-coloured (red, brown, white and black) trituration grit. Wheel-thrown.
Forms. Mortaria with bead and rolled flange (**140**).

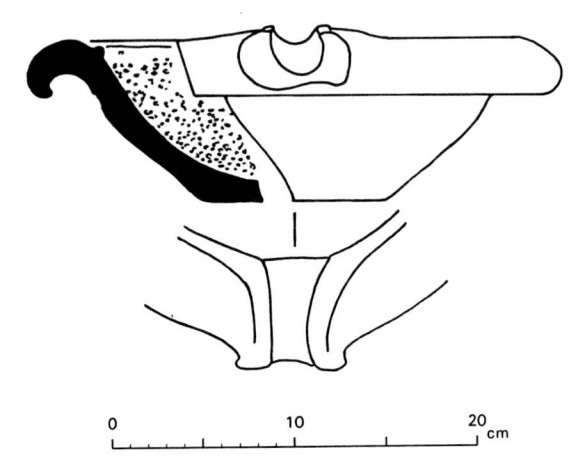

140 *Wilderspool mortaria: Scale 1:4*

Stamps. The Wilderspool potters Austinus, Docci.. and DIS/LDB moved subsequently to the Carlisle (Eden valley) region, where they produced very similar mortaria. It is not always possible to distinguish Wilderspool and Carlisle

IMPORTED WARES

products on fabric grounds alone, but different dies were used in the two workshops.

The potter Nanieco probably originated in the Mancetter-Hartshill potteries. The Scottish potter Emi.., who probably operated from the Newstead area, produced mortaria with the same rim forms as DIS/LDB and Doccius, and probably trained in their Wilderspool or Carlisle workshops (**141, table 41**).

Potter	Date	
AMENUS	-	
AUSTINUS	115–65	→ Carlisle
BRICO	-	
C.C.M	-	
DECANIO	130–65	
DECMITIUS	-	
DIS/LDB	120–50	→ Carlisle
DOCCI..	120–55	→ Carlisle
MIMICIUS	-	
NANIECO	-	← MHMO?
OVID[I]US	-	
REBDECUS(?)	125–60	

Table 41 *Principal Wilderspool mortarium potters*

Chronology. Hadrianic and Antonine.
Source. Wilderspool, Warrington (Cheshire).
Distribution. North-west England, the northern frontier zone, including the Antonine Wall; a few in north Wales.
Aliases. *JRPS bibliography* fabric wpm.
Bibliography. For the Wilderspool kilns: *RCHM gazetteer* F240; K. F. Hartley and Webster 1973. The principal potters, and their Eden valley connections, are discussed in McCarthy 1990, 260–2; Hinchcliffe, Williams and Williams 1992, 73.

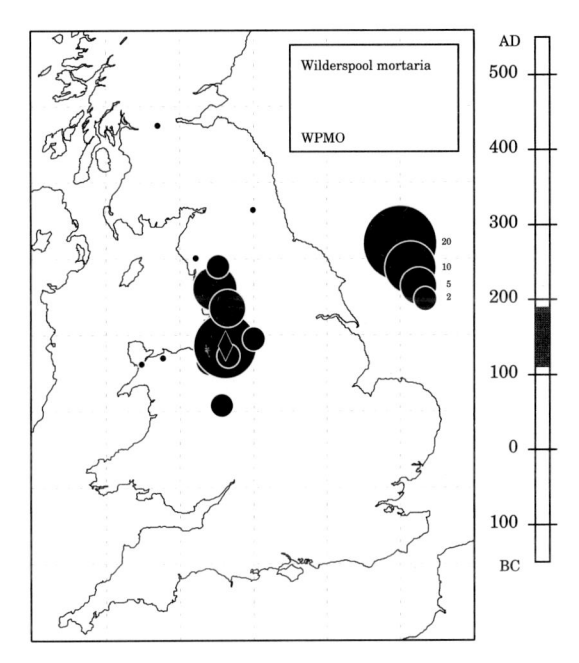

141 *Wilderspool mortaria: distribution of stamps of principal potters*

IMPORTED WARES

In addition to the amphoras, sigillata and mortaria described elsewhere, other classes of pottery were imported into Britain (**142**). These can be considered in two groups.

Tablewares. Imported fine tablewares, particularly plates, cups and beakers. One thread running through this material is the dark-slipped, roughcast or barbotine decorated drinking vessel, in some cases a minor product of the Gaulish sigillata industry. An increasing proportion of such vessels are produced by Romano-British fine-wares industries from the mid-2nd cent. AD, often by potters migrating from the continental centres.

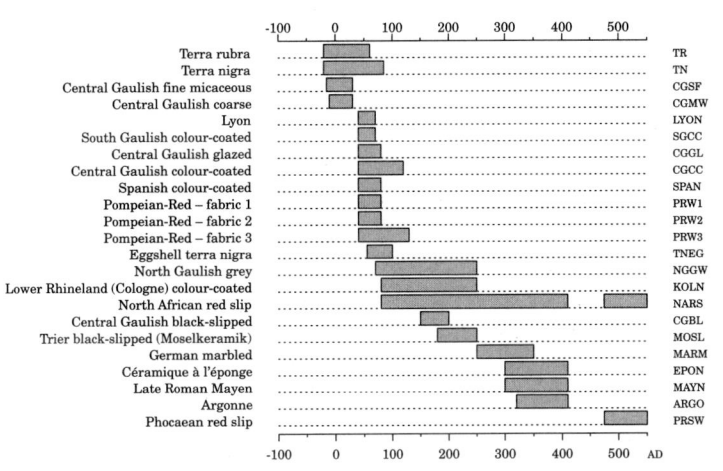

142 *Imported wares: dating of principal classes*

Argonne/IMPORTED WARES

Coarse wares Imported cooking wares or coarse-ware containers. A wide range of types from many sources, but only rarely more than a minor element of the assemblage. Both fine and coarse wares may 'piggy-back' on the trade in the more abundant amphoras and sigillata, or in other commodities, and thus provide useful markers of wider economic activity.

In the Atlas pages the wares are ordered alphabetically.

Argonne ware

Fabric and technology. A fine, hard orange fabric (2.5YR 4/8) with a similarly coloured slip, with a 'soapy' finish. Plain forms occur, but the most distinctive feature is the decoration of horizontal bands of impressed geometric patterns executed with roller stamp. The typology of the roller stamps developed by Chenet (1941) covers the common types and is the basis of most later discussions.

Forms. Principally bowls, especially Chenet form 320 (**143**).

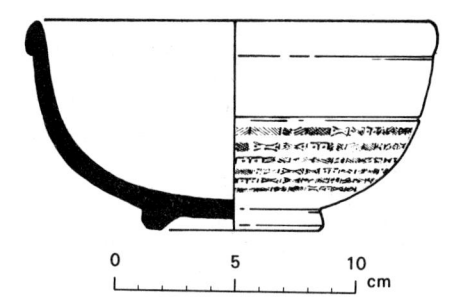

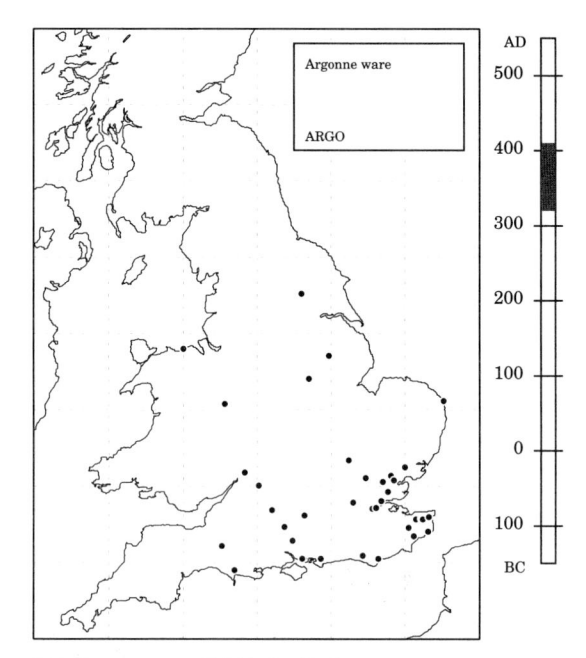

144 Argonne ware: British distribution

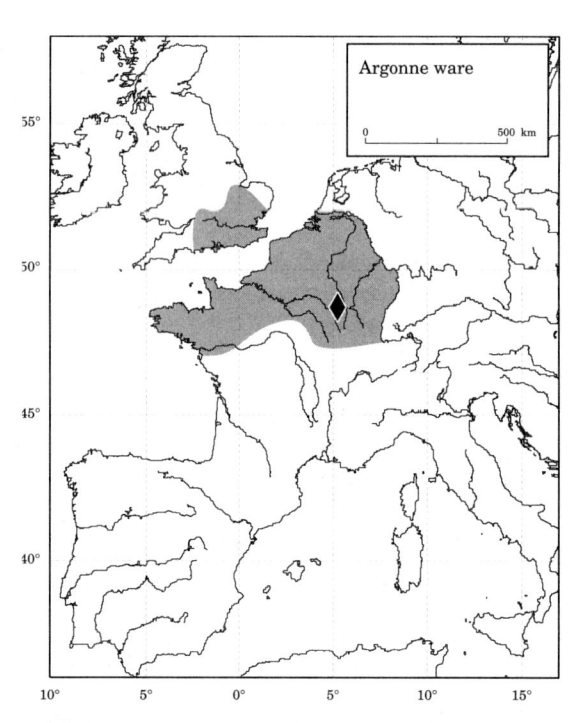

143 Argonne ware: Scale 1:3

Chronology. From late 3rd cent. with production continuing until at least AD 450. Many British pieces are dated to the mid- and late 4th cent. but importation may have started in the later 3rd cent.

Source. The Argonne region of northern France, east of Rheims.

Distribution. Widespread, but sparse, in southern Britain, where it is concentrated around the estuaries of the Thames and Solent. There are also occasional sherds in the north and west. In Gaul the ware is widespread in Gallia Belgica and Upper and Lower Germany, extending south along the Rhine as far as Basel. To the west of Argonne it is widespread north of the Loire, in the Paris basin, Brittany and Normandy. On some sites in this region it is associated with Romano-British pottery imports (**144, 145**).

Aliases. Caister-on-sea fabric ARG. *Gloucester* fabric TF12N. *JRPS bibliography* fabric ats. *Kent* fine fabric 2.

Bibliography. The principal studies of roller-stamped Argonne ware are Unverzagt 1919; Chenet 1941 and Hübener 1968. On the chronology of the decorative styles: Bayard 1990; Feller 1991. The distribution and dating in northern France is described by Blaszkiewicz and Jigan 1991. For British distribution: Fulford 1977b, 39–43, Appendix 1.

145 Argonne ware: overall distribution

Fine black-slipped/IMPORTED WARES

Notes. The Argonne kilns produced standard moulded and plain samian during the 2nd and 3rd centuries at sites such as Lavoye (Bémont and Jacob 1986, 195–207), which occur sporadically in Britain (e.g. Bird and Marsh 1981, 178–9). The importation of Drag 45 mortaria from the Argonne may continue into the later 3rd cent. and some potteries make the transition to roller-stamped wares without a significant break. *See also.* EGTS

Fine black-slipped wares

Fine black-slipped beakers with barbotine or moulded wares were produced and exported widely from the Central Gaulish samian workshops from the early 2nd cent. AD (CGTS, CGCC). By *c.* AD 140 a series of cup and beaker forms had developed in Central Gaulish black wares (CGBL), some mirroring the contemporary sigillata repertoire, and often decorated with combinations of fine barbotine scrollwork and rouletted bands. Some of the beakers are folded or indented.

During the later 2nd cent. black wares were produced and exported from the large workshops at Trier, again a major source of samian. Beakers, flasks and cups were the major forms, but this ware, *Moselkeramik*, is particularly notable for the use of white barbotine decoration, including specimens with short texts or 'mottoes' (MOSL).

Broadly similar black-slipped wares were produced on a small scale at many of the smaller sigillata workshops across Central and Eastern Gaul, but the significance of these at anything more than a local scale is not known. In a wider perspective, dark-coloured slipped wares sharing some of the typological or decorative elements of the Gaulish products are known in the Swiss and Danube provinces, and also in Britain (e.g. NVCC, COLC).

The products of the two major sources, Central and East Gaul, had conventionally been conflated in Britain under the title 'Rhenish ware', a term that is neither used nor understood on the Continent. The distinction between the two groups was highlighted by Greene in 1978 (1978a, 56; 1978b, 18) since when it has been usual to attempt to distinguish between them in British reports.

The background and development of these, and other, fine black-slipped wares is discussed at length in Symonds 1992.

Central Gaulish black-slipped ware

Fabric and technology. Fine-textured fabric; generally pink (2.5YR 6/6) or light red (2.5YR 4/6) with glossy black or dark reddish-brown (10YR 3/1) slip; characteristic micaceous matrix, with fine quartz, limestone and sparse red iron ore inclusions. Decoration includes fine horizontal rouletted lines, barbotine 'ivy scrolls' and animals, and occasional appliqué motifs. Wheel-thrown.

Forms. Beakers and cups. Some overlap with sigillata forms and techniques (**146, table 42**).

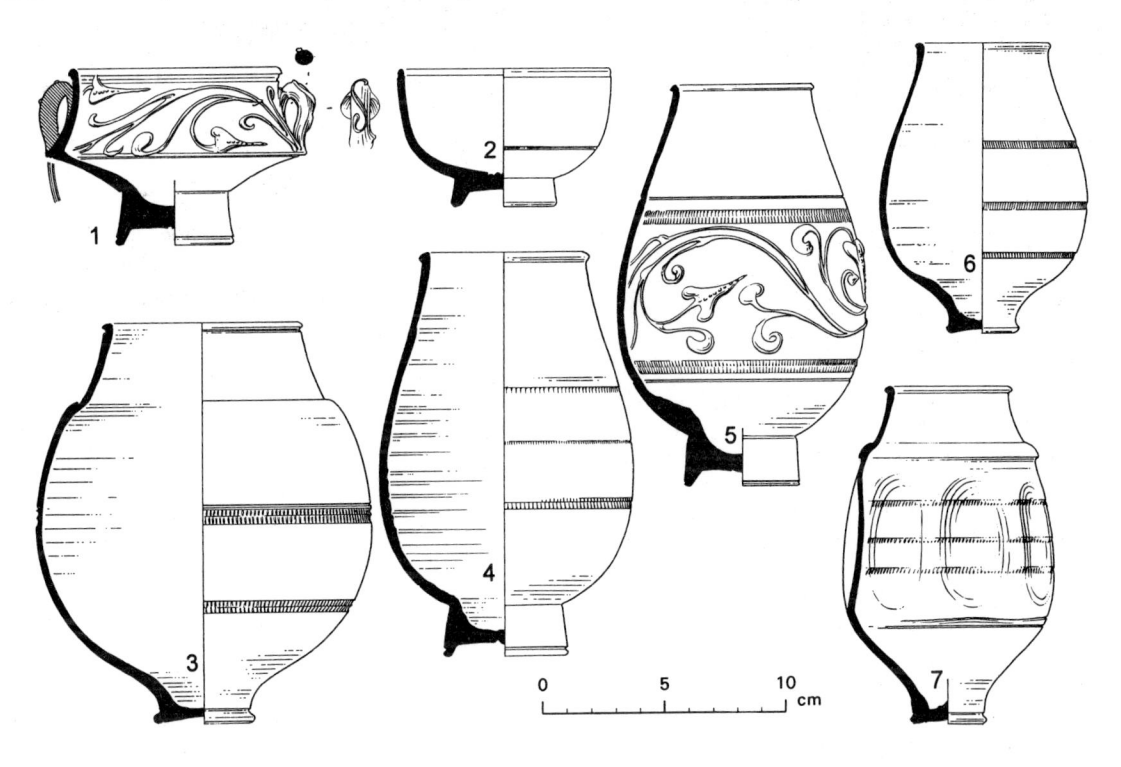

146 *Central Gaulish black-slipped ware: Scale 1:3*

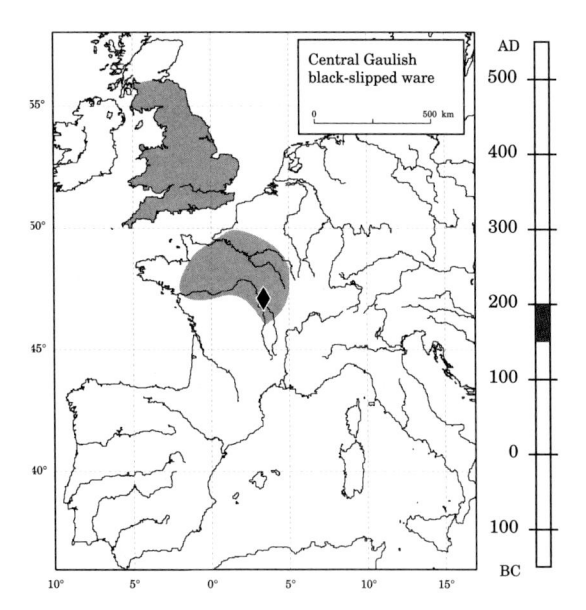

Trier black-slipped ('Moselkeramik')/IMPORTED WARES

147 Central Gaulish black-slipped ware: overall distribution

146	Description	Gillam
1	Two-handled cup	
2	Hemispherical cup (Drag 40)	210
3	Shouldered beaker with plain base	
4–5	Plain beaker with pedestal base	48
6	Plain beaker with plain base	
7	Folded beaker	

Table 42 *Principal Central Gaulish black-slipped forms*

Chronology. Develops from earlier Central Gaulish colour-coated ware traditions by *c.* AD 150, until early 3rd cent.
Source. The Central Gaulish sigillata workshops, including Lezoux.
Distribution. In Gaul, generally distributed east of the Saône (little overlap with Moselkeramik) and noted in Paris basin and along the Loire. In Britain, seems to be present throughout, but inadequate identifications make detailed mapping difficult (147).
Aliases. Caister-on-sea fabric CGBL-30. *Carlisle* fabric 323. *Chelmsford* fabric 8. *Colchester* fabric CLNE. *Gestingthorpe* fabric C2. *Gloucester* fabrics TF12I and TF12J. *Kent* fine fabric 3e. *Lullingstone* fabric 6. *Milton Keynes* fabric 23c. *Old Penrith* fabric 14. *Towcester* fabric 14a. Conflated with Moselkeramik in *JRPS bibliography* as rhn.
Bibliography. For description of fabric and differentiation from Moselkeramik: Brewster 1972; Greene 1978a; Greene 1978b; B. Richardson 1986, 115–18. Lezoux examples illustrated and described in Bet, Gangloff and Vertet 1987.

Symonds 1992, groups 6–15. There is some overlap between CGBL, the earlier colour-coated fabrics of Central Gaul (CGCC) and Central Gaulish 'black samian'.
See also. CGCC CGTS MOSL

Trier black-slipped ware ('Moselkeramik')

Fabric and technology. Very hard, fine-textured fabric; distinct 'sandwich' of dark red (10YR 4/6 to 2.5YR 4/6) with grey margins, with glossy black slip, which may have a dark grey-green metallic lustre; fine white limestone flecks in the matrix, with some quartz sand – not noticeably micaceous (cf. CGBL). Decoration includes fine rouletted bands, white slip or barbotine (applied above the dark slip) and folding or indentations.
Forms. Beakers are most abundant and widespread forms, but flagons, flasks, cups and other more exotic shapes also produced. White-painted scrolls, groups of dots – representing bunches of grapes – wavy lines and other abstract motifs, are particularly characteristic of this group, which may be combined with short texts ('motto beakers') which frequently allude to some aspect of drinking behaviour (e.g. BIBE, MISCE etc.) (**149, table 43**).
Chronology. AD 180–250. Production of black-slipped wares at Trier continues into 4th cent., but not exported.
Source. Principally from workshops at Trier, in the Mosel valley. Oelmann (1914) illustrates material from the production sites.
Distribution. Common in the Mosel valley, middle and lower Rhine, with a scatter to the south and east, but rare west of the Saône. Widespread in Britain, but not consistently distinguished from CGBL in some published reports (148).

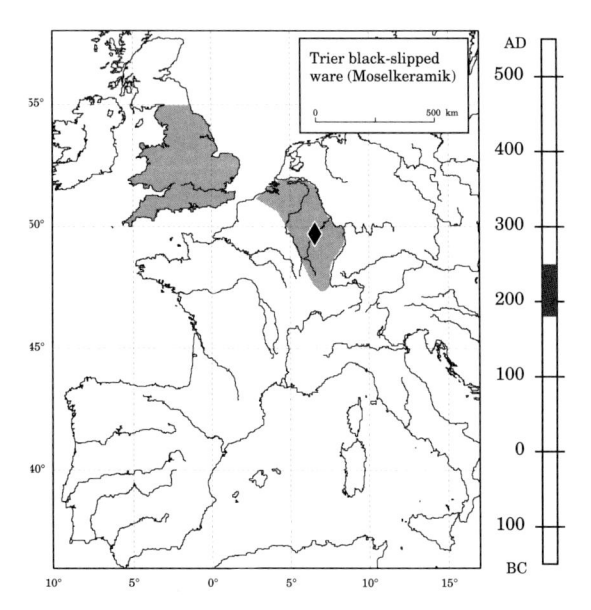

148 Trier black-slipped ware ('Moselkeramik'): overall distribution

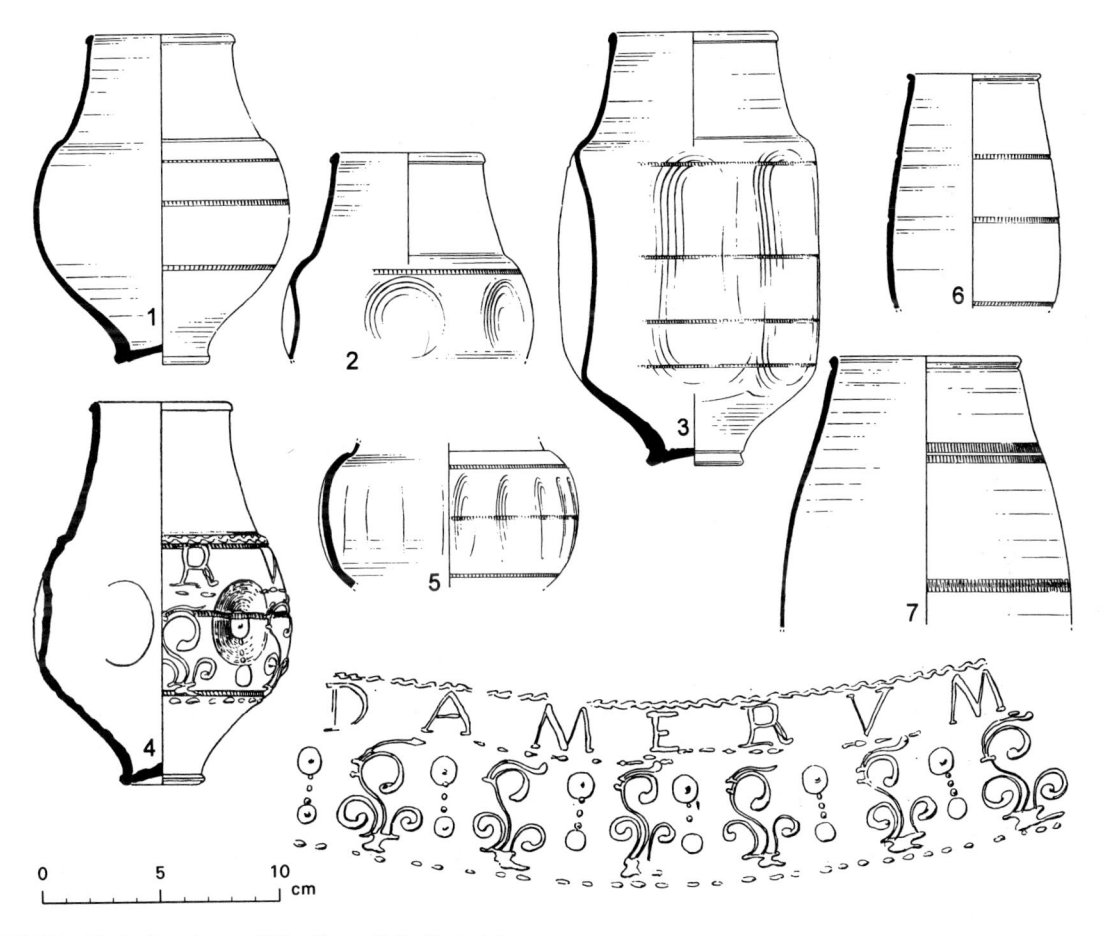

Central Gaulish colour-coated/IMPORTED WARES

149 *Trier black-slipped ware ('Moselkeramik'): Scale 1:3*

149	Description	Gillam
Globular beakers		
1	plain	
2	round/oval indentations	
5	long narrow indentations	44/45
3	folded	46
Beakers with white barbotine decoration		
-	plain	
4	round/oval indentations	
-	long narrow indentations	
Shoulderless beaker		
6–7	plain	

Table 43 *Principal Trier black-slipped ware forms*

Aliases. Caister-on-sea fabric MOSL-31. *Carlisle* fabric 342. *Chelmsford* fabric 9. *Colchester* fabrics CLNF and CLNG. *Gestingthorpe* fabric C1. *Kent* fine fabric 5d. *Lullingstone* fabric 7. *Old Penrith* fabric 13. Conflated with CGBL in *JRPS bibliography* as rhn.

Bibliography. For description of fabric and differentiation from Central Gaulish black-slipped ware: Brewster 1972; Greene 1978a; Greene 1978b; B. Richardson 1986, 118–21; type-series: Symonds 1992, 46–62; for inscriptions: Bös 1958; Symonds 1992, 112–21, with refs. *RIB* ii.6, 2498.

See also. CGBL EGTS

Central Gaulish colour-coated wares

Fabric and technology. There are two fabrics:

1. Hard, almost pure white or cream fabric (2.5Y 9/0) with clean or slightly laminar fracture; sparse red inclusions, clear quartz and mica flakes. Wheel-thrown. Black, dark greenish-brown, (10YR 5/4–3/2) or red (2.5YR 6/4) slip with a metallic sheen; often blood-red (10R 4/8–10) on the interior and lower body. The paste is identical to the principal Central Gaulish glazed ware (CGGL) fabric.

Central Gaulish glazed/IMPORTED WARES

2. Soft, fine pale-buff (10YR 8/4) or buff-brown fabric; slightly sandy and micaceous. Slip ranges from dark chestnut-brown (2.5YR 3/0) or black to orange (5YR 7/8) with a metallic sheen.

Decorated with barbotine, particularly 'hairpin' and 'teardrop' motifs, roughcasting of crushed white clay pellets, or more rarely, rouletting.

Forms. Cups and beakers; the 'hairpin' beakers are particularly characteristic. Rarer types include folded beakers, and shallow tripod dishes. The rims of the beakers are sharply everted and differ from those of the contemporary Rhineland industries (**151**).

Chronology. Produced during the pre-Flavian period, but the floruit of the ware is the Flavian–Trajanic.

Source. Central Gaul. The white fabric may be from the Allier valley, while the buff fabrics are probably from the area of Lezoux and Les Martres-de-Veyre.

Distribution. Gaul, the Rhineland and Britain (**150**).

Aliases. *Gloucester* fabric TF12Q. *JRPS bibliography* fabrics ccc and hpb.

Bibliography. Greene 1979; Bet and Henriques-Raba 1989, summarizes the evidence from Lezoux, with a typology; also Bet, Gangloff and Vertet 1987. Symonds 1992, Group 1 & 2.

See also. CGGL CGBL

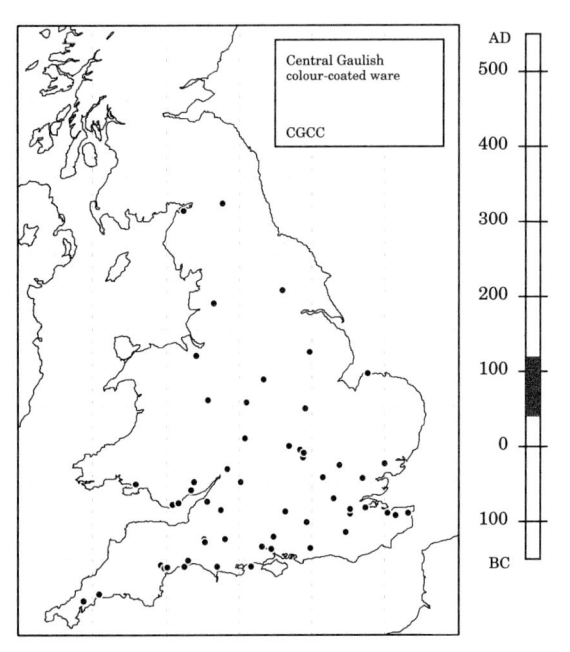

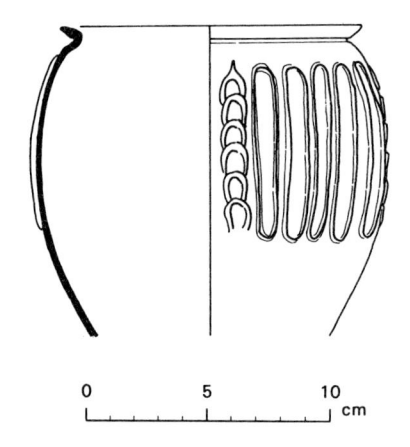

151 Central Gaulish colour-coated ware: Scale 1:3

Central Gaulish glazed ware

Fabric and technology. Most commonly a hard, almost pure white or cream wheel-thrown fabric (2.5Y 9/0) with sparse red inclusions and clean or slightly laminar fracture – identical to that of white central Gaulish colour-coated ware (CGCC). The surfaces are covered with a translucent lead glaze (0.25 to 0.5mm thick) which varies from pale yellow-green to a dark olive green in colour. On cups and beakers the glaze covers the entire surface, but on enclosed flagons only the external surface is covered. Some vessels mould-made, using the same technology (and forms) as contemporary samian wares. Others have appliqué motifs or barbotine decoration.

Forms. Greene's type-series (1979; 1978c) covers the forms found in Britain (**table 44**).

Type	Form	Equivalent
1	Small flagon	Déch 61
2	Flagon	Déch 60
3	Flagon	Déch 62
4	Handled bowl	Déch 59
5	Carinated bowl	Drag 29
6–7	Handled bowls	
8–9	Hemispherical cups	
10	Carinated handled cup	
11	Straight-sided beaker	
12–16	Beakers	
17	Lamp filler	
18	Large bowl	

Table 44 *Classification of Central Gaulish-glazed ware forms (after Greene)*

150 Central Gaulish colour-coated wares: British distribution

Chronology. Generally pre-Flavian in Britain, but a few examples from Flavian sites. Production probably commenced in the Tiberian period.

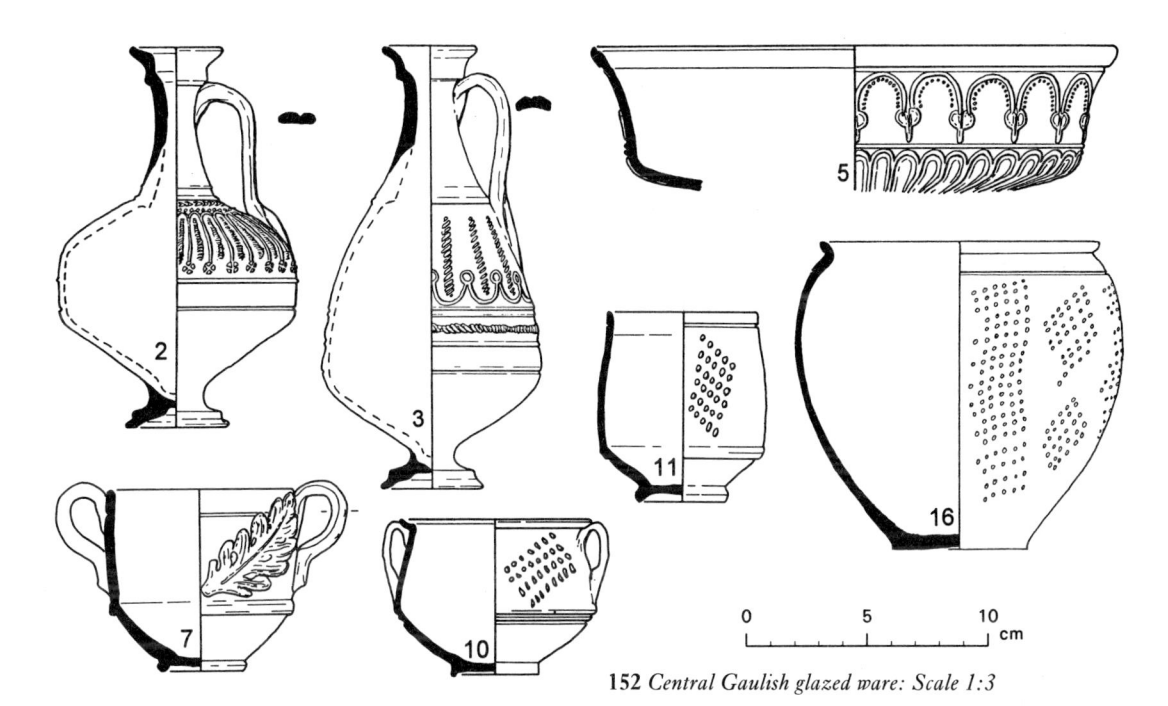

Central Gaulish glazed/IMPORTED WARES

152 Central Gaulish glazed ware: Scale 1:3

Source. Two regions of Central Gaul – the Allier valley and Lezoux. A few vessels from Britain are probably products of Lezoux (e.g. Greene 1978c, 39) but the majority from St Rémy-en-Rollat/Vichy in the Allier valley.

Distribution. Widespread in Britain, but sparse. The continental distribution covers northern France (north and east of the Loire), the Rhineland and western Switzerland (**153, 154**).

Aliases. Cirencester fabrics 60 and 75. *JRPS bibliography* fabric cgg. *Kent* fine fabric 3a. *Leicester* fabric LG1. *Milton Keynes* fabric 13c. *Silchester* fabric E32.

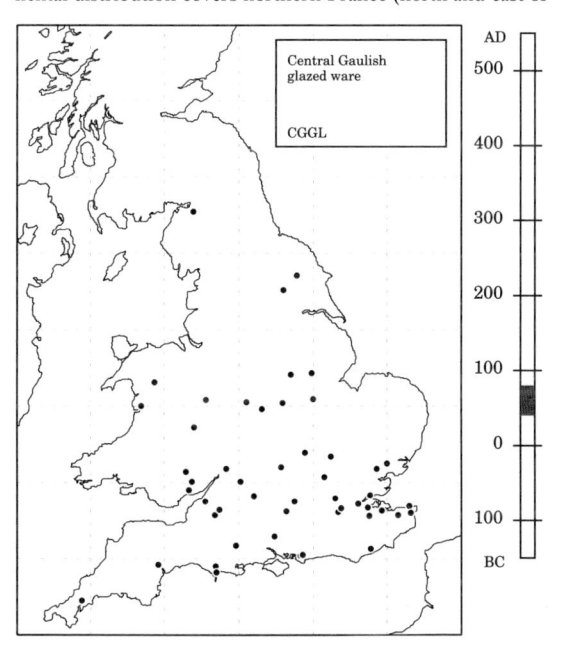

153 Central Gaulish glazed ware: British distribution

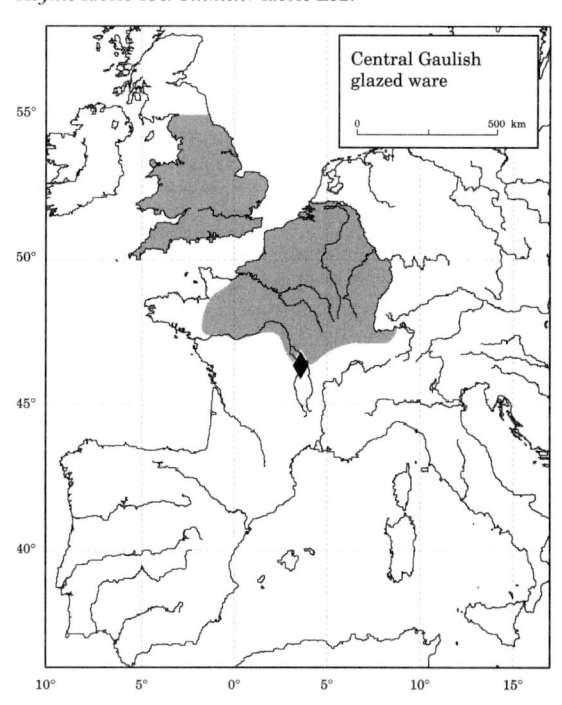

154 Central Gaulish glazed ware: overall distribution

Central Gaulish coarse micaceous/IMPORTED WARES

Bibliography. General introduction to the ware given by Greene (1979, 86–103) who discusses the moulded ware in more detail in Greene 1978c. It has been suggested that the flagons (one of the more widespread forms) may have carried water from the spa at Vichy (Symonds and Wade 1986).
See also. CGCC

Central Gaulish coarse micaceous ware

Fabric and technology. Hard, rough fabric with very irregular fracture; colour ranges from orange- or red-brown through to dark brown, or almost black, but colours towards the middle of the range (2.5YR 6/6 or 2.5YR 4/4) are most common; abundant flakes of biotite mica and very large feldspar inclusions (occasionally over 1cm) prominent in both surface and section; some vessels unevenly smoothed towards rim. Hand-formed.

Forms. Principal form is jar, with moulded rim, *Cam* 262, and there is a single tripod bowl from Sheepen, *Cam* 45A (**155**).

Chronology. Production of this fabric (in larger, heavier forms with incised decorated band on shoulder – class I & II)

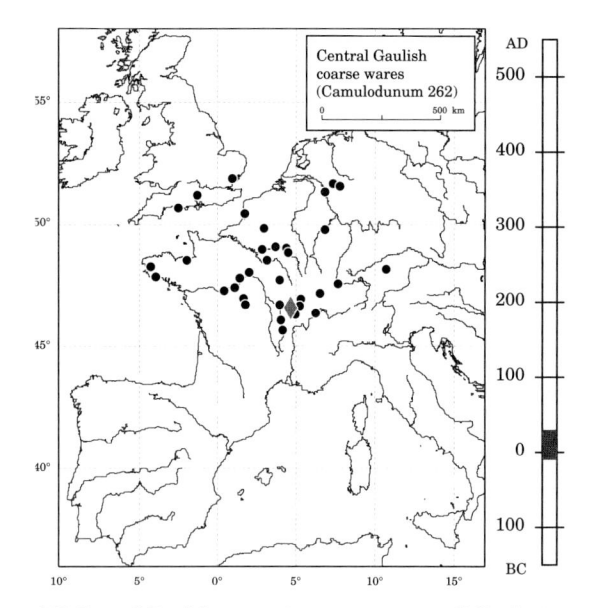

156 Central Gaulish coarse micaceous ware: overall distribution

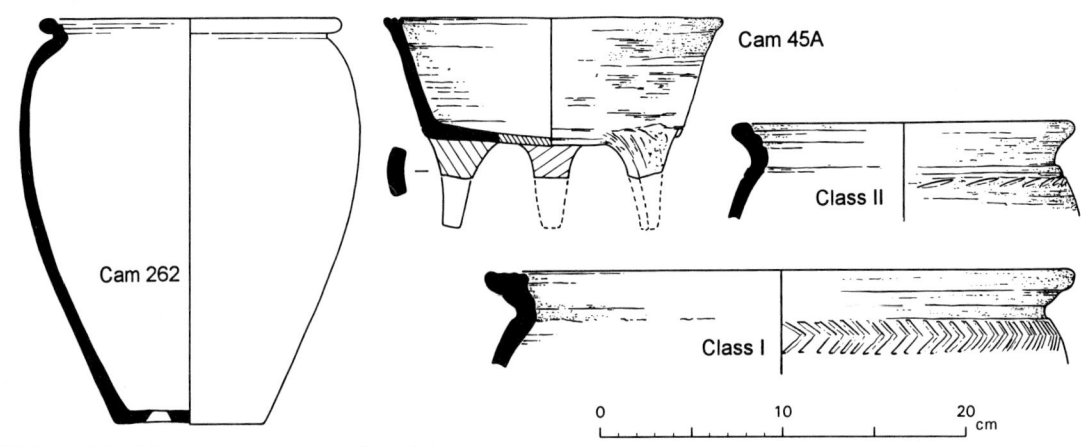

155 Central Gaulish coarse micaceous ware: Scale 1:4

commences before Caesarian period, perhaps as early as 100 BC and reaches Basel and northern Gaul at this period. The *Cam* 262 form develops by *c.* 15 BC, and distribution expands; no evidence for production after early Tiberian period.

Source. Petrology and distribution suggests a source in Morvan, between the Saône and the upper Loire.

Principal contents. Wide distribution of the jar form suggests function as container, and some evidence that they may have contained some form of prepared pig-meat product.

Distribution. Wide but thin distribution across Gaul; most abundant (and highest proportion of the assemblage) in Burgundy and upper Loire valley (**156**).

Aliases. For historical reasons the *Cam* 262 form is known as *le type Besançon* in the French literature, although it is neither made nor found at Besançon.

Bibliography. Tyers (forthcoming) a; on the Besançon 'type' – a conflation of several wares: Ferdière and Ferdière 1972.

Central Gaulish fine micaceous wares

Fabric and technology. Fairly hard, fine-textured, with slightly irregular fracture; red-brown (2.5YR 5/6) with grey core in thicker sherds; inclusions of well-sorted fine sand (containing quartz and feldspar), larger rounded brown clay pellets, and some golden mica (more visible in the surfaces). Wheel-thrown. Three variants: A, red slip; B, cream slip; C, golden micaceous slip.

Forms. The three fabric variants are employed for different forms:

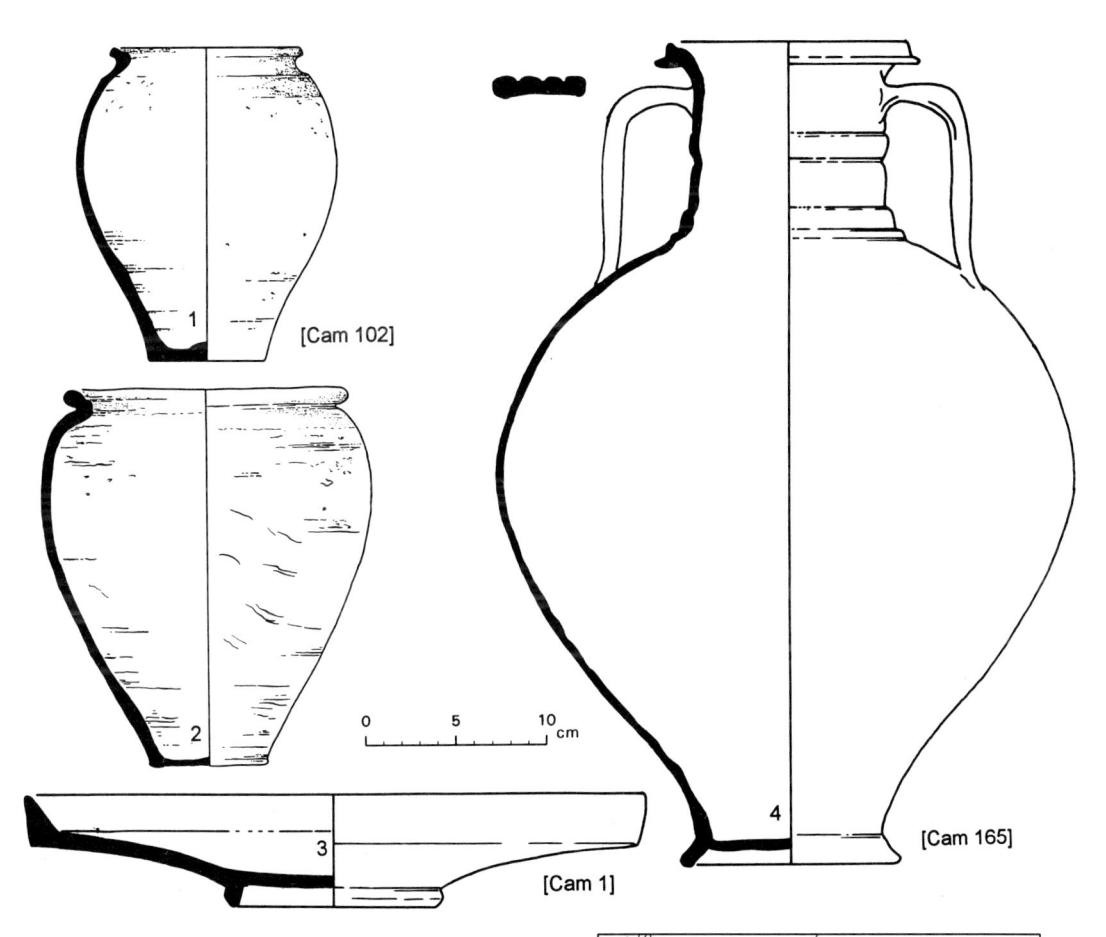

Central Gaulish fine micaceous/IMPORTED WARES

157 *Central Gaulish fine micaceous wares: Scale 1:4*

Fabric	Form	Description	*Cam*
A	P1	Platter	1
B	F1	Flagon	
B	F2	Flagon	
B	F3a	Flagon	
B	F3b	Flagon	165
C	J1	Moulded-rim jar	102

Chronology. Flagon F1 found in early Augustan Welwyn Garden City burial; most other examples pre-Claudian and little evidence of post-conquest importation.

Source. Probably from the middle Loire valley, perhaps the Orléans region where the local assemblage includes a coarser version of the fabric described here, which is not found in Britain (**157**).

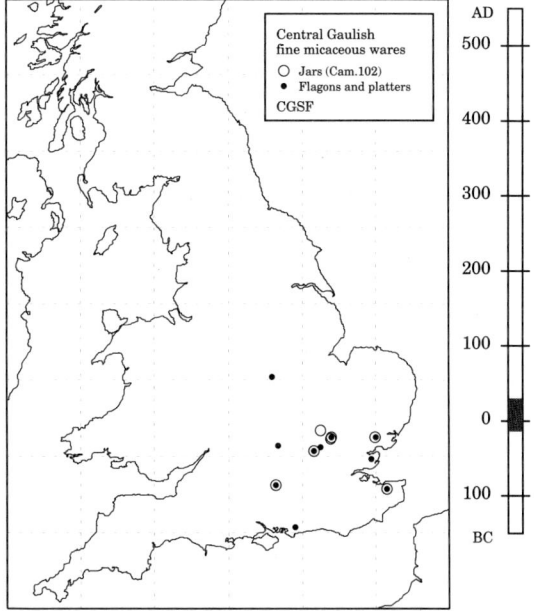

158 *Central Gaulish fine micaceous wares: British distribution*

143

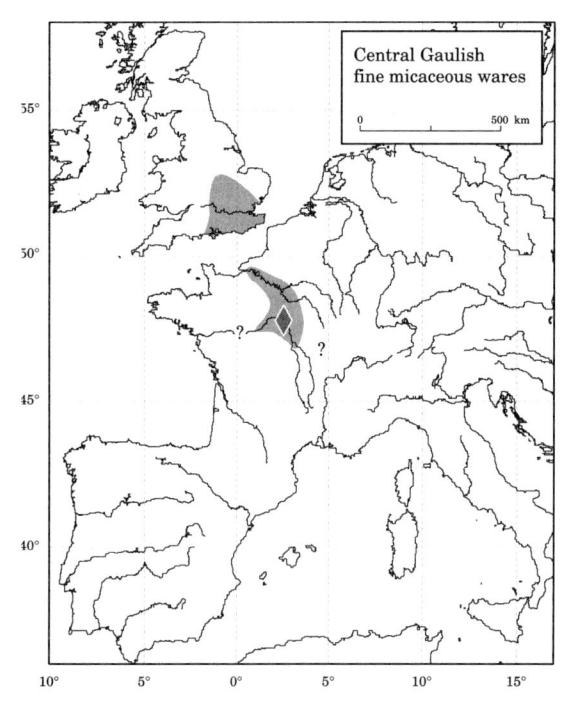

Céramique à l'éponge/IMPORTED WARES

159 *Central Gaulish fine micaceous wares: overall distribution*

Distribution. Common in Orléans region, and north into Paris basin; also at Rouen, suggesting trade along the Seine. In Britain, concentrated in two groups, centered on Hampshire and Herts./Essex (**158, 159**).
Aliases. *Leicester* fabric WS1.
Bibliography. Rigby and Freestone 1986; Stead and Rigby 1989; Tyers (forthcoming) a.

Céramique à l'éponge

Fabric and technology. A pale creamy-yellow fine-textured fabric (7.5YR 7/6) with a smooth glossy yellow-orange or reddish-brown slip, variable in thickness. Wheel-thrown. Upon this is superimposed (in a darker slip) a blurred floral or star pattern, or a simpler marbled effect, hence the French name 'sponged ware'.
Forms. Raimbault (1973) defines twelve principal types. Some are derived from late sigillata prototypes. A general affinity with other late Roman red-slipped traditions of eastern Gaul and Britain (**table 45**).

Type	Form	Prototype
I	Shallow plate	
II	Hemispherical cup	
III	Hemispherical bowl	
IV	Hemispherical bowl	
V	Straight-sided bowl	Drag 44/45
VI	Flanged bowl	Drag 38
VII	Necked bowl	
VIII	Large beaker	Déch 72
IX	Small beaker	
X	Flagon	
XI	Pinch-mouthed flagon	
XII	Face-jug	

Table 45 *Classification of* la céramique à l'éponge *forms (after Raimbault)*

The bowls (V–VII) and jug (X) are the commonest forms, and the most common in Britain (**160**).
Chronology. Production commenced in the early 3rd cent., but initially only for a local market. Wider distribution dates to the 4th cent., but production may continue until *c.* AD 450.
Source. Western France, perhaps near Civaux (Vienne) where there is a particularly wide range of forms and decorative types.
Distribution. Common in western France, between the Loire

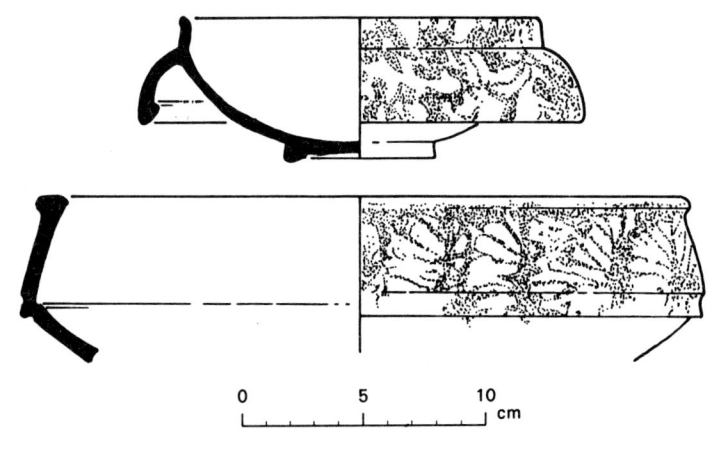

160 *Céramique à l'éponge: Scale 1:3*

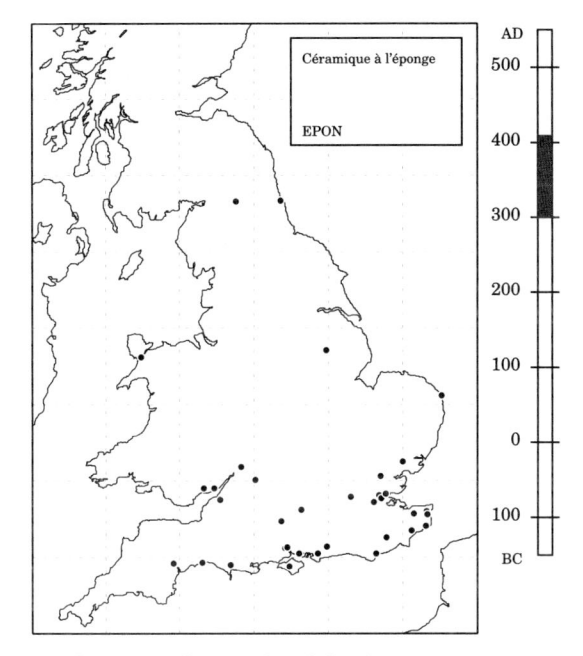

E ware/IMPORTED WARES

161 Céramique à l'éponge: British distribution

and Gironde and scatter of findspots in Brittany and Normandy (as far as the Seine), the Channel Islands and southern Britain (**161, 162**).

Aliases. *Caister-on-sea* fabric EPON-32. *Chelmsford* fabric 22. *Gloucester* fabric TF12M. *Kent* fine fabric 6.

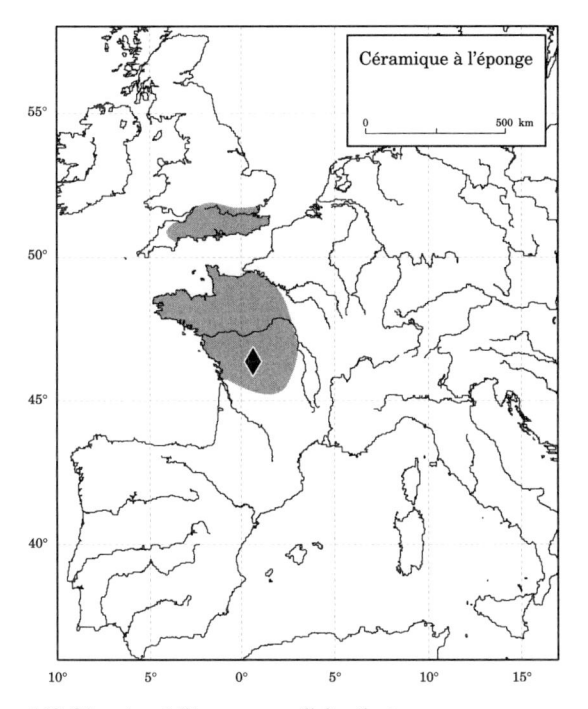

Bibliography. The original typology is Raimbault 1973; British finds listed by Fulford (1977b, 45–7, Appendix 2) and the northern French and British distribution described in Galliou, Fulford and Clement 1980. Simon-Hiernard 1991 discusses source, dating and distribution.

E ware

Fabric and technology. A hard, high-fired granular ware with prominent quartz sand inclusions; varying in colour from dirty white through yellow to dark red or grey. Wheel-thrown, with prominent wheel-marks on the inner surface and a whorl on the underside of the base, caused by the use of a string or wire to detach the vessels from the wheel.

Forms. A very limited range of forms (**164, table 46**):

Form	Description
E1	Necked jars
E2	Small carinated jar or beaker
E3	Carinated bowl with flaring rim
E4	Strap handled jug with pinched or tubular spout
E5	Conical lid

Table 46 *Classification of E ware forms (after Thomas)*

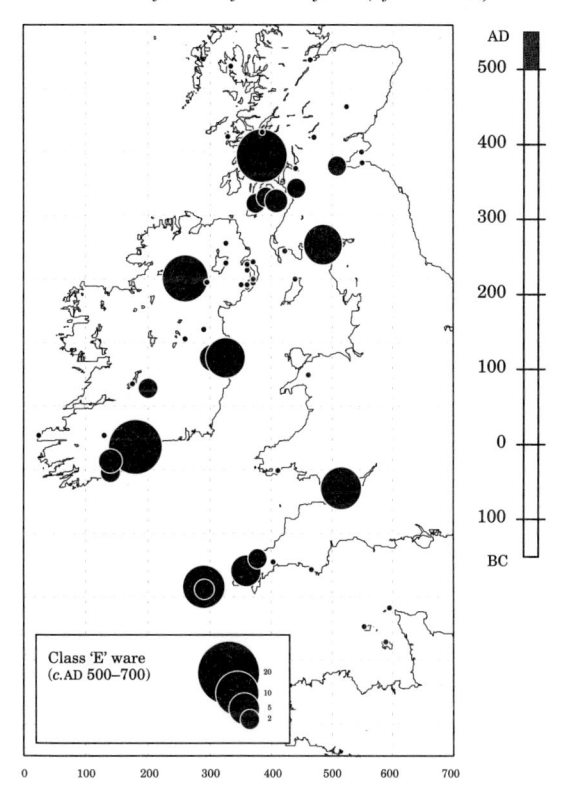

162 Céramique à l'éponge: overall distribution

163 E ware: British and Irish distribution

145

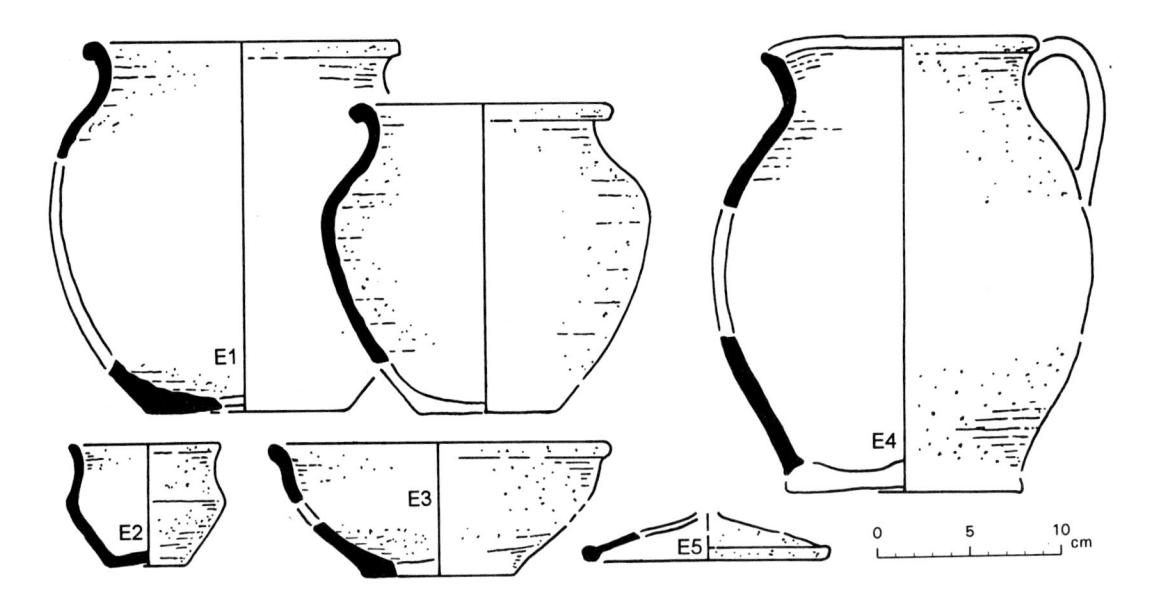

Lower Rhineland (Cologne) colour-coated/IMPORTED WARES

164 *E ware: Scale 1:4*

Chronology. Associated with 6th cent. AD Eastern Mediterranean imports on some sites – perhaps commencing as early as *c.* AD 500 – but importation evidently continues much later than the Mediterranean material, into the 7th cent. AD.

Source. No kilns are known, but the evidence points towards a source in western France, probably somewhere accessible from the Loire or Gironde.

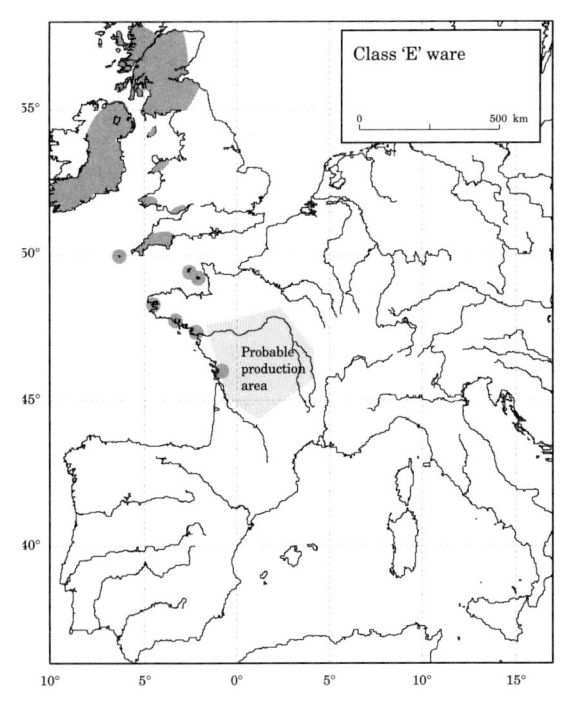

Distribution. South-west England, Wales, western Scotland and Ireland; a few specimens from the Channel Islands and Brittany. There are reports of possible prototypes for E ware of late Roman date from the Bordeaux region (**163, 165**).

Bibliography. For typology and description: C. Thomas 1959; the petrology is described in Peacock and Thomas 1967; Campbell 1984; for distribution: C. Thomas 1981. C. Thomas 1990 discusses the relationship of E ware to the historically attested trading contacts between western Britain, Ireland and Atlantic France.

See also. PRSW

165 *E ware: overall distribution*

Lower Rhineland (Cologne) colour-coated ware

Fabric and technology. A hard, smooth-textured (but occasionally slightly laminar) fabric, containing sparse fine inclusions of colourless quartz, black and red iron and rare fine white mica; almost pure white (2.5YR 9/0) in colour, with a dark brown or black matt colour coat (2.5YR 2.5/0) merging (where the slip is thinner) to a lighter orange-brown. The slip contains minute flakes of red and black iron oxide particles. Wheel-thrown. Principal decorative motifs are roughcasting (with clay particles), barbotine (including hunt cups) and rouletting. The barbotine is made of the same clay as the body.

This ware equates with Anderson's (1980) *Lower Rhineland fabric 1* and is known colloquially as 'Cologne ware' in Britain. The principal differences between this and Central Gaulish colour-coated white ware (CGCC) are its matt slip, slightly

Lower Rhineland (Cologne) colour-coated/IMPORTED WARES

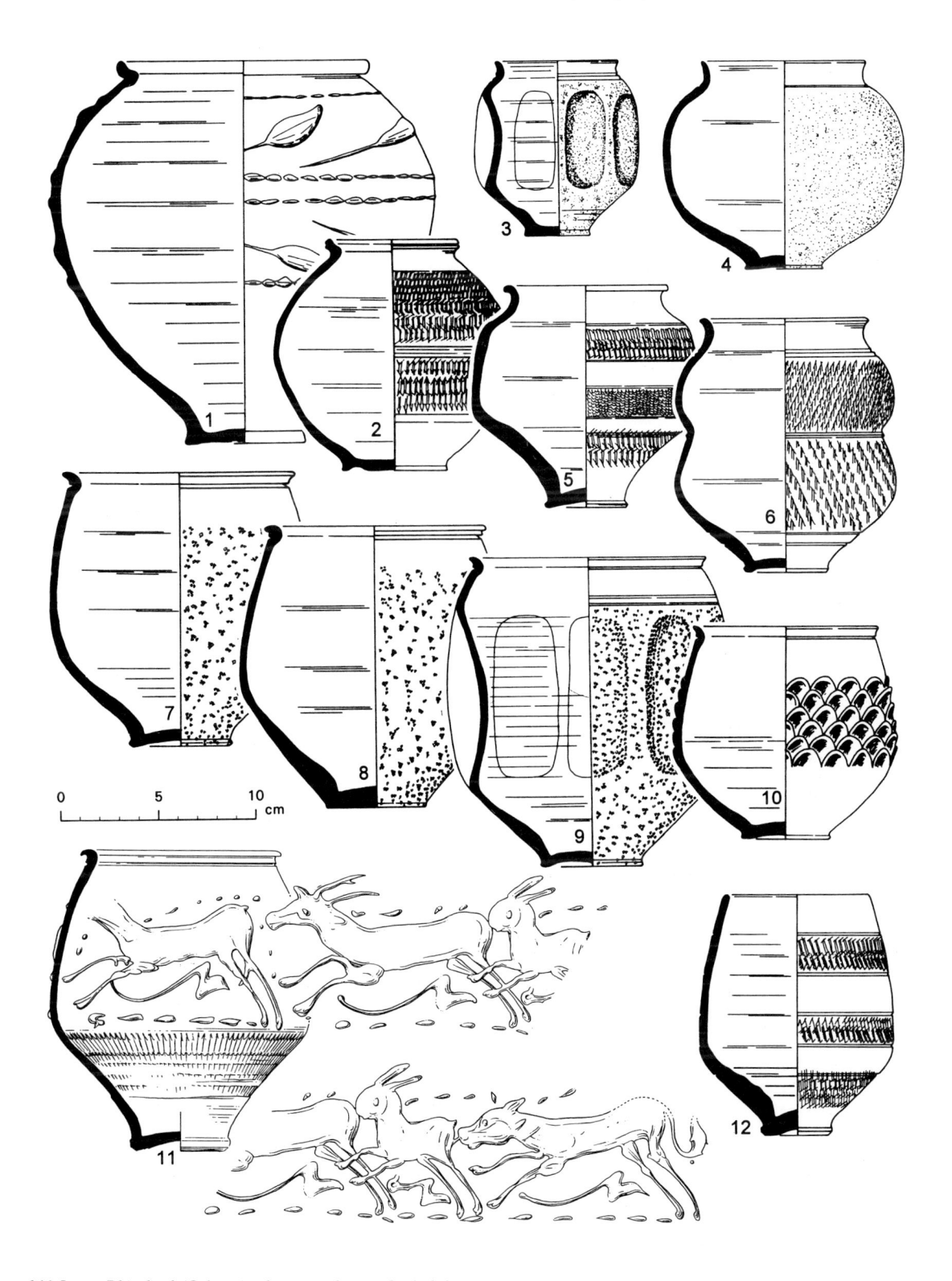

166 Lower Rhineland (Cologne) colour-coated ware: Scale 1:3

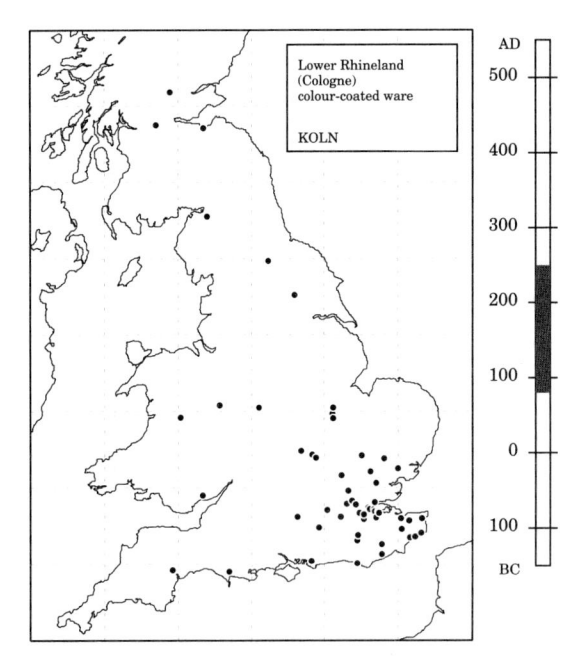

Cups and beakers with barbotine and roughcast decoration (some in a white fabric similar to that described above) are found along the Rhine (and rarely in Britain) during the Claudio-Neronian period (Greene 1979, 56–64). From the Flavian period production concentrated on beakers and this tradition continued to the mid-3rd cent. AD.

Source. Cologne is a major source, where kilns are known (Binsfeld 1964).

Distribution. Principally the Rhineland and Britain (A. C. Anderson 1981, 338, fig. 19.4). There is some risk of confusion between the products of Cologne and those of the Nene valley and Colchester in the hand-specimen, although they may be discriminated with chemical analysis. The distribution is likely to be incomplete due to uncertain identification. Lower Rhineland potters were responsible for the development of the colour-coated industries in the lower Nene valley and Colchester from the early 2nd cent. AD (**167, 168**).

Aliases. Carlisle fabric 318. Chelmsford fabric 6. Gestingthorpe fabric B6. *JRPS bibliography* fabric kww. Kent fine fabric 5b. Lullingstone fabric 2. Milton Keynes fabric 23b. Towcester fabric 14c.

Bibliography. A. C. Anderson 1980; A. C. Anderson 1981. Chemical analysis: A. C. Anderson *et al.* 1982.

See also. COLC NVCC

167 *Lower Rhineland (Cologne) colour-coated ware: British distribution*

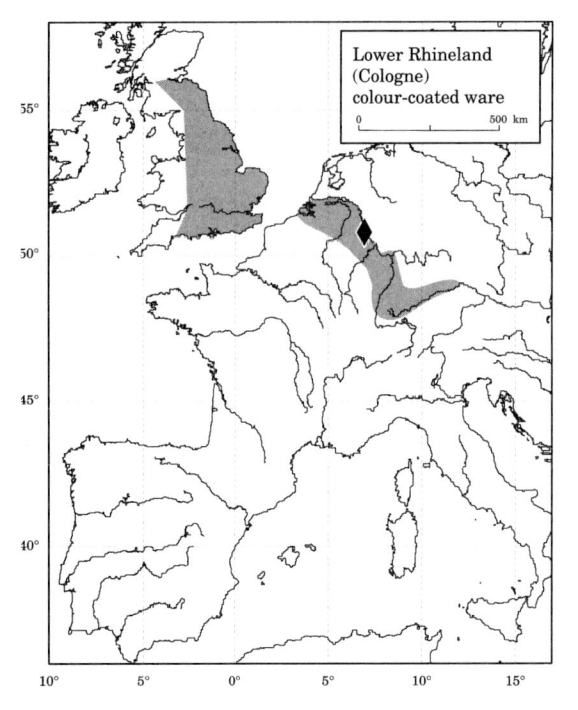

168 *Lower Rhineland (Cologne) colour-coated ware: overall distribution*

166	Type	Form
1–2	1	High shouldered
12	2	Bag-shaped
3–6	3	Globular (high curved neck)
7–11	4	Globular (everted rim)
–	5	Multiple-grooved neck

Table 47 *Classification of Lower Rhineland colour-coated ware forms (after Anderson)*

Lyon ware

Fabric and technology. A fine buff-white fabric with a distinctive greenish tinge (5Y 8/2–9/2) which is usually hard with a fairly clean fracture, although this may have degraded in unfavourable soil conditions. The typical slip is a dark greenish-brown (2.5YR 4/4–4/2) with a lustrous sheen, but may vary from red-brown to almost black. Wheel-thrown.

The commonest decorative technique is a roughcast of quartz sand, which may cover the entire surface of the vessel. A rich variety of rusticated, applied, stamped, rouletted and barbotine motifs is also employed, often in combination with roughcast sand.

Forms. Cups are the commonest type, but beakers occur in smaller numbers and there are other rare forms such as flagons. Some of the rarer cup types imitate the style of contemporary Spanish (SPAN) or Italian colour-coated wares (**169**).

softer, more silty texture and lack of mica.

Forms. Principally beakers (**166, table 47**).

Chronology. Production commences in the Claudian period.

Lyon/IMPORTED WARES

169 *Lyon ware: Scale 1:3*

170 *Lyon ware: British distribution*

171 *Lyon ware: overall distribution*

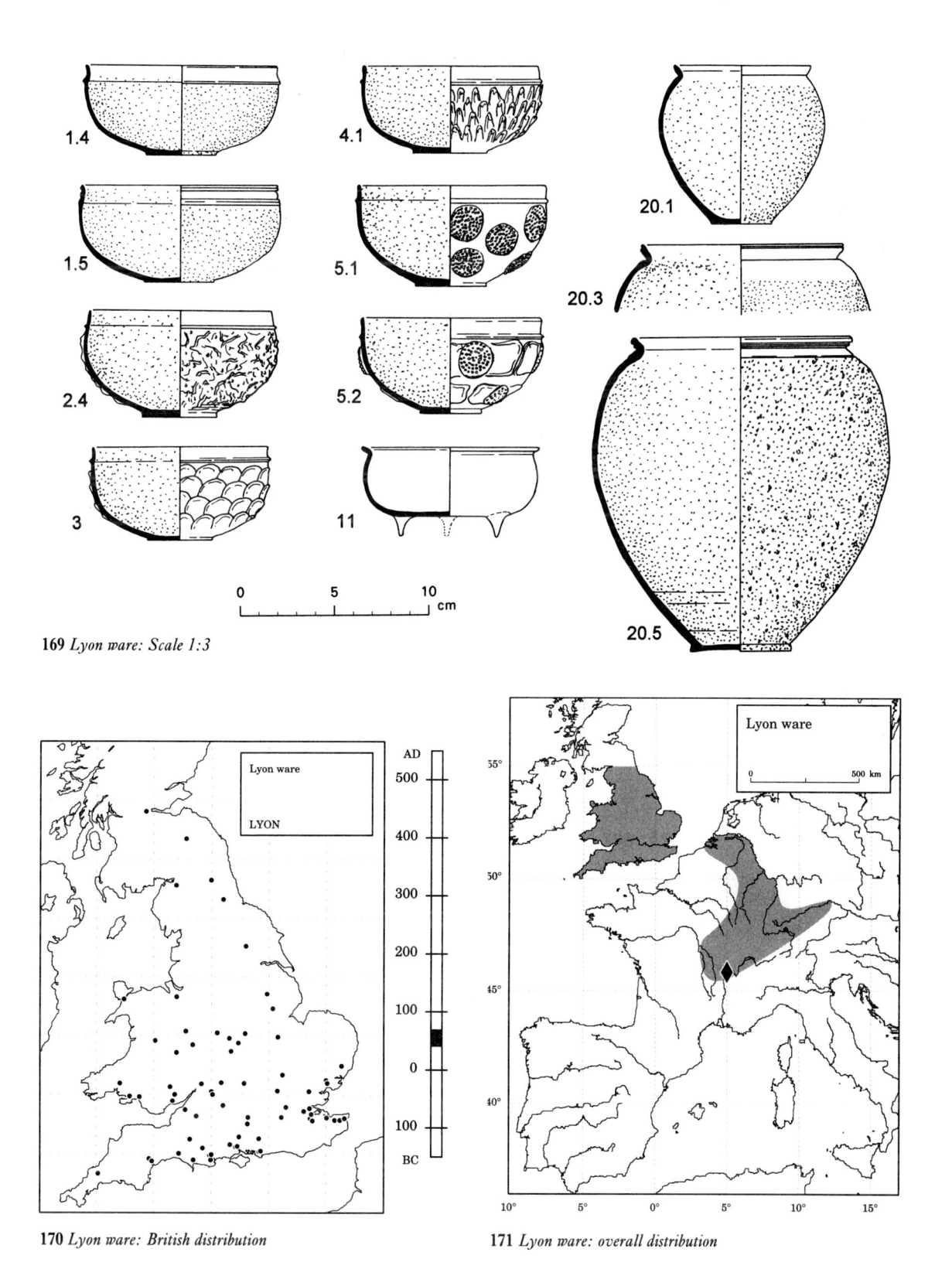

149

German marbled/IMPORTED WARES

Greene's type-series of Lyon ware covers the principal variations (**table 48**).

Type	Decoration
Cups	
1	roughcast
2	rusticated
3	rounded imbricated scales
4	applied scales
5	'raspberry' roundels
Beakers	
20	roughcast
21	folded and roughcast
22	rusticated
23	imbricated scales
24	'raspberry' roundels
25	barbotine hairpins
26	rouletted
Flagon	
40	roughcast

Table 48 *Classification of Lyon ware forms (after Greene)*

Chronology. Production of roughcast cups probably commences in the Tiberian period, but the wide distribution of the ware can be dated to *c.* AD 40–70. Greene suggests that production terminates in AD 69 (Greene 1979). In Britain, Lyon ware is largely confined to pre-Flavian sites, but occurs in small quantities on Flavian foundations, such as York, Caerleon, Chester and Newstead.

Source. Lyon, at the La Butte site.
Distribution. The continental distribution is principally east and north of Lyon, towards the Rhineland and Rhaetia. There are a few vessels from western France, but the fabric is not common south of Lyon (**170, 171**).
Aliases. *Carlisle* fabric 324. *Chelmsford* fabric 5. *Colchester* fabric EB. *Gloucester* fabric TF12H. *JRPS bibliography* fabric lyc. *Kent* fine fabric 11. *Leicester* fabric C14. *Sidbury* fabric 26. *Silchester* fabric E26.
Bibliography. The fundamental study of the ware is by Greene 1979. The evidence from Lyon itself has been described by Grataloup 1988, who also gives valuable descriptions of the Augustan–Tiberian precursors of Lyon ware – not found in Britain. The final reports on all the Lyon kiln sites are anxiously awaited.

German marbled wares

Fabric and technology. A very hard smooth-textured creamy-buff or pink fabric (7.5YR 8/4 to 2.5YR 6/8) perhaps with a grey or orange core, with sparse coarse inclusions of irregular brown clay pellets, glassy quartz and occasional black (volcanic?) grains. Wheel-thrown. The mottled matt slip is normally a shade of orange or red (10R 6/6 to 5/8) but may be lighter (buff) or a darker brownish-black colour; the marbling shows no clear patterning and the slip is often harsh to the touch. Some vessels have white roundels or other motifs (including simple inscriptions) overpainted on the shoulder. In German reports this is described as *marmorierte keramik*.
Forms. The principal forms (**172**) in the ware are flagons:
Gose 262   a two-handled vessel with a collar on the neck.
Gose 265   a one-handled jug with grooves on the body.

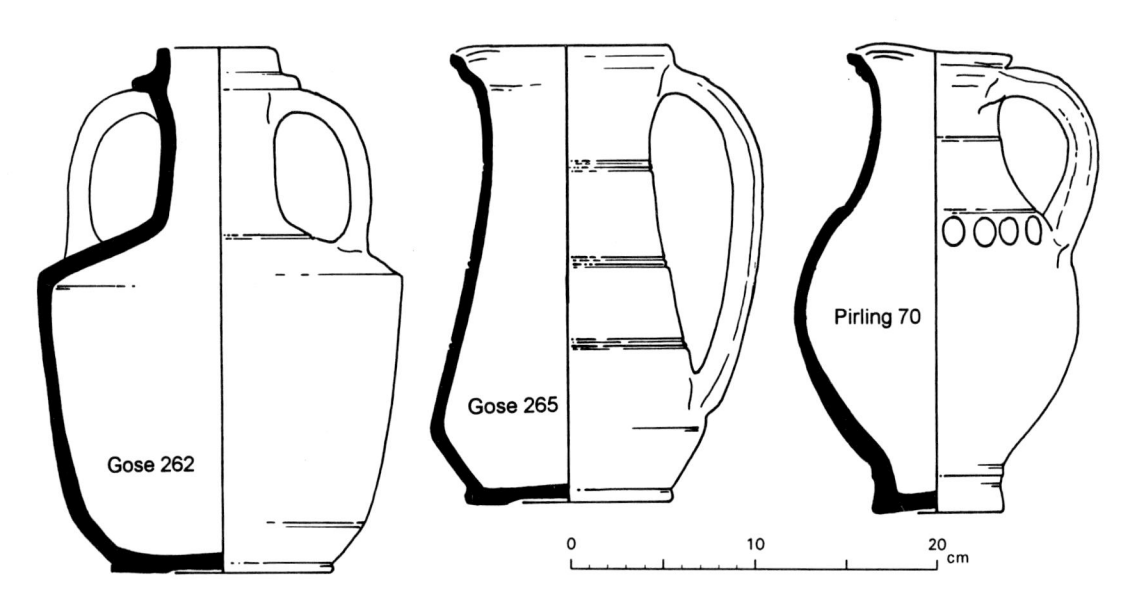

172 German marbled wares: Scale 1:4

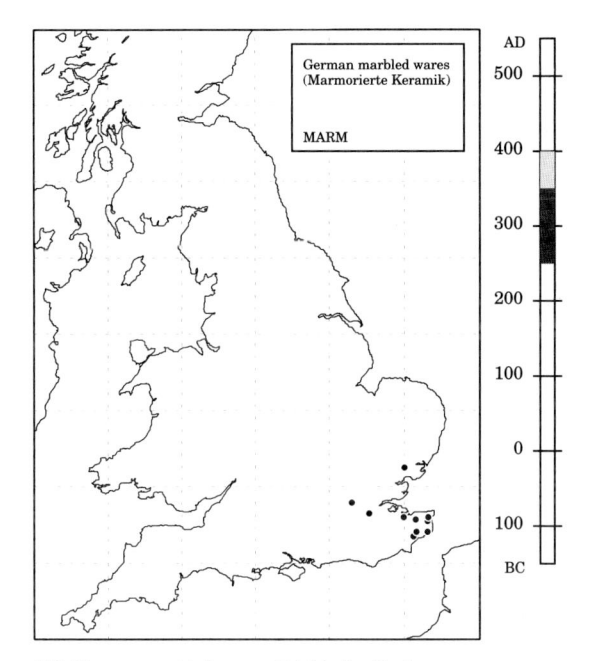

Late Roman Mayen/IMPORTED WARES

173 German marbled wares: British distribution

Pirling 70 a one-handled round-bodied flagon with offset at the shoulder.
Chronology. Early or mid-3rd to late 4th cent.
Source. The middle Rhine or lower Mosel valleys (Oelmann 1914, 50). A second marbled fabric from kilns at Speicher and Trier and described as flamed (*geflammte*) ware is distributed in the Trier area and north into the Ardennes and Belgium; this is not found in Britain.
Distribution. The middle and lower Rhine (from Mainz to Nijmegan), Kent and the London area (**173**).
Aliases. Colchester fabric EESJ. Kent fine fabric 5e. Lullingstone fabrics 8 and 9.
Bibliography. The principal studies of the origin, dating and distribution of the ware are the reports on the Trier Kaiserthermen and Niederbieber (Hussong and Cüppers 1972; Oelmann 1914). The British evidence is described by Bird and Williams 1983 with a report on the petrology.

Late Roman Mayen ware

Coarse pottery was produced at a number of sites in the Eifel mountain region of Germany including Trier, Speicher and Mayen. These wares share certain typological characteristics and are referred to collectively as *Eifelkeramik*. Of these, Mayen ware is the most readily identified due to its distinctive mineral suite, and the only ware exported to Britain in any quantity.
Fabric and technology. A very hard, dense, yellow, brown or purple fabric with a coarse irregular hackly fracture; wheel-thrown, often with heavy rilling on the outer surface and a

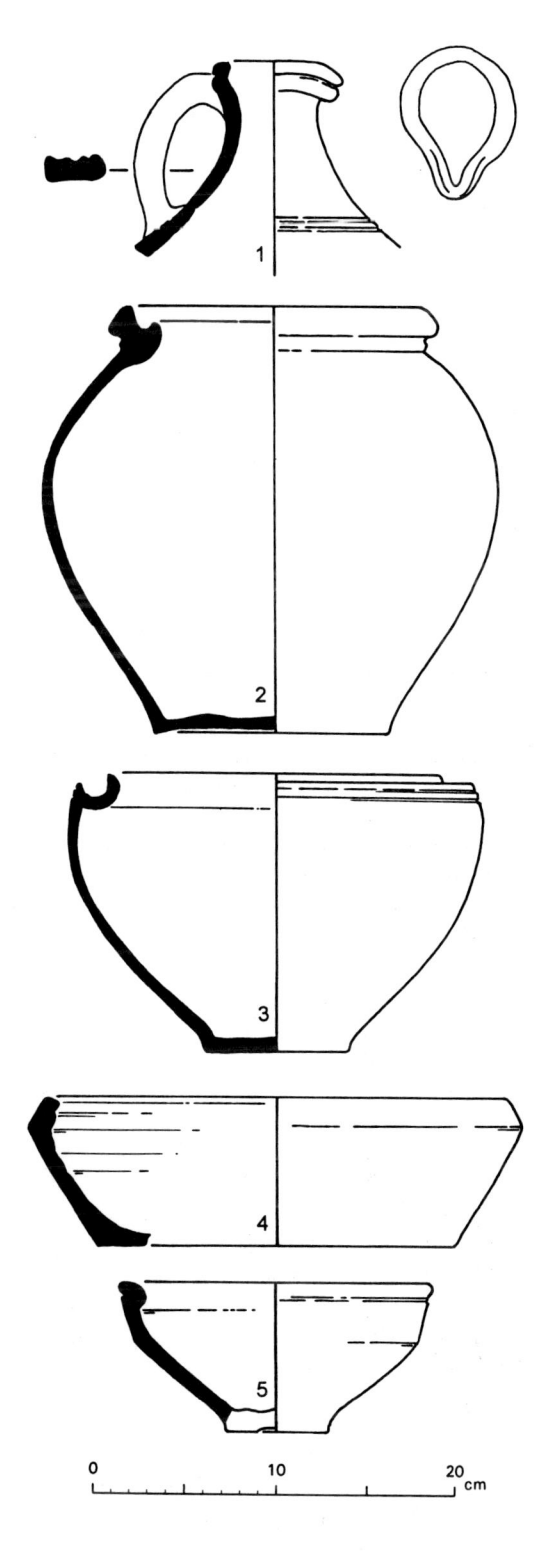

174 *Late Roman Mayen ware*

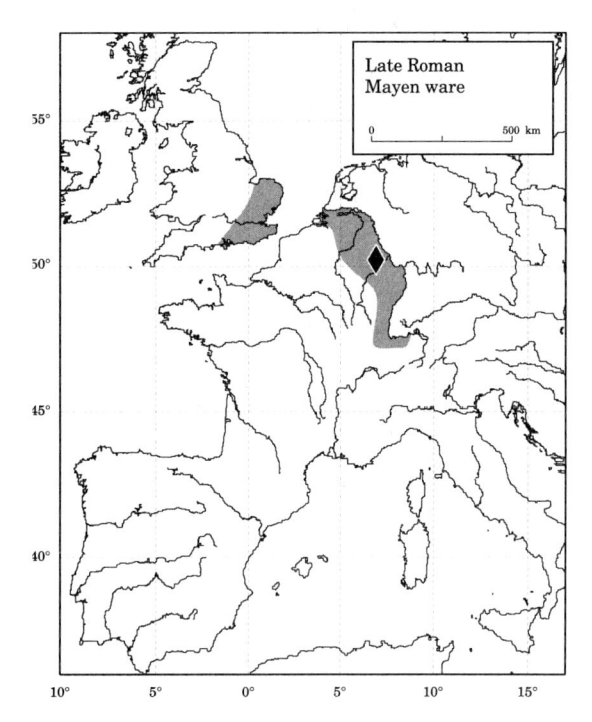

North African red slip/IMPORTED WARES

175 Late Roman Mayen ware: overall distribution

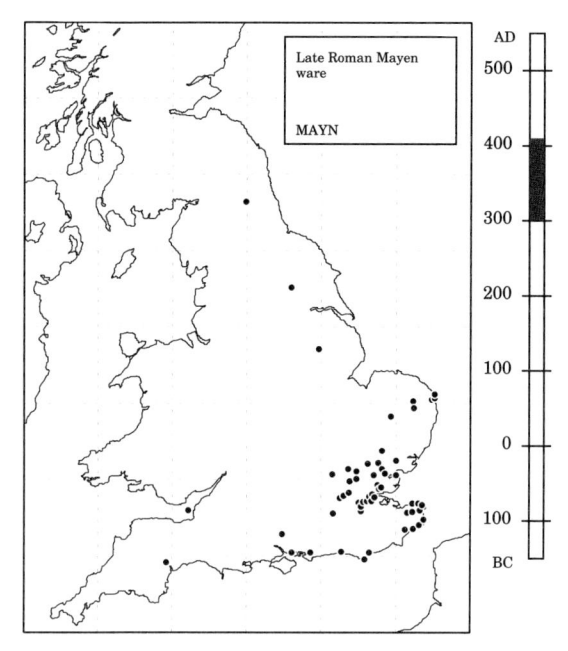

176 Late Roman Mayen ware: British distribution

whorl pattern on the base. Abundant temper of irregular and angular glassy quartz, with occasional black angular (volcanic) inclusions (Fulford and Bird 1975, fabric 1). Sanidine, plagioclase, green augite, barkevitic hornblende, apatite, magnetite and pumice grains can be identified in thin-section.

Forms. Jars, bowls and dishes, and occasional jugs and plates. Unverzagt's typology from Kastel Alzei (Unverzagt 1916) remains a standard reference (table 49).

174	Alzei form	Redknap form	Description
1	30	R29	One-handled jug
2	27	R1	Lid-seated jar
3			Bowl with internal flange
4	34	R6	Plate with angled rim
5	28	R2	Bowl with beaded rim

Table 49 *Classification of Late Roman Mayen ware forms (after Unverzagt and Redknap)*

The distinctive jars with lid-seated rims (the commonest and most widespread form) may have served as containers (**174**).

Chronology. From *c*. AD 300 to 450. In Britain, most are from mid- or late 4th-cent. contexts. Production at Mayen – and typological tradition – continues through into the Frankish and Carolingian period (Redknap 1988, figs 3, 18).

Source. Mayen, in the Eifel mountains.

Distribution. Mayen ware is widespread on the Continent across Belgium and eastern France, through the Rhineland and south into Switzerland. Versions of some of the standard *Eifelkeramik* forms were also produced in the upper Rhineland, and to the east in the Paris basin. In Britain, concentrated in south-east England, with *c*. 90 per cent from Canterbury, Richborough, Colchester and London (**175, 176**).

Aliases. *Caister-on-sea* fabric EIFL-501. *Chelmsford* fabric 54. *Gestingthorpe* fabric I. JRPS bibliography fabric mck. *Kent* coarse fabric 12. Redknap (1987) fabric R.

Bibliography. Redknap 1987; Redknap 1988. For British distribution: Fulford and Bird 1975.

Notes. Other *Eifelkeramik* wares lack the distinctive inclusions of Mayen ware and are tempered with little more than quartz sand. Occasional vessels are recorded from Britain (e.g. an Urmitzer ware jar from a late 2nd- or 3rd-cent. context at Lullingstone; Pollard 1988, coarse fabric 26; Pollard 1987, fabric 77) but there is some risk of confusion in the hand-specimen with other coarse sand-tempered wares, such as Portchester D (Fulford and Bird 1975, fabric 2, 178).

See also. EIMO

North African red slip ware

Fabric and technology. North African wares comprise a series of related fabrics which share some common characteristics. The main variants are:

Early fabrics: Hard granular fabrics with pimply surfaces; brick-red or orange-red with fine quartz, sand and rare mica, with a fine polished glossy slip over all surfaces, similar in

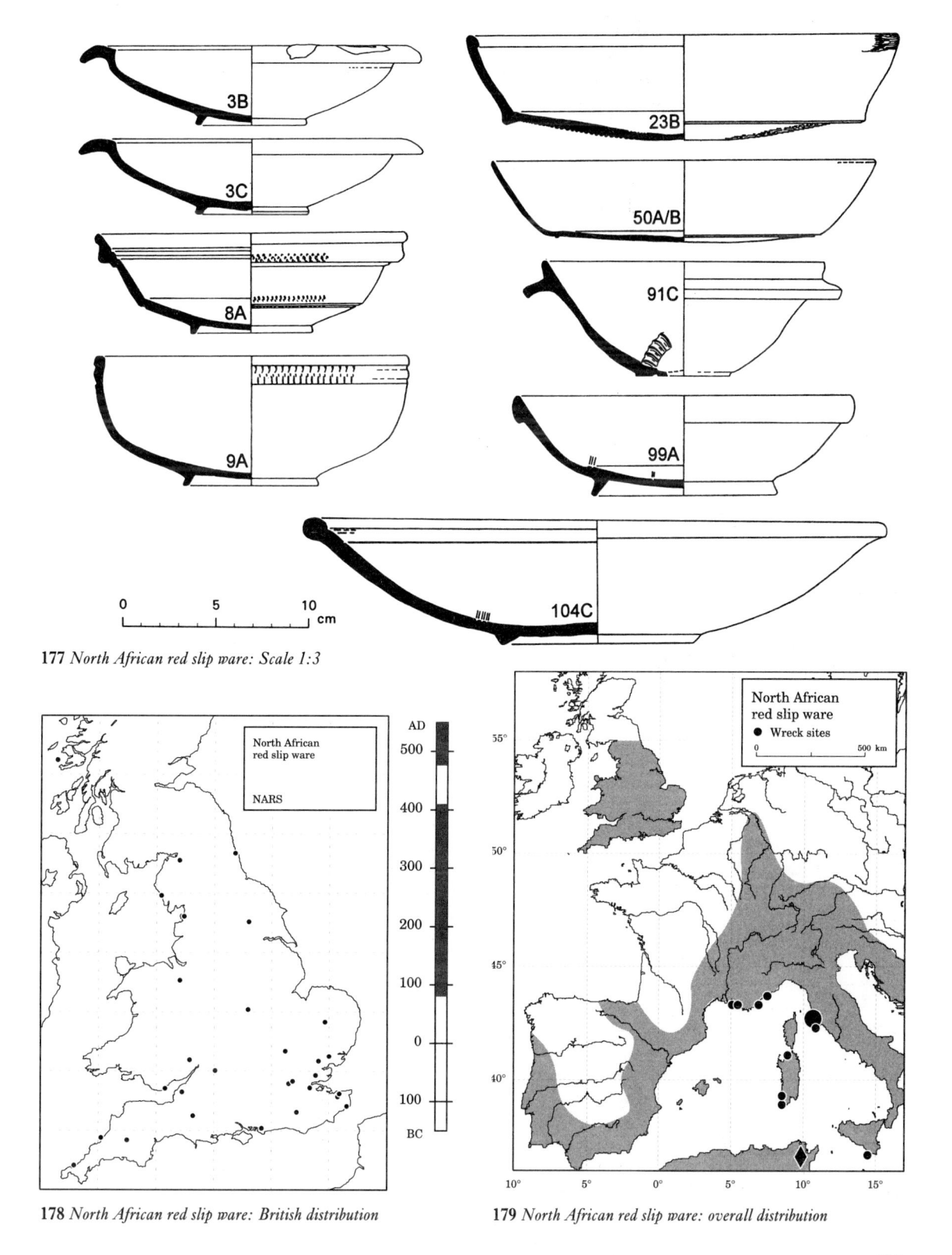

North African red slip/IMPORTED WARES

177 *North African red slip ware: Scale 1:3*

178 *North African red slip ware: British distribution*

179 *North African red slip ware: overall distribution*

North Gaulish grey/IMPORTED WARES

colour to the body. A related cooking-ware has a similar body, but traces of a dull slip (or unslipped) and is frequently blackened near the rim (late 1st–2nd cent).

Later thin fine fabric: A very thin, smooth-textured ware which tends to splinter in the break; thin slip, which may be glossy or matt (3rd cent.).

Later coarser ware: A series of granular wares with pimply surfaces; usually a matt slip, which does not cover all the surfaces (4th–5th cent).

Forms. The full range of forms in North African red slip ware is immense. Some of the earlier plates, cups and bowls (late 1st to mid-2nd cent.) follow Italian and Gaulish sigillata prototypes, but with barbotined or rouletted decoration. The later assemblage includes a variety of large shallow plates or small bowls and coarse-ware bowls with sagging bases (**177**).

Chronology. Production commences in the period *c.* AD 80/100 and continues until Arab invasions of 7th cent. In Britain, a scatter through the 2nd–4th cent. Some importation to western Britain with other Mediterranean imports, *c.* AD 475–550.

Source. Tunisia.

Distribution. Widespread around the western Mediterranean from 2nd to 6th centuries, forming a significant part of assemblages in Provence and the Rhône valley during 3rd–5th cent. AD. Uncommon in northern provinces, although there are an increasing number of identifications from Britain (**178**, **179**).

Influence from African coarse-ware styles can be seen in Gaulish and British industries of the 3rd cent. (e.g. Swan 1994).

Aliases. Carlisle fabric 146. *JRPS bibliography* fabric ars. Kent fine fabric 1. *British* (*Tintagel*) class Aii.

Bibliography. The fundamental study is Hayes 1972, with supplement (Hayes 1980). British distribution catalogued by Bird 1977 and Thomas 1981, 15–16; see also Rahtz *et al.* 1992, 162–5.

See also. NACA

North Gaulish grey wares

Fabric and technology. A hard, light bluish-grey fabric (2.5YR 8/0–7/0) with darker grey (10YR 4/1) surfaces. Wheel-thrown. The main inclusions are abundant clear quartz, occasional black iron-rich particles and sparse fine mica. The most distinctive feature of the jars and bowls are the thin horizontal bands (*bandes lustrées*) on the neck and upper body.

Forms. Jars and bowls. The jars have a truncated conical neck (*vase tronconique*), which changes in shape and proportion through the Roman period. By the Flavian period the height of the neck exceeds that of the body, and it continues to increase through the 2nd and 3rd centuries. The straight wall of the neck of the earlier examples becomes rounded and swells out in later vessels. By the 4th cent. the neck becomes

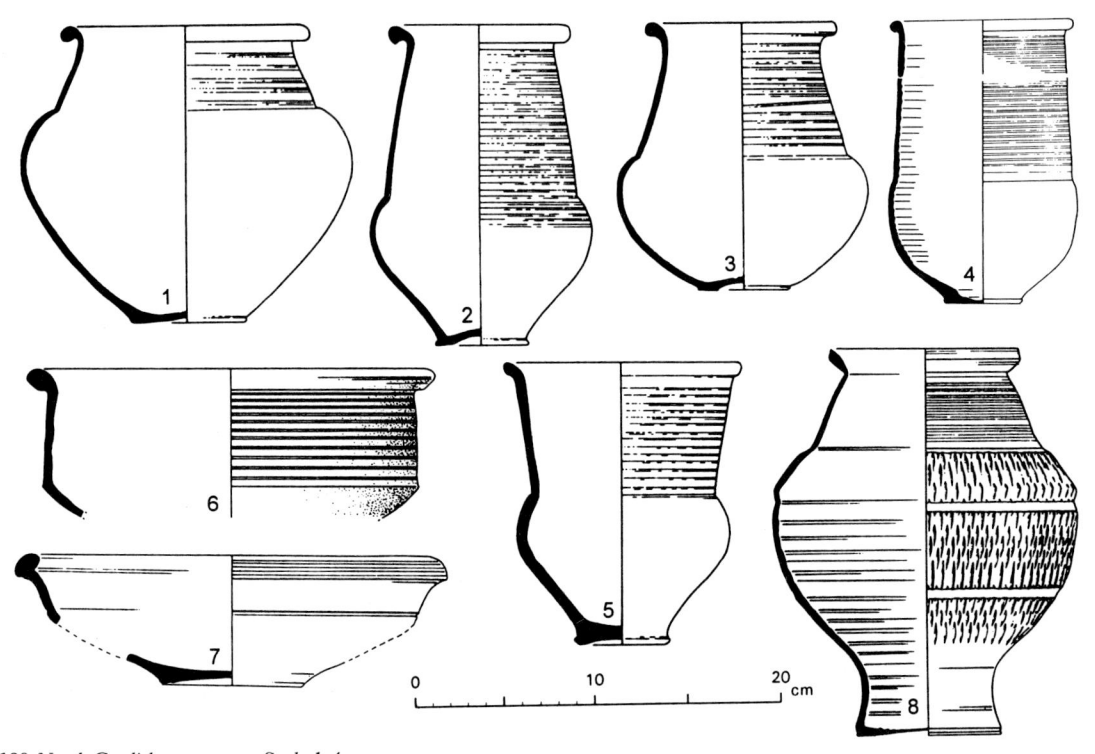

180 *North Gaulish grey wares: Scale 1:4*

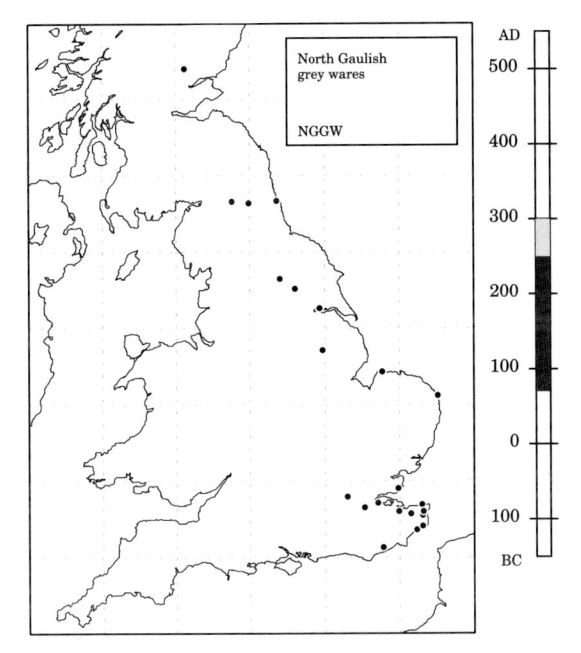

181 North Gaulish grey wares: British distribution

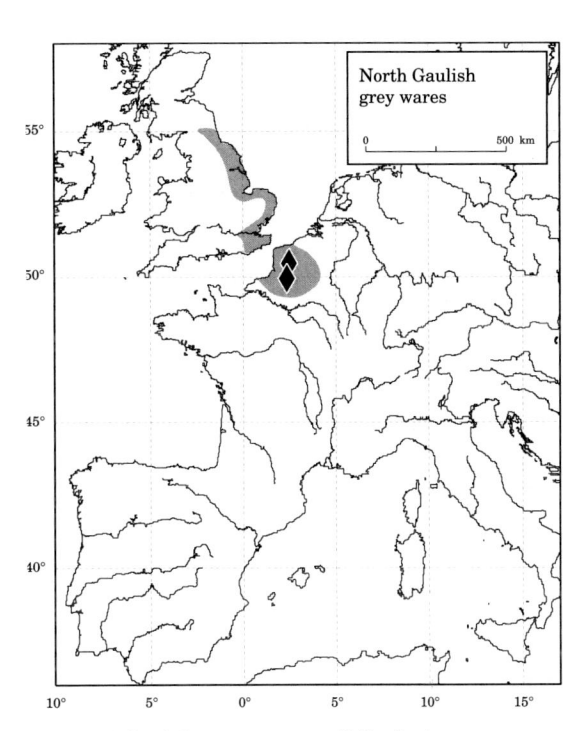

182 North Gaulish grey wares: overall distribution

cylindrical or flares out from the body. There are related (but less common) bowl and dish forms, which have the same burnished horizontal lines (**180**).

Chronology. Production of wheel-thrown grey wares in northern France commenced in the Claudian period. The earliest imports into Britain may be pre-Flavian and there are several examples in groups of Flavian–Trajanic date (including perhaps a vessel from Inchtuthil: Pitts and St Joseph 1985, 326, fig. 99, 35). The taller necks of later vessels are also found in Britain, and may be dated to the 3rd cent.

Source. There are a number of known production sites in the Nord and Pas-de-Calais regions. Similar forms are also common further south in the Somme valley (Bayard 1980).

Distribution. The British distribution is concentrated in the south-east and up the east coast. The ware is found in the New Fresh Wharf waterfront group in London, in association with a wide range of other Gaulish imports, including other coarse wares from Nord and Picardy (B. Richardson 1986). There are particularly large collections from Caister-on-sea (Darling 1993, 161, 166) and York (Perrin 1990b, 268; Monaghan 1993, 717). The *vase tronconique* type is also recorded from Guernsey (Burns 1987, fig. 5, 28; Monaghan 1987b, fig. 7, 51) (**181, 182**).

Aliases. Caister-on-sea fabrics NGCR-3, NGCRa-3a and NGGW-105. *JRPS bibliography* fabric ngg. Kent fine fabric 15b. Kent coarse fabric 16. Lullingstone fabric 25.

Bibliography. The principal synopsis of north Gaulish pottery is Tuffreau-Libre 1980, who gives references to earlier work in the region. The British evidence is summarized in B. Richardson and Tyers 1984.

Notes. (1) A related type in Britain is the pentice beaker, equivalent to *Gillam* 42, **195**, 8. These are found with north Gaulish imports in the New Fresh Wharf group in a similar fabric and some, at least, are likely to be NGGW. However, other pentice beakers found in Britain may not be North Gaulish. (2) Pollard has identified a group of kiln material from Canterbury which seems to represent the movement of potters from the Nord/Pas-de-Calais region into Kent during the Flavian period (Pollard 1988, 177). In addition to the *vase tronconique* form these potters manufactured collared flagons related to north Gaulish prototypes. Some of the Kent examples on the distribution map may be from this source rather than imports.

See also. NGMO

Phocaean red slip ware

Fabric and technology. Hard, fine-textured fabric; brownish-red with purple or maroon tinge, with thin red slip over whole surface; fine white flecks in clean matrix.

Forms. Plates, bowls and dishes; principal form in Britain is Hayes type 3, a shallow bowl with short vertical wall, incorporating slight flange, frequently stamped on inner face with crosses and other motifs (**183**).

Chronology. Post-Roman in Britain, *c.* AD 475–550.

Source. Phocaea, western Asia Minor.

Distribution. Principally the eastern Mediterranean, but with scattered distribution around the west, along the Atlantic seaways, to south-west Britain and Ireland (**184**).

155

Pompeian-Red slip/IMPORTED WARES

183 *Phocaean red slip ware: Scale 1:3*

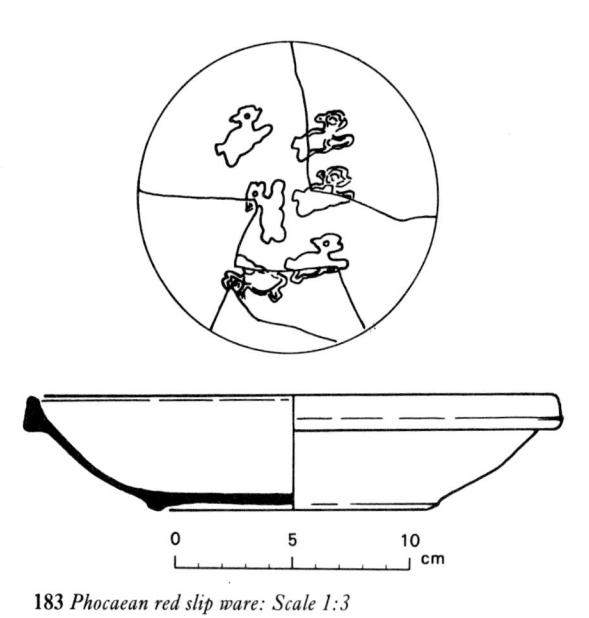

Aliases. British (*Tintagel*) class Ai. Late Roman C.
Bibliography. Source and dating: Hayes 1972, 323–70; Hayes 1980; Mayet and Picon 1986; Empereur and Picon 1986. Distribution in Britain: C. Thomas 1981; Fulford 1989; also Rahtz *et al*. 1992, 161–2.

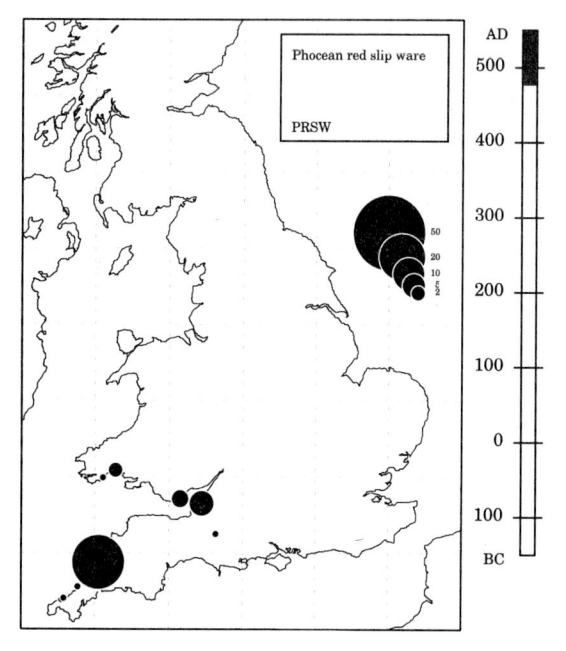

184 *Phocaean red slip ware: British distribution*

Pompeian-Red wares

Simple flat-based dishes with a red slip on the internal surface, known collectively as Pompeian-Red wares (here abbreviated to PRW) are a small but distinctive element of the ceramic assemblage on many sites around both the western and eastern Mediterranean during the 1st cent. BC and 1st cent. AD. The name refers to the colour of the slip and its resemblance to the red paint commonly used as part of the decorative scheme of rooms at Pompeii. Two papers published during the 1970s consider the class in more detail.

Goudineau (1970) surveyed the published literature on Pompeian-Red wares and collected together many of the available illustrations on to a single set of figures. The material from Bolsena, published in this paper for the first time, suggested that the origins of the style should be placed at *c*. 220 BC, and the period of greatest distribution was probably to be dated *c*. 15 BC–AD 80. Goudineau hints that many of the published examples were in a single fabric (ibid., 162–3) but the lack of precision in many of the fabric descriptions did not allow this suggestion to be followed any further.

Fabric	Source	ATLAS
1	Campania	PRW1
2	Mediterranean (?)	PRW2
3	Central Gaul	PRW3
4	Britain (?)	
5	Colchester	
6	Northern Gaul	
7	Northern Gaul	

Table 50 *Pompeian-Red ware fabrics (after Peacock)*

Peacock's study of Pompeian-Red ware, published in 1977, is the classic application of the petrological technique to the problems of a class of early Roman ceramics. The results revealed hitherto unrecognized complexity in the material and laid the groundwork for the future study of the group. Peacock identified seven fabrics, of which three (fabrics 1–3) have a wide distribution in western Europe (Peacock 1977e) (**table 50**).

However, despite Peacock's work, the extent of the distribution of these wares remains uncertain due to the continuing inadequacy of most published fabric descriptions, particularly of the Gaulish material.

In addition to these major 'export' wares, platters with red-slipped internal surfaces, influenced by PRW, were also produced in small numbers by local potters during the 1st cent. AD (e.g. Usk type 29.1; Manning 1993). Despite their classification as a fine ware in most earlier publications, PRW platters were used as a cooking ware – they are now often described as 'cooking plates' or 'frying plates'. The style held

Pompeian-Red fabric 1/IMPORTED WARES

a special place in the ceramic repertoire of the early Roman period, and seems to have its roots in Italian culinary traditions of at least the 2nd cent. BC (Goudineau 1970; Peña 1990).

Pompeian-Red ware – fabric 1

Fabric and technology. Hard reddish-brown fabric (2.5YR 4/6) with inclusions of abundant medium 'black sand' (green augite), occasional white particles and flakes of biotite mica. Distinctive dark-red slip (10YR 4/6–4/8) thickly covers rim and interior of plates. Outer surfaces can be unevenly and coarsely finished. Wheel-thrown.

Forms. Plates with plain rim and flat base. Inside may be decorated with groups of fine concentric rings. The lids are unslipped, but may have single concentric groove or light bead (almost a 'footring') on upper surface (**185**).

Stamps. There are stamps or pre-firing cursive signatures on underside of some plates (Wynia 1979; Grünewald, Pernicka and Wynia 1980). The name Marius appears frequently on both stamps and signatures, in some cases with another name. These are perhaps products of organized workshops and master–slave pairings as attested in the sigillata industry. For total distribution of the stamps and signatures see Wynia 1979, 429, Abb.3 – the majority seem to be on vessels in Peacock's fabric 1. In Britain, signatures are recorded from Colchester (Hawkes and Hull 1947, 221) and London.

Chronology. Present at Haltern, Oberaden and Neuss in Augustan levels, and common on sites of same date in Rhône valley (e.g. Lyon, Valence and Orange). Production in Italy may extend back back into the 2nd cent. BC (Peña 1990, 655). In Britain PRW1 was imported from *c*. AD 40–80, when production may have ceased.

Source. Peacock suggests that PRW1 – and other 'black sand'

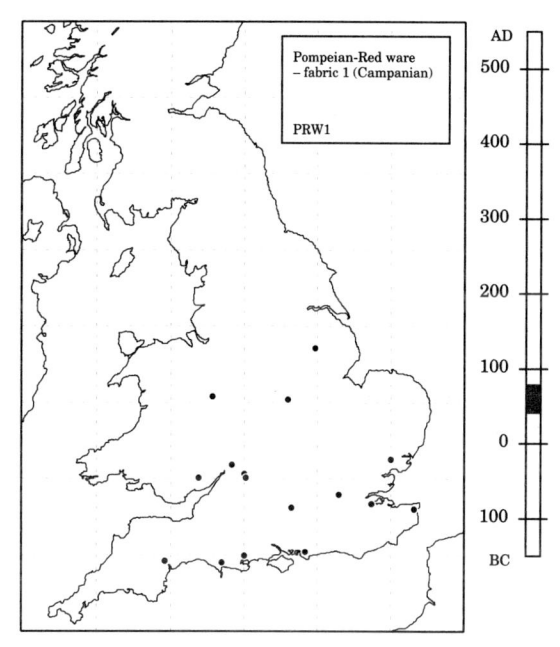

186 *Pompeian-Red ware – fabric 1: British distribution*

fabrics – originates in area of Bay of Naples (1977e, 153; but see Peña 1990, 655, fn. 22 for a contrary view).

Distribution. Very extensive (but patchy) distribution, encompassing Britain, Rhineland, southern Gaul, Italy, Austria and eastern provinces (Peacock 1977e, 152, fig. 2) (**186, 187**).

Aliases. *Cirencester* fabric 153. *Colchester* fabric CSOA. *Gloucester* fabric TF16A. *Silchester* fabric E21.

Bibliography. Peacock 1977e, 149–53; Blakely, Brinkmann

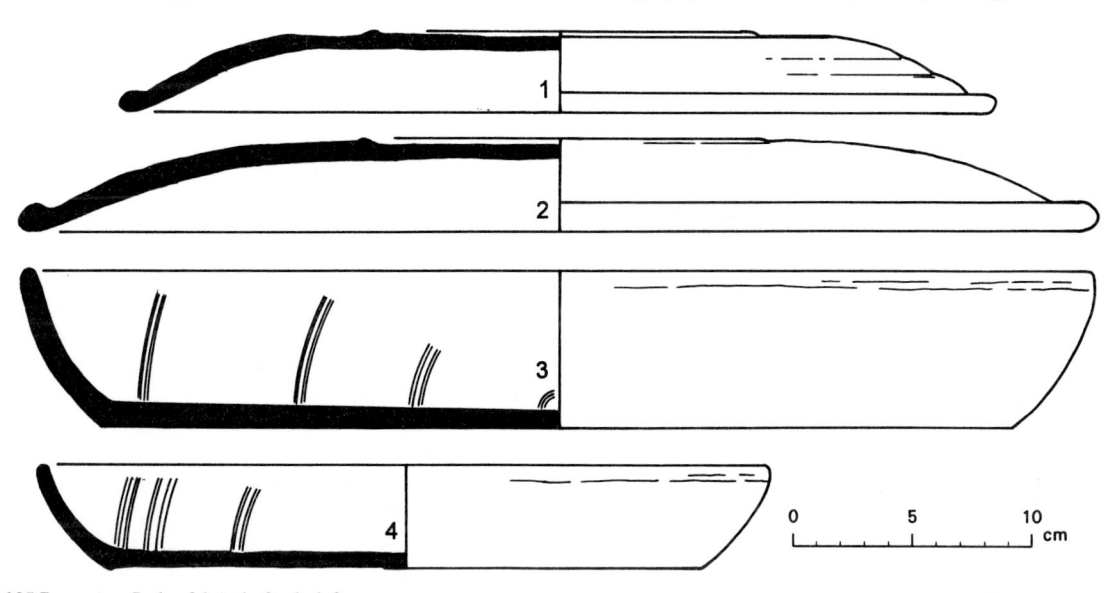

185 *Pompeian-Red – fabric 1: Scale 1:3*

Pompeian-Red fabric 2/IMPORTED WARES

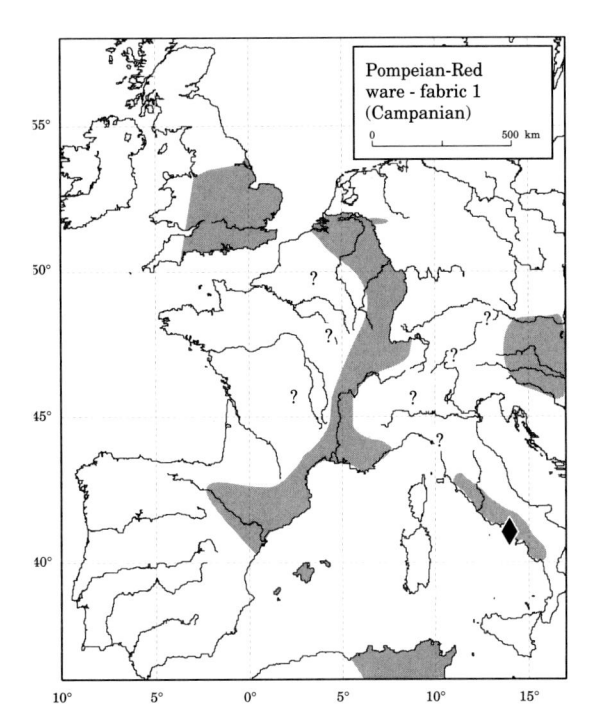

187 Pompeian-Red ware – fabric 1: overall distribution

and Vitaliano 1989; Peña 1990, fabric 2.
See also. DR1 DR2-4 MRCA

Pompeian-Red ware – fabric 2

Fabric and technology. Hard, harsh orange-brown (2.5YR 5–6/8) fabric with hackly texture with patchy red slip (10R 4/6) on smoothed inner face; abundant inclusions of white and glassy quartz, mica and occasional composite rock fragments (a quartz-mica schist). Wheel-thrown.

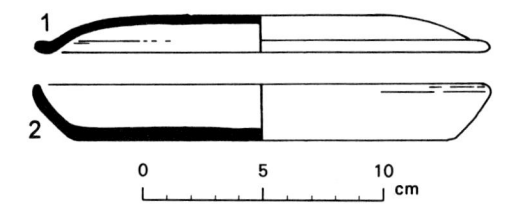

188 Pompeian-Red ware – fabric 2: Scale 1:3

Forms. Plain-rim dishes, some with light concentric grooves on the interior of the base. Lids not slipped (**188**).
Chronology. Perhaps present at Haltern, and certainly in Augustan groups at Valence (Drôme) and Lyon. In Britain, 1st cent. AD, and often associated with PRW1 (**189**).
Source. The least well understood of the widely distributed PRW fabrics. Peacock suggested a Mediterranean source, and further examples have been identified from Sidi Khrebish (Libya): Kenrick 1983, 321, B481.2, B482.2; Settefinestre

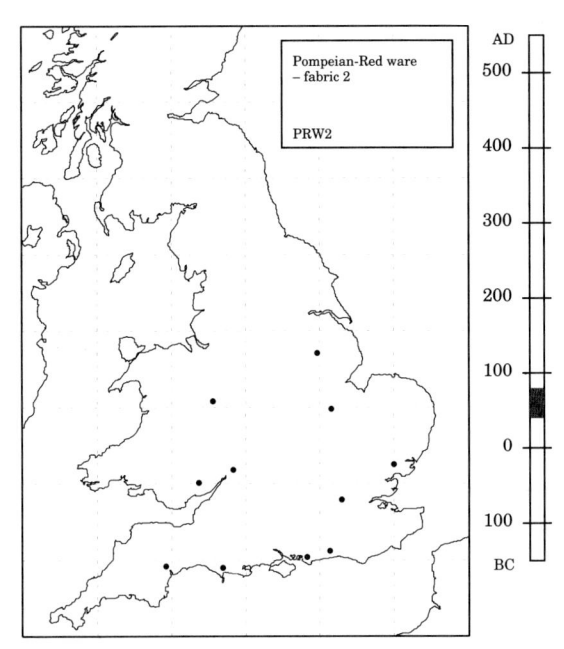

189 Pompeian-Red ware – fabric 2: British distribution

(Italy): Celuzza 1985, tav.31.3; Impasto 3; Lambaesis (Algeria): Unpublished, and Paphos (Cyprus): Hayes 1991, 79. fig. 28 middle, 1.
Aliases. *Colchester* fabric CSOB. *Gloucester* fabric TF16B.
Bibliography. Peacock 1977e, 153.

Pompeian-Red ware – fabric 3

Fabric and technology. Soft pale beige (7.5YR 7/4) micaceous fabric with smooth fracture. Thin glossy red slip (10R 4/8) on interior and rim of plates; thin light brown (10YR 7/4) wash on lids, and outer surface of some plates. Wheel-thrown.
Forms. Plain-rim dishes, up to *c.* 35cm in diameter. Some have elaborate incised grooves and rouletted bands on interior, and footrings. Lids have incised concentric circles on exterior (**190**).
Chronology. In Britain, from *c.* AD 40, and particularly common on Neronian–Flavian sites (e.g. Usk, Gloucester, Exeter). Several from Hadrianic fire deposits in London, including Regis House warehouse (Marsh 1981, 222), and specimens from Hadrianic foundations in the north, suggest production and export continues into 2nd cent.
Source. Petrology, and some similarity to fabric of early micaceous Lezoux samian, may suggest source(s) in central Gaul, but no published evidence suggests production at Lezoux itself. Probably not the product of a single industry.
Distribution. The most extensive British distribution of the PRW fabrics. Predominantly southern, but a scatter in north as far as Inchtuthil. No detailed study of the Gaulish distribution, but micaceous PRW fabrics common in the middle

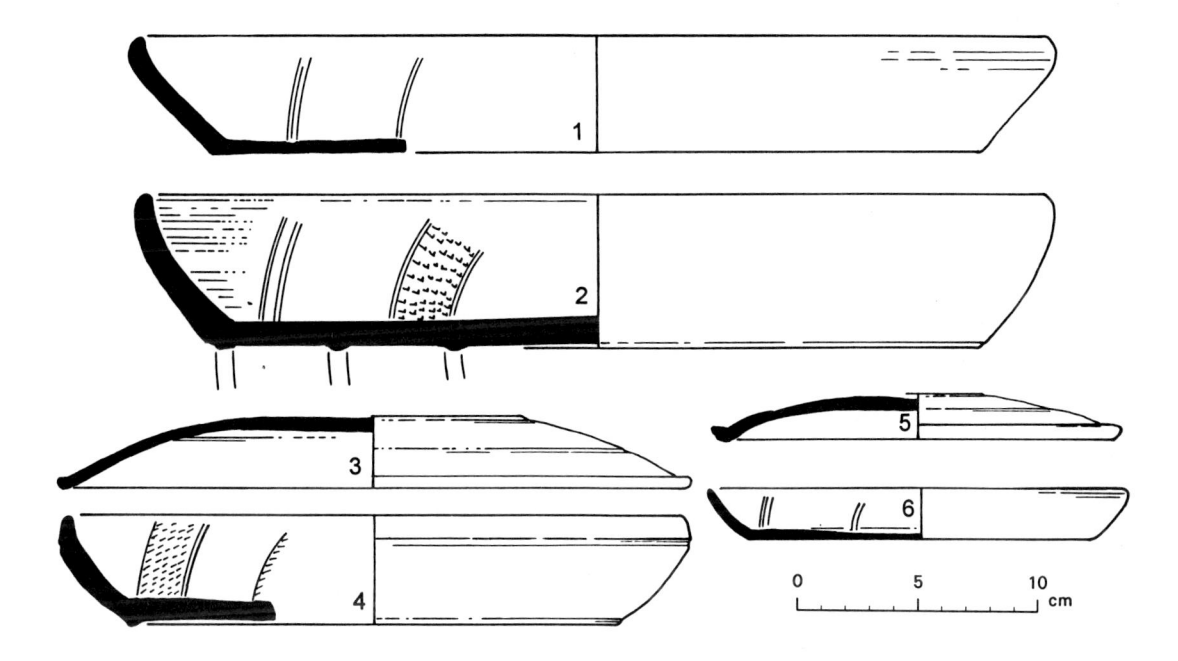

Pompeian-Red fabric 3/IMPORTED WARES

190 *Pompeian-Red ware – fabric 3: Scale 1:3*

Loire valley (e.g. Orléans), and have been observed at Alet (Brittany) and Paris (**191, 192**).
Aliases. *Cirencester* fabric 51. *Colchester* fabric CSOD. *Gloucester* fabric TF16C. *Silchester* fabric E22.
Bibliography. Peacock 1977e, 154.

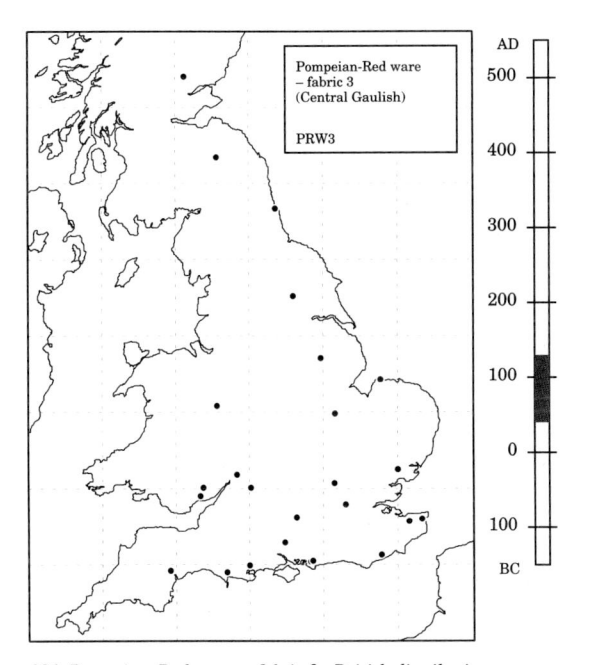

191 *Pompeian-Red ware – fabric 3: British distribution*

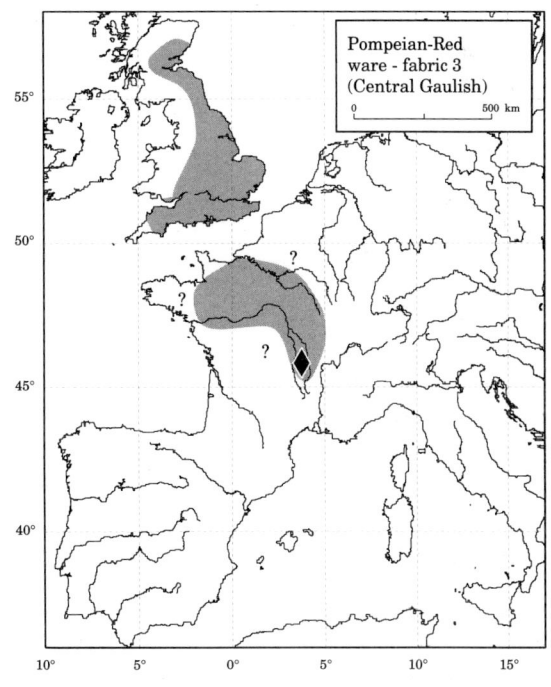

192 *Pompeian-Red ware – fabric 3: overall distribution*

South Gaulish colour-coated/IMPORTED WARES

South Gaulish colour-coated ware

Fabric and technology. Very fine buff or orange-brown fabric (7.5YR 7/4) with thin pale golden-brown (2.5YR 6/6) slip, which usually has a slight metallic sheen. Occasionally slightly micaceous, and with fine sand roughcasting on the interior. Mould-made, with relief decoration on exterior.

Forms. Small cups, *Cam* 62, with a slightly carinated profile, which vary considerably in their details. Some have grooves below the rim, or a slight footring. Decoration in the general style of contemporary sigillata, but with much individual variation (193).

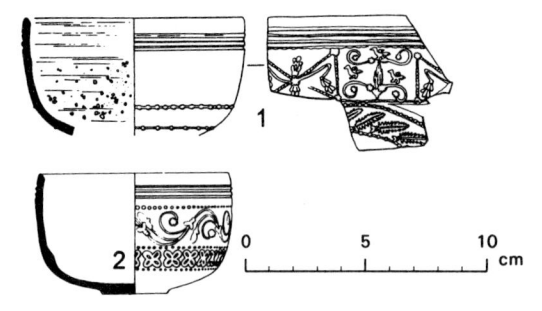

193 *South Gaulish colour-coated ware: Scale 1:3*

Chronology. Production may commence in the Tiberian period, but majority from *c.* AD 40–70.
Source. The southern Gaulish samian factories, particularly La Graufesenque and Montans.

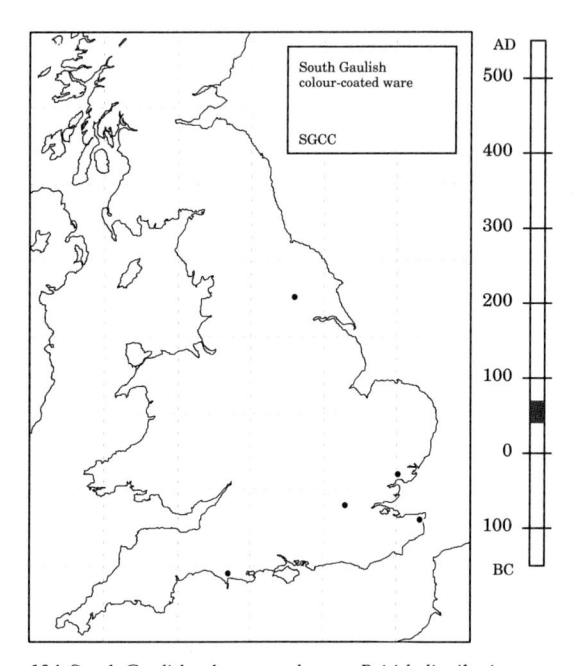

194 *South Gaulish colour-coated ware: British distribution*

Distribution. Wide but thin distribution in Gaul (particularly Aquitaine), the Rhineland and Switzerland; rare in Britain (194).
Aliases. Kent fine fabric 20b.
Bibliography. Greene 1979, 50–5; Greene 1972. Ohlenroth in Ettlinger and Simonett 1952, for the continental distribution. The evidence from La Graufesenque is described in Bémont 1982.
See also. SGTS

Spanish colour-coated ware

Fabric and technology. Hard fine pale brown or orange-brown (10YR 8/4) with orange-brown slip (2.5YR 6/8) with a metallic sheen. Wheel-thrown. Principal decoration is barbotine. Motifs are plant-derived (leaves, buds or ferns) or abstract (dots, lines or scales).
Forms. Cups and cylindrical beakers, sometimes with pairs of small handles (195).

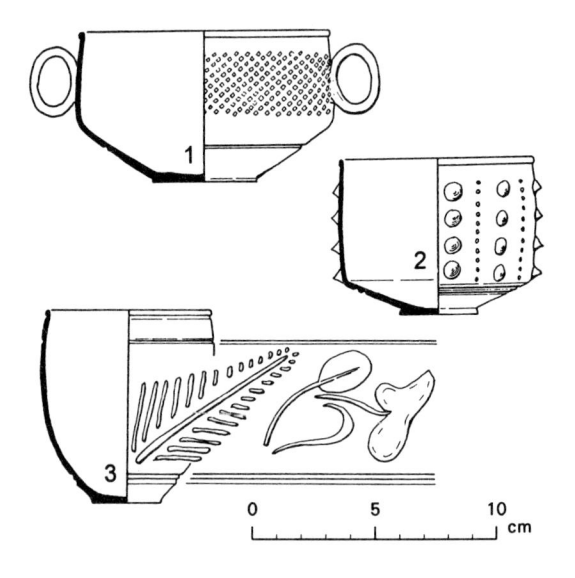

195 *Spanish colour-coated ware: Scale 1:3*

Chronology. Production may commence in the Tiberian period, but principal export is AD 40–80.
Source. Baetica, southern Spain.
Distribution. Southern Spain and Gaul, north Africa, Rhineland. Occasional in southern Britain. The Mediterranean distribution is essentially coastal and riverine (196, 197).
Aliases. *JRPS* bibliography fabric spc. Kent fine fabric 21.
Bibliography. Greene 1979. Mayet (1975, 147–60) discusses the ware as *vases à parois fins de la Bétique*, and suggests that they may be equated with the Saguntum cups mentioned by Pliny and Martial (ibid., 164–9). Source region is close to that

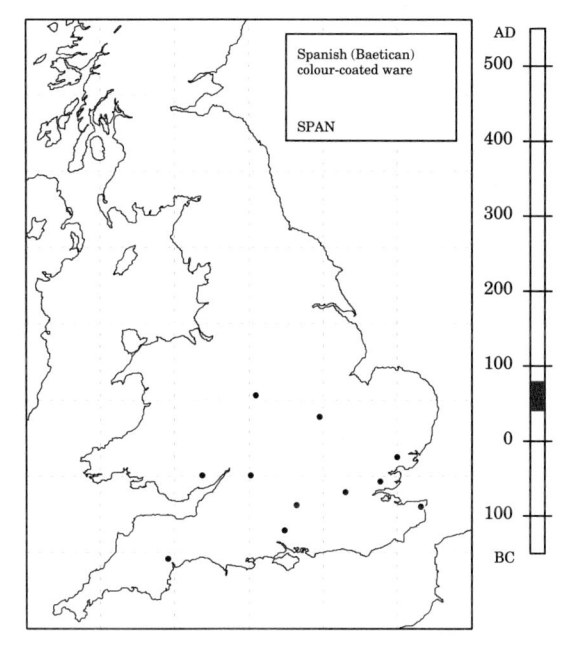

Gallo-Belgic/IMPORTED WARES

of Dressel 20 amphoras, and they were transported in the same ships (Colls *et al.* 1977, 111–14; Parker and Price 1981). *See also.* DR20

Gallo-Belgic wares

Fabric and technology. Three fabric groups, which are discussed below:
- TR   Terra rubra
- TN   Terra nigra
- TNEG Eggshell Terra nigra

Forms. Platters, cups and beakers. The principal forms and their dating are listed in **table 51 (198, 199)**.

Chronology. Early products found on Augustan military sites in Rhineland (e.g. Oberaden and Haltern), and produced into the Flavian.

Source. Principally the Vesle valley, south-east of Rheims (Chossenot and Chossenot 1987 for a summary). Similar wares produced further east, in the Moselle, and smaller sites in north-east Gaul such as Bavay, Blicquy, Arras and Amiens (Neuru 1987).

Distribution. North-east Gaul, between the Seine, Moselle and Rhine. In Britain, principally south and east of the Severn–Humber line **(200)**.

Potters. At least 200 potters are known from name-stamps on the interior of the base of the cups and platters; additionally a large number of illiterate marks. Some 'names' represent more than one individual but some potters probably moved from one production site to another.

Bibliography. The bibliography on Gallo-Belgic wares has increased rapidly in recent years. The study of the Camulodunum assemblage by C. F. C. Hawkes and Hull (1947) remains an important and accessible source. Holwerda's catalogue of the extensive collection of Nijmegan museum, published in difficult circumstances in Holland in 1941 (Holwerda 1941), is still quoted widely. A series of reports by V. Rigby contains much data on the distribution, provenance and dating of the British material, and several alternative typologies: Partridge 1981, 159–95; Niblett 1985, 74–82; Stead and Rigby 1986, 223–31; Potter and Trow 1988, 110–18; Stead and Rigby 1989, 121–37; see concordance, **table 51**.

The proceedings of the *SFECAG* conference at Tournai (Rivet 1992) contains numerous papers describing recent work in France on the various strands of *la céramique gallo-belge* that have now been identified across Gaul, many well beyond any connection with *Gallia Belgica*.

There is no recent synthesis of either the British or continental data.

See also. TR TN TNEG

196 Spanish colour-coated ware: British distribution

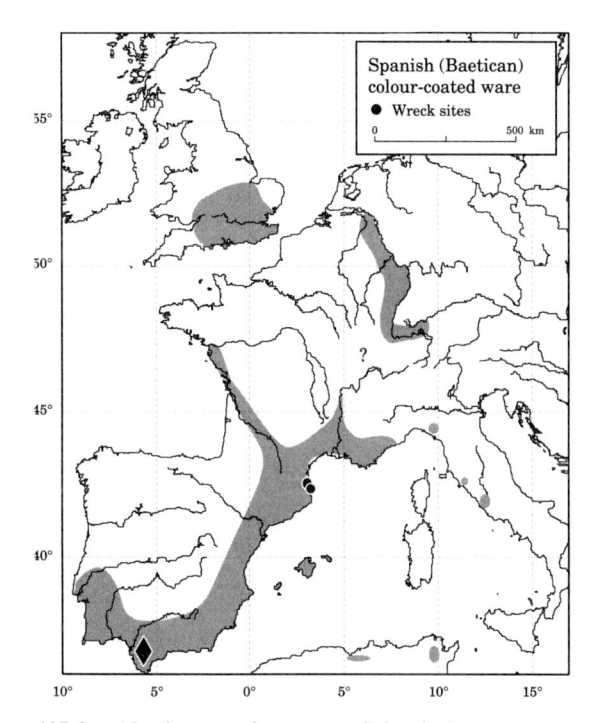

197 Spanish colour-coated ware: overall distribution

Gallo-Belgic/imported wares

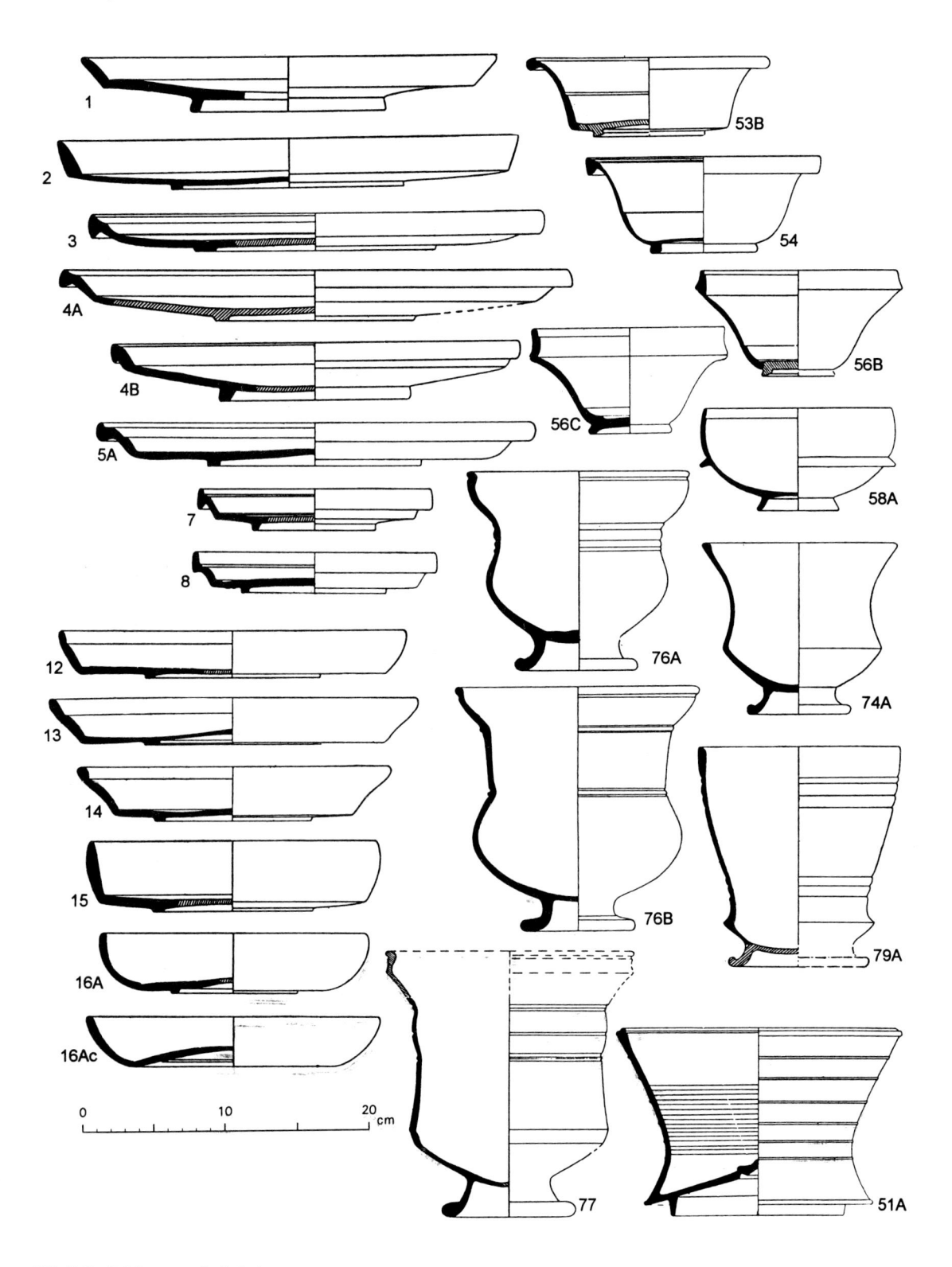

198 *Gallo-Belgic wares: Scale 1:4*

Gallo-Belgic/IMPORTED WARES

199 *Gallo-Belgic wares: Scale 1:4*

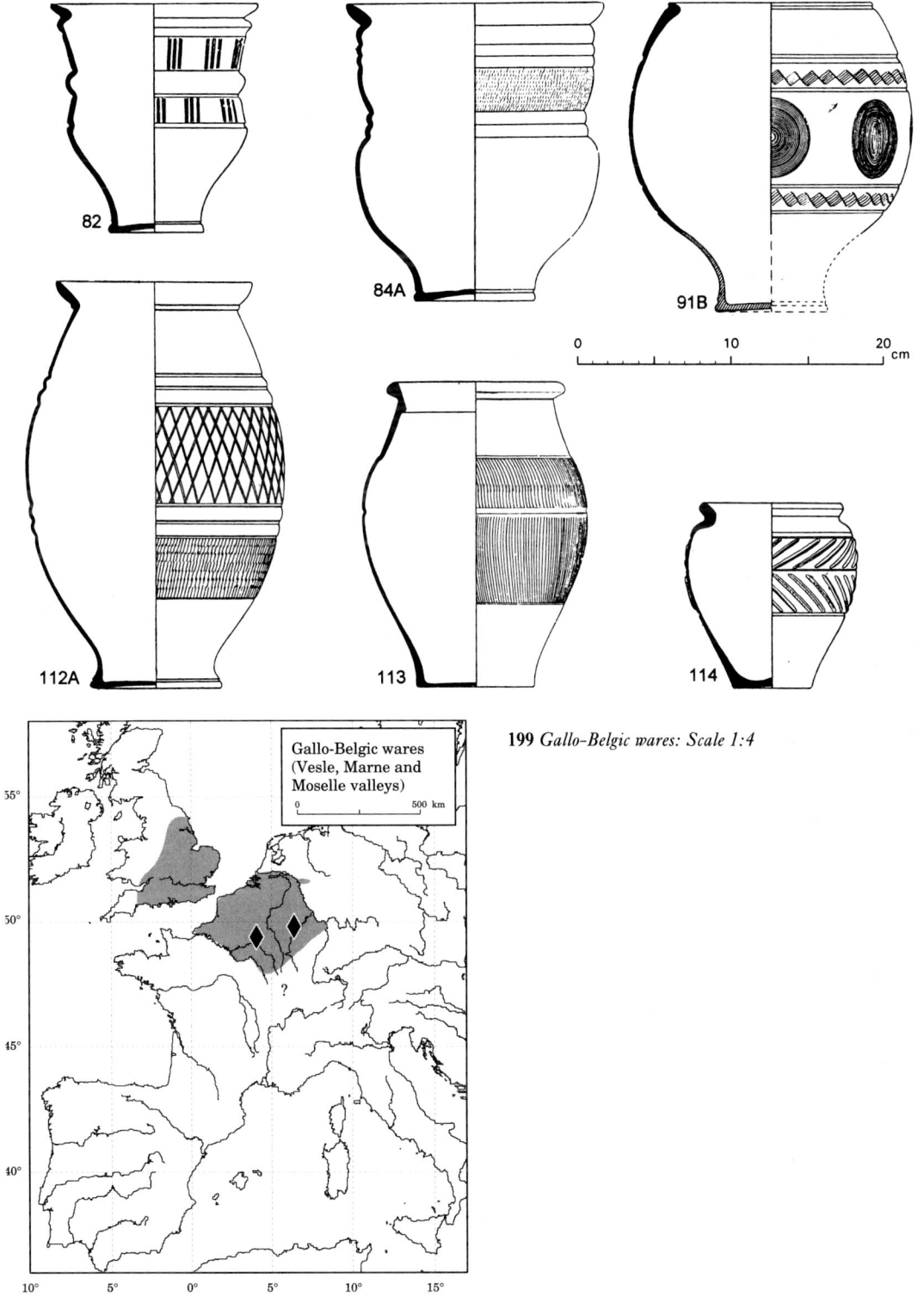

200 *Gallo-Belgic wares: overall distribution*

163

Gallo-Belgic/imported wares

Camulodunum	Date		Baldock	SKG	KHL
Plates					
1	10 BC–AD 25	micaceous	25	22	
2	15 BC–AD 65	Oberaden 96	1a 1b 1c	1	1
3	15 BC–AD 25 (50 TN)	Haltern 72	12	19	5
3/5	10 BC–AD 10		13		
4	10 BC–AD 25	micaceous	26		
4b		micaceous	23		
5	15 BC–AD 25 (40 TR1C; 65 TR2 TN)	Oberaden 88	14a 14b	20	6
5/6	15 BC–AD 25 (40 TR1C; 65 TR2 TN)		15 16	21	
6	AD 1–25		7		
7	AD 1–25		6 9		
7/8	AD 15–60		10	13	
12					
7a					8
7c	15 BC–AD 20		8	8	
8	AD 20–65	Hofheim 97ab	11	15	13
11/12	15 BC–AD 20	Haltern 74		4	2
12	AD 1–25		3		
12/13	AD 10–65		4	5	
13	AD 10–65			6	3
14	AD 40–70		5a 5b 5c 5d	7	
15	?			2	
16	AD 40–85	Hofheim 99	2a 2b 2c	3	4
Cups					
53	15 BC–AD 25	Oberaden 90b		27	15
54	15 BC–AD 25			26	14
56a	10 BC–AD 40		16a	29	16 17
56b	15 BC–AD 25			28	16 17
56c	AD 20–65		16b	32	16 17
58	AD 35–70			18	33
Tazze					
51a/51b				35	
51c				36	
51v				34	
Pedestal cups					
72–79	15 BC–AD 25			42	
74/79	AD 10–50		19		
20					
76	AD 25–50				18
76–77	AD 10–50			43	
79	15 BC–AD 25	Oberaden 95	20	45	19
Girth beakers					
82	10 BC–AD 25	Gose 338	22	38	23
84	AD 1–50	Holwerda 9b/Haltern 87	21	37	22
91	AD 20–50		24		
Ovoid beakers					
112	15 BC–AD 65	Haltern 85	23	39	24
Butt beakers					
113				40	
Barbotine beakers					
114	AD 10–50	Haltern 86	27a	49	25
Carinated beakers					
120				48	

References: Camulodunum (C. F. C. Hawkes and Hull 1947); Baldock (Stead and Rigby 1986); SKG = Skeleton Green, Puckeridge (Partridge 1981); KHL = King Harry Lane, St Albans (Stead and Rigby 1989).

Table 51 *Gallo-Belgic wares: concordance and dating of principal forms*

Terra rubra

Fabric and technology. The TR fabric classification (after C. F. C. Hawkes and Hull 1947) is based on fabric colour and texture, and the extent and colour of the slip.

- TR1(A) Off-white or pink (2.5YR to 10R 8/8) fabric with slightly sandy texture, with occasional rounded red-grog inclusions; polished coral red slip (10R 7/10-5/12) on upper surfaces of cups and platters and outer surface of pedestal cups.
- TR1(B) Pink or buff (10YR 7/4 to 10R 8/8) fabric, slight sandy texture, completely covered with orange or pink (2.5YR 7/12 to 10R 7/10) slip.
- TR1(C) Orange (10YR 6/10) sandy textured fabric, with polished dark red (10R 7/10-5/12) slip on upper surfaces.
- TR2 Similar to TR1(C), with self-coloured, polished surfaces.
- TR3 A variable group of cream to dark red fine-textured fabrics with smooth fracture. Highly polished self-coloured surfaces. Some have dark grey, dark chocolate brown or a lighter smoky grey haze.

Forms. Plates, cups and beakers.
Chronology. Production commences by *c.* 20–10 BC. The proportion of terra rubra in the Gallo-Belgic assemblage drops through the Augustan–Tiberian period, being replaced by terra nigra, and the ware has disappeared by the early Flavian period. The different varieties may be dated thus:
TR1(A) 15 BC–AD 25
TR1(B) 15 BC–AD 15
TR1(C) AD 1–60
TR2 AD 1–65

Source. The principal source is the Vesle valley, near Rheims.
Distribution. North-east Gaul, between the Seine, Moselle and Rhine. In Britain, south and east of the Severn–Humber line, with concentrations in central-southern England, and Herts./Essex region (**201**).
Aliases. Gloucester fabric TF203. *JRPS bibliography* fabric trb. *Kent* fine fabric 7b. *Silchester* fabrics E7, E8, E9, E10, E11, E12 and E44.
See also. TN

Terra nigra

Fabric and technology. A variable series of hard off-white (2.5Y 7-8/0) to dark grey or brown fabrics, with thin darker margins, silty or slightly sandy textured, coated with a darker grey (2.5Y 4/0) or blue-black slip; highly burnished surfaces, sometimes with individual strokes visible. Wheel-thrown. Much variation possible on an individual vessel.
Forms. Plates, cups, beakers and bowls.
Chronology. Augustan to Neronian/early Flavian.
Source. Vesle valley, near Rheims, the Marne valley and the Trier region.
Distribution. North-east Gaul, between the Seine, Moselle and Rhine. In Britain, principally south and east of the Severn–Humber line, with concentrations in central southern England, and Herts./Essex region (**202**).

201 Terra rubra: British distribution, quantified by number of Camulodunum forms

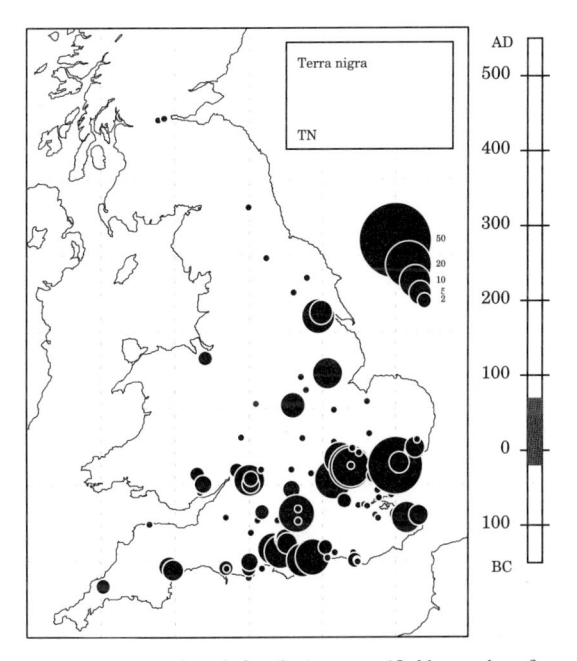

202 Terra nigra: British distribution, quantified by number of Camulodunum types

Aliases. Colchester fabric UR. *Gloucester* fabric TF202. *JRPS bibliography* fabric tng. *Kent* fine fabric 7a. *Silchester* fabric E6. *See also.* TR

Eggshell terra nigra

Fabric and technology. Hard, fine, very thin (1–2mm) fabric, typically a sandwich of grey (7.5YR 4/0) core, brown margins (5YR 7/2) and glossy black (2.5YR 4/0) surfaces; slightly micaceous. Wheel-thrown, with very finely trimmed footrings and smoothed finish.

Forms. Two forms most common in Britain:
Holwerda 26 carinated beaker, equivalent to Cam 120.
Holwerda 27 necked beaker.
Other types of beaker, bowl and flask occur more rarely (Greene 1979, 120). Some vessels stamped on the underside of the base or on the lower body with a name-stamp; occasionally with an intaglio impression (Bushe-Fox 1949, 240–1) (**203**).

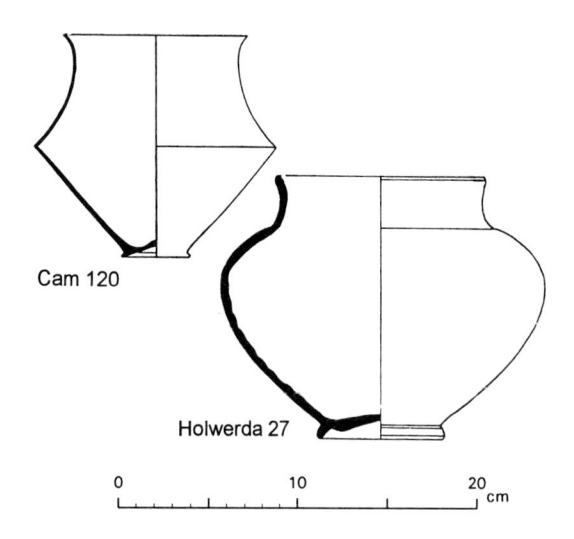

203 Eggshell terra nigra: Scale 1:4

Chronology. Late Neronian and Flavian.
Source. Evidence for production in north-east France, but others may be from Rhineland. Similar forms also made in thicker grey fabrics.
Distribution. North-east Gaul and lower Germany. Widespread, but sparse, in southern Britain and the Midlands; particularly common in London and Southwark (**204**).
Aliases. Gloucester fabric TF219.
Bibliography. Holwerda 1941; Greene 1979, terra nigra group 5; Holbrook and Bidwell 1991, 77–9.

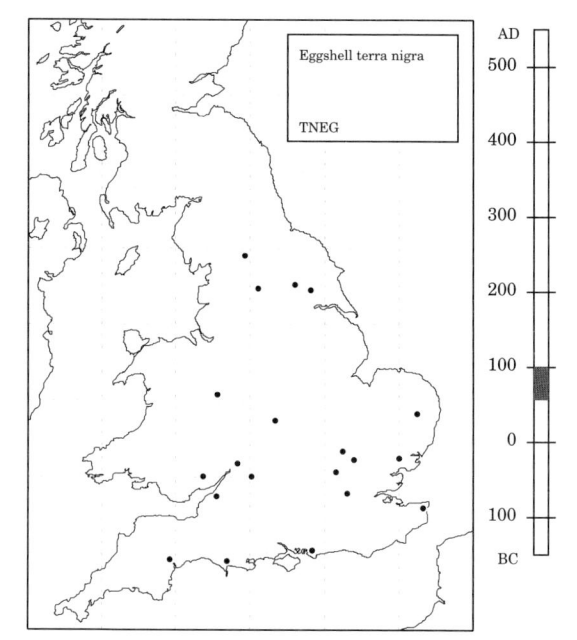

204 Eggshell terra nigra: British distribution

ROMANO-BRITISH FINE WARES

The proportion of imported fine wares in the pottery assemblage declines from the 1st cent., a process accelerated by the collapse of the Gaulish samian industry in the early 3rd cent. AD. The selection described here covers both the major regional industries of the later Roman period and a number of the smaller-scale products of the 1st and 2nd cent. AD (**205**).

In the Atlas pages the wares are ordered alphabetically.

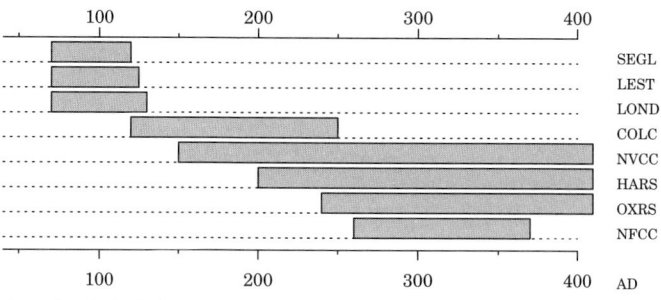

South-east English glazed	SEGL
London–Essex stamped	LEST
London-ware style	LOND
Colchester colour-coated	COLC
Nene Valley colour-coated	NVCC
Hadham red-slipped	HARS
Oxfordshire red/brown-slipped	OXRS
New Forest slipped	NFCC

205 Romano-British fine wares: dating of principal classes

Colchester colour-coated/ROMANO-BRITISH FINE WARES

Colchester colour-coated wares
Fabric and technology. Fine fabric with smooth fracture, but varying from soft to very hard; core pink (5YR 8/4) through light greyish-brown (5YR 6/1-4; 7/1-4) to dark-grey (5YR 4/1) with slipped matt dark-grey or red surfaces; inclusions of black iron ore (may be abundant), mica, quartz sand and calcareous flecks (all fine). Wheel-thrown. Decoration includes barbotine, rouletting, roughcast and appliqué.
Forms. A wide range of tablewares recorded from the kilns, including 'castor boxes' and flagons, but beakers most widespread.
2nd-cent. forms are bag-shaped cornice-rimmed *Colchester* 391, or plain-rimmed beakers *Colchester* 392 with roughcast, rouletted bands or barbotine decoration, including scrolls and 'hunt cups'. Taller, ovoid-folded beakers *Colchester* 406 more typical of 3rd cent. Rare elaborately decorated specimens, combining appliqué and barbotine techniques, feature human figures participating in gladiatorial shows or religious scenes (**206**).
Chronology. Production from *c.* AD 120 until later 3rd cent. Origin probably lies with potters familiar with East Gaulish/Rhineland industry, where most of the forms have their origin. Some contact maintained with these continental industries throughout the 2nd and early 3rd cent.
Source. Colchester, where many kilns have been excavated on the outskirts of the town.
Distribution. Principally East Anglia, the London basin and southern Britain, with some export to the northern frontier during Antonine period (as COMO) – distribution map incomplete due to problems with identification. From early

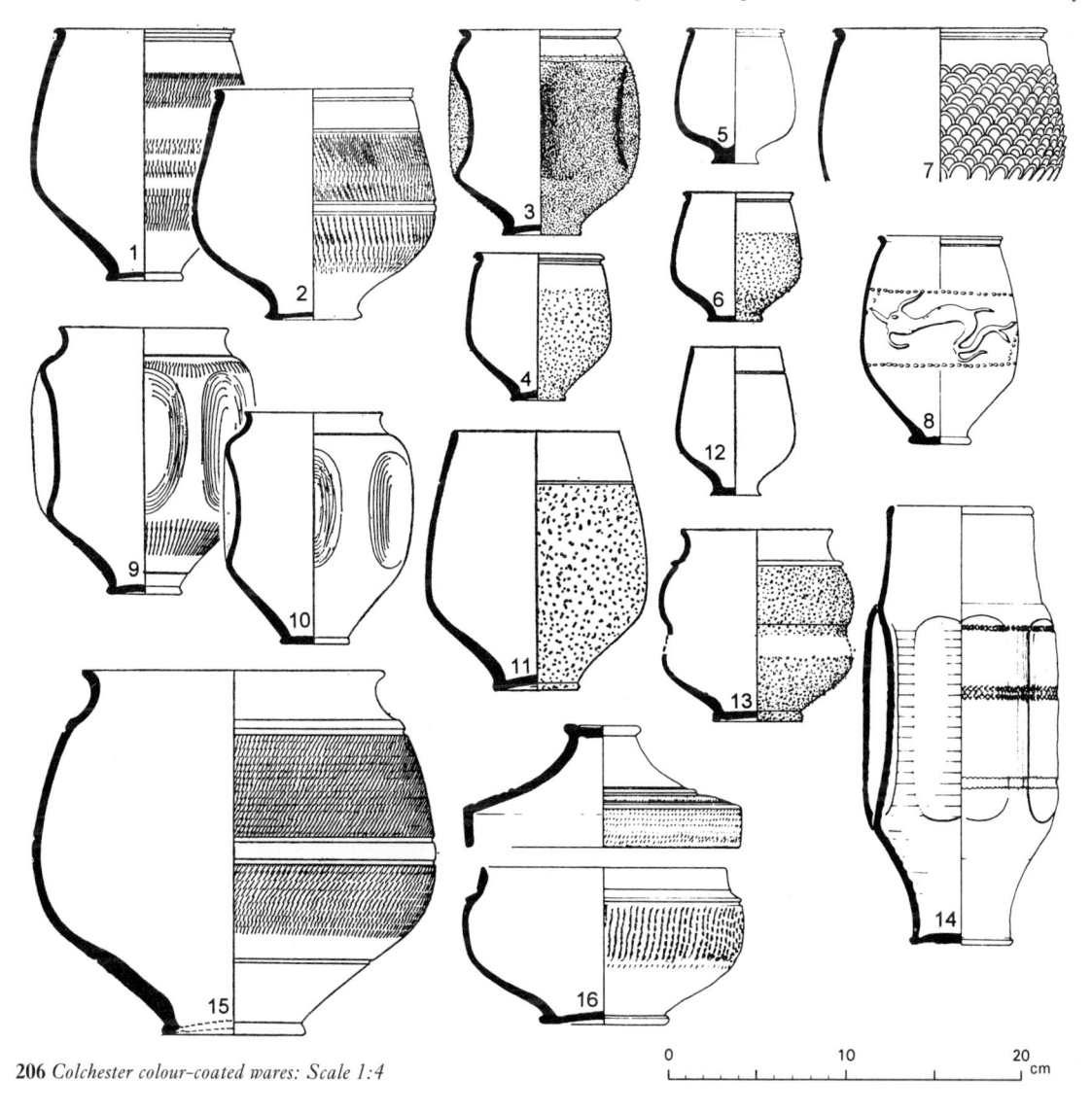

206 Colchester colour-coated wares: Scale 1:4

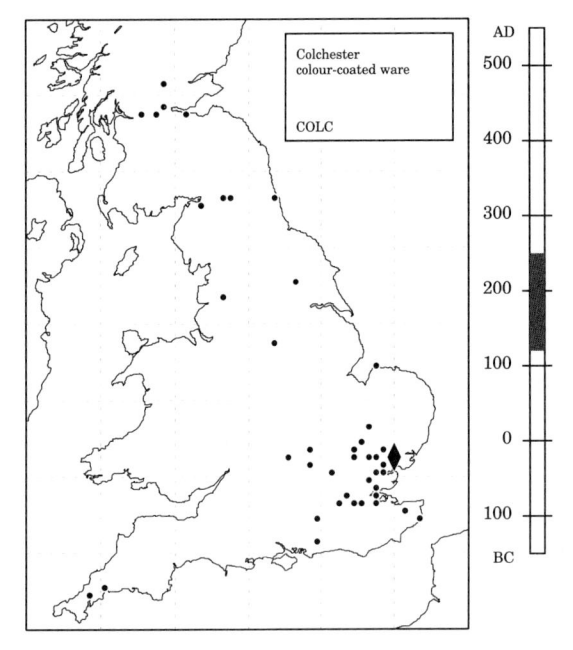

207 Colchester colour-coated wares: overall distribution

206	Colchester type	Body form	Rim form
1–8	391	bag-shaped	cornice
11–12	392	bag-shaped	plain
15	396	globular	curved
13	397	constricted	curved
9–10	406	ovoid folded	curved
14	407	tall	vertical
16	308	castor box	

Table 52 *Classification of Colchester colour-coated forms (after Hull)*

3rd, largely confined to local markets (**207**).
Aliases. Carlisle fabric 300. Chelmsford fabric 1. Chesterfield fabric 30. *Gestingthorpe* fabrics C3–C5. Great Chesterford fabric 30. *JRPS bibliography* fabric clc. Kent fine fabric 4b. Lullingstone fabric 4. Milton Keynes fabric 23a.
Bibliography. For kilns: Hull 1963 (with typology of products); RCHM gazetteer 92–5, F273–88. For fabric: Toller in Draper 1985, 87–8; A. C. Anderson 1980, 37.
Notes. (1) It is not always possible to distinguish consistently between Nene Valley and Colchester colour-coated wares in the hand-specimen (see comments by Toller in Draper 1985 and Orton in Blurton and Rhodes 1977). (2) A small-scale colour-coated industry established in Colchester during the pre-Flavian period (Greene 1978b, 26–7) made cups and beakers loosely modelled on Lyon ware prototypes (LYON). This short-lived enterprise had only limited success outside Colchester and seems to have no connection with the 2nd-cent. industry described above.
See also. COMO COTS

Hadham red-slipped wares

Pottery was produced at the kilns at Hadham (Herts.) from the later 1st cent. Among the most distinctive products of the early phase of the industry are the 'stamped London ware' bowls (Rodwell 1978) described elsewhere (see LEST). The industry expanded significantly from the later 3rd cent. with the production of fine grey and orange-red slipped and burnished wares. Although the orange wares may have formed only a relatively small proportion of the output of the later Hadham industry they are the most widely recognized products of the kilns, and are described further below. Alongside these wares there was some production of grey wares of the standard later-Roman black-burnished derived forms, and jars with rilled surfaces in gritty fabrics reminiscent in form of the jars of the east Midlands shell-tempered industry (LRSH).
Fabric and technology. A range of hard, fine fabrics with sandy texture and finely irregular fracture; bright orange-red (e.g. 2.5YR 6/12) or paler orange-pink or reddish-yellow, distinctively slipped and burnished on exterior of enclosed vessels and (usually) both surfaces of open vessels; tempered with abundant fine quartz sand, moderate fine black and red iron ores and some fine mica. Decoration, other than burnishing, includes stamping, relief-moulded figures, bosses and dimples. Grey (reduced) ware of similar character is less widely recognized.
Forms. No complete typology of Hadham products exists, but wide range of forms are known, including jars, bowls, plates, flagons and flasks. Some follow the common late-Roman imitation red-slipped samian-derived forms, but others are highly decorated in so-called 'Romano-Saxon' style, incorporating stamps and moulding (including anthropomorphic and animal motifs) with bosses and dimples (**208**).
Chronology. Production from mid-3rd, with expanded distribution from the beginning of the 4th cent.
Source. Kilns at Little Hadham and Much Hadham (Herts.).
Distribution. Earlier products have local distribution, but expansion during 3rd cent. Highest proportion of assemblages in Herts./Essex reached during period AD 350–400 (e.g. Going 1987, 115–16) (**209**).
Aliases. Caister-on-sea fabric MHAD-10. Chelmsford fabric 4. Chesterfield fabric 23. Colchester fabric CH. *Gestingthorpe* fabric A1. Great Chesterford fabric 23. *JRPS bibliography* fabric had. Kent fine fabric 12a. Leicester fabric OW9. Lullingstone fabric 19. Milton Keynes fabric 37. Towcester fabric 32.
Bibliography. For kilns: RCHM gazetteer F356–9; Rodwell

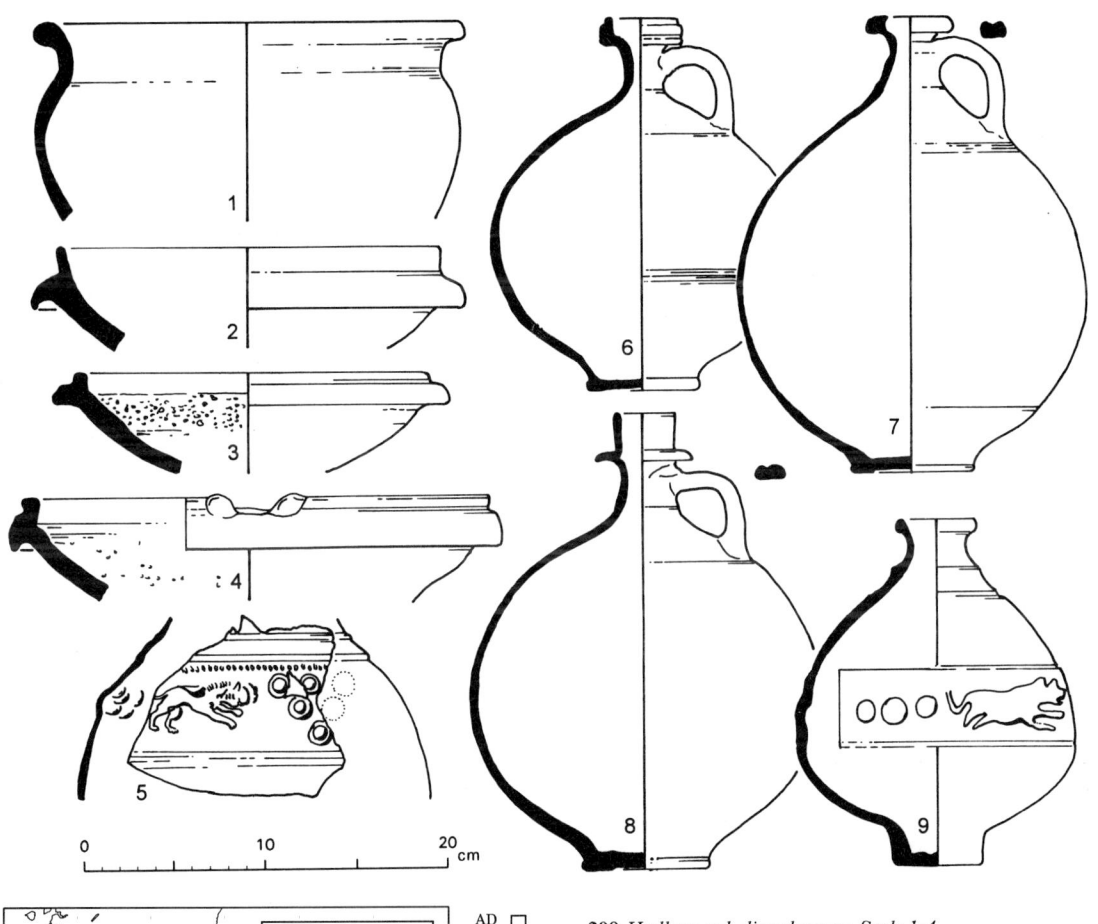

London-Essex stamped /ROMANO-BRITISH FINE WARES

208 Hadham red-slipped wares: Scale 1:4

1982. Final report on kilns and their products by C. Going, forthcoming; for fabrics: Orton in Blurton and Rhodes 1977; discussion of dating of Hadham wares in Harden and Green 1978; Going 1987; for 'Romano-Saxon' style: Roberts 1982 – many are Hadham products.
See also. LEST

London-Essex stamped wares

Fabric and technology. Hard, fine fabric, with slightly laminar fracture; dark grey-brown core (5YR 3/1) with distinct orange margins (2/5YR 5/6) and darker, orange-brown (e.g. 5YR 5/4-4/2) surfaces; tempered with abundant fine quartz and occasional specks of dark-red ironstone in a slightly micaceous matrix. External surface finely burnished; unsmoothed and slightly uneven interior. Traces of thin slip on some specimens. Wheel-thrown.

Forms. Principal form is cylindrical bowl with pedestal foot and projecting flange, but other forms include hemispherical bowl (loosely imitating samian Drag 37). Distinctive decoration of panels of block and circle stamps; also grooves, incised

209 Hadham red-slipped wares: overall distribution

The 'London' style/ROMANO-BRITISH FINE WARES

comb decoration and rouletting. Stamps and die links are described by Rodwell (1978) (**210**).

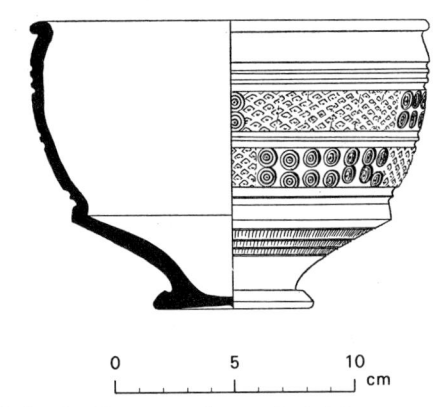

210 London-Essex stamped wares: Scale 1:3

Chronology. Production may commence in the Flavian period, but majority seem to be early 2nd cent.
Source. From the potteries in the region of Little and Much Hadham (Herts./Essex border).
Distribution. The lower Thames basin, with some outliers such as Sea Mills (Rodwell in Bennett 1985, 51) (**211**).
Aliases. *Chelmsford* fabric 19. *Colchester* fabric GQ. *Kent* fine fabric 10e.
Bibliography. Rodwell 1978.
See also. HARS LOND

The 'London ware' style

The 'London ware' style is characterized by incised (including compass-drawn), rouletted and stamped decoration, generally on fine grey or black fabrics and in forms (principally bowls) which loosely follow samian prototypes. Several sources are represented in the group, which is a style rather than a single ware.

Fabric and technology. The London material (the most extensively studied) is typically a hard, fine smooth-textured micaceous fabric, with a slightly laminar fracture; dark grey-brown core with dark-grey or black slip on finely burnished surfaces.

Forms. Bowls are the most common forms (often following the samian prototypes, Drag 37, 29 and 30), but beakers, flasks and plates are known in the same fabrics. The range of 'London ware' from London published by Marsh (1978) is particularly extensive.

The most characteristic decorative element is probably the compass-drawn half-circle, echoing the ovolo of samian ware, which is used in combination with combed lines and rouletting and (in some groups) stamped decoration (**213**).

Chronology. The general style circulates from early Flavian period until the mid-2nd cent., and perhaps beyond in some marginal areas.

Source. Known sources for the 'London ware' style include Upchurch (Kent), Oxford, Ardleigh (Essex), West Stow and Wattisfield (Suffolk), the Nene valley, as well as London itself. Little data available on distribution of many of these producers – most are probably quite restricted.

In some cases (notably London itself), 'London ware' is

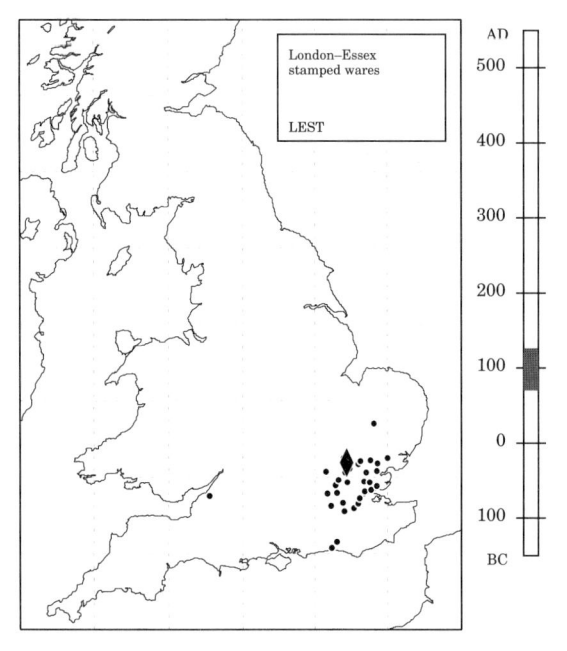

211 London-Essex stamped wares: overall distribution

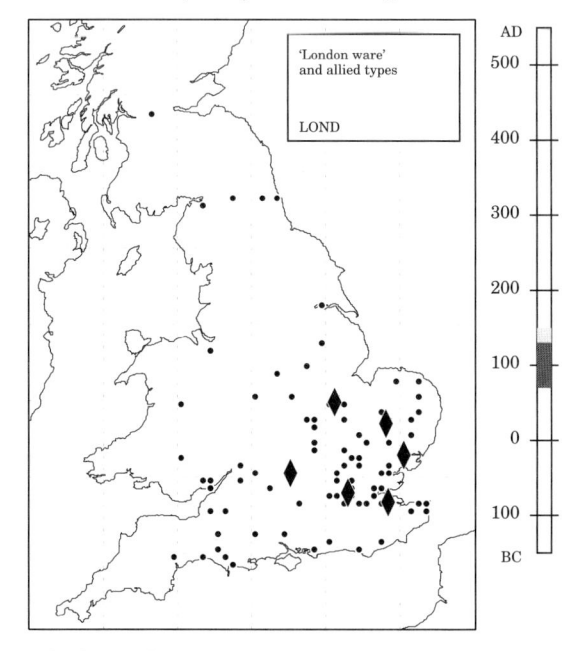

212 The 'London ware' style: overall distribution

New Forest slipped/ROMANO-BRITISH FINE WARES

213 The 'London ware' style: Scale 1:4

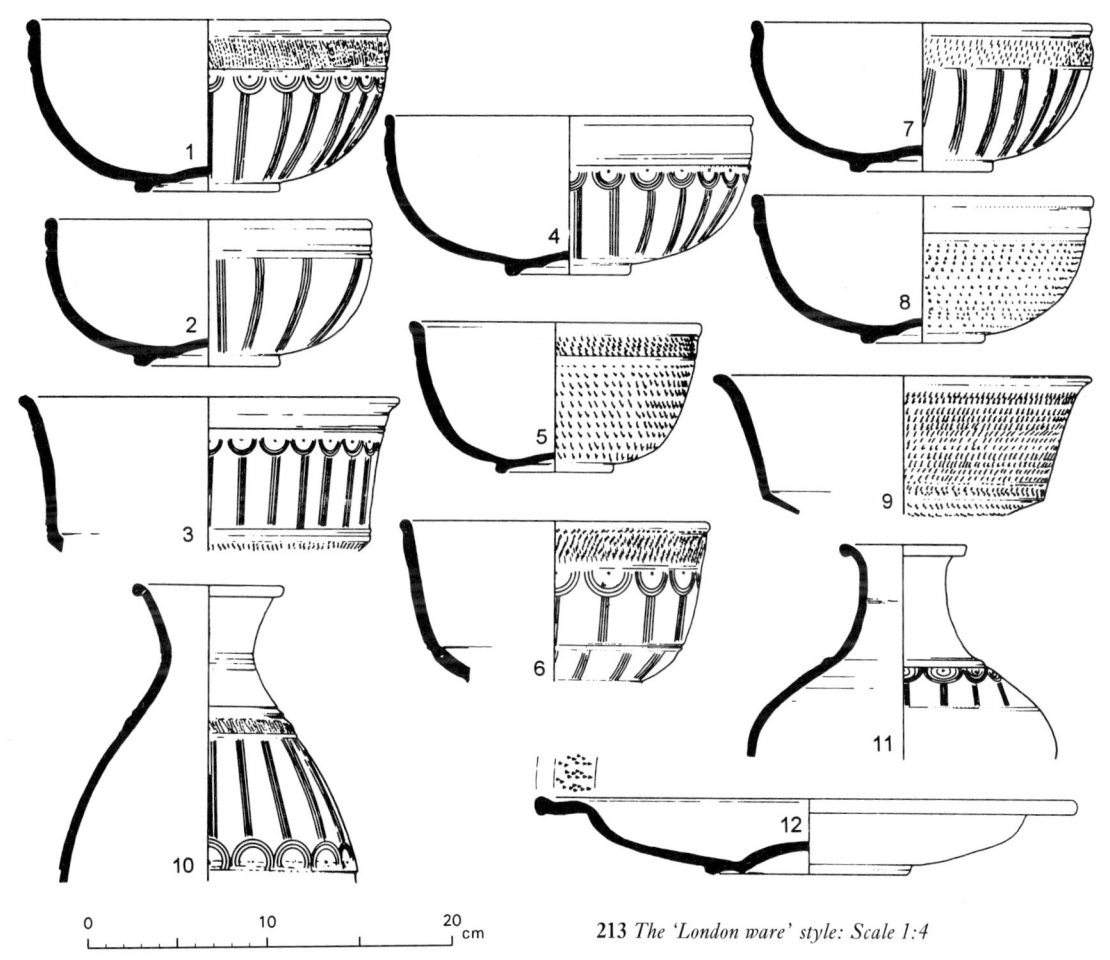

only one element of more extensive fine-ware production (e.g. with mica-dusted, marbled or glazed wares) and there is some sharing of decorative motifs and forms between these groups. Elsewhere, vessels in 'London ware' style are produced alongside coarse wares e.g. at Exeter, 'London ware' is a minor element of local *Exeter micaceous grey ware* (Holbrook and Bidwell 1991, 165, 169); in the Upchurch industry, and perhaps at Ardleigh, 'London ware' was produced alongside coarse wares, and in similar fabrics (Monaghan 1987a, 218).

Distribution. The style has a generally south-eastern distribution, and this is where most of the known producers are located (**212**).

Aliases. *Carlisle* fabric 319. *Chelmsford* fabric 33. *JRPS bibliography* fabric lnd. *Kent* fine fabric 10b. *Milton Keynes* fabric 15.

Bibliography. Marsh 1978 for a survey of the London material and discussion of the background to the style. For Nene valley material: Perrin 1990a. The 'London ware' decorative style is known on the Continent, particularly in the Low Countries, where kilns are recorded at Cuijk: Haalebos 1992, 21–3.

Notes. The term 'London ware' has also been applied to London-Essex stamped wares of the early Hadham industry. *See also.* LEST

New Forest slipped wares

Fabric and technology. A range of dark- or red-slipped wares. Fulford defines three variants:

1a Hard, fine fabric which may be highly fired, up to a 'stone ware' quality; reduced grey or dark-grey core with surface varying from pale yellow-red, through reddish-brown to dark red or purple (often on same vessel), with high-metallic sheen (from 2. 5YR 3.5/2 to 5.5/8; 2.5Y 2/0); rare inclusions of dark iron ores.

1b Similar to 1a, but oxidized; reddish-yellow or reddish-brown (5YR 3.5/3; 2.5YR 5.5/8, 2.5/0) slip.

1c Hard, slightly sandy fabric with granular texture; reddish-yellow (5YR 4.5/6) core with reddish-brown (2.5YR 3.5/6) slip.

All wheel-thrown. Wide range of decorative techniques, including barbotine scales or leaves, white painted, incised,

New Forest slipped/ROMANO-BRITISH FINE WARES

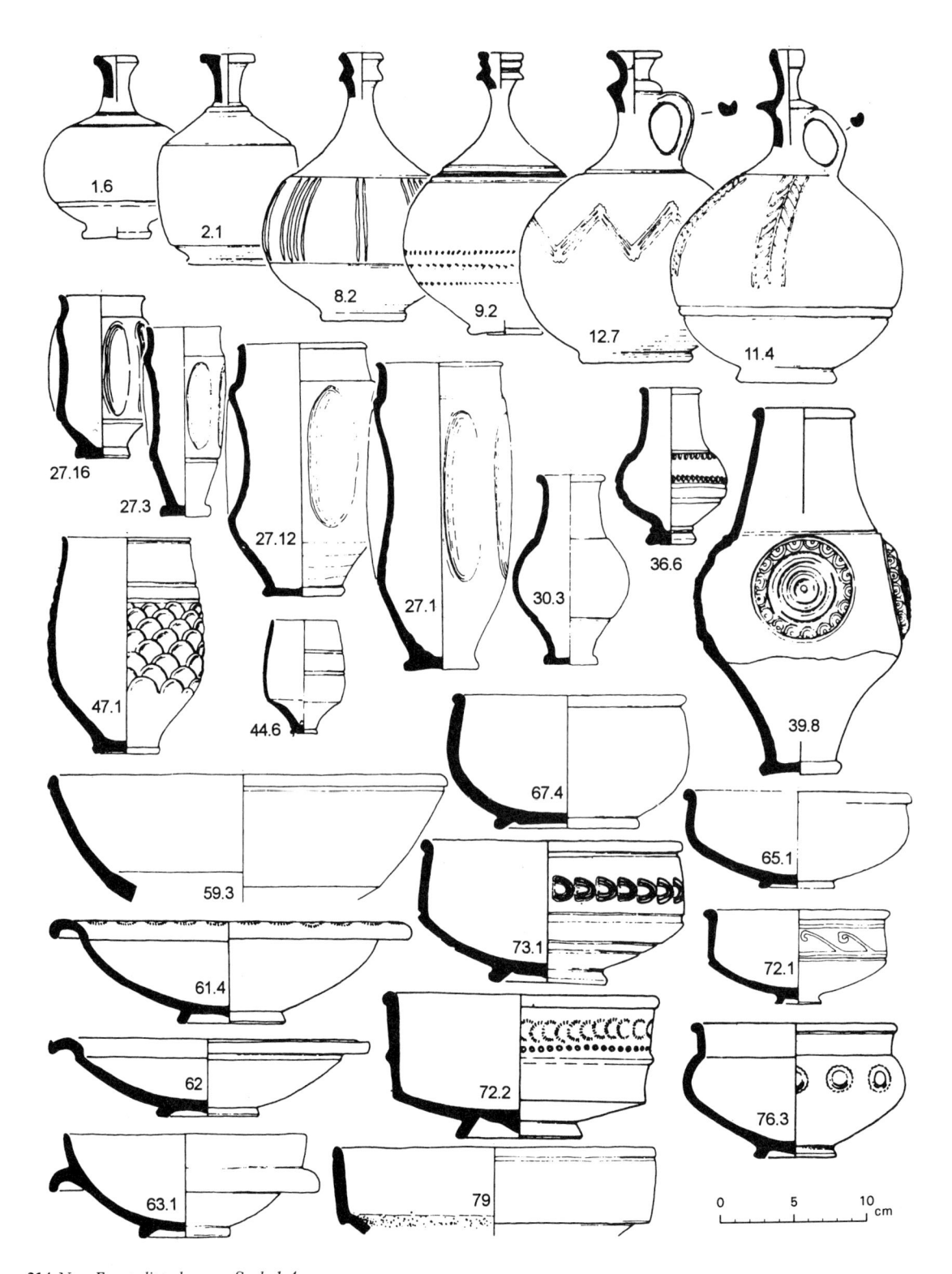

214 *New Forest slipped wares: Scale 1:4*

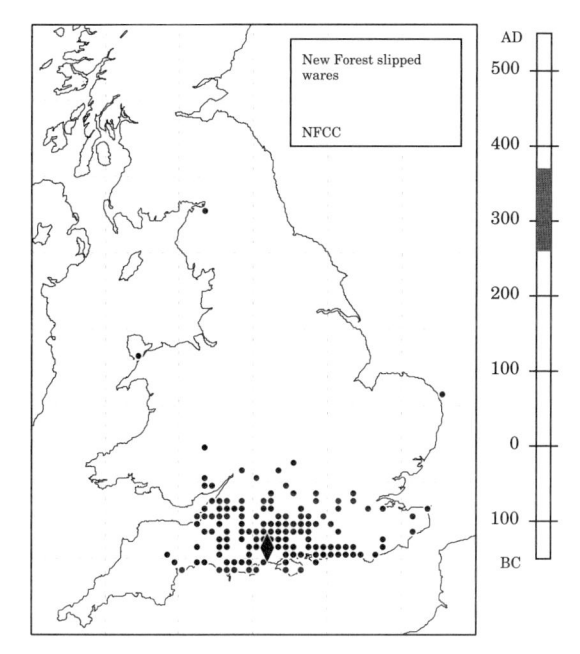

Nene Valley colour-coated/ROMANO-BRITISH FINE WARES

215 New Forest slipped wares: overall distribution

impressed and rouletted.

Forms. Beakers, flasks, jugs and flagons (fabric 1a) and bowls (fabric 1b/c). Many of the red-slipped bowl types follow late sigillata prototypes (Drag 31, 33, 35/36, 38, 44, 45 etc.), but most widely distributed types are beakers (particularly the folded beaker, type 27), flasks and jugs (**214, table 53**)

Form	Description	Fabric
1–26	Flasks and jugs	1a
27–52	Beakers	1a
53	Cup	1a
54–57	Jars or small bowls	1a
58	Lid	1a
59–77	Bowls	1b/c
78–81	Mortaria	1b/c
82–85	Misc. bowls	1b/c

Table 53 *Classification of New Forest slipped ware forms (after Fulford)*

Chronology. c. AD 260–370. Production probably ceased before the end of the 4th cent.
Source. The New Forest industry.
Distribution. Widespread in central-southern England, with a scatter beyond (**215**).
Aliases. Bath fabric 6.2. Caister-on-sea fabric NFCC-29. Carlisle fabric 302. Dorchester fabric 20. Gloucester fabric TF12C. *JRPS bibliography* fabric nfc. Lullingstone fabric 13. Fulford 1975a, fabric 1.

Bibliography. Fulford 1975a; *RCHM gazetteer* 108–9, F322–41, F344.
See also. NFMO

Nene Valley colour-coated wares

Fabric and technology. Hard, smooth-textured fabric with finely irregular fracture; white to off-white (e.g. 7.5YR 7/6-8) orange-yellow (7.5YR 5/6) or darker grey or brown core with variable slip colour, dark brown to black, mottled lighter orange or orange-brown where thinner; abundant very fine quartz sand (visible at x20) and occasional larger quartz grains, red or orange and black flecks and occasional pale clay pellets (some streaking of these, and orange/black flecks, in the matrix); decoration includes barbotine (both under and over the slip), rouletting, grooving, folding and some use of moulds – roughcasting almost unknown.

Forms. Wide range of tablewares, including jugs, flagons and bottles, imitation samian forms, Castor boxes, cups and beakers. The latter are decorated in barbotine with hunting scenes ('hunt cups') or human figures during 2nd and 3rd cent., barbotine scale work (3rd cent.) or white slip scroll and berry motifs (3rd–4th cent.). Some vessels (particularly in the earlier barbotine technique) are very ornate and depict religious scenes (G. Webster 1989). Limited production of stamp-decorated samian-derived forms during early–mid 3rd cent. (Dannell 1973) and plainer vessels from later 3rd (e.g. Drag 31, 36, 37, 45). During 4th cent. some coarse-ware forms produced in colour-coated fabrics (e.g. jars, dishes and flanged bowls) (**216, 217, table 54**).

Form	Description
26–57	Beakers
63–68	Flagons or jugs
75–77	Wide-mouthed jars or bowls
79	Flanged bowl
80–84	Imitation samian
87	Dish
89	Castor box (with lid)

Table 54 *Classification of Nene Valley colour-coated ware (after Howe, Perrin and Mackreth)*

Chronology. Production of colour-coated wares from mid-2nd cent., probably in the hands of immigrant (lower Rhineland?) craftsmen. Some influence from East Gaulish sigillata industries during early 3rd cent. Production continues until end of 4th cent.
Source. The Lower Nene valley, centred on Water Newton.
Distribution. Extent of mapped distribution incomplete due to confusion with other wares (e.g. lower Rhineland imports and Colchester colour-coated wares) in older literature. Has been identified in Antonine groups from Verulamium and

Nene Valley colour-coated/ROMANO-BRITISH FINE WARES

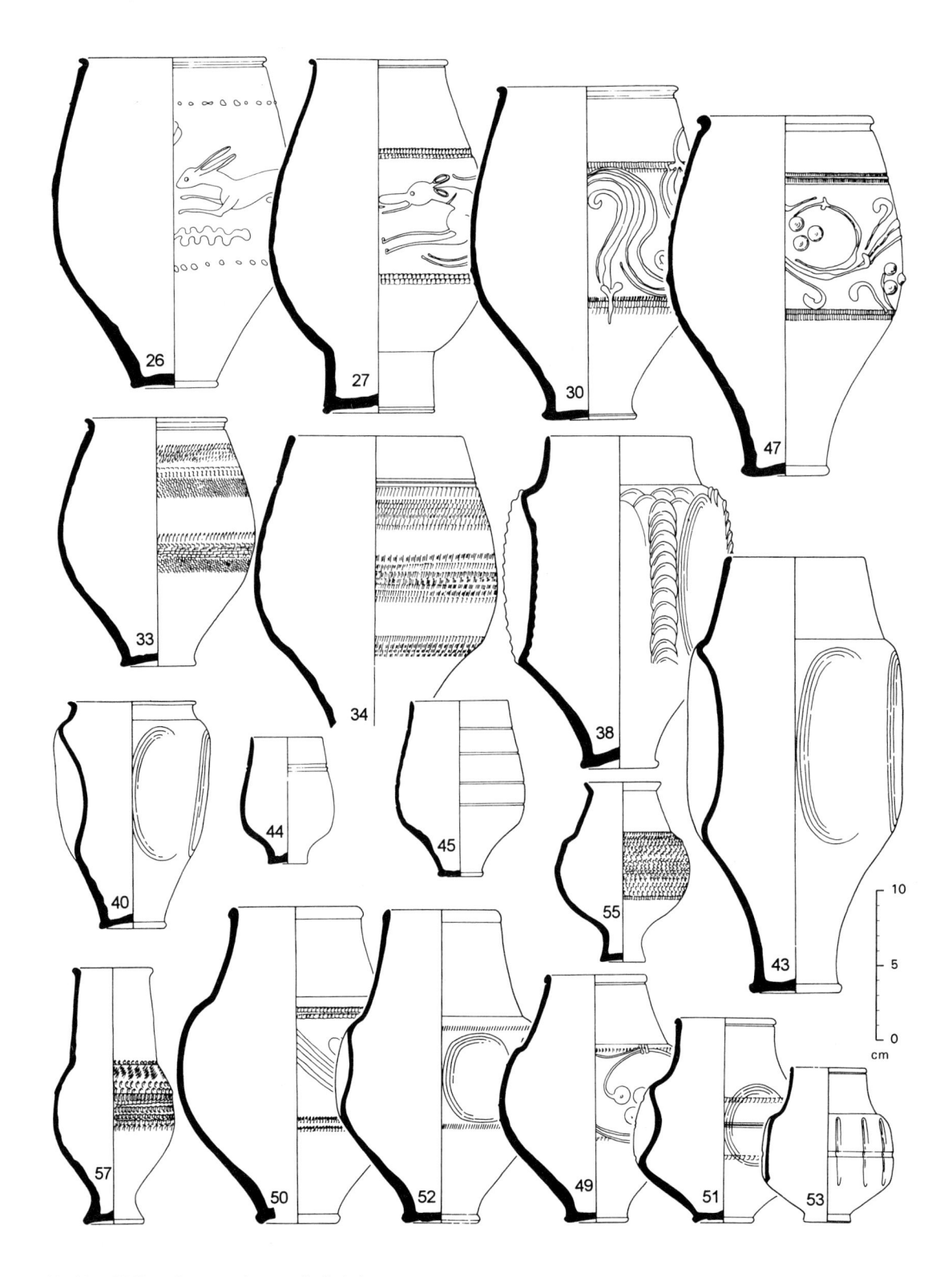

216 Nene Valley colour-coated wares: Scale 1:4

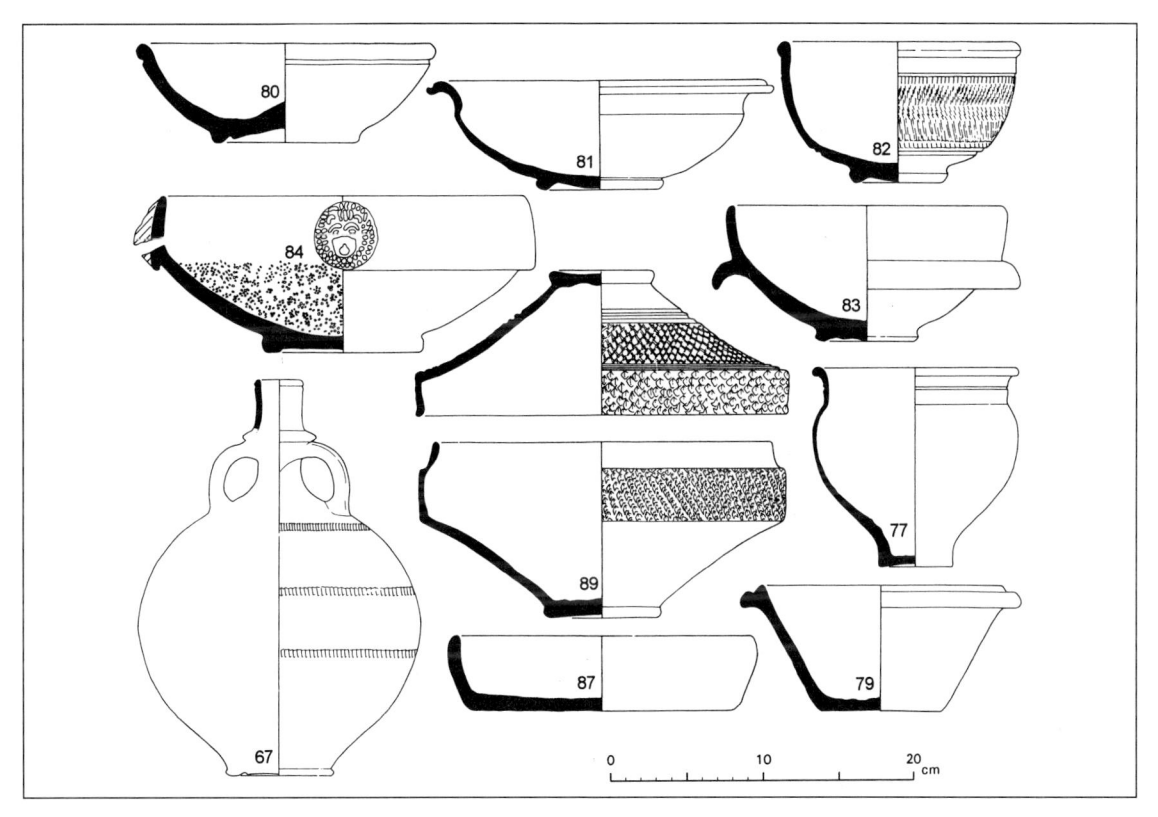

Oxfordshire red/brown-slipped/ROMANO-BRITISH COARSE WARES

217 Nene Valley colour-coated wares: Scale 1:4

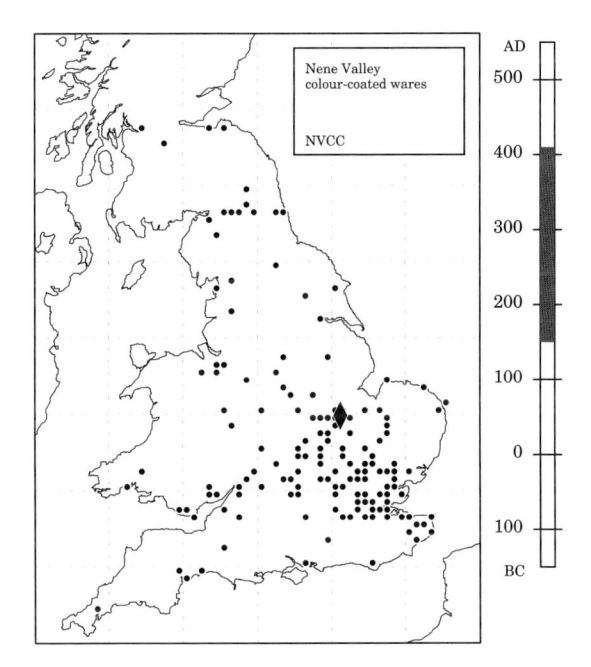

218 Nene Valley colour-coated wares: overall distribution

northern frontier. Probably most extensive during 3rd cent. prior to rise of Oxfordshire industry, but continues to hold large proportion of total market in eastern England into later 4th cent. partly due to production of 'coarse ware' forms (**218**).

Aliases. Bath fabric 6.3. Caister-on-sea fabrics NVCC-20 and NVCC. Carlisle fabric 175. Chelmsford fabric 2. Chesterfield fabric 29. Colchester fabric EA. Gestingthorpe fabrics B1-B3. Gloucester fabric TF12B. Great Chesterford fabric 29. *JRPS bibliography* fabric nvc. Kent fine fabric 13a. Lullingstone fabric 5. Milton Keynes fabric 6. Old Penrith fabric 12. Sidbury fabric 28. Towcester fabric 12. Castor ware.

Bibliography. Howe, Perrin and Mackreth 1980; B. R. Hartley 1960; A. C. Anderson 1980. For kilns: *RCHM gazetteer* 95–7, F366–86.

See also. NVMO KOLN

Oxfordshire red/brown-slipped wares

Fabric and technology. Hard, fine-textured fabric, sometimes with slightly laminar texture; colour varies from orange-buff to red or red-brown, often with grey core; moderate or abundant fine sub-angular red iron ore inclusions (occasionally coarser) and sparse large (up to 5mm) chalk lumps, set in micaceous matrix; smooth slip varies from orange-red to red to dark brown – latter more characteristic

Oxfordshire red/brown-slipped/ROMANO-BRITISH FINE WARES

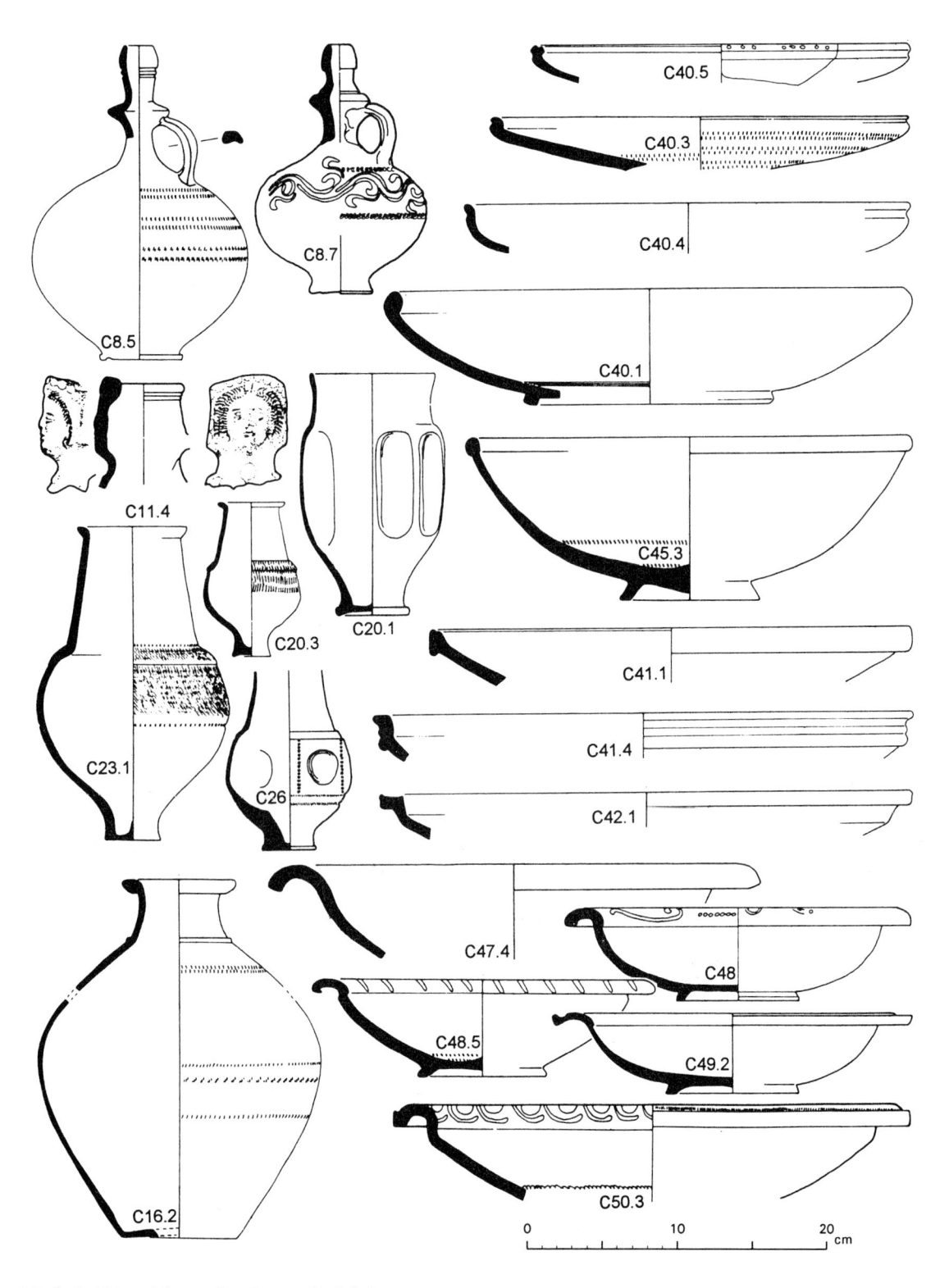

219 *Oxfordshire red/brown-slipped wares: Scale 1:4*

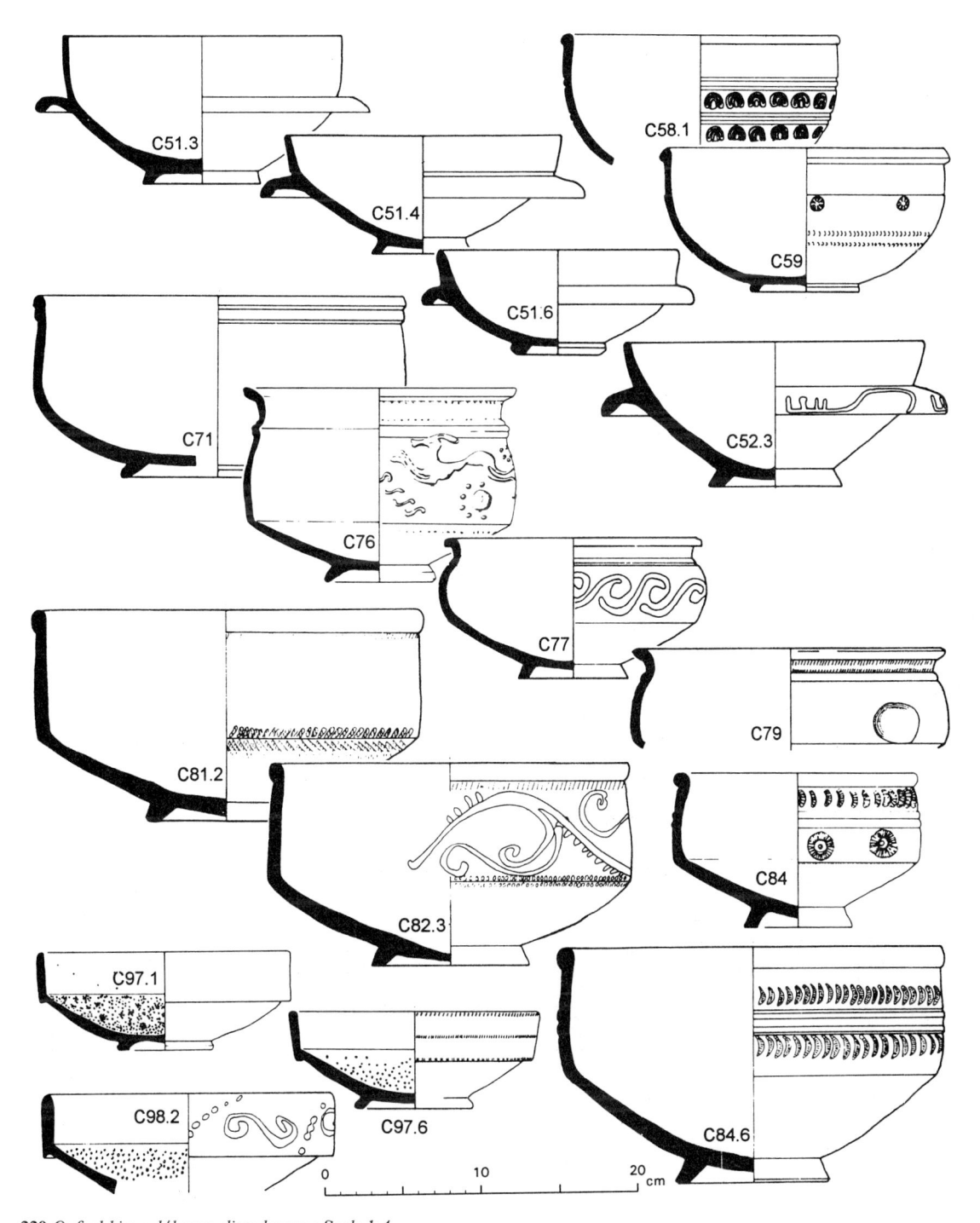

Oxfordshire red/brown-slipped/ROMANO-BRITISH FINE WARES

220 Oxfordshire red/brown-slipped wares: Scale 1:4

of closed forms. Wheel-thrown. Can be soft and powdery, with deteriorating slip, in poor soil conditions, but best examples have high gloss. Commonly decorated with wide variety of techniques, including moulded figures and face masks, bosses and indentations, barbotine, rouletting, stamps and painting.

Forms. Young (1977b) describes the range of forms in this fabric (**table 55**).

Many forms (including many of the commoner types) are

South-east English glazed/ROMANO-BRITISH FINE WARES

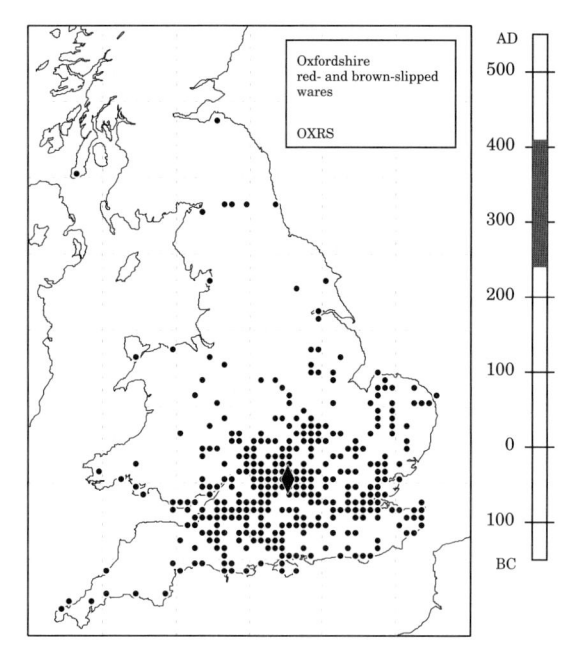

221 Oxfordshire red/brown-slipped wares: overall distribution

derived from late East Gaulish sigillata prototypes, probably by imitation rather than migration of potters (Bird and Young 1981) (**219, 220**).
Stamps. Name-stamps are used on some samian-derived forms (particularly Drag 31 and Drag 36 copies). Most are illiterate combinations of lines and dots, but one reads PATERN (Young 1977b, 176–81).
Chronology. Production of red-slipped wares commences by c. AD 240 and continues until end of 4th cent. Many of the individual forms can be dated more accurately.
Source. The Oxfordshire potteries.
Distribution. Extensive across much of central England, from Severn valley to Thames estuary, by late 3rd cent. Distribution expands and intensifies during 4th cent. Quantified distribution data interpreted by Hodder and Fulford as due to transport costs, but by Millett as result of civitas networks (**221**).
Aliases. *Bath* fabric 6.1. *Caister-on-sea* fabric OXON-50. *Chelmsford* fabric 3. *Colchester* fabric MP. *Dorchester* fabric 18. *Gestingthorpe* fabric A3. *Gloucester* fabric TF12A. *JRPS bibliography* fabrics orc and oxr. *Kent* fine fabric 16a. *Leicester* fabric C13. *Lullingstone* fabric 11. *Milton Keynes* fabric 24. *Sidbury* fabric 29. *Towcester* fabric 13.
Bibliography. Young 1977b; for kilns *RCHM gazetteer* 102–4, F561–73. For relationship with sigillata and derivative industries: Bird and Young 1981; on distribution: Fulford and Hodder 1974; Millett 1990, 171–4.
Notes. Migrant potters from the Oxfordshire industry were responsible for production of red-slipped wares at Hartshill (War.), Harston (Cambs.) and Pevensey (Sussex) during the mid- and late 4th cent. (Bird and Young 1981).
See also. OXMO

Form	Description
C1–C11	Bottles and flagons
C12–C15	Jugs and handled jugs
C16–C19	Jars
C20–C39	Beakers
C40–C96	Bowls
C97–C100	Mortaria
C101–C117	Miniature vessels
C118–C119	Miscellaneous types

Table 55 *Classification of Oxfordshire red/brown-slipped wares (after Young)*

South-east English glazed ware

Fabric and technology. Hard fine fabric; usually grey but occasionally with red-brown margins; silty matrix, slightly micaceous, with occasional iron-rich pellets and mica; surfaces covered with translucent dark-green glaze (e.g. 5YR 4/2-4) which may be over white clay barbotine decoration (which appears light-green or yellow through glaze). Wheel-thrown.

Form	Description	Prototype
1	Pear-shaped flask	
2	Globular beaker with angular shoulder	
3	Globular beaker with everted rim	
5	Cylindrical bowl	Drag 30
7	Hemispherical bowl	Drag 37

Table 56 *Classification of South-east English glazed ware forms (after Arthur)*

Forms. Arthur (1978) identifies 5 principal forms (**table 56**). The imitation samian forms are the most common. Decorative motifs include rows of barbotine circles, lattice, lozenges, dots and vertical lines or hairpins (**222**).
Chronology. Principally AD 70–120.
Source. The large quantities of the ware at Staines suggest one source (see *RCHM gazetteer* F487 for details).
Distribution. Principally the London basin and surrounding counties, with outliers in western Britain (**223**)
Aliases. *Chelmsford* fabric 10. *Kent* fine fabric 22. *Lullingstone* fabric 1. *Milton Keynes* fabric 13a.
Bibliography. Arthur 1978, 298–311.
Notes. Similar wares with mica-dusted or marbled finishes have been identified in the London area, which may be products of the same industry.

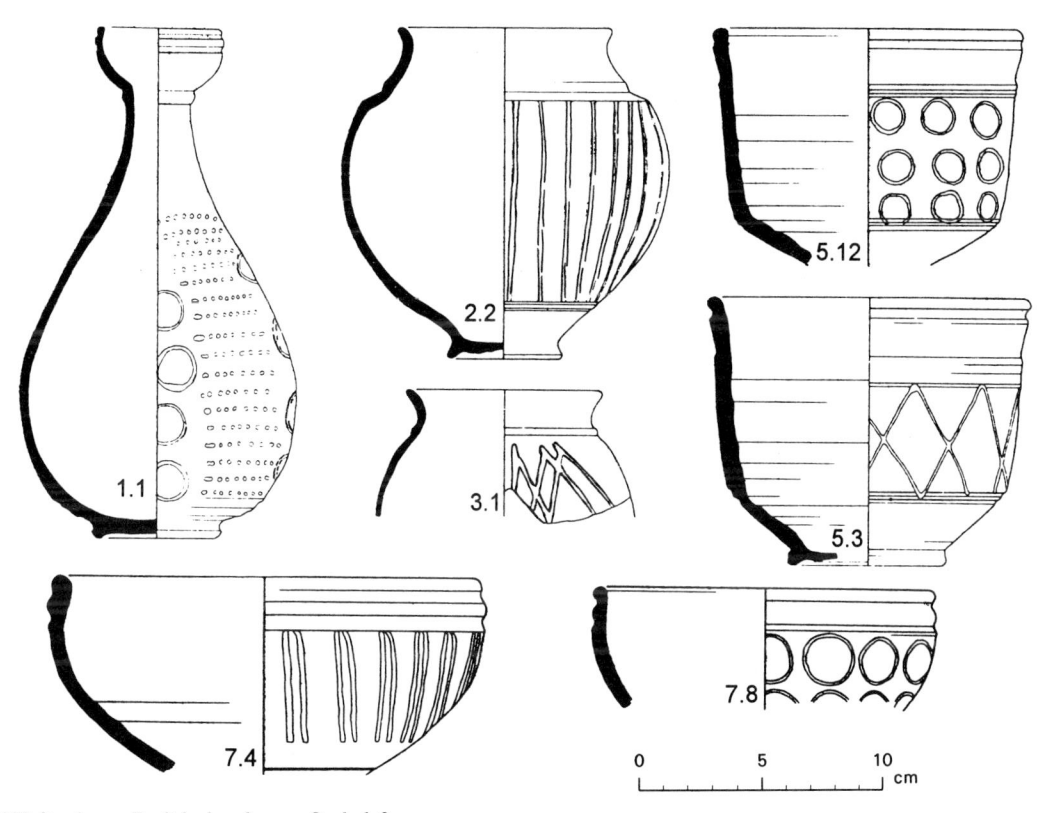

South-east English glazed/ROMANO-BRITISH FINE WARES

222 *South-east English glazed ware: Scale 1:3*

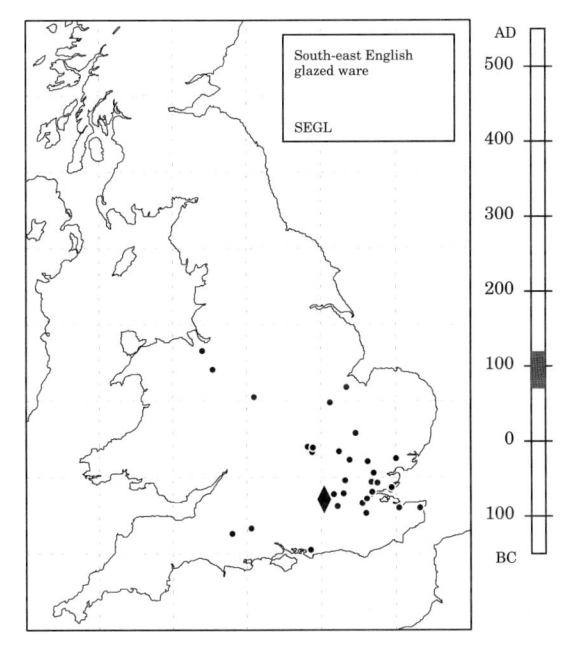

223 *South-east English glazed ware: overall distribution*

ROMANO-BRITISH COARSE WARES

The majority of pottery in most assemblages are locally made coarse wares for food preparation, cooking and storage. The wares selected here include both major regional industries and the products of small potteries. Some, such as black-burnished wares, are highly influential on developments throughout the province (**224**).

224 Romano-British coarse wares: dating of principal classes

In the Atlas pages the wares are ordered alphabetically.

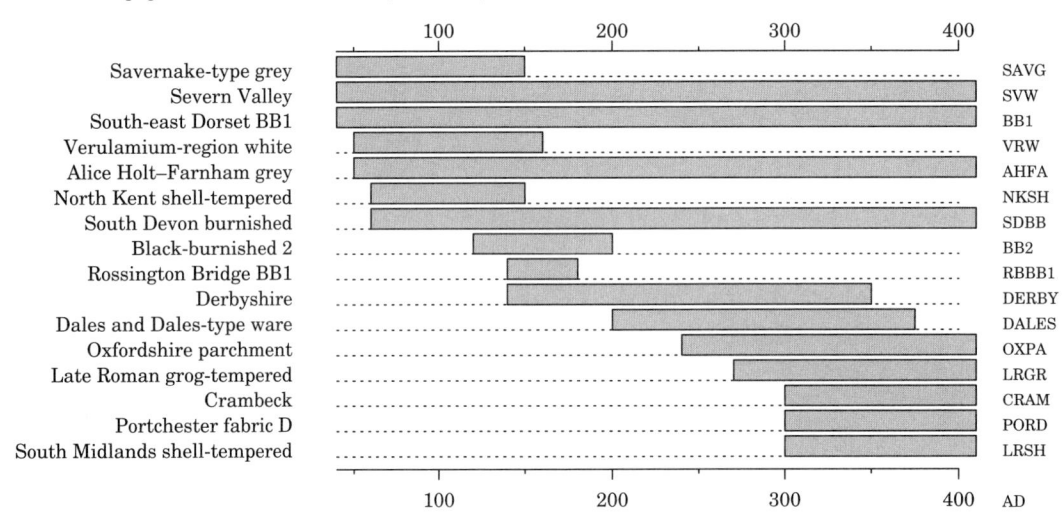

Ware		Code
Savernake-type grey		SAVG
Severn Valley		SVW
South-east Dorset BB1		BB1
Verulamium-region white		VRW
Alice Holt–Farnham grey		AHFA
North Kent shell-tempered		NKSH
South Devon burnished		SDBB
Black-burnished 2		BB2
Rossington Bridge BB1		RBBB1
Derbyshire		DERBY
Dales and Dales-type ware		DALES
Oxfordshire parchment		OXPA
Late Roman grog-tempered		LRGR
Crambeck		CRAM
Portchester fabric D		PORD
South Midlands shell-tempered		LRSH

Alice Holt/Farnham grey wares

Grey wares were produced in the potteries of the Alice Holt/Farnham region throughout the Roman period, production and distribution were most extensive from mid-1st to mid-2nd cent., and from the late 3rd–late 4th cent.

Fabric and technology. Earlier fabrics are hard and rough in texture, with brittle irregular fracture; light grey (e.g. 2.5YR 5/0-6/0) with darker margins and surfaces (2.5YR 2/0-3/0) or may be darker grey throughout; abundant well-sorted quartz (multi-coloured, white and glassy), some fine mica and occasional larger rounded flint inclusions in a silty clay matrix. A rarer variety, with coarse sand temper, is typical of large bead-rim jars. Surfaces burnished externally (and internally on open forms), sometimes in horizontal zones, producing slightly metallic sheen.

From the later 3rd cent. fabrics tend to be hard, dense and smooth textured, decorated with zones of burnishing and combed wavy lines, and zones of slate-grey, white or black slip.

Forms. The earlier assemblage is dominated by necked jars with a carinated shoulder, bead-rim jars and distinctive bowls with moulded lip and cordon or offset half-way down the outer wall known as 'Surrey bowls' or 'Atrebatic bowls'. From the 3rd cent. flanged bowls, dishes and everted-rim jars derived from BB1 prototypes were produced, alongside single-handled jugs and a range of other jar forms (**225**).

Chronology. Production commences by c. AD 50/60 and continues through to end of 4th cent. Chronology of some individual types is disputed, particularly during 3rd cent. (cf. Lyne and Jefferies 1979; Millett 1979a).

Source. The Alice Holt/Farnham region, in the Wey valley on the Surrey–Hampshire border. There is a concentration of c. 80 kilns and waster dumps in an area 2km x 3km in the southern Alice Holt Forest.

Distribution. A major supplier to the London region, Surrey, Hampshire and north Sussex, during the 1st and early 2nd cent., with outliers in the west, as far as Usk and Exeter. Decline from mid-2nd to later 3rd cent. but increased from c. AD 270 to be a major supplier throughout central-southern England and the London region. Occasional examples from beyond, particularly in later 4th-cent. levels (**226**).

Aliases. *Bath* fabric 10.6. *Caister-on-sea* fabric AHF-125. *Chelmsford* fabric 43. *JRPS bibliography* fabric alh. *Kent coarse* fabric 1b. *Lullingstone* fabrics 60 and 61. *Milton Keynes* fabric 31. *Towcester* fabric 31.

Bibliography. Lyne and Jefferies 1979 is the principal recent study of the industry; for kilns: *RCHM gazetteer* F309–21, F623–8. An alternative view of dating of some types, based on the data from local small town of Neatham, is given by Millett 1979a.

See also. PORD

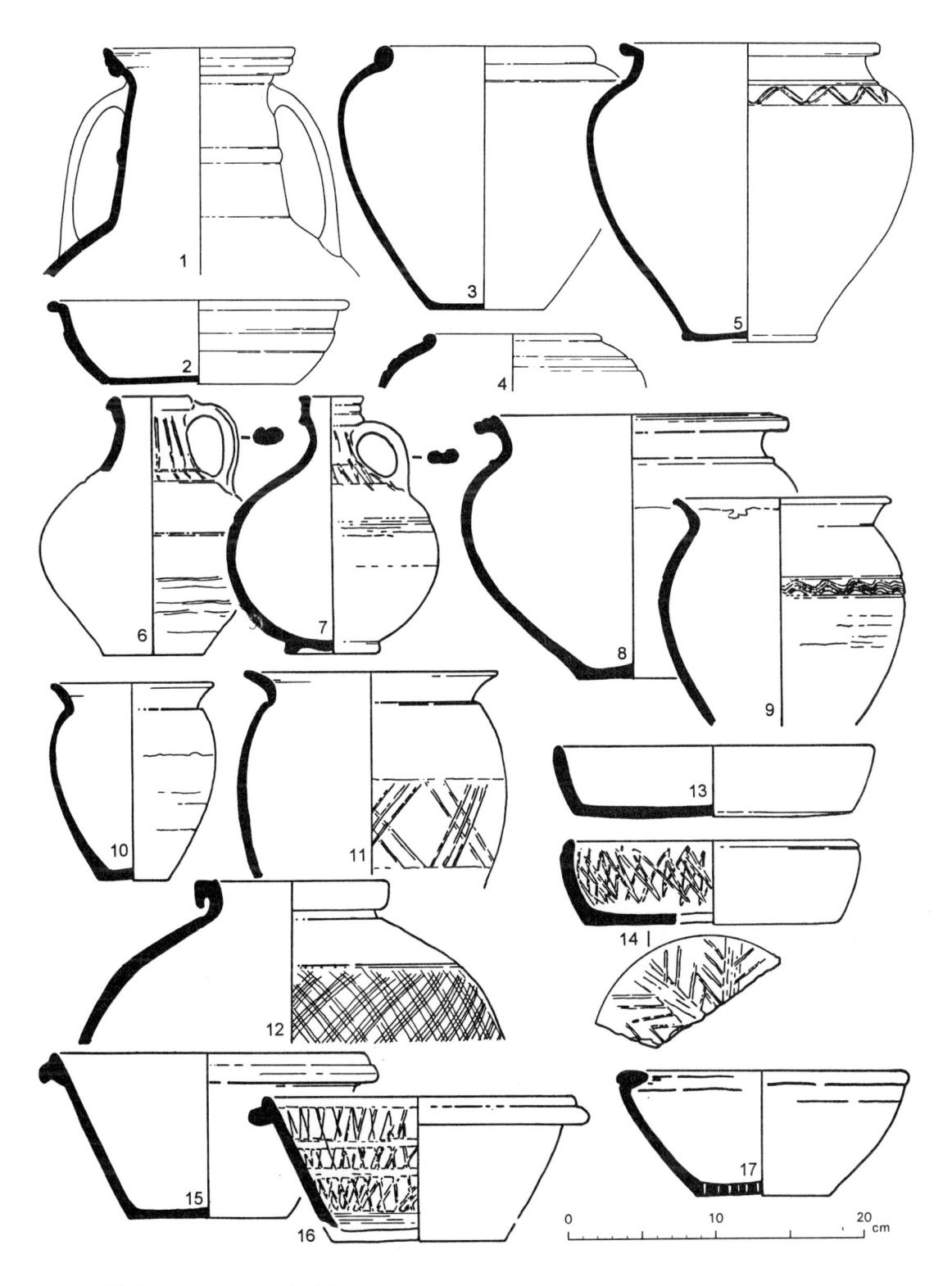

225 *Alice Holt/Farnham grey wares: Scale 1:4*

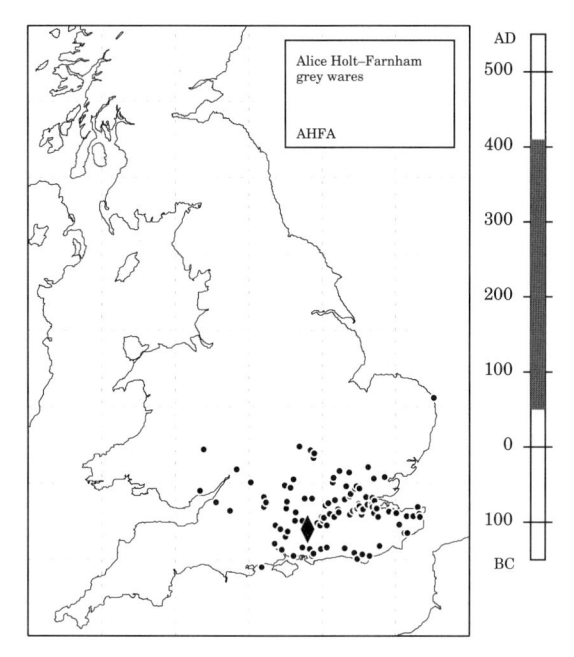

226 Alice Holt/Farnham grey wares: overall distribution

Black-burnished wares

Black or dark-grey cooking pots and bowls, often decorated with burnished lattice decoration, have long been recognized as one of the most significant and widespread elements in Romano-British ceramics from the 2nd cent. onwards. J. P. Gillam published a distribution map of black-burnished wares in 1956 (Gillam 1956, 66) which demonstrated their wide occurrence. However, the significant advance in our understanding of the class came with his description of two distinct varieties of black-burnished wares in the material from Mumrills, in Scotland (Gillam in Steer 1960) which were labelled category 1 and 2 (now universally referred to as black-burnished 1 and 2 and abbreviated to BB1 and BB2). BB1 was a handmade 'gritty' ware, apparently largely from a single source, while BB2 was finer, with a 'silky' texture and wheel-thrown, and included the products of more than one centre. Each group exhibited its own typological characteristics and although the source(s) of neither variety was clear then, the 'cultural' origin of category 1 at least was recognized as lying in the Iron Age pottery of south-western England.

Employing heavy mineral analysis, Peacock (1967b) suggested that BB1 indeed originated in Somerset or Dorset, although the possibility that this ware, a major component of the assemblage in the northern frontier zone, originated in the remote south-west was not received very enthusiastically at the time. The whole problem of the sources of BB1 and BB2 was considered in a major paper by Farrar (1973) and a program of petrological analysis by Williams (1977). BB1 was confirmed as (in large part) the product of a single major industry in south-east Dorset (the Wareham–Poole Harbour area), while BB2, always a looser group, seemed to originate around the Thames estuary. However, it was also clear that some material classifiable as 'BB1' was produced in the north-east, in particular at Rossington Bridge (Yorks.), and in the south-west a number of other 'black-burnished' wares in addition to the principal Wareham–Poole Harbour fabric were circulating. The extent and abundance of these secondary fabrics were unclear at this time.

More recently there have been major studies of the production, typology and chronology of BB1 in the south-west by Holbrook and Bidwell (1991), Seager Smith (in Woodward, Davies and Graham 1993) and Hearne (in Hearne and Smith 1992).

For BB2, the situation is complex. It is apparent that vessels in the black-burnished style were grafted on to many of existing grey-ware industries in the Thames estuary region, but only a selection of these products found their way to the northern frontier where they formed the basis of the original definition of BB2. Attempting to turn this classification back on itself and apply the categories defined at the consumption sites on to the material at its source is at best difficult and at worst misleading. The decision as to whether a particular vessel in southern Britain should be classed as BB2, an 'imitation BB2' or a 'grey ware imitation' is thus coloured by the 'filtering' mechanisms associated with the shipping of goods from the south-east to the north, and the value of 'BB2' as a separate fabric in southern Britain is doubtful – it is a style rather than a ware. Nevertheless, attempts to define separate fabrics and sources within the BB2 group have met with some success and the increasing knowledge of the kiln assemblages from the region will assist in this task.

South-east Dorset black-burnished 1

Fabric and technology. Hard, granular dark-grey or black (2.5YR 3/0–4/0) fabric (occasionally with lighter grey or buff patches); abundant well-sorted translucent quartz (giving distinctive 'cod's roe' fracture) and occasional rounded shale fragments, red and black iron ores and flint, and a little white mica.

Surfaces burnished or smoothed (1st–2nd cent.) or slipped and burnished or wiped (3rd-4th cent.). On closed forms (jars) only outer surface burnished, frequently with decorated (e.g. burnished lattice) band across middle of body; inner surfaces untreated or coarsely wiped, but burnished down inside of everted rims. Both inner and outer surfaces treated on open forms (dishes, bowls). Burnishing frequently shiny, showing individual strokes, but sometimes highly polished and glossy. Slip often difficult to distinguish, but sometimes clear drip-marks visible – some vessels perhaps 'self-slipped'. Hand-formed. (Photographs of BB1 fabric in Farrar 1973, pl. I–V.)

Black-burnished 1/ROMANO-BRITISH COARSE WARES

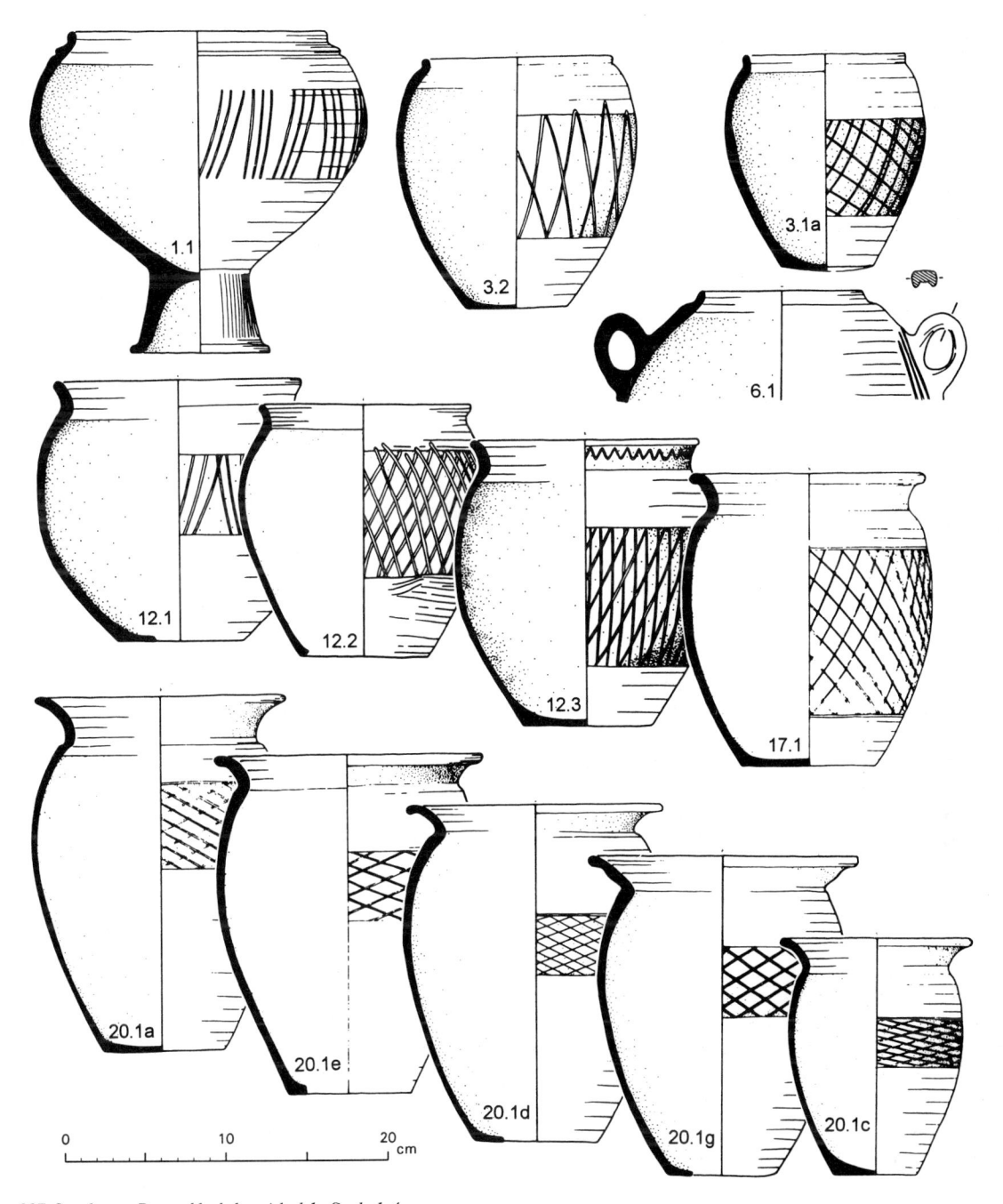

227 *South-east Dorset black-burnished 1: Scale 1:4*

Forms. Bewildering variety of forms apparent at kiln sites and in some south-western assemblages, including copies of Gallo-Belgic plates and bowls, cups, folded beakers, flagons and jugs, *paterae*, candlesticks and ceramic table legs. However, the principal types (and mainstay of the export market) are jars, bowls and dishes (**227, 228, table 57**):

Chronology. Derived from pre-Roman Durotrigian ceramic traditions; production of pottery in Poole Harbour region may commence in middle Iron Age (Holbrook and Bidwell 1991, 90). Production continues until late 4th cent. but with fluctuating distribution pattern (see below).

Gillam (1976) proposed a sequence of constant and even –

Black-burnished 1/ROMANO-BRITISH COARSE WARES

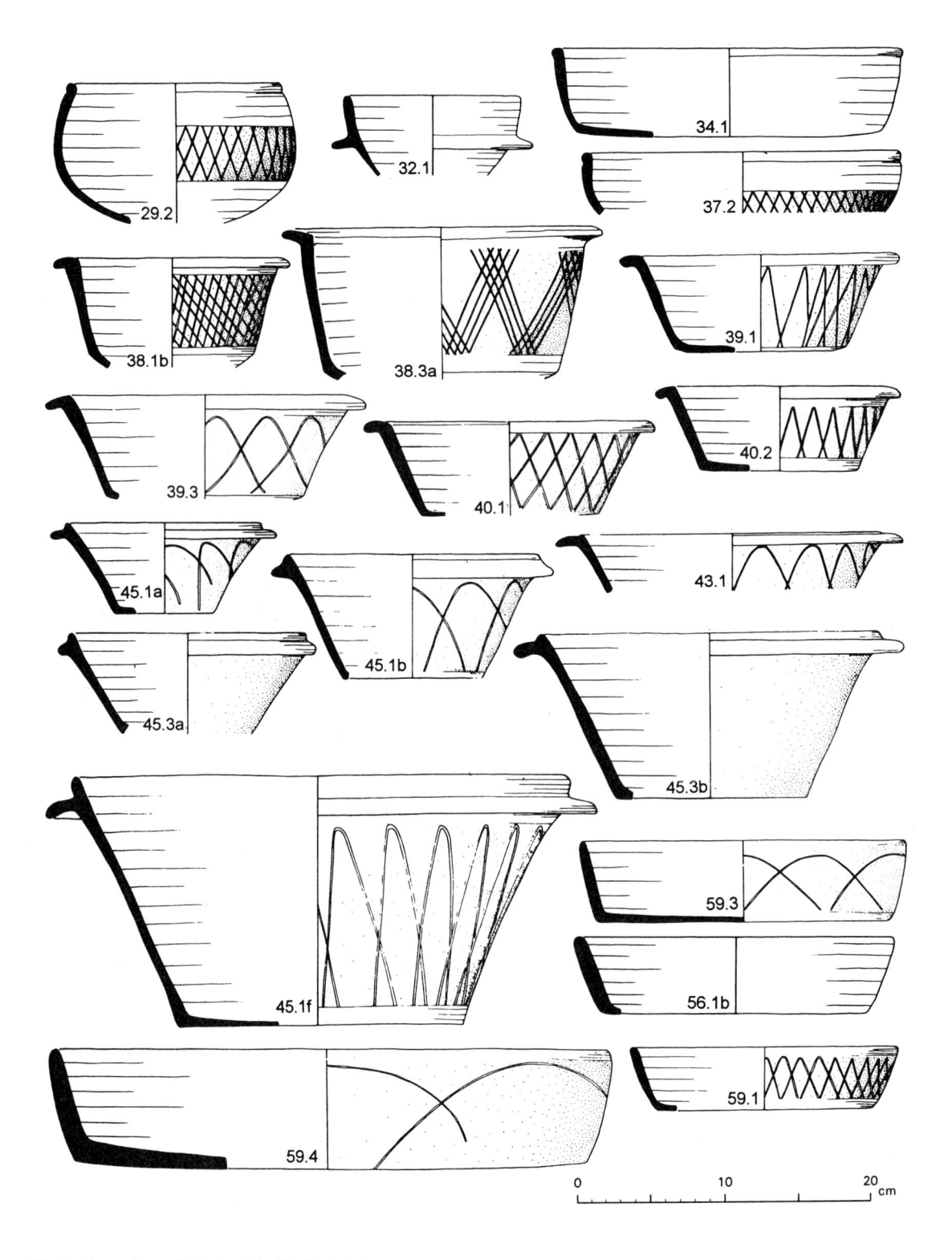

228 *South-east Dorset black-burnished 1: Scale 1:4*

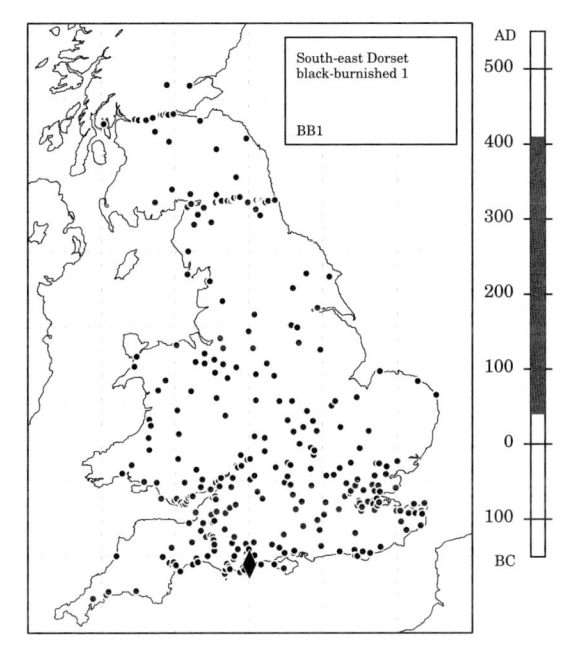

Black-burnished 1/ROMANO-BRITISH COARSE WARES

229 South-east Dorset black-burnished 1: overall distribution

almost mechanical – changes in the principal forms. Subsequent reassessments have suggested periods of relative stasis interspersed by more rapid typological change (Farrar 1981; Holbrook and Bidwell 1991, 94–114). The general sequence is reasonably clear. The everted-rim cooking pots become progressively more slender and the rims move from vertical to become splayed and flared. The decorated lattice band becomes narrower and the angle of intersection of the burnished lines changes from acute to obtuse, with the cross-over point at c. AD 200 and fully obtuse lattice by c. AD 220. In the bowls, the flat-rimmed variant develops by c. AD 120 and the bowl with flat rim and groove dates from late 2nd until mid-3rd cent. AD. The conical flanged bowl probably develops c. AD 250 and, with the obtuse latticed cooking pot, dominates the later assemblage.

Source. The Wareham/Poole Harbour region of south-east Dorset. The petrology of the fabric (D. F. Williams 1977, group I) and the discovery of kiln sites (e.g. Hearne and Smith 1992) confirm the source.

Distribution. Present on pre-Flavian military sites in Dorset and Devon and in Flavian–Trajanic assemblages in the south-west, lower Severn valley and south Wales. Major expansion c. AD 120, when BB1 appears in northern Britain in levels associated with construction of Hadrian's Wall (Holbrook and Bidwell 1991, 92). Appears in south-east at this time (e.g. in London Hadrianic fire deposits) although initially in only small quantities. Major contributor to assemblages in Midlands, south-east and north during 3rd cent. but declining from early to mid-4th cent. (losing northern markets to east Yorkshire grey wares). Distribution retreats to south-west and lower Severn valley and some other coastal sites by later 4th cent. Some small-scale exports to northern France, particularly Normandy and Brittany, during the later 3rd/4th cent. (Pilet 1987; Fulford 1991, fig. 5.7) (**229**).

Aliases. *Bath* fabric 10.3. *Caister-on-sea* fabrics BB1-100 and BB1G-101. *Carlisle* fabric 104. *Chelmsford* fabric 40. *Cirencester* fabrics 49 and 74. *Colchester* fabric GA. *Dorchester* fabric 1. *Exeter* fabric 31. *Gloucester* fabric TF4. *JRPS bibliography* fabric bb1. *Kent* coarse fabric 3. *Lullingstone* fabric 65. *Milton Keynes* fabric 8. *Old Penrith* fabric 43. *Portchester* fabric B. *Sidbury* fabric 22. *Towcester* fabric 15.

Bibliography. For background to study of BB1: Farrar 1973; petrology: D. F. Williams 1977. BB1 in the south-west: Holbrook and Bidwell 1991, 88–114; Woodward, Davies and Graham 1993, 249-58. Kiln assemblages and firing technology: Hearne and Smith 1992; Woodward 1987. For chronology of principal types: Holbrook and Bidwell 1991; Bidwell 1985. *RCHM gazetteer* F259–64.

Type	Description
1	Pedestalled bowls
2–3	Barrel-shaped bead-rim jars
4	Single-handled beakers
5–6	Double-strap-handled beakers
11–20	Cooking pots
23–24	Jars with countersunk-lug handles
29–30	Bead-rim bowls
31	Imitation Drag 37
32.1	Imitation Drag 38
32.2	Imitation *Cam* 58
33–37	Bowls with beaded and plain rims
38–42	Flat-rimmed bowls
43–46	Bowls with flat-grooved rims
56–59	Plain-rimmed dish
61	Handled oval 'fish' dish
62–63	Handled dish

Table 57 *Classification of South-east Dorset BB1 forms (after Holbrook and Bidwell)*

Notes. In addition to the main south-east Dorset production, BB1 style pottery was manufactured at other centres in the south-west, in some cases probably by potters migrating from the Poole Harbour workshops. Some fabrics can be distinguished in the hand-specimen, but others require petrological analysis. Some of these wares (e.g. *South-western BB1*) have also been identified in the north, while others seem to be of purely local significance (Woodward, Davies and Graham 1993, 249–50). The extent and significance of BB1 production in the Brue valley, Somerset, as suggested by

Black-burnished 2/ROMANO-BRITISH COARSE WARES

Farrar (1973, 93–4) but largely discounted by Williams (1977, 192–3) remains unclear (Holbrook and Bidwell 1991, 90). Production of BB1 at Rossington Bridge, Yorkshire, was almost certainly in the hands of migrant Dorset potters, but the extent of the industry remains unclear.

The flanged bowl and everted-rim cooking pot – ultimately derived from BB1 prototypes – become the dominant forms in most coarse-ware industries throughout the province during the later 3rd/4th cent. AD.
See also. RBBB1 BB2

Rossington Bridge BB1
Fabric and technology. A hard sandy ware; dark grey (rather than black) with a slight lustre; less sand temper and burnished decoration has thinner lines than Dorset BB1. Hand-formed.
Forms. Everted-rim jars and pie-dishes (**230**).

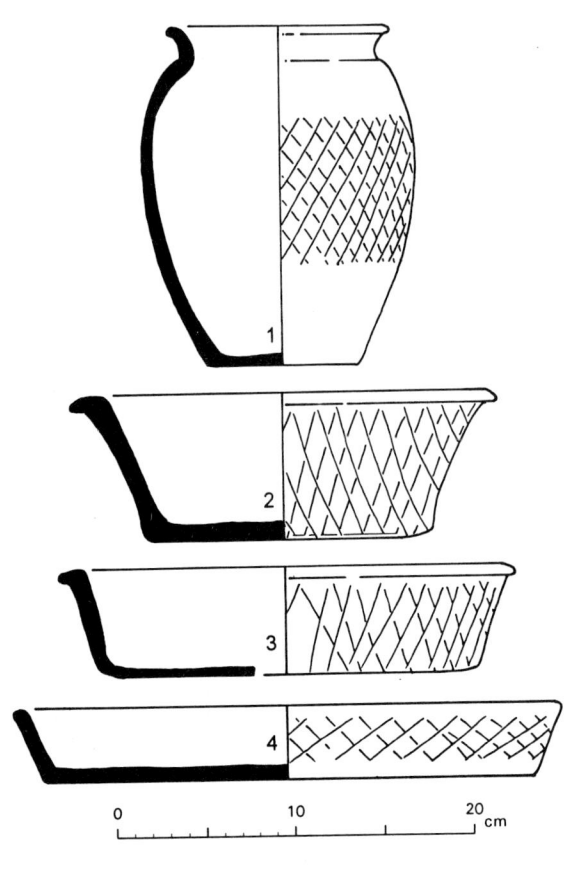

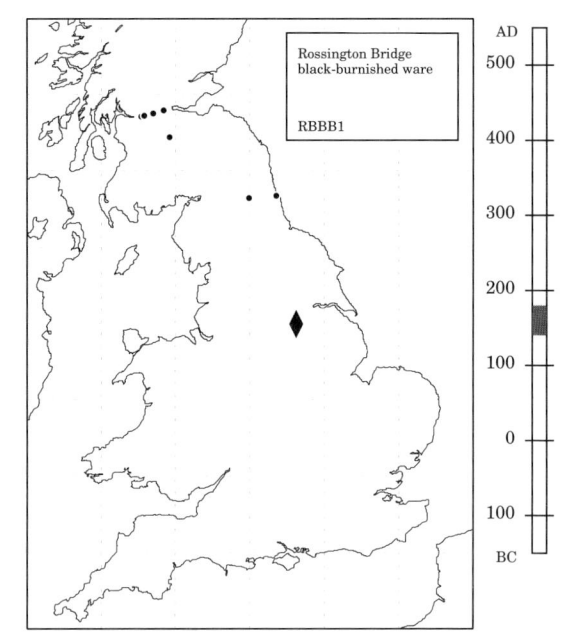

231 Rossington Bridge BB1: overall distribution

nition, but occurs on Antonine Wall and Scottish forts, and Corbridge (**231**).
Bibliography. For kilns: *RCHM gazetteer* F703-4; Buckland, Magilton and Dolby 1980; Buckland 1986, 42–9; for petrology and fabric: D. F. Williams 1977, group II; for distribution: Williams in MacIvor, Thomas and Breeze 1981, 257.
See also. RBMO BB1

Black-burnished 2
Farrar (1973) concluded that the BB2 of the north originated at a number of sites around the Thames estuary, and Williams (1977) subsequently indicated that the petrology suggested Colchester as a major source of the northern assemblage. However, substantial BB2 production assemblages have not yet been identified at Colchester and apparently similar material is present on other Thames-side sites. The principal Hadrianic–Antonine BB2 fabric at London (described below) is apparently identical to the commonest Colchester BB2 fabric, but also very similar to that from some north Kent kiln sites.
Fabric and technology. Hard, sandy fabric, varying in colour from dark grey or black with a brown or reddish-brown core and a reddish-brown, blue-grey, black or lighter ('pearly grey') surface; very finely burnished with a characteristic 'silky' texture; abundant quartz inclusions and some black iron and mica set in a silty matrix. Wheel-thrown.
Forms. Everted-rim jars, bowls and dishes. Jars and bowls have a lattice-decorated band across the body and dishes may have a single horizontal wavy line. The detail of form and

230 Rossington Bridge BB1: Scale 1:4

Chronology. Antonine.
Source. Rossington Bridge (Yorks.). Manufactured alongside the mortarium workshops of Sarrius, probably by migrants (willing or otherwise) from Dorset BB1 industry.
Distribution. Full extent unclear due to difficulties of recog-

232 Black-burnished 2: Scale 1:4

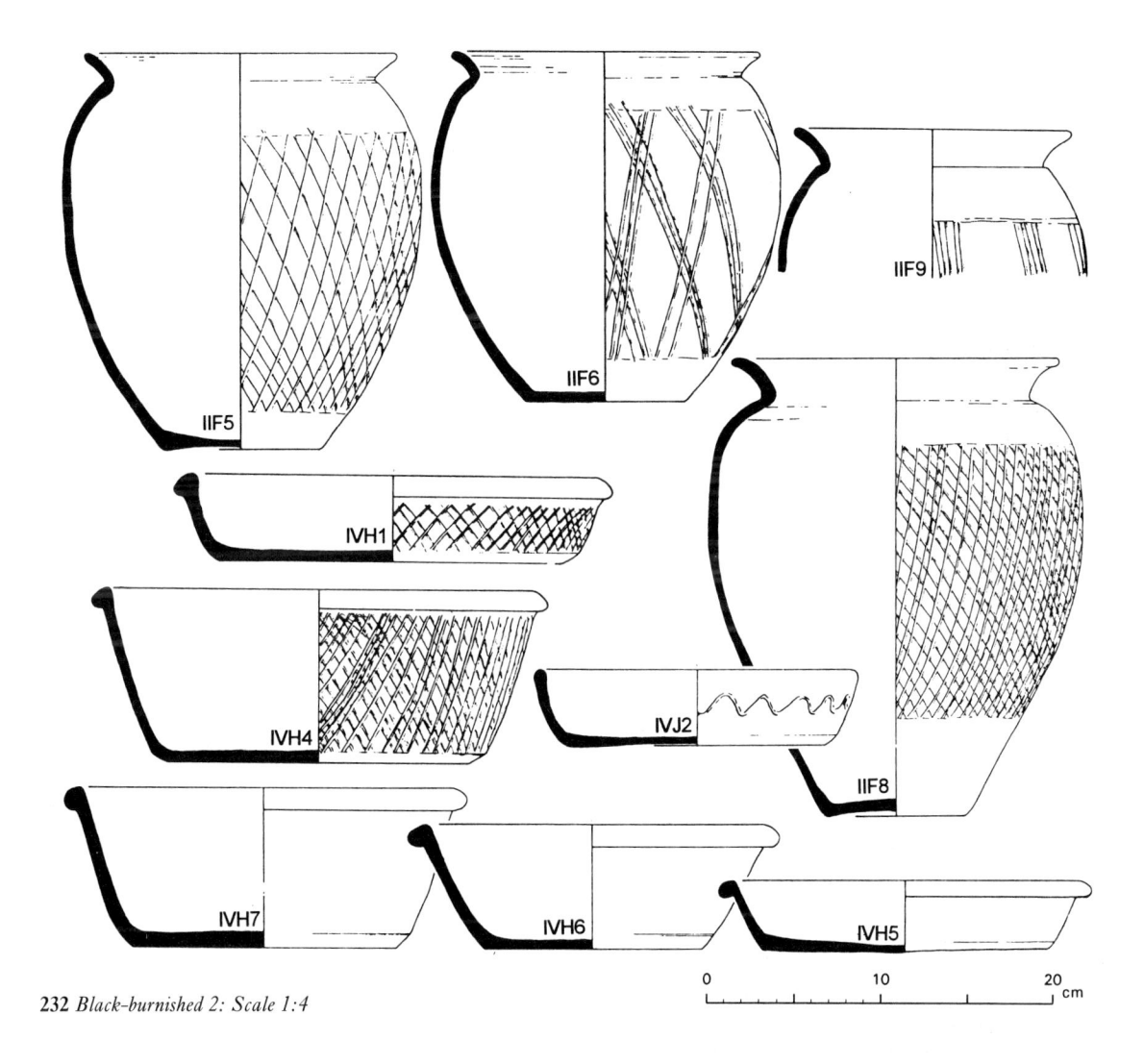

decorative motifs in the assemblage from the north seems more restricted than that from sites in the south-east (**232**).
Chronology. BB2 appears in small quantity below Hadrianic fire levels in London, but no evidence for production much before AD 120 and development of the style in the south-east seems to coincide with the expansion of the distribution of BB1 at that date. The fabric is common throughout the Antonine period.
Source. Colchester, or north Kent.
Distribution. The distribution of this BB2 fabric (as opposed to the other black-burnished wheel-thrown wares which are known to be circulating) in the south-east has not been defined, and is under-recorded on the map (**233**). The general style is abundant in Kent, the London area, Hertfordshire and Essex. In the north BB2 is particularly characteristic of Antonine Wall deposits.

Aliases. Caister-on-sea fabric BB2-102. Carlisle fabric 316. Chelmsford fabric 41. Colchester fabric GB. *JRPS* bibliography fabric bb2. Kent coarse fabric 4. Old Penrith fabric 44.
Bibliography. Farrar 1973; D. F. Williams 1977, group XII. The current state of BB2 studies is discussed by Monaghan 1987a, 171–2; Pollard 1988, 87–91. Monaghan lists 'BB2' fabrics examined in the north and notes possible sources in the south-east (ibid., 256–7).
Notes. From the later 2nd cent. a new range of everted-rim jars and undecorated bowls in finer-textured steely-grey sandy wares (from sources in Essex or Kent) displace the coarser-textured 'Colchester' fabric. These are important local suppliers throughout the 3rd cent. AD (Darling 1993, 207–8), and there is some trade up the east coast to the northern frontier (e.g. B. Richardson 1986, 127; Bidwell and Speak 1994).

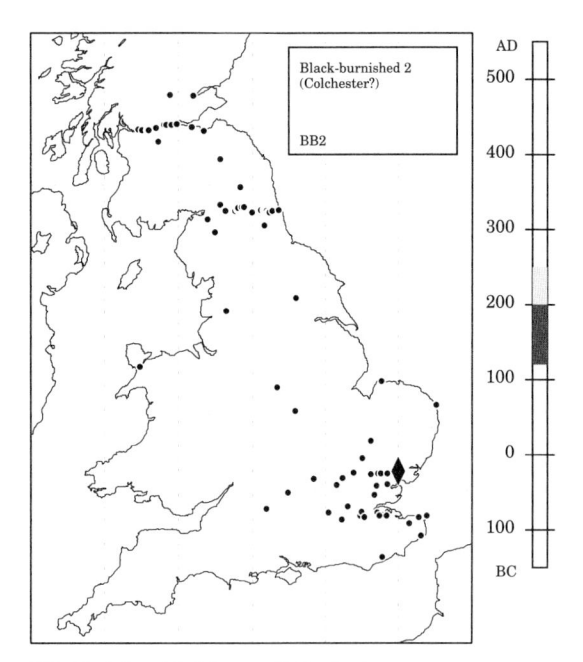

233 Black-burnished 2: overall distribution

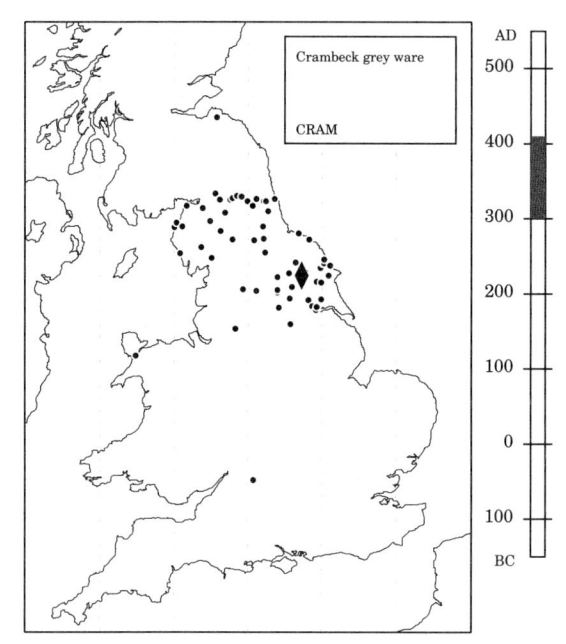

234 Crambeck wares: overall distribution

See also. BB1

Crambeck wares

Fabric and technology. Three distinctive fabrics:

Grey ware: a hard fine-textured fabric; very pale grey core (sometimes almost white) with medium grey surfaces; abundant inclusions of fine quartz sand. Frequent smooth wheel-burnishing on surfaces. Wheel-thrown.

'Parchment' ware: a variable group of hard, brittle, white, buff (through to yellow or orange) fabrics with a laminar fracture; abundant fine sand tempering. Frequent orange- or brown-painted decoration. Iron slag grits on the mortaria.

Red ware: soft fabric with orange core and burnished orange-red surfaces; variable quantities of sand and soft red-brown inclusions.

Forms. The principal forms (**235**) are classified by Corder (1937) (**table 58**).

Chronology. Production commences by early 4th cent. and continues until end of Roman period. Major expansion from mid-4th cent.

Source. Crambeck (Yorks.), which is on the south side of the Howardian Hills, overlooking the Vale of York.

Distribution. The grey ware is the most abundant Crambeck fabric, but both 'parchment' and red ware are found in smaller quantities. Distributed across north-east England during the early to mid-4th cent., but principal market is Malton-York region. Increasing penetration of markets in north-west from *c.* AD 360–70. Small quantities as far as Caernarfon (N. Wales), but distributio to south of Crambeck always restricted. Evans (in Wilson 1989) discusses Crambeck distribution pattern and rehearses arguments for military contracts and social constraints (**234**).

Aliases. Carlisle fabrics 101 and 105. *JRPS bibliography* fabric cra.

Bibliography. Wilson 1989 collects together original reports on the kilns. *RCHM gazetteer* F693–8.

Type	Description	Fabric
1	flanged bowl	G
2	shallow-sided dish	G
3	jar with 2 countersunk handles	G
4	deep wide-mouthed bowl	G
5	hemispherical flanged bowl	GPR
6	hammerhead mortarium	P
7	wall-sided mortarium	P
8	wall-sided mortarium – with double flanged rim	P
9	small bowl with upright rim	P
10	large dish	P
11	small jar/beaker	G
12	beaker	G
13	small bowl.	G
14	bottle or flagon	G
15	jug with pinched spout	G
16	calcite-gritted cooking pot	

Fabric codes: G=grey, P=parchment, R=red.

Table 58 *Classification of Crambeck ware forms (after Corder)*

Crambeck/ROMANO-BRITISH COARSE WARES

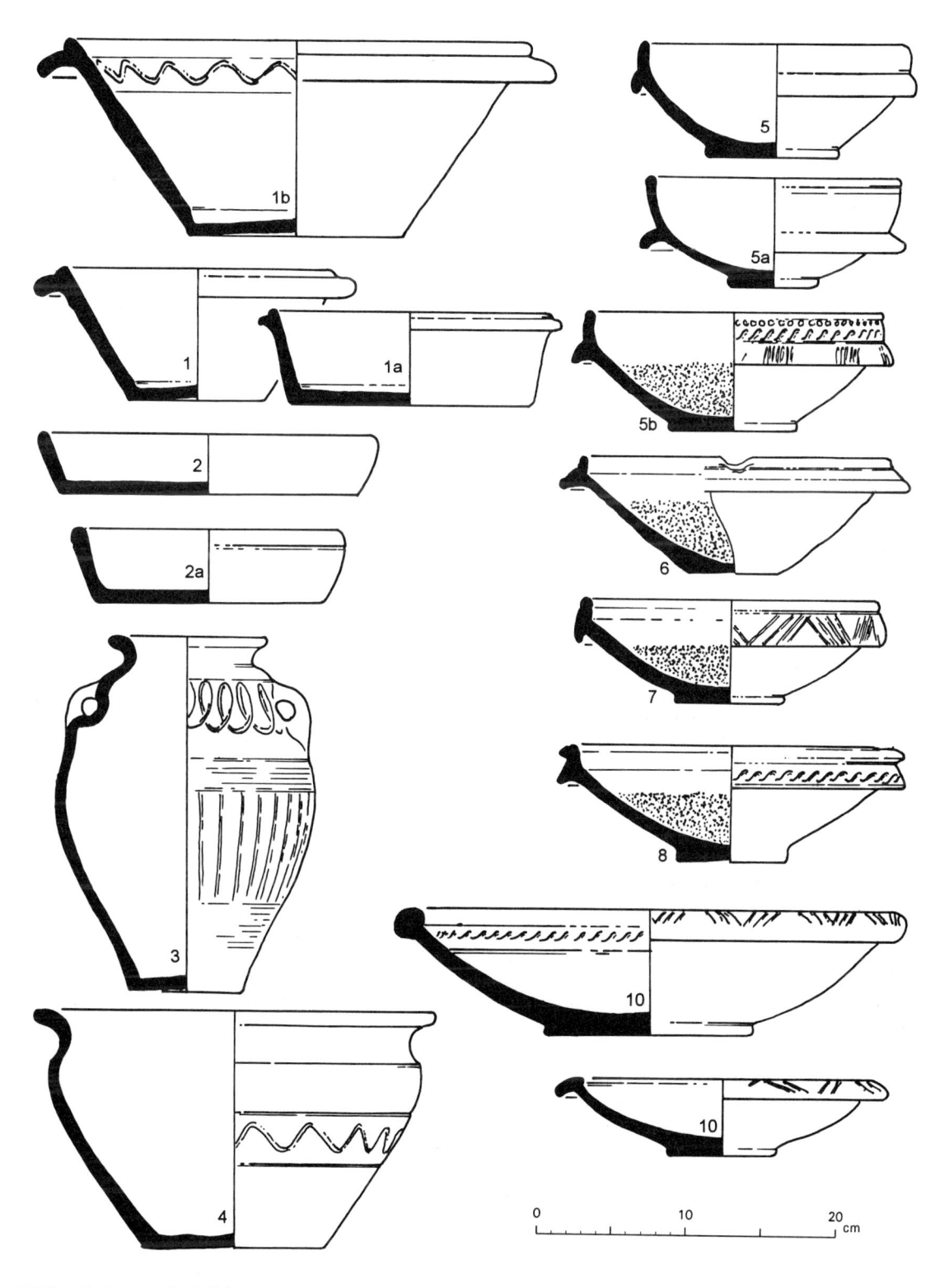

235 Crambeck wares: Scale 1:4

Dales and Dales-type/ROMANO-BRITISH COARSE WARES

Dales ware and Dales-type ware

Forms. Jars with very characteristic rim form, which springs from the shoulder towards a thickened upper lip with inward-sloping top and small sharp internal ridge. *Gillam* 157 (**236**).

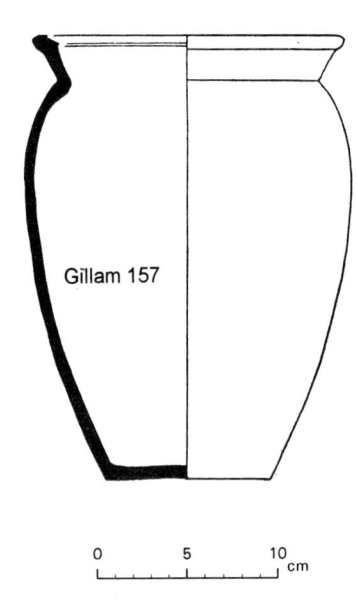

236 *Dales ware and Dales-type ware: Scale 1:4*

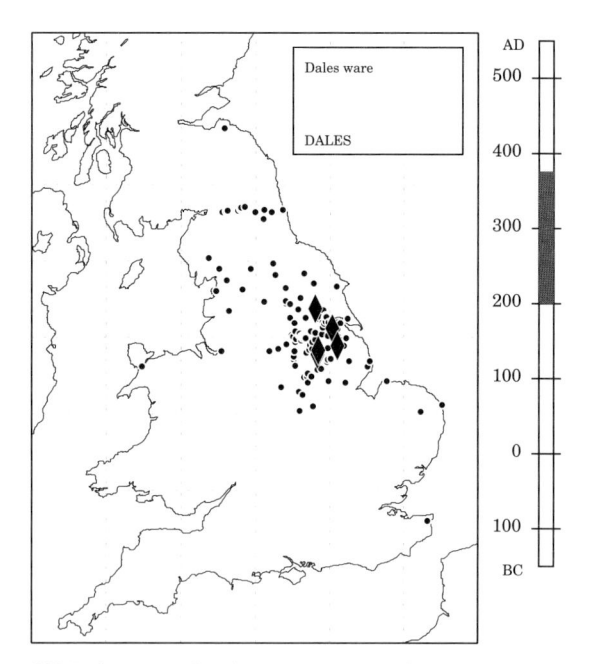

237 *Dales ware and Dales-type ware: overall distribution*

Fabric and technology. The distinctive Dales ware jar form is found in two fabrics – the 'classic' shell-tempered ware and a range of grey sandy wares:

Dales ware: coarse grey, black or brown fabric; tempered with abundant (fossil) shell (sometimes leached out leaving a pitted surface). Irregular finger indentations around the lower body, but generally smoothed towards shoulder and over rim and lip. Hand-formed. In addition to the classic jar form, some larger diameter 'storage jars', dishes, flanged-bowls and lids have been recorded in this ware (Rigby in Stead 1976, 189).

Dales-type ware: several grey sandy fabrics. Wheel-thrown.

Chronology. The classic form probably emerged by the later 2nd cent.; the period of major export to the north, as form *Gillam* 157, is *c.* AD 250–340. The form has blended with other moulded-rim jar forms by later 4th cent.

Source. Firman (1991) suggests that the source of Dales ware lies in the seleniferous clays of Lincolnshire and south Humberside. Dales-type grey-ware jars were produced at several sites in Lincolnshire, Humberside and Yorkshire, alongside a wide range of other coarse-ware types.

Distribution. Abundant in Lincolnshire, Humberside and south Yorkshire (up to 40 per cent of all jars at Doncaster: Loughlin 1977, 129, n. 35); otherwise a thin but wide spread across northern England as far as the Wall. A scatter down the east coast, ending at Richborough (Bushe-Fox 1928, no. 147; Pollard 1988, 24) (**237**).

Aliases. Caister-on-sea fabric SHDW-151. *JRPS bibliography* fabric dal. *Kent* coarse fabric 7. *Leicester* fabric CG1C.

Bibliography. Original study in Gillam 1951b; major reassessment (definition of Dales-type) and distributional studies by Loughlin 1977; on dating in the north: Bidwell 1985, 177; for petrology of Dales ware: Firman 1991. For kilns producing Dales-type jars see *RCHM gazetteer* F443–5, F451–2, F465, F678–80.

Notes. Dales ware has generally been thought to derive from indigenous Iron Age antecedents, although the exact line of descent is difficult to demonstrate. An alternative possibility is that the form derives from continental prototypes. At York, jars with flat-topped rims resembling the Dales ware form in grey wares may be local products of the second half of the 2nd cent. (Gillam in Wenham 1968, 66–8). Potters working in a Mediterranean-inspired tradition, producing 'Eboracum' wares, were operating in York during the 2nd and early 3rd cent. AD (Perrin 1981, 58–60; Monaghan 1993, 705–9) and the distinctive Dales ware rim form strongly resembles that of coarse-ware jars from the western Mediterranean (e.g. Pellecuer and Pomaredes 1991, 369, fig. 4, from Languedoc; Swan 1994, 8–9).

Derbyshire ware

Fabric and technology. Extremely hard, gritty fabric with pimply surface ('like goose-flesh petrified'); varies from buff, through brick-red to dark blue-grey or purple; abundant sand tempering. Surfaces generally unsmoothed, with prominent whorl-marks on base. Wheel-thrown.

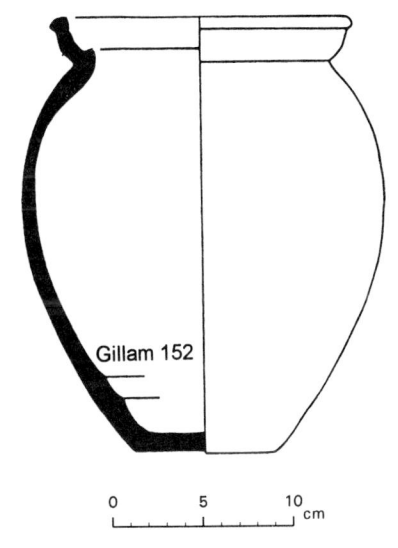

Late Roman grog-tempered/ROMANO-BRITISH COARSE WARES

with distinctive tall kiln structures (Swan 1984, 124–6), perhaps for high-firing temperatures.
Distribution. Abundant on sites in Derbyshire (up to 40 per cent by sherd count at Little Chester), with a scatter in northern frontier zone, including Carpow, and occasional specimens from Wales (P. V. Webster 1970). Bowls and dishes have more local distribution (**239**).
Aliases. JRPS bibliography fabric drb.
Bibliography. Description and sources: Gillam 1939; Kay 1962; G. D. B. Jones and Webster 1969; for kilns: *RCHM gazetteer* F246, F252–5.

Late Roman grog-tempered wares

Fabric and technology. A variety of fabrics, but generally grey, brown or black with frequent inclusions of grog, sand, and occasionally flint and shell; facet-burnished or wiped surfaces, often with 'soapy' finish. Sometimes decorated with lattice or other lines or strokes. Hand-formed.
Forms. Forms follow the common late Roman black-burnished derived models, with flanged bowls, dishes and everted rim jars (**table 59, 240**).

Form	Portchester	Kent
Bowl	86	205–207
Dish	107	204
Jar	123	208–211

Table 59 *Classification of Late Roman grog-tempered forms (after Fulford and Pollard)*

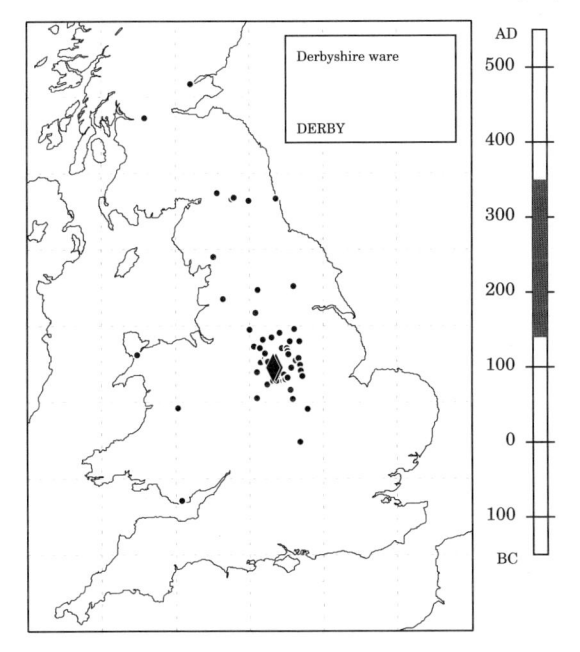

238 Derbyshire ware: Scale 1:4

Forms. Typical form is jar with deep 'bell-mouthed' rim (Kay 1962, type A) or rolled rim (Kay type B). Earlier specimens tend to have more lightly moulded rims, but this develops to deeply dished form by mid-3rd cent., *Gillam 152*. Bowls and dishes also known in same ware (**238**).
Chronology. Production commences by mid-2nd cent., but 'pre-Derbyshire' prototypes at Derby Racecourse kilns from early 2nd cent. Largely 3rd cent. in the north.
Source. Several kilns site in the Holbrook/Hazelwood region,

239 Derbyshire ware: overall distribution

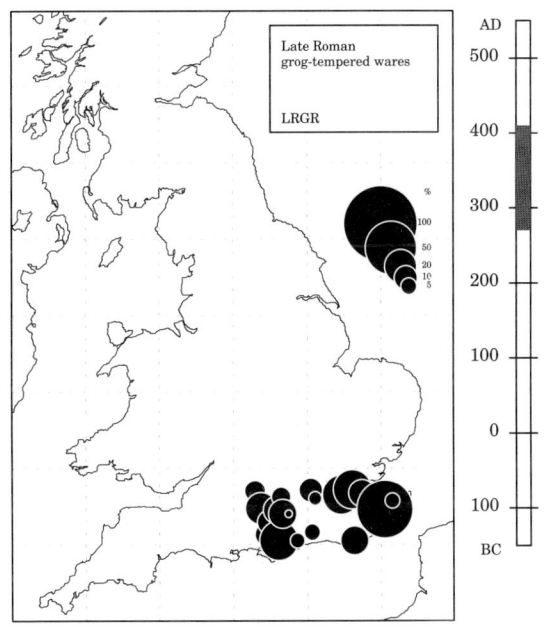

240 Late Roman grog-tempered wares: overall distribution

191

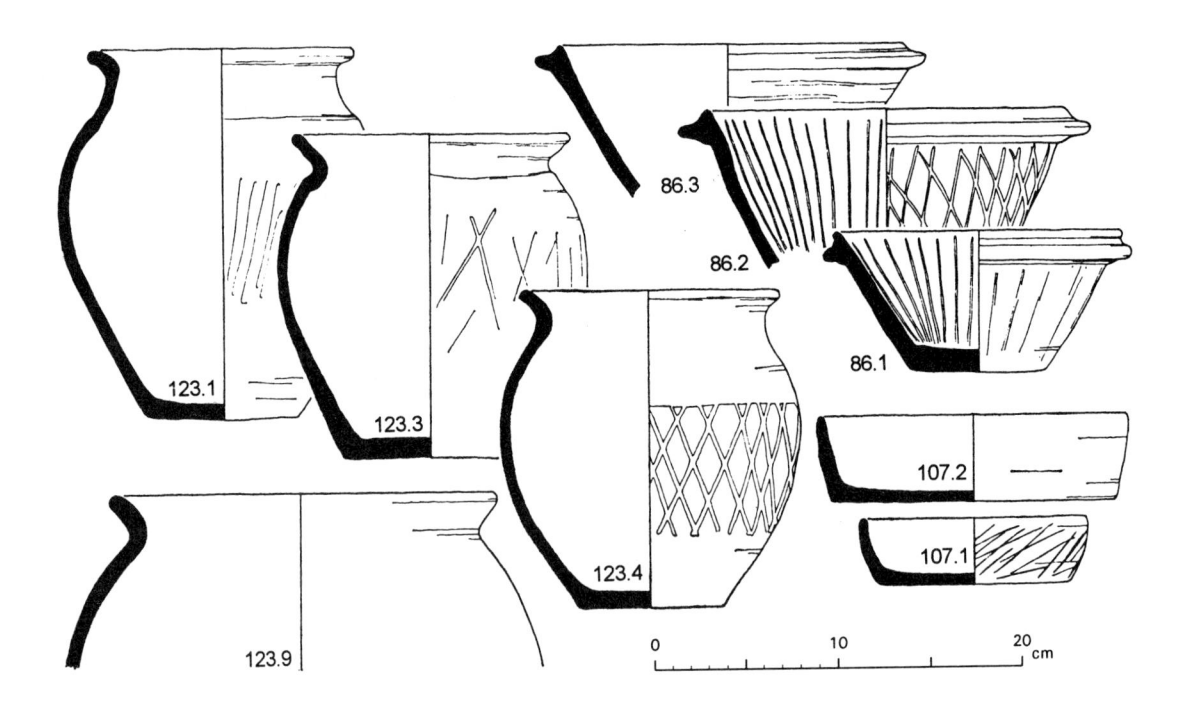

South Midlands shell-tempered/ROMANO-BRITISH COARSE WARES

241 Late Roman grog-tempered wares: Scale 1:4

Chronology. From late 3rd cent. until the end of the Roman period.
Source. A number of sources; the Wessex and Kent material is generally distinguishable, but no kiln sites are known.
Distribution. Hampshire, Sussex, the London region and Kent. High proportions (up to 90 per cent) in some late 4th-cent. contexts in Kent (**240**).
Aliases. *Kent* coarse fabric 11b. *Lullingstone* fabric 66. *Portchester* fabric A.
Bibliography. Fulford 1975b, 286-92; Pollard 1988, 129, 149-50. Quantified data in Pomel 1984.

South Midlands shell-tempered wares

Fabric and technology. Fairly hard, slightly soapy fabric with irregular texture; dark grey or black core with brown or grey margins and black to light brown surfaces (frequently patchy); abundant fine or medium flakes of shell (most < 1mm, but rarely up to 3mm), with occasional fine black and red iron ores and white mica, and rare coarse flint and limestone particles. Wheel-thrown. Surfaces smoothed, and often with horizontal rilling. The shell dissolves out in acid soils leaving a brittle fabric with pitted surface, occasionally described as 'vesiculated ware'.
Forms. Principally necked jars, flanged bowls and plain dishes. Jars and bowls frequently have horizontal rilled surface, occasional scored wavy-lines and 'slashed' rims (**242**, table 60)
Source. Production at Harrold (Beds.), and perhaps Lakenheath (Suffolk), but additional sources likely.
Chronology. The shelly clays at Harrold were exploited from 1st cent. AD but a major expansion in production from early 4th cent. Abundant in late 4th-cent. assemblages in east and south Midlands.

242	Form	Description
-	1	jar with rolled rim
1	2	jar with square-cut rim
2–4	3	jar with undercut rim
7	4	bowl with rounded flange
8	5	bowl with pointed flange
9–10	6	bowl with square-cut flange
6	7	plain dish
5	8	plain dish with thickened lip

Table 60 *Classification of South Midlands shell-tempered ware forms (after Sanders)*

Distribution. A broad belt across southern Britain, north of the Thames and south of the Severn–Humber line. Outliers in Wales and north; relatively uncommon in East Anglia. The jars are the most widely distributed type, and the only form

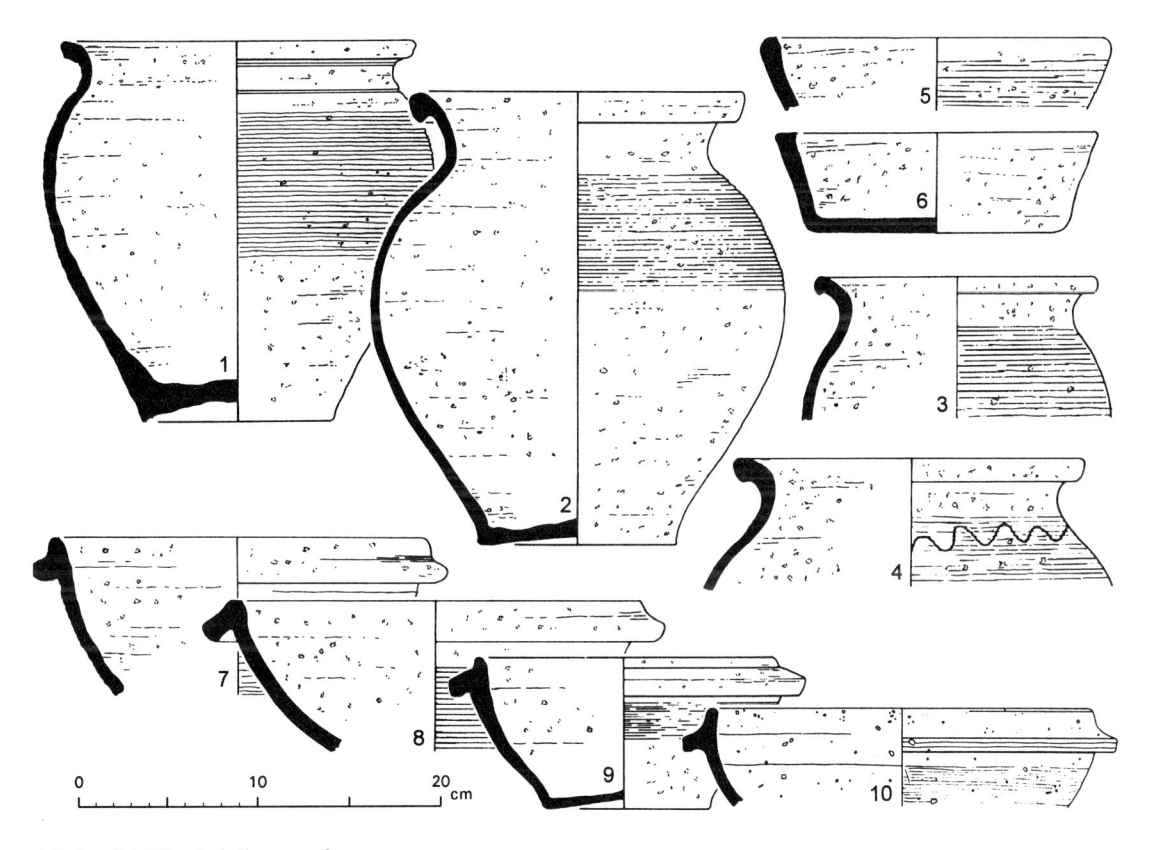

North Kent shell-tempered storage jars / ROMANO-BRITISH COARSE WARES

242 South Midlands shell-tempered wares

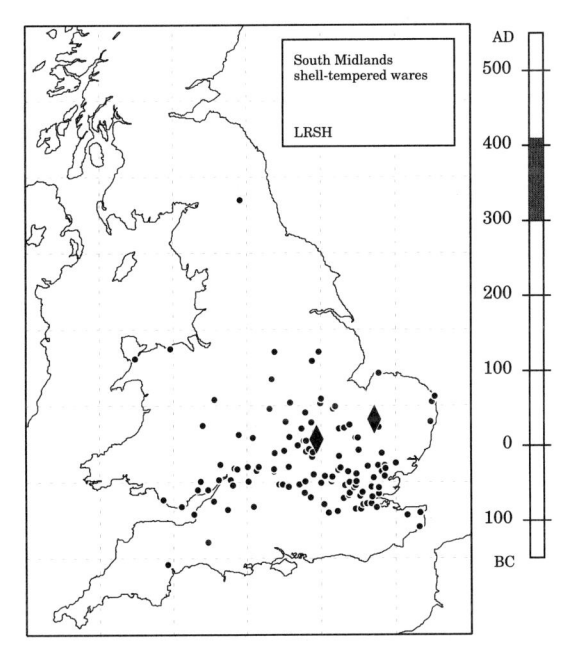

243 South Midlands shell-tempered wares: overall distribution, AD 350–400

found towards the periphery of the distribution (**243**).

Aliases. *Bath* fabric 11. *Caister-on-sea* fabric SHEL-150. *Chelmsford* fabric 51. *Chesterfield* fabric 2. *Gestingthorpe* fabric H. *Gloucester* fabric TF22. *Great Chesterford* fabric 2. *JRPS bibliography* fabric lsh. *Kent* coarse fabric 23c. *Leicester* fabric CG1B. *Lullingstone* fabric 71. *Milton Keynes* fabric 1a. *Towcester* fabric 44b/d. Referred to as 'calcite-gritted wares' in earlier literature.

Bibliography. Principal discussion, with gazetteer of findspots in Sanders 1973. For Harrold kiln site: Brown 1994, especially phases 5–6. Recent discussion of Midlands shelly wares in Marney 1989, 58–64. *RCHM gazetteer* F207–10, F606–8.

North Kent shell-tempered storage jars

Fabric and technology. Fairly hard coarse fabric with irregular fracture; dark-grey (7.5YR 4/0) or reddish-brown (2.5YR 5/4) surfaces, frequently with thick dark-grey or black core; abundant inclusions of shell 'plates' (up to 4mm), which sometimes dissolve out leaving flat voids in surface. Examination of shell suggests derivation from fossil Woolwich Beds.

Forms. Principal form is large jar with rolled rim, with cordons and band of coarse slashed, impressed or incised

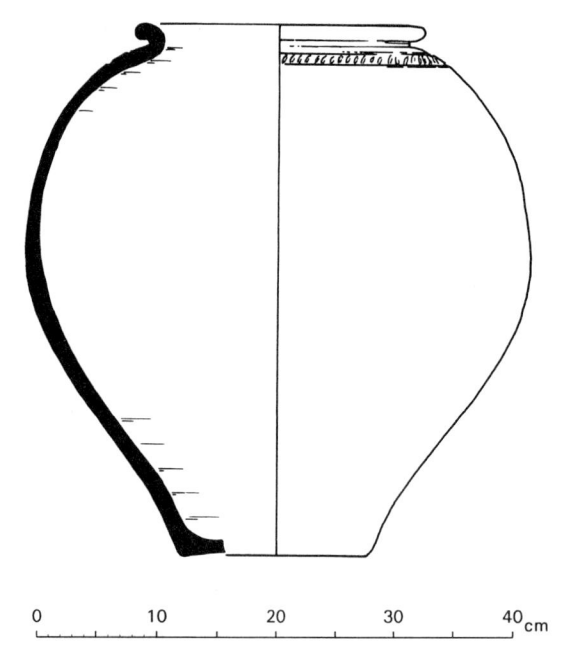

Portchester fabric D/romano-british coarse wares

244 *North Kent shell-tempered storage jars: Scale 1:6*

decoration at the shoulder. Bead-rim jars and other forms also recorded in same ware (**244**).
Chronology. In London, from Neronian period until mid- or late 2nd cent.
Source. The Kent shore of the Thames estuary, probably from the Black Shore area, near Cliffe.
Principal contents. Jars from London frequently have thick black coating on rim and shoulder, identified as pitch made from silver-birch bark. Possibly used as containers for the transport of salt or other products from workings along the Thames shore.
Distribution. Principally the Thames estuary region; common in London. A scatter up the east coast as far as the Antonine Wall fort of Cramond (Rae and Rae 1974, fig. 21, 7; Bidwell and Speak 1994, 230) (**245**).
Aliases. Kent coarse fabric 23b. 'Thames Estuary shelly jars'. Monaghan 1987a, fabric H1/4h.
Bibliography. Pollard 1988, fig. 12, 16; Monaghan 1987a, 32–3, class 3D1, 3D3; C. M. Green 1980b, 80.

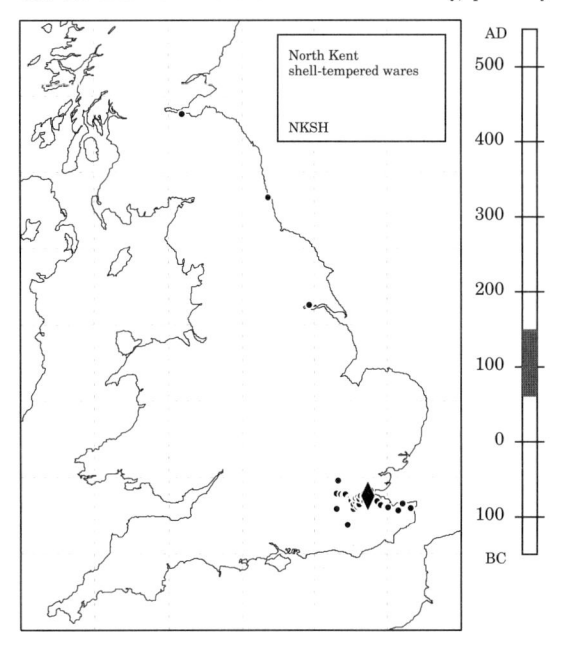

Portchester fabric D

Fabric and technology. Hard, rough, sandy fabric with irregular or hackly fracture, which can be slightly friable; a range of colours but either orange, through yellow/buff to brown, or shades of grey; abundant clear, colourless or reddish quartz, with sparse coarse (or very coarse) red iron ores, fine white mica and occasional large angular chalk inclusions. Some variants show a pale brown slip over the outer surface. Wheel-thrown. Often with smoke-blackened surfaces.
Forms. Principal forms are necked jars with undercut rim and rilled surface, flanged bowls and plain dishes. Minor forms include jugs and moulded-rim jars (**247, table 61**).
Chronology. From early 4th through to the end of the century. Forms 5–10 per cent of late 4th-cent. deposits in London, Surrey and west Kent.

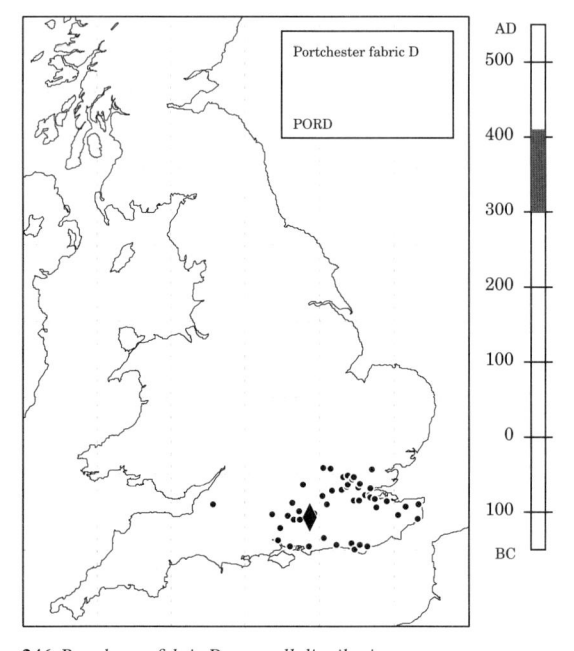

245 *North Kent shell-tempered storage jars: overall distribution*

246 *Portchester fabric D: overall distribution*

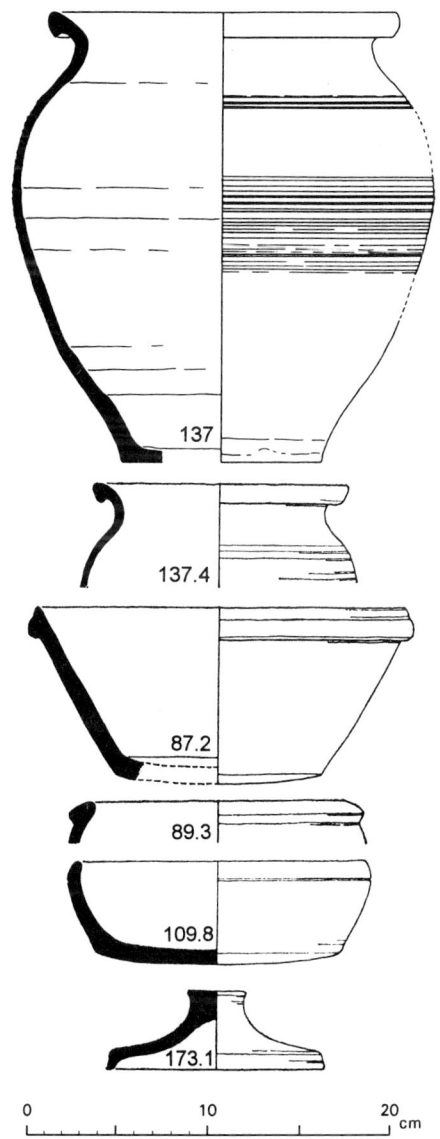

Savernake-type grey/ROMANO-BRITISH COARSE WARES

Form	Portchester	Alice Holt
Flanged bowl	87	5B
Inturned rim bowl	89	5C?
Plain dish	109	6A
Rilled jar	137	3C
Lid	173	7

Table 61 *Classification of Portchester D ware forms (after Fulford, and Lyne and Jefferies)*

Savernake-type grey wares

Fabric and technology. A range of hard, fine-textured fabrics, often with lumpy finish; pale grey, off-white or buff core and surfaces; very little visible sand, but abundant dark blue-grey, or pale grey, grog (up to 4mm) and red-brown iron ores, and occasional brown or white flint. Wheel-thrown. Surfaces often burnished or smoothed.

Forms. Principally necked jars, with characteristic grooves and cordons on shoulder and body, bead-rim jars, storage jars; other minor forms including beakers, bowls and plates. Black-burnished derived jars and bowls from mid-2nd cent (**249**).

Chronology. Commences in Claudian period, and continues into early/mid-2nd cent. AD. Kilns at Lydiard Tregose may be continuation of same tradition (into 3rd/4th cent.?).

Source. Several sources across north Wiltshire, including Savernake Forest (near Mildenhall), Pewsey and Oare.

Distribution. Wiltshire, extending into bordering counties.

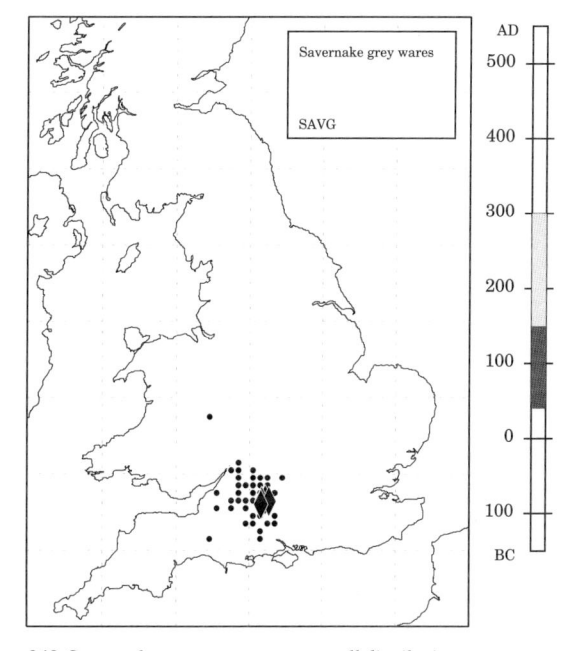

247 *Portchester fabric D: Scale 1:4*

Source. One source is the Overwey kilns, near Tilford (Surrey), but there may be others.
Distribution. Hampshire, Surrey, the London region and Kent (**246**).
Aliases. JRPS bibliography fabric pod. *Kent* coarse fabric 19. *Lullingstone* fabric 63. *Portchester* fabric D. 'Surrey buff ware' and 'fabric C': Lyne and Jefferies 1979. Millett 1979a, fabric 2. Regularly misnamed 'Porchester D' (e.g. *JRPS bibliography* vols 1–5).
Bibliography. Fulford 1975b; Orton in Blurton and Rhodes 1977, 35. For Overwey kilns: Clark 1949, *RCHM* gazetteer F627-8.
See also. AHFA

248 *Savernake-type grey wares: overall distribution*

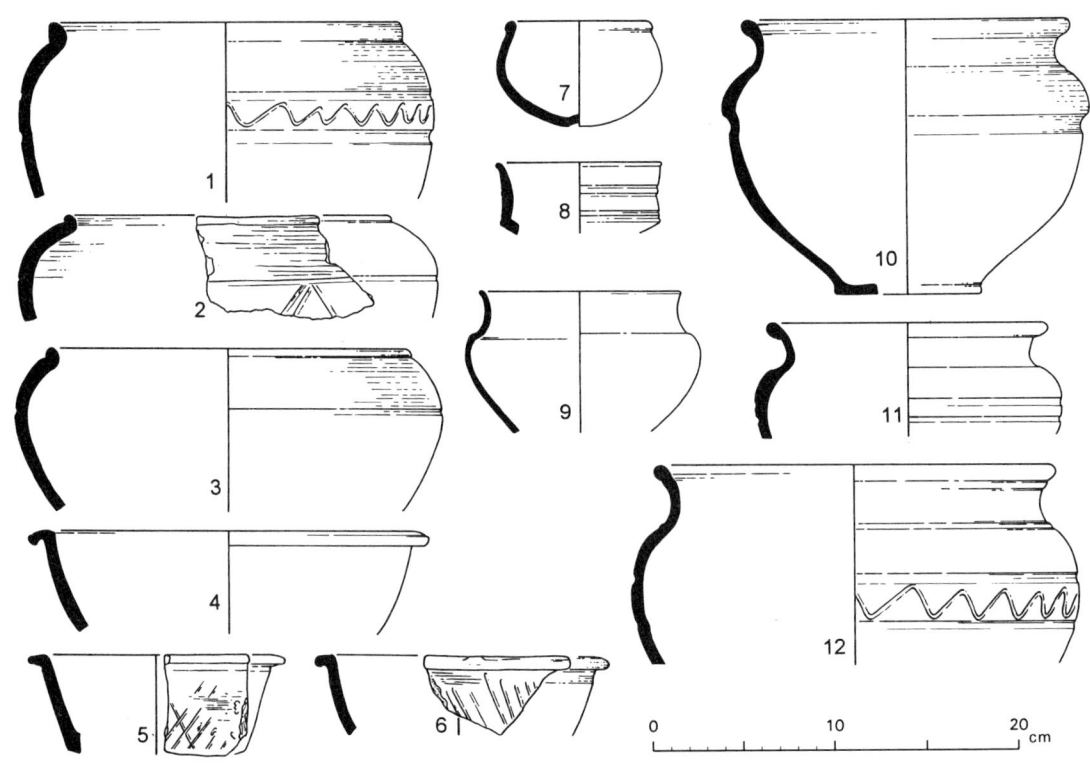

Savernake-type grey/ROMANO-BRITISH COARSE WARES

249 Savernake-type grey wares: Scale 1:4

Large storage jars and bead-rim jars seem to have widest spread. Hodder suggests distribution through market/service area attached to Mildenhall (Hodder 1974, 75–8) (**248**).
Aliases. *Cirencester* fabric 6. *Gloucester* fabric TF6. *JRPS bibliography* fabric svr.
Bibliography. Distribution in Hodder 1974; origins in Swan 1975; Greene 1974, 65–6. For kilns: *RCHM gazetteer* F659–71.
Notes. Small-scale production of lead-glazed wares at Savernake: Arthur 1978, 309, 312.

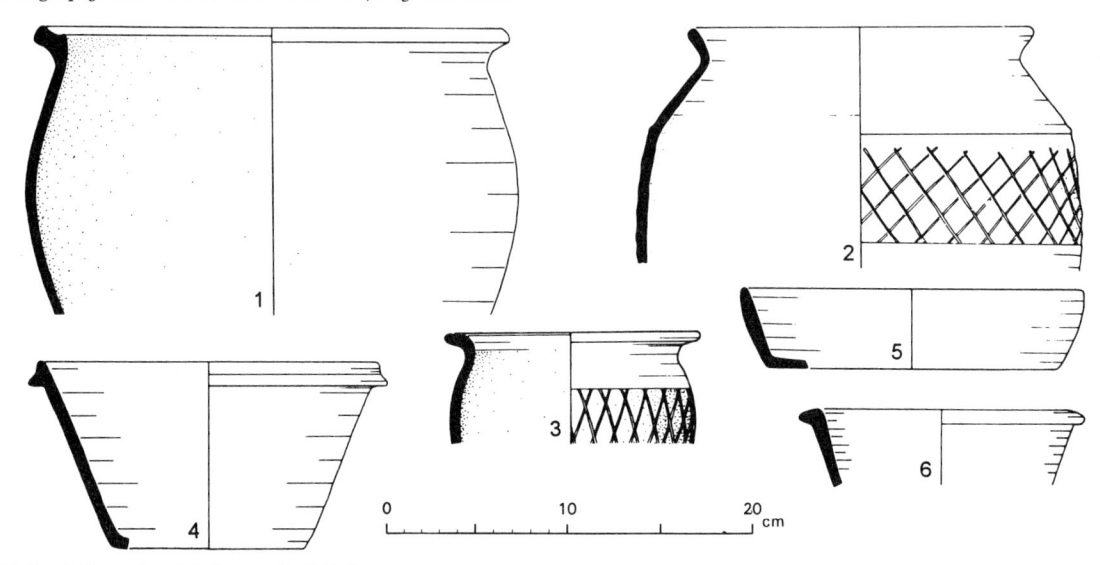

250 South Devon burnished ware: Scale 1:4

196

South Devon burnished ware

Fabric and technology. Hard, with irregular fracture; normally dark grey or black, but occasionally lighter yellow-brown or red-brown; abundant dark mica, and angular feldspar, with sparser quartz sand; exterior surfaces facet burnished. Most wheel-thrown, but some (larger) vessels hand-formed.

Forms. Later assemblage dominated by BB1-derived flanged bowls and everted-rim jars; earlier jar forms with moulded rim may originate from later Iron Age Cornish gabbroic ware prototypes (**250**).

Chronology. Earliest specimens from Neronian deposits, but wide distribution dates from late 2nd cent. to 4th cent.

Source. South Devon.

Distribution. Devon, Cornwall and west Dorset; outliers in London (**251**).

Aliases. Exeter fabric 5. *JRPS bibliography* fabric sdw.

Bibliography. Bidwell and Silvester in Cunliffe 1988, 47–9; Holbrook and Bidwell 1991, 177–81; for London specimens: B. Richardson 1986, 125 (but see comments by M. Wood in Holbrook and Bidwell 1991, 181, no. 18.1 on possible alternative source for some of these vessels).

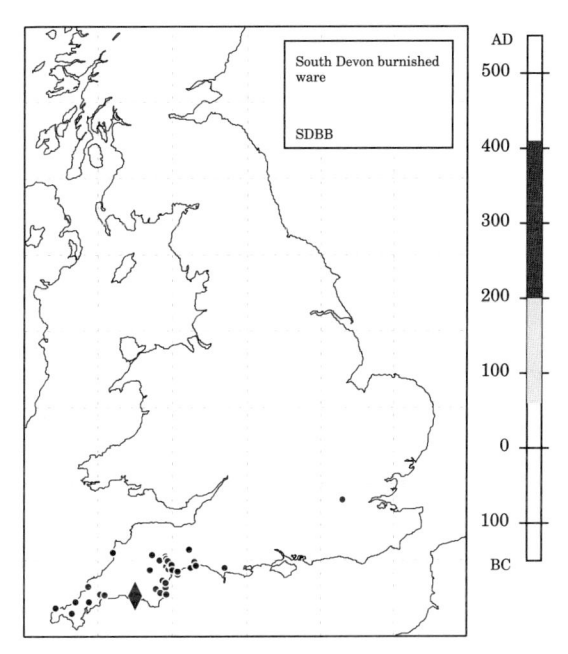

251 South Devon burnished ware: overall distribution

Severn Valley ware

Fabric and technology. A range of hard, fine-textured fabrics; typically brown (5YR 6/6) or reddish-orange (2.5YR 5/8) at the surface, sometimes with a grey core (particularly in the thicker parts), although fully reduced wares also occur; typical ware is slightly micaceous with little visible temper, but coarser 'gritted' (with sand, grog and clay pellets and a little iron ore) or vesicular (?burnt organic) variants known. Surfaces generally burnished, with linear or lattice decorated zones, with grooves and cordons. Usually wheel-thrown, although rare hand-formed variants occur.

Forms. The principal form classes are described by Webster (**table 62**). The handled tankard (class E) is one of the more characteristic forms in SVW. These, with storage and wide-mouthed jars, are most widely distributed forms (**252, 253**).

Chronology. Timby (1990) suggests SVW commences shortly before conquest, although others have preferred a Claudian conception under military influence (P. V. Webster 1976, 40–2). Flourishes during 2nd and early 3rd and continues into 4th cent. AD.

Source. Several 2nd/3rd-cent. kiln sites producing Severn Valley wares are known, extending through Severn valley (Alkington, Ledbury, Malvern, Perry Barr) to Wroxeter. Earliest production centres not yet identified, but perhaps in Gloucester region.

Distribution. Mid-1st-cent. distribution largely confined to sites in Severn valley near Gloucester region, with outliers on Claudio-Neronian military sites such as Usk (S. Wales). Present at Wroxeter and Chester by later 1st cent. AD. Abundant on sites in lower Severn basin through 2nd/3rd cent. (*c.* 70 per cent of all pottery on rural sites in Gloucester region, and at Sidbury, Worcs.). Extension of small-scale supply to north-west England, western sector of Hadrian's Wall and Scotland *c.* AD 120–200. Distribution contracts to Severn basin by 4th cent (**254**).

252–253	Class	Description
8–9 12	A	storage jars
-	B	bead-rim jars
10–11 13–16	C	wide-mouthed jars
-	D	bowls & wide-mouthed jars with beaded/everted rims
4–7	E	tankard
17–18 21–22	F	flanged bowls with internal lip
19	G	flanged bowls with reeded/grooved rims
1–3	H	carinated bowls
23–24	I	samian-derived forms
26	J	segmental bowls
25	K	dishes/platters
27	L	lids

Table 62 *Classification of Severn Valley ware classes (after Webster)*

Aliases. Bath fabric 9.1. *Carlisle* fabric 124. *Dorchester* fabric 37R., *Gloucester* fabrics TF11B, TF11D, TF17 and TF220.

Severn Valley/ROMANO-BRITISH COARSE WARES

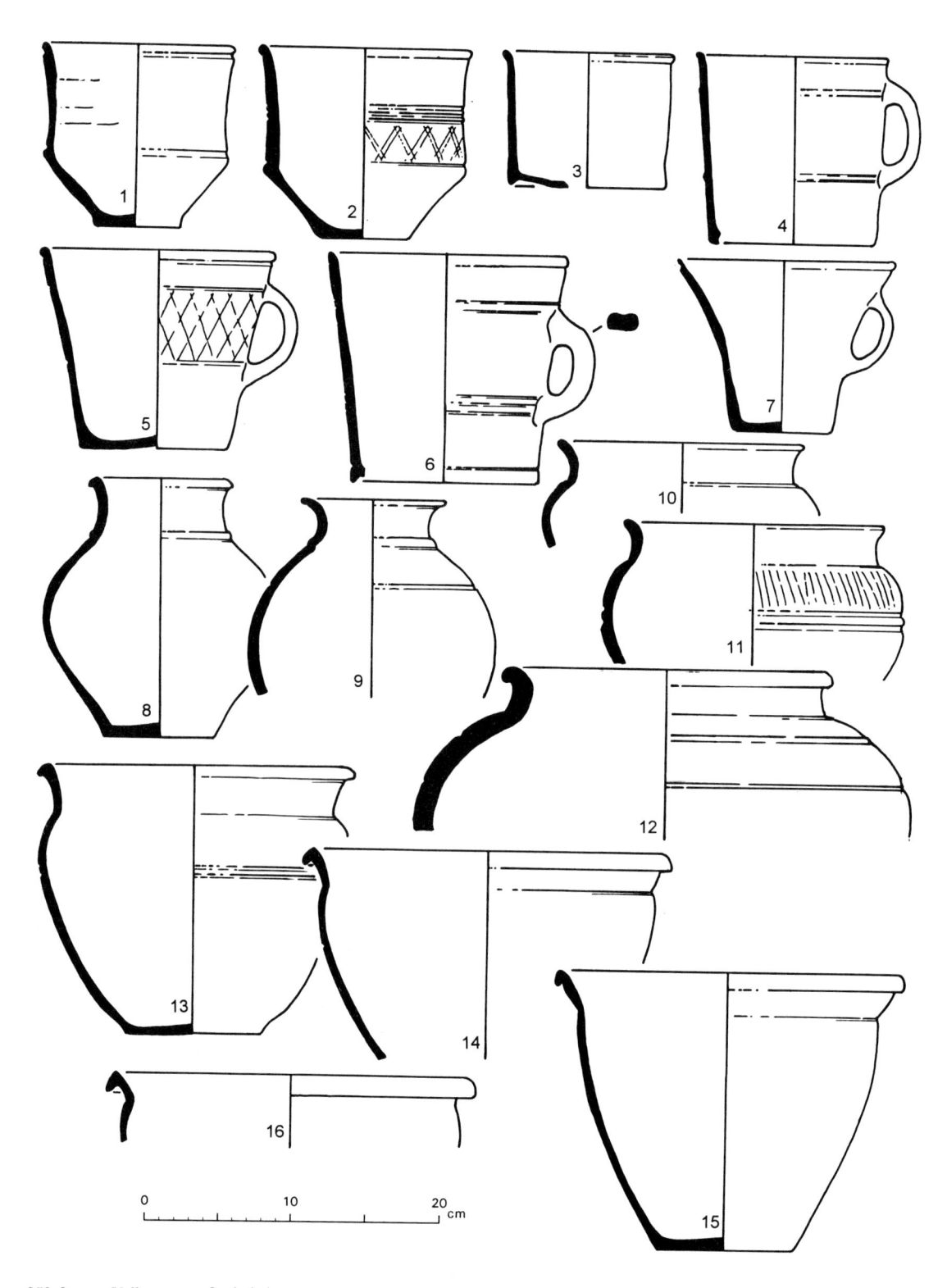

252 *Severn Valley wares: Scale 1:4*

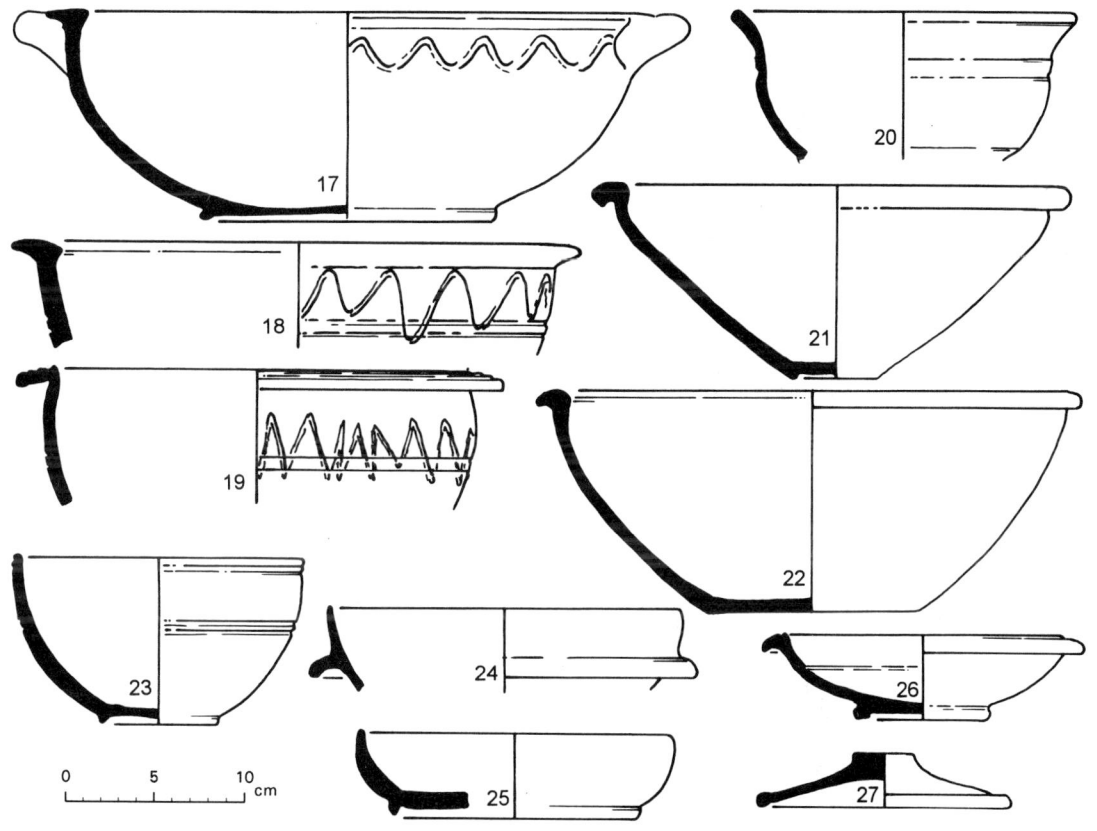

Verulamium-region white/ROMANO-BRITISH COARSE WARES

253 Severn Valley wares: Scale 1:4

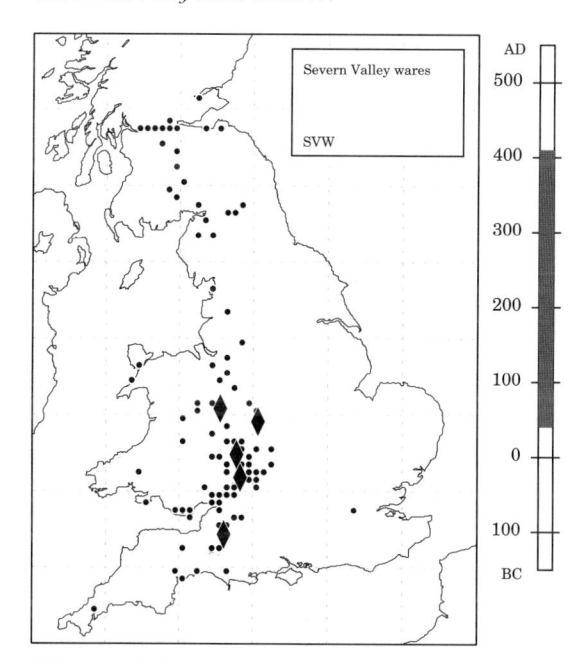

254 Severn Valley wares: overall distribution

JRPS bibliography fabric svv. *Old Penrith* fabric 22. *Sidbury* fabric 12.

Bibliography. For type-series, general development and distribution: P. V. Webster 1976; Rawes 1982; the range of SVW fabrics described in Darlington and Evans 1992, 37–8 and Hurst 1985, 81; for origins and early forms: Timby 1990; for northern distribution: P. V. Webster 1972; P. V. Webster 1977; Bidwell 1985, 171–4. For kilns: RCHM gazetteer F305, F352, F579, F635, F673–6.

Notes. Inspiration from SVW forms seen in many 3rd/4th-cent. industries in south-west and western Britain (Spencer 1988, 114–18); potters working in SVW tradition at Inveresk (Scotland) during the Antonine period (Swan in G. D. Thomas 1989, 167–71).

Verulamium-region white ware

In addition to mortaria, the Verulamium-region potteries produced a range of other vessel types, some of which were widely distributed.

Fabric and technology. Hard, granular fabric with slightly laminar texture; typically white or off-white (2.5YR 9/0–5/0 to 10YR 9/1) through pink to orange (2.5YR 6/8); abundant well-sorted multi-coloured quartz with sparse red iron in a

Verulamium-region white/ROMANO-BRITISH COARSE WARES

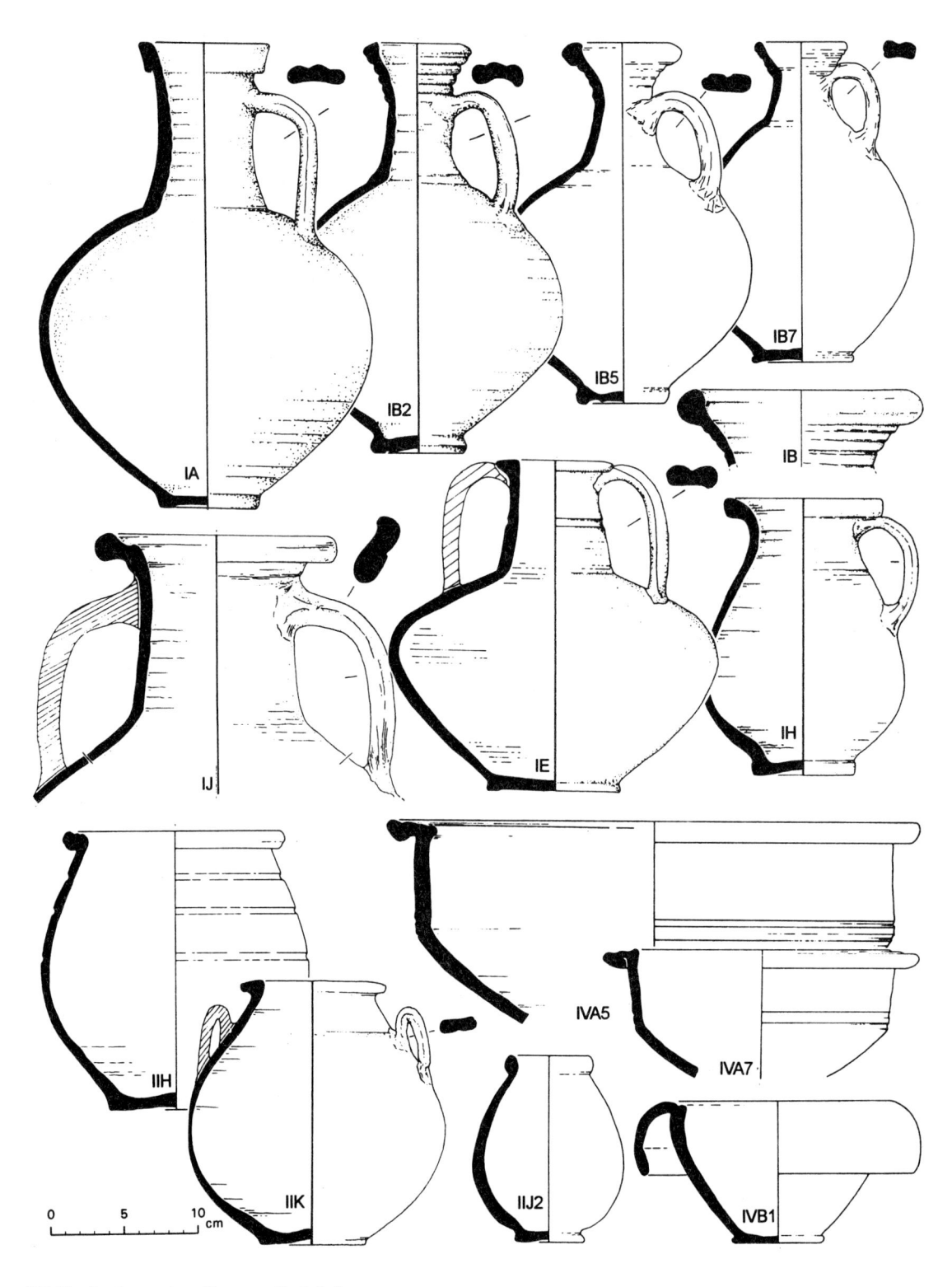

255 *Verulamium-region white ware: Scale 1:4*

clean matrix. Wheel-thrown. Surfaces usually unsmoothed, but trimmed near bases.

Forms. Principal forms (255) covered by Southwark type-series (table 63).

Class	Description
IA	Collared flagon
IB	Ring-necked flagon
IC	Pinch-mouthed flagon
ID	Disc-mouthed flagon
IE	Two-handled flagon
IH	'Concave' neck with rolled-out rim
IJ	Large two-handled flagon
IIG	Necked jar
IIH	'Biconical' urn
IIJ	'Unguent jar'
IIK	Two-handled 'honey-pot'
IVA	Reeded-rim bowls

Table 63 *Classification of Verulamium-region forms (after Marsh and Tyers)*

Additional minor forms known at the kilns or on local sites include dishes, *tazze*, face pots (Braithwaite 1984, 108) lamps, crucibles and beakers.

Cylindrical amphoras of the Dressel 2–4 form stamped by the potter Dares were certainly produced at Brockley Hill (Castle 1978) and the resin on their inner surfaces suggests they were intended to carry local wines (Sealey 1985, 128–30).

The larger specimens of the two-handled flagons, Southwark form IJ, have long been referred to as 'amphora-types' (Corder 1941, 291; K. M. Richardson 1948, 14) and we can now point to some broad typological similarity with the flat-based Gauloise series (see GAUL). A complete specimen with a stamp across the shoulder reading SENECIONIS has been reported (Symonds 1993) although it has not been demonstrated that the VRW vessels were stoppered, sealed and transported with contents.

Chronology. Presence of VRW in pre-Boudiccan groups at both London and St Albans suggests inception in AD 50s; common through to mid-2nd cent. perhaps with some production through to end of 2nd cent. AD. Most common in London during Flavian–Trajanic period, which coincides with production period of the most prolific Verulamium-region mortarium potters.

Source. Watling Street, between London and Verulamium. Major workshops at Brockley Hill, Radlett, Little Munden and St Albans.

Distribution. Major supplier of flagons and bowls to London (over 20 per cent of all pottery during Flavian–Trajanic period = 90 per cent of all oxidized wares) and St Albans; up to 5 per cent at Magiovinium (Bucks.; Parminter in Neal 1987, 91). In Kent – where the data are relatively complete – Pollard demonstrates that the number of VRW forms declines with distance from the source (Pollard 1988, 26–7). Elsewhere recording is irregular, and usually confined to vessels noted for their similarity with the more widely recognized mortarium fabric (VRMO). Flagons seem to be the most widely distributed form, but there are even differences between the VRW assemblage from London and St Albans (see discussion of Marsh and Tyers 1978, form IIH) (256).

Aliases. Carlisle fabric 179. *Chelmsford* fabric 26. *Chesterfield* fabric 25. *Colchester* fabric FJ. *Gloucester* fabrics TF9T and TF209. *Great Chesterford* fabric 25. *JRPS bibliography* fabric vrr. *Kent* coarse fabric 5. *King Harry Lane* fabric VRP. *Leicester* fabric WW5. *Lullingstone* fabric 30.

Bibliography. Summaries of VRW industry: Marsh and Tyers 1978; Swan 1984, 97–8; Seeley and Thorogood 1994. For kilns: RCHM gazetteer F354–5, F359–62, F475–80.

Notes. Small-scale production of minor wares alongside VRW (e.g. grey wares, marbled wares and mica-dusted wares) is indicated by their similar fabric.

See also. VRMO

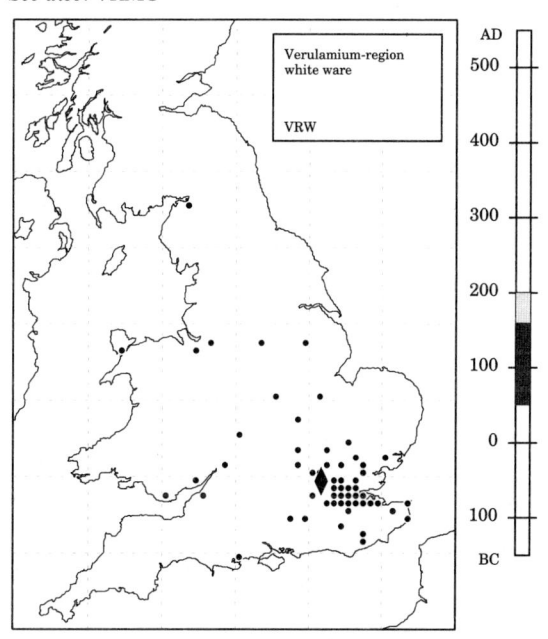

256 *Verulamium-region white ware: overall distribution*

APPENDIX 1
Resources for the study of Romano-British pottery

This appendix lists some of the major resources available to the potential student of Romano-British ceramics. Inevitably this is only a snapshot of a constantly changing picture, but it attempts to give a guide to the resources that are likely to be available to someone faced with the task of preparing a report on a collection of pottery from a site in Britain.

Bibliography

There are a number of introductions to the general study of **archaeological ceramics**, with extensive bibliographies (e.g. Shepard 1956; Rice 1987; Orton, Tyers and Vince 1993). The application of compositional or petrological techniques to Roman and other ceramics is described in the papers in Peacock (ed) 1977; Hughes 1981; Freestone, Johns and Potter 1982; Middleton and Freestone 1991. The current state of the quantfication debate is described in Orton 1993. For a clearly written survey of pottery technology see Rye 1981.

A short, accessible introduction to the potential of **Roman pottery** has been published by Greene (1992b). *Pottery in the Roman World*, by D. P. S. Peacock, combines data from the study of modern and recent pottery manufacturing around the Mediterranean and elsewhere with a survey of production and distribution in the Roman period (1982). Much of the Classical literature on vessel names and function is summarized in Hilgers 1969. An insight into the state of Roman pottery studies in the earlier part of this century is given in a delightful paper by Howard Comfort, which includes a set of photographs showing the principal faces behind the typologies (1979). A detailed bibliography of some of the commoner wares and classes found in Britain will be found with the appropriate Atlas entries.

Romano-British pottery is conveniently introduced in a short study by Swan (several editions: 1988) in the Shire Archaeology series. *The Student's Guide* to Romano-British pottery published by the Council for British Archaeology (G. Webster 1976) contains useful annotated bibliographies, but is now somewhat out of date as it pre-dates the massive expansion of publication of recent years. A new edition is in preparation.

The standard sources for archaeological bibliography in Britain naturally cover material of interest to the student of pottery. These are the Council for British Archaeology's *Archaeological Bibliography of Great Britain and Ireland* (for 1940–80) and *British Archaeological Abstracts* (1968–91), and now the *British Archaeological Bibliography* (from 1992). Earlier reports on Romano-British archaeology (pre-1940) are indexed in Bonsor 1964, especially entries 1403–1622, and under individual sites.

Articles on Romano-British pottery are published regularly in the major national archaeological journals, particularly *Britannia*, *Antiquaries Journal* and the *Archaeological Journal*. The annual summaries of archaeological work published in *Britannia* as *Roman Britain in 19..*, is a source on recent discoveries of interest, particularly of new kiln sites, graffiti and *tituli picti*.

There is now a specialized journal dedicated to Roman ceramics, the *Journal of Roman Pottery Studies* (JRPS), first published in 1986. This incorporates a *Roman pottery bibliography*, an annotated listing of publications on pottery organized by county or region. A typical entry lists the types of pottery covered by the report, using three-letter codes – perhaps rather too abbreviated for comfort. Some entries carry minor editorial essays.

The scope of the bibliography extends beyond Britain, and an increasing number of continental reports are included, particularly from France. The publication of an accumulated bibliography is planned. The maps in the Atlas in this volume are based in part on the data in the JRPS bibliography (see Appendix 3).

Romano-British kiln sites are covered by V. G. Swan's Royal Commission on the Historical Monuments of England (RCHME) volume (Swan 1984). The most valuable part of this work, the gazetteer of kiln sites arranged by county, with full bibliography and references to museum collections, was only published in microfiche in the original volume. A few printed copies of the gazetteer were produced by an enterprising Oxford publisher, but it is unlikely that this data has had the wide distribution that it deserves.

The bibliography on **continental Roman pottery and imports** is vast. There are several journals or occasional series dedicated to Roman ceramics which are of particular interest. The *Société française d'étude de la céramique antique en Gaule* (SFECAG) publishes reports on the proceedings at its annual meetings. An international study group for Roman ceramics, the *Rei Cretariae Romanae Fautores* (RCRF) publishes a biannual journal, the *Acta*, and a series of shorter newsletters which include bibliographies of recent publications. A summary of recent publications on Roman pottery by C. Bémont has been published regularly in the *Revue des Études Anciennes* since the 1970s.

Much of the continental journal literature on Roman ceramics is indexed in the annual bibliography published by the German Archaeological Institute. This is available simultaneously in conventional printed form as the *Archäologisches Bibliographie 19..*, and as a computer database system called DYABOLA, for MSDOS™ systems. Through the latter it is possible to retrieve lists of publications by subject, region and date of publication. This system is particularly valuable for keeping track of the publications on the major traded wares such as sigillata and amphoras. A copy of DYABOLA is held in the library of the Roman Society (Gordon Square, London).

The non-samian Roman pottery industries of Gaul have been surveyed by M. Tuffreau-Libre (1992) with a bibliography. The raw data on Gaulish ceramics is as widely scattered in the literature as that on the Romano-British material. There are a number of useful regional studies (e.g. Tuffreau-Libre 1980; Santrot and Santrot 1979) and a particularly fine survey of the Roman pottery industries in the Ile-de-France region (Paris and its environs) by Dufaÿ, Barat and Veermeersch (1993) employing a methodology closely modelled on British practice. The material from the Rhineland frontier is served by the typology of Gose (1950) and the lavish reports in the *Limesforschungen* and *Materialien zur römisch-germanischen Keramik* series.

Compared to the numerous volumes on pottery, there is relatively little available on the substances that went into the pots, namely the **food and cooking** of the Romans. Discussions of Roman cooking often include comments on cooking and storage vessels, in both ceramics and other materials. Food and table settings shown on wall paintings, for instance, include illustrations of vessels in use (e.g. Blanc and Nercessian 1992). For the recipes themselves, exotic dishes, such as those in the book preserved under the name of Apicius, were probably of direct relevance to only a rather limited sub-set of the population, both socially and geographically (Flower and Rosenbaum 1958). A rather more down-to-earth view of Roman cuisine is given by Giacosa (1992). In the northern provinces, including Britain, the study of food and culinary techniques will be a fruitful area for collaboration between Roman ceramics, zoological and botanical remains, the scientific analysis of deposits and residues on pottery, and the Classical texts (see, for instance, Furger 1985).

Collections

The modern fashion in museum displays is rather against the serried ranks of pots in display cabinets that were once common, and in favour of fewer selected pieces displayed in a more informative tableau. Nevertheless, many museums hold large collections of Roman pottery in their reserves, and are likely to acquire more in the future as part of archaeological archives.

Colchester and Essex Museum, where M. R. Hull was curator, houses one of the country's finest collections of Roman pottery. This includes not only the material from the extensive Colchester potteries, including the sigillata kiln, but also one of the largest collections of Augustan and Tiberian material, from the British pre-conquest capital of Camulodunum.

In Britain, many archaeological units have developed systems for the recording and analysis of Roman ceramics, integrated with their recording systems for other categories of artefact, archaeological contexts, structures and other data. At the core of the pottery records there will usually be some form of fabric type-series, a typology (or at least a set of drawings) and a set of quantified data linked to structural records (see Appendix 2). Such material would usually be the first port-of-call for any comparative data for the Roman pottery of the region.

Other resources

Until recent years the principal resources available to the ceramicist have been a collection of books and papers from journals and the pottery itself. Increasingly, however, the raw data upon which the conclusions in the published report are based is not published in a conventional format, but may be held in centralized archives, increasingly in computerized form. An editorial in the journal *Britannia* in 1986 drew attention to developments in information technology that were then on the horizon, such as electronic journals and on-line databases, and their potential impact on the distribution of archaeological data. Ceramic data is one obvious candidate for distribution on electronic media. A proportion of the data is common to all users, such as the dates of pottery types, or potters, distributions of key wares, core bibliographies and so on. Many archaeological ceramicists seem to be enthusiastic users of databases and spreadsheets, and the comparison between assemblages is obviously a key element of any serious assessment of pottery data; yet relatively little of this is freely available in computerized form and there is no central archive or clearing house.

To take just a simple example, many of the distribution maps in the Atlas contain simple dots which record the presence of a ware on a site. Many of these dots hide further information, such as the proportion of the ware at the site or its distribution in a chronological sequence. It is possible to envisage a system where the user could 'click' on a appropriate dot on the map, and be carried seamlessly into the electronic version of the appropriate report, then back out to the map, and into another report. Most of the tools to create this type of system are freely available, and much of the necessary data – that is the texts and the raw figures – has for at least a decade been available in word-processor files locked up on floppy disks up and down the land. Computerized data needs care and management just as much as a fragile object. If steps are not taken to ensure the survival and archiving of this information it will not survive and it will not be available to future researchers in the form that, by then, will be the natural medium of communication.

APPENDIX 2

The processing of Roman pottery from excavations

A detailed discussion of the processing and recording of archaeological pottery assemblages is not an appropriate topic for this book, and both the theory and practice have been dealt with elsewhere (e.g. Orton, Tyers and Vince 1993; Fulford and Huddleston 1991). Nevertheless, as the discussion of almost any aspect of Roman ceramics is dependent on the quality of the available data, which in part reflects those processing and recording systems, it is appropriate to describe some of the basic guidelines and procedures.

Classification

Although they differ in detail, most pottery processing systems in use in the last decade or so follow broadly similar lines. The aim of the initial sorting of the material is to divide it up into a series of fabrics, and provide a single description of the group which covers the variation within the group, rather than describe every vessel in the assemblage individually. The exact procedure may vary; it may be preferable to survey the larger groups in the assemblage and pull out sherds of the major fabrics to form the basis of the type-series, or it may be preferable to tackle the contents systematically according to the stratigraphic sequence (if that is available).

The usual method is to take representative sherds of all the fabrics that are defined out of their context bags (leaving a proxy card or label behind to record your passing) and keep these sherds separately as a fabric type-series. These are the sherds that will usually be described later for the published descriptions, and they will often be the sherds that are used for further fabric analysis (thin sectioning or compositional analysis) should that prove necessary. Each fabric is given a unique number in a running series, and this number is used as a reference during cataloguing.

The approach taken to a classificatory procedure seems to vary with the individual, and most people will fall into the category of either a 'lumper' or a 'splitter'. Both have their merits, although the splitter at least has the possibility of lumping things together later on; the reverse is rarely the case (Orton, Tyers and Vince 1993, 73, 79). As more of the pottery is processed any decisions made early on will continually be tested against new material. It is important to try and recognize when things are going awry, when some distinction made with one group of material is obviously contradicted by later observations. Reference back to the fabric type-sherds is essential.

Once defined, the fabrics form the framework within which the forms are classified, and illustrated if necessary. At this point it may be preferable to retrieve all the sherds in a particular ware from their contexts and lay them out all at once. Cross-matches between contexts and vessels suitable for total or partial reconstruction should be noted at this stage. The forms present in the ware can be noted and classified at this stage and drawable rims, bases and other diagnostic sherds identified for future action.

Once the number of fabrics that have been defined rises above a certain number – perhaps the number that can fit in a couple of shoe boxes – it is probably time to try and impose some structure over their arrangement. There are several alternative methods, each of which might be appropriate in some circumstances. One is to group the fabrics into their broad classes, such as sigillata, colour-coated wares, amphoras, mortaria, coarse wares (oxidized or reduced), etc. This is probably adequate for a small number of samples, particularly where there are not too many coarse wares. However it may not always be clear which category a new fabric should be placed in, and some of these groupings are functional (e.g. amphoras) rather than technological. For a much larger fabric series with many hundreds of different coarse fabrics (perhaps large, multi-period assemblages with many traded wares) and more users, a more sophisticated system might be appropriate.

The system used in the Department of Urban Archaeology in London in the 1980s for the processing of Roman, medieval and post-medieval pottery was a single-entry key (Orton 1978). To find potential matches for a ware the major inclusions and technological features of the fabric would be listed, and a key constructed with this information. Thus a sherd with organic (C), limestone (L) and quartz sand (S) temper, wheel-made (w), with a slip (s) would be coded CLSsw; the same with no slip, but a glaze (g) would be CLSgw. This key was effectively a pointer to the drawer in a large cabinet containing all similarly coded wares; further progress at that point would require detailed comparison of the details of temper, texture, firing and finish until a matching sherd was found, or until it was clear that a new fabric had been identified.

Quantification

In addition to recording the presence of some combination of fabric and form, we need some measure of the quantity of pottery present in the context. Pottery quantification, 'a subject that has generated more heat than light', is a topic where some admittedly obscure statistical procedures, judgements about what is 'obvious' and practical decisions about how to organize the recording process all rub up against each other. The principal candidates for a measure of pottery in a group are:

1. the minimum number of vessels represented, where each vessel represents 'one'
2. the number of sherds
3. the weight
4. the 'vessels equivalent' value, where a whole pot = 100 per cent, half a pot would be 50 per cent and so on. In practice this measure is usually an estimate by restricting measurement to rims where 360° of a rim would be 100 per cent, 180° = 50 per cent and so on. These are usually known as estimated vessel equivalents or eves.

The relative merits of these measures have been discussed by Orton and others (Orton 1993; Millett 1979b) from both a statistical and a practical viewpoint. Combination of some of these measures provide information on, for instance, the brokenness of an assemblage, which may be used in the study of site-formation processes. It is generally preferable to collect two measures, and my preference is for weights for the fabrics and eves for the forms. Sherd counts, while popular, are perhaps the most time-consuming to collect and certainly the least satisfactory from a statistical viewpoint. Despite their widespread availability (almost universal in the literature on continental and Mediterranean pottery assemblages) they cannot be compared in any meaningful sense (Orton, Tyers and Vince 1993, 168–9).

Recording forms

Pre-printed forms or cards are usual for recording details of both the quantification, and the descriptions of the fabric and form series (Orton, Tyers and Vince 1993, 232–3). The relationship between the forms and the information they contain is shown in 257. Any computerized records will often follow the structure of the forms, but however it is implemented, the basic ideas are the same. Some of the information recorded on the quantification sheets can be thought of as signposts to further data held elsewhere. Thus the fabric reference code or number is a pointer to the fabric recording card (and the sherd) which holds the description of the fabric, and perhaps notes on its source and function (fine ware, cooking ware etc.). Similarly the form reference is a pointer to information on the general class of the vessel (jar, beaker, bowl, etc) and perhaps its function. The context number points to records of the phasing of the site, the type of feature or structure and (indirectly) records of other artefacts in these levels. The analytical phase will often involve the production of summaries of the types of pottery (both fabrics and form) by context, feature, period, or across the whole site. In this case the measures are totalled up for all the selected contexts. Breakdowns of the forms in a single fabric are also a common requirement, when the measures for all the forms in the selected ware will be totalled. Tables showing the sources of the wares or the broad functional classes can be generated by cross-referencing to the files holding details of the forms and fabrics. For computerized data, most simple spreadsheets and database packages are capable of this type of operation and will often allow the production of innumerable varieties of graphs and charts to illustrate the trends.

The form and fabric type-series, and the recording forms and cards are just as much a part of the site archive as the pottery itself, as are any computerized records. They should be documented and copies lodged with the site archives. Future workers will want to see how the pottery from the site was classified and recorded – they may even decide to follow the same systems for any new material.

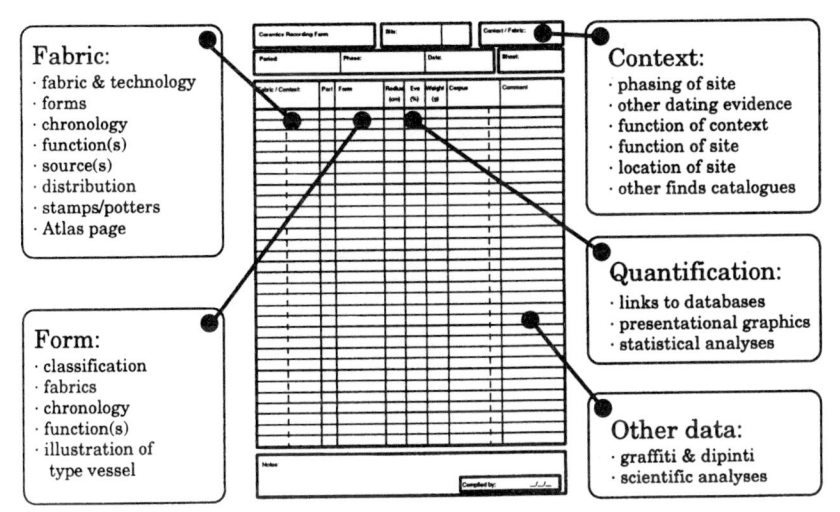

257 Structure of a pottery recording system

Fabric:
· fabric & technology
· forms
· chronology
· function(s)
· source(s)
· distribution
· stamps/potters
· Atlas page

Form:
· classification
· fabrics
· chronology
· function(s)
· illustration of type vessel

Context:
· phasing of site
· other dating evidence
· function of context
· function of site
· location of site
· other finds catalogues

Quantification:
· links to databases
· presentational graphics
· statistical analyses

Other data:
· graffiti & dipinti
· scientific analyses

APPENDIX 3

The Atlas distribution maps

All the maps illustrating pottery distributions in Britain in the Atlas are generated by computer from a simple database. The information was collected and processed on a 486DX33 based system running LINUX, a freely distributable operating system modelled on UNIX™.

The raw data is generally in one of two forms. A survey of the distribution of a particular ware, such as C. J. Young's study of the Oxfordshire industry (1977b) is most efficiently recorded in the order it appears in the printed publication, listing the sites under a heading for each of the pottery types defined:

```
fabric=OXMO
form=m1
offord
cirencester
silchester
st. albans
..
```

In contrast the entries for site reports or the data contained in the *JRPS bibliography* are most efficiently recorded under the heading of the site, with a list of the types present:

```
county="avon"
site="sea mills"
biblio="JRPS-401"
ref="tbgas"
ref2="105"
notes="timby"
AMPH
SPAM
TS
CGCC
LYON
..
```

The files containing this data are managed by a few simple utilities written in a text-processing language called perl, and converted into a unified format, which combines the records from both sources. Using standard UNIX programs such as grep we can now easily retrieve lists of all records which match simple criteria, such as all records containing the keyword BB1. This is converted to a form suitable for plotting by going through the following steps:

1. Extract the site name from the record.
2. Look up the name in a database of sites and National Grid references.
3. Convert the grid references into absolute x/y coordinates from the false origin of the National Grid
4. Check this value against the coordinates of the base map to ensure that it falls within the boundary.
5. Convert the grid coordinates into the local coordinate system of the drawing program.
6. Generate the code in the language of the drawing editor to place the symbol at the local coordinates.

In the case of some dense plots the point is shifted to produce a distribution on a smoothed 10km grid (each point occupies the centre of one 10km square). Where counts are available, the symbol may be scaled to show the numbers or proportion of the assemblage that it represents, and a scale drawn on the margin of the map. All these steps are handled by a single perl script. The drawing program, tgif, merges the base map with the overlay of points, and generates PostScript™ output which can be incorporated directly into finished documents. The maps are generated 'on the fly' when the Atlas entries are printed, so the maps are kept up to date as new data is added to the database.

Acknowledgements

All the software used during the preparation of the maps, and the accompanying text, is freely distributable, and available from Internet sites and elsewhere. I should like to thank the individuals and groups who have developed these programs and made them freely available for others to use. The principal packages are:

linux (operating system, Linus Torvalds and numerous others), **gnu emacs** (text editor, Richard Stallman and the Free Software Federation), **ghostscript** (PostScript interpreter, Aladdin Enterprises), **gnuplot** (interactive plotting program, Thomas Williams and Colin Kelley), **jgraph** (graph plotting filter, Jim Plank), **groff** (text-formatting and bibliography management, James Clark), **perl** (text-processing and report generation, Larry Wall) and **tgif** (interactive drawing editor, William Chia-Wei Cheng).

APPENDIX 4

Principal Roman Emperors from Augustus to Honorius

Ruler	Date	Period
Augustus (Octavian)	27 BC–AD 14	Augustan
		pre-Claudian
Tiberius	14–37	Tiberian
Claudius	41–54	Claudian
		pre-Flavian
Nero	54–68	Neronian
Vespasian	69–79	
Titus	79–81	Flavian
Domitian	81–96	
Trajan	98–117	Trajanic
Hadrian	117–38	Hadrianic
Antoninus Pius	138–61	
Marcus Aurelius	161–80	Antonine
Lucius Verus	161–9	
Commodus	180–92	
Septimius Severus	193–211	
Caracalla	211–17	
Geta	211–12	Severan
Macrinus	217–18	
Elagabalus	218–22	
Severus Alexander	222–35	
Maximinus ('Thrax')	235–8	
Gordian III	238–44	
Philip I ('the Arab')	244–9	
Philip II	244–9	
Valerian	253–9	
Gallienus	253–68	
Postumus	260–9	
Victorinus	269–71	Gallic Empire
Tetricus	271–3	

Ruler	Date	Period
Claudius II ('Gothicus')	268–70	
Aurelian	270–5	
Probus	276–82	
Carus	282–3	
Diocletian	284–305	
Maximian	286–305 & 307–8	Tetrarchy
Constantius I ('Chlorus')	305–6	
Galerius	305–11	
Carausius	287–93	British
Allectus	293–6	usurpers
Constantine I ('the Great')	306–37	
Constantine II	337–40	Constantinian
Constans	337–50	
Constantius II	337–61	
Valentinian I	364–75	
Valens	364–78	Valentinian
Gratian	367–83	
Valentinian II	375–92	
Theodosius I ('the Great')	379–95	Theodosian
Honorius	395–423	

Glossary

This glossary covers both terms used in this book and some which may be encountered in other publications on Romano-British pottery. Useful glossaries of general ceramic terminology, particularly technological terms, are published in Rice (1987) and Rye (1981). Further descriptions of terms employed in the study of Roman ceramics will be found in Swan (1984) and G. Webster (1976).

aceramic region, culture or period in which pottery was not regularly made or used.

amphora (plural amphoras or amphorae) large pottery vessel with handles, for storage and transportation of liquids, especially wine and olive-oil.

ante cocturam pre-firing, usually refers to graffiti, decoration, holes etc.

appliqué decoration, of a figure or motif, made separately (usually in a mould) and fixed to vessel surface.

balsimarium a small narrow-mouthed flask, perhaps for ointments.

barbotine raised decoration produced by applying or trailing a thick clay slip on the vessel surface. May be in contrasting colour to the clay body or slip.

bead rim a rim in the form of a small rounded moulding.

biconical shaped like two truncated cones placed end to end.

block-stamps rectangular dies impressed into a vessel surface, usually in a regular pattern.

boss rounded swelling formed by pushing the vessel wall outwards, perhaps into a mould.

burnish a smooth, shiny surface finish produced on surface of leather-hard pot by rubbing with smooth, hard object.

calcite-gritted ware a general description of fabrics with calcite inclusions; most calcite is crushed shell, and when this dissolves out due to soil conditions the resulting fabrics are referred to as vesicular.

campanulate shaped like an inverted bell (e.g. Drag 27).

carinated a sharp inward angle in the body of a vessel.

cavetto rim *see* everted rim.

ceramicist a student of pottery, particularly archaeological; a harmless drudge.

chamfer a narrow-angled zone between the base and wall of a vessel.

characterization the qualitative and quantitative description of the composition and structure of a material, such as a pottery fabric.

colour-coat *see* slip.

comb-stabbed decoration, made by stabbing surface with toothed implement.

combing/combed decoration made with a toothed implement drawn across the body.

conical shaped like a truncated cone (e.g. Drag 33).

cordon a continuous raised horizontal band on the vessel surface, often between two grooves.

core the central zone in the cross-section of the vessel wall.

cornice rim a finely moulded rim, as in an architectural cornice.

cortex *see* margin.

countersunk handle a rounded handle, partly sunk into the side of a vessel.

cross-hatching *see* lattice.

dipinto (plural *dipinti*) a hand-written inscription or mark, usually in ink or paint.

elemental analysis the determination of the chemical elements present in a material and their proportions.

ethnoarchaeology the study of the culture of living peoples, particularly aspects of the manufacturing, distribution, use and discard of objects, with a view to developing explanations for similar processes in the past.

everted rim a rim which curves out sharply from the shoulder of a vessel; a variant where the curve forms a full quarter-round is referred to as a cavetto rim.

fabric the material from which a pottery vessel is made, usually described in terms of its colours, hardness, feel, texture, inclusion and surface treatments.

face urn (or face jar or face pot) a jar with human face on the neck and shoulder, usually appliqué, incurved, and barbotine techniques.

facet-burnish a variety of burnish where the surface is smoothed with closely spaced short strokes.

finger-marks *see* wheel-marks.

flange a continuous raised projection from the vessel body or rim.

folded *see* indented.

foot (or footring) the base of a vessel, in the form of a projecting ring.

frilled *see* pie-crust.

glaze a glassy coating fused to the surface of the vessel, usually applied as a liquid suspension.

gloss a particularly fine-textured lustrous slip, as on samian wares.

graffito (plural graffiti) an incised or scratched inscription or mark.

grog inclusion of crushed low-fired clay; also sometimes used as a general term for any inclusion.

hand-formed pottery manufacturing using coiling, slab-building or simple turntable.

head-pot *see* face urn.

heavy mineral a mineral with a high specific gravity, present as sparse small dark grains in rocks and sedimentary deposits. Heavy mineral analysis of pottery fabrics uses these minerals as a means of characterization.

Glossary

inclusion aplastic materials in a clay; natural inclusions are a part of the original constituents of the clay, but some inclusions are added by the potter, *see* temper.

indented a vessel where the sides have been pushed in to form a series of depressions, usually evenly spaced around the body.

lattice decoration formed by a criss-cross of diagonal lines. Described as an acute lattice if the angle to the horizontal is greater than 45 degrees, an obtuse lattice is less than 45 degrees.

leather-hard clay that has dried to the point when it is rigid, but before it is fired. Much decoration and secondary forming is carried out at this stage.

marbling variety of slip decoration caused by intermingling of two contrasting colours.

margin the zone in the cross-section of the wall between the core and surfaces.

matrix the finer part of a pottery fabric, originally composed of clay minerals, that surrounds the inclusions.

mica-dusted (or mica-gilt) sheen caused by the application of mica-rich slip. Should be distinguished from micaceous sheen caused by use of mica-rich clays in the fabric.

mortarium (plural mortaria) a hemispherical or conical vessel with a pronounced lip, often with a spout and trituration grits or (more rarely) coarse grooves on the inner surface. Probably used for pounding or mixing foods, as in a mortar.

Munsell Color Charts charts published by the Munsell Color Company of Baltimore, USA, for the standardized description of colours. The description has three components (the hue, value and chroma) which are reported in published descriptions in the form 2.5YR 6/4.

omphalos base a prominent hollow dome, raised in the centre of the base of a vessel.

oxidized fabric a fabric produced when the final stages of firing and cooling are in an atmosphere with an excess of oxygen, usually resulting in a white, buff or red colour.

paint *see* slip.

palaeography the study of the development of hand-writing styles, such as in *dipinti* and graffiti.

petrography the microscopic study and description of rocks and minerals using their optical properties.

petrology the study and description of rocks, their origins, history and structure.

pie-crust decoration formed by pinching a narrow flange between the fingers, as in a pie-crust.

pie-dish a dish with a flat or rounded rim, often in a black-burnished or related fabric.

pinched-mouth flagon (or pinched-neck flagon) a variety of flagon where the mouth is pinched across to form a figure-of-eight shape, to facilitate pouring.

pipe-clay fine-textured pure clays, with low iron content, usually white in colour, as used for manufacture of clay tobacco pipes.

post-cocturam after-firing; usually refers to graffiti, decoration, holes etc.

reduced fabric a fabric produced when the final stages of firing and cooling are in a low-oxygen atmosphere, usually resulting in a grey or black colour.

reeding horizontal grooves on a flange or rim.

rilling close-set horizontal grooves on the body of a vessel.

roller-stamp a repeated sequence of impressed decoration rolled on to a surface with a cylindrical stamp.

rough-cast decoration of small particles of clay or fine sand applied to vessel surface, usually under a slip.

rouletting decoration lightly incised into surface made with toothed or engraved wheel, or flexible blade, held against the vessel while turning on the wheel.

rustication decoration of a thick slip or slurry applied to vessel exterior by hand and worked up into ridges, knobs or lines.

second a vessel marred by firing defects, such as distortion, but still adequately functional (cf. waster).

slip both i) the liquid suspension of fine clay and water used as a coating on pottery and ii) the resulting finish after firing. Finer slips are often described as colour-coats. A slip may be applied with a brush as a paint.

string-marks marks on the underside of the base of a vessel created when the potter removed the pot from a wheel with a string or wire.

tazza (plural tazze) a vessel in the form of a pedestalled cup with a pie-crust or frilled rim (and often with further frilled bands on the body and pedestal). Frequently show signs of burning on the inner surface. Also used as a description of a pedestalled cup with cordons on the body in the 'Belgic' style.

temper material added to a clay to alter its working, drying or firing properties; also the act of mixing such materials with a clay.

thin-section a slice of material (such as rock or ceramic) affixed to a glass microscope slide and ground down to a thin wafer (*c.* 0.03mm thickness). Viewed with a polarizing microscope, the individual mineral inclusions can be identified by their optical properties - one of the basic techniques of petrography.

tituli picti see dipinto.

triple vase a vessel composed of three (occasionally four) small jars attached to a tubular ring, or joined together through the body.

trituration grits the grit embedded on the interior surface of a mortarium, producing a hard grinding surface.

unguent jar (or unguent flask) small, narrow-necked jars, often in coarse fabrics with grooved surfaces. Usually described as imports and containers for ointments and perfumes, although little analytical work has been done.

vesicular ware *see* calcite-gritted ware.

void an open space in a pottery fabric, perhaps caused by chemical leaching or burning out of inclusions.

ware the pottery made at a single production site or region, which may encompass several fabrics.

waster a vessel spoilt or damaged during manufacturing (e.g. under- or over-firing, warping, cracking or distortions). Usually indicative of a production site in the vicinity (cf. second).

waster rate the proportion of vessels damaged during a firing. Important for the interpretation of kiln assemblages.

wheel-marks fine horizontal or spiralling marks, most prominent on the interior of vessels, caused by the potter's fingers when drawing up the clay on the wheel.

wheel-thrown pottery manufacturing using centrifugal force of a wheel to shape the vessel.

Bibliography

Anderson, A. C., *A guide to Roman fine wares*, Vorda Research Series, **1**, Vorda, Highworth, 1980.

Anderson, A. C., 'Some continental beakers of the first and second centuries AD' in *Roman pottery research in Britain and North-West Europe: papers presented to Graham Webster*, ed. A. C. Anderson and A. S. Anderson, British archaeological reports. International series, **123**, BAR, Oxford, 1981, pp. 321–48.

Anderson, A. C., Fulford, M. G., Hatcher, H. and Pollard, A. M., 'Chemical analysis of hunt cups and allied wares from Britain', *Britannia*, **13**, 1982, pp. 229–38.

Anderson, A. S., 'Wiltshire moulded imitation samian' in *Early fine wares in Roman Britain*, ed. P. R. Arthur and G. D. Marsh, British archaeological reports. British series, **57**, BAR, Oxford, 1978, pp. 357–71.

André, P., 'Les amphores cannelées du 1er siècle dans la France de l'ouest' in *Amphores romaines et histoire économique: dix ans de recherche*, Collection de l'École Française de Rome, **114**, École Française de Rome, Rome, 1989, pp. 588–9.

Arnold, D. E., *Ceramic theory and cultural process*, New studies in archaeology, Cambridge University Press, Cambridge, 1985.

Arthur, P. R., 'The lead-glazed wares of Roman Britain' in *Early fine wares in Roman Britain*, ed. G. D. Marsh and P. R. Arthur, British archaeological reports. British series, **57**, BAR, Oxford, 1978, pp. 293–356.

Arthur, P. R., 'On the origins of Richborough form 527' in *Amphores romaines et histoire économique: dix ans de recherche*, Collection de l'École Française de Rome, **114**, École Française de Rome, Rome, 1989, pp. 249–56.

Arthur, P. R. and Williams, D. F., 'Campanian wine, Roman Britain and the third century A.D.', *J Roman Archaeol*, **5**, 1992, pp. 250–60.

Artis, E. T., *Antedeluvian Phytology*, 1825.

Artis, E. T., *The Durobrivae of Antoninus identified and illustrated*, London, 1828.

Artis, E. T., 'Report on recent excavations, made at Sibson, near Wandsford Northamptonshire, on the estate of the Duke of Bedford', *J Brit Archaeol Ass*, **2**, 1847, pp. 164–9.

Atkinson, D., 'A hoard of samian ware from Pompeii', *J Roman Stud*, **4**, 1914, pp. 27–64.

Atkinson, D., 'Three Caistor pottery kilns', *J Roman Stud*, **22**, 1932, pp. 33–46.

Atkinson, R. J. C., 'A Romano-British potters' field at Cowley, Oxon', *Oxoniensia*, **6**, 1941, pp. 9–21.

Austen, P. S., *Bewcastle and Old Penrith. A Roman outpost fort and a frontier vicus: excavations, 1977–78*, Research Series, **6**, Cumberland and Westmorland Antiquarian and Archaeological Society, Kendal, 1991.

Baatz, D., 'Reibschale und Romanisierung', *Acta Rei Cretariae Romanae Fautores*, **17/18**, 1977, pp. 147–58.

Badalona, *Le vi a l'antiguitat. Economia producció i commerç al Mediterrani Occidental*, Monografies Badalonines, **9**, Museu de Badalona, Badalona, 1987.

Baldacci, P., Kapitan, G., Lamboglia, N., Panella, C., Rodríguez Almeida, E., Sciarra, B., Tchernia, A. and Zevi, F., (eds), *Recherches sur les amphores romaines*, Collection de l'École Française de Rome, **10**, École Française de Rome, Paris, 1972.

Baldi, A., 'Elementi di epigraphi Pompeiana', *Latomus*, **23**, 1964, pp. 793–801.

Barley, N., *Smashing pots: feats of clay from Africa*, British Museum Press, London, 1994.

Bats, M., (ed), *Les amphores de Marseille Grecque chronologie et diffusion (VIe-Ier s. av. J.-C.)*, Études Massaliètes, **2**, ADAM éditions & Université de Provence, Lattes & Aix-en-Provence, 1990.

Baudoux, J., 'Production d'amphores dans l'Est de la Gaule' in *Les amphores en Gaule: production et circulation*, ed. F. Laubenheimer, Centre de Recherches d'Histoire Ancienne, **116**, Université de Besançon, Besançon, 1992, pp. 59–69.

Bayard, D., 'La commercialisation de la céramique commune à Amiens du milieu du IIe à la fin du IIIe siècle après J.-C.', *Cahiers Archéologiques de Picardie*, **7**, 1980, pp. 147–209.

Bayard, D., 'L'ensemble du Grand amphithéâtre de Metz et la sigillée d'Argonne au Vème s', *Gallia*, **47**, 1990, pp. 271–319.

Bedaux, R. and van der Waals, D., 'Aspects of life-span of Dogon pottery', *Newsl Pottery Technology*, **5**, 1987, pp. 137–53.

Beltrán Lloris, M., *Las Anforas Romanas en España*, Monografias Arqueológicas, Anejos de Caesaraugusta, 8, Zaragoza, 1970.

Bémont, C., 'Fabrications de vases à parois fines à La Graufesenque', *Acta Rei Cretariae Romanae Fautores*, **21–22**, 1982, pp. 7–15.

Bémont, C. and Jacob, J.-P., *La Terre sigillée gallo-romaine. Lieux de production du Haut Empire: implantations, produits, relations*, Documents d'archéologie française, **6**, Maison des Sciences de l'Homme, Paris, 1986.

Bémont, C., Vernhet, A. and Beck, F., *La Graufesenque: village de potiers gallo-*

Bibliography

romains, Ministère de la Culture et de la Communication, 1987.

Bennett, J., 'A further vessel by the Aldgate-Pulborough potter', *Britannia*, **9**, 1978, pp. 393–4.

Bennett, J., *Sea Mills: the Roman town of Abonae*, Monograph, **3**, City of Bristol Museum and Art Gallery, Bristol, 1985.

Berthault, F., 'Production d'amphores dans la région bordelaise' in *Les amphores en Gaule: production et circulation*, ed. F. Laubenheimer, Centre de Recherches d'Histoire Ancienne, **116**, Université de Besançon, Besançon, 1992, pp. 93–100.

Bertucchi, G., *Les amphores et le vin de Marseille. VIe s. avant J.-C. - IIe s. après J.-C.*, Revue Archéologique de Narbonnaise. Supplément, **25**, Éditions du CNRS, Paris, 1992.

Bet, P., Gangloff, R. and Vertet, H., *Les productions céramiques antiques de Lezoux et de la Gaule centrale à travers les collections du Musée archéologique de Lezoux (63)*, Revue archéologique SITES. Hors-série, **32**, 1987.

Bet, P. and Henriques-Raba, C., 'Les céramiques à parois fines de Lezoux' in *Actes du Congrès de Lezoux. 4–7 Mai 1989*, ed. L. Rivet, SFECAG, Marseille, 1989, pp. 21–30.

Bidwell, P. T., *The Roman fort of Vindolanda at Chesterholm, Northumberland*, Archaeological Report, **1**, Historic Buildings and Monuments Commission for England, London, 1985.

Bidwell, P. T. and Speak, S., *Excavations at South Shields Roman fort. Volume 1*, Monograph series, **4**, Society of Antiquaries of Newcastle upon Tyne with Tyne and Wear Museums, 1994.

Binsfeld, W., 'Zu den römischen Töpfereinen am Rudolfplatz in Köln', *Kölner Jahrbuch für Vor- und Frühgeschichte*, **7**, 1964, pp. 19–32.

Birchall, A., 'The Aylesford-Swarling culture: The problem of the Belgae reconsidered', *Proc Prehist Soc*, **31**, 1965, pp. 241–367.

Bird, J., 'African Red Slip ware in Roman Britain' in *Roman pottery studies in Britain and beyond: papers presented to J. P. Gillam, July 1977*, ed. J. Dore and K. T. Greene, British archaeological reports. International series, **30**, BAR, Oxford, 1977, pp. 269–78.

Bird, J., 'Samian wares' in *The Roman Quay at St Magnus House, London*, ed. L. Miller, J. Schofield and M. Rhodes, Special Paper, **8**, London and Middlesex Archaeological Society, London, 1986, pp. 139–85.

Bird, J., 'Two groups of late Samian from London', *Acta Rei Cretariae Romanae Fautores*, **25–26**, 1987, pp. 325–30.

Bird, J., '3rd-century samian ware in Britain', *J Roman Pottery Stud*, **6**, 1995, pp. 1–14.

Bird, J. and Marsh, G. D., 'The samian ware' in *The excavation of the Roman forts of the Classis Britannica at Dover 1970–77*, ed. B. Philp, Dover, 1981, pp. 178–202.

Bird, J. and Williams, D., 'German Marbled Flagons in Roman Britain', *Britannia*, 14, 1983, pp. 247–52.

Bird, J. and Young, C. J., 'Migrant potters - the Oxford connection' in *Roman Pottery research in Britain and North-West Europe: papers presented to Graham Webster*, ed. A. C. Anderson and A. S. Anderson, British archaeological reports. International series, **123**, BAR, Oxford, 1981, pp. 295–312.

Birley, A., *The people of Roman Britain*, Batsford, London, 1979.

Birley, E., 'A ceramic pilgrim's progress: the growth of Roman pottery studies in northern Britain' in *Roman pottery studies in Britain and beyond: papers presented to J. P. Gillam, July 1977*, ed. J. Dore and K. T. Greene, British archaeological reports. International series, **30**, BAR, Oxford, 1977, pp. 1–4.

Bishop, M. C. and Dore, J. N., *Corbridge: excavations of the Roman fort and town, 1947–80*, Archaeological Report, **8**, Historic Buildings and Monuments Commission for England, London, 1989.

Bittner, F.-K., 'Zur Forsetzung der Diskussion um die Chronologie der Rhienzaberner Reliefftöpfer', *Bayerische Vorgeschichtsblätter*, **51**, 1986, pp. 233–59.

Blakely, J. A., Brinkmann, R. and Vitaliano, C. J., 'Pompeian red ware: processing archaeological ceramic data', *Geoarchaeology*, **4**, 1989, pp. 201–28.

Blanc, N. and Nercessian, A., *La cuisine romaine antique*, Glénat, Grenoble, 1992.

Blaszkiewicz, P. and Jigan, C., 'Le problème de la diffusion et de la datation de la céramique sigillée d'Argonne décorée à la molette des IVème-Vème siècles dane le nord-ouest de l'Empire' in *Actes du Congrès de Cognac. 8–11 Mai 1991*, ed. L. Rivet, SFECAG, Marseille, 1991, pp. 385–415.

Blurton, R. and Rhodes, M., 'Excavations at Angel Court, Walbrook, 1974', *Trans London Middlesex Archaeol Soc*, **28**, 1977, pp. 14–100.

Bonsor, W., *A Romano-British bibliography (55BC–AD449)*, Blackwell, Oxford, 1964.

Boon, G. C., 'Micaceous sigillata from Lezoux at Silchester, Caerleon and other sites', *Antiquaries J*, **47**, 1967, pp. 27–42.

Borgard, P., 'L'origine liparote des amphores Richborough 527 et la détermination de leur contenu' in *Actes du Congrès de Millau. 12–15 Mai 1994*, ed. L. Rivet, SFECAG, Marseille, 1994, pp. 197–204.

Borgard, P. and Gateau, F., 'Des amphores canneleés à Cavaillon (Vaucluse) à la fin du 1er siecle avant notre ère. Nouveaux éléments pour l'étude des "Richborough 527"' in *Actes du Congrès de Cognac. 8–11 Mai 1991*, ed. L. Rivet, SFECAG, Marseille, 1991, pp. 311–28.

Bös, M., 'Aufschriften auf rheinischen Trinkgefässen der Römerzeit', *Kölner Jahrbuch für Vor- und Frühgeschichte*, **3**, 1958, pp. 20–5.

Bowden, M., *Pitt Rivers: the life and archaeological work of Lieutenant-General Augustus Henry Lane Fox Pitt Rivers, DCL, FRS, FSA*, Cambridge University Press, Cambridge, 1991.

Bowman, A. K., Thomas, J. D. and Adams, J. N., 'Two letters from Vindolanda', *Britannia*, **21**, 1990, pp. 33–52.

Bradley, R. and Fulford, M. G., 'Sherd size in the analysis of occupation debris', *Bull Inst Archaeol Univ London*, **17**, 1980, pp. 85–94.

Braithwaite, G., 'Romano-British face pots and head pots', *Britannia*, **15**, 1984, pp. 99–131.

Brassington, M., 'A Trajanic kiln complex at Little Chester, Derby, 1968', *Antiquaries J*, **51**, 1, 1971, pp. 36–69.

Brewis, P., 'Roman Rudchester: report on excavations, 1924', *Archaeol Aeliana (4th series)*, **1**, 1925, pp. 93–120.

Brewster, N. H., 'Corbridge: it's significance for the study of Rhenish ware',

Bibliography

Archaeol Aeliana (4th series), **50**, 1972, pp. 205–16.

Britnell, J., *Caersws Vicus, Powys: excavations at the Old Primary School, 1985–86*, British archaeological reports. British series, **205**, BAR, Oxford, 1989.

Brodribb, G., *Roman tile and brick*, Alan Sutton, Gloucester, 1987.

Brodribb, G. and Cleere, H., 'The Classis Britannica bath-house at Beauport Park, East Sussex', *Britannia*, **19**, 1988, pp. 217–74.

Brown, A. E., 'A Romano-British shell-gritted pottery and tile manufacturing site at Harrold, Beds', *Bedfordshire Arch J*, **21**, 1994, pp. 19–107.

Brown, A. E. and Sheldon, H. L., 'Highgate Wood: the pottery and its production', *London Archaeol*, **2**, 9, 1974, pp. 223–31.

Browne, Sir T., *Concerning some urnes found in Brampton-Field, in Norfolk, Ann. 1667*, London, 1712.

Bryant, G. F., 'Experimental Romano-British kiln firings' in *Current research in Romano-British coarse pottery: papers given at a C.B.A. Conference held at New College, Oxford, March 24 to 26, 1972*, ed. A. Detsicas, Research reports/Council for British Archaeology, **10**, Council for British Archaeology, London, 1973, pp. 149–60.

Buckland, P. C., *Roman South Yorkshire: a source book*, Department of Archaeology and Prehistory. University of Sheffield, Sheffield, 1986.

Buckland, P. C. and Magilton, J. R., *The archaeology of Doncaster, 1. The Roman civil settlement*, British archaeological reports. British series, **148**, Oxford, 1986.

Buckland, P. C., Magilton, J. R. and Dolby, M. J., 'The Roman pottery industries of South Yorkshire: a review', *Britannia*, **11**, 1980, pp. 145–64.

Bulmer, M., *An introduction to Roman samian ware: with special reference to collections in Chester and the North West*, Chester Archaeological Society, Chester, 1980.

Burns, R. B., 'L'époque gallo-romaine: un nouveau chapitre de l'histoire de Guernsey' in *Actes du Congrès de Caen. 28–31 Mai 1987*, ed. L. Rivet, SFECAG, Marseille, 1987, pp. 29–38.

Bushe-Fox, J. P., *Excavations on the site of the Roman town at Wroxeter, Shropshire, in 1912*, Reports of the Research Committee of the Society of Antiquaries of London, **1**, Oxford, 1913.

Bushe-Fox, J. P., 'The use of samian pottery in dating the early Roman occupation of the north of Britain', *Archaeologia*, **64**, 1913, pp. 295–314.

Bushe-Fox, J. P., *Second report on the excavations on the site of the Roman town at Wroxeter, Shropshire, 1913*, Reports of the Research Committee of the Society of Antiquaries of London, **2**, Oxford, 1914.

Bushe-Fox, J. P., *Excavations at Hengistbury Head, Hampshire in 1911–12*, Reports of the Research Committee of the Society of Antiquaries of London, **3**, Oxford, 1915.

Bushe-Fox, J. P., *Third report on the excavations on the site of the Roman town at Wroxeter, Shropshire, 1914*, Reports of the Research Committee of the Society of Antiquaries of London, **4**, Oxford, 1916.

Bushe-Fox, J. P., *Excavation of the Late-Celtic urn-field at Swarling, Kent*, Reports of the Research Committee of the Society of Antiquaries of London, **5**, Oxford, 1925.

Bushe-Fox, J. P., *First report on the excavation of the Roman fort at Richborough, Kent*, Reports of the Research Committee of the Society of Antiquaries of London, **6**, Oxford, 1926.

Bushe-Fox, J. P., *Second report on the excavation of the Roman fort at Richborough, Kent*, Reports of the Research Committee of the Society of Antiquaries of London, **7**, Oxford, 1928.

Bushe-Fox, J. P., *Fourth report on the excavation of the Roman fort at Richborough, Kent*, Reports of the Research Committee of the Society of Antiquaries of London, **16**, Oxford, 1949.

Calkin, J. B., 'An early Romano-British kiln at Corfe Mullen, Dorset', *Antiquaries J*, **15**, 1935, pp. 42–55.

Callender, M. H., *Roman amphorae: with an index of stamps*, University of Durham publications, Oxford University Press, London, 1965.

Campbell, E., 'E ware and Aquitaine: a reappraisal of the petrological evidence', *Scottish Archaeol Review*, **3**, 1, 1984, pp. 38–41.

Carre, M.-B., 'La banque de données "timbres sur amphores romaines" du Centre Camille Jullian' in *Les amphores en Gaule: production et circulation*, ed. F. Laubenheimer, Centre de Recherches d'Histoire Ancienne, **116**, Université de Besançon, Besançon, 1992, pp. 225–30.

Casey, P. J., *Excavations at Segontium (Caernarfon) Roman fort, 1975–1979*, Council for British Archaeology Research Report, **90**, Council for British Archaeology, London, 1993.

Castle, S. A., 'Trial excavations in field 410 Brockley Hill: Part I', *London Archaeol*, **2**, 2, 1973, pp. 36–9.

Castle, S. A., 'Amphorae from Brockley Hill, 1975', *Britannia*, **9**, 1978, pp. 383–92.

Cavalier, M., 'Les amphores Richborough 527: decouverte d'un atelier à Portinenti (Lipari, Italie)' in *Actes du Congrès de Millau. 12–15 Mai 1994*, ed. L. Rivet, SFECAG, Marseille, 1994, pp. 189–96.

Celuzza, M. G., *Settefinestre. Una villa schiavistica nell'Etruria romana. La villa ei suoi reperti*, Edizioi Panini, Modena, 1985, pp. 107–15.

Chadburn, A. and Tyers, P. A., 'The Roman ceramics from Fenchurch Street', DUA Archive Report, 1984.

Chenet, G., *La céramique gallo-romaine d'Argonne du IVe siècle et la terre sigillée décorée à la molette*, Mâcon, 1941.

Chossenot, M. and Chossenot, D., 'Introduction à l'étude de la céramique gallo-belge dans la vallée de la Vesle (Marne)', *Revue Archéologique de l'Est et du Centre-Est*, **38**, 1987, pp. 113–23.

Clark, A. J., 'The Fourth-century Romano-British pottery kilns at Overwey, Tilford', *Surrey Archaeol Collect*, **51**, 1949, pp. 29–56.

Coatts, M. and Lewis, E., *Heywood Sumner: artist and archaeologist. 1853–1940*, Winchester City Museum, Winchester, 1986.

Collingwood, R. G., *The archaeology of Roman Britain*, Methuen, London, 1930.

Collingwood, R. G. and Richmond, I. A., *The archaeology of Roman Britain*, Methuen, London, 1969.

Collingwood, R. G., Wright, R. P., Frere, S. S. and Tomlin, R. S. O., *The Roman* inscriptions of Britain. Volume II, Fascicule 5, Alan Sutton Publishing, Stroud, 1993.

Collingwood, R. G., Wright, R. P., Frere, S. S. and Tomlin, R. S. O., *The Roman inscriptions of Britain. Volume II, Fascicule 6*, Alan Sutton Publishing, Stroud, 1994.

Collis, J. R., 'Pre-Roman burial rites in north-western Europe' in *Burial in the Roman world*, ed. R. Reece, Research reports/Council for British Archaeology, **22**, Council for British Archaeology, London, 1977, pp. 1–12.

Colls, D., Étienne, R., Lequément, R., Liou, B. and Mayet, F., 'L'Épave Port-Vendres II et le Commerce de la Bétique à l'Époque de Claude', *Archaeonautica*, **1**, 1977, pp. 1–143.

Comas Solà, M., 'Importació i exportació de vi a Baetulo: l'estudi de les àmfores' in *Le vi a l'antiguitat. Economia producció i commerç al Mediterrani Occidental*, Monografies Badalonines, **9**, Museu de Badalona, Badalona, 1987, pp. 161–75.

Comas Solà, M., 'Les amphores de M. PORCIUS et leur diffusion de la Léetanie vers la Gaule' in *Actes du Congrès de Cognac. 8–11 Mai 1991*, ed. L. Rivet, SFECAG, Marseille, 1991, pp. 326–46.

Combe, C. and Jackson, J., 'Account of the discoveries in digging a sewer in Lombard-street and Birchin-lane, 1786', *Archaeologia*, **8**, 1787, pp. 116–32.

Comfort, H., *Notes on Roman ceramic archaeology, 1928–1978*, Rei Cretariae Romanae Fautorum Acta. Supplementa, **4**, Rei Cretariae Romanae Fautores, Augst, 1979.

Corder, P., *The Roman pottery at Crambeck, Castle Howard*, Roman Malton and District report, **1**, Roman Antiquities Committee of the Yorkshire Archaeological Society, Leeds, 1928.

Corder, P., *The Roman pottery at Throlam, Holme-on-Spalding-Moor, East Yorkshire*, Roman Malton and District report, **3**, Roman Antiquities Committee of the Yorkshire Archaeological Society, Hull, 1930.

Corder, P., 'A pair of fourth century Romano-British pottery kilns near Crambeck', *Antiquaries J*, **17**, 1937, pp. 392–413.

Corder, P., 'A Roman pottery of the Hadrianic-Antonine period at Verulamium', *Antiquaries J*, **21**, 1941, pp. 271–98.

Corder, P., *Structure of Romano-British pottery kilns*, Research report/Council for British Archaeology, **5**, Council for British Archaeology, [London], 1957.

Corder, P. and Kirk, J. L., *A Roman villa at Langton, near Malton, East Yorkshire*, Roman Malton and District report, **4**, Roman Antiquities Committee of the Yorkshire Archaeological Society, Leeds, 1932.

Crowther, P., 'Edmund Artis: the obituary of 1849', *Durobrivae*, **9**, 1984, pp. 14–15.

Cuming, H. Syer, 'On some recent discoveries of Roman remains at Wilderspool', *J Brit Archaeol Ass*, **27**, 1871, pp. 430–7.

Cuming, H. Syer, 'On vessels of samian ware', *J Brit Archaeol Ass*, **47**, 1891, pp. 277–85.

Cunliffe, B. W., *Fifth report on the excavation of the Roman fort at Richborough, Kent*, Reports of the Research Committee of the Society of Antiquaries of London, **23**, Society of Antiquaries, Oxford, 1968.

Cunliffe, B. W., *Excavations at Fishbourne 1961–1969. Volume II: The finds*, Reports of the Research Committee of the Society of Antiquaries of London, **27**, Society of Antiquaries, Leeds, 1971.

Cunliffe, B. W., *Iron Age communities in Britain*, Routledge and Kegan Paul, London, 1974.

Cunliffe, B. W., *Hengistbury Head, Dorset. Volume 1: The prehistoric and Roman settlement 3500BC–AD500*, Oxford University Committee for Archaeology. Monograph, **13**, Oxford, 1987.

Cunliffe, B. W., *Mount Batten, Plymouth. A prehistoric and Roman port*, Oxford University Committee for Archaeology. Monograph, **26**, Oxford, 1988.

Cunliffe, B. W. and Davenport, P., *The Temple of Sulis Minerva at Bath, Volume 1: The site*, Oxford University Committee for Archaeology. Monograph, **7**, Oxford, 1985.

Curle, J., *A Roman frontier post and its people: the fort of Newstead in the Parish of Melrose*, Glasgow, 1911.

Dangréaux, B. and Desbat, A., 'Les amphores du dépotoir flavien du Bas-de-Loyasse à Lyon', *Gallia*, **45**, 1988, pp. 115–53.

Dangréaux, B., Desbat, A., Picon, M. and Schmitt, A., 'La production d'amphores à Lyon' in *Les amphores en Gaule: production et circulation*, ed. F. Laubenheimer, Centre de Recherches d'Histoire Ancienne, **116**, Université de Besançon, Besançon, 1992, pp. 37–50.

Dannell, G. B., 'The potter Indixivixus' in *Current research in Romano-British coarse pottery: papers given at a C.B.A. Conference held at New College, Oxford, March 24 to 26, 1972*, ed. A. Detsicas, Research reports/Council for British Archaeology, **10**, Council for British Archaeology, London, 1973, pp. 139–42.

Dannell, G. B., 'The samian from Bagendon' in *Roman pottery studies in Britain and beyond: papers presented to J. P. Gillam, July 1977*, ed. J. Dore and K. T. Greene, British archaeological reports. International series, **30**, BAR, Oxford, 1977, pp. 229–35.

Dannell, G. B. and Wild, J. P., *Longthorpe II. The military works-depot: an episode in landscape history*, Britannia. Monograph series, **8**, Society for the Promotion of Roman Studies, London, 1987.

Darling, M. J., 'Pottery from early military sites in western Britain' in *Roman pottery studies in Britain and beyond: papers presented to J. P. Gillam, July 1977*, ed. J. Dore and K. T. Greene, British archaeological reports. International series, **30**, BAR, Oxford, 1977, pp. 57–100.

Darling, M. J., *Roman Pottery from the Upper Defences*, Monograph series/Lincoln Archaeological Trust. Monograph, 16/2, Council for British Archaeology for the Lincoln Archaeological Trust, London, 1984.

Darling, M. J., 'Nice fabric, pity about the form', *J Roman Pottery Stud*, **2**, 1989, pp. 98–101.

Darling, M. J., *Caister-on-Sea excavations by Charles Green, 1951–55*, E. Anglian Archaeol. Report, **60**, 1993.

Darlington, J. and Evans, J., 'Roman Sidbury, Worcester excavations 1959–1989', *Trans Worcestershire Archaeol Soc*, **13**, 1992, pp. 5–104.

Darvill, T. and Timby, J. R., 'Textural analysis: a review of limitations and possibilities' in *Current research in ceramics: thin-section studies*, ed. I. C. Freestone, C. Johns and T. Potter, British Museum Occasional Paper, **32**, British Museum,

Bibliography

London, 1982, pp. 73–87.

Déchelette, J., *Les vases céramiques ornés de la Gaule romaine*, Paris, 1904.

De la Bédoyère, G., *Samian ware*, Shire archaeology, **55**, Shire, Princes Risborough, 1988.

Desbat, A., 'Les importations d'amphores vinaires à Lyon et Vienne au début de l'Empire' in *Le vi a l'antiguitat. Economia producció i commerç al Mediterrani Occidental*, Monografies Badalonines, **9**, Museu de Badalona, Badalona, 1987, pp. 407–16.

Detsicas, A., 'First-century pottery manufacture at Eccles, Kent' in *Roman pottery studies in Britain and beyond: papers presented to J. P. Gillam, July 1977*, ed. J. Dore and K. T. Greene, British archaeological reports. International series, **30**, BAR, Oxford, 1977, pp. 19–36.

Detsicas, A., (ed), *Current research in Romano-British coarse pottery: papers given at a C.B.A. Conference held at New College, Oxford, March 24 to 26, 1972*, Research reports/Council for British Archaeology, **10**, Council for British Archaeology, London, 1973.

Doran, J. E. and Hodson, F. R., *Mathematics and computers in Archaeology*, Edinburgh University Press, Edinburgh, 1975.

Down, A., *Chichester excavations III*, Philimore, Chichester, 1978.

Down, A., *Chichester excavations VI*, Philimore for Chichester District Council, Chichester, 1989.

Dragendorff, H., 'Terra sigillata', *Bonner Jahrbücher*, **96**, 1895, pp. 18–155.

Draper, J., *Excavations by Mr. H. P. Cooper on the Roman site at Hill Farm, Gestingthorpe, Essex*, E. Anglian Archaeol. Report, 25, Archaeology Section. Essex County Council, 1985.

Draper, J., 'Excavations at Great Chesterford', *Proc Cambridge Antiq Soc*, **75**, 1986, pp. 3–41.

Drower, M. S., *Flinders Petrie: a life in archaeology*, London, 1985.

Drury, P. J. and Wickenden, N. P., 'An Early Saxon settlement within the Romano-British small town at Heybridge, Essex', *Medieval Archaeol*, **26**, 1982, pp. 1–40.

Dufaÿ, B., Barat, Y. and Veermeersch, D., *Trésors de terre: céramiques et potiers dans l'Ile-de-France Gallo-Romaine*, Service Archéologique Départemental, Conseil Général des Yvelines, Versailles, 1993.

Duncan, R. J., Hodson, F. R., Orton, C. R., Tyers, P. A. and Vekaria, A., *Data analysis for archaeologists: the Institute of Archaeology programs*, Institute of Archaeology, London, 1988.

Duncan-Jones, R., *The economy of the Roman Empire: quantitative studies. 2nd edition*, Cambridge University Press, Cambridge, 1982.

Edwards, N. and Lane, A., (ed), *Early Medieval settlement in Wales AD 400-1100*, Research Centre Wales and Department of Archaeology, University College, Cardiff, Cardiff, 1988.

Ellis, P., 'Roman Chesterfield: excavations by T. Courtney 1974-1978', *Derbyshire Archaeol J*, **109**, 1989, pp. 51–130.

Elsdon, S. M., *Parisian ware: a study of stamped wares of the Roman period in Lincolnshire, Humberside and South Yorkshire*, Vorda research series, 4, Vorda, Highworth, 1982.

Empereur, J. Y. and Picon, M., 'A propos d'un nouvel atelier de Late Roman C', *Figlina*, **7**, 1986, pp. 143–6.

Empereur, J.-Y. and Picon, M., 'Les régions de production d'amphores impériales en Méditerranée orientale' in *Amphores romaines et histoire économique: dix ans de recherche*, Collection de l'École Française de Rome, **114**, École Française de Rome, Rome, 1989, pp. 223–48.

Esmonde Cleary, S., *The ending of Roman Britain*, Batsford, London, 1989.

Ettlinger, E., 'Legionary pottery from Vindonissa', *J Roman Stud*, **41**, 1951, pp. 105–11.

Ettlinger, E., Hedinger, B., Hoffmann, B., Kenrick, P. M., Pucci, G., Roth-Rubi, K., Schneider, G., Schnurbein, S. von, Wells, C. M. and Zabehlicky-Scheffenegger, S., *Conspectus formarum terrae sigillatae Italico modo confectae*, Materialien zur römisch-germanischen Keramik, 10, R. Habelt, Bonn, 1990.

Ettlinger, E. and Simonett, C., *Römische Keramik aus dem Schütthugel von Vindonissa*, Veröff. Ges. Vindonissa, 3, Basel, 1952.

Evans, A. J., 'A Late Celtic urn-field at Aylesford, Kent', *Archaeologia*, **90**, 1890, pp. 315–88.

Evans, A. K. B., 'Pottery and history' in *Roman pottery research in Britain and north-west Europe; papers presented to Graham Webster*, ed. A. C. Anderson and A. S. Anderson, British archaeological reports. International series, **123**, BAR, Oxford, 1981, pp. 517–35.

Evans, J., 'Graffiti and the evidence of literacy and pottery use in Roman Britain', *Archaeol. J*, **144** pp.191–204.

Evans, J. and Millett, M., 'Residuality revisited', *Oxford J Archaeol*, **11**, 2, 1992, pp. 225–40.

Fabroni, A., *Storia degli antichi vasi fictile aretini*, Arezzo, 1841.

Farrar, R. A. H., 'The techniques and sources of Romano-British black-burnished ware' in *Current research in Romano-British coarse pottery: papers given at a C.B.A. Conference held at New College, Oxford, March 24 to 26, 1972*, ed. A. Detsicas, Research reports/Council for British Archaeology, **10**, Council for British Archaeology, London, 1973, pp. 67–103.

Farrar, R. A. H., 'The first Darfield hoard and the dating of black-burnished ware' in *Roman pottery research in Britain and north-west Europe: papers presented to Graham Webster*, ed. A. C. Anderson and A. S. Anderson, British archaeological reports. International series, **123**, BAR, Oxford, 1981, pp. 417–30.

Feller, M., 'Classification et datation des molettes d'Argonne: problèmes et méthodes' in *Actes du Congrès de Cognac. 8–11 Mai 1991*, ed. L. Rivet, SFECAG, 1991, pp. 161–9.

Ferdière, A. and Ferdière, M., 'Introduction à l'etude d'un type céramique: les urnes à bord mouluré Gallo-Romaines précoces', *Revue Archéologique de l'Est et du Centre-Est*, **22**, 1972, pp. 77–88.

Firman, R. J., 'The significance of anhydrite in pottery as exemplified by Romano-British Dales ware', *J Roman Pottery Stud*, **4**, 1991, pp. 45–50.

Fitzpatrick, A. P., 'The distribution of Dressel 1 amphorae in north-west Europe', *Oxford J Archaeol*, **4**, 3, 1985, pp. 305–40.

Fitzpatrick, A. P., 'La place des amphores dans l'approvisionnement militaire de l'Écosse romaine' in *Les amphores en Gaule: production et circulation*, ed. F. Laubenheimer, Centre de Recherches d'Histoire Ancienne, **116**, Université de Besançon, Besançon, 1992, pp. 179–83.

Fletcher, M. and Lock, G. R., *Digging numbers: elementary statistics for*

Bibliography

archaeologists, Oxford University Committee for Archaeology. Monograph, **33**, Oxford, 1991.

Flower, B. and Rosenbaum, E., *The Roman cookery book: a critical translation of The Art of Cooking by Apicius for use in the study and the kitchen*, Harrap, London, 1958.

Forster, R. H. and Knowles, W. H., 'Corstopitum: report on the excavations in 1911', *Archaeol Aeliana (3rd series)*, **8**, 1912, pp. 137–263.

Freestone, I. C., 'Applications and potential of electron microprobe analysis in technological and provenance investigations of ancient ceramics', *Archaeometry*, **24**, 1982, pp. 99–116.

Freestone, I. C., Johns, C. and Potter, T., (eds), *Current research in ceramics: thin-section studies*, British Museum Occasional Paper, **32**, British Museum, London, 1982.

Frere, S. S., *Verulamium excavations. Volume I*, Reports of the Research Committee of the Society of Antiquaries of London, **28**, Oxford, 1972.

Frere, S. S. and Wilkes, J. J., *Strageath: excavations within the Roman fort 1973-1986*, Britannia. Monograph series, **9**, Society for the Promotion of Roman Studies, London, 1989.

Fulford, M. G., New Forest *Roman pottery: manufacture and distribution, with a corpus of pottery types*, British archaeological reports, **17**, BAR, Oxford, 1975.

Fulford, M. G., 'The pottery' in *Excavations at Portchester Castle. Volume I: Roman*, ed. B. W. Cunliffe, Reports of the Research Committee of the Society of Antiquaries of London, **32**, Society of Antiquaries, London, 1975, pp. 270–367.

Fulford, M. G., 'The location of Romano-British pottery kilns: Institutional trade and the market' in *Roman pottery studies in Britain and beyond: papers presented to J. P. Gillam, July 1977*, ed. J. Dore and K. T. Greene, British archaeological reports. International series, **30**, BAR, Oxford, 1977, pp. 301–16.

Fulford, M. G., 'Pottery and Britain's foreign trade in the later Roman period' in *Pottery and early commerce: characterization and trade in Roman and later ceramics*, ed. D. P. S. Peacock, Academic Press, London, 1977, pp. 35–84.

Fulford, M. G., 'The interpretation of Britain's late Roman trade: the scope of medieval historical and archaeological analogy' in *Roman shipping and trade: Britain and the Rhine provinces*, ed. J. du Plat Taylor and H. Cleere, Research reports/Council for British Archaeology, **24**, Council for British Archaeology, London, 1978, pp. 59–69.

Fulford, M. G., 'Pottery production and trade at the end of Roman Britain: the case against continuity' in *The end of Roman Britain*, ed. P. J. Casey, British archaeological reports. British series, **71**, BAR, Oxford, 1979, pp. 120–32.

Fulford, M. G., 'Berenice, Carthage, Ostia: the amphoras of three cities', *Acta Rei Cretariae Romanae Fautores*, **25–26**, 1987, pp. 155–9.

Fulford, M. G., 'Byzantium and Britain: a Mediterranean perspective on post-Roman Mediterranean imports in western Britain and Ireland', *Medieval Archaeol*, **33**, 1989, pp. 1–6.

Fulford, M. G., 'Britain and the Roman Empire: the evidence for regional and long distance trade' in *Britain in the Roman period: recent trends*, ed. R. F. J. Jones, J. R. Collis Publications, Sheffield, 1991.

Fulford, M. G. and Bird, J., 'Imported Pottery from Germany in Late Roman Britain', *Britannia*, **6**, 1975, pp. 171–81.

Fulford, M. G. and Hodder, I., 'A regression analysis of some later Romano-British pottery: a case study', *Oxoniensia*, **39**, 1974, pp. 26–33.

Fulford, M. G. and Huddleston, K., *The current state of Romano-British pottery studies: a review for English Heritage*, English Heritage Occasional Papers, **1**, English Heritage, London, 1991.

Furger, A. R., 'Vom Essen und Trimken im römischen Augst Kochen, Essen und Trinken im Spiegel einiger Funde', *Archäologie der Schweiz*, **8**, 3, 1985, pp. 168–84.

Galliou, P., *Les amphores tardo-républicaines*, Corpus des amphores découvertes dans l'ouest de la France, **2**, Brest, 1982.

Galliou, P., Fulford, M. G. and Clement, M., 'La diffusion de la céramique "à l'éponge" dans le Nord-Ouest de l'empire romain', *Gallia*, **38**, 1980, pp. 265–78.

Garnsey, P., Hopkins, K. and Whittaker, C. R., (eds), *Trade in the Ancient Economy*, University of California Press, Berkeley and Los Angeles, 1983.

Giacosa, I. G., *A taste of Ancient Rome*, University of Chicago Press, Chicago, 1992.

Gillam, J. P., 'Roman-British Derbyshire ware', *Antiquaries J*, **19**, 1939, pp. 429–37.

Gillam, J. P., 'Dating second-century pottery in northern Britain', *Trans Dumfriesshire Galloway Natur Hist Antiq Soc*, **28**, 1949–50, pp. 190–8.

Gillam, J. P., 'Dating fourth-century pottery in northern Britain', *Archaeol Newsl*, **3**, 1951, pp. 171–2.

Gillam, J. P., 'Dales wares: a distinctive Romano-British cooking pot', *Antiquaries J*, **31**, 1951, pp. 154–64.

Gillam, J. P., 'Roman pottery in the north of Britain' in *Carnuntina. Ergebnisse der Forschung über die Grenzprovinzen des römischen Reiches. Vorträge beim internationalen Kongress der Altertumsforscher. Carnuntum 1955*, ed. E. Swoboda, Römische Forschungen in Niederösterreich, **3**, Hermann Böhlaus Nachf., Graz, 1956, pp. 64–77.

Gillam, J. P., 'Types of Roman coarse pottery vessels in northern Britain', *Archaeol Aeliana* (4th series), **35**, 1957, pp. 180–251.

Gillam, J. P., 'Sources of pottery found on northern military sites' in *Current research in Romano-British coarse pottery: papers given at a C.B.A. Conference held at New College, Oxford, March 24 to 26, 1972*, ed. A. Detsicas, Research reports/Council for British Archaeology, **10**, Council for British Archaeology, London, 1973, pp. 53–62.

Gillam, J. P., 'Coarse fumed ware in northern Britain', *Glasgow Archaeol J*, **4**, 1976, pp. 57–80.

Gillam, J. P., 'Romano-Saxon pottery, an alternative explanation' in *The end of Roman Britain*, ed. P. J. Casey, British archaeological reports. British series, **71**, BAR, Oxford, 1979, pp. 103–18.

Gillam, J. P. and Greene, K. T., 'Roman pottery and the economy' in *Roman pottery research in Britain and north-west Europe: papers presented to Graham Webster*, ed. A. C. Anderson and A. S. Anderson, British archaeological reports. International series, **123**, BAR, Oxford, 1981, pp. 1–24.

Going, C. J., *The Mansio and other sites in the south-eastern sector of Caesaromagus: the Roman pottery*, Research

Bibliography

reports/Council for British Archaeology, **62**, Chelmsford Archaeological Trust; Council for British Archaeology, London, 1987.

Going, C. J., 'Economic "long-waves" in the Roman period? A reconnaisance of the Romano-British ceramic evidence', *Oxford J Archaeol*, **11**, 1, 1992, pp. 93–117.

Gose, E., *Gefässtypen der römischen Keramik im Rheinland*, Beihefte der Bonner Jahrbücher, **1**, 1950.

Goudineau, C., 'Note sur la céramique à engobe interne rouge-pompéien (Pompejanisch-roten platten)', *Memoires de l'École Française de Rome*, **82**, 1970, pp. 159–86.

Grace, V. R., *Amphoras and the ancient wine trade*, Princeton, 1961.

Grataloup, C., *Les céramiques à parois fines, Rue des Farges à Lyon*, British archaeological reports. International series, **457**, Oxford, 1988.

Green, C., *Excavations in the Roman kiln field at Brampton*, E. Anglian Archaeol. Report, **5**, 1977.

Green, C. M., 'Handmade pottery and society in Late Iron Age and Roman East Sussex', *Sussex Archaeol Collect*, **118**, 1980, pp. 69–86.

Green, C. M., 'Roman pottery' in Excavations at *Billingsgate Buildings Triangle, Lower Thames Street, 1974*, ed. D. M. Jones, Special Paper, **4**, London and Middlesex Archaeological Society, London, 1980, pp. 39–80.

Green, L. S., 'The Roman pottery manufacturing site at Between Towns Road, Cowley, Oxford', *Oxoniensia*, **48**, 1983, pp. 1–11.

Greene, K. T., 'Seven pre-Flavian moulded cups from Britain', *Acta Rei Cretariae Romanae Fautores*, **14–15**, 1972–3, pp. 48–54.

Greene, K. T., 'A group of Roman pottery from Wanborough, Wiltshire', *Wiltshire Archeaol Natur Hist Magazine*, **69**, 1974, pp. 51–66.

Greene, K. T., 'Legionary pottery, and the significance of Holt' in *Roman pottery studies in Britain and beyond: papers presented to J. P. Gillam, July 1977*, ed. J. Dore and K. T. Greene, British archaeological reports. International series, **30**, BAR, Oxford, 1977, pp. 113–32.

Greene, K. T., 'Roman trade between Britain and the Rhine provinces: the evidence of pottery to *c.* AD 250' in *Roman shipping and trade: Britain and the Rhine provinces*, ed. J. du Plat Taylor and H. Cleere, Research reports/Council for British Archaeology, **24**, Council for British Archaeology, London, 1978, pp. 52–8.

Greene, K. T., 'Imported fine wares in Britain to AD 250: A guide to identification' in *Early fine wares in Roman Britain*, ed. G. D. Marsh and P. R. Arthur, British archaeological reports. British series, **57**, BAR, Oxford, 1978, pp. 15–30.

Greene, K. T., 'Mould-decorated central Gaulish glazed ware in Britain' in *Early fine wares in Roman Britain*, ed. P. R. Arthur and G. D. Marsh, British Archaeological Reports. British Series, **57**, BAR, Oxford, 1978, pp. 31–60.

Greene, K. T., *The pre-Flavian fine wares*, Report on the excavations at Usk, 1965-1976, 1, University of Wales Press [for] the Board of Celtic Studies of the University of Wales, Cardiff, 1979.

Greene, K. T., *The archaeology of the Roman economy*, Batsford, London, 1986.

Greene, K. T., 'Review of M. G. Fulford and K. Huddleston *The current state of Romano-British pottery studies: a review for English Heritage 1991*', Britannia, **23**, 1992, pp. 362–5.

Greene, K. T., *Roman Pottery: interpreting the past*, British Museum Press, London, 1992.

Griffiths, K. E, 'Marketing of Roman pottery in second-century Northamptonshire and the Milton Keynes area', *J Roman Pottery Stud*, **2**, 1989, pp. 66–76.

Griffiths, K. E. and Greene, K. T., 'Pottery, history and ethnoarchaeology', *Scottish Archaeol Review*, **2**, 2, 1983, pp. 183–7.

Grimes, W. F., 'Holt, Denbighshire; the works-dêpot of the Twentieth Legion at Castle Lyons', *Y Cymmrodor*, **41**, 1930, pp. 1–235.

Grünewald, M., Pernicka, E. and Wynia, S. L., 'Pompejanisch-rote Platten - Patinae', *Archäologisches Korrespondenzblatt*, **10**, 1980, pp. 259–60.

Guillaume, A., 'The Phoenician graffito in the Holt collection of the National Museum of Wales', *Iraq*, **7**, 1940, pp. 67–8.

Gurney, D., 'Settlement, religion and industry on the Fen-edge; Three Romano-British sites in Norfolk', *E Anglian Archaeol Report*, **31**, 1986.

Haalebos, J. K., 'La céramique belge à Nimègue' in *Actes du Congrès de Tournai. 28–31 Mai 1992*, ed. L. Rivet, SFECAG, Marseille, 1992, pp. 17–28.

Hamerow, H., *Excavations at Mucking. Volume 2: The Anglo-Saxon settlement*, Archaeological Report, **21**, English Heritage, London, 1993.

Hampe, R. and Winter, A., *Bei Töpfern und Zieglern in Süditalien Sizilien und Greichenland*, Römisch-Germanisches Zentralmuseum, Mainz, 1965.

Harden, D. B., 'Two Romano-British potters'-fields near Oxford', *Oxoniensia*, **1**, 1936, pp. 81–102.

Harden, D. B. and Green, C. M., 'A late Roman grave-group from the Minories, Aldgate' in *Collectanea Londiniensia: studies in London archaeology and history presented to Ralph Merrifield*, ed. J. Bird, H. Chapman and J. Clark, Special Paper, **2**, London and Middlesex Archaeological Society, London, 1978, pp. 163–76.

Hartley, B. R., *Notes on the Roman pottery industry in the Nene valley*, Occasional papers – Peterborough Museum Society, **2**, The Museum, Peterborough, 1960.

Hartley, B. R., 'Samian ware or Terra sigillata' in *The archaeology of Roman Britain*, ed. R. G. Collingwood and I. A. Richmond, Methuen, London, 1969, pp. 235–51.

Hartley, B. R., 'The samian ware' in *Verulamium excavations. Volume I*, ed. S. S. Frere, Reports of the Research Committee of the Society of Antiquaries of London, **28**, Oxford, 1972, pp. 216–62.

Hartley, B. R., 'The Roman Occupation of Scotland: the evidence of samian ware', *Britannia*, **3**, 1972, pp. 1–55.

Hartley, B. R., 'Some wandering potters' in *Roman pottery studies in Britain and beyond: papers presented to J. P. Gillam, July 1977*, ed. J. Dore and K. T. Greene, British archaeological reports. International series, **30**, BAR, Oxford, 1977, pp. 251–62.

Hartley, K. F., 'The kilns at Mancetter and Hartshill, Warwickshire' in *Current research in Romano-British coarse pottery: papers given at a C.B.A. Conference held at New College, Oxford, March 24 to*

Bibliography

26, 1972, ed. A. Detsicas, Research reports/Council for British Archaeology, **10**, Council for British Archaeology, London, 1973, pp. 143–7.

Hartley, K. F., 'The marketing and distribution of mortaria' in *Current research in Romano-British coarse pottery: papers given at a C.B.A. Conference held at New College, Oxford, March 24 to 26, 1972*, ed. A. Detsicas, Research reports/Council for British Archaeology, **10**, Council for British Archaeology, London, 1973, pp. 35–91.

Hartley, K. F., 'La diffusion des mortiers, tuiles et autres produits en provenance des fabriques italiennes', *Cahiers d'Archéologie Subaquatique*, **2**, 1973, pp. 49–60.

Hartley, K. F., 'Were mortaria made in Roman Scotland?', *Glasgow Archaeol J*, **4**, 1976, pp. 81–9.

Hartley, K. F., 'Two major potteries producing mortaria in the first century A.D.' in *Roman pottery studies in Britain and beyond: papers presented to J. P. Gillam, July 1977*, ed. J. Dore and K. T. Greene, British archaeological reports. International series, **30**, BAR, Oxford, 1977, pp. 5–18.

Hartley, K. F., 'The mortarium stamps' in *Verulamium Excavations Volume III*, ed. S. S. Frere, Oxford University Committee for Archaeology. Monograph, **1**, Oxford, 1984, pp. 280–91.

Hartley, K. F. and Richards, E. E., 'Spectrographic analysis of some Romano-British mortaria', *Bull Inst Archaeol Univ London*, **5**, 1965, pp. 25–44.

Hartley, K. F. and Webster, P. V., 'Romano-British pottery kilns near Wilderspool', *Archaeol J*, **130**, 1973, pp. 77–103.

Haselgrove, C., 'Inference from ploughsoil' in *Archaeology from the ploughsoil*, ed. C. Haselgrove, M. Millett and I. Smith, Department of Archaeology and Prehistory, University of Sheffield, Sheffield, 1985, pp. 7–30.

Haupt, D., 'Römischer Töpfereibezirk bei Soller, Kreis Düren' in *Beiträge zur Archäologie des römischen Rheinlands, 4*, ed. D. Haupt, Rheinland-Verlag, Ausgrabungen, **23**, Rheinland-Verlag, Bonn/Köln, 1984.

Haverfield, F., 'Notes on samian ware', *Trans Cumberland Westmorland Antiq Archaeol Soc*, **15**, 1898, pp. 191–6.

Haverfield, F., 'The Corbridge pottery shop and other notes on samian ware', *Proc Soc Antiq London*, **32**, 1911, pp. 112–21.

Haverfield, F., *The Romanization of Roman Britain. 3rd edn.*, Oxford University Press, Oxford, 1915.

Hawkes, C. F. C. and Hull, M. R., *Camulodunum: first report on the excavations at Colchester, 1930–39*, Reports of the Research Committee of the Society of Antiquaries of London, **14**, Society of Antiquaries, Oxford, 1947.

Hawkes, J., *Mortimer Wheeler: adventurer in archaeology*, Weidenfeld and Nicolson, London, 1982.

Hayes, J. W., *Late Roman pottery*, British School at Rome, London, 1972.

Hayes, J. W., *A supplement to Late Roman pottery*, British School at Rome, London, 1980.

Hayes, J. W., *Paphos III: the Hellenistic and Roman pottery*, Department of Antiquities, Cyprus, Nicosia, 1991.

Hearne, C. M. and Smith, R. J. C., 'A late Iron Age settlement and Black Burnished ware (BB1) production site at Worgret, near Wareham, Dorset (1986–7)', *Proc Dorset Nat Hist Archaeol Soc*, **113**, 1992, pp. 55–105.

Hermet, F., *La Graufesenque (Condatomago)*, Librairie Ernest Leroux, Paris, 1934.

Heron, C. and Pollard, A. M., 'The analysis of natural resinous materials from Roman amphorae' in *Science and archaeology, Glasgow, 1987*, ed. E. A. Slater and J. O. Tate, British archaeological reports. British series, **196**, BAR, Oxford, 1988, pp. 429–47.

Hesnard, A., Ricq, M., Arthur, P. R., Picon, M. and Tchernia, A., 'Aires de production des gréco-italiques et des Dr. 1' in *Amphores romaines et histoire économique: dix ans de recherche*, Collection de l'École Française de Rome, **114**, École Française de Rome, Rome, 1989, pp. 21–65.

Heukemes, B., *Römische Keramik aus Heidelberg*, Materialien zur römisch-germanischen Keramik, **8**, Habelt, Bonn, 1964.

Hilgers, W., *Lateinische Gefässnamen*, Beihefte Bonner Jahrbucher, **31**, Düsseldorf, 1969.

Hinchliffe, J., Williams, J. H. and Williams, F., *Roman Warrington: excavations at Wilderspool 1966–9 and 1976*, Brigantia Monograph, **2**, Dept. of Archaeology, University of Manchester, Manchester, 1992.

Hodder, I., 'The distribution of Savernake Ware', *Wiltshire Archeaol Natur Hist Magazine*, **69**, 1974, pp. 67–84.

Hodges, H. W. M., 'Thin sections of prehistoric pottery: an empirical study', *Bull Inst Archaeol Univ London*, **3**, 1962, pp. 58–68.

Holbrook, N. and Bidwell, P. T., *Roman finds from Exeter*, Exeter Archaeological Reports, **4**, Exeter City Council and the University of Exeter, Exeter, 1991.

Holwerda, J. H., *De Belgische Waar in Nijmegen*, The Hague, 1941
Howard 1981.

Howard, H., *In the wake of distribution: towards an integrated approach to ceramic studies in prehistoric Britain*, British archaeological reports. International series, **120**, BAR, Oxford, 1981, pp. 1–30.

Howe, M. D., Perrin, J. R. and Mackreth, D. F., *Roman pottery from the Nene valley: a guide*, Occasional paper, **2**, Peterborough City Museum and Art Gallery, Peterborough, 1980.

Hübener, W., 'Eine Studie zur spätrömischen Rädchensigillata (Argonnensigillata)', *Bonner Jahrbücher*, **168**, 1968, pp. 241–98.

Hughes, M. J., (ed), *Scientific studies in ancient ceramics*, British Museum Occasional Papers, **19**, British Museum, London, 1981.

Huld-Zetsche, I., 'Glatte Sigillaten des "Massenfundes" aus Trier', *Acta Rei Cretariae Romanae Fautores*, **13**, 1971, pp. 21–39.

Huld-Zetsche, I., 'Zum Forschungsstand über Trierer Reliefsigillaten', *Trierer Zeitschrift*, **34**, 1971, pp. 233–45.

Huld-Zetsche, I., *Trierer Reliefsigillata: Werkstatt I*, Materialien zur römisch-germanischen Keramik, **9**, R. Habelt, Bonn, 1972.

Huld-Zetsche, I., *Trierer Reliefsigillata: Werkstatt II*, Materialien zur römisch-germanischen Keramik, **12**, R. Habelt, Bonn, 1993.

Hull, M. R., 'The pottery from the Roman signal-stations on the Yorkshire coast', *Archaeol J*, **89**, 1932, pp. 220–53.

Hull, M. R., 'Eine Terra-Sigillata-Töpferei in Colchester (Camulodunum)', *Germania*, **18**, 1934,

Bibliography

pp. 27–36.
Hull, M. R., *Roman Colchester*, Reports of the Research Committee of the Society of Antiquaries of London, **20**, Society of Antiquaries and the Corporation of the Borough of Colchester, Oxford, 1958.
Hull, M. R., *The Roman potters' kilns of Colchester*, Reports of the Research Committee of the Society of Antiquaries of London, **21**, Society of Antiquaries and the Corporation of the Borough of Colchester, Oxford, 1963.
Hurst, H. R., *Kingsholm*, Gloucester Archaeological Reports, **1**, Gloucester Archaeological Publications, Gloucester, 1985.
Hussong, L. and Cüppers, H., *Die Trierer Kaiserthermen. Die spätrömische und frühmittelalterliche Keramik*, Trieren Grabungen und Forschungen, **1**, P. von Zabern, Mainz am Rhein, 1972.
Jacob, E., 'Observations on the Roman earthen ware taken from Pudding Pan Rock', *Archaeologia*, **6**, 1782, pp. 121–4.
Jefferson, T. O., Dannell, G. B. and Williams, D. F., 'The production and distribution of Terra Sigillata in the area of Pisa, Italy' in *Roman pottery research in Britain and north-west Europe: papers presented to Graham Webster*, ed. A. C. Anderson and A. S. Anderson, British archaeological reports. International series, **123**, BAR, Oxford, 1981, pp. 161–72.
Jewitt, L., 'On Roman remains, recently discovered near Headington, near Oxford', *J Brit Archaeol Ass*, **6**, 1851, pp. 52–67.
Jobey, I., 'Housesteads ware – a Frisian tradition on Hadrians Wall', *Archaeol Aeliana (5th series)*, **7**, 1979, pp. 127–43.
Johns, C., *Arretine and samian pottery*, British Museum, London, 1971.
Joncheroy, J.-P., 'Etude de l'epave Dramont D', *Cahiers d'Archéologie Subaquatique*, **1**, 1972, pp. 11–33.
Jones, G. D. B. and Webster, P. V., 'Derbyshire ware – a reappraisal', *Derbyshire Archaeol J*, **89**, 1969, pp. 19–24.
Jones, M. U., 'Potter's graffiti from Mucking', *Antiquaries J*, **52**, 1972, pp. 335–8.
Jones, M. U. and Rodwell, W. J., 'The Romano-British pottery kilns at Mucking', *Essex Archaeol Hist*, **5**, 1973,

pp. 13–47.
Kay, S. O., 'The Romano-British pottery kilns at Hazelwood and Holbrook, Derbyshire', *Derbyshire Archaeol J*, **82**, 1962, pp. 21–42.
Keate, G., 'Observation on the Roman earthen ware in the sea on the Kentish coast between Whitstable and Reculver on the banks of the Isle of Thanet', *Archaeologia*, **6**, 1782, pp. 125–9.
Keay, S. J., *Late Roman amphorae in the western Mediterranean: a typology and economic study. The Catalan evidence*, British archaeological reports. International Series, **196**, BAR, Oxford, 1984.
Keay, S. J. and Jones, L., 'Differentiation of early Imperial amphora production in Hispania Tarraconensis' in *Current research in ceramics: thin-section studies*, ed. C. Johns and T. Potter, British Museum Occasional Paper, **32**, British Museum, London, 1982, pp. 45–61.
Kendall, D. G., 'Seriation from abundance matrices' in *Mathematics in the archaeological and historical sciences*, ed. F. R. Hodson, D. G. Kendall and P. Tautu, Edinburgh University Press, Edinburgh, 1971, pp. 215–52.
Kennett, D. H., 'Shale vessels of the Late pre-Roman Iron Age: context, distribution and origins', *Bedfordshire Arch J*, **12**, 1977, pp. 17–22.
Kenrick, P. M., *Excavations at Sidi Khrebish Benghazi (Berenice). III, Part 1: The fine pottery*, Supplements to Libya Antiqua, **5**, Department of Antiquities, Tripoli, 1983.
Kenrick, P. M., 'Hommage au Professeur H. Comfort: la suite du *Corpus Vasorum Arretinorum*' in *Actes du Congrès de Millau. 12–15 Mai 1994*, ed. L. Rivet, SFECAG, Marseille, 1994, pp. 175–82.
Kenyon, K. M., *Excavations at the Jewry Wall site, Leicester*, Reports of the Research Committee of the Society of Antiquaries of London, **15**, Society of Antiquaries, London, 1948.
Keppie, L. J. F., 'Excavations at the Roman fort of Bar Hill, 1978–1982', *Glasgow Archaeol J*, **12**, 1985, pp. 49–81.
King, A., 'The decline of samian manufacture in the north-west provinces: problems of chronology and interpretation' in *The Roman West in the third century: contributions from archaeology and history*, ed. A. King and M. Henig,

British archaeological reports. International series, **109**, BAR, Oxford, 1981, pp. 55–78.
Knorr, R., *Töpfer und Fabriken verzierter Terra–Sigillata des ersten Jahrhunderts*, Kohlhammer, Stuttgart, 1919.
Knorr, R., *Terra Sigillata Gefässe des ersten Jahrhunderts, mit Töpfernamen*, Kohlhammer, Stuttgart, 1952.
Lang, M., 'Dated jars from early Imperial times', *Hesperia*, **24**, 1955, pp. 277–85.
Laroche, C., 'Aoste (Isère): un centre de production de céramiques. Fin du Ier siècle avant J.–C. – fin du Ier siècle après J.–C. Fouilles récentes, 1983–1984', *Revue Archéologique de Narbonnaise*, **20**, 1987, pp. 281–348.
Laubenheimer, F., *La production des amphores en Gaule Narbonnaise*, Centre de Recherches d'Histoire Ancienne, **66**, Paris, 1985.
Laubenheimer, F., 'Les amphores gauloises sous l'Empire: recherches nouvelles sur leur production et leur chronologie' in *Amphores romaines et histoire économique: dix ans de recherche*, Collection de l'École Française de Rome, **114**, École Française de Rome, Rome, 1989, pp. 105–38.
Laubenheimer, F., *Le temps des amphores en Gaule: vins, huiles et sauces*, Collection des Hesperides, Errance, Paris, 1990.
Laubenheimer, F., *Sallèles d'Aude: un complexe de potiers gallo–romain. Le quartier artisanal*, Documents d'archéologie française, **26**, Maison des Sciences de l'Homme, Paris, 1990.
Laubenheimer, F., 'Les amphores à l'époque romaine' in *Bibliographies sur l'époque romaine*, ed. M. Feugère, Bibliographies Thématiques en Archéologie, **16**, Monique Mergoil, Montagnac, 1991.
Laubenheimer, F. and Rodriguez, C., *Les amphores de Bibracte: le matériel des fouilles anciennes*, Documents d'archéologie française, **29**, Maison des Sciences de l'Homme, Paris, 1991.
Laubenheimer, F., Gebara, C. and Beraud, I., 'Production d'amphores à Fréjus' in *Les amphores en Gaule: production et circulation*, ed. F. Laubenheimer, Centre de Recherches d'Histoire Ancienne, **116**, Université de Besançon, Besançon, 1992, pp. 15–24.
Laubenheimer, F. and Lequoy, M.-C., 'Les amphores Gauloise 12 de Normandie: le matériel de la nécropole

Bibliography

de Vatteville-la-Rue' in *Les amphores en Gaule: production et circulation*, ed. F. Laubenheimer, Centre de Recherches d'Histoire Ancienne, **116**, Université de Besançon, Besançon, 1992, pp. 75–92.

Laubenheimer, F. and Notet, J.–C., 'Les amphores produites a Gueugnon (S. et L.) et les debuts du vignoble Bourguignon', *Dialogues d'histoire ancienne*, **12**, 1986, pp. 431–53.

Laubenheimer, F., Odiot, T. and Leclère, H., 'Sous Auguste, un atelier de potiers italianisant à Saint–Just (Ardèche)' in *Mélanges P. Lévêque* **2**, 1989, pp. 295–329.

Laubenheimer, F., (ed), *Les amphores en Gaule. Production et circulation*, Centre de Recherches d'Histoire Ancienne, **116**, Université de Besançon, Besançon, 1992.

Leech, R., 'The excavation of a Romano-Celtic temple and a later cemetery on Lamyatt Beacon, Somerset', *Britannia*, **17**, 1986, pp. 259–328.

Lenoir, M., Manacorda, D. and Panella, C., (eds), *Amphores romaines et histoire economique: dix ans de recherche*, Collection de l'École Française de Rome, **114**, École Française de Rome, Rome, 1989.

Lepper, F. and Frere, S. S., *Trajan's Column: a new edition of the Chichorius plates. Introduction, commentary and plates*, Alan Sutton, Gloucester, 1988.

Lewis, N. and Reinhold, M., *Roman civilization. Sourcebook II: The Empire*, Harper Torchbooks, New York, 1966.

Lewis, P. H. and Goodson, K. J., 'Images, databases and edge detection for archaeological object drawings' in *Computer applications and quantitative methods in archaeology 1990*, ed. K. Lockyear and S. P. Q. Rahtz, British archaeological reports. International series, **565**, BAR, Oxford, 1991, pp. 149–53.

Liou, B. and Morel, M., 'L'orge des Cavares: une amphorette à inscription peinte trouvée dans le port antique de Marseille', *Revue Archéologique de Narbonnaise*, **10**, 1977, pp. 189–97.

Loeschcke, S., 'Keramische Funde in Haltern', *Mitteilungen der Altertums–Kommission für Westfalen*, **5**, 1909, pp. 103–322.

Loughlin, N., 'Dales ware: a contribution to the study of *Roman coarse pottery*' in *Pottery and early commerce: characterization and trade in Roman and later ceramics*, ed. D. P. S. Peacock, Academic Press, London, 1977, pp. 85–146.

Ludowici, W., *Stempel–Namen und Bilder römischer Töpfer, Legions-Ziegel-Stempel, Formen von Sigillata- und anderen Gefassen aus meinen Ausgrabungen in Rheinzabern 1901–1914*, Katalog, **5**, Carl Ludowici, Speyer, 1927.

Ludowici, W. and Ricken, H., *Die Bilderschüsseln der römischen Töpfer von Rheinzabern: Tafelband*, Katalog, **6**, Speyer, 1948.

Lutz, M., 'Etat actuel de nos connaissances sur la céramique sigillée de la Gaule de l'Est', *Revue Archéologique du Centre de la France*, **5**, 1966, pp. 130–57.

Lutz, M., 'La puissance attractive de l'Est', *Dossiers de l'Archéologie*, **9**, 1975, pp. 51–8.

Lyne, M. A. B. and Jefferies, R. S., *The Alice Holt/Farnham Roman pottery industry*, Research reports/Council for British Archaeology, **30**, Council for British Archaeology, London, 1979.

MacIvor, I., Thomas, M. C. and Breeze, D. J., 'Excavations on the Antonine Wall fort of Rough Castle, Stirlingshire, 1957–61', *Proc Soc Antiq Scot*, **110**, 1981, pp. 230–85.

Manning, W. H., 'Excavations on Late Iron Age and Saxon sites at Ufton Nervet, Berks in 1961–3', *Berkshire Arch J*, **67**, 1974, pp. 1–62.

Manning, W. H., *The Roman pottery*, Report on the excavations at Usk, 1965–1976, University of Wales Press [for] the Board of Celtic Studies of the University of Wales, Cardiff, 1993.

Marichal, R., *Les graffites de la Graufesenque*, Supplément à Gallia, **47**, Éditions du CNRS, Paris, 1988.

Marney, P. T., *Roman and Belgic pottery from excavations in Milton Keynes, 1972–1982*, Buckinghamshire Archaeological Society. Monograph, **2**, Buckinghamshire Archaeological Society, Aylesbury, 1989.

Marsh, G. D., 'Early second century fine wares in the London area' in *Early fine wares in Roman Britain*, ed. P. R. Arthur and G. D. Marsh, British archaeological reports. British series, **57**, BAR, Oxford, 1978, pp. 119–223.

Marsh, G. D., 'London's samian supply and its relationship to the development of the Gallic samian industry' in *Roman pottery research in Britain and north-west Europe: papers presented to Graham Webster*, ed. A. C. Anderson and A. S. Anderson, British archaeological reports. International series, **123**, BAR, Oxford, 1981, pp. 173–238.

Marsh, G. D. and Tyers, P. A., 'The Roman pottery from Southwark' in *Southwark Excavations 1972–74*, ed. J. Bird, A. H. Graham, H. L. Sheldon and P. Townend, Joint Publication (London and Middlesex Archaeological Society and Surrey Archaeological Society), **1**, London, 1978, pp. 530–607.

Martin-Kilcher, S., *Die römischen Amphoren aus Augst und Kaiseraugst. Ein Beitrag zur römischen Handels- und Kulturgeschichte. 1, Die südspanischen Ölamphoren, Gruppe* 1, Forschungen in Augst, **7**, Römermuseum, Augst, 1987.

Martin-Kilcher, S., 'Fischsaucen und Fischconserven aus dem römischen Gallien', *Archéologie Suisse*, **13**, 1990, pp. 37–44.

Martin-Kilcher, S., *Die römischen Amphoren aus Augst und Kaiseraugst. Ein Beitrag zur römischen Handels- und Kulturgeschichte. 2, Die Amphoren für Wein, Fischsauce, Südfrüchte (Gruppen 2–24) und Gesamtauswertung*, Forschungen in Augst, **7**, Römermuseum, Augst, 1994.

Massy, J. L. and Molière, J., 'Céramiques sigillées aretines precoces à Amiens', *Cahiers Archéologiques de Picardie*, **6**, 1979, pp. 109–29.

Matthews, C. L., *Occupation sites on a Chiltern ridge: excavations at Puddlehill and sites near Dunstable, Bedfordshire. Part 1: Neolithic, Bronze Age and Early Iron Age*, British archaeological reports, **29**, BAR, Oxford, 1976.

May, T., *The Roman altar and other relics found at Wilderspool (1895–6)*, reprinted from the Transactions of the Historic Society of Lancashire and Cheshire, **48**, Liverpool, 1897.

May, T., *Warrington's Roman remains*, Warrington, 1904.

May, T., 'The Roman pottery in York Museum', *Report of the Yorkshire Philosophical Society*, 1909.

May, T., 'The Roman pottery in York Museum', *Report of the Yorkshire Philosophical Society*, 1910.

May, T., 'The Roman pottery in York Museum', *Report of the Yorkshire Philosophical Society*, 1911.

May, T., *The pottery found at Silchester*,

Bibliography

County Borough of Reading. Museum and Art Gallery Silchester Department, Reading, 1916.

May, T., *Catalogue of the Roman pottery in the Colchester and Essex Museum*, Borough of Colchester, Cambridge, 1930.

McCarthy, M. R., *A Roman, Anglian and medieval site at Blackfriars Street, Carlisle: excavations 1977–79*, Research series, **4**, Cumberland and Westmorland Archaeological and Antiquarian Society, Kendal, 1990.

McVicar, J., 'Review of *D. P. S. Peacock, Pottery in the Roman world*', *Archaeological Review from Cambridge*, **2**, 2, 1983, pp. 106–8.

Mayet, F., *Les céramiques à parois fines dans la peninsule iberique*, Publications du Centre Pierre Paris, 1, Université de Bordeaux III, Centre Pierre Paris; diffusion, E. de Boccard, Talence; Paris, 1975.

Mayet, F. and Picon, M., 'Une sigillée phocéenne tardive (Late Roman C ware) et sa diffusion en Occident', *Figlina*, **7**, 1986, pp. 129–34.

Meffre, J.-C. and Meffre, P., 'L'atelier augustéen d'amphores et de céramiques de Sainte-Cécile-les-Vignes (Vaucluse)' in *Les amphores en Gaule: production et circulation*, ed. F. Laubenheimer, Centre de Recherches d'Histoire Ancienne, **116**, Université de Besançon, Besançon, 1992, pp. 25–35.

Middleton, A. P. and Freestone, I. C., (eds), *Recent developments in ceramic petrology*, British Museum Occasional Paper, **81**, British Museum, London, 1991.

Miller, D., *Artefacts as categories: a study of ceramic variability in central India*, New studies in archaeology, Cambridge University Press, Cambridge, 1985.

Millet, M., 'Boudicca, the first Colchester potters' shop, and the dating of Neronian Samian', *Britannia*, **18**, 1987, pp. 93–123.

Millett, M., 'The dating of Farnham (Alice Holt) pottery', *Britannia*, **10**, 1979, pp. 121–37.

Millett, M., 'How much pottery?' in *Pottery and the archaeologist*, ed. M. Millett, Institute of Archaeology Occasional Publications, **4**, University of London Institute of Archaeology, London, 1979, pp. 77–80.

Millett, M., *The Romanization of Roman Britain*, Cambridge University Press, Cambridge, 1990.

Milne, G., *The Port of Roman London*, London, 1985.

Miró, J., 'Vi català a França (segle I a.C–I d.C), una síntesi preliminar' in *Le vi a l'antiguitat. Economia producció i commerç al Mediterrani Occidental*, Monografies Badalonines, **9**, Museu de Badalona, Badalona, 1987, pp. 249–68.

Monaghan, J., *Upchurch and Thameside Roman pottery. A ceramic typology for northern Kent, first to third centuries A.D.*, British archaeological reports. British series, **173**, Oxford, 1987.

Monaghan, J., 'Découvertes maritimes provenant du baillage de Guernsey' in *Actes du Congrès de Caen. 28–31 Mai 1987*, ed. L. Rivet, SFECAG, Marseille, 1987, pp. 39–45.

Monaghan, J., *Roman pottery from the Fortress: 9 Blake Street*, The Archaeology of York, **16**, Council for British Archaeology for the York Archaeological Trust, London, 1993.

Morel, J.-P., 'Observations sur les céramiques à vernis noir de France et d'Espagne', *Archéologie en Languedoc*, 1, 1978, pp. 149–58.

Munsell Color Company, *Munsell soil color charts*, Munsell Color Company, Baltimore, Md, 1975.

Myres, J. N. L., 'Wingham villa and Romano-Saxon pottery in Kent', *Antiquity*, **18**, 1944, pp. 52–5.

Myres, J. N. L., 'Romano-Saxon Pottery' in *Dark Age Britain*, ed. D. B. Harden, London, 1956, pp. 16–39.

Myres, J. N. L., *Anglo-Saxon pottery and the settlement of England*, Oxford University Press, Oxford, 1969.

Myres, J. N. L., *The English settlements*, 1986.

Myres, J. N. L. and Green, B., *The Anglo–Saxon cemeteries of Caistor-by-Norwich and Markshall, Norfolk*, Reports of the Research Committee of the Society of Antiquaries of London, **30**, Society of Antiquaries, London, 1973.

Neal, D. S., 'Excavations at Magiovinium, Buckinghamshire, 1978–80', *Rec Buckinghamshire*, **29**, 1987, pp. 1–124.

Neuru, L. L., 'Les potiers gallo-belges de la période augustéenne en Gaule Belgique: etat de la question', *Revue Archéologique de l'Est et du Centre-Est*, **38**, 1987, pp. 197–200.

Niblett, R., *Sheepen: an early Roman industrial site at Camulodunum*, Research reports/Council for British Archaeology, **57**, Council for British Archaeology, London, 1985.

Oakley, K. P., 'The pottery from the Romano-British site on Thundersbarrow Hill', *Antiquaries J*, **13**, 1933, pp. 134–51.

Oelmann, F., *Die Keramik des Kastells Niederbieber*, Materialien zur römisch-germanischen Keramik, 1, 1914.

Orton, C. R., *Pottery archive: user's handbook*, DUA Publication, 1, DUA, London, 1978.

Orton, C. R., 'Dealing with the pottery from a 600 acre urban site' in *Pottery and the archaeologist*, ed. M. Millett, Institute of Archaeology Occasional Publications, **4**, Institute of Archaeology, London, 1979, pp. 61–71.

Orton, C. R., 'How many pots make five? – An historical review of pottery quantification', *Archaeometry*, **35**, 2, 1993, pp. 169–84.

Orton, C. R. and Tyers, P. A., 'Statistical analysis of ceramic assemblages', *Archeologia e Calcolatori*, **1**, 1990, pp. 81–110.

Orton, C. R., Tyers, P. A. and Vince, A. G., *Pottery in archaeology*, Cambridge Manuals in Archaeology, Cambridge University Press, Cambridge, 1993.

Oswald, A., *The Roman pottery kilns at Little London, Lincs Wellow, Notts*, Rock House, 1937.

Oswald, F., *Index of potters' stamps on terra sigillata*, Hand-printed and published by the author, East Bridgford, Notts, 1931.

Oswald, F., *Index of figure-types on terra sigillata*, University Press, Liverpool, 1936–7.

Oswald, F., 'The mortaria of Margidunum and their development', *Antiquaries J*, **24**, 1944, pp. 48–63.

Oswald, F. and Davies Pryce, T., *An introduction to the study of terra sigillata treated from a chronological standpoint*, Longmans, Green and Co, London; New York, 1920.

Oxé, A. and Comfort, H., *Corpus Vasorum Arretinorum: a catalogue of the signatures, shapes and chronology of Italian sigillata*, Antiquitas, 3.4, R. Habelt, Bonn, 1968.

Page, W., 'A Romano-British pottery lately found at Radlett, Herts', *Proc Soc Antiq*

London, **17**, 1898, pp. 261–70.

Parker, A. J., *Ancient shipwrecks of the Mediterranean and the Roman provinces*, British archaeological reports. International series, **580**, Tempus Reparatum, Oxford, 1992.

Parker, A. J. and Price, J., 'Spanish exports of the Claudian period: the significance of the Port-Vendres II wreck reconsidered', *Int J Naut Archaeol Underwater Explor*, **10**, 1981, pp. 221–8.

Partridge, C., *Skeleton Green: a Late Iron Age and Romano-British site*, Britannia. Monograph series, **2**, Society for the Promotion of Roman Studies, London, 1981.

Pascual Guasch, R., 'Las anforas de la Layetania' in *Méthodes classiques et méthodes formelles dans l'etude des amphores*, ed. G. Vallet, Collection de l'École Française de Rome, **32**, École Française de Rome, Rome, 1977, pp. 47–96.

Peacock, D. P. S., 'Romano-British pottery production in Malvern district of Worcestershire', *Trans Worcestershire Archaeol Soc*, **1**, 1967, pp. 15–28.

Peacock, D. P. S., 'The heavy mineral analysis of pottery: a preliminary report', *Archaeometry*, **10**, 1967, pp. 97–100.

Peacock, D. P. S., 'Roman amphorae in pre-Roman Britain' in *The Iron Age and its hill forts: papers presented to Sir Mortimer Wheeler*, ed. M. Jesson and D. Hill, University of Southampton Monograph Series, **1**, University of Southampton, Southampton, 1971, pp. 161–88.

Peacock, D. P. S., 'Amphorae and the Baetican fish industry', *Antiquaries J*, **54**, 1974, pp. 232–43.

Peacock, D. P. S., 'Ceramics in Roman and medieval archaeology' in *Pottery and early commerce: characterization and trade in Roman and later ceramics*, ed. D. P. S. Peacock, Academic Press, London, 1977, pp. 21–33.

Peacock, D. P. S., 'Recent discoveries of Roman amphora kilns in Italy', Antiquaries J, **57**, 1977, pp. 262–9.

Peacock, D. P. S., 'Roman amphorae: typology, fabric and origin' in *Méthodes classiques et méthodes formelles dans l'etude des amphores*, ed. G. Vallet, Collection de l'École Française de Rome, **32**, École Française de Rome, Rome, 1977, pp. 261–78.

Peacock, D. P. S., 'Late Roman amphoras from Chalk, near Gravesend, Kent' in *Roman pottery studies in Britain and beyond: papers presented to J. P. Gillam, July 1977*, ed. J. Dore and K. T. Greene, British archaeological reports. International series, **30**, BAR, Oxford, 1977, pp. 295–300.

Peacock, D. P. S., 'Pompeian red ware' in *Pottery and early commerce: characterization and trade in Roman and later ceramics*, ed. Peacock, Academic Press, London, 1977, pp. 147–62.

Peacock, D. P. S., 'The Rhine and the problem of Gaulish wine in Roman Britain' in *Roman shipping and trade: Britain and the Rhine provinces*, ed. J. du Plat Taylor and H. Cleere, Research reports/Council for British Archaeology, **24**, Council for British Archaeology, London, 1978, pp. 49–51.

Peacock, D. P. S., *Pottery in the Roman world: an ethnoarchaeological approach*, Longman archaeology series, Longman, London, 1982.

Peacock, D. P. S., 'Appendix 1. Seawater, salt and ceramics' in *The Avenue du President Habib Bourguiba, Salammbo: the pottery and other ceramic objects from the site*, ed. M. G. Fulford and D. P. S. Peacock, Excavations at Carthage: The British Mission, I, **2**, British Academy, 1984, pp. 263–4.

Peacock, D. P. S., (ed), *Pottery and early commerce: characterization and trade in Roman and later ceramics*, Academic Press, London, 1977.

Peacock, D. P. S. and Thomas, C., 'Class E imported post-Roman pottery; a suggested origin', *Cornish Archaeol*, **6**, 1967, pp. 35–46.

Peacock, D. P. S. and Williams, D. F., *Amphorae and the Roman economy: an introductory guide*, Longman archaeology series, Longman, London, 1986.

Pellecuer, C. and Pomaredes, H., 'La céramique commune "Brune Orangé Biterroise" (B.O.B.): une production Languedocienne des IIème-IIIème siècles après J.–C.' in *Actes du Congrès de Cognac. 8–11 Mai 1991*, ed. L. Rivet, SFECAG, Marseille, 1991, pp. 365–83.

Peña, J. T., 'Internal red-slip cookware (Pompeian Red Ware) from Cetamura del Chianti, Italy: mineralogical composition and provenience', *American Journal of Archaeology*, **94**, 1990, pp. 647–61.

Perrin, J. R., *Roman pottery from the Colonia: Skeldergate and Bishophill*, The Archaeology of York, **16**, Council for British Archaeology for the York Archaeological Trust, London, 1981.

Perrin, J. R., 'Pottery of "London Ware" type from the Nene valley', *Durobrivae*, **8**, 1990, pp. 8–10.

Perrin, J. R., *Roman pottery from the Colonia, 2: General Accident and Rougier Street*, The Archaeology of York, **16**, Council for British Archaeology for the York Archaeological Trust, London, 1990.

Petrie, W. M. F., 'Sequences in prehistoric remains', *J Royal Anthropological Institute*, **29**, 1899, pp. 295–301.

Philp, B., *The excavation of the Roman forts of the Classis Britannica at Dover 1970–77*, Dover, 1981.

Pilet, C., 'La céramique britanno-romaine et anglo-saxonne découverte dans les nécropoles bas-normandes' in *Actes du Congrès de Caen. 28–31 Mai 1987*, ed. L. Rivet, SFECAG, Marseille, 1987, pp. 97–4.

Pitt Rivers, A. H. L. F., 'Typological museums', *J. Royal Soc. of Arts*, **40**, 1891, pp. 115–22.

Pitts, L. F. and St Joseph, J. K., *Inchtuthil: the Roman legionary fortress. Excavations 1952–65*, Britannia. Monograph series, **6**, Society for the Promotion of Roman Studies, London, 1985.

Pollard, R. J., 'The other pottery' in *The Roman villa at Lullingstone, Kent, 2: the wall paintings and finds*, ed. G. W. Meates, Monograph series of the Kent Archaeological Society, **3**, Kent Archaeological Society, Maidstone, 1987, pp. 164–306.

Pollard, R. J., *The Roman pottery of Kent*, Monograph series of the Kent Archaeological Society, **5**, Kent Archaeological Society, Maidstone, 1988.

Pomel, M. G., 'A study of later Roman pottery groups in southern Britain: fabrics, form and chronology', M. Phil. thesis, Institute of Archaeology, University of London, 1984.

Ponsich, M., *Implantation rural antique sur le bas-Guadalquivir. I*, Collection de la Casa de Velázquez, **3**, Madrid, 1974.

Ponsich, M., *Implantation rural antique sur le bas-Guadalquivir. II*, Collection de la Casa de Velázquez, Madrid, 1979.

Ponsich, M., *Implantation rural antique sur*

Bibliography

le bas-Guadalquivir. IV, Collection de la Casa de Velázquez, **33**, Madrid, 1991.

Potter, T. W. and Johns, C., *Roman Britain*, Exploring the Roman world, British Museum Press, London, 1992.

Potter, T. W. and Trow, S. D., 'Puckeridge-Braughing, Herts: the Ermine Street excavations, 1971–1972', *Hertfordshire Archaeol*, **10**, 1988, pp. 1–191.

Pownall, T., 'Memoire on the Roman earthen ware fished up within the mouth of the River Thames', *Archaeologia*, **5**, 1779, pp. 282–90.

Pownall, T., 'Account of some Roman pottery, found at Sandy, in Bedfordshire, and at Lincoln, together with a Roman speculum', *Archaeologia*, **8**, 1787, pp. 377–83.

Pryor, F. M. M., *Excavation at Fengate, Peterborough, England, the fourth report*, Northamptonshire Archaeology Society Monograph, **2**, 1984.

Pucci, G., 'Cumanae Testae', *La Parola del Passato*, **30**, 1975, pp. 368–71.

Rae, A. and Rae, V., 'The Roman fort at Cramond, Edinburgh: excavations 1954–1966', *Britannia*, **5**, 1974, pp. 163–224.

Rahtz, P. A., Woodward, A., Burrow, I., Everton, A., Watts, L., Leach, P., Hirst, S., Fowler, P. and Gardner, K., *Cadbury Congresbury 1968–73. A late/post-Roman hilltop settlement in Somerset*, British archaeological reports. British series, **223**, Tempus Reparatum, Oxford, 1992.

Raimbault, M., 'La céramique gallo-romaine dite "à l'éponge" dans l'ouest de la France', *Gallia*, **31**, 1973, pp. 185–206.

Rawes, B., 'Gloucester Severn valley ware', *Trans Bristol Gloucestershire Archaeol Soc*, **100**, 1982, pp. 33–46.

Redknap, M., 'Mayenerware and Eifelkeramik: the Roman and medieval pottery industries of the West German Eifel', Ph.D. Thesis, Institute of Archaeology, University of London, London, 1987.

Redknap, M., 'Medieval pottery production at Mayen: recent advances, current problems' in *Zur Keramik des Mittelalters und der beginnenden Neuzeit im Rheinland*, ed. D. R. M. Gaimster, M. Redknap and H.-H. Wegner, British archaeological reports. International series, **440**, BAR, Oxford, 1988, pp. 3–37.

Remesal Rodríguez, J., 'Die Ölwirtschaft in der Provinz Baetica: neue Formen der Analyse', *Saalburg-Jahrbuch*, **38**, 1982, pp. 30–71.

Remesal Rodríguez, J., *La annona militaris y la exportacion de aceite bético a Germania*, Universidad Complutense, Madrid, 1986.

Reusch, W., 'Kleine, spitzkonische amphoren', *Saalburg-Jahrbuch*, **27**, 1970, pp. 54–62.

Rice, P. M., *Pottery analysis: a sourcebook*, University of Chicago Press, Chicago, 1987.

Richards, E. E., 'Preliminary spectrographic investigation of some Romano-British mortaria', *Archaeometry*, **2**, 1959, pp. 23–31.

Richardson, B., 'Pottery' in *The Roman Quay at St Magnus House, London*, ed. L. Miller, J. Schofield and M. Rhodes, Special Paper, **8**, London and Middlesex Archaeological Society, London, 1986, pp. 96–138.

Richardson, B. and Tyers, P. A., 'North Gaulish pottery in Britain', *Britannia*, **15**, 1984, pp. 133–41.

Richardson, K. M., 'Report on the excavations at Brockley Hill, Middlesex, August and September 1947', *Trans London Middlesex Archaeol Soc*, **10**, 1, 1948, pp. 1–23.

Ricken, H. and Fischer, C., *Die Bilderschüsseln der römischen Töpfer von Rheinzabern: Textband mit Typenbildern zu Katalog VI der Ausgrabungen von Wilhelm Ludowici in Rheinzabern 1901–1914*, Materialien zur römisch-germanischen Keramik, **7**, Habelt, Bonn, 1963.

Rigby, V., 'The coarse pottery' in *Early Roman occupation at Cirencester*, ed. J. S. Wacher and A. D. McWhirr, Cirencester, 1982, pp. 153–200.

Rigby, V. and Freestone, I., 'The petrology and typology of the earliest identified Central Gaulish imports', *J Roman Pottery Stud*, **1**, 1986, pp. 6–21.

Riley, J. A., 'The coarse pottery from Benghazi' in *Excavations at Sidi Khrebish, Benghazi (Berenice). II*, ed. J. A. Lloyd, Supplements to Libya Antiqua, **5**, Department of Antiquities, Tripoli, 1979, pp. 91–497.

Ritterling, E., *Nr. 31. Das Kastell Wiesbaden*, Obergerm.-Raet. Limesforschungen, **31**, 1909.

Ritterling, E., 'Das frührömische Lager bei Hofheim im Taunus', *Annalen des Vereins für nassauische Altertumskunde*, **40**, 1913.

Rivet, L., (ed), *Actes du Congrès de Tournai. 28–31 Mai 1992*, SFECAG, Marseille, 1992.

Rivet, L., (ed), *Actes du Congrès de Millau. 12–15 Mai 1994*, SFECAG, Marseille, 1994.

Roberts, W. I., *Romano-Saxon pottery*, British archaeological reports. British series, **106**, BAR, Oxford, 1982.

Robertson, A. S., *Birrens (Blatobulgium)*, Dumfriesshire and Galloway Natural History and Antiquarian Society, Edinburgh, 1975.

Rodríguez Almeida, E., *Il Monte Testaccio: ambiente, storia*, materiali, Rome, 1984.

Rodríguez Almeida, E., *Los Tituli Picti de las ánforas olearias de la Bética. I*, Universidad Complutense, Madrid, 1989.

Rodwell, W. J., 'Coinage, oppida and the rise of Belgic power in south-eastern Britain' in *Oppida: the beginnings of urbanisation in barbarian Europe*, ed. B. Cunliffe and T. Rowley, British archaeological reports. Supplementary series, **11**, BAR, Oxford, 1976, pp. 181–367.

Rodwell, W. J., 'Stamp-decorated pottery of the early Roman period in eastern England' in *Early fine wares in Roman Britain*, ed. G. D. Marsh and P. R. Arthur, British archaeological reports. British series, **57**, BAR, Oxford, 1978, pp. 225–92.

Rodwell, W. J., 'The production and distribution of pottery and tiles in the territory of the Trinovantes', *Essex Archaeol Hist*, **14**, 1982, pp. 15–76.

Rogers, G. B., *Poteries sigillées de la Gaule centrale*, Supplément à Gallia, **28**, Éditions du CNRS, Paris, 1974.

Rogers, G. B., 'Marbled samian from Fréjus (Var)' in *Roman pottery research in Britain and north-west Europe: papers presented to Graham Webster*, ed. A. C. Anderson and A. S. Anderson, British archaeological reports. International series, **123**, BAR, Oxford, 1981, pp. 257–64.

Rothschild-Boros, M. C., 'The determination of amphora contents' in *Archaeology and Italian society: prehistoric, Roman and medieval studies*, ed. G. Barker and R. Hodges, British archaeological reports. International series, **102**,

Bibliography

1981, pp. 79–89.

Rule, M. and Monaghan, J., *A Gallo-Roman trading vessel from Guernsey: the excavation and recovery of a third century shipwreck*, Guernsey Museum Monograph, **5**, States of Guernsey, 1993.

Rye, O. S., *Pottery technology: principles and reconstruction*, Manuals on archaeology, **4**, Taraxacum Inc, Washington DC, 1981.

Rye, O. S. and Evans, C., Traditional pottery techniques in Pakistan: field and laboratory studies, Smithsonian Contributions to Anthropology, **21**, Smithsonian Institution Press, Washington DC, 1976.

Sabir, A., Laubenheimer, F., Leblanc, J. and Widemann, F., 'Production d'amphores vinaires republicaines en Gaule du Sud', *Documents d'Archéologie Méridionale*, **6**, 1983, pp. 109–13.

Sanders, J., 'Late Roman shell-gritted ware in Southern Britain', B.A. dissertation, Institute of Archaeology, University of London, 1973.

Santrot, M.-H. and Santrot, J., *Céramiques commune gallo-romaines d'Aquitaine*, CNRS, Paris, 1979.

Saunders, C. and Havercroft, A. B., 'A kiln of the potter Oastrius and related excavations at Little Munden Farm Bricket Wood', *Hertfordshire Archaeol*, **5**, 1977, pp. 109–56.

Schiffer, M. B., *Behavioral archaeology*, Academic Press, New York, 1976.

Sciallano, M. and Sibella, P., *Amphores: comment les identifier*, Edisud, Aix-en-Provence, 1991.

Sealey, P. R., *Amphoras from the 1970 excavations at Colchester Sheepen*, British archaeological reports. British series, **142**, BAR, Oxford, 1985.

Sealey, P. R. and Tyers, P. A., 'Olives from Roman Spain: a unique amphora find in British waters', *Antiquaries J*, **69**, 1, 1989, pp. 53–72.

Seeley, F. and Thorogood, C., 'Back to Brockley Hill', *London Archaeol*, **7**, 9, 1994, pp. 223–8.

Seillier, C. and Thoen, H., 'Céramique d'une fosse-dépotoir du camp de la Classis Britannica à Boulogne-sur-Mer', *Septentrion*, **8**, 1978, pp. 62–7.

Shackley, M. L., *Archaeological sediments: a survey of analytical methods*, Butterworths, London, 1975.

Shepard, A. O., *Ceramics for the archaeologist*, Publication, **609**, Carnegie Institute of Washington, Washington D.C., 1956.

Simon-Hiernard, D., 'Du nouveau sur la céramique à l'éponge' in *Actes du Congrès de Cognac. 8–11 Mai 1991*, ed. L. Rivet, SFECAG, 1991, pp. 61–76.

Simpson, G., 'The Aldgate potter: a maker of Romano-British samian ware', *J Roman Stud*, **42**, 1952, pp. 68–71.

Simpson, G., 'Decorated terra sigillata at Montans (Tarn) from the manuscript of Elie Rossignol at Albi', *Britannia*, **7**, 1976, pp. 244–73.

Simpson, G., 'A revised dating for the Colchester samian kiln', *Essex Archaeol Hist*, **14**, 1982, pp. 149–53.

Simpson, G. and Rogers, G., 'Cinnamus de Lezoux et quelques potiers contemporains', *Gallia*, **27**, 1969, pp. 3–14.

Siraudeau, J., *Amphores romaines des sites Angevins et leur contexte archéologique*, Corpus des amphores découvertes dans l'ouest de la France, **2**, 1988.

Smith, C. Roach, 'On Roman potters' kilns and pottery, discovered, by Mr E. T. Artis, in the county of Northampton', *J Brit Archaeol Ass*, **1**, 1, 1845, pp. 1–9.

Smith, C. Roach, 'Roman potters' kilns discovered near Colchester', *Collecteana Antiqua*, **7**, 1, 1880, pp. 1–11.

Smith, C. Roach, *Retrospections, social and archaeological. Vol 1*, Privately published, London, 1883.

Spencer, B., 'The Late Roman grey-ware industry in south Wales' in *Biglis, Caldicot and Llandough: three Late Iron Age and Romano-British sites in south-east Wales. Excavations 1977-79*, ed. D. M. Robinson, British archaeological reports. British series, **188**, BAR, Oxford, 1988, pp. 114–17.

Stanfield, J. A., 'Unusual forms of terra sigillata', *Archaeol J*, **86**, 1929, pp. 113–51.

Stanfield, J.A., 'Unusual forms of terra sigillata: second series', *Archaeol. J*, **93**, pp. 101–16.

Stanfield, J. A. and Simpson, G., *Central Gaulish potters*, Oxford University Press, London, 1958.

Stanfield, J. A. and Simpson, G., *Les potiers de la Gaule centrale*, Revue Archeologie Sites, Gonfaron, 1990.

Stead, I. M., 'A La Tène III burial at Welwyn Garden City', *Archaeologia*, **101**, 1967, pp. 1–62.

Stead, I. M., *Excavations at Winterton Roman villa and other sites in north Lincolnshire 1958–1967*, Department of the Environment Archaeological Reports, **9**, HMSO, London, 1976.

Stead, I. M. and Rigby, V., *Baldock: the excavation of a Roman and pre-Roman settlement, 1968–72*, Britannia. Monograph series, **7**, Society for the Promotion of Roman Studies, London, 1986.

Stead, I. M. and Rigby, V., *Verulamium: the King Harry Lane site*, English Heritage Archaeological Report, **12**, HMSO, London, 1989.

Steer, K., 'Excavations at Mumrills Roman Fort, 1958–60', *Proc Soc Antiq Scot*, **94**, 1960–61, pp. 86–132.

Steinby, M., 'Ziegelstempel von Rom und Umgebung' in *Paulys Encyclopädie der classichen Altertumswissenschaft*, Supplementband, **XV**, München, 1978. cols 1489–1531.

Storey, J. M. V., Symonds, R. P., Hart, F. A., Smith, D. M. and Walsh, J. N., 'A chemical investigation of Colchester samian by means of inductively-coupled plasma emission spectrometry', *J Roman Pottery Stud*, **2**, 1989, pp. 33–43.

Suggett, P. G., 'The Moxom Collection (a Romano-British pottery group from Brockley Hill Middlesex)', *Trans London Middlesex Archaeol Soc*, **18**. 1, 1955, pp. 60–4.

Swain, H., 'Pottery survival in the field: some initial results of experiments in frost shattering', *Scottish Archaeol Review*, **5**, 1988, pp. 87–90.

Swan, V. G., 'Aspects of the New Forest late-Roman pottery industry' in *Current research in Romano-British coarse pottery: papers given at a C.B.A. Conference held at New College, Oxford, March 24 to 26, 1972*, ed. A. Detsicas, Research reports/Council for British Archaeology, **10**, Council for British Archaeology, London, 1973, pp. 117–34.

Swan, V. G., 'Oare reconsidered and the origins of Savernake ware in Wiltshire', *Britannia*, **6**, 1975, pp. 36–61.

Swan, V. G., 'Relief decorated imitation samian cups from Wanborough, Wiltshire' in *Roman pottery studies in Britain and beyond; papers presented to J. P. Gillam, July 1977*, ed. J. Dore and K. T. Greene, British archaeological reports. International series, **30**, BAR, Oxford, 1977, pp. 263–6.

Bibliography

Swan, V. G., 'Review of *M. A. B. Lyne and R. S. Jefferies, The Alice Holt/Farnham Roman pottery industry (1979)*', Rescue News, **20**, 1979, p. 9.

Swan, V. G., 'Caistor-by-Norwich reconsidered and the dating of Romano-British pottery in East Anglia' in *Roman pottery research in Britain and north-west Europe: papers presented to Graham Webster*, ed. A. C. Anderson and A. S. Anderson, British archaeological reports. International series, **123**, BAR, Oxford, 1981, pp. 123–56.

Swan, V. G., *The pottery kilns of Roman Britain*, Royal Commission on Historical Monuments: Supplementary Series, **5**, HMSO, London, 1984.

Swan, V. G., *Pottery in Roman Britain. 4th edn*, Shire archaeology, 3, Shire, Princes Risborough, 1988.

Swan, V. G., 'Legio VI and its men: African legionaries in Britain', *J Roman Pottery Stud*, **5**, 1994, pp. 1–34.

Symonds, R. P., *Rhenish wares: fine dark coloured pottery from Gaul and Germany*, Oxford University Committee for Archaeology. Monograph, **23**, Oxford, 1992.

Symonds, R. P., 'Amphores Romano-Britanniques' in *Actes du Congrès de Versailles. 20–23 Mai 1993*, ed. L. Rivet, SFECAG, Marseille, 1993, pp. 281–91.

Symonds, R. P. and Wade, S. M., 'A large Central Gaulish glazed vessel with applied-moulded decoration from Colchester', *J Roman Pottery Stud*, **1**, 1986, pp. 55–7.

Tchernia, A., *Le vin de l'Italie romaine*, Rome, 1986.

Terrisse, J. R., *Les céramiques sigillées gallo-romaines des Martres-de-Veyre (Puy-de-Dome)*, Supplément à Gallia, **19**, Éditions du CNRS, Paris, 1968.

Thomas, C., 'Imported pottery in Dark-Age western Britain', *Medieval Archaeol*, **3**, 1959, pp. 89–111.

Thomas, C., *A provisional list of imported pottery in post-Roman Britain and Ireland*, Special report, **7**, Institute of Cornish Studies, Redruth, 1981.

Thomas, C., 'Gallici Nautae de Galliarum Provinciis', *Medieval Archaeol*, **34**, 1990, pp. 1–26.

Thomas, G. D., 'Excavations at the Roman civil settlement at Inveresk, 1976–77', *Proc Soc Antiq Scot*, **118**, 1989, pp. 139–76.

Thompson, I., *Grog-tempered 'Belgic' pottery of south-eastern England*, British archaeological reports. British series, **108**, BAR, Oxford, 1982.

Timby, J. R., 'The distribution of terra nigra and terra rubra to Britain', *Acta Rei Cretariae Romanae Fautores*, **25–26**, 1987, pp. 291–310.

Timby, J. R., 'Severn Valley wares: a reassessment', *Britannia*, **21**, 1990, pp. 243–51.

Tomber, R. and Williams, D. F., 'Late Roman amphoras in Britain', *J Roman Pottery Stud*, **1**, 1986, pp. 42–54.

Tomlin, R. S. O., 'The Roman "carrot" amphora and its Egyptian provenance', *J Egyptian Archaeol*, **78**, 1992, pp. 307–12.

Tomlinson, S., 'Edmund Artis, antiquary', *Durobrivae*, **2**, 1974, pp. 22–3.

Tuffreau-Libre, M., 'La céramique de l'officine gallo-romaine du Pont-Rouge à Bourlon', *Bull. Com. dép. Mon. hist Pas-de-Calais*, **10**, 1, 1976, pp. 1–20.

Tuffreau-Libre, M., 'La céramique gallo-romaine dorée au mica dans le nord de la France (Nord et Picardie)', *Hélinium*, **18**, 1978, pp. 105–205.

Tuffreau-Libre, M., *La céramique commune gallo-romaine dans le nord de la France*, Lille, 1980.

Tuffreau-Libre, M., *La céramique en Gaule romaine*, Errance, Paris, 1992.

Tyers, P. A., 'Central Gaulish coarse wares', forthcoming (a).

Tyers, P. A., 'Rhône valley mortaria', forthcoming (b).

Tyers, P. A., 'The poppy-head beakers of Britain and their relationship to the barbotine decorated beakers of the Rhineland and Switzerland' in *Early fine wares in Roman Britain*, ed. P. R. Arthur and G. D. Marsh, British archaeological reports. British series, **57**, BAR, Oxford, 1978, pp. 61–107.

Tyers, P. A. and Vince, A. G., 'Computing the DUA Pottery', *London Archaeol*, **4**, 11, 1983, pp. 299–305.

Unverzagt, W., *Die Keramik des Kastells Alzey*, Materialien zur römisch-germanischen Keramik, **2**, J. Baer, Frankfurt a. Main, 1916.

Unverzagt, W., *Terra sigillata mit Rädchenverzierung*, Materialien zur römisch-germanischen Keramik, **2**, 1919.

Vallet, G., (ed), *Méthodes classiques et méthodes formelles dans l'etude des amphores*, Collection de l'École Française de Rome, **32**, École Française de Rome, Rome, 1977.

van der Werff, J. H., 'Roman amphoras at Nijmegen – a preliminary report', *Berichten van de Rijksdienst voor het Oudheidkundig Bodemonderzoek*, **34**, 1984, pp. 347–87.

Varone, A., 'Voices of the ancients. A stroll through public and private Pompeii' in *Rediscovering Pompeii*, L'Erma di Bretschneider, Rome, 1992, pp. 27–41.

Wallace, C. R., 'Roman pottery studies in Britain 1890–1919', *J Roman Pottery Stud*, **3**, 1990, pp. 80–7.

Walters, H. B., *Catalogue of the Roman pottery in the Department of Antiquities, British Museum*, British Museum, London, 1908.

Ward, J., *The Roman fort of Gellygaer in the county of Glamorgan*, London, 1903.

Ward, J., *The Roman era in Britain*, Methuen, London, 1911.

Warner, R. B., 'Some observations on the context and importation of exotic material in Ireland from the first century BC to the 2nd century AD', *Proc Roy Ir Acad J*, **76**, C, 1976, pp. 267–92.

Webster, G., 'A Roman pottery at South Carlton, Lincs', *Antiquaries J*, **24**, 1944, pp. 129–43.

Webster, G., *Romano-British coarse pottery: a student's guide*, Research reports/Council for British Archaeology, **6**, Council for British Archaeology, London, 1964.

Webster, G., *Romano-British coarse pottery: a student's guide. 3rd edn*, Research reports/Council for British Archaeology, **6**, Council for British Archaeology, London, 1976.

Webster, G., 'Reflections on Romano-British pottery studies, past, present and future' in *Roman pottery studies in Britain and beyond: papers presented to J. P. Gillam, July 1977*, ed. J. Dore and K. T. Greene, British archaeological reports. International series, **30**, BAR, Oxford, 1977, pp. 317–33.

Webster, G., 'Deities and religious scenes on Romano-British pottery', *J Roman Pottery Stud*, **2**, 1989, pp. 1–28.

Webster, P. V., 'A sherd of Derbyshire ware from south Wales', *Derbyshire Archaeol J*, **90**, 1970, p. 31.

Webster, P. V., 'Severn Valley ware on Hadrian's Wall', *Archaeol Aeliana (4th series)*, **50**, 1972, pp. 191–203.

Bibliography

Webster, P. V., 'More British samian ware by the Aldgate-Pulborough potter', *Britannia*, 6, 1975, pp. 163–70.

Webster, P. V., 'Severn Valley ware: a preliminary study', *Trans Bristol Gloucestershire Archaeol Soc*, 94, 1976, pp. 18–46.

Webster, P. V., 'Severn Valley ware on the Antonine frontier' in *Roman pottery studies in Britain and beyond: papers presented to J. P. Gillam, July 1977*, ed. J. Dore and K. T. Greene, British archaeological reports. International series, 30, BAR, Oxford, 1977, pp. 163–76.

Webster, P. V., *Roman samian pottery in Britain*, CBA Practical Handbook, 1996.

Wells, C., *The German policy of Augustus: an examination of the archaeological evidence*, Oxford University Press, Oxford, 1972.

Wells, P. S., *Culture contact and culture change: early Iron Age central Europe and the Mediterranean world*, New Studies in Archaeology, Cambridge University Press, Cambridge, 1980.

Wenham, L. P., *The Romano-British cemetery at Trentholme Drive, York*, Ministry of Public Buildings and Works. Archaeological Reports, 5, HMSO, London, 1968.

West, S. E., *West Stow: the Anglo-Saxon village*, E. Anglian Archaeol. Report, 24, 1985.

Wheeler, R. E. M., *An inventory of the historical monuments of London Volume III. Roman London*, HMSO for Royal Commission of Historical Monuments (England), London, 1928.

Wheeler, R. E. M. and Wheeler, T. V., *Verulamium: a Belgic and two Roman cities*, Reports of the Research Committee of the Society of Antiquaries of London, 11, Oxford, 1936.

Wickenden, N. P., 'Prehistoric settlement and the Romano-British "small town" at Heybridge, Essex', *Essex Archaeol Hist*, 17, 1986, pp. 7–68.

Will, E. L., 'The Roman amphoras from Manching: a reappraisal', *Bayerische Vorgeschichtsblätter*, 52, 1987, pp. 21–36.

Williams, D. F., 'The Roman-British black-burnished industry: an essay on characterization by heavy-mineral analysis' in *Pottery and early commerce: characterization and trade in Roman and later ceramics*, ed. Peacock, Academic Press, London, 1977, pp. 163–220.

Williams, D. F., 'The Roman amphorae trade with Late Iron Age Britain' in *Production and distribution: a ceramic viewpoint*, ed. E. Morris and H. Howard, British archaeological reports. International series, 120, BAR, Oxford, 1981, pp. 123–32.

Williams, D. F., 'Preliminary petrological analysis of Italian sigillata' in *Roman pottery research in Britain and north-west Europe: papers presented to Graham Webster*, ed. A. C. Anderson and A. S. Anderson, British archaeological reports. International series, 123, BAR, Oxford, 1981, pp. 169–71.

Williams, D. F., *Late republican Roman amphorae from the Airport Catering Site, Stanstead, Essex*, Report, 84/90, Ancient Monuments Laboratory, London, 1990.

Williams, D. F. and Dannell, G. B., 'Petrological analysis of Arretine and early samian: a preliminary report' in *Early fine wares in Roman Britain*, ed. P. R. Arthur and G. D. Marsh, British archaeological reports. British series, 57, BAR, Oxford, 1978, pp. 5–13.

Williams, D. F. and Peacock, D. P. S., 'The importation of olive-oil into Iron Age and Roman Britain' in *Producción y commercio del aciete en la antugüedad. II Congresso Internacional*, Universidad Complutense, Madrid, 1983, pp. 263–80.

Williams, R. J., *Pennyland and Hartigans: Two Iron Age and Saxon sites in Milton Keynes*, Buckinghamshire Archaeological Society. Monograph, 4, Buckinghamshire Archaeological Society, Aylesbury, 1993.

Wilson, P. R., (ed), *Crambeck Roman pottery industry*, The Roman Antiquities Section, Yorkshire Archaeological Society, Leeds, 1989.

Woimant, G.-P., 'Un site de La Tène à Beauvais (Oise), Les Aulnes du Canada', *Revue archéologique de Picardie*, 1, 1983, pp. 219–25.

Woods, A. J., 'An introductory note on the use of tangential thin sections for distinguishing between wheel-thrown and coil/ring built vessels', *Bull Experimental Firing Group*, 3, 1984–5, pp. 100–14.

Woods, P. J., 'Types of late Belgic and early Romano-British pottery kilns in the Nene valley', *Britannia*, 5, 1974, pp. 262–81.

Woods, P. J. and Hastings, S., *Rushden: the early fine wares*, Northamptonshire County Council, 1984.

Woodward, P. J., 'The excavation of a Late Iron-Age trading settlement and Romano-British pottery production site at Ower, Dorset' in *Roman-British industries in Purbeck*, Dorset Natural History and Archaeological Society. Monograph series, 6, Dorset Natural History and Archaeological Society, 1987, pp. 44–123.

Woodward, P. J., Davies, S. M. and Graham, A. H., *Excavations at the Old Methodist Chapel and Greyhound Yard, Dorchester, 1981–84*, Dorset Natural History and Archaeological Society. Monograph series, 12, Dorset Natural History and Archaeological Society, 1993.

Wright, R. P., Hassall, M. W. C. and Tomlin, R. S. O., 'Roman Britain in 1975. II. Inscriptions', *Britannia*, 7, 1976, pp. 378–92.

Wright, T., 'Wanderings of an antiquary. VI. The Roman potteries on the banks of the Medway', *Gentleman's Magazine*, 38, 1852, pp. 364–7.

Wright, T., *Uriconium: a historical account of the ancient Roman city*, Longmans, London, 1872.

Wynia, S. L., 'Töpfersignaturen auf Pompejanisch-roten Platten: quantité négligeable?', *Berichten van de Rijksdienst voor het Oudheidkundig Bodemonderzoek*, 29, 1979, pp. 425–32.

Young, C. J., 'Oxford ware and the Roman army' in *Roman pottery studies in Britain and beyond: papers presented to J. P. Gillam, July 1977*, ed. J. Dore and K. T. Greene, British archaeological reports. International series, 30, BAR, Oxford, 1977, pp. 289–94.

Young, C. J., *The Roman pottery industry of the Oxford region*, British archaeological reports, 43, Oxford, 1977.

Young, C. J., *Guidelines for the processing and publication of Roman pottery from excavations*, Directorate of Ancient Monuments and Historic Buildings. Occasional Paper, 4, Department of the Environment, London, 1980.

Zienkiewicz, J. D., *The legionary fortress baths at Caerleon. II. The finds*, Cardiff, 1986.

Index

Aldgate-Pulborough potter, 69
Alice Holt-Farnham grey wares (AHFA), 59, 64, 71, 77, 180-182; exports of, 73
amphoras, 40, 85-105; Algerian, 72; Almagro 55, 73; Baetican, 87, 98,99; Bi, 81; Bii, 81; capacity of, 86; Catalan, 92, 99; classification of, 86; Eastern Mediterranean, 72, 81, 101; economic history and, 87;Egyptian, 101; Etruscan, 49; Gaulish, 48, 90, 93-94, 96; Gauloise, 94;Gaza, 72; Graeco-Italic, 49; importance of, 85; Italian, 49, 89-91, 99;Kingsholm 117, 101; 'Koan', 90; Lyon, 94, 98, 99; Massiolite, 48, 95;Mauretanian, 72, 73; North African, 81, 104; resin coatings on, 35;Rhodian, 93; Rhône valley, 98; Romano-British, 90, 201; Spanish, 51, 52,61, 73, 87, 90, 92, 97, 98; Verulamium-region, 90
'amphorology', 87
Anglo-Saxon pottery,75, 78
Antonine Wall, 67, 118, 120, 186, 187
Aoste mortaria (AOMO), 13, 58, 117-118, 125
Archaeology of Roman Britain, The, (1930), 15; (1969), 21
Argonne ware (ARGO), 71, 72, 114, 136-137
Arretine wares, 9, 17, 37, 47, 51, 111, see also Italian-type terra sigillata
Artis, Edmund Tyrell (1787-1847), 2-4, 34
Asia Minor, imports from, 102, 155
Atlas, 83-201; abbreviations used in, 85; introduction to, 83
'Atrebatic', bowls, 180; pottery, 55
Augst, type-series, 31-32, 99; 20, 98; 21, 98
Aylesford-Swarling style, 16, 53

B4 amphoras (B4), 72, 79, 81, 102-104
'Belgic' pottery, 53, 64
Besançon, le type, see Central Gaulish coarse micaceous ware
'black samian', see Central Gaulish black-slipped ware
'black sand fabric', 89-91, 157
Black-burnished 1 (South-east Dorset) (BB1), 32, 59, 64, 66-67, 71, 73,74, 77, 79, 182-186; deposits on, 43; exports of, 73, 81
Black-burnished 2 (BB2), 38, 67, 182, 186-188; difficulties in definition of, 67, 182; exports of, 73
black-burnished wares, 19, 21, 32, 66-68, 182-188; Brue valley, 186;influence of, 67, 74, 77, 173, 180, 186, 188, 191, 195, 197; original definition of, 182; resistance to, 75; South-east Dorset, 183; South-western, 185; Yorkshire, 186

Boudiccan destruction horizon, x, 37
British Archaeological Reports, 22
British fleet, 73
Brittany, coarse wares from, 49, 56
brokenness, 79, 205
Burkitt, Alexander Horace (engraver), 5
Bushe-Fox, Jocelyn Plunket (1880-1954), 11-13, 16, 49
Byzantine pottery, 80-82

'calcite-gritted ware', see South Midlands shell-tempered wares
Campanian wares, 9, 50, 51
Camulodunum (1947), 18, 161
Camulodunum 189 'carrot' amphoras (C189), 57, 101
Castor ware, 3, 14, 16, 19, 32
CBA10, 21
Celtic, personal names, 46
Central Gaulish black-slipped ware (CGBL), 137-138
Central Gaulish coarse micaceous ware (CGMW), 50, 51, 142
Central Gaulish colour-coated ware (CGCC), 57, 61, 137, 138, 139-140,146, 148
Central Gaulish fine micaceous wares (CGSF), 51, 53, 142-144
Central Gaulish glazed ware (CGGL), 139, 140-142
Central Gaulish terra sigillata (CGTS), 61, 71, 105, 113, 137
Céramique à l'éponge (EPON), 72, 73, 81, 144-145
Christian motifs, on pottery, 81
classification, of amphoras, 86; of assemblages, xi, 38, 42; of fabrics,30-33, 86, 204; of forms, xi, 30, 44; of function, xii, 42, 45; of mortaria, 116; of terra sigillata, 105
clay, potting, 28, see also scientific techniques
coarse wares, 63-64, 66-68, 74-75, 151; Gaulish, 142, 145, 154, 158;Italian, 50, 157; 'Italian-derived', 51, 58; Mediterranean, 158; North African, 152; Romano-British, 180, 182, 186, 188, 190-195, 197, 199; study of, 11
coinage, 80; Roman, 78
Colchester colour-coated ware (COLC), 18, 68, 69, 137, 167-168
Colchester mortaria (COMO), 18, 45, 46, 61, 69, 116, 119-120, 167
Colchester terra sigillata (COTS), 18, 69, 105, 114-116; difficulties in identification of, 115
'Cologne wares', see Lower Rhineland colour-coated ware
computers, 23, 30, 87, 111, 203, 205, 206; Internet, 203
containers, pottery, 85
Conyers, John (apothecary), 1
cooking, 42, 43, 52, 77, 116, 157, 203

Corbridge mortaria (CBMO), 69, 118-119
Corpus Inscriptionum Latinarum, 20, 86
correspondence analysis, 38, 45
Crambeck wares (CRAM), 19, 74, 77, 78, 116, 188-189
Current Research in Romano-British coarse pottery (1973), 21
'cycles', in pottery supply, 41

Dales ware and Dales-type ware (DALES), 19, 75, 190
dating, 36-38; and supply, 37, 42; by coinage, xi, 78; by stratigraphic analogy, 78; ceramic phases, 37; historical, x; problems of, 56, 72, 79
Déchelette, Joseph (1862-1914), 9
decorative techniques, appliqué, 76, 137, 140; block stamps, 170; eggshell, 66; glazed, 22, 61, 65-67, 140, 171, 178, 196; marbled, 65,66, 112, 144, 150, 171, 178, 201; mica-dusted, 61, 65,66, 142, 178,201; moulded, 66, 69, 76, 140, 160, 168, 173, 177; roller-stamped, 71,136; stamped, 66, 71, 72, 168, 177
defrutum, 89, 90, 97, 98; identification of, 97; Spanish, 52, 57
Department of Urban Archaeology (DUA), London, 84, 204
deposits, on pots, 43, 203
Derbyshire ware (DERBY), 16, 19, 64, 71, 75, 190-191
dérivées de sigillée paléochrétienne, 80, 81
die stamp, mortaria, 20; terra sigillata, 69
dipinti, 86, 87, 89, 95, 98, 99; Greek, 101
distribution maps, 16, 19, 37, 182; generation of, 206; reliability of, 85; sources for, 84
Dragendorff, Hans (1870-1941), 8, 105
Dressel 1 amphoras (DR1), 18, 49-51, 53, 57, 89-90, 94
Dressel 2-4 amphoras (DR2-4), 57, 89, 90, 94, 201
Dressel 7-11 'salazon' amphoras (SALA), 51, 57, 94, 98-99
Dressel 20 amphoras and allied types (DR20), 57, 87-89
Dressel, Heinrich (1845-1920), 86
Durobrivae of Antoninus, The (1828), 3
Durotrigian wares, 58, 59, 64, 66, 183

'E' ware (EWARE), 81, 82, 145-146
East Gaulish terra sigillata (EGTS), 71, 105, 113-114
Eastern Mediterranean, imports from, 72, 81, 101
Eboracum ware, 70, 190
Eggshell terra nigra (TNEG), 166
Egypt, imports from, 101

Eifel region mortaria (EIMO), 58, 120
Eifelkeramik, see Mayen ware
entrepreneurs, in pottery industry, 67
EPON, see Céramique à l'éponge
estimated vessel equivalent (eve), 205
ethnography, 25, 29, 30, 33-35, 42, 202
Ettlinger, Elisabeth, 65
everted-rim jars, 58, 67, 74, 75, 183, 186; development of, 71
Excavations in Cranborne Chase (1887-1898), 7
Exeter micaceous grey ware, 171
experimental archaeology, 33-35
exported pottery, from Britain, 73

fabric analysis, 22, 31-33, 204
fabric, description of, 84
field survey data, interpretation of, 41
fine wares, 64-66, 68-69, 74, 138; from Asia Minor, 81, 155; Gaulish,81, 136, 137, 139, 140, 142, 144, 146, 148, 160, 165, 166; German, 150;influence from continent, 61, 65; Italian, 50; North African, 81, 152;Romano-British, 167-171, 173, 175, 178, 188; Spanish, 160
fish-sauces, 52, 85, 90, 94; North African, 104; Spanish, 51, 52, 57, 99
flanged bowls, 183; origin of, 74; producers of, 75
fluctuations, in pottery industry, 41, 77-79; in pottery industry,cyclic, 23; in pottery supply, xi, 40-42; in terra sigillata supply, 56,66
foodstuffs, carried in pots, xi, 40, 43, 47, 52, 57, 85, 101, 103, 142,194; imported, influence of, 52; sealed samples of, 43
form, see typology
fortress horizon (on Rhine), 51
Frisian pottery, 76
fruit, dates, 90, 101; figs, 93; palm, 57, 101
Fulford/Huddleston report (1991), 23
function, of amphoras, 85; of mortaria, 116; of pottery, 42-45

Gallo-Belgic wares, 51, 55, 58, 161-164; imitation of, 65, 66;influence of, 59, 183
garum, see fish-sauces
Gaul, imports from, 51-53, 55-58, 61, 68, 71, 90, 94, 96, 112, 113, 116,117, 125, 130, 136, 137, 139, 140, 142, 144-146, 148, 154, 156, 158,160, 165, 166; post-Roman pottery of, 80; trade routes across, 49, 57
Gauloise 12 amphoras (G12), 94, 96-97
Gauloise flat-based amphoras (GAUL), 57, 72, 94-96, 201
German marbled wares (MARM), 72, 150-151
Germanic pottery, 76-77

226

Index

Germany, imports from, 57, 58, 68, 71, 113, 120, 131, 138, 150, 151; military units from, 76; publications from, 9, 11, 14
Gillam, John Pearson (1917-86), 16, 19-21, 67, 71, 75, 76, 182, 183
glass vessels, imitated in pottery, 65
graffiti, 116; capacity, 43, 87, 95; dated, 47, 87; from kiln sites, 46;Greek, 65, 103; Neo-Punic, 65; on amphoras, 86; on mortaria, 117, 129;on tiles, 47, 65; pre-firing, 42, 47, 112, 157; study of, 44; 'tare and weight', 43
graffito jars, 47
Greek, amphoras stamps, 95; graffiti, 103; influence in southern France,48; measures of capacity, 86
Greene, Kevin T., 21, 22, 51, 58, 65
Guidelines for the Processing and Publication of Roman Pottery (1980),23

Hadham red-slipped wares (HARS), 76, 77, 168-169
Hadrian's Wall, 9, 16, 17, 38, 74, 76, 78, 190, 197; BB1 on, 185; influence on pottery industry, 66
'hairpin beakers', see Central Gaulish colour-coated ware
Haltern 70 amphoras (H70), 57, 97
hand-formed wares, 76; Late Iron Age, 56; late Roman, 78, 80
Hartley, Katherine F., 21, 22, 85, 117
Haverfield, John Francis (1860-1919), 9, 11
HOFA ('Hollow foot amphoras'), see Kapitän II amphoras
Housesteads ware, 76
Hull, Mark Reginald (Rex) (1897-1976), 16, 17, 69, 114
Huntcliff ware, 16, 78

imported pottery, 56-58, 61, 72, 135-166; amphoras, 51, 52, 57, 80;coarse wares, 80; containers, 51, 52; cooking wares, 57, 157; copied inBritain, 29, 51, 53, 55, 56, 59, 64, 156; fine wares, 51-53, 57, 80; mortaria, 52, 57, 58; post-Roman, 80; pre-conquest, 48-52; table ware,51
Introduction to the study of Terra sigillata, An (1920), 11, 107
Ireland, post-Roman pottery in, 80; Roman pottery in, 1
iron working, 47
Italian mortaria (ITMO), 121-122
Italian-type terra sigillata (ITTS), 51, 105, 111-112
Italy, imports from, 50, 51, 57, 89-91, 99, 111, 121, 156, 157

Journal of Roman Pottery Studies, 83, 85, 202

Kapitän II amphoras (HOFA), 72, 101-102
KOLN, see Lower Rhineland colour-coated ware

lamps, pottery, 66
Late Iron Age, Hertfordshire, 53, 58; pottery, 16-17, 48-56; potterykilns, 28; Southern central England, 55; see also pre-conquest
Late Roman grog-tempered wares (LRGR), 77, 78, 191-192
Latin, names of pottery types, 42, 117, 202; personal names, 45, 46
ledge-rim jars, 55, 58, 64, 67, 75
Leeds Index (terra sigillata stamps), 106
Legio II Augusta, role in development of BB1, 66
legionary wares, 65-66
Lincolnshire mortaria (LIMO), 47, 122-123
liquamen, see fish-sauces
London 555 amphoras (L555), 97-98
'London ware' (LOND), 64, 66, 170-171; origin of style, 171
London-Essex stamped wares (LEST), 65, 168, 169-170
Lower Rhineland colour-coated ware (KOLN), 32, 61, 146-148
LRSH, see South Midlands shell-tempered wares
Lugudunum mortaria, 20, 132
Lyon ware (LYON), 57, 59, 61, 148-150, 168

Mancetter-Hartshill mortaria (MHMO), 61, 69, 77, 123-124, 132
MARM, see German marbled wares
May, Thomas (186?-1931), 13-15
Mayen ware (MAYN), 72, 80, 151-152
Med, imports from, 158
metal vessels, 56; imitated in pottery, 51, 53, 55, 59, 65, 76; Italian, 53
Mid Roman Campanian amphoras (MRCA), 72, 91-92
migration of potters, 47, 51; from Arezzo, 51; from continent, 28, 40,46, 56, 58-59, 65, 68, 69, 72, 74, 76, 115, 116, 118, 155, 173, 190;within Britain, 28, 45, 58, 61, 63, 67, 69, 74, 116, 117, 119, 123, 129,132, 135, 178, 180, 185, 186, 199; within Gaul, 125; within terra sigillata industry, 107
military, production, 35, 58; supply, xi, 28, 47, 55, 59, 61, 63, 66, 67,69-70, 76, 78, 197
modes of pottery production, 34
Montans terra sigillata (MOTS), 105, 112-113
mortaria, 2, 6, 19-21, 38, 42, 58, 61-63, 74, 116-135; East Anglian grey, 73; Eden valley, 135; function of, 116; Gaulish, 52, 57, 58, 61,117, 125, 130; German, 120, 131; history of, 116; Italian, 121;production of, 116, 117; raetian, 13; Romano-British, 118, 119, 122,123, 125, 127, 129, 132, 134, 188; Scottish, 69; sources of, 117; stamps, 45, 117; terra sigillata, 116; trade in, 69; typology of, 12
MOSL, see Trier black-slipped ware
motto beakers, 137, 138
Munsell colours, 33, 84
museum catalogues, British Museum, 9, 13; Carlisle, 13; Colchester andEssex, 13, 15; Nijmegen, 161; Reading, 13, 15; York, 13
museum collections, 203
Myres, J. N. L., 75, 78

Nene Valley colour-coated wares (NVCC), 22, 32, 68, 73, 74, 78, 79, 137,148, 173-175
Nene Valley mortaria (NVMO), 47, 74, 127-129
New Forest mortaria (NFMO), 74, 77, 125
New Forest slipped wares (NFCC), 16, 74, 77, 171-173; exports of, 73
North Africa, imports from, 104, 152; influence in Britain, 70, 154
North African cylindrical amphoras (NACA), 72, 79, 81, 104-105
North African red slip ware (NARS), 81, 152-154
North Gaulish grey wares (NGGW), 72, 73, 127, 154-155

North Gaulish mortaria (NGMO), 45, 58, 61, 116, 118, 125-127, 131
North Gaulish white wares, 51
North Kent shell-tempered wares (NKSH), 47, 193-194

olive-oil, 43, 52, 85, 90; Baetican, 57; Eastern Mediterranean, 81;North African, 72, 81, 104; Spanish, x, 52, 57, 72, 87
olives, in *defrutum*, 97, 98; introduction to Gaul, 48; Italian, 89; Spanish, 87
organic residues, in pots, 43
Oxford conference (1972), 21, 22
Oxfordshire red- and brown-slipped wares (OXRS), 72, 77-79, 175-178;exports of, 73
Oxfordshire white-ware mortaria (OXMO), 63, 74, 77, 78, 116, 129

parallel searching, 18
Parisian wares, 65, 130
Pascual 1 amphoras (PAS1), 57, 92-93, 94
Peacock, David P. S., 22, 31, 156, 182
personal names, Celtic, 46; graffiti, 44; Latin, 45, 46
Pevensey ware, 74
Phocaean red slip ware (PRSW), 81, 155-156
pie-dishes, 67, 74, 183, 186
pie-slice, 38
Pitt Rivers, Augustus Henry Lane Fox (1827-1900), 7-8, 16
Pompeian-Red ware-fabric 1 (PRW1), 42, 57, 59, 61, 89, 156, 157-158
Pompeian-Red ware-fabric 2 (PRW2), 57, 61, 156, 158
Pompeian-Red ware-fabric 3 (PRW3), 57, 156, 158-159
Pompeian-Red wares, 156-157
poppy-head beaker, 65
Portchester fabric D (PORD), 77, 78, 180, 194-195
post-Roman, imports, 80
potter, Abducius, 96; Acceptus, 69, 114, 120; Aesico, 122; Albanus, 132; Albinus, 20, 46, 61, 132; Amandinus, 114; Amenus, 135; Amminus, 120;Anaus, 118; L Arrius Caludus, 132; Ateius, 47; Atepacius, 122; G AtisiusGratus, 118; G Atisius Sabinus, 13, 118; L Atisius Secundus, 118;GAttius Marinus, 45, 61, 123, 132; Austinus, 135; Baro, 120, 130;Bellicus, 135; Biiji, 126; Bilicedo, 122; Biso, 122; Bonoxus, 123;Boriedo, 126; Brariatus, 96; Brico, 135; Bruccius, 132; Bruscius, 123;Buccus, 126; C.C.M., 135; Cacumattus, 126; Camulorix, 127; Candidus,123, 132; Castus, 132; Cavarius, 126; Cettus, 113; Cevanos, 123; Cicro|Cicrus, 123; Cinnamus, 71, 113; Cintugnatus, 114; Coertutinus,123; Crico, 122; Cunoarda, 127; Cunopectus, 69, 114, 120; Cupitus, 122;Dares, 201; Decanio, 135; Decanius, 122; Decmitius, 135; Devalus, 132;DIS/LDB, 135; Doballus, 123, 127; Doccas, 123, 132; Docci.., 135;Doinus, 132; Driccius, 132; Dubitatus, 120; Erucanus, 123; Fronto, 126;Gabrus, 114; Gissus, 132; Gracilis, 126; Gratinus, 123; Icotagus, 123; TIulius Afer, 126; C Iulius Privatus, 126; Iunius, 123; Iunius Loccius,123; Q Iustius Cico, 122; Q Iustius Crescens, 122; Junius, 132;Lallaius, 132; Latinus, 114; Lipuca,

114; T Littera, 114; Litugenus,114, 120, 126; Loccius Pro.., 123; Loccius Vibius, 123; Lossa, 126;Marcus, 118; Mariaus, 120; Marinus, 132; Marius, 157; Martic, 122;Martinus, 120, 132; Matuacus, 114; Matugenus, 20, 46, 132;Matutinus,118; Maurius, 123; Melus, 132; Mertucus, 132; Messor, 120;Miccio, 114; Mimicius, 135; Minomelus, 123; Minuso, 114; Moco|Mocus,123; Modestus, 36; Moricamulus, 132; Morina, 132; Mossius, 123; MottiusBollius, 126; Nanieco, 123, 135; Nidus, 123, 132; Nsro, 132;Oastrius, 58, 132;Orbissa, 126; Orgilus, 126; Ovidius, 135; Ovidus, 132; Patern.., 178; Paullus, 126; M Porcius, 93; Prasso, 126; Ramotus, 132;Rebdecus(?),135; Regalis, 120; Regu.., 114; Roa, 132; Ruicco|Rutico, 123; Q RutiliusRipanus, 132; Sarrius, 67, 123, 130, 186; Saturninus, 118, 132;GSe-Veranius, 69; Secundua, 130; Secundus, 132; Senico, 122;Senilis,114; Sennienius, 128; Sennius, 123; Septuminus, 67, 123;Setibogius, 130; Similis, 123; Sollus, 132; Sulloniacus, 118; Summacus, 126; Surus, 123; Thamesubugus, 47, 129; TMH, 132; G Valerius Esunertus, 126; S Valerius Iv.., 132; Q Valerius Sc.., 126; Q ValeriusSuriacus, 126; Q Valerius Veranius, 126; Variatus, 46; Vassonus, 126;Vediacus, 127; Verecundus,131; Viator, 127; Victor, 123; Videx, 132;Virrinus, 74; Vitalis, 122,123; Vorolas, 122; Vossullus, 129
potters, career development of, 46; conservatism of, 29; families of,46; freedmen, 45; Greek (operating in France), 48; masters and apprentices, 47; names on stamps, 45; Roman citizens, 45; slaves, 46,47, 66; status of, 45
pottery, as container, xi; as marker of trade, 40; dating of, x, 9, 17,18, 20; description of, 2; function of, xii; illustration of, 4, 9, 11;life-spans, 24; site formation processes and, xii; social context of,xii, 42
Pottery in the Roman World (1982), 35, 202
pottery industry, economics of, xi, 23, 38-42; organization of, 46, 47; ruralization of, 29
pottery kilns, 3, 5, 16, 20, 22, 23, 26-29, 34, 53, 58, 80
Pottery Kilns of Roman Britain, The (1984), 22, 85, 202
pottery processing systems, x, 23, 29, 203-205; discarding pottery, 45
pottery studies, history of, 1-23, 202; methodology of, 8, 14, 18, 20,22, 23, 202; role in archaeology, x-xii, 5, 8, 36-47; scientific techniques in, 20-22; sources for, 24-35
Pownall, Thomas (antiquarian), 2
pre-conquest, imports, 116; wine imports, 53
procuratorial stamps, on mortaria, 132
production assemblage, 29

quantification, 22, 25, 37, 40, 42, 202, 204; comparison between techniques, 25

Red-glazed pottery of the Romans, The (1848), 4, 9
residuality, 26, 38

227

Index

residues, organic, on pots, 43
'Rhenish' wares, 137
Rhineland, see Germany
Rhodes, imports from, 57, 93
Rhodian amphoras (RHOD), 57, 93-94
Rhône valley mortaria (RVMO), 58, 125, 130-131
Richborough 527 amphoras (R527), 57, 99-101
Roach Smith, Charles (1806-1890), 3-6, 9
Roman, character of economy, 38; map of Empire, 84; measures of capacity, 86; taxation, role of, 39
Roman era in Britain, The (1911), 11
Romanization, 11; of culinary habits, 52, 64, 116, 157
Romano-British pottery, Claudio-Neronian, 56-61; coarse wares, 179-201; collapse of industry, 78; divergence from continental styles, 63; end of, 77-80; exported to the continent, 73-74; fifth century, 78-80; finewares, 166-179; Flavian-Trajanic, 61-66; Hadrian to Severus, 66-70; history of, 48-82; influence of continental styles on, 64; Iron Age traditions in, 64, 77; on post-Roman sites, 79-80; origins of style, 58;third and fourth centuries, 70-77
Romano-Frankish wares, 80, 152
Romano-Saxon wares, 75-76, 78
Rossington Bridge black-burnished ware (RBBB1), 67, 130, 186
Rossington Bridge mortaria (RBMO), 67, 123, 129-130
Rustic ware, 16

SALA, see Dressel 7-11 'salazon' amphoras
salt, 194; production of, 47
samian, see terra sigillata
Savernake grey wares (SAVG), 59, 195-196
scientific techniques, compositional, 32, 37, 87, 115, 202, 204; geological techniques; 31; heavy mineral, 32, 67, 78, 182; petrology, 21, 31, 53, 86, 87, 90, 93, 94, 100, 101, 112, 131, 142, 146, 151, 156,186, 190, 202, 204; spectrographic, 21; textural, 31; thin-section, 21,31
Scotland, 19, 28, 61; dating of occupation of, 13, 16, 37; mortarium production in, 69; post-Roman pottery in, 80; supply to forts in, 69
seriation, 12, 37, 38
Severn Valley wares (SVW), 59, 64, 69, 197-199
Severus, campaigns in Britain, 70
sherd size, 26
shipwrecks, 49, 73, 85, 88, 90, 93, 99, 101, 102, 104, 122; pottery in, 40
site assemblages, xii, 24-26, 43
site formation, 26
Soller mortaria (SOMO), 131-132
sources, bibliographic, 87, 107, 117, 161, 202, 203; classical literary, 2, 4, 7, 11, 35, 42, 117
South Devon burnished ware (SDBB), 196-197
South Gaulish (La Graufesenque) terra sigillata (SGTS), 46, 51, 56, 61,71, 105, 112, see also Montans terra sigillata
South Gaulish colour-coated ware (SGCC), 57, 169
South Midlands shell-tempered wares (LRSH), 75, 77-79, 168, 192-193
South-east English glazed ware (SEGL), 65, 178-179

Spain, imports from, 51, 52, 57, 87, 90, 92, 97, 98, 160
Spanish colour-coated ware (SPAN), 57, 148, 160-161
stamps, on amphoras, 86, 88, 89, 95, 100; on Gallo-Belgic wares, 161; on mortaria, 63, 117, 118, 120-123, 125, 127, 129, 131, 132, 134; on Pompeian-Red ware, 157; on terra sigillata, 106
Structure of Romano-British pottery kiln, The (1957), 20
Student's Guide to Romano-British coarse pottery (1964), 21, 202
Study Group for Romano-British Pottery, 21, 23
sub-Roman pottery, 80, 82
Syer Cuming, H., 7

Terra nigra (TN), 51, 165-166
Terra rubra (TR), 51, 165
terra sigillata, 1, 2, 4, 7, 15, 18, 21, 34, 37, 105-116, 136, 137; calibration curve, 40; chronological distribution of, 40; classification of, 105; Colchester, 18, 28, 69, 114; dating of, 71, 107, 114; definition of,105; dies, 106; Gaulish, 112, 113; German, 113; influence of, 64-66, 69,71, 80, 125, 140, 144, 154, 168, 170, 173, 178, 183; Italian, 111; Lyon,51, 111; moulds, London, 69; moulds, York, 69; production in Britain,69; Romano-British, 69, 114; role in dating, 36; stamps, 4; stamps on, 106; study of, 8-11; successors of, 71-72
Terra sigillata (1895), 8
third century, problem of, 70
tin trade, 50, 81
TNEG, see Eggshell terra nigra
tools, moulds, 69, 114, 116; potters, 28
trade, xi, 22, 23, 39, 40, 73, 81; patterns, 85; 'piggy-back', 66, 82,136, 161; pottery as marker of, 40; routes across Gaul, 50; routes through Atlantic seaways, 81; silence of classical authors on, 35; with Rhineland, 40; within Britain, 20, 40
traders, Roman, in Gaul, 50; role of, 66
Trier black-slipped ware (MOSL), 137, 138-139
Turkey, imports from, 103
type-series, Africana, 86, 104; alternatives to, 30; Augst; 87; Beltrán, 86, 98; Camulodunum, 18, 85, 86, 161; Chenet, 136; Conspectus, 105;Curle, 11, 105; development of, 30; Dragendorff, 9, 105; Dressel, 86; Déchelette, 9, 105; Gauloise, 86, 94; Gillam, 19, 85, 116; Gose, 151; Haltern, 86, 105; Hayes, 104; Holwerda, 161; Knorr, 9, 105; Ludowici,105; Ritterling, 105; Southwark, 201; Tintagel, 81; Tripolitana, 86; Walters, 9, 105; Wroxeter (mortaria), 12, 116
Types of Roman Coarse Pottery Vessels in Northern Britain (1957), 19,38, 71
typology, 7, 18, 22, 29-30; and dating, xi; stagnation in, 77

Upchurch ware, 14, 16

vase tronconique, see North Gaulish grey wares
Verulamium-region mortaria (VRMO), 2, 20, 46, 61, 63, 116, 118, 119,123, 129, 132-134, 201
Verulamium-region white ware (VRW), 61, 199-201; amphoras, 90

Wales, 188; BB1 in, 66, 67, 185; post-Roman pottery in, 80, 146, 156; south, SVW influence in, 199
Walters, H. B., 9
Ward, John, 11
wear marks, on pots, 43
weathering, of pottery, 25
Welwyn Garden City (Herts), 53
wheel thrown pottery, derived from hand-formed style, 58; introduced into Britain, 53, 56
Wheeler, Sir Robert Eric Mortimer (1890-1976), 13, 17
wheels, potters, 28, 46
Wilderspool mortaria (WPMO), 134-135
wine, 85; Celtic appetite for, 50; drinking of, 138; Eastern Mediterranean, 81; from Asia Minor, 93, 103; Gaulish, 57, 72, 90, 95; Gaulish, in barrels, 82; in pre-conquest Britain, 53; introduction to Gaul, 48; Italian, 49-51, 53, 56, 57, 89-91; Rhodian, 57, 93;Romano-British, 90, 201; Spanish, 57, 90, 93, 99

Young report (1980), 2

INDEX OF PLACES IN BRITAIN

CHANNEL ISLANDS; Guernsey, 73, 155

ENGLAND; Ardleigh (Essex), 170; Aylesford (Kent), 16; Baldock (Herts),53; Bath (Avon), 77, 79; Beauport Park (Sussex), 73; Brampton (Norf), 1;Bricket Wood (Herts), 28, 58, 61, 132, 134, 201; Brockley Hill (Middx), 20, 58, 61, 90, 134, 201; Brue valley (Somer), 186;Cadbury-Congresbury (Somer), 79, 81; Caister-on-Sea (Norf), 155;Caistor-by-Norwich (Norf), 16, 28, 58, 78; Canterbury (Kent), 58,77, 78, 152, 155; Cantley (Yorks), 74, 130; Carlisle (Cumbr), 101,135; Castor (Hunts), 3; Catterick (Yorks), 40; Chelmsford (Essex), 22,37, 43, 76; Chester (Ches), 65, 150, 197; Chester-le-Street (Durham),26; Chesterholm (Northum), 40, 43, 71, 74, 76; Chichester (Sussex), 58; Cliffe (Kent), 194; Colchester (Essex), 5, 9, 17, 18, 28, 37, 46,58, 59, 61, 67-69, 72, 115, 120, 126, 152, 157, 167, 186; Corbridge (Northum), 12, 69, 118, 126, 186; Corfe Mullen (Dorset), 16, 58; Cowley (Oxon), 16; Crambeck (Yorks), 16, 74, 78, 188;Cranborne Chase (Dorset), 8; Derby (Derby), 191; Doncaster (Yorks),190; Dorchester (Oxon), 16; Dover (Kent), 73; Eccles (Kent), 58, 59;Eden valley (Cumbr), 69, 135; Ellingham (Norf), 120; Elslack (Yorks),13; Exeter (Devon), 22, 64, 71, 126, 158; Gloucester (Glos), 22, 64,158; Great Casterton (Rutland), 68, 69; Hadham (Herts), 76, 168, 170; Hambleden (Bucks), 13; Harpenden (Herts), 55; Harrold (Beds), 192;Harston (Cambs), 74, 178; Hartshill (Warw), 74, 123, 178; Hayton (Yorks), 126; Hazelwood (Derby), 191; Headington (Oxon), 5, 6, 13; Hengistbury Head (Dorset), 13, 49, 56; Hertfordshire, 53, 58; Heybridge (Essex), 79; Highgate Wood (London), 46, 64, 67; Holbrook (Derby),191; Housesteads (Northum), 76; Inworth (Essex), 76;

Knapton (Yorks),16; Lakenheath (Suff), 192; Lamyatt Beacon (Somer), 44; Leicester (Leic), 18; Lincoln (Lincs), 122; Lincolnshire, 74; Little Chester (Derby), 64, 67, 191; Little London (Notts), 16; Littlemore (Oxon),69; London, 1, 2, 4, 5, 9, 37, 40, 58, 66, 69, 71, 94, 96, 101,113, 114, 126, 131, 152, 155, 157, 158, 166, 170, 185, 187, 197, 201; Longthorpe (Cambs), 58, 59; Lullingstone (Kent), 152; Lydiard Tregoze (Wilts), 195; Mancetter (Warw), 28, 61, 63, 71, 123; Margidunum (Notts), 20; Midlands, 64; Mildenhall (Wilts), 196; Milton Keynes (Bucks), 22, 79; Morley St Peter (Norf), 28; Mount Bures (Essex), 52; Mucking (Essex), 78, 79; Nene valley (Northants), 2, 5, 28, 64, 68,71, 75, 76, 78, 128, 170; New Forest (Hants), 5, 16, 22, 125,173; Oare (Wilts), 61, 195; Ospringe (Kent), 13; Overwey (Tilford,Surrey), 195; Oxfordshire, 16, 22, 28, 63, 71-72, 75, 129, 178; Pan Sand (nr. Whitstable, Kent), 98; Peterborough (Hunts), 69; Pevensey (Sussex), 74, 178; Pewsey (Wilts), 195; Poole Harbour (Dorset), 183;Portchester (Hants), 78; Prae Wood (Herts), 17, 55; Pudding Pan Sand (nr. Whitstable, Kent), 1-2; Puddlehill (Beds), 55; Pulborough (Sussex),69; Purbeck (Dorset), 32; Radlett (Herts), 20, 134, 201; Richborough (Kent), 13, 126, 152, 190; Rossington Bridge (Yorks), 67,130, 182, 186; Rudchester (Northum), 17; Rushden (Northants), 58;Sandford (Oxon), 13; Sandy (Beds), 2; Savernake Forest (Wilts), 195; Sea Mills (Avon), 170; Severn valley, 197; Sheepen (Colchester, Essex), 17, 18, 37, 57; Skeleton Green (Herts), 51, 101; South Carlton (Lincs),16, 68, 122; South Devon, 197; Southern central, 55; St Albans (Herts), 16, 37, 46, 53, 58, 61, 134, 201; Staines (Middx), 178; Sugar Loaf Court (London), 58; Swarling (Kent), 13, 16; Templeborough (Yorks), 13; Thralom (Yorks), 16; Thurrock (Essex), 76; Tiddington(Warw), 11; Tintagel (Corn), 80; Ufton Nervet (Berks), 56; Upchurch marshes (Kent), 5, 22, 47, 67, 71, 170, 186; Warrington (Ches),13, 135; Wattisfield (Suff), 170; Welwyn (Herts), 53; Welwyn GardenCity (Herts), 51, 144; West Stow (Suff), 79, 170; Wheathampstead(Herts), 17; Wilderspool (Ches), 7, 13, 135; Wiltshire, 55; Winchester (Hants), 43; Wroxeter (Salop), 12, 63, 197; Wye (Kent), 78; York (Yorks), 66, 69, 70, 150, 155, 190; Yorkshire signal-stations,16, 17

SCOTLAND; Bar Hill (Strath), 69; Camelon (Central), 126; Carpow (Tays), 97, 191; Cramond (Lothian), 69, 194; Inchtuthil (Tays), 61, 155, 158; Inveresk (Lothian), 69, 120, 199; Mumrills (Central), 67, 182; Newstead (Borders), 11, 69, 115, 135, 150; Rough Castle (Central), 69,120

WALES; Caerleon (Gwent), 44, 65, 66, 70, 150; Caernarfon (Gwynedd), 43,188; Dinas Powys (S Glam), 81; Gellygaer (Mid Glam), 11; Holt (Clywd), 22, 66, 70; Usk (Gwent), 22, 42, 58, 59, 71, 158, 197

228